# NATURAL REASONS

# NATURAL REASONS

## PERSONALITY AND POLITY

S. L. Hurley

New York   Oxford
OXFORD UNIVERSITY PRESS

Oxford University Press

Oxford   New York   Toronto
Delhi   Bombay   Calcutta   Madras   Karachi
Kuala Lumpur   Singapore   Hong Kong   Tokyo
Nairobi   Dar es Salaam   Cape Town
Melbourne   Auckland

and associated companies in
Berlin   Ibadan

First published in 1989 by Oxford University Press, Inc.,
200 Madison Avenue, New York, New York 10016

First issued as an Oxford University Press paperback, 1992

Oxford is a registered trademark of Oxford University Press

Library of Congress Cataloging-in-Publication Data
Hurley, S.L. (Susan L.)
Natural reasons : personality and polity / S.L. Hurley
p.   cm.   Bibliography: p.
Includes index.   ISBN 0-19-505615-9
ISBN 0-19-508012-2 (PBK.)
1. Decision-making (Ethics)   2. Jurisprudence.   I. Title
BJ1419.H87   1989   170-dc19   88-37967

2   4   6   8   9   7   5   3   1

Printed in the United States of America
on acid-free paper

*To my mother, and the memory of my father.*

# ACKNOWLEDGMENTS

I would like to thank St. Catherine's College and All Souls College for their generous support of this work in its early stages. I would also like to thank Edward McClennan and the National Science Foundation for the opportunity and funding to attend the Public Choice Institute, held at Dalhousie University in Halifax in the summer of 1984, during which the seeds of some of the ideas developed here were planted.

My greatest thanks, for inspiration, comments, and encouragement over many years, are due to Ronald Dworkin, John McDowell, Derek Parfit, Amartya Sen, and Charles Taylor. I am also grateful to many other people for extremely helpful criticisms of various drafts and sections of this material and comments in conversation, including Michael Bacharach, Simon Blackburn, David Braybrooke, John Broome, David Charles, Gerald Cohen, Robin Cubitt, Donald Davidson, William Ewald, Elizabeth Fricker, Rai Gaita, Peter Gardenfors, Richard Gaskin, Allan Gibbard, James Griffin, Justin Gosling, Samuel Guttenplan, Jean Hampton, John Harsanyi, Steven Holtzman, Mark Johnston, Lewis Kornhauser, David Lewis, Sabina Lovibond, John Mackie, David Mitchell, Thomas Nagel, Martha Nussbaum, David Owens, Christopher Peacocke, David Pears, Nicholas Rawlins, Donald Regan, Hugh Rice, Kevin Roberts, Paul Seabright, Martin Slater, Michael Smith, John Vickers, David Wiggins, Bernard Williams, and the members of my seminars at U. C. Berkeley, 1984, at Harvard, 1987, and at Princeton, 1988. Needless to say, all remaining errors are my own.

Earlier versions of some the material in the book were published in four articles: "Frege, the Proliferation of Force, and Non-Cognitivism", in *Mind*, 1984; "Objectivity and Disagreement", in *Morality and Objectivity: Essays in Honour of John Mackie*, Ted Honderich, editor (Routledge & Kegan Paul, London, 1985); "Supervenience and the Possibility of Coherence", in *Mind*, 1985; and "Conflict, Akrasia and Cognitivism", in *Proceedings of the Aristotelian Society*, 1985–86. I'm grateful to the editors concerned for permission to use revisions of previously published material.

*Princeton, N.J.*                                                                S.L.H.
*January 1989*

# CONTENTS

## Part IV.   Knowledge of What Should Be Done

# NATURAL REASONS

The student of politics, then, must study the soul . . .
Aristotle, *Nicomachean Ethics* I.13

# 1

# Introduction

*Natural Reasons* is about the rationality of the decisions and actions of persons, and illustrates the continuity of philosophy of mind, on the one hand, and ethics and jurisprudence, on the other. It is not about morality, and indeed rejects the traditional conception of morality and self-interest as substantially independent of one another. Rather, it is about ethics, or rationality on the part of self-interpreting and self-determining agents. A major thesis of the book is that arguments drawn from the philosophy of mind may be used to undermine widely-held subjectivist positions in ethics and associated positions in politico-economic theory. The book is broadly inspired by the philosophies of Wittgenstein and Davidson, but goes on to connect their arguments about interpretation with formal work in decision theory and social choice theory and with the theory of adjudication. Throughout the book runs a thematic consideration of the analogies and disanalogies between interpersonal and intrapersonal relationships, between the resolution of conflicts between persons and the resolution of conflicts faced by one person. In the final chapter this theme culminates in an examination of the close relationships between the values of personal autonomy and of democracy.

The book falls into four parts. A brief sketch of the contents of each part is followed by more general remarks about the structure of the book and its intended audience.

Part I, containing chapters on Objectivity, Disagreement, Preference, Interpretation, and Subjectivism, is about the relations between mind and value. Arguments about interpretation drawn from the philosophy of mind are focussed on the concept of preference, in the context of formal decision theory. Decision theory presupposes that mistakes and disagreements about what should be done are possible. But if they are to be possible, there must be constraints on the eligibility of interpretations of action in terms of beliefs and preferences. The constraints needed are substantive as well as formal, and they include evaluative constraints. Separate issues about objectivity, realism, and cognitivism are distinguished, and the subjectivist view that values are determined by conceptually prior and independent preferences is criticized. It is argued that certain theories of higher-order preference and

3

interpersonal comparison depend on theories of human nature which are in part evaluative; the importance of articulating disagreements about such evaluative theories is emphasized. The constitutive role of values in interpretation undermines the subjectivist's attempt to use individuals' preferences as the unproblematic building blocks of theories of value. The objectivist conception of preference as value-laden is distinguished from Platonism and is located in relation to a more general conception of the mind as world-laden that emerges from contemporary critiques of psychological individualism.

Part II, containing chapters on Conflict, *Akrasia*, and Cognitivism, is about conflicting reasons and values. The grounds for resistance to a view of conflicts of reasons for action as merely apparent are considered. An evidential model of conflict is distinguished from a subsystems model, according to which conflicts within persons are analogous in certain respects to conflicts between persons. The relationships of the evidential and subsystems models of conflict to attributions of attitudes with the akratic structure are examined. The rationality of intrapersonal and interpersonal coordination and the inadequacy of individualism about agency, which takes the unit of agency as fixed, are urged. Persons are understood to be self-interpreting and self-determining animals, whose attitudes, characters, and identities are not fixed, but are in part their own creation; a theory of rationality for persons is an ethic. Conflicts of values understood according to the subsystems model are argued to be compatible with ethical cognitivism, and a Fregean argument against noncognitivism is pressed.

Part III, containing chapters on Theory, Deliberation, Coherence, and Commensurability, is about rationality in the face of conflicting reasons. On the basis of legal and ethical examples, deliberation about what should be done, all things considered, is characterized as the search for a coherent set of relationships among the relevant conflicting reasons. In ethical contexts deliberation may be understood as a kind of self-interpretation and self-determination on the part of persons. A theory that displays the coherence sought in deliberation can be represented by a coherence function, from orderings of alternatives by conflicting reasons to judgments about what should be done, all things considered. However, social choice theory demonstrates the impossibility, given certain constraints, of social welfare functions that rationally resolve conflicts of different agents' preferences. The analogy between conflicts faced by one person and conflicts between persons suggests the question whether analogues of certain impossibility results in social choice theory apply to the situation of the deliberator who faces conflicting reasons and seeks coherence. To understand why they do not, the modal structure of deliberation is examined; deliberation involves appeals to counterfactual possibilities, but not counterevaluative possibilities, and the search for coherence is constrained both by specific values and by the formal requirement of the supervenience of evaluative concepts. The features of deliberation that are discovered rebut the skeptical suggestion that analogues of certain theorems of social choice theory show that coherence is impossible and thus that there is no such thing as what should be done, all things considered. Moreover, coherence is possible without commensurability.

Part IV, containing chapters on Skepticism and on Autonomy and Democracy, is about knowledge of what should be done and the relationship of personal autonomy and democracy to such knowledge. A discussion of realism and a critique of the error theory about values lead into consideration of epistemological skepticism and a defense of the possibility of "tracking the truth" about what should be done. The skeptic tries to debunk evaluative beliefs; that is, he or she tries to explain evaluative beliefs in a way that shows that if they were not true they would still be held. The understanding of the modal structure of deliberation and the role of supervenience achieved in Part III is brought to bear in resisting the skeptic's insufficiently discriminating efforts to debunk. Some explanations of evaluative beliefs that do not cite values do positively debunk those beliefs, but others do not; a democratic division of epistemic labour may provide a means of avoiding debunking influences. The social choice conditions are reinterpreted as conditions on beliefs about what should be done rather than preferences, and are found to have epistemological significance. The close relationships between cognitive conceptions of self-determination, or autonomy, and of democracy are examined, and the idea of a fully structured social theory, which holds intrapersonal relations and interpersonal relations to be equally basic, is developed as a natural extension of the idea of an ethic. Finally, the bearing of decision-theoretic issues about intrapersonal structure on issues about distributive justice is displayed.

The organization of the book is more in the nature of a spiral, or even several interwoven spirals, than a linear progression; in this sense the book illustrates its own coherentist theme. Certain ideas and analogies are approached several times, from various directions, as the strands of argument that make up the book are woven together. The analogy between intrapersonal and interpersonal relations is an example that will be evident just on the basis of the sketch above. There are several others. Various Aristotelian themes surface regularly. The naturalness of rationality is emphasized: the naturalness of eligible contents, the naturalness of personality and of the capacity for self-interpretation and self-determination. And it is a possibility of naturalism overlooked by the undiscriminating debunker that proves his undoing. Moreover, the divide-and-conquer strategy that is implicit in the teasing apart of issues about centralism, subjectivism, cognitivism, realism, and skepticism, and in the explicit scrutiny of the relationships between them, is essential to the argumentative structure of the book. Too often, I suggest, these issues are run together, as if there were some one big (though perhaps ineffable, or only metaphorically expressible) issue standing behind all of them.

The complexity of structure that results from this interweaving of themes makes for occasional repetition. I have not tried to eliminate all repetition because I hope that it will make certain chapters more self-contained than they would be if they required readers to refer to, or recall material from, other chapters. This should make for easier reading even for those reading straight through. But it is also intended to accommodate those who only read certain chapters, or who skim through some and read others. I hope that ample cross-referencing of chapters will also be helpful to some readers, though others may find it distracting.

Readers are encouraged to skim and to dip into chapters that most interest them. There is always a danger of misunderstanding in doing this, of course, especially with respect to a book whose parts are highly interdependent; but there is also a particular reason to encourage it here. The book is doggedly interdisciplinary. It is aimed at an audience of professional academics and graduate students, but from several different fields: economics, law, political theory, and decision theory as well as philosophy. As a result, practitioners in each field will find some material that is thoroughly familiar and standard, which they can skim through, other material that bears on their field and may be of immediate interest, and perhaps other material which is too far from their field, or too technical, for it to be of interest to follow in detail (though in general I have deliberately avoided formal presentations of technical material in favour of prose, for the sake of accessibility). Philosophers, for example, may find parts of Part I thoroughly familiar and think that much more could have been taken for granted; but perhaps nonphilosophers will not. Decision theorists will find the exposition in the chapter on Preference unnecessary; but again, others will not. Political theorists may wish to read through the long final chapter, the only one focussed on political theory, first, so that they can estimate what material in preceding chapters may be of most interest to them. Similarly, economists may wish to begin by skimming through Chapters 4, 6 and 12, and lawyers by skimming through Chapters 10 and 11. I hope that readers will be willing to bear with my efforts to make the book accessible from various disciplines and will read accordingly.

# I

# RELATIONS BETWEEN MIND AND VALUE

# 2

# Objectivity

## 1. Terminology and Distinctions: Cognitivism, Realism, Centralism, and Objectivism About Reasons for Action

In his lucid and influential book on ethics Mackie appealed to the existence of ethical disagreement as one of two major sources of support for ethical skepticism and subjectivism. The view that disagreement undermines claims to objectivity, however, is not independent of the way in which objectivity is conceived; one of the many salutary effects of Mackie's skepticism has been to stimulate explicit consideration of conceptions of objectivity. A distinctive conception of objectivity is suggested by Wittgenstein's later work and by certain of Davidson's writings. In this chapter I shall sketch the way in which a view about reasons for action may be in this sense objectivist, and in the next I shall go on to challenge the view that disagreement undermines an objectivism conceived along these lines. In the following three chapters I shall develop the argument for objectivism about reasons for action.

Several caveats are in order: First, I shall distinguish a certain issue about objectivity from other issues that cut across it and shall try to defend objectivism against arguments from disagreement, but I'll here take the general interest of such an objectivism for granted. I shall only argue in detail for such an objectivism in later chapters, in particular in the chapters on preference, interpretation, and subjectivism. Second, I must assume general familiarity with the views of the later Wittgenstein and of Davidson which I invoke, and shall not here offer a systematic exposition or defense of them. I assume that these views are of sufficient currency, influence, and power for the availability of a view of reasons for action that develops out of them to be of interest, although it is subject to whatever objections the original views are subject to. What I hope to show in this chapter and the next is that the view about reasons for action is not subject to a further difficulty, special to itself, on the score of disagreement. Thus, much of the expository material concerning the views of Wittgenstein and Davidson is intended to remind and highlight and interpret for present purposes, but not to initiate a novice or to bring an adamant opponent of their philosophies to his or her knees; my arguments are rather about the *connections* between their views and a certain view about reasons for action. Third, my development of a view about reasons for action out of certain views of the later Wittgenstein and of Davidson is not intended to describe a position that might be attributed to these philosophers.

At least two issues have frequently been treated as bearing on the objectivity of the values that govern action. The first, the issue of what I shall call *cognitivism*, turns on whether judgments about what should be done carry assertoric force or imperatival force, and accordingly express beliefs about the way things are that may be true or false and may, under the right conditions, constitute knowledge, or instead express attitudes of some other kind, in particular, some kind of preference. The second, the issue of what I shall call *scientific realism*, turns on whether evaluative concepts have explanatory primacy, in the sense that they are used in ideal, scientific, causal theories of the world[1], where the latter *explanandum* is understood to include our uses of evaluative concepts. If causal explanation of the world, including our uses of certain concepts, itself depends on uses of such concepts, then a realistic view, in this sense, is warranted of the subject matter of claims that use those concepts; if such concepts do not feature in ideal theories of the world, then realism is not warranted.

The issue of objectivity, in the sense I shall be concerned with, will turn out to cut across the issues of cognitivism and realism. Though denials of objectivity in this sense are often made in the wake of arguments against cognitivism or realism, when the three issues have been clearly distinguished it is not obvious why the success of such arguments should be assumed to support the denial of objectivity. And this is as it should be, since, intuitively, it seems possible to maintain the objectivity of claims about what ought to be done while admitting that such claims are conceptually tied to action, entail imperatives, express preferences, and do not employ explanatorily primary concepts. These remarks will be pursued and confirmed in later material, after the issue of objectivity has been made out (see especially section 3 of this chapter, and the chapters on cognitivism and on skepticism).

The possibility of objectivity, in the sense I am concerned with, is closely connected to an issue of conceptual priority and independence. A conceptual account of $X$ is an account of what we mean, understand, and intend ourselves to be talking or thinking about, when we talk or think about $X$. If $X$ is not correctly thus accounted for in terms of $Y$, then $X$ is conceptually independent of $Y$; if $Y$ is accounted for in terms of $X$, where $X$ is not in turn accounted for in terms of $Y$, then $X$ is both conceptually prior to and independent of $Y$. Conceptual priority and independence issues are closely related to issues about what things are and in what constitutive relationships they stand, and are contrasted with issues of epistemic priority and issues about how we can tell what things are. (To take an example that will be familiar to most philosophers, Putnam's claim that meanings aren't in the head involves denying the conceptual independence of meanings in relation to the world. It is a claim about what we mean, understand, and intend ourselves to be talking or thinking about, when we talk or think about what we mean. It also a constitutive claim, about *what it is* to mean such-and-such by the term 'water', for example. It is not a claim about how we know what we mean or understand, or how we can tell what meanings are.) To deny a claim of conceptual independence is to deny that someone could correctly understand what is postulated using one concept or set of concepts without understanding what is postulated using the other concept or set of concepts. (For example, it might be claimed that understanding what it is to mean something in particular presupposes understanding what it is to stand in certain relationships to the world.) Someone need not be invariably correct in his applications of a concept in order to be said to understand what is postulated when it is used, but he does need to be able to apply it correctly in some possible cases. So, a denial of independence involves saying that correct uses of the concepts depended on are not irrelevant to the question of whether someone understands the concept that depends. And a denial of priority need not involve an assertion of the reverse priority; the two concepts or sets of concepts may be interdependent. In most of this book, except where I indicate to the contrary (as, for example, in Chapter 15 section 3), when I talk about independence and priority I mean to be addressing issues about conceptual and constitutive relations, not epistemic relations.

A feature common to many philosophical accounts of ethical concepts is that the general concepts, such as *right* and *ought*, are taken to be conceptually prior to and independent of the specific concepts, such as *just* and *unkind*. According to such accounts, the general concepts carry a core meaning, which may be associated with either assertoric or imperatival force, that also provides the specific concepts with reason-giving status, relating, for example, to their tendency to pick out the right thing to do or to provide evidence about the right thing to do. I shall refer to accounts that take the general concepts in some category to be conceptually prior to and independent of the specific as *centralist*.[2] An example of a cognitivist version of centralism is found in the work of Ross; an example of a non-cognitivist version of centralism is found in the work of Hare.

*Non-centralism* about reasons for action rejects the view that the general concepts such as *right* and *ought* are conceptually prior to and independent of specific reason-giving concepts such as *just* and *unkind*. Instead it may take the identification of discrete specific values such as justice and kindness as a starting point, subject to revision, and give an account of the relationships of interdependence between the general concepts and specific reason-giving concepts. *Coherentist* views provide examples of non-centralism.[3] According to such a view, to say that a certain act ought to be done is to say that it is favoured by the theory, whichever it may be, that gives the best account of the relationships among the specific values that apply to the alternatives in question; such a view must, at least implicitly, characterize the conditions that must be met by a theory about the relationships among specific values.

Note in passing at this point that a non-centralist coherence account is not a form of reductionism, and that it avoids reductionism while respecting the conceptual requirement that evaluative concepts supervene on non-evaluative concepts, that is, that the former be used consistently with respect to the latter in the sense that, necessarily, if two objects are the same with respect to all relevant non-evaluative concepts, they are the same with respect to evaluative concepts as well. Indeed, a coherence account provides a natural explanation of the compatibility of supervenience and irreducibility, which some have found puzzling. Here is a sketchy preview of the explanation. According to a coherence account, to claim that a certain act ought to be done is *not* to say that it is favoured by any given theory, or to say which theory does the best job of displaying coherence, but rather that the act is favoured by the theory that best displays coherence; which theory this is must be discovered *a posteriori*, and is subject to disagreement. It is a concomitant of the theoretical status of the general concepts that they supervene on the concepts whose applications provide the subject matter of the theory in question. The best theory (or theories, in the case of a tie) cannot vary independently of what it is a theory about; to the extent it does, it does no explanatory work. If the general concepts express claims about what is required by the best theory about the relationships among specific values in the circumstances at hand, then we should expect the general concepts to supervene on specific evaluative concepts and the concepts needed to describe the circumstances in which they apply. If in turn specific evaluative concepts supervene on (or perhaps reduce to as well—I do not take a position on the issue of reductionism for specific values) non-evaluative concepts, then we should expect the general concepts to supervene on non-evaluative concepts. Supervenience is thus a mark of the theoretical, the explanatory. But since the appeal to theory does nothing in itself to answer the question of which theory is in fact the best theory, a requirement of supervenience whose source is an appeal to theory has no need of reductionist (or non-cognitivist[4]) underpinning. It is a further, substantive question, open to disagreement, which theory is the best theory, and the answer to it is not given by the appeal to the best theory, whichever that may be.

I shall not be in a position to develop the explanation of supervenience more fully until much later in the book, in the chapter on skepticism. For present purposes, of understanding the way in which a coherence account constitutes an alternative to centralism, it will be useful to explain one point more formally, by means of a scope distinction. A coherentist holds that when we say that a particular alternative would be right, it is part of what we mean that there is some theory which is the best theory about the specific values that apply to the alternatives at hand and that this theory favours a particular alternative. This claim must be distinguished from the stronger, reductionist claim that there is some theory which is the best theory about the specific values that apply to the alternatives at hand and such that, when we say that a particular alternative would be right, it is part of what we mean that it is favoured by this theory. The former claim preserves supervenience without entailing the reductionism of the latter claim by exploiting the distinction between the claim that: necessarily there is some theory such that . . . , and the claim that: there is some theory such that necessarily. . . . In each possible world there may be some theory that does the requisite job, while there is no one theory (except, perhaps, a gimmicky disjunctive theory or list of theories, which provides a "reduction" of little interest) such that in every possible world that theory does the requisite job.[5]

I'll now fill in the sketch of centralism a bit further. Consider a specimen centralist account of a specific reason-giving concept, such as *just,* in terms of a purely descriptive component, e.g., *'just'*, plus a general evaluative component *O*, representing the standard deontic operator, which carries claims about what ought to be the case.[6] The inverted commas serve to detach and suspend the evaluation carried by the concept *just,* thus to map *just* onto a co-extensive purely descriptive concept. Of course, inverted commas merely provide a means of symbolizing the purely descriptive component; if there is such a component, it must be capable of being understood other than merely as a function of the full-fledged evaluative concept.[7] This is simply to say that the notion of suspended evaluation can't be used to explicate the notion of evaluation. The general evaluative component is attached to alternatives in virtue of their purely descriptive, i.e., non-evaluative, characteristics. According to some non-cognitivist centralist accounts, the general evaluative component expresses imperatival rather than assertoric force. What makes an account centralist is not its non-cogntivism, *per se*, however, but the conceptual independence and priority it allows to the general evaluative component in relation to specific reason-giving concepts: *just,* in the example I gave, is accounted for in terms of the general *O* plus a purely descriptive component. A coherence account, by contrast, would hold the general and the specific concepts to be conceptually interdependent.

One of the attractions of centralism is that it facilitates an account of the criticism of particular ethical standards. The unparadoxical status of "It may have been rude/unchaste/unpatriotic, but it wasn't wrong" is readily accounted for if *right* and *wrong* are conceptually independent of specific values and we may freely and intelligibly attach them to whatever purely descriptive characteristics we please so long as we do so consistently. One of the challenges for non-centralism is thus to frame its account of the conceptual relationships between specific reason-giving concepts and the general concepts so as to avoid rendering such claims paradoxical. The challenge may be met, however, by the coherentist view that *right* and *wrong* reflect status under the best theory about the relationships among various values. There is no appearance of contradiction in claims to the effect that some specific value condemns an alternative but that the best theory about the relationships among all the relevant specific values does not.[8]

The crucial difference between centralism and non-centralism, then, is over the priority and independence of the general: whereas the centralist takes the general evaluative concepts to be prior to and independent of familiar specific reason-giving concepts, and explains the reason-giving status of the latter in terms of the general concepts, the non-centralist rejects this claim of priority and independence and as a result must give an account of the conceptual relationships between familiar specific reason-giving concepts and the general concepts. In the case of coherentist views in particular, the relationships in question are held to be those of subject matter and theory; in the chapter on coherence I consider precisely how these relationships should be characterized. But from the denial that the general concepts are prior it doesn't follow that the specific must be prior, any more than it follows that data must be entirely independent of theory because theory is not independent of data. Data may be theory-laden; reflective equilibrium may be wide; the specific and the general concepts may be interdependent.

So far I've claimed that the issues of cognitivism and realism are distinct from the issue of objectivism, and that the latter is closely related to the issue of centralism. But I haven't said *how* centralism and objectivism are related. In a sense the rest of this chapter and the next four will be taken up with saying how they are related. But a nutshell account at this point will help to follow the details to come.

There is *something* plausible about the view that there is a conceptual link between the general evaluative concepts and preferences; one, non-cognitivist, version of this view holds that the general evaluative concepts serve to express preferences. (There is more on what is plausible about this view and on non-cognitivism to follow, in section 3 of this chapter and in the chapters on subjectivism and cognitivism. I shall suggest that the appeal of the view that there is a conceptual link can be secured within cognitivism.) Now non-cognitivism does not entail centralism. But if we do combine the non-cognitivist view that the general concepts express preferences with centralism (as is commonly done), we get *subjectivism* about reasons for action: the view that preferences are prior to and independent of specific values, and indeed, in some way, determine values. *Objectivism* about reasons for action is the denial of subjectivism: the denial that preferences determine values or are prior to or independent of values. Thus a coherence account is a version of objectivism, one which holds, by contrast to subjectivism, that preferences and values are, as a constitutive matter, interdependent. (Note that we can deny subjectivism without denying non-cognitivism, if we instead deny the centralist claim about the conceptual independence of preferences from values; I shall discuss this possible kind of objectivism in section 3.)

The *contrary* priority, independence and determination claims, namely, that values are prior to, independent of, and determining with respect to preferences, I shall refer to, in so far as I do at all, as *Platonism*. Platonism is strictly speaking a kind of objectivism, but when I mean Platonism I shall call it that; when I speak of objectivism I shall *not* mean Platonism. Of all the possible objectivist positions available in the logical space left by the denial of subjectivism, Platonism is one of the least tempting. Hardly anyone holds it, there is little point in arguing against it, and there is not very much to say about it. Any subjectivists who take it to be their most serious opposition are wasting their time on a straw man, and underestimating the strength of their objectivist opposition. The interdependence doctrine with which I associate objectivism rejects the conception of preference or value as independent of the other, a conception which gives rise to the issue between subjectivism and Platonism and which they share; it holds that subjectivism and Platonism are equally wrong in this respect. This rejection may be viewed as part of the rejection of a larger conception of the relations between the mind and the world which gives rise to a host of traditional skeptical challenges and counter-moves.[9] But I argue against subjectivism, and assume that in ethics, at least, Platonism is not a live option, so that the case for an interdependence doctrine is made out by making out a case against subjectivism. (If anyone objects to my pre-empting the term "objectivism" in this way, and would prefer that it be reserved for what I call "Platonism", I do not mind having the issues I am concerned with systematically relabelled. It is the substance of the interdependence view for which I am arguing, rather than its label.)

## 2. Parallels: Centralism About Colour, Law, and Logic, and Some Prelimary Doubts

We can compare centralism about reasons for action to several other kinds of centralism, including centralism about colours, law and logic, in order to realize that the issue about centralism is not as obscure or unfamiliar as it may seem at first. The immediate appeal of centralism about reasons, whether ethical, legal, or logical, is perhaps stronger than that of centralism about colour. But there are certain familiar grounds for doubt even about centralism about reasons. I shall make a few preliminary comments as I set out the parallels to convey, unsystemically, some of these grounds for doubt and to set the context for later discussions. Then in the following section I shall begin considering the way in which arguments of Wittgenstein and Davidson can be applied to oppose certain centralist positions, the possibility of analogous opposition to centralism about reasons for action, and its relation to objectivism.

First, consider the parallel for colours. Centralism about colours would hold that the general concept of colour is prior to and independent of specific colour concepts. Consider an account of specific colour concepts like *red* and *green* that represents their colour-giving status by means of a general colour-giving component of their meaning that's prior to and independent of particular colour concepts. Let applying inverted commas to a specific colour concept such as *red* produce a non-colour description (in terms of wavelengths, say) co-extensive with *red*, in the way that applying inverted commas to *just* produced '*just*'. Thus, centralism would account for what it is for an object to be red in terms of its being 'red' plus its being the case that anything that is 'red' has what human beings under the right conditions experience as coloured.

What motivation might there be for centralism about colours? The inverted commas suggest a kind of detached reflectiveness about the ability to perceive colour directly, a savvy awareness of the secondary status of colour concepts and their conceptual ties to experience. Perhaps what we mean when we talk about colours does reflect their secondary status. However, a centralist account of colours reflects their secondary status in a particular way: it doesn't leave at large the contribution to being red that is made by the perceptual apparatus that happens to be sensitive to colour, but rather rounds it up and isolates it in the colour-giving component. Thus, if the goal is to reflect the secondary status of colour concepts, centralism constitutes overkill. We may grant as a general thesis about colour that an object of any colour must have a tendency to produce experiences as of that colour in normal people under normal conditions; if they didn't they wouldn't be objects of that colour. (Similarly, we may grant that there is something plausible in the view that there are conceptual links between the general evaluative concepts and preferences.) But we can grant this without admitting that the character of an experience *as of colour* is independent of the various specific colour concepts of red, yellow, blue, etc. (Similarly, the admission that there are conceptual links between the general evaluative concepts and preferences doesn't entail centralism.) This is to say that the secondariness of colour concepts does not determine the issue about colour centralism. Despite our having learned that specific colours are associated with positions on a single spectrum of wavelengths, to say that something is red, yellow, or blue isn't simply to assign it status and degree in respect of some unitary quality of experience as of colour; nor can the qualitative distinctions and relationships among specific colours be understood in terms of some general colour-giving status. Our understanding of what it is to be coloured isn't independent of our understanding of discrete specific colours such as red, yellow, and blue, and of the relationships among them that, for example, make it possible to combine primary colours such as red and blue to get secondary colours such as purple and impossible for there to be such a colour as purplish-yellow. Indeed, it's in terms of such relationships that we're able to conceive of the possibility of unfamiliar colours and to consider on what grounds we might attribute experiences of them.[10] (I shall say more about this possibility in the next chapter.)

Consider next the parallel for law. Legal centralism would hold the general concept of law to be prior to and independent of specific legal concepts and associated principles, as determined by various specific legal practices, such as those of contract. We can follow the centralist recipe to get an account of specific legal concepts. A centralist account of a legal concept such as *contract*, for example, would represent its status as providing reason for a legal decision one way or another in terms of a general concept of law that is prior to and independent of specific legal concepts, principles, and associated practices, perhaps in terms of the endorsement of rules by something like Hart's rule of recognition. Let applying inverted commas to a specific concept like *contract* produce a legally neutral co-extensive concept or behavioural rule. Thus centralism might account for what it is for there to be a contract in terms of satisfaction of the rule setting out conditions for a 'contract' plus endorsement of that rule by the rule of recognition.[11]

Consider the following claims made in opposition to legal centralism. Understanding of the general concept of law requires understanding of at least some specific legal concepts and associated practices. Correspondingly, recognition of certain substantive principles as binding on courts is direct and doesn't depend on recognition of some central reason-giving status, such as having been endorsed by a rule of recognition. A judgment of law that's backed by a rule of recognition may at the same time be accountable to specific legal practices that have not been validated by the master rule but are nonetheless legal practices. So the general conception of law in terms of a rule of recognition is alloyed by its accountability to specific legal practices, and can't be identified with the reason-giving status of the concepts these practices determine. If, on the other hand, the general reason-giving component is extended so as to apply to customary practices as well, it avoids adulteration at the price of redundancy.

These points are familiar from Ronald Dworkin's discussion of H. L. A. Hart's version of legal positivism. Dworkin considers Hart's view in application to difficult cases such as the *Riggs* and *Henningson* cases, in which the court cites principles as its justification for adopting and applying a new rule. As Dworkin explains, the *Riggs* court cited the principle that no one may profit from his own wrongdoing in justifying a new interpretation of the statute of wills; the *Henningson* court cited several intersecting principles and policies in justifying a new rule about manufacturer's liability for automobile defects.[12] According to Hart, rules of law are valid because they have been validated by a rule of recognition, which is itself not valid, but merely accepted. Dworkin objects:

> But this test of pedigree will not work for the *Riggs* and *Henningson* principles. The origin of these as legal principles lies not in a particular decision of some legislature or court, but in a sense of appropriateness developed in the profession and the public over time. Their continued power depends on this sense of appropriateness being sustained. If it no longer seemed unfair to allow people to profit by their wrongs, or fair to place special burdens upon oligopolies that manufacture potentially dangerous machines, these principles would no longer play much of a role in new cases, even if they had never been overruled or repealed.... Hart does say that a master rule might designate as law not only rules enacted by particular legal institutions, but rules established by custom as well.... Many of our most ancient legal rules were never explicitly created by a legislature or a court. When they made their first appearance in legal opinions and texts, they were treated as already being part of the law because they represented the customary practices of the community, or some specialized part of it, like the business community. (The examples ordinarily given are rules of mercantile practice, like the rules governing what rights arise under a standard form of commercial

paper.) . . . The master rule, Hart says, might stipulate that some custom counts as law even before the courts recognize it. But he does not face the difficulty this raises for his general theory because he does not attempt to set out the criteria a master rule might use for this purpose. It cannot use, as its only criterion, the provision that the community regard the practices as morally binding, for this would not distinguish legal customary rules from moral customary rules, and of course not all of the community's long-standing customary moral obligations are enforced at law. If, on the other hand, the test is whether the community regards the customary practice as legally binding, the whole point of the master rule is undercut, at least for this class of legal rules. The master rule, says Hart, marks the transformation from a primitive society to one with law, because it provides a test for determining social rules of law other than by measuring their acceptance. But if the master rule says merely that whatever other rules the community accepts as legally binding are legally binding, then it provides no such test at all, becomes (for these cases ) a non-rule of recognition; we might as well say that every primitive society has a secondary rule of recognition, namely the rule that whatever is accepted as binding is binding.[13]

Finally, consider the parallel for logic. A logically valid inference preserves truth in moving from premises to conclusion: if the premises are true and the inference is valid, the conclusion is true. However, there are various specific kinds of valid inference. For example, when we infer from the premises "$p$" and if "$p$ then $q$" to the conclusion "$q$", we're following the rule known as *modus ponens*. Logical centralism would hold the general concept of validity, or truth-preservingness, to be prior to and independent of specific logical characterizations of inferences such as " . . . is a case of *modus ponens*". Consider an account of the specific characterization " . . . is a case of *modus ponens*" that represents its status as validating inferences in terms of a general concept of validity or truth-preservingness that's conceptually prior to and independent of specific characterizations of inferences. This general concept of validity might be held, by a conventionalist, for example, to express the community's conventional endorsement of all instances of a certain neutrally described inference pattern. Let applying inverted commas to a specific logical characterization of an inference, say, as a case of *modus ponens*, produce a semantically neutral co-extensive characterization in purely syntactic terms. Then centralism would account for what it is for an inference to be a case of *modus ponens* in terms of its satisfying the rule for '*modus ponens*' plus endorsement of whatever satisfies that rule by the convention that determines the central concept of validity.

Wittgenstein's view that meanings are determined by practices, applied to the logical constants and to mathematical concepts, leads to what Crispin Wright describes as the doctrine of the antecedence of logic and mathematics to truth, which entails the denial of such logical centralism. According to the antecedence doctrine, "there is . . . no content to the idea of something's really being a consequence of some set of statements over and above its following from them by our procedures of inference"; "there is no ulterior concept of correct inference lurking behind our actual procedures of inference to which they are answerable."[14] Thus Wittgenstein writes:

> The steps which are not brought in question are logical inferences. But the reason why they are not brought in question is not that they 'certainly correspond to the truth'—or something of the sort,—no, it is just this that is called 'thinking', 'speaking', 'inferring', 'arguing'. There is not any question at all here of some correspondence between what is said and reality; rather is logic antecedent to any such correspondence; in the same sense, that is, in which the establishment of a method of measurement is antecedent to the correctness or incorrectness of a statement of length.
>
> —"But isn't there a truth corresponding to logical inference? Isn't it true that this follows from that?"
>
> —The proposition: "It is true that this follows from that" means simply: this follows from that.
>
> ... 'calculating right' ... means calculating like *this*.[15]

While the doctrine that logic is antecedent to truth entails the denial of logical centralism, Wittgenstein does not restrict the view that practices determine meanings to the meanings of logical and mathematical concepts; indeed, the view extends to contents in general. The view that practices determine contents admits of no residue or slack in terms of which a practice can be challenged or justified solely by applications of the very concept whose content it determines: "If you measure a table with a yardstick, are you also measuring the yardstick? If you are measuring the yardstick, then you cannot be measuring the table at the same time."[16] The question does not arise whether our conceptual scheme, our determination of meanings corresponds to the facts conceived as including not only the objects we talk about but also whatever it is we can truthfully say about them.[17] It does not arise because it is no part of a defensible theory of objective truth and correspondence that "meanings take care of themselves", in independence from their contexts, in particular, our practices.[18]

> The words "right" and "wrong" are used when giving instruction in proceeding according to a rule. The word "right" makes the pupil go on, the word "wrong" holds him back. Now could one explain these rules to a pupil by saying instead: "this agrees with the rule—that not"? Well yes, if he has a concept of agreement. But what if this has yet to be formed? (The point is how he reacts to the word "agree".)
>
> One does not learn to obey a rule by first learning the use of the word "agreement".
>
> Rather, one learns the meaning of "agreement" by learning to follow a rule.[19]

On this generalized non-centralist view, it makes no sense to suppose that there is some criterion of using an expression in the same way that is independent of all our various specific ways of going on in particular environments, some standard of meaning the same thing which is independent of all our context-embedded practices and to which they strive to conform.[20]

### 3. Wittgensteinian and Davidsonian Arguments Applied Against Centralism, and How the Issue About Centralism Cuts Across the Issue About Cognitivism

In the rest of this and several following chapters I shall try to explain how a conception of reasons for action as objective is connected with resolution of the issue about centralism in a Wittgensteinian spirit, namely, in favour of non-centralism about reasons for action. In doing so I shall be drawing out the implications of the thought that the way in which meaning guides linguistic utterances may fruitfully be regarded as a special case of the way in which reasons guide intentional action more generally. Thus I shall be trying to apply Wittgenstein's considerations about the way in which meanings are determined and their normative relation to linguistic action in particular to the way in which reasons in general are determined and their normative relation to action in general. I shall also pursue the analogy Davidson suggests between the problem of the interdependence of belief and meaning in interpreting linguistic action and the problem of the interdependence of belief and desire in interpreting action in general. And I shall draw connections between the Wittgensteinian and Davidsonian concerns: The conception of objectivity that emerges is represented by a generalized principle of charity; I address the problem that disagreement poses for a Wittgensteinian view of reasons for action by interpreting the need for agreement in form of life in terms of the necessary role of charity.[21]

The way in which considerations about meaning and its relation to belief may be applied to questions about desire and its relation to belief is brought out by considering how non-cognitivism may be compatible with non-centralism. The view that, as a conceptual matter, claims about what ought to be done entail imperatives, express attitudes toward action which are preferences rather than beliefs, does not settle the further question, of what the relationship is of this whole conceptual complex (of what ought to be done, preference and action) to specific values. As noted above, since the combination of centralism and non-cognitivism yields subjectivism, one could reject subjectivism by rejecting its centralist component rather than its non-cognitivist component (though ultimately I shall come down against non-cognitivism as well, for reasons not discussed until Chapter 9). Consider the way in which this claim might be developed.

Michael Dummett has suggested that there is an alternative to the interpretation of Wittgenstein as denying "the idea, common to most philosophers who have written about meaning, that the theory of meaning has some one key concept", "that there is some one feature of a sentence which may be identified as determining its meaning." The alternative is the less radical view that Wittgenstein does not reject the idea that there is a key concept, but takes "the key concept not to lie, as it were, on the side of the grounds for an utterance, as do the concepts of truth, verification, confirmation, etc., but, rather, on that of its consequences. To know the meaning of a sentence, on such a theory, would be to know what the conventional consequences of uttering it are, both in the sense of the appropriate response, linguistic and non-linguistic, to it by the hearers, and in that of what the speaker commits himself to by uttering it."[22]

Similarly, the view that reason-giving concepts are unified by their consequences, for example, by the entailment of imperatives, at least under certain conditions, might be urged as an alternative to the rejection of centralism about reasons for action altogether. Of course the view that reason-giving concepts entail imperatives may take a centralist form. It doesn't have to, however; a non-centralist need not deny that reason-giving concepts entail imperatives which express attitudes toward action. What follows, however, is that the very concept of action that informs expressions of imperatival force is not conceptually prior to and independent of specific reason-giving concepts.

But this is not a surprising or outlandish view. Indeed, it runs parallel in certain respects to views that are familiar in the philosophical literature. Those already acquainted with some of the relevant literature will perhaps be best able to see the parallels if we first roughly set out the motivation for the view in several stages, which will be elaborated and refined upon in later chapters. I shall first given an exceedingly abstract and programmatic three-stage sketch of the strategy, which will then be partially illustrated at once, and will eventually be illustrated many times over in succeeding chapters. Those not at all familiar with the background literature may not find the sketch helpful, and may have to wait on the illustrations that follow. In the three-stage sketch that follows here, and throughout later chapters, we shall be trying to map out several sets of interconnected relationships: between what ought to be done, all things considered, action and preference (the issue of cognitivism); between what ought to be done, all things considered, and specific values (the issue of centralism); between action, preference, belief, meaning, i.e., the mind, and natural and social environments, i.e., the world (issues about objectivity and the dependence or independence of mind and world); and between the world and values (issues about ethical realism and ethical skepticism). (See Figure 2.1.)

*First*, we reject the assumption that the concept of intentional action is primitive and unproblematic in a way that, say, linguistic action in particular is not. As persons, we interpret the world in order to understand events as intentional action, expressive of preference, no less than we interpret the world in order to understand events as linguistic action, expressive of belief. As Christopher Peacocke writes: "Preferences as expressed in behaviour yield actions, that is, token events: and these token events, being each one an instance of ever so many types, in advance of a theory of interpretation give no clue as to the type (or indeed believed type) for which the behaviour expresses preference."[23] We *are* capable of interpreting token events as action,

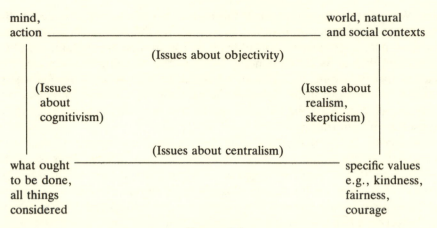

FIGURE 2.1

that is, of coming to understand them as expressive of beliefs, desires, and intentions with determinate content, but how do we do it? How is it determined what type of action a token event is? Intentional action in general is no more self-interpreting than linguistic action in particular is, and a parallel problem arises as to how radical underdetermination, or indeterminacy, of interpretation is avoided. Some of the details of the way in which this problem arises for preference and action in the context of decision theory are presented in the chapter on preference.

As we shall see, Wittgenstein and Davidson share an absolutely sharp appreciation of questions about how the contents of the mind are determined, and of the inadequacy of various popular answers, especially in terms of experience. Both relentlessly avoid the temptation to postulate self-interpreting entities of any kind to solve the problems. Indeed, they seem to have most in common at this first, negative stage; Wittgenstein's positive suggestions as to how the problems are to be overcome are far harder to pin down (though, as I shall argue, they seem to anticipate certain of Davidson's views). What is clear is that Wittgenstein's appeals to practices to determine contents cannot charitably be interpreted to have overlooked the point that action is no more self-interpreting than linguistic action or anything else. If practices are conceived as somehow self-interpreting, they will be subject to all the same objections he brings against other candidate determinants of contents, such as particular feelings or experiences, sense data, etc.

Practices do the trick, for Wittgenstein, not because they are self-interpreting—*nothing* is—but because they are conceived as essentially identified in relation to their contexts, the agent's natural and social environments. An intention, he remarks, "is embedded in its situation, in human customs and institutions"; "what, in a complicated surrounding, we call "following a rule", we should certainly not call that if it stood in isolation"; "we refer by the phrase 'understanding a word' not necessarily to that which happens while we are saying or hearing it, but to the whole environment of the event of

saying it."[24] The constitutive engagement of practices with the world constrains interpretation, thus making it possible; such constraint is not itself the
product of interpretation. "There is a way of grasping a rule which is not
interpretation"[25], not because interpretation has no role to play—it is itself
one of our practices—but because it must be subject to at least partially
exogenous constraints in order to be possible at all. The *second* stage of the
parallel, then, is the stage at which agents' normal relations to their natural
and social environments are invoked as constitutive constraints on interpretation; psychology is naturalized, and the mind and action are conceived as
essentially world-involving; this stage is the focus of the chapter on interpretation, below. The second stage, in a sense, constitutes a diagnosis of the
problem faced at the first stage: its source is the supposed independence
of mind from world. Reject this supposition, and you trade mythical self-
interpreting entities on the mental side, which fail to solve the problem, for
the constitutive engagement of the mind with the world, which prevents the
problem from arising to begin with by providing constraints on interpretation.
As Davidson puts it, "we can't in general first identify beliefs and meanings
and then ask what caused them. The causality plays an indispensable role in
determining the content of what we say and believe".[26] We've now made the
transition from appreciation of the problem to a gesture toward its solution.

To use terminology made familiar by Tyler Burge, the second stage of
argument leads to the rejection of *psychological individualism*, about intention
and preference as well as belief and meaning.[27] Individualism holds that there
is no necessary, constitutive, individuative relationship between the contents
of someone's mind and what someone does, on the one hand, and the character of his natural or social environments, on the other; an individual's mental
states and actions are conceptually independent of the world. Thus the problem arises of how his mind and the world ever manage to connect up, so that
his mental states represent determinate states of the world and his acts are
of determinate types. With the problem comes the temptation to offer spurious
solutions by assuming intermediate entities at some point along the way that
are magically self-interpreting and thus evade the indeterminacy problem.
Note that, while at the second stage individualism is ruled out, it is ruled out
as a consequence of rejecting the indepedence of mind from world. A socialized version of the independence view might avoid individualism but ultimately would not keep the problem from arising again in socialized form,
as a consequence of the collective independence of mind from world. For
Davidson, however, no element of the basic triangle of agent-speaker(s),
interpreter(s), and world can be omitted. Thus Davidson's way of rejecting
the independence of mind from world entails but is more radical than the
rejection of individualism by itself, as Davidson's view would also entail
rejection of a socialized version of the dualism of mind and world.[28] I think
that to the extent Wittgenstein is attracted to the view that social practices
play an important role in determining contents, this is as a consequence of a
conception of practice, activities, and capacities in general as world-
embedded, as identified in terms of their worldly roles, causes, effects, and
functions, and, more generally still, of a position quite close in important

respects to Davidson's more explicit rejection of the independence of mind from world. Only the latter more radical moves will keep Wittgenstein's main problem about rule-following from arising again in relation to practices. Thus it will be beside the point to criticize Wittgenstein, or interpretations of him, for appealing to social practices to solve his problem, while not recognizing the radical source of the appeal. The second stage will be elaborated in the chapter on interpretation.[29]

Granted that the individuation of the contents of preferences and intentions is no more world-independent than that of meanings and beliefs, we still have to see what the relation of preference and action to value is, i.e., to address the issue of subjectivism. This latter issue is the focus of the *third* notional stage of argument, and of the chapter below on subjectivism, in which I view the value-ladenness of preference as a species of the world-ladenness of the mind in general. Consider the question whether theories of interpretation necessarily depend on constitutive normative constraints on the contents of the attitudes in question. A familiar answer is given by, among others, David Lewis, who explains that a principle of charity constrains the relationship between the agent as a physical system (described in terms of bodily movements and the like, not yet in terms of his intentional actions) and the attitudes we ascribe to him: he "should be represented as believing what he ought to believe, and desiring what he ought to desire. And what is that? In our opinion, he ought to believe what we believe, or perhaps what we would have believed in his place; and he ought to desire what we desire, or perhaps what we would have desired in his place. (But that's only our opinion! Yes. Better we should go by an opinion we don't hold?)"[30]

On this kind of view, the concepts of preference and intentional action, rather like those of meaning, belief, and linguistic action and unlike those of bodily motion and brain processes, are normatively constrained concepts; susceptibility to the influence of certain reasons or values[31] is a constitutive feature of intentional action, intelligible in terms of the agent's beliefs and preferences, in the somewhat the same sort of way that susceptibility to the influence of truth-related reasons is a constitutive feature of linguistic action, intelligible in terms of the speaker's beliefs and meanings. (I say "somewhat" because the constraints on preference must be loose enough to accommodate conflict among the reasons and values governing action, akratic action, as well as disagreement between persons about how such conflict should be resolved, as discussed in the chapters on interpretation and subjectivism; I shall argue in the chapters on conflict and *akrasia* that the constraints on belief are not exactly parallel to those on preference in these respects.) If this view is correct, we should expect that just as the interpretation of a particular linguistic action as deviant, reflecting an unfamiliar concept or an intention to deceive, is parasitic on charity at large, so interpretation of a particular intentional action as deviant, reflecting an unfamiliar value or an intention that gerrymanders familiar reasons, is parasitic on charity at large.

As indicated, I shall only argue fully for a thus value-laden conception of preference and action in the chapters on preference, interpretation, and subjectivism that follow. Moreover, the full argument against subjectivism will make important use of the higher-order attitudes characteristic of persons, the role of which I do not attempt to sketch here. Here my purpose is merely to convey the gist of the argument so as to help make out the conception of objectivity in question. The general strategy of argument is suggested by Davidson's comments on Ramsey's proposal about the roles of belief and preference in the interpretation of behaviour, which provides the preliminary illustration that immediately follows.

First, the problem. Davidson holds that "an event is an action if and only if it can be described in a way that makes it intentional". We interpret an agent's behaviour as action by ascribing beliefs and preferences to the agent in terms of which it may be understood as intentional; happenings that cannot be rendered intelligible in this way do not count as actions. However, the possibility of rendering action intelligible by ascribing beliefs and preferences to agents requires that we have some way in principle of sorting out the contribution of beliefs to determining behaviour from the contribution of preferences; many possible combinations of beliefs and preferences could explain the same behaviour. Holding behaviour constant, we can infer beliefs from preferences or preferences from beliefs; but since behaviour is "the resultant of both factors, how can either factor be derived . . . until the other is known?"[32]

Ramsey's proposal is that we can tell that someone believes an event is as likely to happen as not if he is indifferent about whether an attractive or an unattractive outcome is tied to it.[33] For example, his behaviour may reveal his indifference between option 1 and option 2:

|  | Option 1 | Option 2 |
|---|---|---|
| If it rains, you get: | $10 | nothing |
| If it doesn't rain, you get: | nothing | $10 |

Having fixed the agent's belief about the probability of this one event, the theory goes, we can use it to measure his preferences, and then fill in his other beliefs.

However, built into Ramsey's proposal that someone believes an event is as likely to happen as not if he is indifferent between option 1 and option 2 is the assumption that the attractiveness of the outcomes used to construct the options does not vary with the occurrence of the event. Consider option 3 and option 4:

|  | Option 3 | Option 4 |
|---|---|---|
| If it rains, you get: | an umbrella | no umbrella |
| If it doesn't rain, you get: | no umbrella | an umbrella |

If we assume that an umbrella is more attractive to someone if it rains than if it doesn't, then his indifference between option 3 and option 4 does not suggest that he believes it is as likely to rain as not to rain, but that he believes it is more likely not to rain. This assumption is natural to make, but any behavioural basis for it that doesn't in turn depend on other assumptions about the contents of the agent's preferences is obscure.[34] If we are able to control whether it rains or not and we give the subject instead a choice between an umbrella and rain and an umbrella and no rain, can we still be trying to determine his beliefs about whether it will rain or not? If we make this assumption, we arrive at a different description of the agent's indifference: it is indifference between a small chance of winning the prize when it would be more needed and a large chance of winning it when it would be less needed, rather than indifference between equal chances of winning it in each of two cases when it would be equally useful. In order to apply Ramsey's method of interpreting behaviour we must already be making assumptions about what is attractive to the agent, namely, that the options we construct to determine his beliefs are like options 1 and 2 and not like options 3 and 4.[35]

Second, the general form of the solution. Davidson claims that "if we are intelligibly to attribute attitudes and beliefs, or usefully to describe motions as behaviour, then we are committed to finding, in the pattern of behaviour, belief, and desire, a large degree of rationality and consistency".[36] The nature of the assumptions we must make in order to apply Ramsey's method of ascribing beliefs and preferences and hence to entitle ourselves to apply the concept of action to certain happenings warrants a strong interpretation of this claim. We must make assumptions about the content of the agent's preferences as well as their consistency; the solution to the problem involves embracing this necessity. That is, the interpretation of action is dependent on a non-optional principle of charity that reaches to the substantive rationality of desires as well as to their consistency.[37] Finally, moreover, it is natural for values to influence what counts as substantive rationality; that is, in conceiving of happenings as action, we naturally make assumptions about the agent's susceptibility to the influence of various specific values. As Davidson writes, in interpreting someone's action we "will try for a theory that finds him consistent, a believer of truths, and a lover of the good (all by our own lights, it goes without saying)".[38]

Davidson urges that the problem of the interdependence of belief and preferences in interpreting action has an analogue in the problem of the interdependence of meaning and belief in interpreting utterances, and that the latter problem is to be solved by assigning meanings to alien sentences "that make native speakers right as often as plausibly possible, according, of course, to our own view of what is right." Charity here reaches to substance as well, in that it imports our conception of truth and truth-related reasons for belief into the enterprise of ascribing meaningful assertions to others. Davidson cautions:

The methodological advice to interpret in a way that optimizes agreement should not be conceived as resting on a charitable assumption about human intelligence that might turn out to be false. If we cannot find a way to interpret the utterances and other behaviour of a creature as revealing a set of beliefs largely consistent and true by our own standards, we have no reason to count that creature as rational, as having beliefs, or as saying anything.[39]

We might hold, similarly, that the charitable ascription of preferences informed by familiar specific reasons in interpreting the behaviour of other people does not rest on an assumption about human motivation that could turn out to be false. On such a view, the concept of preference as applied to persons, like that of belief, is essentially value-laden; the will, like the intelligence, can fall short only against the right sort of background, recognition of which is a condition of conceiving someone as a rational agent at all.

Thus, the non-cognitivist view that claims about what ought to be done entail imperatives, which express attitudes toward action, does not rule out the view that the very concept of intentional action we invoke in deploying imperatival force is responsible to a set of specific reasons, or values; decentralization might proceed through action to imperatival force itself. Even without abandoning the former view, then, we may abandon subjectivism, along with the centralist independence and priority claims. (However, there are further reasons for abandoning the non-cognitivist view of the conceptual link between ethical concepts and expressions of preference, as I shall argue in Chapter 9.) Even if there are conceptual links between the general ethical concepts and preference, rejection of the centralist view that the general concepts are independent of specific evaluative concepts amounts to rejection of the subjectivist view that prior and independent preferences determine values.

Note that one can be an objectivist about the relation between preference and values without being committed to scientific realism about either preference or values, i.e., to the view that either propositions about preference or about values feature in ideal, scientific, causal explanations. The conceptual indeterdependence thesis about preference and value is only committed to the claim that, at whatever point for purposes of the realism issue personal preferences and values arrive in the world, they arrive together. Persons' preferences don't exist independently of values and in turn determine values. (The references to persons are needed to respect the role in my later arguments against subjectivism of the higher-order attitudes characteristic of persons; see Chapter 6.)

To claim that the general concept of what ought to be done, all things considered, is not conceptually prior to and independent of specific reason-giving concepts such as *just* and *unkind*, is to claim in effect that what ought to be done, all things considered, stands in some relationship to specific reasons, or values, that is constitutive, not merely epistemic, in nature. Thus, while non-centralism allows that our concepts give us the freedom to deny, for example, that one ought to do the just thing, it does imply that our freedom is limited. The theory about specific reasons postulated by a coherence account may be represented by a function, so that what ought to be done, all things considered, is, as a conceptual matter, some function of the specific reasons that apply to the alternatives at issue. Thus, in order to deny that one ought to do what a particular reason demands, one must still depend in some way on those specific reasons. The concept of what one ought to do does not afford a content to the denials of the external skeptic, who wishes to express global or arbitrary doubts from a standpoint outside the entire system of specific reasons, but only to those of the internal skeptic, whose doubts operate within the system of specific reasons.[40] The limitation is not avoided by insistence on some form of conceptual link between claims about what ought to be done and action, as the concept of intentional action itself may not be conceptually independent of specific reasons: if charity is not an option in interpreting events as intentional action by attributing meanings, beliefs, and preferences, then the concept of objective reasons for action, no less than "the concepts of objective truth, and of error, necessarily emerge in the context of interpretation."[41]

### 4. A Coherence Account and the Threats of Overdetermination and of Indeterminacy

What can we say about the function from specific reasons to what one ought to do, all things considered, whose existence is implied by a non-centralist coherence account? What properties should it have? Are they consistent with one another, so as to avoid the possibility, in effect, of overdetermination? A skeptic about what ought to be done, all things considered, may raise this threat, which will be addressed later in the book, in the chapter on coherence. There I shall argue that what at first looks an alarmingly strong case for their inconsistency, and hence for the non-existence of such a function, does not in the end succeed. As a result we can at least make the cautious claim that, if efforts to show that such a function does not exist fail, then an obstacle to believing that there is such as thing as what one ought to do, all things considered, that there are right answers to questions about what ought to be done, has been removed. In this sense, by proceeding from a non-centralist position we may provide resistance to ethical skepticism.

However, another threat must be avoided if we are to make out an objectivist position, a threat of radical underdetermination, or indeterminacy. Even if we agree that a function from specific reasons to all-things-considered evaluations must meet certain conditions and that the existence of a function that meets those conditions is not threatened, we nevertheless disagree widely in our all-things-considered evaluations, or, according to a non-centralist coherence account, about which of the possible functions that meet these conditions constitutes the best theory about the relationships among the relevant specific reasons in the circumstances at hand. Moreover, we may not even agree about which specific reasons are in play. What, then, guarantees that we are seeking the same thing to begin with? Isn't the attempt to found a decentralized account of what one ought to do, all things considered, on Wittgensteinian considerations vitiated by this disagreement? After all, it is a central tenet of the philosophy of the later Wittgenstein that "the practice has to speak for itself".[42] Can the Wittgensteinian conception of practices, in virtue of which we are able to use words with determinate meaning, accommodate the disagreement that is characteristic of issues about what one ought to do so as to allow us to be talking about the same thing, even though we disagree? If not, the existence of a function that meets the agreed-on conditions will not be enough to support the view that there are right answers; those who appear to be disagreeing about the right answer to a question would in fact be answering different questions. The challenge is to defend our right to regard certain of our practices as expressive of open-ended theoretical disagreement, rather than of theoretical indeterminacy. I emphasize, however, that the threat of indeterminacy that I will be concerned to resist is that of radical theoretical indeterminacy, based on a certain kind of *a priori* skepticism. It is not the mere possibility of moderate occasional *a posteriori* underdetermination, which I do not regard as a threat to the very point or rationality of theoretical activity and disagreement, and which is an hypothesis that must be supported in particular cases by engaging in the relevant practice of theorizing to the extent necessary to support a view of the equal actual and projected success of particular theories. The following chapter will address the threat of indeterminacy while further developing the sense in which a non-centralist position constitutes a kind of objectivism.

# 3

# Disagreement

## 1. A Coherence Account and the Locus of Disagreement

The concepts that provide us with reasons for action permit us to communicate, disagree, and sometimes even argue across the boundaries between paradigms of the good life for human beings. Members of different cultures or subcultures may in normal circumstances participate in rather different specific reason-giving practices, and yet they do stand substantively opposed to one another when one claims that an action is right and another claims that it is wrong. Thus, as Bernard Williams has put it, there must be some element of their claims "which can be identified as the *locus* of exclusivity", such that they are not from every point of view incommensurable.[1] How is this *locus* of substantive disagreement to be accounted for?

On a centralist view of reason-giving concepts, disagreement is located in some general evaluative concept that is prior to and independent of specific reason-giving concepts. But on the non-centralist view that the general evaluative concepts are not prior to the specific and that claims about what ought to be done, all things considered, are claims about the relationships among specific values, if one creature does not possess the specific reason-giving concepts of another, then the minimal element of conceptual congruence that is a prerequisite of substantive disagreement between them may fail to obtain. Non-centralism claims that there are conceptual connections between claims about what ought to be done, all things considered, and a list of certain familiar specific values; the sense of *ought* that is a function of the specific values on the list can be used to challenge and revise views about the relationships among those values, but it cannot be used to endorse an entirely unfamiliar list. Thus, non-centralism threatens to deprive us of a sense in which to disagree about things we seem to want to disagree about. In what sense can we disagree with someone who does not share our specific reason-giving practices? Even if someone does share our specific reason-giving practices, in what sense are we talking about the same thing when we disagree about what ought to be done, all things considered, when our specific values conflict?[2]

36

## 2. Disagreement in Form of Life and Substantive Disagreement

Wittgenstein suggests that a certain kind of disagreement, disagreement in form of life, precludes the use of language as a means of communication. He illustrates disagreement in form of life by describing people who go through motions that are puzzling in the following way: while we can understand the descriptions, which contain no hidden contradictions, and thus we must admit that what is described is possible, we cannot understand what reason anyone could have to act in the particular ways described. The procedures described do not make sense, and yet we are reluctant to dismiss them as perverse or idiotic. Disagreement in form of life is not substantive disagreement, which is a kind of communication, but lack of conceptual common ground; it precludes substantive disagreement by ruling out the possibility of identifying what a particular dispute is about in a manner common to the different forms of life.[3]

According to Barry Stroud, the point of Wittgenstein's examples of peculiar behaviour is to show "only that 'the formation of concepts different from the usual ones' is intelligible to us; but it does not follow from this that those concepts themselves are intelligible to us". The possibilities of language and communication, calculation and inference depend on certain contingent facts, such as the fact that we have certain mathematical and logical concepts, that we naturally continue a series or go on from examples in certain ways. But

> ... we can understand and acknowledge the contingency of this fact, and hence the possibility of different ways of calculating, and so forth, without understanding what those different ways might have been. If so, then it does not follow that those rules by which calculating, and so forth, might have been carried out constitute a set of genuine alternatives open to us among which we could choose, or even among which we could have chosen.[4]

Stroud suggests that the possibility of language and communication, dependent as it is on our conceptual agreement, our shared sense of the necessity of going on in some ways rather than others, is not incompatible with the contingency, for each way of going on, of the fact that we do share a sense of its necessity.

The contingency claim supported by Wittgenstein's examples is: For any of our concepts or forms of life, it is possible that others do not share it. It does not follow from this, as I shall emphasize below, that it is possible that others share none of our concepts but have an entirely alien conceptual scheme (though of course there is ample room for creatures that entirely lack a conceptual scheme); the possibility of local differences in concepts or forms of life does not entail the possibility of globally different conceptual schemes. It does follow, however, that agreement in specific forms of life need not be sheltered or isolated from knowledge of or contact with other forms of life; the notion of forms of life admits of a conception of the world in which there is variation among specific forms of life. If it is a contingent fact that we do find it natural and necessary to go on in a particular way, then it is possible that others do not. If recognition of this possibility does not undermine our agreement in form of life, it is hard to see how recognition of the actual existence of others, who do not find it natural and necessary to go on in this way, could do so. Nor should the determinacy of our concepts be undone by contact with creatures some of whose specific forms of life differ from ours, or who entirely lack a conceptual scheme; we might observe regularities in their unintelligible procedures that enable us to interact with them profitably, without thereby eroding our own forms of life.

Given that some variation among forms of life seems to be possible, should we say that this possibility is in fact realized in our world by various co-existing schemes of reason-giving concepts? In particular, is this the consequence of the view that reason to act, like meaning, is "embedded in its situation, in human customs and institutions",[5] that the way in which meaning guides linguistic action is a special case of the way in which reasons guide action generally? As linguistic practices rather than some central intention to go on in the same way determine that we mean *blue* and not *grue*, *plus* and not *quus*,[6] and constitute the "bedrock" of logical necessity, so, on such a view, specific reason-giving practices, rather than some central commitment to do *this*, to go on in the same way, constitute the "bedrock" of practical necessity. The existence of certain shared practices, any of which might not have existed, is all that our having determinate reasons to say or do anything rests on. Still, as we've seen, it is compatible with their existence that other different forms of life also exist.

However, the price of regarding distinctive reason-giving schemes as different forms of life may be to deprive ourselves of a sense in which they are in competition with one another, and of the *locus* of substantive disagreement that we started out to account for. It may be correct to regard some apparent disagreements about what ought to be done, all things considered, as differences in form of life, and our opponents as "different sorts of beings from us",[7] with whom we do not stand in substantive disagreement because they do not have the concepts necessary for them to stand in disagreement with us. There may also be borderline cases between differences in form of life and substantive disagreement. However, *some* disputes about what ought to be done are substantive, and if the practice account is to succeed, it must make clear logical space for them. That is, it must make it possible to distinguish substantive disagreement within a given form of life from disagreement in form of life.

A closely related problem arises in other areas for Wittgenstein's views: there is tension between the doctrine of the antecedence of logic and mathematics to truth and the intelligibility of the supposition made by Wittgenstein that we can describe practices that are in some sense of the same general kind—logical or mathematical—as our own practices, yet constitute alternatives to them, that embody competing views about how to do the same thing. As Wright explains, " 'Calculating', 'inferring', 'measuring' are, for us, determined by the methods we use; there is no residue in these concepts in terms of which the adequacy of our methods might be questioned". But, he asks, "if there is nothing further to our understanding of these concepts, how can it be coherent to suggest that other people might measure differently, might calculate in accordance with other rules, etc?"[8]

Wittgenstein is well aware of this tension and addresses many remarks to the problem is various contexts. In this chapter I shall try to develop a framework in which many of his remarks about agreement and disagreement, and his suggestions about how this tension may be resolved, can be located. This framework will show how there is room within a non-centralist view of reasons for action for disagreement about the right answer to a given question. Although my purpose is interpretative, the interpretation is admittedly speculative: it does, I think, help to account for many of Wittgenstein's remarks taken together, but it goes well beyond anything that can be explicitly attributed to him, most obviously with respect to the connections suggested between a practice account and Davidson's views on interpretation and disagreement.

### 3. Practices as Criteria of Agreement in Form of Life; Constraints on Interpretation vs. Ultra-interpretations

Critics of what is taken to be Wittgensteinian "conceptual relativism" have tended to assume that the practice account must assimilate persistent disagreement to difference in form of life, and hence be landed with the unacceptable consequence that such disagreement does not amount to substantive disagreement at all, so that argument is futile, misconceived in principle.[9] But it cannot be a consequence of the role of practices, customs, or institutions in determining meaning that all disagreements and mistakes threaten conceptual divergence; substantive disagreement and argument may themselves be practices or customs, as in ethics and law. I shall argue that to attribute such an assimilation, and the consequent conceptual relativism, to Wittgenstein is to make a fundamental mistake in interpreting his views. As well as his remarks rejecting the identification of agreement in form of life with substantive agreement, we have strategic reasons not to make this identification if we are to make sense of Wittgenstein's central concerns.

The identification would seem to be the result of an attempt to account for such remarks as:

> If language is to be a means of communication there must be agreement not only in definitions but also (queer as this may sound) in judgments. This seems to abolish logic, but does not do so.—It is one thing to describe methods of measurement, and another to obtain and state results of measurement. But what we call "measuring" is partly determined by a certain constancy in results of measurement.[10]

> We say that, in order to communicate, people must agree with one another about the meanings of words. But the criterion for this agreement is not just

agreement with reference to definitions, e. g., ostensive definitions—but also an agreement in judgments. It is essential for communication that we agree in a large number of judgments.[11]

However, the correct interpretation of these remarks must at least reconcile them with remarks such as the following:

"So you are saying that human agreement decides what is true and what is false?"—It is what human beings say that is true and false; and they agree in the language they use. That is not agreement in opinions but in form of life.[12]

The agreement of humans that is a presupposition of logic is not an agreement in opinions, much less in opinions on questions of logic.[13]

It is obscure how we are to regard these remarks on any interpretation that identifies agreement in form of life with substantive agreement.

Indeed, the role that the notion of agreement in form of life is invoked to play in Wittgenstein's thought cannot be played by substantive agreement. Wittgenstein challenges the private language theorist to show how it is possible for a concept to have determinate meaning, such that mistaken attempts to apply it can be distinguished from the results of a failure to grasp its meaning and from applications of other concepts:

What is the difference between inferring wrong and not inferring? between adding wrong and not adding?

What I always do seems to be—to emphasize a distinction between the determination of a sense and the employment of a sense.[14]

Someone can only be mistaken in his use of a concept, however, if he stands in substantive disagreement with one who applies it correctly, as someone who is trying to apply a different concept does not. Thus, the challenge to the private language theorist is to distinguish same-meaning-different-belief cases, cases of substantive disagreement, from different-meaning cases, cases of conceptual difference; only if this distinction can be made out against the threat of radical indeterminacy is it possible to regard the use of language as a rational activity, one that permits us to speak of right and wrong ways of going on. Private ostensive definition or private experience or representation is incapable of meeting this challenge, not simply because of the inaccessibility of the crucial intentions to go on in the same way, but because we do not and cannot have intentions the content of which establishes, rather than presupposes, the determination of content;[15] to suppose we could is to suppose that representations might be somehow, intrinsically or—what comes to the same thing—magically, self-interpreting. Our minds do not and cannot race ahead to decide of each possible case whether or not it falls under the concept whose meaning is supposedly thus determined. Not only can we not peer into our own minds in order to fix our meanings, but "If God had looked into our minds, he would not have been able to see there" what we meant.[16] As Kripke has emphasized, this claim does not depend on any behaviouristic premise that dismisses the inner, but rather on a proper respect for what inner life is really like. The difficulty it raises does not stem from a denial that there is something that it is like in there. Rather, what it is like "in there" does not answer the question; in particular, we do not and could not have special self-interpreting experiences of meaning this or that. Experiences alone cannot determine that we mean this or that by what we say or do, and thus how it would be correct to go on in further cases, because they in turn are subject to multiple interpretations. Nowhere among the facts about what someone feels like is there to be found a rule that applies itself, or an idealized, self-sufficient interpretation of a rule that does not in turn permit of interpretation; and no such thing could determine the contents of our minds or guide our uses of concepts.[17]

The criticisms Wittgenstein makes of the experientialist approach to the problem of how the contents of the mind are determined, so that same-meaning-different-belief cases can be distinguished from different-meaning cases, can be generalized in at least two broad ways. *First*, the problem Wittgenstein is addressing is in essence the same problem as that Davidson is addressing, and if experiences won't solve Wittgenstein's problem, they won't solve Davidson's—as indeed Davidson clearly recognizes—either.[18] *Second*, the essence of Wittgenstein's criticism of the experientialist approach to the problem has applications beyond the experientialist approach. The essential point is not merely that experiences are not self-interpreting, and so can't solve the problem, but that *nothing could possibly be self-interpreting*.

> However many rules you give me—I give a rule which justifies my employment of your rules.[19]

> I can of course paraphrase the rule in all sorts of different forms, but that makes it more intelligible only for someone who can already follow these paraphrases.[20]

> . . . any interpretation still hangs in the air along with what it interprets, and cannot give it any support. Interpretations themselves do not determine meanings.[21]

The point is quite general, and applies to anything, including states, dispositions, practices, capacities, etc., as well as experiences, *in so far as they might be put forward in a self-interpreting role*.[22] I shall refer to any entity supposed to be self-interpreting, to point in virtue of its intrinsic qualities to something outside itself which it represents, as an *ultra-interpretation*. I shall explain shortly how this terminology will be useful in avoiding a certain ambiguity. But first it is worth emphasizing the second generalization. There are many possible kinds of candidate for ultra-interpretations as well as experiences, including individualistically identifed physiological states and behaviour patterns; not even an extended forefinger carries its meaning intrinsically.[23] It should not be imagined that Wittgenstein has overlooked this, or thought that behaviour might magically interpret itself where experience could not. His point is not simply that experiences can't interpret themselves, but that it is a mistake to conceive of the relation between the mind and the world in such a way that the need to postulate intrinsically self-interpreting entities of any kind arises, because there can't be such entities. He appeals to practices and capacities *not* as ultra-interpretations, but because he conceives them as identified in relation to and constitutively engaged with the world. His appeal to them is in effect a repudiation of the conception of the mind as independent of the world that gives rise to the problem which makes ultra-interpretations seem necessary. As has been pointed out explicitly by others since, it is far easier to relinquish this dualistic conception of mind and world with respect to activity than with respect to experience. (This is not to admit that the conception is correct for experience either, however.) *Which* practice a given bodily event belongs to, *what* a capacity is a capacity for, are questions that it is hardly tempting to answer without reference to the world.[24] In the next chapter, on preference, I shall pursue the themes that behaviour does not interpret itself, and that the interpretation of behaviour is only possible given constraints on interpretation, in decision-theoretic terms.

Back to how the "ultra-interpretation" terminology will be useful in avoiding a certain ambiguity. I shall be developing in later chapters the idea that persons are distinctive in that they are self-interpreting and self-determining animals. These phrases, however, are ambiguous. A self-determining preference, for example, may be a preference that determines *itself*, or a preference that determines *the self*. The latter preferences, I shall argue, exist and are importantly distinctive of persons. The former, however, would constitute ultra-interpretations, and do not exist. Similarly, the phrase "self-interpreting belief" may suggest a belief that interprets *itself*, or a belief that interprets the *self*. Again, the latter are not repudiated in repudiating the former. When I refer to self-interpretation and self-determination, I shall do so in the latter sense, rather than in the sense that involves ultra-interpretation.

How are self-interpretation and self-determination on the part of persons possible without ultra-interpretation? This is a particular version of the question, how is interpretation possible without ultra-interpretation? The general answer to the latter question involves distinguishing constitutive constraints on interpretation from ultra-interpretations. That is, constitutive constraints on interpretation make possible interpretation without ultra-interpretation. The answer to the particular version of the question, about how self-interpretation and self-determination on the part of persons is possible, also depends on constraints on interpretation; but in a sense the entire rest of this book will be taken up with answering the question in detail. The answer will involve developing a coherence account of deliberation conceived as a kind of self-interpretation, and, in the final chapter, exploring its relation to the concepts of self-determination or autonomy, and of democracy.

The challenge to be met, then, is to distinguish same-meaning-different-belief cases from different-meaning cases. Only if this distinction can be made out, can someone be mistaken in his or her applications of a concept, or stand in substantive disagreement with someone else about how it should be applied. Only if this distinction can be made out will content be determined to an extent that makes interpretation, understanding, and rationality possible. The parallel problem for belief and preference is to distinguish same-desire-different belief cases from different desire cases. Only if this distinction can be made out will it be possible for someone to be practically irrational; if he can always insist that he is merely following a different rule, mistakes and disagreement cannot obtain. What Wittgenstein shows, negatively (in what is in effect the first of the three stages of argument I sketched above in Chapter 2 section 3), is that ultra-interpretations cannot meet these parallel challenges. What he suggests, positively, and what Davidson shows (in the second stage of argument sketched above), is that we do not need ultra-interpretations to meet these challenges; rather, we need constraints on interpretation, which are not up to us, optional, or themselves the products of interpretation. (In making out the positive side of the argument, I shall below connect what Davidson says about charity in interpretation with what Wittgenstein says about forms of life.) It is conceiving the relation between mind and world in such a way that ultra-interpretations seem to be needed, which gives rise to the problem, and which prompts the view that all disagreements or mistakes are symptoms of conceptual difference. The way to meet the challenge is to repudiate the conception that gives rise to the problem:

> This was our paradox: no course of action could be determined by a rule, because every course of action can be made out to accord with the rule. The answer was: if everything can be made out to accord with the rule, then it can also be made out to conflict with it. And so there would be neither accord nor conflict here.

> It can be seen that there is a misunderstanding here from the mere fact that in the course of our argument we give one interpretation after another, as if each one contented us at least for a moment, until we thought of yet another standing behind it. What this shews is that there is a way of grasping a rule which is not an interpretation, but which is exhibited in what we call "obeying the rule" and "going against it" it actual cases.

> Hence there is an inclination to say: every action according to the rule is an interpretation. But we ought to restrict the term "interpretation" to the substitution of one expression of the rule for another.

> And hence also 'obeying a rule' is a practice. And to think one is obeying a rule is not to obey a rule. Hence it is not possible to obey a rule 'privately': otherwise thinking one was obeying a rule would be the same thing as obeying it.[25]

Clearly, any positive account proposed in place of the private-experience or other ultra-interpretationalist approaches must be able to make some progress toward meeting the challenge the ultra-interpretationalist approaches fail to meet, or no ground is gained. This is true even if the positive proposal is skeptical in the sense Kripke suggests, that is, even if it concedes that we cannot "speak of a single individual, considered by himself and in isolation, as ever meaning anything", and goes on to claim that we don't need to after all.[26] Wittgenstein suggests that we do not need to speak of an individual meaning something privately because what an individual means is not determined by any kind of ultra-interpretations, but by the practices, customs, and institutions in which he participates, which provide a context that constrains interpretation.[27] Such an appeal to practices must be viewed as an attempt to meet the challenge despite the concession, not as an admission that it cannot be met. Otherwise the arguments against a private language lose their point, which derives from the assumption that the rational use of language *is* possible; the challenge is to explain *how* it is possible. For Wittgenstein to succeed in showing how it is possible by reference to practices and without invoking the ultra-interpretations shown to be mythical, the view that meanings are determined by practices must allow us to distinguish substantive from conceptual difference, to answer the question: "In what does your having meant this in particular, rather than nothing in particular, or something slightly different, consist?", in terms of participation in the relevant practices. It is this participation that Wittgenstein calls agreement in form of life.

If agreement in form of life, identified in terms of practices, is to provide the conceptual common ground on the basis of which we may be entitled to regard ourselves as standing in substantive disagreement with someone who has made a mistake, it cannot amount to substantive agreement. The point of invoking practices is to account for the possibilities of substantive *dis*-agreement and mistake, as distinct from the possibility of conceptual difference. Davidson makes a related point on the method of charity in interpreting behaviour: "The method is not designed to eliminate disagreement, nor can it: its purpose is to make meaningful disagreement possible, and this depends entirely on a foundation—some foundation—in agreement".[28] Thus, the problem that disagreement presents for a non-centralist coherentist view of reasons for action is an instance of the general problem of how to accommodate the possibility of substantive disagreement and mistake among participants in a common form of life. If the notion of agreement in form of life is to do the work it is intended to do, it must accommodate the possibility of substantive disagreement wherever our concepts admit of it.

## 4. The Antecedence Doctrine and Substantive Disagreement; Disagreement About Colours?

Above I described Wittgenstein's doctrine that logic is antecedent to truth as the rejection of logical centralism, and I noted the tension between this doctrine and the intelligibility of the supposition made by Wittgenstein that we can describe logical practices that are in some sense alternatives to our own, that embody different views about how to do the same thing. Crispin Wright has described this tension between two strands off Wittgenstein's thought in detail. He complains that "Wittgenstein's soft-ruler people are merely stipulated as doing a kind of measuring; and the wood-sellers likewise are stipulated as determining quantity by area.... [W]hat is not clear", he says, "is what justifies the description of such people as employing different concepts of length, or of quantity. Where are the analogies anchored? What are the points of similarity? ... [I]t has still to be made out that there is in what they do anything which may rightly be regarded as the use of any such concepts; nothing has been done to distinguish their performance from mere ceremony".[29] A parallel tension may be traced between a non-centralist conception of colour and the possibility of alternative ways of seeing and responding to colours. How can we admit that alternative practices may compete with our own, let alone that we are able to have substantive disagreements about the correct application of a given concept and to criticise mistaken attempts to apply it, without positing some conceptually central concept, prior to and governing specific practices, to carry the content of our disagreement? Participation in practices that constitute a common form of life was invoked, in lieu of the mythical ultra-interpretations by which the private-experience theorist purported to anticipate reality, with the aim of meeting the challenge to distinguish substantive from conceptual difference. But we have yet to see just how practices and forms of life help in meeting the challenge.

As I've indicated, Wittgenstein explicitly recognises this tension and is crucially concerned to resolve it. He considers the problem in particular detail in relation to colour concepts and to logical and mathematical concepts. Since the identification of agreement in form of life with complete agreement in application gains appeal from consideration of observational concepts like *red* and *green*, I shall first examine Wittgenstein's remarks about specific colours. The importance of the practice of theorizing with respect to complex, articulable concepts, which is highlighted by a coherence account, will emerge in the rest of this chapter, in which I shall set out the general framework which gives theorizing an important role in explaining how substantive disagreement and mistake within a form of life are possible. The way in which theorizing and constraints on interpretation work together in my overall account of practical rationality will only emerge gradually, in later chapters (especially those on preference, interpretation, *akrasia*, and coherence).

That someone groups a green object in good light and plain view with a series of red objects in good light and plain view is the best kind of evidence one could want that he is not applying our concept *red*. We do not articulate reasons for applying *red* or *green*. Hence, it is difficult to conceive of questions about someone's reasons for his grouping the answers to which would reveal him to stand in substantive disagreement with us in asserting the redness of a green object, rather than not to be talking about its redness at all.

> Someone asks me: What is the colour of this flower? I answer: "red".—Are you absolutely sure? Yes, absolutely sure! But may I not have been deceived and called the wrong colour "red"? No. The certainty with which I call the colour "red" is the rigidity of my measuring-rod, it is the rigidity from which I start. When I give descriptions, that is not to be brought into doubt. This simply characterizes what we call describing.

> (I may of course even here assume a slip of the tongue, but nothing else.)[30]

It is simply the normal case, to be incapable of mistake about the designation
of certain things in one's mother tongue.[31]

Nevertheless, Wittgenstein goes on to ask:

Is it not difficult to distinguish between the cases in which I cannot and those
in which I can hardly be mistaken? Is it not always clear to which kind a
case belongs? I believe not.[32]

It is clear that we are not entitled to regard ourselves as disagreeing with
someone about whether or not a red object is *red*, so long as both have a
plain view of the object in good light. If he does not recognize that it is red
he must either not have understood what it is to be red or not have the ability
to perceive redness. It is less clear that we are not entitled to regard ourselves
as disagreeing with someone who groups a green object with a series of red
ones about the *colour* of the object. Whether we are or not depends on
further context and circumstances, on how much of the structure of the relationships among various specific colours he recognizes. But if we were to
stand in substantive disagreement with him, it would not be because the
general concept *colour* is conceptually prior to and independent of the specific
concepts *red* and *green*—it is not. Specific colour concepts may be concepts
of secondary qualities, but they nonetheless have conceptual ties to distinct
qualities of experience, not to some common quality of experience as of
colour. Rather, *colour* has an abstract and theoretical status in relation to
specific colours that allows us to discuss, for example, the relationships among
the primary and secondary colours, or to consider whether reddish-green is
a possible colour. It is because we conceive colour to have an articulable
structure that Wittgenstein is able to claim that there is "a geometrical gap
. . . between green and red", and that the sentence " 'There is no such thing
as a reddish green' is akin to the sentences that we use as axioms in mathematics" in its contribution to the logic of colour concepts.[33] The articulability
of the concept of colour in terms of the relationships among specific colour
concepts, rather than some uniform central component in the meaning of the
specific concepts, makes it intelligible for Wittgenstein to consider the possibility of unfamiliar colours and on what grounds we might attribute experiences of them:

"Can't we imagine certain people having a different geometry of colour than
we do?" That, of course, means: Can't we imagine people having colour
concepts other than ours? And that in turn means: Can't we imagine people
who do not have our colour concepts but who have concepts which are related
to ours in such a way that we would also call them "colour concepts"?

We will, therefore, have to ask ourselves: What would it be like if people
knew colours which our people with normal vision do not know? In general
this question will not admit of an unambiguous answer. For it is by no means
clear that we must say of this sort of abnormal people that they know other
colours. There is, after all, no commonly accepted criterion for what is a
colour, unless it is one of our colours.

And yet we could imagine circumstances under which we would say, "These people see other colours in addition to ours."

The difficulty is, therefore, one of knowing what we are supposed to consider as the analogue of something that is familiar to us.[34]

Wittgenstein is well aware of the lack of definitive criteria for circumstances that support the alternative colourist hypothesis. Nevertheless, he does think it conceivable that such circumstances might be found, and suggests that we might identify them in terms of the relationship between the "geometry" of our colour concepts and the geometry of the alternative colour concepts: for example, is the latter isomorphic to the former, or perhaps even a refinement of it?

But even if there were also people for whom it was natural to use the expressions "reddish-green" or "yellowish-blue" in a consistent manner and who perhaps also exhibit abilities which we lack, we would still not be forced to recognize that they see colours which we do not see. There is, after all, no commonly accepted criterion for what is a colour, unless it is one of our colours.

'The colours' are not things that have definite properties, so that one could straight off look for or imagine colours that we don't yet know, or imagine someone who knows different ones than we do. It is quite possible that, under certain circumstances, we would say that people know colours that we don't know, but we are not forced to say this, for there is no indication as to what we should regard as adequate analogies to our colours, in order to be able to say it. This is like the case in which we speak of infra-red 'light'; there is a good reason for doing it, but we can also call it a misuse.

Can't we imagine people having a geometry of colours different from our normal one? And that, of course, means: can we describe it, can we immediately respond to the request to describe it, that is, do we know unambiguously what is being demanded of us?

The difficulty is obviously this: isn't it precisely the geometry of colours that shows us what we're talking about, i. e. that we are talking about colours?[35]

Let *colour'* be the predicate used by a group of people who may have an alternative set of colour concepts, and let *primary colours'* be colours' that cannot be obtained by combining other colours'. Circumstances that would support the claim that they are alternative-colourists, rather than that they are onto something other than colour, might include, as a limiting case, those in which they typically assert that no colour' can be the result of combining more than two primary colours'. Since our primary colours are red, blue, and yellow, the parallel claim for us would imply that there is no such colour as reddish-green, yellowish-purple, or bluish-orange. Now we might be unable to learn to apply the specific colour' concepts these people use, and yet be able to identify the predicates *R*, *B* and *Y*, which they use to stand for colours' they regard as unobtainable by combination, or primary. If they were in fact to assert that there is no such colour' as *R*-ish-*B*-*Y*, *Y*-ish-*R*-*B*, or *B*-ish-*R*-

*Y*, the isomorphism might be regarded as providing some, though rather weak, support for the alternative colourist claim—at least, say, in the context that members of the group display interest in which particular combinations of *R*, *B* and *Y* occur in cloth, paintings, and flower gardens. On interpretative grounds such as these we might work our way towards a basis for supposing that they have an alternative conception of colour rather than no conception of colour at all.

Stronger support would be found in the circumstances Wittgenstein describes, in which members of some group make all the specific colour discriminations we make, but more as well, so that the geometry of their colour concepts is a refinement on that of ours:

> Let us imagine men who express a colour intermediate between red and yellow, say by means of a fraction in a kind of binary notation like this: R, LLRL and the like, where we have (say) yellow on the right, and red on the left.—These people learn how to describe shades of colour this way in the kindergarten, how to use such descriptions in picking colour out, in mixing them, etc. They would be related to us roughly as people with absolute pitch are to those who lack it. They can do what we cannot.[36]

> The logic of the concept of colour is just much more complicated that it might seem.[37]

Members of such a group would bear the same relation to us as we bear to persons who are blind to some colour distinctions but not others. We may not be able to disagree with a red-green colour-blind person about whether a red object and a green object are the same colour, but it does not follow that we cannot have any disagreements about colour with such a person. Just as we are able to disagree with someone who is *red-green* colour-blind about whether two *purple* objects are the same colour or not, we would be able to have substantive disagreements with the alternative colourists. According to a decentralized conception of colour, any disagreement about colour requires that there be some conceptual *locus* of disagreement, but there need not be one conceptual *locus* of all disagreements about colour. Thus, just as we would also able to disagree with someone who was *blue-orange* colour-blind about whether two *purple* objects are the same colour or not, we would be able to have substantive disagreements with two different groups of alternative colourists, whose candidate colour concepts bore different similarities to ours.

In looking for circumstances that would support the alternative-colourist claim, we are looking for examples of cases in which agreement in form of life with respect to the use of the concept *colour* is compatible with substantive disagreement about particular applications of it. That is, we are trying to discover the nature of the agreement in form of life that characterizes the use of our concept *colour* and makes it possible to distinguish agreement over its proper use from use of another concept. We have found that this agreement in form of life is not monolithic; several practices, which need not go hand in hand, contribute to it. Among them are our activities of applying specific colour concepts such as *red* and *green* as well as our claims about the relationships among certain specific concepts. To be a colour is to be one of the things on our list of specific colours, related to one another as they are. The example of isomorphism we considered occupies a borderline position at best between conceptual and substantive difference; the relationships among specific concepts were familiar, but the specific component concepts were not. If we change the example so that most of the specific component concepts are familiar as well, as in Wittgenstein's example, the alternative colourist claim gains support; we could have a substantive disagreement with these people about whether two objects are the same colour—and we might well be mistaken. Such people would not be failing to perceive colour at all, but would be better at perceiving colour than we are.

## 5. Uncontestable Concepts

Wittgenstein explicitly suggests that the distinction between conceptual and substantive difference with respect to the general concept of colour is not absolute but admits of differences of degree, and that this is also the case for the general concepts of calculation and thinking:

> Does it make sense to say that people generally agree in their judgments of colour? What would it be like for them not to?
> —One man would say a flower was red which another called blue, and so on.—But what right should we have to call these people's words "red" and "blue" our 'colour-words'?"—
>
> How would they learn to use these words? And is the language-game which they learn still such as we call the use of 'names of colour'? There are evidently differences of degree here.
>
> This consideration must, however, apply to mathematics too. If there were not complete agreement, then neither would human beings be learning the technique which we learn. It would be more of less different from ours up to the point of unrecognizability.[38]
>
> (There is a continuum between an error in calculation and a different mode of calculating.)[39]
>
> ... it is for us an essential part of 'thinking' that—in talking, writing, etc.,—he makes this sort of transition. And I say further that the line between what we include in 'thinking' and what we no longer include in 'thinking' is no more a hard and fast one than the line between what is still and what is no longer called "regularity".[40]

I claimed above that the practice account ought to be viewed as an attempt to meet the challenge to distinguish conceptual and substantive difference and thus to show how language conceived as a rational activity is possible, rather than as a concession that the challenge cannot be met. To hold that the distinction between conceptual and substantive difference admits of degrees and borderline cases is not to concede that the challenge cannot be met.

Rather, it is another aspect of the strategy of rejecting assumptions that give rise to the problem. The importance of Wittgenstein's exercises in imagining strange ways of going on is not that they reveal a sharp boundary between conceptual and substantive difference or some underlying ultra-interpretative basis for the distinction. Rather, they show us that the distinction does not depend on sharp boundaries any more than on an underlying ultra-interpretative basis. And they help us to develop a sense of how to place instances of strange ways of going on on a spectrum that ranges from cases of radical conceptual disparity at one extreme to cases of purely sustantive disagreement at the other. We learn to place cases on the spectrum by looking at the variety of ways in which the contexts and uses of words can be different from ours and akin to ours; we break our practices down by imagining small deviations against which to test and develop our awareness of which aspects contribute to "the determination of a sense" and which to "the employment of a sense." By contrast, the self-interpreting intentions invoked by the private language theory to go on using a word *like this*, are no less mythical for purposes of developing such means of placement than for purposes of fixing absolutely clear conceptual boundaries.

Thus, "it is not clear that the general agreement of people doing calculations is a characteristic mark of all that is called 'calculating' ".[41] This admission is compatible with the antecedence doctrine, that *calculating* means calculating *like this*, because *calculating* doesn't only mean calculating *like this*, but *like that*, and *like this*, and *like that* as well; *derivation* is like an artichoke:

> ...we told ourselves that this was only a quite special case of deriving; deriving in a quite special garb, which had to be stripped from it if we wanted to see the essence of deriving. So we stripped those particular coverings off; but then deriving itself disappeared.—In order to find the real artichoke, we divested it of its leaves. For certainly [a case considered in a previous section] was a special case of deriving; what is essential to deriving, however, was not hidden beneath the surface of this case, but this 'surface' was one case out of the family of cases of deriving.[42]

Because of this complexity of structure, practices of articulating the relationships among specific criterial instances of calculation and derivation may also contribute to determining what we mean by *calculation* and *derivation*.

The concept of calculation is related to the concept, say, of adding 1 to 4 as is the concept of colour to the concept of redness: just as someone's grouping a green object with a series of red objects shows that he is not applying red, someone's getting a result other than 5 shows that he hasn't understood what it is to add 1 to 4:

> Thus the truth of the proposition that 4 + 1 makes 5 is, so to speak, over-determined. Overdetermined by this, that the result of the operation is defined to be the criterion that this operation has been carried out.

> The proposition rests on one too many feet to be an empirical proposition. It will be used as a determination of the concept 'applying the operation + 1 to 4'.[43]

The concepts of redness and of adding 1 to 4 are among those that do not admit of substantive disagreement. I shall refer to such concepts as *uncontestable concepts*. Concerning uncontestable concepts it is correct to say that complete agreement in application characterizes agreement in form of life. Strange ways of extending a series of applications of such a concept are located at one end of the spectrum we are concerned to fill out, and indicate conceptual disparity. People who persist in these strange ways of going on are not making mistakes, or disagreeing with us; rather they do not have our concepts or our perceptual capacities. With respect to these cases, the sense in which the practice "speaks for itself" in enabling us to distinguish conceptual from substantive difference is clear: no persistent substantive difference, or mistake, is possible; persistent differences must be conceptual.


## 6. Conceivably Contestable Concepts

Further along the spectrum we find strange ways of extending series of applications of concepts such as *colour*, *calculation*, *thinking* and *measurement*. These are concepts that do not normally, but might conceivably, admit of alternative conceptions or substantive disagreement. I shall refer to them as *conceivably contestable concepts*. While uncontestable concepts include specific sensory concepts and the concepts of particular calculations, conceivably contestable concepts include categorial concepts that subsume uncontestable concepts of one or another sort, in the way that *colour* subsumes *red*, *green*, etc. and *calculation* subsumes *4 + 1*, *add 2*, etc. With respect to conceivably contestable concepts, it is normal for complete agreement in application to characterize agreement in form of life, and hence difference in application constitutes *prima facie* evidence of conceptual difference. However, such evidence is conceivably defeasible; we can imagine circumstances, as Wittgenstein does, in which we would hesitate to claim that the deviant application is not an attempt to apply our concept.

That such circumstances are conceivable is due to the complex and articulable structure of conceivably contestable concepts. Someone can make certain criterial applications of such a concept correctly and construct a theory about the relationships that obtain among his applications. Yet he may go on to make eccentric applications of it, based, perhaps, on extrapolation from the relationships he recognizes.[44] That such circumstances are not normal is due to the fact that the criteria for applying conceivably contestable concepts do not conflict among themselves: Correct uses of *red* do not compete with correct uses of *green* to tell us the colour of an object in the way that correct uses, for example, of *just* may compete with correct uses of *unkind* to tell us what we ought to do, all things considered. Similarly, the laws of arithmetic reflect harmony among particular calculations rather than the resolution of conflict.

Again, it is by reference to practices that we attempt to identify circumstances in which contest is conceivable and to locate contested applications on the spectrum from conceptual to substantive difference. Extent of agreement or disagreement in form of life is signalled by a variety of uses. If complete agreement in application is the normal expression of agreement in form of life, nevertheless it might conceivably be expressed by agreement about certain criterial applications of a concept and the relationships among them, which provides a springboard for intelligible mistakes:

> In order to make a mistake, a man must already judge in conformity with mankind.

> Can we say: a mistake doesn't only have a cause, it also has a ground? i. e., roughly: when someone makes a mistake, this can be fitted into what he knows aright.[45]

> Whether a thing is a blunder or not—it is a blunder in a particular system. Just as something is a blunder in a particular game and not in another.[46]

And again, the admission that the division between conceptual and substantive difference is not sharp does not undermine the point of Wittgenstein's enterprise, which is to understand how meanings are determined to the extent they are, to an extent that makes understanding and communication possible. If meanings turn out *a posteriori* not to be completely determinate, we want our account to reflect this, without thereby going to the other extreme and making it impossible ever to distinguish conceptual from substantive difference. The practice account allows some concepts a measure of indeterminacy, as their uses and possible uses indicate. But this is moderate underdetermination with a good conscience, and concomitant with the firm determinations that practices also effect. The radical indeterminacy the private language theory involved, on the other hand, was disguised by the pretense that we have special ultra-interpretative experiences or intentions capable of determining meanings to the extent they are determined; when this pretense is exposed as false, the private language theorist has no explanation of how meanings are determined at all.

## 7. Essentially Contested Concepts

At the other end of the spectrum we find divergent applications of what I shall call, following W. B. Gallie, *essentially contested concepts*. These are concepts that characteristically admit of substantive disagreement.[47] Gallie describes essentially contested concepts as appraisive and applicable to objects of an internally complex character that may be described in various ways by altering one's view of the significance of descriptions of their component features.

In my taxonomy, essentially contested concepts differ from conceivably contestable concepts in that correct descriptions of component features characteristically compete with one another to influence applications of the former. Examples are the general concepts of what ought to be done, all things considered, and of what the law requires, all things considered, as well as many specific ethical and legal concepts. (Distributive justice, for example, may be conceived either in terms of equality of welfare or in terms of equality of resources; and there are competing theories of contract.[48]) Conceivably contestable concepts may be appraisive, but it is not characteristic of the criteria to which they are responsible to conflict with one another. Consider, for example, the concept *valid* as applied to inferences. We require any given formalization of logic to be consistent. Nevertheless, disagreement exists, based on theoretical considerations, about the validity of the law of the excluded middle.

Gallie asks how we are able to distinguish cases in which the correct application of a single concept is contested from cases in which the dispute only serves "to confuse two different concepts about whose proper application no one need have contested at all".[49] A variety of practices contribute to agreement in form of life; Gallie makes two suggestions. First, each party to a disagreement about the correct application of an essentially contested concept "recognises the fact that its own use of it is contested by those of other parties, and . . . each party must have at least some appreciation of the different criteria in the light of which the other parties claim to be applying the concept in question", even though they differ as to the relative contribution made by the different criteria to an all-things-considered judgment. Second, a substantive disagreement about the correct application of an essentially contested concept involves appeals to exemplary applications that display relationships, which the disputants claim to be extrapolating, among the criteria that conflict in the case at hand.[50]

If there is some list of specific values such that what ought to be done, all things considered, is some function of those specific values, then both specific reason-giving practices and practices of theorizing about specific values contribute to agreement in form of life. Accordingly, Gallie's two suggestions about how to recognize agreement in form of life may be applied at both levels. That is, in attempting to distinguish divergences that indicate substantive disagreement from divergences that indicate conceptual difference we may ask the following four questions:

1. Do our opponents recognize the force of the various conflicting criteria our essentially contested concept is responsible to? When they conflict as well as when they apply in isolation? Do they recognize the force of specific reason-giving concepts in the cases in question?

2. Can we agree with our opponents on normal and exemplary applications of the essentially contested concept, in instances in which the various conflicting criteria that apply to the cases in question also apply? Can we agree on the resolution of conflicts among the relevant specific reason-giving concepts in some actual or hypothetical cases?

3. Are our opponents able to deliberate when criteria conflict, and do they recognize the force of the theoretical considerations that we bring to bear in arguments about the proper relationships among conflicting criteria? In constructing theories about the relationships among conflicting values, for example, do they respect the rule of dominance and the requirements of

supervenience and transitivity? (See the chapter on coherence below.) Do they recognize that the simplicity and comprehensiveness of an account of the relationships among specific values count in its favour?

4. Can we agree with our opponents on an exemplary instance of an account of the relationships within a group of conflicting criteria? (These should preferably be criteria to which the same essentially contested concept is responsible in different circumstances so that the exemplary account is subject to the same theoretical constraints as the one we are concerned with in the case at hand.) Can we find examples of ethical or legal deliberation and theorizing that we agree are decisive?

If we weren't to repeat the questions at the theoretical level, the question of whether there exists a practice of theorizing that "speaks for itself", in addition to the specific practices it is about, would remain open; both types of practice contribute to agreement in form of life with respect to an essentially contested concept. But once again, the distinction between conceptual and substantive difference is drawn by reference to practices. By participating in such practices, our opponents reveal their competence at using the concept our applications of which they contest. Moreover, the practices that contribute to agreement in form of life need not go hand in hand. Any disagreement about what ought to be done, all things considered, requires that there be some conceptual *locus* of disagreement, but there need not be one conceptual *locus* of all such disagreements.

Consider two possible objections to what I've said about essentially contested concepts. First, it might be objected that the challenge to distinguish substantive from conceptual difference can be raised again with respect to the claim to theoretical favour, which a non-centralist coherence account associates with the central concepts *right* and *ought*. If so, perhaps the appeal to theory only puts the radical threat to the possibility of substantive disagreement at one step's remove, but does not really avert it. We can only understand substantive disagreement about applications of essentially contested concepts by reference to theoretical coherence if we share a conception of theoretical coherence; but the challenge we started out to meet can now be raised again. How can someone's mistaken perceptions of theoretical coherence be distinguished from his failure to understand what he is supposed to be doing, or from an intention to do something else? What keeps theoretical differences in particular from threatening conceptual divergence? For example, suppose that we share specific reason-giving concepts and that we agree on certain conditions that a theory about the relationships between specific values and what ought to be done must meet, in order to be in the running as a theory. Nevertheless, we may differ about which of the possible theories that meet this description do the best job of accounting for the settled cases of conflict whose resolution we agree about. What guarantees then that we have the same interpretation of what it is to do the best job of accounting for the cases?

This objection misconstrues the role of the appeal to theory. Theoretical coherence does not permit us to resurrect the repudiated conception of content as determined by ultra-interpretations and go on to solve the problem of distinguishing substantive from conceptual difference in terms of this conception. Even at the level of theory, the way to meet the threat of radical indeterminacy is to reject the assumption that underwrites the suggestion that any difference threatens conceptual divergence. But the objection we are considering adheres to the assumption that there must be matching ultra-interpretations of some kind at the meta-level, guiding our efforts to achieve theoretical coherence if we are to be capable of substantive theoretical disagreements. It is this assumption that a practice account rejects; not only are there no such meta-ultra-interpretations guiding our behaviour about which we can ask: "Do they match up?", but they are not needed. At the level of theory again, the conceptual *locus* of disagreement is participation in world-embedded practices and customs and the criterion of conceptual divergence is inability to participate in those practices. There is a spectrum ranging from participation to inability to participate, on which we may learn to place instances of different ways of going on. By rejecting the assumption that there needs to be some other kind of basis for the distinction between substantive and conceptual difference we undermine the suggestion that any difference threatens conceptual divergence.

However, the response to this first objection to the role of theoretical coherence may prompt a second objection. It may be objected that there is a general tension between Wittgenstein's views about following rules and the role given by a non-centralist coherence account to theoretical coherence. The thrust of Wittgenstein's considerations of what it is to follow a rule is to deny that any kind of ultra-interpretation is needed to determine our meanings or guide our uses of concepts. But isn't the pursuit of theoretical coherence the pursuit of just such an interpretation, an interpretation of what we have done in the past that will guide our efforts to go on in the same way? Isn't interpreting just a kind of theorizing? How is the view that "interpretations themselves do not determine meanings", as Wittgenstein puts it, consistent with the role of theorizing in a coherence account?

Again, we must distinguish the practices of interpretation and theorizing, to which Wittgenstein is not hostile, from the idea of ultra-interpretation, to which he is hostile; ultra-interpretations cannot explain how interpretation and theorizing are possible, and, given constraints, interpretation and theorizing are possible without ultra-interpretations. Wittgenstein's views about what it is to follow a rule apply no less to the second-order concepts of coherence and interpretion, as applied to sets of practices, than to any other concept; they apply both to the understanding of reasons and to the understanding of the relationships among reasons. Our exercise of the technique of bringing considerations of coherence to bear in difficult cases is itself a practice, a custom. Interpretative theorizing when we are in doubt about what ought to be done, all things considered, or what the law requires, is one of the things that we, as persons and members of communities, "simply . . . do".[51] But for such interpretation to play the role it does for persons (as we shall see in further detail in the chapters on preference, interpretation, *akrasia* and coherence) it must be (charitably) constrained. It's the aspiration of ultra-interpretations somehow to constrain themselves in independence from the world, from the agent's natural and social environments, that damns them; Wittgenstein is hostile to this aspiration, not to interpretation *per se*. Indeed, it is one of his aims, as it is one of Davidson's, to understand how interpretation and theorizing, with their attendant characteristic disagreements, are possible. As I mentioned above, we will only see exactly how theorizing and the needed constraints on interpretation work together in later chapters, which will demonstrate various points at which constraints on interpretation anchor and render determinate the theoretical deliberative framework. Thus the answer to this second objection is in part a promissory note. But we can already see that it is one thing to admit that by making claims about what ought to be done or what the law requires we leave ourselves susceptible to the influence of deliberation and theorizing, which involve explicit interpretation of settled cases, and another to claim that ultra-interpretations must be the source of the determinacy of any concept, must guide all our applications. Sometimes we simply do go in for interpretation; a denial that we have interpretative practices is no part of Wittgenstein's views about what it is to follow a rule. In allowing efforts at interpretation their proper place among our practices we do not deny that there is a way of grasping a rule which is not an interpretation, or assert that when we do interpret meta-ultra-interpretations are needed to guide us and to determine what it is we are doing; the possibility of interpretation is, so to speak, secured by practices from the bottom up, and anchored by them again at each level. Application of Wittgenstein's views about how rule-following is possible to our efforts at interpretation themselves averts any danger of a fruitless regress.

## 8. The Shifting Locus of Substantive Disagreement and the Limits of Substantive and Conceptual Difference

Wittgenstein's examples of strange ways of going on involve extending a series of applications of an uncontestable or conceivably contestable concept; they provide us with exercises in delimiting our own form of life from within. Bernard Williams writes: "the business of considering them is part of finding our way around inside our own view, feeling our way out to the points at which we begin to lose our hold on it (or it, its hold on us), and things begin to be hopelessly strange to us. The imagined alternatives are not alternatives to us; they are alternatives for us, markers of how far we might go and still remain within our world—a world leaving which would not mean that we saw something different, but just that we ceased to see".[52] We might think that comparable exercises in delimiting our own form of life with respect to essentially contested concepts are not far to seek, that we have only to look in the daily papers to find the practical and ethical analogues of the student learning to add 2, the soft-ruler people, the woodcutters, the people with absolute colour vision. However, if we seek a *locus* of substantive disagreement by asking questions 1 through 4 above, we find that examples of the sort provided by current events and recent history—crimes of passion, mercy killings, acts of political terrorism—or even the more bizarre cases found in science fiction stories, *can* be made sense of, and only rarely approach the horizon of intelligibility. Indeed, as particular acts in our midst move toward this horizon our sense of the futility of attempts to communicate that the acts are wrong increases, as does our tendency to regard them as lacking the elements of intent required for responsibility, as manifestations of insanity. Consider cases in which persons go to great lengths for no intelligible reason: to acquire saucers of mud, or to avoid even very mild pain on days other than Tuesday at the cost of agony on Tuesdays.[53]

A practice account allows us to place particular examples of divergent series of applications on a conceptual/substantive difference spectrum. Questions 1 through 4 seek out shared practices that might underwrite substantive disagreements about applications of an essentially contested concept. Such practices might underwrite disagreements, for example, about political terrorism, marital fidelity, vegetarianism. The conceptual *locus* of substantive disagreement is not constant from example to example. We are free to move around within our forms of life and to criticize one aspect of them on the basis of another; indeed, it is characteristic of certain forms of life that we do so. On a coherentist view, deliberation requires abilities of more than one kind. We should expect some people to be better at the sympathetic and imaginative scrutiny of alternatives that is needed to discover and illuminate the values at stake in the first place, to see all that it is possible to see about how an alternative might make sense, and others to be better at the more abstract and theoretical thinking that is needed to arrive at all-things-considered judgments. The responsibility of essentially contested concepts to structured sets of conflicting criteria thus makes deliberation, argument, and criticism not only intelligible but inevitable.

A practice account does not, however, allow us to have things both ways: it does not allow us to imagine ourselves as standing in substantive disagreement on certain points with those whose forms of life differ sufficiently from ours. Moreover, we cannot stand in substantive disagreement of any kind with creatures whose forms of life are entirely alien to us, such that we cannot regard their forms of life as expressive of concepts at all. We cannot make sense of the supposition that they make mistakes in virtue of the fact that their forms of life are mistaken, and ours correct.[54] A practice account denies that there could be a residual content to our concepts that transcends all the uses to which we put them, a slack that carries a claim about these uses themselves: that, as a matter of fact, they collectively succeed in delineating the contours of reality, as if their uses did not already embed them within a network of constitutive relationships to the world in virtue of which they carry the determinate information they carry.[55] Some such slack would be needed to make sense of the supposition that our forms of life are right and alien forms of life are wrong, to serve as the conceptual *locus* of their purported opposition to one another. But no such slack is needed to make sense of substantive disagreements; the articulable complexity of our concepts and their susceptibility to theorizing fills this need. The agreement in form of life that bears the weight of substantive disagreement may be preserved through various changes of perspective on the criteria to which essentially contested concepts are responsible and the relationships among them.

To reject this sense of the claim that our concepts succeed as a matter of fact in delineating the contours of reality is to reject what Davidson has called the third dogma of empiricism: the dualism of mind and world, of conceptual scheme and empirical content, of organizing system and something—the Great Fact—waiting to be organized. The effect of this rejection is a large-scale version of the effect of a non-centralist view of reason-giving concepts, which I described in the last chapter: namely, to deny a sense to the challenges of the radical external skeptic. In constraining skepticism to operate within the conceptual scheme we have, we achieve a kind of objectivism. Davidson writes:

> In giving up dependence on the concept of an uninterpreted reality, some-thing outside all schemes and science, we do not relinquish the notion of objective truth—quite the contrary. Given the dogma of a dualism of scheme and reality, we get conceptual relativity, and truth relative to a scheme. Without the dogma, this kind of relativity goes by the board. Of course truth of sentences remains relative to language, but that is as objective as can be. In giving up the dualism of scheme and world, we do not give up the world, but reestablish unmediated touch with the familiar objects whose antics make our sentences and opinions true or false.[56]

Davidson rejects the third dogma on grounds that "charity is not an op-tion" when doing interpretation; "whether we like it or not, if we want to understand others, we must count them right in most matters". "Given the underlying methodology of interpretation, we could not be in a position to judge that others had concepts or beliefs radically different from our own."[57] Before reaching anything that would count as a radically different conceptual scheme, we lose our grip on the very idea of a conceptual scheme, on the very notion of belief. We might come across beings whose alien forms of life we could not interpret at all, but then there would be no basis for attributing a conceptual scheme and beliefs to them at all; not all differences between forms of life express differences between concepts. This is not a verificationist point, about what grounds we might have for believing that others have beliefs. It is rather a point about what beliefs *are*: that it is their nature, given the way in which they get the content they have, to be, in general, true. (Davidson's arguments here, like Wittgenstein's, are in the constitutive rather than the epistemic mode.) Thus there are limits to conceptual difference, to the possibility of conceiving of alternative concepts. Alternatives must be local; we cannot make sense of the possibility of an entirely alien conceptual scheme. *A fortiori*, we cannot stand in substantive disagreement with those who do not share 'our' conceptual scheme:

It would be wrong to summarize by saying we have shown how communication is possible between people who have different schemes. ... For we have found no intelligible basis on which it can be said that schemes are different. It would be equally wrong to announce the glorious news that all mankind—all speakers of language, at least—share a common scheme and ontology. For if we cannot intelligibly say that schemes are different, neither can we intelligibly say that they are one.[58]

To hold, as Wittgenstein does, that for any of our concepts, it is possible for language users not to have it but some other concept or concepts, is not to hold that it is possible for language users to have none of our concepts but an entirely alien conceptual scheme. Given Wittgenstein's prolific efforts at interpretation, of the soft-ruler people, the woodcutters, and so on, it is not surprising that he should anticipate the view that we do not choose to be charitable:

To say: in the end we can only adduce such grounds as we hold to be grounds, is to say nothing at all.[59]

I argued above that, if the interdependence of belief and meaning is analogous to the interdependence of belief and desire in the way Davidson suggests, then charity constrains our efforts to interpret events as action generally, as well as our efforts to interpret events as linguistic action in particular. Our response to the challenge to distinguish same-desire-different-belief cases from different-desire cases must be of the same form as our response to the challenge to distinguish same-meaning-different-belief cases from different-meaning cases. The alternative reason-giving concepts, which express the content of the different desires, must be local alternatives; we cannot make sense of the possibility of an entirely alien scheme of reasons for action, without losing our grip on the very idea of intentional action. To be a reason for action just is to be one of our reasons, related to one another in roughly the ways they are. The problem that essentially contested concepts present for a practice account is that of explaining the sense in which those with whom we disagree actually do share our reason-giving practices, our forms of life; a problem of how to justify our forms of life to those who do not share them cannot arise. Far from leading to relativism, a practice account denies the availability of a detached standpoint from which judgments about what ought to be done might be relativized. We cannot disagree or argue about whether something ought to be done with creatures to whom we cannot attribute the reason-giving concepts that would make the doing of it intelligible as intentional action of a particular type rather than, say, as a series of muscular contractions. The very concept of the will and hence expressions of intention are conceptually if holistically tied to the specific reasons that make it possible for us to understand others as wanting, intending and doing at all.

In the next chapter we shall begin to look at the interpretation of action in detail, in decision-theoretic terms, in order to display the need for constraints on interpretation and the way in which theory and constraints work together to make mistakes, substantive disagreement and practical rationality possible.

# 4

# Preference

## 1. Survey of the Arguments of Three Chapters and Introduction to the 'Problem' of the Eligibility of Interpretations

This chapter and the following two develop in detail the three-part argument indicated in the sketch given above in Chapter 2 section 3. The general aim is to investigate the relationships between preference and value, and to undermine the subjectivist view of that relationship, which I suspect is often underwritten by lack of attention to the role of preference, by contrast to other contentful mental states, within conceptions of the mind. The view I argue for, of course, is that preference and value are constitutively interdependent. I shall begin these three chapters by reminding readers of the three-part strategy of argument.

First, in the present chapter, I shall set out the problem about the determination of content for preference in particular, and show in detail how it arises within the context of formal behavioural decision theory. (I hope I have made the exposition of decision theory accessible to those who know no decision theory; as a result, much of what I say will be obvious to those who do know it.) Decision theories are, after all, attempts to interpret and understand behaviour in terms of beliefs—probabilities—and desires—utilities; they are formalized versions of the interpretative concerns of previous chapters. As many decision theorists themselves recognize, behaviour does not interpret itself, and constraints on interpretation, substantive as well as formal, are necessary if we are to be able to interpret someone as having behaved irrationally, as having made a mistake in following one rule rather than merely having been following a different rule.

The second stage of argument, developed in the following chapter on interpretation, will survey various views about the interdependence of mind and world, and the nature and sources of constraints on interpretation in general, and will draw out their implications for the case of preference in particular. The world, the natural and social environment of the agent, including evolutionary context, human nature, needs, functions, and forms of life, provide substantive constraints on preference. This is a claim about constitutive constraints on preference, not merely one about how we know what the contents of preferences are, nor merely one about the causal influences on preferences, though normal causal interactions between the subject and his environment may themselves provide constitutive constraints on his mental states, via their role in individuating the contents of mental states.[1](Chapter 5 presupposes some familiarity with the relevant literature in philosophy of mind, but does not pretend to make novel contributions to that literature. It occupies a half-way position that may make it largely unnecessary for those who do know the literature and barely comprehensible to those who do not. Nevertheless, it represents the kind of compromise necessary in work that hopes to engage readers from various disciplines. My hope is that it provides sufficient clues and references to make it easy for an interested reader to pursue the relevant sources.)

Each of the two chapters just surveyed essentially summarizes a body of argument; the next chapter, on subjectivism, brings these two bodies of argument together to address, finally, the relationship between mind and values in particular. My argument in the chapter on subjectivism draws heavily on material from the two preceding chapters, applying it to the consideration of the higher-order attitudes that play a distinctive role in personality and in ethics. It is perhaps most straightforward to hold a subjectivist view about the relationship between values and preference in combination with a view of the mind, including preference, as independent of the world. However, one might give up the latter view while holding onto subjectivism, if one thinks that the constraints on preference do not include values, that the natural and social environments of the agent, which one admits may provide constitutive constraints on preference, leave values out. Perhaps it can be shown that preferences in some form, granting the ways in which they are naturalistically and socially constrained, nevertheless determine values; perhaps an account can be given of what values are in terms of preference conceived as value-free. I shall argue that, for persons at least, this is not the case. In this sense, my use of the term *natural* is intended to have Aristotelian rather than reductionist associations; I do not take nature to exclude values, but regard values themselves as natural.[2] At whatever point, conceptually speaking, personal preferences and values arrive in the world, they arrive together; values are as fundamental, for persons, as preferences are. That is, I argue against the view that the constraints on preference should be taken to exclude values, and against what I take to be the best version of the subjectivist view that values are determined by preferences conceived as prior and independent of values.

These claims will only strike someone as circular or vacuous if he is so wedded to the subjectivist project of accounting for values in terms of preferences than he cannot see that this very project is what is under attack. There is no circularity in a different choice of primitives, nor is there vacuity in the rejection of the subjectivist value-free conception of preference in favour of a claim of structured interdependence. (The structure is to come.) And it is still important to keep in mind that in denying one priority or determination claim one need not necessarily assert the contrary priority or determination claim; I do not put forward the Platonistic claim that values are prior to and independent of preferences, but merely deny that preferences are prior to and independent of values. In order to rebut subjectivist reductions of value to preference it is sufficient to show that values may provide constitutive constraints on preference; it is not necessary to deny what I indeed hold to be the correct view, that preference and values are conceptually interdependent and that neither can be reduced to the other.

The topic of the present chapter, then, is one of the central theoretical 'problems' in the foundations of decision theory and its philosophical significance. Borrowing a term from David Lewis, I shall call it *the 'problem' of the eligibility of interpretations*. In the particular manifestations of it which will be discussed here, the 'problem' has been recognized for a long time, at least since the fifties among economists and decision theorists, such as Allais, Savage, and Samuelson, and has been the object of a great resurgence of interest in recent years. However, there is no generally-used label for the 'problem', perhaps because it arises in various contexts in somewhat different forms. Hence I take the liberty of generalizing and labelling the common pattern as the 'problem' of the eligibility of interpretations. There are inverted commas around the word "problem" because I want to try to show that it isn't really a problem, though something important is learned by going through the process of thinking it is and then seeing why it is not.

I shall illustrate the 'problem' by means of simpler, and then progressively more complicated, examples. Three different formal decision-theoretic principles will be in play in this chapter. First, I shall discuss examples involving transitivity, then examples involving the independence of different criteria of desirability from one another given certainty ('Mutual Preferential Independence'), and finally examples involving the independence of preferences that relate to given possible states of affairs from what would be the case in other possible states of affairs ('Independence'). All the while I shall maintain a rather lofty perspective that purposefully leaves some of the technical details of the issues obscure; my purpose is to convey a general view of the landscape, and to leave interested readers to check the sources for details. This is because I think it may be more difficult to see why certain apparently rather technical issues in decision theory are of any philosophical significance, why they should matter to philosophers, than it is to work through the details. The examples in each of these three categories are subjected to what is basically the same argument, the conclusion of which is that substantive constraints on the eligibility of contents are necessary in order for it to be possible for formal constraints to 'bite' and for individuals to violate them, that is, to make mistakes. The examples illustrate with respect to preference in particular general Wittgensteinian and Davidsonian considerations already expounded about the way in which constraints are needed in order for it to be possible to distinguish between someone who makes a mistake or disagrees in "following one rule" and someone who "follows a different rule". The purpose of the discussion is to show how mistakes and disagreement are possible in the realm of reasons for action, and why it isn't always possible to interpret them away.

## 2. Conceptions of the Preference Relation, and Examples of the 'Problem' Involving Transitivity

The examples to be considered concern the conditions that characterize the preference relation, either actual preferences or the preferences of a rational agent. The preference relation may be understood in several different ways, each of which are connected to the 'problem' of eligibility, as I'll try to show in this section. Some take preference to be a relation between *objects*, commodities: I prefer that apple to that orange. This way of thinking is often handy in economics. Some take it to be a relation between *possible actions*: I prefer my eating of that apple in two minutes to my eating of that orange in two minutes. Actions may include accepting a particular gamble among the ones you're offered. This way of thinking is the dominant one in decision theory. These first two conceptions of the preference relation have an advantage that appeals to those with behaviourist leanings, including most economists and decision theorists: such preferences are supposed to be observable, revealed in choices. Others take preference to be a relation between *propositions*: I prefer that it be true that I eat that apple rather than that it be true that I eat that orange. This way of thinking seems natural to many philosophers, and Jeffrey recasts decision theory taking propositions as the objects of preference. Since propositions are much more finely individuated than objects that are chosen, Jeffrey's system works with much richer data than the former systems: it helps itself to the difference between preferring both red and green apples to oranges and preferring green apples but not red to oranges, even when all we are able to observe are choices between green apples and oranges. That is, it helps itself to data about preferences with respect to possibilities, even though the corresponding choices may not be observed. Finally Davidson suggests that a radical decision theory take, in the first instance, uninterpreted *sentences*—patterns of noise, or marks—as the objects of preference. I prefer that the sentence 'je mange le pomme' be true, rather than that the sentence 'je mange l'orange' be true. It's not clear whether this move restores a measure of observability: can one *observe* that someone prefers one sentence rather than another to be true when one does not yet understand the language the sentences are in? Davidson thinks one can at least make an educated guess, subject to revision. On the basis of this data we calculate how probable and how desirable someone thinks the truth of various sentences is, and we only then proceed to interpret the sentences, find out what they are about. If we can't make sense of the person at this stage, we presumably go back and revise our 'observations' of which sentences he or she prefers true. Keeping in mind these last ways of conceiving the preference relation—Jeffrey's and Davidson's—will help in understanding parallels between the issues about the attribution of beliefs and meanings and issues about the attribution of beliefs and desires, or subjective probabilities and utilities.

Let's begin with one of the simplest manifestations of the 'problem'. It is widely held that the preference relation, however it is understood, should not be intransitive. If I prefer apples to oranges and prefer oranges to pears, I do not, or should not, prefer pears to apples. Decision theories, whether used descriptively or normatively, commonly (though not without exception) take transitivity to be an axiom. Now a descriptive theory should be refutable, or it will lack empirical content, and a normative theory should be possible to violate, or it will not provide any constraint on behaviour. Is a descriptive theory postulating transitivity refutable on this point? Suppose I do make several choices which together seem to be intransitive; has the theory been refuted? Not necessarily; the proponent of the theory can point out that I chose a *green* apple instead of an orange, an orange instead of a pear, and a pear instead of a *red* apple. At least he can if I did. What if I didn't; has the theory then been refuted? No; he can surely find some other distinction: I chose an apple with several leaves attached over an orange, but a pear over an apple with no leaves. I evidently found the leaves attractive, and a relevant point of difference. What if neither apple has leaves? Perhaps I made one choice in a shop which also had bananas, and another in a shop which didn't; I chose an apple-in-the-presence-of-bananas over an orange, but a pear over an-apple-not-in-the-presence-of-bananas. At some point however, even allowing for the understandable taste for variety, and for changes of taste, we're likely to balk at the theorist's shameless ad-hoc reinterpretation of the data to get it to fit his theory. At some point we cross a line between interpretations we regard as eligible and those we regard as ineligible. The possibility of empirically refuting the theory depends on our ability to draw this distinction. But what does it amount to? How do we know which interpretations are eligible? What makes them eligible?

Notice that there is a version of the 'problem' that arises for a normative use of the transitivity principle. Suppose the theorist admits that my preferences are intransitive, but says that this shows that I am being irrational, inconsistent, that I've made a mistake. Now I claim in my own defense that my preferences are *not* intransitive, that one apple was green, or had some leaves, or whatever. What further light does my claim throw on the transitivity issue? Of course, my linguistic behaviour itself must be interpreted, and its interpretation is not achieved in isolation from the interpretation of my behaviour in general;[3] there is scope for insincerity, self-deception, and so on. But, even more fundamentally, if it's to be possible for me to make mistakes at all, as people often do, there must be limits to how far I can go in casting about for distinctions; and these limits are not provided by anything in the way of my current experience, or by a neurophysiological description of my brain and/or my bodily movements in making choices. In trying to determine whether my choices are consistent, I look out, at the objects of choice; the limits to eligible interpretation apply to efforts to understand and justify oneself as well as others.[4] In order for me to be convicted of making a mistake, of having intransitive preferences and hence of being inconsistent, we again need to be able to distinguish eligible from ineligible interpretations of my actions and of the contents of the preferences my actions express. Otherwise, as Wittgenstein remarks, whatever is going to seem right to me is right. And that only means that here we can't talk about 'right'—even in the weak form of consistency.[5]

In Table 4.2, Observed Violations of Conditions, to be found at the end of this chapter, there are two somewhat more elaborate examples involving transitivity. In John Broome's example, George prefers staying at home to visiting Rome and visiting Rome to mountaineering, but prefers mountaineering to staying at home. However, he justifies himself by distinguishing four possibilities rather than merely three; staying at home when one has not rejected a mountaineering trip is different from staying at home when one has. Mountaineering frightens him, so he prefers visiting Rome; sightseeing bores him, so he prefers to stay at home; but to decide to stay at home when he could have gone mountaineering strikes him as cowardly. If this is an acceptable distinction between the characters of possible actions and thus an eligible interpretation of his preferences—and who are we to say it shouldn't be, given that how *cowardly* a course of behaviour is may vary with the available alternatives to it, and given that a desire not to be *too* cowardly is perfectly intelligible?—then there is no violation of transitivity.

An example due to Raiffa is also in the table. Many subjects of psychological experiments prefer A, a lottery with a 50% chance of losing $100 and a 50% chance of losing nothing, to B, which is losing $45 for certain. They also prefer B to C, paying $45 in order to be offered a lottery with a 50% chance of winning $45 and a 50% chance of losing $50. However, they prefer C, which is equivalent to a 50% chance of losing nothing and a 50% chance of losing $95, to A, with its 50% chance of losing $100.[6] It would seem that C dominates A, so that if you prefer A to B, you must prefer C to B; but the subjects don't (see Figure 4.1). Thus, one way of interpreting their preferences makes them intransitive. However, again the subjects may be distinguishing four possibilities instead of only three. What they say is that the lottery contained within C is *unfair*, and they would rather not play even after paying $45 to have the chance. But C as a whole is less unfair than A, and A is less unfair than B. This suggests the following: C, a quite unfair gamble, is preferred to A, an even more unfair gamble; but A, an unfair gamble, is still preferred to B, outright robbery. But B, robbery, is better than robbery plus a slightly unfair gamble, which we can call B plus B' (see Figure 4.2).

Whether an action counts as C, getting the best of a bad situation, or B plus B', letting them get away with insult as well as injury, seems here to depend on what the alternatives to it are. If the option is A, it counts as C; but if the option is B, it doesn't. Again, doing-such-and-such-when-you-could-do-one-thing may not be doing the same thing as doing-such-and-such-when-you-could-do-something-else. Is this an eligible interpretation? It does at least make sense to suppose that the subjects might not only be interested in how much money they stand to win or lose, but also in the character of the process

A > B > C

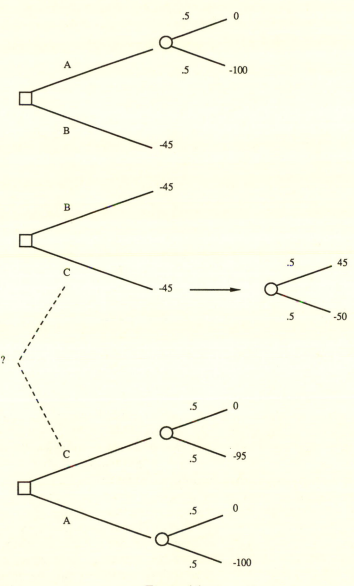

FIGURE 4.1

that is offered them as a means to the possible end of winning money; if the process can be made out as unfair, or in some other way distasteful, they may be willing to pay for the privilege of not playing. That is, they may conceivably care about the character of the games they play to an extent that

$$C > A > B > B \& B'$$
$$B \& B' \neq C$$

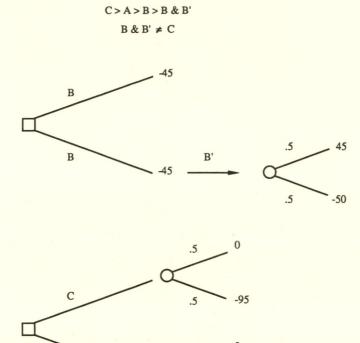

FIGURE 4.2

affects what they choose when actually presented with offers they regard as unsavoury, as well as which offers they'd prefer to be presented with; they may care about the processes which lead to outcomes as well as the outcomes.[7] But even the subjects themselves have to *think* about the fair or unfair character of the alternatives in order to draw these distinctions; and not just any arbitrary distinction they might draw among alternatives will make for an eligible interpretation. Moreover, there is no such thing as an intrinsically self-validating interpretation of the choices they're offered; the money-only interpretation is one possible interpretation, but it is not somehow 'neutral', or exclusively built into the nature of the offered choices, or what would be revealed from a God's-eye view of the 'brute facts' about the distribution in space-time of certain flat rectangular pieces of botanically derived material ('money'), etc. It is an eligible interpretation, but its eligibility equally derives from its context in human institutions and forms of life. This is just to say, again, that there are no such things as ultra-interpretations.

Notice that if we help ourselves to data about the exact propositional contents of preferences to begin with, regardless of whether these contents are reflected in what the agent does, we may seem to avoid the need to interpret, to make decisions about what counts as an eligible content. But if any possible propositional content may be the object of preference, the scope for finding violations of transitivity is severely reduced, since any difference between two possibilities will make them different objects of preference.[8] The conception of preference as relating propositions, unsupplemented by criteria of eligibility, does not put us in a strong position either to make falsifiable empirical predictions or to give binding normative advice.

If we now consider Davidson's scheme, we can see how a variation on Jeffrey's theory to recognize explicitly the role of criteria of eligibility might work. After we have 'observed' preferences that sentences be true, and have applied the formal conditions which yield degrees of belief and desirability that attach to sentences, so that we have an uninterpreted structure of logical relationships, then we must look at the world and see what in it might fit the structure we've got; the world includes facts about values. In doing so, we apply criteria of eligibility to various possible interpretations. Davidson writes: "As with belief, so with desire or evaluation. Just as in coming to the best understanding I can of your beliefs I must find you coherent and correct, so I must also match up your values with mine; not of course, in all matters, but in enough to give point to our differences."[9] Davidson is here sounding his familiar theme that only against a background of agreement does the possibility of disagreement, and of mistake, make sense. It should be emphasized that Davidson does not claim that this three-stage schematization— first, the preferences that sentences be true, second, the formal relationships among them, third, the interpretation of the sentences, what they are about— represents a procedure that is actually gone through, or ought to be. In practice no doubt the stages get mixed together as one tinkers and revises and tries to achieve reflective equilibrium.[10]

Thus, whichever view one takes of the preference relation, the question of the eligibility of interpretations arises. The rest of the examples I shall consider in this chapter will not involve violations of transitivity, but of other conditions; I began with violations of transitivity for the sake of providing a simple and dramatic illustration of the way in which to give formal, or consistency, conditions on preferences either empirical or normative bite we must implicitly depend on substantive constraints as well, that is, on some more or less articulate conception of which interpretations of the contents of preferences are eligible. (Broome puts the point in terms of whether differences between possibilities count as justifiers.)

However, there is another reason for beginning with a discussion of the way in which the problem arises even for the transitivity axiom, which relates to a point made in Chapter 2 section 3. There, I illustrated the need to make assumptions about the substance of an agent's desires as well as their consistency, such as the assumption that an umbrella is more attractive to someone if it rains than if it doesn't, in order to apply Ramsey's method of separating the contribution of belief to determining behaviour from that of desire. In reply it might have been said that Ramsey's method was proposed in service of the project of *measuring* subjective probability and utility, and he simply took it for granted that a mere transitive preference *ordering* of alternatives was given. But the need to make determinations of eligibility cannot be avoided merely by not going in for the measuring project; it arises even for the project of establishing a transitive preference ordering. We shall return to violations of transitivity in Chapters 8, 12, and 13, where we'll be looking in some detail at the way in which intransitivities may result in the presence of conflicting criteria of choice.

### 3. An Intuitive Introduction to the General Idea of Independence Conditions

Next we'll introduce the general idea of independence conditions. In this chapter we'll consider two broadly different kinds of independence conditions, one of which concerns the independence of preferences with respect to certain conflicting criteria from the level of satisfaction of other criteria, and the other of which concerns the independence of preferences given certain possibilities from what would be the case were other possibilities to obtain. Both kinds of independence involve assumptions of separability, non-complementarity, or non-interaction: between the values of the satisfaction of different criteria, in the first case, and between the values of what happens in different possible states of affairs, in the second case. Independence conditions may be unfamiliar to many readers. Thus, before discussing the way in which the 'problem' of eligibility arises with respect to independence conditions, I will try to make their role somewhat more intuitive than it might otherwise be.

Many readers will already be familiar with the issues about distributive justice that arise within the welfarist tradition. In particular, issues arise about the socially preferable distribution of resources (e.g., income and wealth), as opposed to the distribution of utility or welfare, across persons. Classical utilitarians admit that individual utility may decline at the margin with additional units of income, and that such declining marginal utility of income tends, within the additive framework of classical utilitarianism, to favour equalizing the distribution of income across persons. But they resist the further concern with the distribution of utility itself across persons. For this concern to be valid, one would have to depart from the additive character of classical utilitarianism: social welfare, that is, would have to be conceived not simply as the sum of individual utilities, but as itself a function of individual utilities that declines at the margin. One such function, for example, would involve maximizing the product, rather than the sum, of individual utilities. (We can speak of such a non-additive function as non-linear.) If we are maximizing a non-additive social welfare function, social preferences as to how to redistribute income between certain members of society may not be independent of the levels of income of other members of society. This suggests that the total quantity of utility present in society is not all we care about; we also care about how it is distributed, or arranged, with respect to persons. Our concern is such that one person's utility may in effect interact with, or complement, another person's utility; our concern with some person or persons may not be separable from our concern with other persons.

I have introduced in the above paragraph, purposely in a very loose way, various closely related concepts that have application in the intrapersonal decision-theoretic context as well as in the interpersonal context of distributive justice: concepts of distribution, additivity, linearity, independence, interactivity, complementarity. (I have not tried to capture such subtleties as the distinction between weak and strong separability, etc., which are not necessary for my purposes.) In particular, I hope by introducing them in a context that may be relatively familiar to many philosophical readers I serve my aim of making their decision-theoretic applications somewhat more intuitive than they might otherwise be. Issues analogous to those about whether it may be appropriate to depart from the interpersonally additive character of classical utilitarianism arise in at least two separate ways in the intrapersonal context. These issues are raised by what are generally referred to as *independence conditions*.[11] The two separate ways in which analogous intrapersonal issues arise may be understood by setting up two different analogies between interpersonal and intrapersonal decisions. (It should be kept in mind that these are only heuristic analogies; I do not suggest that consistency requires one to resolve the parallel issues the same way in the different contexts.)

First, for the different individuals of classical utilitarianism, substitute different values, attributes, or criteria of choice, all of concern to one person, who must weigh them against one another when they conflict in application to the alternatives he or she faces. Are such different values additively related, or do they interact with one another, so that the distribution of satisfaction across them, in effect, is a matter of concern? These are the issues raised under the heading of *Mutual Preferential Independence* below (which are discussed in greater detail in section 4 of this chapter). Note, however, that for this way of setting up the analogy to issues about distributive justice, no uncertainties or probabilities are involved. The individual knows the consequences of each alternative open to him with certainty; his problem is one of weighing the conflicting values, which definitely apply, against one another.

In the second way of setting up an analogy to issues about distribution between persons, we substitute for different persons not different values, but consequences in different possible states of the world, or, more briefly, different possible worlds. The decision-maker is uncertain about how the world will turn out; the various alternative actions open to him will have different consequences depending on which possible world actually obtains. Now he in effect weighs the consequences of each act in different possible states of the world against one another. He will compare the consequences of various alternatives in each possible world. The question is: do, or should, the preferences he has with respect to consequences of alternatives given one possible world depend on what the consequences of his alternatives are in other possible worlds? That is, does how valuable certain consequences are in one possible world depend on what the consequences would be in other possible worlds, given that the possible worlds in question are mutually exclusive? Can consequences in different possible worlds interact, or complement one another? Can the distribution of utility across different, mutually exclusive, possible worlds *per se* be a matter of concern to the rational decision-maker, in a way that does not reduce to concern with the total amount of utility of the various consequences? If the answer to these questions is *no*, then the decision-maker's utility function has the familiar additive form of expected utility theory: for each act, he weights each possible consequence by its probability, or multiplies the probability of each possible world by the utility of the consequences of that act in that world, and then *adds* these products together. He then does the act which maximizes this *sum* (rather than some other function). This is in effect the requirement imposed by the *Independence Axiom* and the *Sure-Thing Principle* of expected utility theory (which are discussed in section 5 and in Chapter 6, section 1—and see Table 4.1, at the end of this chapter).[12]

It may help to understand (in certain respects, at least) the current debate within decision theory over the Independence Axiom, to pursue a bit further the analogy to issues about whether the distribution of utility across persons may in itself be a matter of concern, independently of the distribution of resources or income. The Independence Axiom, which entails that preferences are "linear in the probabilities", as it is sometimes put[13], demands that the distribution of utility across various possible outcomes is not in itself, *independently of risk aversion*, a matter of concern. As I suggested briefly above, in certain respects, this is similar to requiring that the distribution of utility across persons is not in itself, *independently of dimininishing marginal utility*, a matter of concern. When the latter is required, the overall function the maximization of which is sought has the additive, or linear, form found in classical utilitarianism: one maximizes the sum, or average, of individual utilities, but is not concerned with the distribution of utilities across persons. Distributional concerns must be confined to those representable in terms of the diminishing marginal utility of income, such that the total amount of individual utility is, formally, all that matters.

Why might a classical utilitarian adhere to this requirement? Intuitively, the source of the requirement may seem to be thoughts like these: individuals are the only possible containers, so to speak, of value; their utilities are supposed to be measured so as already to reflect all that is valuable, including the way in which utility diminishes at the margin with increases in income; further value can't somehow hover in the air, inhering in the mere relationships between the utilities of different persons. In particular, the weight we give to one person's utility should not depend on how much utility other people have. Distributional concerns with respect to resources or income are properly absorbed into the measurement of utility and none survive with respect to utility itself. (I am not endorsing this view, merely trying to express intuitions that may lie behind it.) If this were not the case, it might be argued, individual utility would not be a measure of all that really matters; its distribution would matter as well, and that would not be captured by the measure of individual utility. On the other hand, one might take the view that no matter how accurately we measure value to individuals, we cannot rule out the possibility that issues about the sheer distribution of such value across persons will also turn out to be of intrinsic concern to us.

Now consider why one might want to require that the distribution of utility across different possibilities not be a matter of concern. We are substituting consequences in possible worlds for people as the only possible containers, so to speak, of utility. (This kind of substitution should not be unfamiliar; consider approaches to the problem of distributive justice that require one to choose principles of distribution not knowing who one will be, or having an equal chance of being any of the people in society.[14]) The utility one would obtain in different possible worlds of course should affect one's decisions; and utility is measured so as already to reflect one's 'attitudes to risk' with respect to goods. As Deaton and Muellbauer emphasize, a crucial assumption is that "consequences be fully specified so as to contain everything of interest to the agent". But if we have fully specified and accurately measured the value of consequences of acts in possible worlds, how could the mere distribution of this value across possible worlds be of intrinsic concern to us, given that only one possibility will be realized? For example, why should my marginal utilities with respect to the fully specified set of goods available if I should draw a spade vary with how well off I would be if I do not draw a spade? Since only one possibility—I draw a spade or I do not—will actually be realized, why should choices that relate just to the possibility in which I do draw a spade be affected by what might have been the case if various other possibilities had been realized instead? If goods are received together, they may well interact, as white burgundy and salmon trout do (see section 4 below); but how can goods received in different possible worlds interact with one another? I will receive either one lot or the other; never both.[15]

The intuition here is that utilities in different possible worlds should no more be given complementary or interactive importance than should, on the classical utilitarian view, the utilities of different persons. Concerns about risk with respect to goods are absorbed into the measurement of utility, and none survive with respect to utility itself. This seems to be what Tversky is getting at when he comments:

> In utility theory, risk aversion is explained by the concavity of the utility function for money. Once the monetary scale is properly transformed, no risk aversion remains. (In this respect is it somewhat misleading to refer to the measurement of the utility for money as 'the measurement of attitudes towards risk'. One's utility function reflects one's attitude toward money, not toward risk. Risk aversion is an epiphenomenon in utility theory).[16]

However, if we depart from "linearity in the probabilities", the phrase "attitudes towards risk" takes on a more robust sense. The distribution of utility across possible worlds immediately reflects the probabilities of various outcomes; this distribution is equal, for example, in the case of certainty, where the utilities of all possible outcomes are the same. Because of this, when we bring Independence across possible worlds into question, we also raise questions about the ultimate independence of probability and utility, the measures of belief and desire. When the Independence condition is not met, possibilities seem not to be mere containers of utility; the distribution of utility across different possible worlds seems to be taking on the role of an object of preference in itself. If this is so, how can the consequences in each possible world be, as Deaton and Muellbauer put it, "fully specified so as to contain everything of interest to the agent"? In these circumstances one may perhaps wonder whether probability and utility, or belief and desire, constitute wholly distinct, or distinguishable, influences on action.

Tversky writes: "The fundamental assumption of all psychological expectation models, which is independent of any particular measurement method, is that utility and subjective probability contribute independently to the overall "worth" of a gamble. That is, judgments of desirability of outcomes are independent of judgments of likelihoods of events. More specifically, utility and subjective probability are compensatory but non-interacting."[17] Of course, what one does depends both on what one desires and on what one believes, so that beliefs only explain actions in conjunction with desires and desires in conjunction with beliefs; this is the doctrine of the holism of the mental.[18] The fundamental assumption of expected utility theory that Tversky refers to, that utility and probability are independent, is one about the pattern of relationships desires and beliefs are held to *within* the holistic scheme. Granted that the contents of beliefs and desires derive in part from their places in a pattern of attitudes and actions, one may require that these contents be identified in such a way that what one believes does not properly (or at least not normally) depend on what one desires; self-deceptive 'beliefs', held for reasons that are not truth-related reasons for belief but rather for reasons for desiring to believe, are defective *qua* beliefs. And there is a sense in which the converse requirement may seem reasonable as well, though care must be taken in stating it.

The probability of a state of affairs may certainly be used to weight its intrinsic desirability in a variety of ways corresponding to different attitudes to risk, to get the desirability of a whole gamble, as in expected utility theory. Nevertheless, one may require, for example, that the utility of a fully specified positive outcome not "be greater when it is certain than when it is embedded in a gamble", as Tversky puts it.[19] Such an effect cannot be explained in terms of risk aversion as understood in expected utility theory; it violates the Independence Axiom. More generally, it may seem reasonable to require that the relative values of certain fully specified states of affairs in which various goods have been obtained not vary with the lottery structure or probabilistic context in which choices between them are set.

On the other hand, perhaps the rational influences of belief and of desire on action cannot be sharply distinguished, any more than can the respective contributions of the way the world is and of meaning to the truth of sentences. If not, perhaps the holistic pattern in terms of which belief and desire are identified should reflect this by not treating Independence as axiomatic. Theoretical alternatives might be a rebuttable presumption of Independence, so that violations at least have to be the exception rather than the rule (as it can be argued self-deception and *akrasia* must be—see Chapter 8), or simply dispensing with Independence in favour of other weaker axioms, as non-expected utility theorists do (see below, this chapter, section 5).[20] In this chapter I discuss, but do not take a position on, the issue about the normative status of the Independence axiom.

To recapitulate: In the rest of this chapter we'll examine in some detail two kinds of independence condition, the way in which they are related in the decision-theorist's efforts at prediction or recommendation, and the way in which they raise the 'problem' of the eligibility of interpretations. The first kind of independence condition to be considered concerns the relations between the conflicting criteria of desirability and choice that apply simultaneously to given alternatives. It is called *Mutual Preferential Independence* in the table, and involves consequences that occur with *certainty*, but in which various *conflicting criteria* are met to various degrees by the alternatives, as they are in cases involving applications of essentially contested concepts. It tells us that trade-offs between the conflicting criteria in any subset do not depend on the level to which other criteria not in that subset are satisfied. Because the consequences with respect to these criteria of alternative actions are certain, rather than probable or uncertain, we are dealing with *value functions* rather than with cardinal *utility functions* as they are understood in expected utility theory. (In the standard framework, probabilities, either objective or subjective, are used to obtain a measure of cardinal utility, as illustrated in section 5 below, and thus to effect the move from ordinal preference rankings to utility.) The second kind of independence condition we'll consider is simply called *Independence* in the table of conditions, and concerns the independence of preferences about goods received in some possible worlds from what is the case in other possible worlds. It constrains cardinal utility functions, and only comes into play when the alternatives involve known *risk*. The *Sure-Thing Principle* is a counterpart of Independence when instead of known risk we are dealing with *uncertainty*, and thus must derive subjective probabilities as well as utilities, rather than assuming objective probabilities or known risks. (None of these decision-theoretic independence conditions should be confused with the social-choice-theoretic condition, the Independence of Irrelevant Alternatives, which figures in Chapter 12 and which I refer to there as *Condition I*.) To summarize the contexts in which the various pieces of decision-theoretic terminology feature:

> *Independence*: constrains utility functions in the presence of *known risk*.
> *Sure-Thing*: constrains utility functions in the presence of *uncertainty*.
> *Mutual Preferential Independence*: constrains value functions in the presence of *certainty* and *conflicting criteria* (or component value functions).

## 4. Mutual Preferential Independence and the Individuation of Criteria

Given certain consequences and conflicting criteria, decision-makers must arrive at trade-offs between the various conflicting criteria, or values, in-

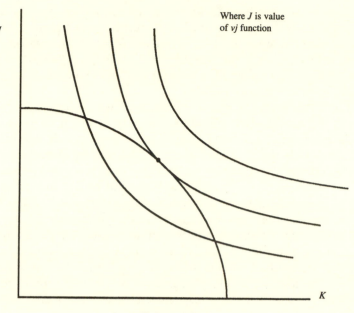

FIGURE 4.3

volved. Multi-attribute decision theory helps the decision maker to articulate the complex decision he faces and to find a value function, which weights and combines the various conflicting component values, to maximize. Or, in geo-metrical rather than algebraic terms, it helps him to construct indifference curves or surfaces on the basis of a few hypothetical preferences he's certain of, as reflected by settled actual and hypothetical choices, then uses these to determine which of the actual alternatives he faces reaches the highest in-difference curve or surface. If the indifference curves were extremely quirky, with all sorts of dips and ripples, this would be a near-impossible task. Decision theory is able to extrapolate from the few preferences the decision maker is certain of to a whole preference structure, embodied in the indifference curves or surfaces that sum up all possible trade-offs among the conflicting values, only by depending on certain formal conditions which impose more or less structural uniformity on the preference space. I shall illustrate with the case of only two such conflicting values, for the sake of simplicity, and then gen-eralize to the case of more than two.

The case of only two conflicting criteria or values, call them $J$ and $K$, can be illustrated, as in Figure 4.3, by a set of indifference curves and a set of actual alternatives, where the goal is to find the actual alternative that reaches the highest indifference curve (the point marked in Figure 4.3). In order to find this point we need to know exactly how the indifference curves are shaped. So we ask the decision maker for a few preferences to get started. But we obviously can't ask him for all of them; if he knew that already there would be no problem to solve. We've somehow got to extrapolate from the few he does know and some general properties to the rest.

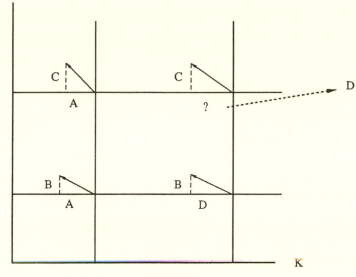

FIGURE 4.4

The basic theorem in this area[21] says that just when a certain condition holds we can get the answer by maximizing some additive value function governing trade-offs between various amounts of $J$ and $K$ that is simply the sum of two separate component value functions, one for $J$ and one for $K$:

$$v(x_j,x_k) = v_j(x_j) + v_k(x_k)$$

The condition that secures this simple structure is a kind of independence condition, where the independence is between the contributions of $J$ and $K$ to overall worth. It says that if at a given level of $K$, one improvement in $J$ is worth the same sacrifice of $K$ as another improvement in $J$, then for all other levels of $K$, these two improvements in $J$ will be worth equal sacrifices of $K$. There may be some ambiguity in the wording of the condition, which can be clarified by reference to Figure 4.4. The condition entails that if, at one level of $K$, improvement $B$ in $J$ will compensate for sacrifice $A$ in $K$ and improvement $C$ in $J$ will compensate for sacrifice $A$ in $K$, and if, at another level of $K$, improvement $B$ in $J$ will compensate for sacrifice $D$ in $K$, then, also at that second level in $K$, improvement $C$ will just compensate for sacrifice $D$ in $K$.

What this means in part is that the indifference curves should not contain eddies, as in Figure 4.5. If they contain such irregularities, it's not possible to generalize from a few preferences to a whole preference structure in such a way that the preference structure can be captured by a simple additive function. However, the relationship between many different goods is *not* such as to meet this condition. Consider the trade-offs one might make between the number of right shoes one possesses and the number of left shoes. Or between the degree of autonomy in a child's character and her level of achieve-

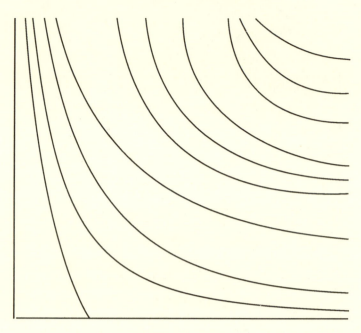

FIGURE 4.5

ment (e.g., excellence at the violin or at mathematics). Or between the degree
to which one's work is flourishing and the degree to which one's family life
is flourishing, as illustrated in Figure 4.6. Whether publishing one's fifth article
is worth the same sacrifice of domestic happiness as publishing one's tenth
may depend on how much domestic happiness one's family enjoys already.
If it's a great deal, publishing one's tenth article may be just as important as
publishing one's fifth; but if it's very little, publishing one's tenth article may
be less important than publishing one's fifth, because at least one has made
a start professionally, and one's family badly needs attention.

The generalization of the additive value function result to more than three
criteria requires Mutual Preferential Independence, which says in effect that
for a set of criteria $[J, K, \ldots N]$, preference trade-offs within each subset of
these criteria do not depend on the level of satisfaction of the criteria not in
that subset. So, for example, preferences between consumption of red burgundy and of white burgundy that depend on how much salmon trout happens
to be available don't meet the condition. Nor do preferences between consumption of vanilla ice cream and of strawberry that depend on how much
hot fudge sauce there is. There is an additive value function for a set of criteria
if and only if they are mutually preferentially independent.

I am *not* claiming that if these independence conditions are not met,
decision theory has nothing to say. That claim would not be true. There are
weaker conditions that still give us quite a bit of information about the preference structure and suppress some irregularities. And perhaps we can divide
the domain up so that the conditions hold in the subdomains. But if it does

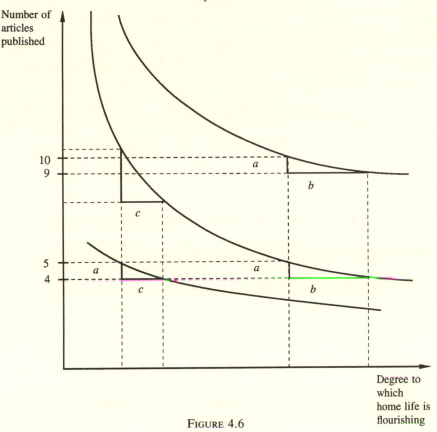

Number of
articles
published

Degree to
which
home life is
flourishing

FIGURE 4.6

happen to be the case that the preference structure is so convoluted that *no* such conditions are met, then what? We can still try to construct indifference curves, or surfaces in the case of more than two dimensions, or to find more complicated value functions to maximize, rather than simple additive ones, but we will have to take many more preference samples to establish these as an appropriate representation of the person's preferences, and many of these hypothetical preferences we ask the decision-maker for may be just as difficult for him to determine as the decision we're trying to help him with.

In fact this would probably not be the procedure recommended by a decision theorist. Rather, the next step would probably be to move straight-away from considering consequences known with certainty to risky conse-quences, from ordinal value functions to cardinal utility functions, in order to make available the many powerful techniques of expected utility the-ory, which ultimately depend on the Independence Axiom introduced in sec-tion 3.[22]

However, before we follow the recommended route let's consider another possible response to the problem: the reindividuation-of-criteria response. If Preferential Independence is not met for given criteria, nevertheless we might be tempted to try to reanalyze the problem in order to find new criteria for which Preferential Independence is met.[23] Let's pursue the suggestion in order to see where it gets us.

Perhaps the failure of preferences as between criteria in a given set to meet the Preferential Independence condition suggests that that those are not really the relevant criteria, that we have not yet drawn the right distinctions among the various objects of preferences. Right shoes and left shoes aren't the relevant categories, but pairs of shoes; and vanilla-ice-cream-with-hot-fudge-sauce forms a unitary attribute, or object of desire, to be compared *en masse* with strawberry ice cream. Perhaps the distinctions between different values, or objects of preference, like those between attitudes of belief and of desire, are bound up with the applicability of an independence condition. If the relationship between the values in one set seems not to be characterized by Independence, then you haven't individuated the values correctly; go back and try to find some other way of interpreting the objects of preference so that the condition does hold. If you succeed, you'll have drawn the right distinctions, found the right interpretation.

This brings us back to the issue about eligible interpretations of the contents of preferences: constraints on eligibility are needed if the Preferential Independence condition is to be falsifiable. I shall spell out the way the eligibility issue arises for the case of apparent violations of Preferential Independence given certainty, and show how, if the Preferential Independence condition is falsified, this first approach may lead us back to plain Independence, where the eligibility issue arises again. I'll then consider the parallel points about apparent violations without certainty.

Note that Preferential Independence does not have the status of an axiom of normative decision theory, as transitivity does, so the issue about eligible interpretations arises in a somewhat different form within a normative version of decision theory; the argument must be conditionalized, so to speak. Preferential Independence is a empirical condition which, *if* it holds, allows the decision theorist either to make predictions about behaviour or to give advice about rational choices. We've already seen that in many cases it seems implausible. If the condition does not hold, the decision maker has not done anything wrong *per se*, as he has when he violates transitivity; it's just that no solution to the problem has been determined—predictions can't yet be made, nor advice be given. (Of course, given a descriptive conception of decision theory, transitivity and other axioms may be treated this way as well.) We're considering the recourse of reanalyzing the problem to find a set of criteria that do meet the condition and thus do yield a solution.

Suppose we start out trying to verify Preferential Independence by checking a few hypothetical preferences and establishing, say, three indifference curves, which do conform to the condition. Now we look at the actual alternatives, interpolate another curve, and predict or advise that decision-maker should do A (as in Figure 4.7). Suppose in fact he does B, which means that Preferential Independence is not met by the curves between two of our initial curves. Is he being irrational? This doesn't follow; nothing says he has to meet Preferential Independence. Without it, however, the problem may not

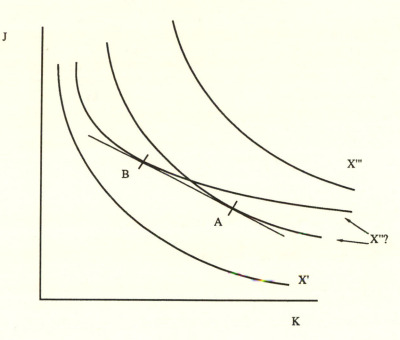

FIGURE 4.7

have a determinate solution. But we can try to reinterpret the original hypothetical preferences by recasting them as preferences between different aspects or combinations of the goods involved, such that the newly individuated criteria do meet Preferential Independence for the cases we've checked. Now, looking back to the choice that caused the problem with the benefit of hindsight, we see that if we'd had our present interpretation of the explananda in the first place, we would have made the right prediction. Or, in the normative case, the decision-maker can look back and say: See, I wasn't being inconsistent at all; I was just interested in something other than what you took me to be interested in.

But now suppose the same thing happens all over again? And what if it's again possible to tailor the new criteria to accommodate the decision-maker's non-conformity, perhaps with the help of Goodmanesque predicates?[24] It may not be obvious how to do so; but equally it may be, as in the examples I gave. If for a large range of possible choices a reinterpretation of the relevant criteria can be found such that prefential Independence is met and the choice is as predicted on that basis, the empirical content of the condition is correspondingly reduced. It rules out only those choices that enterprising reinterpretation of the data cannot squeeze into the framework the condition imposes. To avoid this diminishing of the theory's empirical content, at some point we shall have to resist excessively accommodating reinterpretations. That is, we shall have to distinguish between eligible and ineligible reinterpretations. Having done so, we may find that the condition is in fact sustained empirically. But suppose that a decision-maker makes a further non-conforming choice, and that we cannot reinterpret to accommodate this choice while respecting constraints on eligibility. We can't say he's being irrational if his preferences aren't correctly characterized by Preferential Independence in the first place. Preferential Independence has been refuted, given the eligible interpretation we've fixed on, and we need to look for a new descriptive condition as a basis for further predictions. Moreover, from the perspective of normative decision theory, we're still without determinate recommendations or advice; we can't say whether the decision was consistent or inconsistent with past decisions, right or wrong. Let's now turn to expected utility theory.

### 5. The Argument Yet Again, This Time Concerning Independence and the Individuation of Alternatives: Axiom-conservatism vs. Data-conservatism

At this point we introduce risk and the Independence Axiom, which allows us to attach cardinal utilities as well as probabilities to possible states of affairs. Now the many additional techniques of multi-attribute expected utility theory, the development of expected utility theory that deals with conflicting criteria, are at our disposal to help resolve the problem. There are new, cardinal versions of inter-criterial independence; instead of Preferential Independence, we now try to verify Mutual Utility Independence or the even stronger condition of Additive Independence, which allow us to assess the shape of the whole multi-attribute utility function on the basis of a few determinations of preference.[25] However, I am not going to describe these techniques, because they all ultimately depend on the Independence Axiom, which is what allows us, within expected utility theory, to measure cardinal utility with respect to any attribute in the first place. When we consider the Independence Axiom, we find that another version of the 'problem' of the eligibility of interpretations arises.

The basic idea of expected utility theory is to use probabilities to obtain a cardinal measure of strength of someone's preferences. Suppose we know that someone prefers alternative $a$ to alternative $b$, and alternative $b$ to alternative $c$. Let us assign the value 1 to alternative $a$ and the value 0 to alternative $c$. (For reasons which I will not go into here, there is a great deal of flexibility about how we assign these starting values.[26]) Then our measurement problem is one of determining where in the interval between the value of $a$ and the value of $c$ to locate the value of $b$. This is done, in effect, by creating a series of new alternatives of the form, $a$ with probability $p$ plus $c$ with probability $(1 - p)$, and varying the probability $p$ until we find a point at which the person is indifferent between the new alternative and alternative $b$. We then use the probability $p$ for which this indifference is achieved as the weight or measure of $b$'s utility for this person. We can proceed in a similar way to locate the values of other alternatives in relation to $a$, $b$, and *c*. In general, the expected utility of getting a certain outcome with probability *p* is equal to *p* times the utility of that outcome. For this procedure to work systematically, however, the overall preference ordering must meet certain formal conditions, such as transitivity. Another condition standardly imposed in expected utility theory is the Independence Axiom, which says that *a* is at least as highly ranked as *b* if and only if *a* with probability *p* plus *c* with probability (1 − *p*) is at least as highly ranked as *b* with probability *p* plus *c* with probability (1 − *p*). (Again, Savage's Sure-Thing Principle plays a similar role if we are trying to measure subjective probabilities at the same time as utilities, rather than taking probabilities as given.[27])

However, the Independence Axiom has been repeatedly tested and is claimed to be dependably and systematically violated by experimental subjects—by rats as well as people![28] Some of the 'observed violations' are given in Table 4.1. (The inverted commas around "observed violations" are of course there because the data can be reinterpreted to avoid violating the Independence Axiom.) There are many fascinating discussions of these results and their interpretation in the literature.[29] I cannot discuss a large number of examples in this context, and the points I want to make are quite general. Thus, while certain of Allais' examples are probably the best known, an example of Tversky's is simpler and involves a related certainty effect, and I shall concentrate on that.

In Tversky's example,

> *A* is: 50% chance of $1000, 50% chance of nothing
> *B* is: $400 for certain
> *C* is: 10% chance of $1000, 90% chance of nothing; i.e., 20% chance of A, 80% chance of nothing
> *D* is: 20% chance of $400, 80% chance of nothing; i.e., 20% chance of B, 80% chance of nothing.

Tversky finds that the great majority of experimental subjects prefer B to A and C to D. This pattern of choices violates the Independence Axiom, and is inconsistent with expected utility theory.[30] Since C and D embed A and B, respectively, in what is otherwise the same gamble, this suggests that B in itself—not merely a given chance of B!—may be "more desirable when it is certain than when it is embedded in a gamble".[31]

However, there's a very natural way to reindividuate the states of affairs the subjects are expressing preferences about so that their preferences do not violate the Independence Axiom.[32] On this view, choosing A when one could have had B, or $400 for sure, is not simply the choice of a 50% chance of $1000 and a 50% chance of nothing, but of a 50% chance of $1000 and a 50% chance of nothing plus reactions of regret, disappointment, and/or foolishness at having been greedy and foregone a benefit to be had with certainty. Such reactions of regret, disappointment, and/or foolishness, or concerns with the qualities of character one's act manifest, do not accompany the zero outcomes in C and D, because no *certain* prize is offered as an alternative to C or D. Thus, C is not equivalent to a 20% chance of A plus an 80% chance of nothing; it does not raise the concerns of regret, disappointment, foolishness, or shame at one's greed that A may raise, in virtue of competing with a certain prize, B, so is better than A in that respect. If, with these concerns taken into account, the equivalence does not hold, then the Independence Axiom does not apply and hence is not violated.

In another example, due to Sen, I prefer to review a paper when I get home from work, rather than go to a movie. But if I run a large risk of a serious accident in getting home, I may prefer that if I get home without an accident I go to the movie rather than reviewing the paper; self-indulgence may be an appropriate way to celebrate or express relief, in the circumstances.[33] If my mental states are regarded as part of the outcomes in such a case, it can be argued that there is no violation of Independence, because it doesn't apply to the case so regarded. And it can be argued in defense of Expected Utility Theory and the Independence Axiom that an adequate interpretation of the contents of preferences must take *all* such differentiating reactions into account; thus that the evidence of supposed violations of the axiom is no such thing, but merely reveals that some interpretation other than the one assumed is in fact appropriate. This line urges conservativism about the axioms but flexibility about the interpretations of the data. However, the 'problem' of the eligibility of interpretations now arises again, and again there is a version of the 'problem' for descriptive purposes and a version of it for normative purposes.

The obvious objection for descriptive purposes is made by Samuelson, and by Tversky. Samuelson points out that the Independence Axiom must always be applied to a definite set of entities; it "then has implications and restrictions upon choices among such entities; but, strictly speaking, it need not impose restrictions upon some different . . . set of entities." He then goes on to query "In what dimensional space are we "really" operating? If every time you find my axiom falsified, I tell you to go to a space of still higher dimensions, you can legitimately regard my theories as irrefutable".[34] And Tversky writes:

> One way to interpret the utility for gambling within the classical framework is to redefine the consequences so that winning a certain amount in a gamble is regarded as a different consequence from receiving the same amount as a sure-thing. In spite of its apparent plausibility, this approach does not yield testable predictions because consequences cannot be identified independently of gambles. Furthermore, according to this approach utility has to be defined not on monetary outcomes but on abstract consequences which depend on subjective probabilities as well. This renders the experimental identification of consequences practically unfeasible and the SEU [subjective expected utility] model virtually invulnerable. Thus, although it is possible to argue that the experimental identification, rather than the SEU model, is in error, the fruitfulness of such an approach is questionable."[35]

Parallel to the objection that too much flexibility about the data makes descriptive theories irrefutable and unempirical is the objection concerning normative uses of axioms: too much flexibility about the contents of preferences makes it impossible for someone to be held to a binding standard of consistency that he may conceivably fail to meet. That is, it allows someone always to wriggle out of an accusation of inconsistency, having made a mistake, having violating a normatively binding axiom. By the same token, it makes it impossible for people to disagree about what the normatively binding axioms should be, in the way that non-expected utility theorists wish to disagree with expected utility theorists. Disagreement about axioms requires that interpretation of consequences be constrained and held in common to some extent. Otherwise the disagreement will simply dissolve, as theorists will be talking past one another, about different things; each theorist's assertions in favour of his axioms will hold only relative to the interpretations he favours. Again, the aim of substantive constraints on eligibility is to make mistake and disagreement possible.

Arguments such as these suggest that the correct response to the experimental evidence may be conservativism about the interpretations of the data but a different attitude toward the axioms. Consider first the descriptive alternative, then the normative alternative.

Suppose we retain standard interpretations of the contents of preferences for purposes of a descriptive theory, but consider whether revised axioms might do a better job of prediction than those of expected utility theory. Some non-expected utility theories abandon transitivity as well as Independence, some only Independence, and impose weaker coherence conditions. One theory, for example, which retains transitivity, requires instead of Independence the axioms of mixture-dominance and symmetry, which are not falsified by Tversky's data under their original interpretation.[36]

Next, consider the normative version of data-conservatism. Suppose our interest in the axioms is not descriptive or predictive, but normative. People do make mistakes, and we want to be able to give people advice about what it would be rational for them to do, and to correct their mistakes when they behave irrationally. (In many cases we may do best merely to attribute sheer unstructured confusion to subjects, or failure to keep track of the alternatives and their relationships to one another; but we cannot hold such confusion to be the normal state of affairs without undermining the general supposition that subjects are capable of making mistakes.) Of course, it's critical, if we're going to identify and correct people's mistakes, that we've first identified the normatively correct axioms, and there may conceivably be some theoretical disagreement about which axioms are normatively correct. Even if the theoreticians who disagree with us about a given axiom are *wrong*, for them to be wrong they must at least be talking about the same thing as we are. If each theorist is unconstrained in interpreting the data, they will simply be talking past one another again, not talking about the same thing at all. Thus, for normative purposes we need to secure the possibility of mistake, and of disagreement; and this requires substantive constraints on eligibility. Mistake and disagreement are only possible against the background of agreement that such substantive constraints reflect.

|  | DESCRIPTIVE/PREDICTIVE PURPOSES | NORMATIVE PURPOSES |
|---|---|---|
| AXIOM-CONSERVATISM | old axioms plus ever-new interpretations: axioms not falsifiable | old axioms plus ever-new interpretations: no mistakes or disagreements |
| DATA-CONSERVATISM | constrained interpretations, possibility of false predictions, leading to revised axioms | constrained interpretations, possibility of mistakes, disagreements |

FIGURE 4.8

The theoretical options we face can be summarized as in Figure 4.8. My conclusion is that, whether our purposes are normative or descriptive, substantive constraints on the eligibility of interpretations are needed as well as formal, consistency constraints such as the Independence Axiom. Principles of charity must include, in Davidson's terms, norms of correspondence as well as norms of pattern.

Note that the argument applies quite generally, not just to the Independence Axiom; if we were to abandon that axiom, new versions of the same problem might arise with respect to purported violations of whatever weaker axioms of non-expected utility theory we favoured.[37] Thus the argument I've given does not constitute an argument for abandoning Independence in particular. I emphasize that, for my purposes in demonstrating the need for substantive constraints on eligibility in this chapter, there is no need to take sides in the debate over the Independence Axiom, and I do not do so. My argument in this chapter in no way depends on casting doubt on the axiom as a normative principle. Perhaps among our general guiding principles is a presumption in favour of the Independence Axiom, or indeed some other particular consistency axiom or axioms; but the point is that no such consistency constraint alone is enough to resolve the difficulty. We still have in effect a radically underdetermined system; if our overall decision theory is to be either refutable or normatively binding, we still need further guidance in the form of some independent purchase on which interpretations are eligible. Decision-theoretic efforts at the interpretation of behaviour in terms of beliefs and desires need substantive as well as formal constraints. Only in the light of such substantive constraints on content, constraints on the eligibility—as Lewis puts it—of interpretations, can the empirical or normative adequacy of expected utility theory, or any other formal decision theory, be judged. Only given such constraints can there be a difference between having preferences with a given content that violate some particular consistency condition and preferences that simply have a different content, so that the threat of radical indeterminacy as it arises in this context is dispelled. Or, as

Wittgenstein might put it, only in the context of a shared form of life can there be a difference between making a mistake in following one rule, and following a different rule.

I hope that in this chapter I have at least begun to pay another promissory note, made in Chapter 3, by casting some light on the relationship between the need for constraints and the role of theory in the presence of articulable complexity. In the following chapter we shall move on the the second stage of argument: we'll consider the nature and source of constraints on the eligibility of the contents of preference, and place our considerations within the general context of discussion of the determination of content in the philosophy of mind.

TABLE 4.1   Table of Conditions

---

*Transitivity:*

If you're indifferent between A and B and between B and C, you should be indifferent between A and C; and if you prefer A to B and B to C, you should prefer A to C.

*Mutual Preferential Independence* (of different attributes given certainty) (see Keeney and Raiffa, *Decisions with Multiple Objectives*, pp. 90ff, 111ff):

For a set of criteria, {J, K, . . . N}, preference trade-offs within each subset of criteria do not depend on the levels of satisfaction of the criteria not in that subset.

*Independence* (assuming known risk, i.e., values of probabilities taken by $p$ independently determined):

Lottery $A$ is at least as good as lottery $B$ iff a $p$ chance of $A$ plus a $1 - p$ chance of $C$ is at least as good as a $p$ chance of $B$ plus a $1 - p$ chance of $C$, for all $A$, $B$, $C$, $p$.

(How desirable a consequence is and how probable it is contribute independently to the worth of gambles; the desirability of a given consequence does not depend on which gambles it appears in.)

*Sure-Thing* (assuming uncertainty instead of known risk, i.e., subjective probability of $s$ not already determined) (Savage's P2):

Suppose s and $-s$ are two mutually exclusive and exhaustive states of nature.
A is: if s, then you get W; if $-s$, then you get Y.
B is: if s, then you get X; if $-s$, then you get Y.
C is: if s, then you get W; if $-s$, then you get Z.
D is: if s, then you get X; if $-s$, then you get Z.

Then, if you prefer A to B, you should prefer C to D.

*Substitution* (Raiffa, *Decision Analysis*, p. 62):

If a lottery is modified by substituting for one of its prizes another prize, everything else remaining fixed, and if you are indifferent between the original prize and its substitute, then you should be indifferent between the original lottery and the modified lottery.

(Independence, Sure-Thing and Substitution are closely related.)

---

TABLE 4.2    Examples of 'Observed Violations' of Conditions

---

*Transitivity:*

Broome's example ("Rationality and the Sure-Thing Principle"): George prefers staying at home to visiting Rome and visiting Rome to mountaineering, but prefers mountaining to staying at home. (Mountaineering frightens him, so he prefers visiting Rome; sightseeing bores him, so he prefers to stay at home; but to decide to stay at home when he could have gone mountaineering strikes him as cowardly.)

Raiffa's example (*Decision Analysis*, p. 75):

Many subjects of psychological experiments prefer A, a lottery with a 50% chance of losing $100 and a 50% chance of losing nothing, to B, which is losing $45 for certain. They also prefer B to C, which is paying $45 in order to be offered a lottery with a 50% chance of winning $45 and a 50% chance of losing $50. However, they prefer C, which is equivalent to a 50% chance of losing nothing and a 50% chance of losing $95, to A, with its 50% chance of losing $100.

(The lottery contained within C is unfair, and they would rather not play even after paying $45 to have the chance. But C as a whole is less unfair than A, and A is less unfair than B.)

*Preferential Independence* (of different attributes under certainty):

Number of right shoes and number of left shoes.

Amount of white burgundy as opposed to red burgundy and amount of salmon trout.

Degree of autonomy in a child's character and her level of achievement (e.g., excellence at violin, or at mathematics)

Flourishing of one's work and flourishing of one's family life.

*Independence/Sure Thing:*

Tversky's example:

A is:  50% chance of $1000, 50% chance of nothing

B is:  $400 for certain

C is:  10% chance of $1000, 90% chance of nothing; i.e., 20% chance of A, 80% chance of nothing

D is:  20% chance of $400, 80% chance of nothing; i.e., 20% chance of B, 80% chance of nothing

Many experimental subjects prefer B to A and C to D.

Allais' example:

A: $500,000 for certain

B: 10% chance of $2,500,000; 89% chance of $500,000; 1% chance of status quo

C: 11% chance of $500,000; 89% chance of status quo

D: 10% chance of $2,500,000; 90% chance of status quo

Most prefer A to B and D to C.

Savage's version of Allais' example (*Foundations of Statistics*, p. 103):

Subjects draw from an urn containing 100 tickets, numbered 1 to 100.

A: ticket 1 pays $500,000; tickets 2–11 pay $500,000; tickets 12–100 pay $500,000

B: ticket 1 pays $0; tickets 2–11 pay $2,500,000; tickets 12–100 pay $500,000

C: ticket 1 pays $500,000; tickets 2–11 pay $500,000; tickets 12–100 pay nothing

D: ticket 1 pays nothing; tickets 2–11 pay $2,500,000; tickets 12–100 pay nothing.

Diamond's example:

I must decide which child gets the one piece of candy; the coin is fair.

A: heads and Johnny gets it; tails and Mary gets it.

B: heads or tails and Mary gets it.

C: heads or tails and Johnny gets it.

D: heads and Mary gets it; tails and Johnny gets it.

Even if the child who loses won't know the other child has won, I may prefer A to B and D to C, because A and D are fairer, respectively. (Discussion in Chapter 6.1)

TABLE 4.2 (*continued*)

Ellberg's example (concerns distinction between known risk and uncertainty):

Subjects are asked to draw a ball from an urn known to contain 30 red balls and 60 balls that are black and/or yellow, in unknown proportions (there could be 60 black, 60 yellow, or any combination of black and yellow).

A: red pays $100; black pays $0; yellow pays $0.

B: red pays $0; black pays $100; yellow pays $0

C: red pays $100; black pays $0; yellow pays $100

D: red pays $0; black pays $100; yellow pays $100

Most subjects prefer A to B and D to C; B and C involve greater 'epistemic' risk than A and D. (For discussion, see, e.g., Gardenfors and Sahlins; Eells, p. 39; Chapter 15.6 below.)

# 5

# Interpretation

## 1. The Need for Substantive as Well as Formal Constraints on Eligibility: a Sample of Views

What can be said about the nature and source of the constraints on the eligibility of interpretations? In Chapter 3 I argued that they cannot be solely the products of interpretation itself; to think they could be is to slip into supposing there could be ultra-interpretations of some kind. Any interpretation is itself susceptible to multiple further interpretations; to end the regress we can't appeal to mythical intrinsically self-interpreting entities but must reject the conception of the contents of the mind as independent of the world which gives rise to the problem of radical indeterminacy to begin with. This is to recognize constitutive constraints on interpretation, provided in part by the normal relations of the mind to the world, in virtue of which mental states have the contents they have and which furnish the framework within which interpretation is possible. These points are familiar applied to sense-data, private representations, special experiences of supposedly meaning this or that, but they apply equally to practices (whether individual or social), behaviour, dispositions, and capacities if someone is tempted to individuate the latter independently of their worldly context. The way in which the problem of eligibility arises in decision theory demonstrates that bodily movements, dispositions, and capacities, individualistically characterized, are no more capable of interpreting themselves than anything else. The needed constraints on interpretation still leave ample room for interpretation, for disagreement, and for there to turn out to be a degree of underdetermination in the relations of mind to world. But the *a priori* threat of radical indeterminacy is averted by constitutive constraints on interpretation in a way that it can never be by appeal to ultra-interpretations. Whatever the normal relations of mind to world are, they're not up to us.

The problem of eligibility with respect to the propositional attitudes in general is widely recognized, and it is also widely held that the constraints on eligibility are not, to borrow a phrase made famous by Hilary Putnam, in the head.[1] Not a great deal has been said, however, about the nature of

84

constraints on eligibility with respect to preference in particular. A sample of relevant comments, from Savage, Samuelson, Broome, Davidson, and Lewis, follows, after which we'll be in a position to raise some general issues about eligibility with respect to preference. Recall that my aim in this chapter is not to make novel contributions to the existing philosophical literature but rather to survey and highlight relevant parts of it in order to make certain applications of it with respect to preference. Those to whom the positions characterized are thoroughly familiar should skim through to the following chapter.

In Savage's classic work on the foundations of statistics we find the following comments. "In general, the reinterpretation needed to reconcile various sorts of behavior with the utility theory is sometimes quite acceptable and sometimes so strained as to lay whoever proposes it open to the charge of trying to save the theory by rendering it tautological. The same sort of thing arises in conection with many theories, and I think there is general agreement that no hard-and-fast rule can be laid down as to when it becomes inappropriate to make the necessary reinterpretation."[2] Samuelson is willing to say a bit more on Savage's behalf, in answer to his own challenge, which I cited toward the end of the last chapter. He thinks we may hope to find a significant range of human behaviour that can approximately be accounted for by expected utility theory applied to a specifiable and convenient set of entities, and suspects that while we will not succeed in understanding gambling and risk-taking in general merely in terms of monetary prizes, we may be more successful along these lines with certain areas of corporate behaviour.[3]

John Broome takes a bolder and philosophically more interesting line, in the course of defending Savage's Sure-Thing Principle against apparent violations by reindividuating alternatives. (Recall from the last chapter that the Sure-Thing Principle is closely related to the Independence Axiom, although Sure-Thing does not assume known probabilities but merely uncertainty, and it permits the determination of a decision-maker's subjective probabilities along with his utilities. The principle is set out, along with 'observed violations', in Tables 4.1 and 4.2 at the end of the last chapter.) Broome recognizes that critics of the Sure-Thing Principle may regard his defense of it by reindividuating the alternatives as achieving only a hollow victory. The critics may worry that as the alternatives are individuated more and more finely, axioms of coherence such as transitivity and the Sure-Thing Principle become easier and easier to satisfy, finally providing no constraint at all on behaviour. And they may fear that once we depart from the most familiar, coarse schemes of individuation, in monetary terms, there will be no place to stop short of the finest scheme of individuation. Broome responds as follows:

The correct place to draw the line is between justifiers and non-justifiers, between propositions that justify a preference and those that do not. Drawing the boundary itself amounts to setting up some principles of rationality: rationality requires a person to be indifferent between classes of worlds that differ only in non-jusitifiers. These principles of indifference are logically prior to the principles of coherence because they determine precisely what the principles of coherence mean.

Broome allows that justifying differences between alternatives include certain differences with respect to the agent's or anyone else's feelings or reactions, such as regret, foolishness, anxiety, exhilaration, etc., and also differences with respect to the ethical characteristics of the alternatives—some decisions may be cowardly, others virtuous in various ways. Justifying differences between alternatives are distinctions with respect to some intelligible reason-giving characterization of the alternatives. (I will of course hold, following Wittgenstein, that an experience or feeling by itself could not provide the needed constraints on eligible distinctions; although of course it may characteristically be present in reaction to an intelligible difference between the alternatives.) He continues:

> I imagine that the critics of the STP may be sceptical about the existence of these principles of indifference. They may doubt the distinction between justifiers and non-justifiers. But then they will have to allow that any difference at all can justify a preference. . . . In that case the principles of coherence will indeed be empty of practical significance, and this is true not just of the STP but of transitivity also. So in repudiating principles of indifference the critics are repudiating coherence altogether.[4]

This line of thought doesn't by itself constitute a complete defense of the Sure-Thing Principle in particular. The implicit further claim, which restores the refutabilility and bindingness of expected utility theory, must be that in fact we will not need to draw impermissible distinctions in order to account for intuitively acceptable apparent violations of the Sure-Thing Principle; the permissible distinctions will not fall short but will account for the problematic cases. If there were problematic cases that the permissible distinctions could not handle, then doubt would be cast on the Sure-Thing Principle. Broome doubts that there are such cases; but if there were they might, given the principles of indifference, constitute evidence in favour of one of the non-expected utility theories. Again, it would not serve my purposes in this chapter to take a side in the debate about the Sure-Thing Principle. The point for present purposes is that only given substantive constraints on the eligibility of interpretations does a real issue re-emerge between the alternative formalizations given by expected and non-expected utility theories. And only together do formal and substantive constraints on the interpretation of behaviour produce refutable or normatively binding decision theories.

Notice that, following Broome, we have worked around by a different route to a conclusion in harmony with Davidson's views on charity in interpretation. Davidson's own scheme, as I explained earlier, involves substituting for Jeffrey's preferences between propositions, preferences that uninterpreted sentences be true. The formal constraints of Jeffrey's theory are then applied to yield measures of the desirabilities and subjective probabilities of the truth of these still uninterpreted sentences. Only at the last notional 'stage' in the procedure Davidson describes do we depend on substantive constraints, principles of charity, when we finally look at the world and determine which of the many possible ways of carving it up and assigning contents to the formal structure of desired and believed sentences is indeed the way that makes best sense. In Davidson's scheme as in Broome's, we need to distinguish between, on the one hand, characterizations of alternatives or states of affairs that are intelligibly related to values and human goods, thus potentially reason-giving, with respect to which distinctions between alternatives may be justified, in Broome's terminology, and, on the other hand, characterizations that are none of these things. Such intelligibility makes for eligibility. The shared values by reference to which we are able to draw this line are ultimately among the substantive constraints in both schemes.

Finally, in two recent articles, David Lewis elaborates the notion of eligibility as it emerges quite generally from considerations about interpretation, which our worries about transitivity and independence merely provide illustrations of. He writes of the need, to avoid radical indeterminacy of interpretation, for principles of charity which "impose *a priori*—albeit defeasible— presumptions about what sorts of things are apt to be believed and desired; or rather, about what dispositions to develop beliefs and desires, what inductive biases and basic values, someone may rightly be interpreted to have". He continues:

> It is here that we need natural properties. The principles of charity will impute a bias toward believing that things are green rather than grue, toward having a basic desire for long life rather than for long-life-unless-one-was-born-on-Monday-and-in-that-case-life-for-an-even number-of-weeks. In short, they will impute eligible content, where ineligibility consists in severe unnaturalness of the properties the subject supposedly believes or desires or intends himself to have.

Concerning the status of the principles that constrain interpretation, in particular the charitable presumption in favour of eligible content, he cautions:

> We must shun several misunderstandings. It is not to be said (1) that as a contingent psychological fact, the contents of our [mental] states turn out to be fairly eligible, we mostly believe and desire ourselves to have not-too-unnatural properties. Still less should it be said (2) that we should daringly presuppose this in our interpreting of one another, even if we haven't a shred of evidence for it. Nor should it be said (3) that as a contingent psychological fact we turn out to have states whose content involves some properties rather than others, and that is what makes it so that the former properties are more natural. . . . The error is the same in all three cases. It is supposed, wrongly as I think, that the problem of interpretation can be solved without bringing to it the distinction between natural and unnatural properties; so that the natural properties might or might not turn out to be the ones featured in the content of thought according to the correct solution, or so that they can afterward be defined as the ones that are so featured. I think this is over-optimistic. We have no notion of how to solve the problem of interpretation while regarding all properties as equally eligible to feature in content. For that would be to solve it without enough constraints. Only if we have an

independent, objective distinction among properties, and we impose the presumption in favour of eligible content *a priori* as a constitutive constraint, does the problem of interpretation have any solution at all. If so, then any correct solution must automatically respect the presumption. There's no contingent fact of psychology here to be believed, either on evidence or daringly. . . . The reason natural properties feature in the contents of our attitudes is that naturalness is part of what it is to feature in them. It's not that we're built to take a special interest in natural properties, or that we confer naturalness on properties when we happen to take an interest in them.[5]

Both Lewis and Davidson emphasize the constitutive character of the needed constraints, or principles of charity; it is an *a priori* matter, and not up to us, that mental states are thus constrained, as without the constraints, determinate content would not be possible at all.

This brief survey of views already raises large issues about how natural constraints on the eligibility of content should be generally characterized, which would require at least an entire book to discuss adequately. The remarks that follow merely try to clarify certain points about their characterization that may be liable to misunderstanding, and do not pretend to be a substitute for some familiarity with the literature. I shall make free expository use of points made by various philosophers whose work is relevant, especially Burge, Davidson, Lewis, and Wittgenstein, with apologies in advance for slurring over the (sometimes large) differences between them about the nature of the needed constraints (some of which I shall signal in notes). Despite the differences, there is extremely significant common ground in the recognition of the need for constraints on content, which is pertinent to my purposes in this chapter.

## 2. Special Feelings Don't Help

Constraints on the eligibility of content are needed if we are to be able to say what is wrong with a kind of radical skepticism about the contents of the mind, which lands us with a paradox to the effect that even when all the evidence is in, (individual–dispositional, instrospective, qualitative, etc.), there can be no determinate fact of the matter about whether someone means one thing or another, whether the content of his attitude is one thing or another. And if there is no such thing as determinate content, there is no difference between consistency or inconsistency. A classic modern statement of this skepticism is found in Chapter 2 of Kripke's *Wittgenstein on Rules and Private Language*. Kripke's skeptic challenges us to say what it is in virtue of which someone means *plus* by 'plus', rather than, say, *quus*, a function that takes him to the number 5 for any arguments greater than a certain number (choose a number large enough so that the person whose meaning is in question has never applied the function to arguments larger than it). It is controversial whether Wittgenstein accepts the skeptical paradox, as Kripke suggests, or rather regards it as an absurdity that we only fall into if we have an erroneous conception of content to begin with.[6] I subscribe to the latter view. Either way, however, the negative force of Kripke's interpretation of Wittgenstein stands: he shows that the skepticism can be neither responded to nor avoided *ab initio* by a conception of content as determined by the subject's dispositions, by considerations of simplicity, by introspection, or by the subject's experiences, as none of these can constrain what he goes on to do so that it is possible for him to go on inconsistently.

We have already, in preceding chapters, rehearsed Wittgensteinian arguments supporting these points. Kripke's account, however, is particularly illuminating about why no ground is gained against the skeptic by invoking first-person introspection of what it feels like inside. Thus it may be helpful to those not familiar with his account to suggest a bit more of what he has to say on this point in particular, about why what it feels like inside doesn't, and couldn't, determine content:

> The idea that we lack 'direct' access to the facts whether we mean plus or quus is bizarre in any case. Do I not know, directly, and with a fair degree of certainty, that I mean plus?
>
> . . . Why not argue that "meaning addition by 'plus' " denotes an irreducible experience, with its own special *quale*, known directly to each of us by instrospection?
>
> I referred to an introspectible experience because, since each of us knows immediately and with fair certainty that he means addition by 'plus', presumably the view in question assumes we know this in the same way we know that we have headaches—by attending to the 'qualitative' character of our own experiences. Presumably the experience of *meaning addition* has its own irreducible quality, as does that of feeling a headache. The fact that I mean addition by 'plus' is to be identified with my possession of an experience of this quality.

However, even if I had such a 'feeling' of addition, how could it determine what I mean about cases I have never considered? It could not provide the normative constraint needed to underwrite the possibility of mistakes. In fact it would leave me free to go on in any way I pleased in each new case, and would give me no basis for rejecting the skeptic's claim that when all the facts are in I may just as well mean *quus* as *plus*.

> So: If there were a special experience of 'meaning' addition by 'plus', analogous to a headache, it would not have the properties that a state of meaning addition by 'plus' ought to have—it would not tell me what to do in new cases. In fact, however, Wittgenstein extensively argues in addition that the supposed unique special experience of meaning (addition by 'plus', etc.) does not exist. His investigation here is an introspective one, designed to show that the supposed unique experience is a chimera.
>
> . . . Wittgenstein does not base his considerations on any behavioristic premise that dismisses the 'inner'. On the contrary. . . . Careful consideration of our inner lives, he argues, will show that there is no special inner experience of 'meaning' of the kind supposed by his opponent.[7]

Neither could introspection of a special inner experience of preferring this or that, even if there were one, by itself provide constraints on the eligibility of content or constitute the difference between having inconsistent preferences with one content and consistent preferences with a different content. Any such feeling will leave me free to interpret it as I please and hence to go on as I please in new cases, so that anything I do will count as 'consistent'.

The negative part of Kripke's interpretation is in harmony with the arguments I've made above, to the effect that interpretation itself cannot be the sole source of the needed constraints on contents. He shows that the needed constraints cannot be provided by dispositions, considerations of simplicity, or special inner experiences. But how *is* determinate content possible, then? What *are* the character and sources of the needed constraints?

### 3. Constraint by Physical and Social Environment: The Rejection of Psychological Individualism

Perhaps the most widely discussed constitutive constraints are those that concern the relations in which the contents of a subject's mind stand to his natural and social environments, as illustrated by Twin Earth thought experiments in which the contents of a subject's mental states are found to vary counterfactually along with aspects of his environment, while his physiological/bodily states and the immediate causal impacts of his environment on his body are held constant. The Twin Earth-style of argument applied to meanings, and the slogan that meanings aren't in the head, are of course due to Putnam, whose thought experiments demonstrate constitutive links between the meanings of natural kind terms, such as "water" and "gold", and the subject's physical environment. In a series of articles Burge has employed the Twin Earth-style of argument as a basis for rejecting psychological individualism.

The cases discussed in the earlier of Burge's articles, involving uses of the terms "arthritis", "contract", "sofa", etc. in counterfactually varying social contexts, emphasize constitutive links between the contents of someone's beliefs and his *social* environment.[8] For instance, someone generally competent in English who would assent to many true sentences containing the term "contract" is reasonably credited with propositional attitudes the content of which involves contracts. If he asserts "Contracts must be written agreements", whereas in fact contracts may perfectly well be unwritten, he would reasonably be held to have a false belief about contracts; he can have the concept of a contract and beliefs about contracts even though his understanding is deficient in that he draws distinctions that don't in fact apply to contracts.[9] But now consider another possible world in which the subject's physiological history, sensory intake, motions, utterances, are exactly the same in physical terms, in which his "dispositions to respond to stimuli are explained in physical theory as effects of the same proximate causes" and "all of this extends to his interaction with linguistic expressions". The counterfactuality of the second possible world concerns only the subject's social environment; in it, "contract" only applies to written agreements. In the counterfactual world, the subject's utterance expresses a true belief the content of which does not involve the concept of contract at all, but some more restricted notion. The content of his belief is sensitive, though not via the intrinsic character of proximal causal impacts, to his social environment. It varies with the relations he stands in to his linguistic community, which make it possible to distinguish the same-meaning-different-belief case from the different meaning case.

The moral of the examples is, in effect, that the difference between making a mistake in following one rule—in the example, a false belief about contracts—and following a different rule, or none at all, is not to be found among the intrinsic, non-relational, individualistically identified properties, movements, or states of an individual; "What, in a complicated surrounding, we call 'following a rule' we should certainly not call that if it stood in isolation"[10]—or in a different surrounding. Moreover, Burge has emphasized in recent work that his style of argument, and his consequent rejection of psychological individualism, does not depend on incomplete understanding on the part of the subjects; there are further examples which rather involve theoretical disagreement on the part of competent speakers about what sofas,—or, to take a case somewhat closer to my concerns, contracts—, really are.[11]

In Burge's more recent work his examples have given greater emphasis to the subject's *physical* environment as a source of constitutive constraints. About perceptual representation he writes:

> Not only do our perceptual presentations or experiences have the qualitative features that they have because of the law-governed ways that our sense organs and neural system interact with the physical environment. But their giving empirical information to conscious beings about the environment—their representing it—depends on their qualitative features being regularly and systematically related to objective features of the environment.[12]

Burge emphasizes the importance of distinguishing the causation of *particular* mental states from the individuation of their contents in terms of *normal* causal relations to environment:

> Variations in the environment that do not vary the impacts that causally 'affect' the subject's body may 'affect' the individuation of the information that the subject is receiving, of the intentional processes he or she is undergoing, or of the way the subject is acting.

> We may agree that a person's mental events and behavior are causally affected by the person's environment only through local causal effects on the person's body. Without the slightest conceptual discomfort we may individuate mental events so as to allow distinct events (types or tokens) with indistinguishable chemistries, or even physiologies, for the subject's body. Information from and about the environment is transmitted only through proximal stimulations, but the information is individuated partly by reference to the nature of normal distal stimuli.[13]

Thus different *normal* causal relations may individuate contents differently in counterfactual cases despite the stipulation of intrinsically indistinguishable causal impacts on the subject in the *particular* case. When this view is applied to perception, a familiar point about systematic error emerges:

> The methods of individuation [of intentional content] are governed by the assumption that the subject has adapted to his or her environment sufficiently to obtain veridical information from it under certain normal conditions. If the properties and relations that *normally* caused visual impressions were regularly different from what they are, the individual would obtain different information and have visual experiences with different intentional content. If the regular, law-like relations between perception and the environment were different, the visual system would be solving different information-processing problems; it would pass through different informational or intentional states; and the explanation of vision would be different.
>
> When we seek to determine the intentional content or representational types in a creature's perceptual experience, we determine what objective properties are discriminated by its perceptual apparatus. That is, we build up intentional type attributions by determining the types of objective entities whose instances regularly causally affect the creature's sense organs and are normally discriminated perceptually by the creature—or at least by creatures of the same species.
>
> This fact about perception constitutes, I think, a qualified basis for the oft-repeated slogan that error presupposes a background of veridicality.
>
> . . . It makes no sense to attribute systematic perceptual error to a being whose perceptual representations can be explained as the results of regular interaction with a physical environment and whose discriminative activity is reasonably well adapted to that environment.[14]

Thus features of the subject's world, both physical and social, may determine, in a constitutive sense, i.e., may individuate, the content of his mental states. There are certainly differences between the physical and social cases,[15] but they both provide the needed constraints and there is no essential tension or incompatibility between them. We can recognize the need for constraints on contents while nevertheless aiming to be reasonably liberal and pluralistic in recognizing sources of the needed constraints. Nor is there any reason someone's social environment should count as any less part of his natural surroundings, part of the world he finds himself in, than his physical environment does. That is, we find no necessity in Burge's views about the constitutive constraints on content to postulate or accept a dichotomy between the natural and the social.[16]

## 4. The Mind as World-laden: Naturalism vs. Idealism

Burge often argues by appealing to intuitions in thought experiments, rather than by offering a general and abstract argument about the nature of interpretation. However, the argument now familiar about the threat of indeterminacy and the need for constraints on interpretations is very close to the surface of some of his work.[17] Moreover, his use of thought experiments helps to guard against certain misunderstandings of more general and abstract arguments that have been offered for related conclusions by Davidson and Wittgenstein. I have in mind misunderstandings of these latter arguments as idealist or verificationist in tendency. In essence, the misunderstanding involves seeing these arguments as merely another attempt to show the world to depend on the mind, rather than as an attempt to show the mind as, in effect, naturalized, by denying the independence of the mind from the world, or, more radically, by rejecting the dualism of mind and world altogether.

As discussed in Chapters 2 and 3, Davidson argues for principles of charity, which give truths about the world as well as requirements of consistency— "norms of correspondence" as well as "norms of pattern"—a constitutive role in relation to the contents of mental states. Thus, as we've seen, only against a background of veridality and agreement do the possibilities of error and disagreement make sense. Davidson writes:

> What stands in the way of global skepticism of the senses is, in my view, the fact that we must, in the plainest and methodologically most basic cases, take the objects of a belief to be the causes of that belief. And what we, as interpreters, must take them to be is what they in fact are. Communication begins where causes converge: your utterance means what mine does if belief in its truth is systematically caused by the same events and objects.[18]

This type of view has sometimes been regarded as verificationist in spirit, for example, by Blackburn, who interprets it as involving an argument to the effect that if we couldn't recognize something as a particular mental state it couldn't be such, or idealist in tendency, for example, by Nagel, who regards it as a way of cutting the world down to the size of our minds (rather than as a way of conceiving our minds as world-involving); Williams and Nagel similarly cast aspersions of idealism on Wittgenstein's views about rule-following.[19]

However, in the light of the common emphasis placed by Davidson, Burge, and Lewis on the *objectivity* of the properties and relations that individuate content, we can see how this kind of reading goes wrong. Davidson contrasts his view of the causal constraints governing interpretation with Quine's by commenting that "Quine makes interpretation depend on patterns of sensory stimulation, while I make it depend on the external events and objects the sentence is interpreted as being about" and that "Quine's proposal, like other forms of verificationism, makes for skepticism".[20] Davidson argues in effect that if principles of charity or constitutive constraints on content do not hold, then radical indeterminacy of content does and it is not possible for us to understand one another. However, understanding *is* possible, and radical indeterminacy does *not* obtain; in order to explain how, we must thus concede that constitutive constraints do hold.[21] And Wittgenstein argues that what saves us from the intolerable paradox that no course of action can be determined by a rule, because every course of action can be made out to accord with the rule, and also to conflict with it, is that there is a way of grasping a rule which is not an interpretation, that obeying a rule is a practice. What someone is doing, which practice he is participating in, is determined by the forms of life that provide the normal context of his activity and the contraints on interpretation which make possible a distinction between mistakenly applying one rule and applying a different rule. Engagement with the world and other people, the speaker's natural—physical and social—environment, is what saves the mind from the threat of indeterminacy posed by a certain kind of skepticism about the contents of the mind.[22] If determinacy of content and hence rule-following and understanding are possible, and indeed they are, then there must be constitutive constraints on the relations in which the mind stands to the world, where the direction of individuation may be from world to mind, but not wholly *vice versa*. This is not idealism, but in some sense just the denial of it!

The rejection of the independence of mind from world has the effect of silencing radical external skepticism, which is also an ambition of idealism. But this does not make the former view a kind of idealism.[23] Idealism attempts to silence skepticism through a revisionary conception of reality, which cuts it down to the size of our minds so that some kind of general contact between our minds and reality is guaranteed; this is altogether different from a conception of our minds as, so to speak, world-laden—even if the effect is to guarantee such general contact, *given* that mental states with determinate content, minds capable of understanding and being understood, exist. It remains altogether possible that there are forms of life interpretation of which is not possible, forms of life without contentful mental states at all. And nothing *guaranteed* that there would be any minds, determinate content, or understanding at all. There might not have been. But in fact there are; the aim is to explain how this is possible.[24]

In general, however, it is important to avoid spurious dichotomies here, and not to overstate the contrast in direction of determination. What's in question is a denial that the contents of the mind are given in some way independently of the subject's environment and his relations to it; from the denial of one independence claim the contrary independence claim does not necessarily follow (though in particular cases it may be appropriate). When the contents in question are those of preferences and the relevant features of the environment are the reason-giving characteristics of the alternatives the agent faces, the contrary independence claim, which I labelled earlier as Platonistic, is not appropriate, and it is no part of my position to make it. Rather, here an interdependence claim seems appropriate, and allows sufficient constraints for decision-theoretic determinacy. Reflection on the discussion in earlier sections of the interaction between constraints and settled cases in decision theory makes this clear; constraints on interpretation are necessary, but at no point is it suggested that decision theory could possibly do without the brute input of activity to be interpreted, taken at least *prima facie* to be expressive of preference.

### 5. The Role of Empirical Information: The Causation of Particular Mental States vs. the Individuation of Their Contents in Terms of Normal Causal Relations

That constraints on interpretation, principles of charity, give the world a constitutive role in relation to the mind and are imposed *a priori* does not of course mean that the way the world is is an *a priori* matter. (Otherwise, Lewis' emphasis on the *a priori* status of the presumption in favour of eligible contents, and his claim that "there's no contingent fact about psychology here to be believed", would be transparently inconsistent with his naturalism.) What is *a priori* is not (necessarily) the way the world is (certainly not in the case of perception, but possibly so in other cases, e.g., involving mathematical entities), but the relation between the mind and the world, where the direction of individuation may be from world to mind.

It would be to miss this point to suppose that empirical investigation could resolve the question of whether the world stands in a constitutive relation to the mind. (—As if one were to resolve the question of whether someone on Twin Earth has a belief about water or not by making a survey of what others similarly situated believe; one cannot see possible worlds through telescopes![25]) However, the point must be put more carefully where the constraints are social, as in Burge's example about whether someone believes falsely that contracts require written agreements or rather has a true belief that is not about contracts at all. In a sense here the answer *is* given, at least in part,[26] by considering how the word is used by those in the community at large. But properly understood this is analogous to its being *a priori* in the natural kind case that the answer is given by empirical investigation within the envisaged possible world, rather than being an empirical question to be answered by seeing what the contents of our mental states turn out to be generally like. The point is that we can't get hold of the contents first, then look to see how they relate to their worldly contexts. In the contract, and other social cases, discussed by Burge, it is *a priori* that what the subject means is constitutively affected by aspects of his social context (given the social division of linguistic labour and the existence of experts in social practices such as law), within the envisaged possible world. The mistake would be to suppose the answer is given by *somehow* first determining what others in exactly his position, considered in isolation from social context, do in fact mean, and then inductively generalizing to cover the case in question. This would be to suppose we have a way of determining contents in the absence of the needed constitutive constraints.

Thus, the results of empirical, and specifically psychological, investigation may well be of constitutive relevance to the contents of the mind,[27] but it will not be empirical investigation that takes a particular form: it will not be empirical investigation that presupposes prior determination of content and formulates 'psychological laws' correlating contents thus determined and the world. The world gets in, so to speak, at an earlier conceptual stage than this; the contents of the mind are not conceptually prior to and independent of the way the world is, so that it can turn out as a matter of empirical fact that they are correlated. Normal interactions with the world may individuate the very states the mind is in.

Applied to preference in particular, this is to say that constraints on eligibility cannot be provided by empirical correlations between characteristics of alternatives and the contents of preferences somehow independently determined. Preferences aren't in the head either; the very determination of the contents of preference already requires worldly constraints. This also rules out enterprising attempts to provide constraints on preference by reference to consideration of which constraints, if adopted, would maximize total welfare or utility, conceived as a function of preference; embedding the problem of the determination of content more deeply in this way does not make it go away. (I have heard discussed, for example, the view that whether to admit distinctions between alternatives with respect to counterfactuals about further alternatives, or with respect to feelings of regret, for purposes of defending against consistency violations, should be determined by utilitarian evaluation of what the consequences would be if such distinctions were generally recognized!)

Once the role of empirical information in relation to contents is properly understood, it should readily be admitted that constitutive constraints on the contents of preferences are naturalistic, and physical as well as social. Teleological consideration of biological fitness and function, as well as consideration of specifically human nature, needs, and functions may properly be taken to constrain the eligibility of contents with respect to preference.[28] Care must be taken to account not only for the animal nature of human beings, but also for what is distinctively human about them, and for what makes human beings persons—sometimes, plausibly, claimed to be the capacity for self-interpretation and for certain complex rational structures of higher-order attitudes, which capacity is the ground of human interests in autonomy, or self-determination, and knowledge.[29] However, this capacity needn't be regarded as anything occult, but may be admitted to be in some way a product of the natural and social contexts of human life. The important thing here is to eschew both attempts to exclude any concern with biological function and attempts to restrict or reduce human good, concerns, and values, to biological function. It is reasonable to admit that evolution may be responsible for certain complex capacities of human beings, but it is not reasonable to look to the theory of evolution to tell us the answers to specific questions those capacities enable us to pose, such as questions of grammar, logic, legal interpretation, or ethics.

## 6. Causal Relations, Causal Explanations, and Rational Explanations

From this point on in this chapter I shall be raising issues that seem to be left open in the philosophical literature, in preparation for the arguments of the next chapter. The positions I will take should not necessarily be attributed to the philosophers whose views I've been appealing to up to now, nor should they be regarded as mere straightforward applications of their views to my problems.

First, there is an important ambiguity is the above summary of views about constraints on content, which reflects, I believe, an ambiguity in the literature—or at least in parts of it. This corresponds to the distinction drawn by Davidson between causal relations and causal explanations. According to Davidson, the relation of cause to effect is extensional, and not sensitive to ways in which the events related as cause and effect are described. The relation of causal explanation, however, holds between sentences, and *is* sensitive to the way in which cause and effect are described. If an event is a cause of another event, it is so no matter how described. Nevertheless, the event described in one way may provide a causal *explanation*, while the same event described in another way may not.

We have seen that both Davidson and Burge hold that normal causal relations may individuate contents. In this context Davidson usually speaks of causal relations, whereas Burge sometimes speaks of causal relations and sometimes of causal explanations.[30] It is important, I suggest, that no implication be drawn that *only* causal explanations, let alone only ideal, scientific, causal explanations, can contribute to the individuation of contents. Such a view would be excessively restrictive, for many reasons. I here sound again a theme that will return: we must be liberal about our constraints. This may sound paradoxical at first, but it will easily be seen than the paradox is a shallow one. And the pluralism implied will be important when we come to develop ethical and political theories in harmony with the arguments in the philosophy of mind that we've been considering.

The cases in which social environment provides constraints immediately give the lie to any such restriction; concepts like *contract* and *sofa* don't get very far in the scientific, causally explanatory enterprise. Furthermore, many of the qualities we perceive, such as colour qualities, play no indispensable role in causal explanation. Yet agents may stand in normal causal relations to instances of such qualities in their environments. We *don't* want to have to say that they are not really perceiving that objects have particular colours but instead, whatever the concepts needed in the relevant causal explanations, that objects are characterized by those concepts.

In fact, we need also to distinguish between causal explanation and rational explanation, in order to do justice to the nature of the constraints on interpretation. Reasons may be causes; and whether something is a cause of something else or not does not depend on how it is decribed. But we should not expect that reason-giving descriptions, which provide rational explanations of why people do things, will be those appropriate to scientific, causal laws and explanations. Causal explanatory force depends on the right description of the cause, as rational explanatory force does; but the descriptions may be different, as the kinds of explanation, and understanding sought, are different. The difference between acting in the presence of a reason and acting for a reason may be that in the latter case the reason is also a cause (in the "right sort of way", i.e., nondeviantly) of what is done. And if a reason is a cause, that may entail that *there is* a causal law (even if we don't know what it is) that the reason, under some causally explanatory (even if unknown) description, provides an instance of. Causal explanations explain by hitting on, or approximating to, the right description for purposes of causal understanding and prediction. But rational explanations also explain in a way that is sensitive to description; rational explanatory force may be lost by redescription, even if the redescription brings us closer to the causally explanatory description. The right description for the purposes of rational explanation and understanding may not be the right description for the purposes of causal explanation and understanding.[31]

## 7. Constraint by Reasons and Values: Interpretation Does Not Compete with Science

The problem of the determination of contents that prompts recognition of constraints on interpretation is a special case of a more general problem, about the radical underdetermination of theories in general—not just theories, or interpretations, of rational agents. Goodman and others raise the problem in its more general form.[32] But theories may have different subject matters, and may be of different kinds, seeking different kinds of understanding, even in relation to the same subject matter. The need for constraints on theorizing is perfectly general, but the nature of the constraints needed will vary with the subject matter and the kind of explanation sought. The constraints needed for purposes of physical explanation may not be sufficient for purposes of causal understanding of biological systems, for example. And the constraints needed for causal understanding of biological systems in general may not be sufficient for purposes of causal understanding of rational, language-using creatures with higher-order attitudes, such as human beings. Finally, the constraints needed for causal understanding of human beings may not be sufficient for rational understanding of human beings and their institutions and societies. The normal relations of human beings to reasons and values may play a constitutive constraining role in the rational explanation and understanding—interpretation—of human beings, that they do not play in a purely causally explanatory, strictly scientific enterprise. Rational explanation does not provide the kind of understanding and predictive power the latter enterpise seeks; but neither does the latter enterprise provide the kind of understanding and insight that rational explanation seeks.[33] There is no reason why we shouldn't go in for both kinds of explanation, and recognize in each case the appropriate constitutive constraints, so long as we don't confuse the two enterprises. They do not compete with one another, nor is there any incompatibility between them.

We have seen that decision theory and economics, as they for the most part are (namely, blithely extensionalist), tacitly recognize a variety of naturalistic and social substantive constraints on preference, in addition to formal principles of rationality such as the principles of transitivity and Independence. (Thus decision theory is a branch of 'naturalistic psychology', in Fodor's sense.[34]) Witness, for example, Tversky's comments, quoted in the last section of the previous chapter, concerning the "experimental identification of consequences", which support the need for some substantive constraints on interpretations of the contents of preferences, and in particular support adherence to monetary interpretations for the cases he is concerned with.

However, explicit awareness that substantive as well as formal constraints must inevitably be in play should lead to an enhanced concern that assumptions not be one-sided, that they not dismiss part of the fully pluralistic range of intelligible goods. It should not be assumed *in general*, for example, that admissible basic distinctions must:

—concern the possession of money or consumer goods;
—concern only outcomes as opposed to processes, activities, or states of character which result in them;
—not concern counterfactual characterizations of alternatives;
—not concern agent-relative characterizations of alternatives;
—not concern agents' feelings and reactions;
—not treat certainty *per se*, as as opposed to any degree of uncertainty or risk, as a matter of specific concern;
—be solely in service of scientific explanation, or articulable by concepts with causal explanatory primacy.

Some of the issues raised under these heads will be discussed more fully in various later chapters. But for present purposes the point is simply that, while these assumptions may well be appropriate to particular disciplines, such as decision theory in some of its uses, or economics, and for particular purposes and circumstances, they would be unwarranted as perfectly general constraints on the ascription of preferences. There are intelligible goods, the objects of familiar forms of life and successful reason-giving practices, which do not respect these assumptions.[35] (Of course, to say such goods are intelligible is to say nothing whatsoever about their weight relative to other goods or their authority in particular cases, all things considered; again, explicit recognition of substantive constraints, properly understood, is hospitable, not hostile, to pluralism.)

We have, in particular, no reason for excluding from the class of distinctions that respect constraints on eligibility those provided by applications of evaluative or reason-giving concepts to the alternatives the agent faces. The supposition that such concepts play no role in ideal, scientific causal explanations of the behaviour that expresses someone's preferences would not justify such an exclusion; the fact that causal explanations provide constitutive constraints on the eligibility of contents provides no basis for supposing they do so exclusively and so for denying rational and evaluative constraints on eligibility. This is just to say that *objectivism* about values does not depend on or presuppose scientific *realism* about values, in the senses I have given these terms. (See Chapter 2 section 1; see also Chapter 14.)

As well as being interested in strictly causal explanation, persons are interested in making sense of themselves and one another, in trying to find one another intelligible; they are rational and self-interpreting animals. Applications of reason-giving and evaluative concepts make an essential contribution to the kind of intelligibility and understanding that we seek as persons. To eschew the use of these concepts, or to insist on universally mentioning rather than using them—to give them the 'inverted commas' treatment— would be to frustrate this interest, and at the same time to distort the attitudes to be understood, which are constitutively informed by this interest.[36] It would be to declare oneself, for no apparent reason, simply not interested in this kind of intelligibility or understanding. We are under no kind of obligation— methodological, rational, ethical, or whatever—to do so.

I have already argued that respect for science and strictly causal explanation provides no reason to do so, as the intelligibility sought by rational explanation in no way conflicts with or renders unavailable scientific understanding. The point is not that doing strictly causal super-psychology is impossible, but that it constitutes changing the subject. An analogy may help. Suppose someone were to say, about a piece of music: "I'm only interested in the musical relations of so-called 'harmony' and 'modulation' if they have predictive value; if not, I only want the hard facts, the frequencies of the sounds, and their causes and effects!" But the music is there to be understood, whether one ignores it or not. Understanding it as music will not enable one to deduce or predict accurately which sounds, or which frequencies, will occur in which order. Nevertheless, there is a kind of understanding that someone who attends to a piece of music as music can achieve, which someone who refuses to, or who gives it the inverted commas treatment, cannot. The value of musical understanding does not depend on prediction or causal understanding.

When insistence on an exclusive interest in causal understanding is explicitly considered, its motivation becomes extremely obscure. The claims that commonsense attitude ascriptions *ought* to be solely in aid of causal explanation, that people *ought not* to be interested in a kind of understanding of one another in terms of shared values that is not solely causal, cannot be supported. Some of our practices are not attempts to do science, and it would be unreasonable to claim that science is all we should do. Our other practices are not dispensable; their suppression would impoverish our lives, just as the suppression of science would. Science may tell us how to achieve our ends, but it will be of little help in determining what our ends are, or should be, and how they are related in particular cases.[37] It would be quixotic, as a judge trying to arrive at a decision in a hard case, or as someone trying to deliberate about conflicting ends, to assume that distinctions that do not pull scientific weight are irrelevant. Moreover, in the absence of a general and principled basis for the exclusion of values from the role of providing eligible distinctions, their exclusion in specific cases would be in a sense self-defeating: it would count as just as evaluative as their inclusion would be. (An example of this point is given at the beginning of the next chapter, in application to Diamond's case.)

In casting reasons and values among the natural sources of constraints on interpretation, I am suggesting that reason and nature should no more be opposed than society and nature. In appealing to nature in our investigations of rationality, we do not leave rationality behind, but reveal what rationality *is*, and that it is human nature to be rational. To oppose reason and nature, in the style of Hume, is already to be insufficiently compatibilist in one's view of rationality, to make a mistake about what reasons and values might intelligibly be supposed to be (perhaps out of a lingering disappointment with the supernatural). The point of the Wittgensteinian appeal to human nature isn't so much to correct an unduly rationalistic conception of the mind as to correct an untenable—because insufficiently naturalistic—conception of rationality.[38]

I said in the introduction to the previous chapter that one might give up the independence of the mind from the world and individualism about preferences while nevertheless holding onto subjectivism about the relations between preference and value. One could do so by taking the position that constraints on preference do not include reasons and values, that the natural and social environments of the agent, which one admits may provide constitutive constraints on preference, leave reasons and values out. So far I have argued that the supposition that values don't feature in ideal causal explanations provides no reason to hang on to subjectivism in this way, since our explanatory practices in attributing content are not solely in aid of causal explanation, and are, at least partly, in aid of understanding one another by reference to reasons and values. It might also be thought that skepticism about values in general provides support for subjectivism; I argue against such skepticism in Chapter 14. But not only is there no reason to hang on to subjectivism in this way; there is also positive reason not to do so. In the next chapter I shall develop a positive argument for abandoning subjectivism, which takes the form of criticizing what I take to be the best, most highly developed and representative form of it. And I shall argue that it is only in the context of the distinctions provided by evaluative concepts that the higher-order preferences distinctive of persons can be understood.[39]

# 6

# Subjectivism

## 1. Preference as Value-laden

In this chapter, finally, I shall bring together the concerns of the previous two chapters to argue against subjectivism. The argument will ultimately depend on examples that illustrate what's wrong with the subjectivist conception of the determination of values by preferences. In a nutshell, the only credible subjectivist accounts of this determination depend on some notion of higher-order preference; but it is precisely in understanding how the contents of the higher-order preferences characteristic of persons are determined that subjectivism is least adequate. That is, it is precisely here that it is most unreasonable and distorting to exclude values from the role of providing constitutive constraints on preferences; only prior theoretical commitments could recommend the exclusion. The strategy of argument will be to examine explicitly and critically the subjectivist exclusion, and its surprisingly anti-democratic effects, in application to higher-order preferences.

We shall begin by reviewing the way in which values may play a role in the determination of first-order preferences. We've already come across an example in which an evaluative concept provides an eligible distinction: Broome's example about George's concern not to be a cowardly sort of person. Another example, in which an eligible interpretation is provided by distinctions with respect to the value of fairness, was originally given by Diamond (though for a different purpose); a variation is discussed by Broome. In this case, to be found in Table 4.2, at the end of Chapter 4, I must determine which of two children gets the one piece of candy; I have a fair coin. I prefer a gamble in which if heads, Johnny gets the candy, if tails Mary gets it, to a degenerate gamble in which Mary gets it either way; but I prefer a gamble in which if heads, Mary gets the candy, if tails Johnny gets it, to a degenerate gamble in which Johnny gets it either way. That is, referring to the example as set out in the table, I prefer A to B and D to C, because A and D are fairer than B and C, respectively. Do these preferences violate the Sure-Thing Principle, as they might seem to if we insist that the only thing I can be interested in is who gets the candy—the outcome, as opposed to the character of the process by which the outcomes are arrived at? No; as Broome argues, distinctions with respect to the fairness of the process provide an eligible interpretation of my preferences which shows that they do not after all violate the Sure-Thing Principle.[1]

It would be absurd to reject the eligibility of the fairness distinction because it plays no role in scientific explanation. However, it is certainly possible to argue in defense of the Sure-Thing Principle on normative grounds without accepting the relevance of the fairness distinction in cases like Diamond's. Harsanyi, for example, gives an ethical argument against the relevance of the distinction, to the effect that the person who draws it does indeed violate the Sure-Thing Principle, and in doing so is irrational. He imagines two societies. Society A has an extremely unequal income distribution, revolting even to politically conservative observers. B is exactly like it except that by old custom all babies born are randomly distributed by bureaucrats among all the families who had a baby in the same month, so that every baby born in any month has the same chance of ending up in any given family. Harsanyi asks whether B is less morally objectionable than A because each individual in B has a 'fair' chance of ending up in a privileged position, even though the final distribution is just as unfair in B as in A, and any individual's position just as insensitive to merit and just as much a matter of 'luck' in B as in A:

> In A it depends wholly on the accident of birth—on the 'great lottery of life' which decides who is born into what particular family. In contrast, in B it depends wholly on a government-conducted lottery. Why should we assign higher moral dignity to a lottery organized by government bureaucrats than we assign to the 'great lottery of life' which chooses a family for each of us without the benefit of government intervention? Why should a bureaucratic lottery be regarded as being a 'fairer' allocative mechanism than the great biological lottery produced by nature?

He concludes:

> Diamond's suggestion that economic and social privileges allocated by government policies with random components are morally more acceptable than social and economic privileges allocated by the accidents of birth and of personal life history—i.e., the suggestion that the first kind of personal 'luck' is morally superior to the second kind—is wholly without merit. Therefore, his claim that social choices are not subject to the sure-thing principle falls to the ground.[2]

There are several things to note about this argument, without passing on the merits of it as an ethical argument for an ethical conclusion, about which I take no position. First, it seems to involve an unfortunate assumption that persons can be identified independently of who their parents are, such that the conception of a 'lottery of life' is intelligible. The persons whose genetic constitution is mere accident must be something like featureless bare egos or noumenal selves, and it would be a pity if an ethical argument were to turn on their postulation. Perhaps in the present context this objection can be rebutted, but since no weight will be placed on it in what follows, I shall not pursue the matter further here.

Second (and this is not an objection to the argument), the argument is an ethical one, for an evaluative conclusion. The question of whether the person whose preferences are in question has violated the Sure-Thing Principle or not, and thus whether his preferences are inconsistent or consistent, given the normative status of the Sure-Thing Principle, depends on whether the interpretation of the content of his preferences that Broome gives is eligible. If the distinction it draws with respect to fairness is ineligible, then he cannot defend his preferences against the accusation that he has violated Sure-Thing by reference to it. And there must be some point at which it would be held that a distinction someone might draw to defend his *prima facie* inconsistent preferences is ineligible; otherwise, whatever is going to seem right to someone will be right, and Sure-Thing will have no normative force. But the question of whether the fairness distinction is eligible or not is an ethical question; Harsanyi in effect argues for a negative answer to it on ethical grounds. The needed constraints on interpretation in cases like this are provided by reference to ethical values, whether the answer is positive or negative; the judgment that the fairness distinction should be excluded is just as much an evaluative judgment as the judgment that it should be included. Indeed, if someone were to argue, however implausibly, that the answer is provided by the theory of evolution, he would nevertheless be taking a substantive and debatable ethical position. The very business of ascribing content to the preferences of the person in question is a value-laden business.

Third, however, perhaps for *our* purposes at present (as opposed to Harsanyi's *own* purposes in making his argument—more on this below) Harsanyi's argument constitutes ethical overkill. That is, it seems to result in a higher-order ethical judgment than is necessary to resolve the question of interpretation needed to determine whether someone's first-order preferences violate Sure-Thing. At present, we are only trying to determine whether a distinction someone might draw is eligible, that is, intelligible, and thus what the content of his preferences is, so that we can determine whether or not he has violated the Sure-Thing Principle; not whether correct judgments about what should be done, all things considered, respect this distinction. *It is essential to recognize that values may have constitutive relevance to the former question without depending on an answer to the latter question.* The former may be, in certain cases, an evaluative question, to be answered, for example, by reference to the shared value of fairness that renders the distinction in question intelligible, but it is not such a difficult question as the question about whether the person whose preferences are in question has arrived at the correct judgment about what should be done, all things considered—which is what Harsanyi seems to be answering. (Harsanyi's *own* purpose in giving his argument seems to be, in effect, to determine an extended preference ordering, and for this purpose his argument is appropriate; see below, this chapter, section 3.) The business of ascribing preferences is where ethics begins, but not where it ends; it may require the use of specific reason-giving concepts to individuate alternatives, but it doesn't require judgments of right and wrong, all things considered. An ascription of content may fall within the constraints on eligible interpretation by reference to the value of fairness even though the person's preferences reflect an ethical belief that is incorrect, all things considered.[3] Evaluative constraints on eligibility operate at the level of *pro tanto* intelligibility, not correctness, all things considered; otherwise they would be illiberal to an extent incompatible with the variety of preferences we must allow for, given the actual choices we observe in trying to ascribe preferences. There is no assumption that the choices people make, and the preferences they reflect, must always be correct, all things considered. Again, correctly understood, evaluative constraints on eligibility are hospitable, not hostile, to pluralism.

Note that my argument about the relationship between Diamond's example and Harsanyi's argument is strictly a meta-argument; it does not depend on whether Harsanyi's argument is ultimately correct or incorrect at the all-things-considered level, but rather is about what kind of argument his argument is. It is beside the point with respect to my purposes in this chapter to pass on whether or not his argument is correct, which is why I am do not.

## 2. Extended Preference and Interpersonal Comparisons

Let's return to question: Is the 'problem' of the eligibility of interpretations really a problem? Or rather, for whom is it a problem? It is *not* a problem for formal decision theory; as I've pointed out, formal decision theory already more or less tacitly recognizes the need for substantive constraints on eligibility and their extra-individual sources. Witness the harmony between the views of Davidson and Tversky. Davidson writes that "A radical theory of decision must include a theory of interpretation and cannot presuppose it."[4] And Tversky writes:

> . . . normative decision theory is concerned only with the consistency of preferences, not with their justification. Put differently, decision theorists are eager to tell people how to act, in light of their values, but they are very reluctant to tell people how to feel, or what values they should have. I believe that an adequate analysis of rational choice cannot accept the evaluation of consequences as given, and examine only the consistency of preferences.

And also:

> . . . it is not possible to evaluate the normative adequacy of the axioms of utility theory in the absence of a specific interpretation of the consequences. The criteria for the selection of such an interpretation, and for evaluating its appropriateness, however, are not part of expected utility theory. In this respect utility theory provides only a partial analysis of the problem of rational choice. A comprehensive analysis of rational choice under risk should face the interpretation problem as well as the problem of the legitimacy of values.[5]

Both Davidson and Tversky are claiming, in effect, that decision theory is incomplete in the absence of some means of determining the eligibility of interpretations. This claim is surely correct. But this does not mean that the 'problem' of eligibility is a problem *for* formal decision theory. Whether what is needed should count as part of decision theory, so that we talk about substantive decision theory as distinct from formal decision theory, or be given a different name, or be regarded as part of a theory of the naturalness of properties, or even a theory of human nature, or flourishing, or function, the fact that a complete theory of the rationality of action must address the matter of substantive constraints as well as the matter of formal constraints does not pose any threat to the value and importance of formal decision theory. The power, elegance, and sheer interest of its results are unchallenged, and there is no suggestion that the complete theory could do without the formal component.

The 'problem' of the eligibility of the content of preference makes trouble not for those committed to the importance of investigation of the formal conditions on preference, but rather for those who in some way or another are committed to the subjectivist view that all substantive evaluative questions may be reduced to formal problems about the relations among preferences, that solutions to the latter, as a conceptual matter, determine answers to the former: if values are among the substantive constraints on the content of preference, then preference cannot be conceived as prior to and independent of values, as the subjectivist would have it. But such subjectivism is itself a substantive, not a formal stance; formal decision theory neither entails nor presupposes such subjectivism. The most plausible and attractive form of ethical subjectivism, in particular, holds that ethical questions are determined by preferences with a special kind of content, which are variously called extended preferences, highest order preferences, fundamental preferences, or preferences at the third level of universalizability.[6] I shall explain this terminology shortly. But we shall find that values are also among the substantive constraints on preferences of this kind, and thus that the most sophisticated, plausible, and attractive kind of account of how preference conceived as prior and independent might determine values, does not succeed.

What I have just said entails that my argument is not exhaustive. I do not attempt to show that no other kind of subjectivism could possibly succeed, only that what I regard as the most sophisticated, plausible, and attractive kind, which appeals to higher-order preferences, does not; certain crude versions of subjectivism have been so often and thoroughly refuted that I do not attend to them here at all. Nor do I suggest that theories of higher-order or extended preference must be subjectivist. On the contrary; I would support the view that theories of higher-order attitudes are of great importance and interest in the absence of any alliance to subjectivism; see especially Chapter 15 section 1. In particular I would suggest that the attractions of Harsanyi's position are independent of its alliance to subjectivism; I argue in this chapter against the subjectivist elements of that position only, which I regard as inessential to it. However, I go on to argue in Chapter 9 against non-cognitivism, with the result that I cast the coherence account developed in subsequent chapters as a kind of cognitivism rather than as a non-subjectivist theory of higher-order preference.

The view that ethical questions are determined by higher-order preferences may be introduced as an attempt to improve upon certain aspects of Kant's view of the way in which ethical questions are determined by the autonomous will. From a subjectivist point of view—which, as we shall see, should not be assumed to be Kant's—there are difficulties with Kant's notion of the autonomous will, which the appeal to higher-order preferences offers the hope of remedying. However, I shall argue that the theory of higher-order preference no more provides a refuge for subjectivism than Kant's theory does.

In Kant's scheme, the heteronomous will reflects the preferences determined by merely contingent, hence not rational, influences; the autonomous will is determined by reason alone, by the pure form of universal lawfulness, and is the source of ethical judgments.

> Autonomy of the will is that property of it by which it is a law to itself independently of any property of objects of volition.

> But for reason to be legislative, it is required that reason need presuppose only itself, because the rule is objectively and universally valid only when it holds without any contingently subjective conditions which differentiate one rational being from another.

> If a rational being can think of its maxims as practical universal laws, he can do so only by considering them as principles which contain the determining grounds of the will because of their form and not because of their matter.

> The sole principle of morality consists in independence from all material of the law (i.e. a desired object) and in the accompanying determination of choice by the mere form of giving universal law which a maxim must be capable of having.[7]

However, Kant has well-known difficulties when he tries to show how, through reason alone, we may become "conscious of a law to which all our maxims are subject as though through our will a natural order must arise".[8] He explains that

> The rule of judgment under laws of pure practical reason is: Ask yourself whether, if the action which you propose should take place by a law of nature of which you yourself were a part, you could regard it as possible through your will. Everyone does, in fact, decide by this rule whether actions are morally good or bad. Thus people ask: If one belonged to such an order of things that anyone would allow himself to deceive when he thought it to his advantage, or felt justified in shortening his life as soon as he was thoroughly weary of it, or looked with complete indifference on the needs of others, would he assent of his own will to being a member of such an order of things?[9]

But it is of course a standard point in critiques of Kant's ethical views that a sense in which "the mere form of a law . . . limits its material" cannot be got from logical possibility alone. It is notoriously unclear how the autonomous will is supposed to be determined to follow one consistent and universal course rather than another among the many that are merely logically possible, how the autonomous agent determines whether he could regard this or that universal state of affairs as possible through his own will.[10] Purely formal considerations leave indeterminate the answers to ethical questions, in part because they may support different conclusions applied to different true descriptions of the alternatives; considerations of logical consistency do not determine which descriptions are the relevant ones. In her admirable book *Acting on Principle*, Nell surveys the difficulties and then proceeds to show how surprisingly far a Kantian formalism can get. But even her explication of Kant's position is subject to the kind of arguments recently made, for example, by Herman. Herman argues for the view that Kant's conception of the autonomous will as the source of ethical judgments cannot succeed unless rational agents are allowed some prior ethical understanding of the alternatives in the form of "rules of moral salience," which structure the agent's perceptions of his situation so that what he perceives is a world with ethically relevant, rather than ethically Goodmanesque, features. It should be noted that Herman puts forward her argument not as a critique but as a speculative interpretation of Kant; hence my earlier claim that Kant's position should not be assumed to be subjectivist, as it would not be if Herman's view that it at least tacitly involves appeal to rules of moral salience is correct.[11]

Herman's appeal to rules of moral salience may thus, arguably, suit Kantians; but it cannot suit subjectivists. To avoid the indeterminacy of the purely formalistic interpretation of Kant's account of ethics, subjectivists must look in another direction. It has seemed appropriate to many to escape from this difficulty by allowing that, while the autonomous will which is the source of ethical judgments does not merely reflect the contingent personal preferences of the agent whose will it is, its determining grounds may include such mere preferences, so long as they are taken into account via their necessary influence on the hypothetical higher-order preferences of the agent in circumstances in which knowledge of his own identity among all those affected, and hence his tastes and ideals and the contents of his personal preferences, is suspended. Such higher-order preferences are in effect preferences over *extended alternatives*, understood to include not only features of the environment the persons affected are in but also all differentiating features of those persons—including their tastes, ideals, capacities, preferences. Such preferences, which I shall call, following Harsanyi, *extended preferences*,[12] are thus at least second-order preferences, between alternative packages of preferences and objective circumstances; they are supposedly contrasted with personal preferences, which range over non-extended alternatives. The contrast between personal and extended preferences cannot be drawn by reference to whether the agent actually faces the alternatives, since personal preferences certainly do range over hypothetical as well as actual alternatives, and indeed neither decision theory nor garden variety deliberation would get very far if they did not, since appeal to preferences about hypothetical alternatives is standard procedure in both.[13] The distinguishing feature of extended preferences is rather that they are preferences the content of which concerns the various features that differentiate agents from one another, including their differing first-order preferences and the factors that causally account for the differences, as well as features of their environments. (As we shall see, the distinction may not be sharp, in that personal preferences may also be higher-order; but at least they are not so ambitiously higher-order as extended, or 'highest-order', preferences.) An extended preference is a preference between being in one person's objective situation with all his subjective features, including his preferences, and being in another person's objective situation with all his subjective features, including preferences. It is argued by proponents of the extended preference approach that, since all differentiating features of agents have been extracted from the subjects of extended preference and incorporated into the contents of extended preference, the extended preferences of all subjects must coincide; that which determines this shared extended preference ordering Kolm refers to as 'human nature', while Harsanyi appeals to 'basic psychological laws'.[14] It is the extended preference ordering which is supposed, in the versions of subjectivism I shall be concerned with, to determine the all-things-considered answers to ethical questions, and to be expressed by the general ethical concepts, such as *ought* and *right*, and the central evaluative components of specific ethical concepts.

An example of the way in which extended preferences may be claimed to determine ethical questions is given by Harsanyi's theory, within which it can be proved as a theorem that "In making moral value judgments, i.e., in judging alternative social situations from a moral . . . point of view, a rational individual will rank these situations according to the arithmetic mean of the utility levels that the individual members of society would enjoy in this situation."[15] To make an ethical judgment, the rational individual must choose among alternatives as if he were ignorant of his own position among those the choice concerns, or as if he were to have an equal probability of occupying the position of any one of them. In order to do this, however, a rational individual must make interpersonal comparisons of utility, which he does through a process of imaginative empathy that involves imaginatively putting himself into the objective and subjective positions of other people. Harsanyi holds that "The interests of each individual must be defined fundamentally in terms of his own personal preferences and not in terms of what somebody else thinks is 'good for him' "; and that "in deciding what is good and what is bad for a given individual, the ultimate criterion can only be his own wants and his own preferences".[16] Thus, trying to make an interpersonal utility comparison between two persons' objective and subjective positions really amounts to trying to decide whether one would prefer one extended alternative, the first person's objective and subjective situation, to another, the second person's objective and subjective situation, that is, to arrive at the relevant extended preferences. A measure of interpersonal utility is determined by extended preferences that meet the consistency axioms of expected utility theory, analogously to the way in which a measure of personal utility is determined by personal preferences that meet the axioms of expected utility theory.[17]

In practice, extended preference orderings may differ, so that there may be disagreement about interpersonal comparisons. However, the true extended preference orderings of all persons must coincide. Kolm writes:

> If two persons have preferences which appear to differ, there is a reason for this, there is something which makes them different from each other. Let us place this "something" within the object of the preferences which we are considering, thereby removing it from the parameters which determine the structure of these preferences. The preferences of these two persons defined in this way are necessarily identical.

> . . . that which discerns this common preference is at bottom 'human nature'.[18]

Harsanyi argues that if different individuals' preferences are determined by the same basic psychological laws and causal variables, then differences between the preferences of different persons can be predicted at least in principle from differences in, e.g., biological inheritance, past history, current environment, etc. This means that if one person were subject to all the same causal influences as another is, then he or she would have the same preferences as well. Thus, even though different people's personal utility functions may differ, their extended utility functions must be identical, and in principle it is possible to reduce any interpersonal utility comparison to an intrapersonal utility comparison with respect to extended alternatives. Differences between different person's extended utility functions must be due to ignorance of the relevant psychological laws and causal influences, in a way somewhat analogous to the way in which differences between person's subjective probabilities are due to ignorance of objective probabilities. However, the "psychological difficulty is accessible to direct empirical solution to the extent to which these psychological differences between people are capable of change, and it is therefore possible for some individuals to make direct comparisons between the satisfactions open to one human type and those open to another". Thus, "given enough information about the relevant individuals' psychological, biological, social, and cultural characteristics, as well as about the general psychological laws governing human behavior, *inter*personal utility comparisons in principle should be no more problematic than *intra*personal utility comparisons are between the utilities that the same person would derive from various alternatives under different conditions".[19]

Hare's approach involves a closely related effort to reduce ethical problems that involve the conflicting preferences of different persons or groups to the form of a rational decision problem for one person, in which he must treat the conflicting preferences of others as if they were conflicting preferences of his own. According to Hare, it follows from the doctrine of universalizability that if I now say I ought to do a certain thing to a certain person, I am committed to the view that the same thing should be done to me, were I in exactly his situation, with his traits and motivations. If I am thus left with conflicting prescriptions, how should I resolve the conflict? Hare writes:

> I can see no reason for not adopting the same solution here [in cases of interpersonal conflict] as we do in cases where our own preferences conflict with one another. . . . we have in effect not an interpersonal conflict of preferences or prescriptions, but an intrapersonal one; both the conflicting preferences are mine. I shall therefore deal with the conflict in exactly the same way as with that between two original preferences of my own. . . . [in multilateral cases too] the interpersonal conflicts, however complex and however many persons are involved, will reduce themselves, given full knowledge of the preferences of others, to intrapersonal ones. And since we are able, in our everyday life, to deal with quite complex intrapersonal conflicts of preferences, I can see no reason why we should not in the same way deal with conflicts of this special sort, which have arisen through our awareness of the preferences of others combined with the requirement that we universalize our moral prescriptions.[20]

Thus the extended preference approach to determining ethical questions yields a special version of the individual decision problem addressed by multi-attribute decision theory (an exposition of which was given in Chapter 4 sections 4–6), a version that involves higher-order preferences; the assumption seems to be that the problem of how to make interpersonal comparisons is in principle solved once it is thus reduced to a problem of intrapersonal comparison of extended alternatives.[21] But what *is* the way in which we make intrapersonal comparisons when we have conflicting preferences? I have claimed that intrapersonal comparisons are already value-laden; this is where ethics, a concern with fairness, virtue, etc., the qualities of one's character, begins. Extended preferences are required to meet the same formal conditions as personal preferences; and we have seen, in preceding sections, that formal decision theory by itself is incomplete; solutions to formal problems in multi-attribute decision theory are only determined relative to constitutive, substantive constraints on the eligibility of interpretations. If ethical values, such as courage and fairness in the examples we have considered, contribute to distinguishing between eligible and ineligible interpretations, they are already playing a constitutive role in determining solutions to individual decision problems, and values are not determined by individual preference conceived as prior and independent. Theorists not committed to the latter conception can happily admit all this and get on with whichever branch of the subject, ethics or formal decision theory, happens to interest them. And consideration of extended alternatives or of alternatives under conditions of ignorance of one's own identity may be an important method of ethical deliberation in the hands of non-reductionists: consider Rawls' use of the veil of ignorance, in conjunction with the Thin Theory of the Good and an index of primary goods, as a means of arriving at reflective equilibrium. But those committed to the subjectivist reduction have a problem.

### 3. Substantive Constraints on Extended Preference, Human Nature, and Ethical Disagreement

Is there any reason to think that determinations of eligibility by reference to ethical values are excluded when the intrapersonal comparison is of extended alternatives and hence involves higher-order preferences? That is, is there any reason to think that the theory of 'human nature' that determines the one correct extended preference ordering does not include evaluative distinctions? If so, then perhaps the subjectivist could generate the evaluative distinctions relevant to considerations of first-order preference from the theory of extended preference. A subjectivist theory with this kind of structure could concede that values affect the eligibility of the contents of ordinary preferences, while still holding that values are ultimately determined by extended preferences, and thus preserve the ultimate independence of preference from values. I shall argue, however, that explicit consideration of extended preference, far from providing a safe if rarified haven for subjectivism, actually gives us further reason to reject it. The needed theory of human nature is in part an evaluative theory, in at least two ways: first, values influence issues of eligibility, and, second, even given determinations of eligibility issues, ethical arguments about what should be done when values conflict influence the final ranking of alternatives by extended preference.

We must ask with respect to the content of extended preference: what is the difference between making a mistake in following one rule, and following a different rule? What is the difference between having extended preferences with given contents, which violate some axiom, and having extended preferences with different contents, which do not? For extended preferences to provide a measure of interpersonally comparable utility and hence the answers to ethical questions they must be subject to substantive as well as formal constraints on eligibility. This is true even if there is only one true and universal extended preference ordering once everything that might cause people to disagree in their ordering of alternatives has been placed into the extended alternatives. Thus we must be careful to leave something other than featureless bare egos to be the representatives of 'human nature', which determines the extended preference ordering; they could not be the subject of empirical theories or 'basic psychological laws', and it is doubtful that they could be the subject of ethical or any other kind of theory either. We cannot incorporate the sources of concern with all possible distinctions among alternatives into the extended alternatives, leaving nothing to constrain the eligibility of the contents of the extended preference ordering, for then the extended preference ordering will be completely indeterminate. Featureless bare egos cannot determine the content of the extended preference ordering.[22]

Properly understood, however, the notion of extended preference does not depend on this easily-parodied idea of extensionless points ineffectually leaping into the void. Consider the alternatives. Perhaps what Kolm calls 'human nature', conceived as held in common by all persons once we have abstracted from *all* sources of disagreement, is the source of constraints on the eligibility of the contents of extended preference. Perhaps eligible distinctions are those that are *universally* recognized in the human community as relevant; any distinction that someone could be found not to recognize, no matter how many others did, would be ineligible. This unanimity requirement would maximally constrain eligible distinctions; there may be very few distinctions that no one could be found not to recognize. The result would be a maximally coarse individuation of extended alternatives. Consider how this suggestion would work.

It would rule out George's distinction between decisions that are cowardly and those that are not, as well as Diamond's distinction between fair methods of the allocation of benefits and unfair methods, so long as someone could be found not to draw these distinctions. But it would also rule out a great many other distinctions. So long as some eccentric, austere, perverse, disturbed, or wicked person could be found who did not recognize, respond to, or care about some characteristic, it would not provide eligible distinctions between extended alternatives, no matter how many other people did care about it. Indeed, it is not clear that any distinctions at all would survive as eligible, and we would be back in the situation of appealing to an utterly featureless human nature to determine extended preferences.

This can't be right. Not *everyone* has to recognize a distinction in order for it to be eligible; given a background of agreement, we can disagree even about issues of mere intelligibility. As I argued at length in the chapter on disagreement above, different people are free to move around within our form of life or to occupy different corners of it, and accordingly to be differentially perceptive with respect to various evaluative aspects of alternatives, to participate to different degrees in various specific reason-giving practices. But from the fact that we can dislodge particular planks from our raft while afloat on it, it of course does not follow that we can get off it altogether. Neither the lowest common denominator (if there is one) nor featureless disembodied egos (if there isn't) can represent human nature or determine the content of the extended preference ordering. We need a theory of human nature that allows determinations of eligibility with respect to extended preference to be sensitive to distinctions that it is *normal and natural* (in a sense familiar from the considerations of the last chapter) to recognize or care about, in the context of familiar human reason-giving practices and forms of life, or which have an intelligible function in relation to human society or human flourishing; we do not want a theory of human nature to give insensitive, unperceptive, abnormal, and other unusual persons a veto over eligible distinctions. Rather than treating only universally recognized distinctions as eligible, we must treat such normally recognized distinctions and distinctions with intelligible functions as eligible, and incorporate the influences upon unusual persons that cause them to differ from the norm into the extended alternatives. The constraints must reflect concerns that are representative of human nature rather than universal.[23] Such a theory will have empirical and,

I argue below, evaluative elements. It will not, however, be a matter of observing or predicting the content of any one 'representative person''s extended preferences.

Now we have a much more liberal individuation of extended alternatives. Now the concern with certainty *per se* which Allais, Tversky, and others demonstrate to be widely shared provides eligible distinctions, as in Tversky's case, discussed in Chapter 4. The concern Ellsberg, Fellner, and others demonstrate to be widely shared with the difference between uncertainty and known risk, and with the quality of the information on which subjective probability judgments are based, provides eligible distinctions (for discussion, see Chapter 15 section 6).[24] Diamond's concern with fair methods of allocation, and perhaps even George's with courage and cowardice, would seem to be fairly normal. (Need I re-emphasize that to admit the eligibility of these distinctions is not necessarily to hold that it is right, all things considered, to respect them?) In particular, it is normal for a person—some would say it is one of the distinguishing features of persons, or one of the distinctive functions of human beings as rational animals[25]—to draw evaluative distinctions among his conflicting first-order preferences, which rank alternatives with respect to specific concerns he has, and to form higher-order preferences about what sort of character to have, what sort of person to be, and to participate in the formation of his own character. Similarly, someone can know that if he were to be in a certain situation with a certain character, he would prefer that $p$, without prefering that if he were to be in that situation with that character, then $p$. He may prefer not to have that character, or to gratify that character, should he have it, since, as Aristotle saw, "states of character arise out of like activities", and we become, for example, courageous by doing courageous acts.[26] While the sense in which extended preferences express the autonomy of the agent is not Kant's sense, there is a sort of rough analogy between Kant's distinction between the autonomous will and the heteronomous will, and the distinction between extended and non-extended preferences. In fact, extended preferences are a special kind of *self-determining* preference, about what kind of person to be, what kind of character and preferences to have and to act on; higher-order self-determining preferences in general are quite familiar.

(Again, the phrase 'self-determining preference' may be ambiguous, as *between preference that determines itself*, and *preference that determines the self*, i.e., what kind of person one is. In Chapter 3 I introduced the term "ultra-interpretation" to disambiguate in favour of the former sense. Here, and in later chapters when I speak of "self-interpretation" and "self-determination" in association with deliberation and the value of autonomy, I intend the latter sense. As we shall see by developing a coherence account subject to constraints on interpretation, self-interpretation in the latter sense—that of deliberated self-determination and autonomy—is possible without ultra-interpretation. Indeed, I shall in effect argue in later chapters that it can only be understood how deliberated self-determination in the face of conflicting reasons, or autonomy, is possible, by recognizing constitutive constraints on interpretation. See especially Chapter 15.)

Thus, what emerges as a part of our theory of human nature is something like a theory of primary goods, including goods such as self-respect and self-determination. Distinctions drawn by reference to these goods provide eligible distinctions. However, there is still a line past which distinctions cease to be intelligible and contents become Goodmanesque; there are still constraints on eligibility. Perhaps one should speak of differences of degree rather than of boundaries; the distinction between long life and long-life-unless-one-was-born-on-Monday-and-in-that-case-life-for-an-even-number-or-weeks is still relatively ineligible. As is the distinction between a cowardly decision and a cowardly decision made while wearing sunglasses and eating a banana. Thus, someone's higher-order preferences may be deemed inconsistent (or consistent), in the light of constraints on eligible distinctions provided by the theory of human nature, even though his own perceptions about the relevant distinctions are extremely quirky (or simply lacking, respectively).[27]

Consider, for example, various extended alternatives of the following kinds:

> A. being deprived of music with the tastes of one who is a lover and connoisseur of music,
> B. being deprived of a temple with the faith of one who is a true believer, and
> C. being deprived of a substance with the physiological states and associated cravings of one who has a strong physiological need to ingest the substance in question.

Suppose that, among the various extended alternatives of these kinds, those of kind A are ranked above those of kind B, and some of those of kind C are ranked above those of kind A while others of kind C are ranked below those of kind B. Is this extended preference ordering intransitive? It depends on whether the differences among alternatives of kind C accord with eligible distinctions. Alternative C1, ranked above alternatives of kind A, is being deprived of a drug given that one is physiologically addicted to it and withdrawal is extremely unpleasant (and to simplify matters we can add that one has no family or responsibilities and a small private fortune sufficient to support the addiction for one's lifetime in seclusion in a country in which the drug is freely available). Alternative C2, ranked below alternatives of kind B, is being deprived of food when one is hungry. If someone were both hungry and addicted, and for some reason could satisfy only one craving or the other but not both, he might well prefer to deprive himself of the drug, suffer withdrawal, and give himself nourishing food instead, on the grounds that although his desire for the drug is at least as strong as his desire for food, he has a higher-order desire not to desire the drug, and not to act on his desire for it, because he regards the life and character of an addict as unworthy, undignified, and ignoble, even when it harms no one else. He might act so as to identify himself with the desire for wholesome nourishment rather than the desire for the drug, and thus play an active role in the formation of his own character. The distinction he draws is perfectly intelligible, and it is in fact characteristic of human beings as autonomous persons to draw distinctions of this kind (as opposed to what Harry Frankfurt calls *wantons*, who take their own preferences as given and have no interest in the activity of self-determination). Thus the distinction is eligible, and the extended preference ordering that reflects it is not inconsistent.[28] This is not to say that it is necessarily correct, all things considered; that is a further question, and one that demands substantive evaluative argument. But it is not in violation of substantive constraints on eligibility, and it cannot be faulted on formal grounds.

Consider also Sen's suggestions about how his Paretian liberal paradox might be resolved. Sen illustrates the incompatibility of an unrestriced Paretian principle and a liberal principle with the case of Prude and Lewd and a risqué book such as *Lady Chatterley's Lover*.[29] There are three alternatives: no one reads the book, Prude reads it, or Lewd reads it. The Paretian criterion says that if everyone prefers one alternative to another, the first should be socially preferred. But the liberal principle says that issues that strictly concern one individual's personal affairs should be decided by his own preferences. Prude prefers that no one read the book, of course, but if someone has to read it he would rather suffer through it himself than let poor misguided Lewd get his hands on it. Lewd would rather read the book himself, of course, than have no one read it and have it be wasted; but most of all he would like that stuffy Prude to have to read it. By the liberal principle, Prude's preferences should govern the choice between no one's reading the book and Prude's reading it, and Lewd's preferences should govern the choice between no one's reading the book and Lewd's reading it; these are strictly personal matters. Thus it's better for Lewd to read it than no one, and better for no one to read it than Prude. However, by the Paretian criterion, since Prude and Lewd both prefer Prude's reading the book to Lewd's reading it, it would be better for Prude to read it than Lewd. Thus we have an intransitivity.

Suppose we try to resolve this problem by using the extended preference approach. We must establish a preference ordering over extended alternatives that include Prude's and Lewd's preferences about who reads the book. Is it better that Prude, with his preferences, be forced to read the book rather than simply leaving it unread; or that Lewd, with his preferences, be forcibly kept from reading the book when no one else will read it otherwise; or that Lewd be given the book to read rather than Prude, given both their meddlesome (if not spiteful) preferences that Prude read it rather than Lewd? There is no reason to assume that Prude and Lewd are wantons. As Sen suggests, they may have liberal higher-order preferences that draw a distinction between preferences to which the Paretian criterion should apply, and preferences to which it should not apply; that is, they may prefer that the Pareto principle not apply to meddlesome or spiteful preferences, even when these are their own. Sen asks how, given that each of them 'prefers' that Prude read the book rather than Lewd, either could say that Lewd 'should' read it rather than Prude. He writes that "The answer lies in his evaluation of his own preference. Suppose we are concerned with A [Lewd]. He can now argue:

> I do prefer that prude B reads it; it will do him a lot of good. But he does not want to. And I am liberal enough to believe that if he does not want to then he should not. So given his preference, I should not really prefer that he should read the book. I must rank my preferences, and my preference that he reads it is of a lower moral order than what my preference would be if I took his views into account.[30]

Moreover, higher-order preference need not passively reflect the strength of first-order preferences. Prude's first order preferences, for example, rank no one's reading the book above his own reading it, and his own reading it above Lewd's reading it. But even if Prude's preference that no one read the book rather than Lewd is thus stronger than his preference that no one read the book rather than he himself, Prude may nevertheless have a liberal higher-order preference that his stronger first-order preference not be fulfilled. Taking such second-order preferences into account would allow us to avoid the intransitivity, by in effect reindividuating the extended alternatives: what we have is a case of applying the Paretian criterion to 'other-regarding' (to use Mill's term), and in particular meddlesome or even possibly spiteful preferences, and that is different from applying the Paretian criterion to non-meddlesome, non-spiteful preferences.

Does this resolution of the problem depend on whether Prude and Lewd actually have these second-order preferences? It may be hard to defend if they both actually have the *contrary* second-order preferences, and endorse their meddlesome or spiteful preferences even at the cost of sacrificing fulfillment of their own personal preferences. However, even if we grant that point, for the sake of argument, what are we to say about the other cases? (We don't need *every* case to prove our point, only a few.) What if they are both wantons, or what if they have opposed higher-order preferences? The problem is still unresolved; what in these cases is to determine the extended preference ordering that provides a measure of interpersonally comparable utility? We must fall back on our theory of human nature. But why should it not recognize the very fact that Sen's enlightened Lewd recognizes, namely, that the protection of a personal sphere in which one's own personal preferences govern is more valuable for human beings than the fulfillment of meddlesome or spiteful preferences—even if Prude and Lewd themselves were to fail to recognize this? An extended preference ordering that reflected this evaluative judgment by reindividuating the extended alternatives as I described above to reflect this distinction could meet the formal constraints on utility functions and provide an interpersonal measure. There is no reason to regard the distinction thus drawn as ineligible; it is perfectly intelligible. Of course, whether this evaluative judgment is ultimately correct, all things considered, is again a further matter, a matter for ethical argument; the contrary view, the view that the protection of a personal sphere is less valuable

than the fulfillment of meddlesome or spiteful preferences, would determine
a different extended preference ordering, and a different measure of interpersonally comparable utility. But the liberal resolution of the problem cannot
be faulted as inconsistent; it avoids inconsistency by drawing an eligible distinction. And the further issue among alternative, consistent extended preference orderings and thus between alternative measures of interpersonally
comparable utility may depend in part on how the ethical issue between the
liberal view and competing views is resolved. If our theory of human nature
is to resolve the latter issue, it must be at least in part an ethical theory, and
must reflect the results of substantive ethical argument. Evaluative constraints
on eligibility, reflecting specific reason-giving practices, make disagreement
and argument at the all-things-considered level, when values conflict, possible.
As I shall argue in later chapters, such disagreement and argument should
not be suppressed, but articulated within a deliberative democratic framework; the needed theory of human nature must itself be, in part, the product
of deliberative democracy. (Note, again, that such issues cannot be resolved
by an appeal to maximum total utility; the measure of interpersonal utility,
provided by the extended preference ordering, is just what is in question.)

It may help to reiterate at this point the important difference between
appealing to evaluative considerations to justify certain distinctions as eligible,
and appealing to all-out ethical arguments for all-things-considered conclusions. The issue as to how the extended alternatives should be individuated
in the previous paragraph depends on considerations of eligibility, not on all-
things-considered conclusions. But even holding considerations of eligibility
and the individuation of extended alterantives fixed, there is more than one
way of ordering the extended alternatives—the liberal way, for example, and
the contra-liberal way. My claim is that the theory of human nature needed
to determine the extended preference ordering will have ethical components
at both these levels.

There are again several points to note. First, we have now dismissed the
spectre of the bare person or featureless abstract ego, who would indeed be
ineffectual at constraining eligibility or determining extended preference. We
have admitted the need for a theory of human nature. The theory should
reflect our shared forms of life in at least two ways: it should reflect constraints
on eligibility as well as the debate and argument about what should be done,
all things considered, which such constraints make possible.

Second, ethical reasons and values are again among the factors that distinguish eligible and ineligible contents for self-interpreting animals, and they
will naturally play a part in the needed theory of human nature; the extended
preference device, useful as it may be as a way of thinking about ethical
problems, does not avoid the interdependence of preference and value. To
exclude evaluative considerations from our theory of human nature would be
to fail to understand something important about what human beings, as partly
constituted by their self-interpretations, are like.[31]

Third, even if we grant for the sake of argument that there is one correct
extended preference ordering, we now see that there is plenty of room for

theoretical disagreement about human nature, and about what the true extended preference ordering is (even taking the point that many extended alternatives may be tied), and that these disagreements will be resolved not just by discovery of empirical psychological laws, but also, in part, by ethical argument.[32] And when all that's required to determine the extended preference ordering is made explicit, and the scope for ethical disagreement is recognized, it becomes extremely obscure how science alone could serve to resolve such disagreements, or how any particular resolution of them might count as the scientific way of resolving them. The questions raised simply go beyond the subject matter of science; they could of course be suppressed, but the suppression of questions seems intuitively to count more as undemocratic than as scientific. Given a set of eligible distinctions drawn, in part, by reference to shared values, it will nevertheless still be a subject for ethical argument how conflicts among the values should be resolved, and hence what the extended preference ordering should be. However, the kinds of ethical arguments that are needed are themselves only possible given a set of constraints on eligibility, which will themselves be, in part, ethical. We can move around within these constraints, but we cannot dispense with them or reject them entirely.

Thus Harsanyi's ethical argument concerning Diamond's example, which I said constituted ethical overkill if the ascription of preference to someone on the basis of his choices is in question, does not constitute overkill when the determination of the extended preference ordering is in question. (Which, as I noted, seems to be the way Harsanyi was treating Diamond's example.) There is more than one way to rank extended alternatives, even given a fixed way of individuating them; Harsanyi's ethical argument seems to be addressed to an issue at this level, rather than to an issue of eligibility. Open argument is needed here; there is no one representative individual whose choices we can observe as part of the enterprise of determining the extended preference ordering, in the way that we observe an ordinary person's choices in trying to determine his preference ordering.[33] The danger of supposing that the extended preference ordering can be determined by a theory of human nature that is in no part an ethical theory is that what are in effect ethical conclusions are passed off under another guise, without properly ethical scrutiny, consideration and argument. In particular, automatic deference to the course or extrapolated thrust of evolution cannot do the work of the needed theories of human nature and ethics. Evolution neither operates upon nor determines a unique and extremely fine-grained theoretical entity such as the extended preference ordering. But even if it did, such deference would in effect constitute a substantive stance whose ethical implications would be open to challenge by more pluralistic theories of human nature and ethics; it would not be automatically justified.

Thus extended preferences look, in the end, at least as much like highly theoretical *beliefs* about human nature and about what ought to be done, all things considered—subject, as theoretical beliefs are, to disagreement and argument—as like garden-variety preferences. Not that a great deal turns at this point on whether we say that extended preferences are *really* beliefs or *really* preferences; the distinction between belief and preference, especially higher-order preference, may not be absolutely sharp.[34] Either way, preference and value turn out to be interdependent, and the place of preference is no longer as it was conceived to be by subjectivism. I shall have more to say in later chapters about what ought to be done, all things considered, and about self-determination, autonomy and democracy.

It should hardly be surprising that the determination of the extended preference ordering may depend on ethical argument, given that intrapersonal comparisons and higher-order preferences arrived at when interests conflict that are all one's own to begin with, such that there is no problem about fully identifying with all of the interests in question, often turn on ethical deliberation. Thus the reduction of interpersonal comparison to intrapersonal comparison should not be conceived as a basis for ethical subjectivism. Someone may of course assert that considerations only become ethical, by definition, when the interests of more than one person are involved; but this is a substantive issue between the subjectivist tradition and some of its rivals, such as the classical tradition and the view (neo-Aristotelian in certain respects) which I am developing here. Pulling definitional stops achieves nothing, given that we have an established understanding of certain concerns, with qualities of character, virtue, autonomy, and the identification with certain aspects of oneself rather than others, as ethical.[35] The subjectivist cannot define these concerns away; he must show that we *ought not* (in some mysterious sense) to have them, and of this I see little hope.

Finally, the fact that there is plenty of room for disagreement and argument about human nature underscores the *epistemic* (if not metaphysical) possibility that, in particular respects (though not all), human nature could have been other than what it is. If someone were to disagree that it is characteristic of human beings as persons to form self-determining preferences of the kind we have considered, and to hold instead that human beings are by nature wantons, he might be very badly wrong, but he doesn't seem to be out of order *a priori*. That is, perhaps it is the nature of human beings to be persons, in Frankfurt's sense, rather than wantons, perhaps their personality is an essential property and could not have been otherwise as a matter of metaphysics. But it would not follow that this holds *a priori*.[36]

## 4. Disagreement and Democracy

I have set out arguments against psychological individualism with respect to preference in particular, and against subjectivism about the relation between preference and values. The undermining of subjectivism invites us to theorize about why some interpretations are more eligible than others in terms of the greater naturalness of some contents of desire than others, where some of the dimensions of naturalness are unabashedly evaluative; and it lends itself to the development of theories of shared fundamental human responses, forms of life and reason-giving practices, and of human nature, functions and flour-ishing.[37] It is not my purpose to develop such a theory here, but rather to indicate the general character and role in practical rationality of such theories. Suppose we were to grant, for the sake of argument, Harsanyi's claims, that "in deciding what is good and what is bad for a given individual, the ultimate criterion can only be his own wants and preferences" and that "the only way we can make sense of the claim that that someone irrationally wants what is bad for him is by interpreting it as claiming that his own preferences at some deeper level are inconsistent with what he is now trying to achieve".[38] Even so, the application of these criteria will naturally assume the relevance of certain evaluative characteristics of alternatives, so that what counts as a consistent set of preferences is not determined independently of evaluative assumptions. That is, what counts as the set of someone's consistent pref-erences is not ultimately independent of the way the world is carved up in evaluative respects, any more than what counts as the set of concepts someone possesses or what he means by an utterance is independent of his context. With willing as with meaning: "An intention is embedded in its situation, in human customs and institutions".[39] The value-ladenness of preference is a species of the world-ladenness of the mind in general.

Should this displacement of a primitive notion of preference, constrained only by requirements of consistency, from a central place in ethics, worry those who value individual autonomy highly? What is the bearing of the rejection of psychological individualism and subjectivism on ethical and po-litical individualism, and on liberal democratic theory? These questions can only be addressed fully in Chapter 15, after further theoretical resources have been developed. There I shall argue that new, and indeed firmer, foundations for democracy and respect for individual autonomy can be provided in the absence of psychological individualism and subjectivism. But at this point it is worth pointing out again that, properly understood, the rejection of sub-jectivism has been shown to be hospitable, not hostile, to pluralism, and indeed to avoid certain dangers of tyranny implicit in subjectivism. Superficial appearances may be misleading; one should not be drawn to subjectivism because one applauds tolerance and autonomy. I have tried to suggest the way in which the subjectivist program might motivate the suppression of ethical disagreement at crucial points, perhaps in favour of 'science'. By contrast, the objectivist and cognitivist theory I shall develop takes such disagreement seriously, contributes toward its articulation through deliber-ation, and gives it, along with individual autonomy, critically important roles to play in the life of a democracy. (For further discussion of this contrast, see Chapter 15 section 4.) The evaluative assumptions about eligibility we have needed to make are not of controversial solutions to ethical problems in which fundamental values conflict, but are rather assumptions that it is correct to describe the problems in those value-laden terms in the first place. Specific reason-giving concepts are appealed to in order to arrive at a deter-minate conception of the issue to be addressed, to determine, for example, whether the problem is one of how to balance a desire for a long life against a desire to avoid pain, or one of how to balance a desire for a long life unless one was born on Monday and in that case life for an even number of weeks against a desire to avoid pain except on Tuesdays. Or to determine, as in Tversky's case, whether the problem is one of how to balance possible monetary benefits against a desire not to be a certain sort of person, a greedy one, or against a desire for certainty *per se*, or is adequately described merely in terms of possible monetary benefits. Or to determine, as in Diamond's case, whether the problem is one of which child should get the candy, or of how to treat both children fairly while not wasting the candy. But there is no suggestion that *solutions* to these problems must be assumed; their solution is a matter for the kind of ethical and political argument that it is a central task of democracy to foster and protect. (If the extended preference ordering is held to determine the solutions to ethical issues, it can hardly be objectionable that ethical argument, carried on under democratic conditions, may be needed to determine the extended preference ordering.) Of course, the way we conceive the alternatives affects the solutions we eventually arrive at, but without some constraints on the way we conceive the alternatives we won't arrive at solutions at all. There is still great scope and need for guidance by considerations of consistency relative to eligible interpretations of the alternatives, which is, after all, what formal decision theory gives us.

# II

# CONFLICTING REASONS
# AND VALUES

# 7

# Conflict

## 1. Conflict of Reasons: Real or Apparent?

Throughout the last chapter I emphasized that the evaluative constraints on eligibility do not impose controversial solutions to ethical problems in which fundamental values conflict, but rather provide a way of determining what the alternatives and hence the issues are to begin with. Properly understood, evaluative constraints on eligible distinctions between alternatives support rather than threaten democratic recognition of a plurality of conflicting values. In later chapters we shall be concerned with how, when values conflict, judgments about what should be done, all things considered, may be arrived at, through deliberation, and with the relationship of democracy to deliberation and disagreement. However, the ground must be laid for these later concerns by considering first (in this chapter and the following two chapters) what reason we may have to suppose that the values which provide substantive constraints on eligible distinctions do conflict, and indeed what we are claiming when we claim that values conflict. Some apparent conflicts of values may be merely apparent; in what sense may any conflicts be more than merely apparent?

We can approach the matter by considering the inconsistency among the following three claims:

> A. *Ought*s are agglomerative: if one ought to do one thing and one ought to do another thing, then one ought to do both.
> B. Reasons for action can really conflict (not merely seem to): sometimes it's not possible to do both of the things one ought to do.
> C. *Ought* implies *can*: if it's not possible to do both of the things one ought to do, then it can't be the case that one ought to do both of them.[1]

Which of these claims should be abandoned? I shall suggest that the answer turns on distinctions within the category of reasons for action and on disambiguation of the *ought*s to which various reasons give rise.

Consider claim B. What does it mean to say that reasons conflict? Imagine a conflict between kindness and justice—though nothing turns on the choice of these reasons; we might just as well consider a conflict between the different kinds of self-interested reasons someone has. A straightforward way to represent the claim that a certain alternative, $X$-ing, would be kind, is as saying that some specification, call it '$K$', of the relevant purely descriptive features of the alternative is such that there's a reason to do any alternative with the property so specified. And to say that $X$-ing would be unjust would be to say that some specification, call it '$-J$', of the relevant purely descriptive features of the alternative is such that there's a reason not to do any alternative with the property so specified.

But a problem arises for this way of describing conflicting reasons if we represent both reasons by the standard monadic deontic operator "it ought to be that . . . ". By making the conflicting reasons logically detachable, this description entails that the alternative ought to be done and that it ought not to be done. As Lemmon points out, the price of denying that these are contradictory is either to deny that *ought* implies *can* (even in the sense of logical possibility) or to deny that ought obeys what Williams calls *the agglomeration principle*, namely that "it ought to be that $p$" and "it ought to be that $q$" entail "it ought to be that $p$ and $q$".[2] If we want to retain the possibility of conflict and the principle that *ought* implies *can*, the fact that we can derive a contradiction from the description of conflicting reasons may prompt a restriction of agglomerativity. That is, we can respect claims B and C by restricting the scope of claim A.

The range of application of the agglomeration principle seems to reflect distinctions between different kinds or sources of reasons (related points might be made about the transitivity and independence conditions discussed in Chapter 4). For any given period of application, for any kind of reason $R$ with that period of application, if $R$ gives a reason for $p$ and $R$ gives a reason for $q$, then $R$ gives a reason for $p$ and $q$.[3] If agglomeration seems to fail because $p$ and $q$ turn out to be incompatible, we have two options (these brief sketches are filled out as the chapter proceeds):

  1. We can say: we're not dealing with one kind of reason but with two different kinds of reason, so the principle doesn't apply and thus is not violated; reasons that conflict do detach, but since they are of different kinds the conflict involves no contradiction. Conflict between reasons of two different kinds no more casts doubt on their existence than conflict between two different wills would cast doubt on theirs.[4]

  2. Or, we can say: we're dealing with one kind of reason but we're wrong to think it ultimately favours both $p$ and $q$; it may appear to, but it doesn't really. Reasons of a given kind favouring both $p$ and $q$ aren't both detachable; one or both is merely *prima facie*. To be a reason of one kind is not to conflict, other than apparently, with other reasons of that kind.[5] So, agglomerativity is unrestricted among ultimate, detachable reasons, though it may be restricted among *prima facie* reasons. (I shall explain just what I mean by "*prima facie*" in section 3 below. For the present it is sufficient to think of *prima facie* reasons as like pieces of evidence, subject to being overriden by better evidence.)

How do we decide between these two options when the agglomeration principle seems to fail? We might always choose the second option and claim that there aren't any real, other than apparent, conflicts of reasons. While we could restrict the agglomerativity of *prima facie* reasons, we would preserve unrestricted agglomerativity, and lack of conflict, among detachable reasons. Or we might go to the other extreme, treat all apparent conflicts as real and allow kinds of reason to proliferate. But both extremes have an artificial air. The latter extreme offends theoretical norms that favour simplicity and economy. But the former begs substantive theoretical questions that shouldn't be answered by mere fiat. It doesn't follow from the admission that some reasons are merely *prima facie* that at least one reason in any conflict of reasons must be merely *prima facie*. Unlike the principle that *ought* implies *can*, unrestricted agglomerativity can't be postulated as a formal feature of any acceptable theory of reasons for action.[6]

If the decision between these two options has a substantive air, just what are the matters of substance at issue? The issue of whether conflicts of reason are real or only apparent involves two questions, a preliminary question and a question of detailed theory. The preliminary question aims to establish whether the possibility is admitted that reasons in some general category may stand in ultimate conflict with one another, that the first option might ever be correct. If the possibility is admitted, then the question of detailed theory aims to establish whether conflict in fact obtains between specific reasons, which option is justified in particular cases. It asks: what is the best theory about specific reasons and their relationships to one another, and what does it say about the relationship between the reasons that feature in this candidate case of real conflict? A detailed theory might show that most conflicts are actually only apparent, even though we admit the possibility that they are real. General familiarity with the successes and failures of various attempts to reduce reasons of one kind to reasons of another and so to eliminate the appearance of conflict suggests that neither extreme view will emerge as correct but rather that there is a limited number of different kinds of reason, capable of coming into real conflict with one another. At least occasionally, such attempts fail; and their success is seldom uncontroversial.[7]

When consideration of theories about specific reasons suggests that a reduction of one to the other won't succeed, then we're justified in taking the first option and recognizing different kinds of reason. We could do this by indexing the deontic operator to distinguish kinds of reason, so that we are in effect operating with as many distinct deontic operators as there are discrete kinds of reason. Assuming we could rank alternatives under them, justice and kindness would be represented in a way reminiscent of the way economists represent the preferences of different people. The agglomeration principle would hold for each kind of reason but not across different kinds of reason: if justice requires that $p$ and justice requires that $q$, then justice requires that $p$ and $q$; but if justice requires that $p$ and kindness requires that $q$, there may not be any reason requiring that $p$ and $q$. By restricting agglomerativity, we could make the existence of conflicting reasons compatible with the principle that *ought* implies *can*.[8]

Perhaps we don't need to wait on substantive theoretical grounds to make this move, as there are pragmatic grounds for it as well. If we start out with the expressive power to mark all the candidate distinctions, we facilitate the theoretical process, that is, the explicit formulation of the relationships among various kinds of reason and their contribution to all-things-considered judgments.[9] There would be no loss of simplicity in substance, since by building too much expressive power into the account at the beginning we merely make ourselves explicitly accountable for moves that would have to be implicit on a simpler account anyway. So, perhaps we should start by treating apparently conflicting reasons as distinct and proceed through deliberation to try to find successful reductions of one kind to another. We could then adjust our distinctions in accord with our successes. The deliberative basis for the adjustments would be exposed, but they wouldn't be otherwise inhibited.

There's a burden of proof objection to this view, though: why should the no-real-conflict position have the burden? This brings us back to the preliminary question, about whether we admit in principle the possibility of real conflicts of reason. The answer to this question determines whether we register preliminary distinctions among reasons and defer to the result of theorizing, or go straight for the view that all conflicts involve merely *prima facie* reasons. I shall suggest that the answer to this question stands in an explanatory relation to the answer to another question: Concerning the reasons in some candidate conflict, is it possible to be akratic with respect to these reasons? The two issues, about the relations between reasons and about the relations between attitudes, are interdependent.

## 2. Restricted Agglomerativity: The Relational Form vs. the Indexed Form

I began by claiming that, in order to hold on to the principle that *ought* implies *can*, we have to abandon either the view that sometimes we really do have conflicting reasons for action, and don't merely seem to, or the view that reasons are agglomerative. This was borne out by the first account of conflict we considered, but there may be various ways in which the first account could be improved on. Perhaps a better account could avoid rendering conflict as contradiction without restricting agglomerativity by distinguishing between different kinds of reason.

There are various alternatives, but I shall concentrate on the one that is probably most attractive.[10] Davidson and Chisholm have suggested representing reasons for action in terms of a relation analogous to the probability or confirmation relation, which does not license the detachment of conclusions about what is probable absolutely. As Chisholm explains, by doing so we can describe conflicts of reasons without contradiction. To avoid contradiction in describing relations of probability, we have to respect the logical rule that $q$

and $-q$ can't both be probable in relation to the same body of evidence $r$. However, $q$ can be probable in relation to $e$ while $-q$ is probable in relation to another piece of evidence $r$. Hence Davidson's example of rain ($q$) probable in relation to a falling barometer ($e$) and no rain ($-q$) probable in relation to a red sky ($r$): it can be held, without contradiction, both that $e$ & ($ePq$) and that $r$ & ($rP-q$).[11]

The suggestion is that conflict between reasons for action is analogously possible, so long as the grounds in favour of the alternative and those against it are not of the same sort. The alternative may be kind but unjust, and there may be different sorts of grounds for doing the kind thing and against doing the unjust thing, say, that it would be '$K$' and '$-J$', respectively, analogous to the different pieces of evidence about whether or not it will rain. Let $q$ now say that the particular act in question is done, instead of that it will rain. The fact that the act in question would be '$K$' plays a positive role in relation to $q$, analogous to that of the falling barometer, so I'll let $e$ express the fact that the act would be '$K$' in the context of reasons for action. Similarly, the fact that the act in question would be '$-J$' plays a negative role in relation to $q$, analogous to that of the red sky, so I'll let $r$ express the fact that the act would be '$-J$' in the context of reasons for action. Again, there's no contradiction in holding both that $e$ & ($eOq$) and that $r$ & ($rO-q$): $q$ ought to be the case in relation to $e$ but $-q$ ought to be the case in relation to $r$.[12]

The relational model avoids rendering conflict as contradiction by, in effect, restricting agglomerativity: if some characteristic gives a reason for $X$-ing and also gives a reason for not $X$-ing, then it gives a reason for both $X$-ing and not $X$-ing. But nothing can give a reason for doing the impossible; the reasons given by any one characteristic must be for alternatives that are at least possibilities. So, if some characteristic of $X$-ing gives a reason for $X$-ing and some characteristic of $X$-ing gives a reason for not $X$-ing, they must be different characteristics; and the principles of the relational model don't license the agglomeration of different reason-giving characteristics. Moreover, the relational model can restrict agglomerativity without distinguishing among kinds of reason. Instead it can distinguish among non-evaluative character-istics to which reasons attach and restrict agglomerativity accordingly (hence the use of inverted commas to specify the different grounds in the previous paragraph).

However, there's an alternative that preserves the virtues of the relational model of conflicting reasons for action while improving on it. Davidson says that the thing that makes trouble for descriptions of conflicting reasons for action is the assumption that the universally quantified conditional form is appropriate.[13] But it isn't this form *per se* that is the cause of the trouble, but rather the unrestricted agglomerativity it normally imports. However, we don't have to move from a conditional to a relational form in order to restrict agglomerativity and avoid rendering conflict as contradiction. While the re-lational form has this effect, we also get it by distinguishing the requirements of different kinds of reason. As I suggested before, we can do this by indexing and permitting agglomeration only when indices match. So, it ought to be the case with respect to kindness that $q$, while it ought to be the case with respect to justice that $-q$; that is, $e$ & $(e \rightarrow O_k q)$ and $r$ & $(r \rightarrow O_j - q)$. The indexed reasons, $O_k q$ and $O_j - q$, that detach from this description of conflict are no more contradictory than reasons expressed in relational form are, or than judgments about the conflicting interests of different persons are. Moreover, while the description of conflict in terms of indexed reasons is compatible with the existential claim that there are non-evaluative characteristics on which reasons supervene, it needn't depend on the independent specifiability of such non-evaluative characteristics as the basis for the distinction among reasons.[14]

But is there really an issue between the relational form and the indexed form? Why depart from the more economical relational form? Both avoid rendering conflict as contradiction by restricting agglomerativity to cases in which the characteristics and indices match, respectively. They differ, supposedly, in that the indexed form does and the relational form does not distinguish kinds of reason *per se*. Also, the indexed form allows us to detach modal conclusions and the relational form does not. But perhaps when the modal conclusions are indexed to kinds of reason, this is a distinction without a difference.

### 3. *Prima Facie* Reasons vs. *Pro Tanto* Reasons, and the Absence of Evidential *Akrasia*

What's at issue here is in effect the answer to the preliminary question I raised in section 1, about whether we admit in principle the possibility of real conflicts of reasons. I believe that there's an important distinction to be drawn and I suggest that we take the distinction between the relational and the indexed forms to mark it. This is the distinction between reasons in relation to which *akrasia* is not possible, which I suggest we refer to as *prima facie* reasons and represent as having the relational form, and reasons in relation to which it is possible, which I suggest we refer to as *pro tanto* reasons and represent as having the indexed form. These suggestions may seem curious, in that Davidson has argued that an analogy between specific reasons for action and relational probabilities shows us how weakness of will is possible. But there are prior grounds for curiosity about how such an analogy shows how weakness of will is possible when the relational form of probability judgments doesn't seem to make a corresponding evidential form of 'weakness of belief' possible.

*Akrasia*, or weakness of the will, occurs when, in the face of conflicting reasons for and against $X$-ing, someone makes an all-things-considered judgment that he ought not to $X$, but $X$'s anyway and does so for a reason, namely, for whatever the reason in favour of $X$-ing was (which was included in the basis of the all-things-considered judgment). For example, he may judge that, all things considered, he ought to do what justice requires and not what kindness requires, but may do what kindness requires anyway, and for a reason, namely, because kindness requires it. Or the conflict may be between an ethical reason and a self-interested reason. As Davidson points out, however, the akratic structure doesn't have to involve ethical reasons, but can occur with respect to one person's different pleasures and interests. He gives the marvellous example of someone who akratically gets back out of bed to brush his teeth even though he judges that all things considered he should neglect his teeth on this occasion and stay in bed.

Davidson's view of *akrasia* in his earlier article "How Is Weakness of the Will Possible?" is, in effect, as follows: There's a conflict of reasons in relational form. The *akrates* makes the judgment that in relation to all the relevant features of the alternatives, he should refrain. This all-things-considered judgment remains insulated from action in relational form, is, as Davidson puts it, "practical only in its subject, not in its issue",[15] while somehow the reason for doing the act gets itself into all-out, detachable form. Since the antecedent condition obtains, this latter detaches and the *akrates* does the act, and for a reason:

$e$ & $(eOq)$
$r$ & $(rO-q)$
$e$ & $r$ encompass all the relevant features of the alternatives
$(e$ & $r)O-q$
$e \rightarrow Oq$
$Oq$
$q$

This description of *akrasia* depends on what I shall call *the evidential account* of conflict, which employs the relational form; thus we may refer to it as *the evidential account of akrasia*. There's no contradiction in this description, but it doesn't parallel any familiar structure of probability or evidential judgments and associated beliefs. This is worrying, since an analogy between relational probability and specific reasons for action is supposed to help explain how weakness of will is possible.

In fact I want to claim that there's no such thing as evidential *akrasia*, which would be a phenomenon strictly parallel to acting against one's better judgment and on a subset of one's reasons, but involving evidential reasons, reasons for belief, and that the unavailability of the akratic structure is partly constitutive of belief and helps us in attributing attitudes to distinguish between beliefs and desires (which is not to say this distinction is always sharp; my claim does not involve a denial that there may be some degree of indeterminacy). That is, the claim that there is no such thing as evidential *akrasia* is put forward as part of a theory of interpretation.

Consider someone who makes two relational probability judgments, $ePq$ and $rP-q$, and goes on to judge that in relation to all the relevant evidence there is, namely $e$ and $r$, $-q$ is probable. He couldn't, despite having made the more inclusive relational judgment conjoined with the judgment of no better evidence, believe that $q$ is probable *because of the evidence provided by e*; $e$'s evidential force has been subsumed without remainder by the more inclusive evidence *(e & r)*. Less inclusive probabilistic evidence has no constitutive reason-giving force that could hold out in the face of recognition that it's subsumed by the best probabilistic evidence, which favours the opposite conclusion. He might believe that probably $q$ anyway, but his irrationality in doing so wouldn't be a case of probabilistic *akrasia*, but a case of wishful thinking or self-deception: he might have strong reasons for wanting to believe that $q$. But his reason for believing that probably $q$ cannot be the reason given by $e$ once he recognises that in relation to all the evidence, including $e$, $-q$ is probable.

Self-deception isn't evidential *akrasia*. Self-deception occurs when reasons for action influence beliefs, by means of desires to believe something because of the beneficial or comfortable consequences of so believing, or by means of techniques applied to get oneself to believe something. It belongs with the cases David Pears refers to as the *hot cases* of irrationality, which are motivated by desires, and illustrates conflict between reasons for belief and for action just as *akrasia* illustrates conflict between reasons for action. (The possibilities of conflict between reasons for belief and for action, and of self-deception, reveal what is already implicit in my account of the *prima facie/pro tanto* distinction: that reasons are *prima facie* or *pro tanto* not intrinsically, but in relation to other reasons; reasons for belief may be *prima facie* in relation to other reasons for belief, but *pro tanto* in relation to reasons for action.[16]) Evidential *akrasia*, by contrast to self-deception, would involve no crossing of the categories of reason for action and reason for belief; it would be restricted to probabilistic or truth-related reasons for belief proper and would belong with the *cold cases* of irrationality, not motivated by desires, which have been studied by attribution and decision theorists. So, if it occurred, it would have the form of belief that probably $q$, held for the reason given by less inclusive evidence in relation to which $q$ is probable, and maintained in the face of recognition that $-q$ is probable in relation to more inclusive evidence, which subsumes the evidence for $q$ and which is all the evidence there is.

But beliefs about what is probable that are motivated by evidence don't display this structure of irrationality; if we met a case that seemed to have this structure we'd immediately suspect the influence of reasons of the wrong sort, reasons for action; the very structure sends us looking for a desire to attribute. An attribution of wishful thinking of some kind, or some other attribution, will always be better than one of evidential *akrasia*. We could be justified in attributing either the belief that $-q$ is probable in relation to all the evidence, or the belief, held for a reason given by some piece of the evidence, that probably $q$; but we couldn't be justified in attributing both. Cases of deception and self-deception aside, whatever grounds would justify attributing the latter belief, that probably $q$, and an associated reason, would also justify revising the former attribution, so as to describe the case, for example, as one of simple mistake, such as a failure to recognize or remember that $-q$ is probable in relation to all the evidence. As Pears comments, if the operation of a wish is detected and the resulting belief recognized as irrational, it may still retain some of its power to delude and fascinate. But cold illusions, produced, for example, by the salience of a piece of information, have no residual force after they have been unmasked. The explanation is that in the case of what should be done there may be conflict within an agent, there may be conflicting reasons competing for authority. But in the case of what should be believed, truth alone governs and it can't be divided against itself or harbour conflicts.[17] It makes sense to suppose that something is, ultimately, good in some respects but not others (even if this turns out not to be true in particular cases), in a way that it does not make sense to suppose that something is, ultimately, true in some respects but not others.

This, then, is the answer to the preliminary question: We do admit the possibility in principle of real conflicts between reasons for action, and between reasons for action and for belief, but not between reasons for belief. There may be alternatives to attributing *akrasia*, which would avoid the akratic structure, but it is just because the reasons in terms of which we make sense of events as actions can come into conflict, that it sometimes makes more sense to attribute *akrasia* in relation to familiar reasons than to avoid attributing *akrasia* at the expense of distortion of the operative reasons. Thus the relations among familiar reasons and values provide substantive constraints on the eligibility of interpretations that sometimes outweigh the constraint which favours interpreting agents as acting in accord with their all-things-considered judgments. I shall elaborate this point in the next chapter.

The term *"prima facie"* seems appropriate for reasons that are like the reasons given by relational probabilities in that they can't come into ultimate conflict with one another or be the operative reasons in cases of *akrasia*. *Prima facie* reasons are like rules of thumb, that give us reasons provisionally but may turn out not to apply when we learn more about the situation at hand, in which case they have no residual reason-giving force. The relational form is well suited to express *prima facie* reasons for belief, just because it doesn't allow the detachment of modal conclusions, because it insulates *prima facie* judgments of probability from beliefs about what's probable absolutely. And the absence of ultimate conflict among reasons for belief and hence of evidential *akrasia* is reflected in the relationship between relational and absolute probabilities (again, cases of self-deception aside). As Chisholm writes, "*q* is *prima facie* probable for *S* if there is a *e* such that *e* is evident to *S* and *q* is probable in relation to *e* (*e* confirms *q*); and *q* is absolutely probable for *S* if there is a *e* such that *e* is evident to *S* and *q* is probable in relation to *e*, and if there is no *r* such that *r* is evident to *S* and *q* is not probable in relation to *e* & *r*".[18]

If uses of the relational form are to remain true to the model of relational probability, they should represent reasons that are *prima facie*. Conflicting reasons for action such as justice and kindness aren't *prima facie* in the sense that, like rules of thumb, they seem to give reasons to do acts that would be just or kind, but may turn out not to when we learn more about the situation.[19]One could do the kind act because kindness requires it, even in the face of one's better judgment, namely, that all things considered one ought not to do the kind act but rather the just act. In doing so, one would be acting irrationally, in the way that the *akrates* acts irrationally. But one would still be acting for a reason, namely, because of the kindness of the act. The term *"pro tanto"* seems appropriate to describe such reasons, which might conceivably come into ultimate conflict with one another and can thus be the operative reasons in cases of *akrasia*.

The relationship between *pro tanto* and all things considered reasons for action has a more complicated structure than the relationship between relational and absolute probabilities. *Pro tanto* reasons for action allow the detaching of modal conclusions just as readily as all things considered reasons do; neither sort of reason for action "is practical only in its subject, not in its issue", as Davidson puts it. One does better to do the act favoured by one's all things considered judgment rather than to act on a conflicting *pro tanto* reason because one's all things considered judgments are some theoretically significant function of one's *pro tanto* reasons, expressive of one's personal coherence and autonomy (in the sense to be elaborated in Chapters 12, 13, and 15). But nevertheless one can just as much act on any of one's *pro tanto* reasons as one can act on one's all-things-considered judgment; unkindness is no more eliminated by theoretical favour, or by considerations of coherence or autonomy, than by justice. There is an overabundance of detachable reasons for action; the sense in which one of them may outrank the others provides the sense of the supposition that one would be irrational not to follow its recommendation, but it doesn't mean that *pro tanto* reasons no longer conflict with that recommendation. Hence the circumstances of *akrasia* (I use "$O_t$" here to express judgments about what should be done, all things considered):[20]

$$e \ \& \ (e \to O_k q)$$
$$r \ \& \ (r \to O_j - q)$$
$$O_k q$$
$$O_j - q$$
k and j are all the relevant reasons
$$O_t \ldots = f( \ldots, O_k \ldots, O_j \ldots, \ldots )$$
$$O_t - q$$
$$O_k q$$
$$q$$

This model of *akrasia* depends on what I shall call *the subsystems account* of conflict, which employs the indexed form; we may thus refer to it as *the subsystems account of akrasia*. The indexed form permits detachment of reasons that may conflict but, since they are of different kinds, will not contradict one another. It reflects the view that conflicts within persons, between reasons, are, in some interesting ways, like conflicts between persons, a view that takes seriously the qualitative distinctions between reasons as starting points for reflective self-determination and declines to accept the envelope provided by "the poor empirical self" as the only or prior source of significant unity.[21] The relationships between different *pro tanto* reasons are, in interesting ways, like relationships between individuals whose wills clash. Indeed, their role in interpretation is such that they guide us in drawing the boundaries between the functional subsystems of the agent described in Davidson's later article and by Pears.[22] So the agglomeration principle reappears in its role of reflecting distinctions between different kinds or sources of reasons; the indices by which *pro tanto* reasons are distinguished indicate that agglomeration is restricted between subsystems but not within them, and consistency is maintained within subsystems.

In the next chapter I shall press further the analogy between different reasons and different persons, to see what light it may shed on the nature of individual irrationality and on why interpretations of persons as irrational are nevertheless sometimes more eligible than the alternatives. I shall then go on to defend the claim that there is no such thing as evidential *akrasia* by reference to several examples.

# 8

# *Akrasia*

## 1. Irrational Systems and Rational Subsystems: Conflicts Within Persons and Conflicts Between Persons

In the last chapter I distinguished the evidential account of conflict, in which conflicting *prima facie* reasons are represented in relational form, from the subsystems account of conflict, in which conflicting *pro tanto* reasons are represented in indexed form. I also suggested an analogy between conflicting *pro tanto* reasons and individuals whose wills clash. Perhaps the analogy can be extended to the level of all-things-considered reasons.

Here is a first try at the extension: the relationship between specific *pro tanto* reasons and all-things-considered reasons is like the relationship between the individuals in society, each of whom tries to get his own way, and someone (or some institution) in authority over them. It's a necessary (but not sufficient) condition for attributing authority over others to someone that he generally gets his way. Nevertheless, each individual tries to get his way and there's no guarantee that authority will always prevail.

Aristotle writes: "And thus the incontinent man is like a city which passes all the right decrees and has good laws, but makes no use of them, as in Anaxandrides jesting remark, 'The city willed it, that cares nought for laws'; but the wicked man is like a city that uses its laws, but has wicked laws to use."[1] However, this way of setting out the analogy fails to register that cases of flouting authority have to be the exception rather than the rule if attributions of authority aren't to be undermined. Similarly, cases of *akrasia* have to be the exception rather than the rule if attributions to the agent of judgments about what he should do, all things considered, aren't to be undermined. We can, and should, recognize a general link between all-things-considered judgments and action without regarding the link as holding without exception and so regarding *akrasia* as impossible. Thus it's more accurate to compare judgments about what should be done, all things considered, as functions of *pro tanto* reasons, to the laws of a representative government. Then the function from *pro tanto* reasons to all-things-considered judgments (which I shall call in Chapter 12 a *coherence function*) would be in certain respects analogous to a social welfare function or democratic constitution.[2]

The analogy is reinforced by the possibility of a failing on the part of democratic societies with the akratic structure, which would be as follows: Society is divided into class *r* and class *e*. Class *r* wants a certain outcome *q*, say, that the members of a certain ethnic group are discriminated against, and appeals for support to certain precedents or principles. Class *e* wants a different outcome, that −*q*, no discrimination, and appeals to other precedents or principles. An election is held in which the members of classes *e* and *r* vote; the elected representatives pass a law requiring that −*q*. Nevertheless, *q* is the actual result and it comes about because the members of class *r* want this result. Their power in society is such that they're able to find ways of getting around the law and neither the members of class *e* nor the elected representatives prevent them from doing so, even though what is happening is clear to everyone.

This is a description of a familiar enough failing of democratic societies. In the absence of dictatorial power, it may be extremely difficult to enforce laws even though they are supported by a majority of the voters. When this happens, we're not forced to revise our assessment of the validity of the law or our description of its content so that what the law actually requires is always aligned with political realities, to say that the real government of the society is a peculiar coalition between the apparent government and class *r*, which allows class *r* to have its way in certain circumstances. We understand without difficulty that members of society may try to get what they want, and may sometimes succeed, even though their wants have already received fair expression through voting, along with the wants of others, and have been denied. Only if the requirements of most laws passed by the representatives are flouted do we have to reassess their status as the laws of the society. We may sometimes attribute a peculiar coalition rather than a series of cases of flouting, depending on whether the hypothesized complicity makes sense, given what we know about class relations and interests and the workings of the government. But the possibility of flouting the law isn't difficult to understand. We can imagine cases in which the best theory about a democratic society would describe it in this way.

The possibility of *akrasia* can be similarly understood. The capacity of *pro tanto* reasons to influence what an agent does is no more exhausted by their contribution to his deliberated all-things-considered evaluations than the capacity of interest groups to influence what a democratic society does is exhausted by their contribution to its government and laws: each may go on trying to get its way in the face of legitimate authority. *Pro tanto* reasons are manifestations of the conflicting values that may continue to exert their discrete influences over us even when we have arrived at all-things-considered judgments; they're not like pieces of evidence or rules of thumb about what ought to be done, all things considered, that yield automatically to better evidence.

(The question of precisely how various *pro tanto* reasons for action determine what ought to be done, all things considered, is the question that deliberators try to answer. Their efforts to answer it are what we attend to in order to determine whether there is what I referred to in Chapter 3 as a practice of theorizing that speaks for itself, so that deliberators are disagreeing about the right answer to a theoretical question rather than talking about different things. In later chapters I will develop the view that what ought to be done, all things considered, is some function of the *pro tanto* reasons that apply to the alternatives in question, and will consider what conditions such a coherence function must meet.)

What I have done in pursuing the analogy between *pro tanto* reasons and individuals whose wills may clash is to develop in one possible direction the suggestions made by Davidson in "Paradoxes of Irrationality" to the effect that we may be able to understand irrational systems in terms of rational subsystems. There are several other possible ways in which his extremely interesting suggestions in that article might be pursued further. We are familiar with many variations on the theme of how many instances of individual rationality may amount to group irrationality; possible intrapersonal analogues of these variations may be considered, and may enable us to understand various kinds of individual irrationality. I shall briefly discuss three kinds of case. I do not claim that these cases illustrate *akrasia* in particular, only that they illustrate the ways in which irrational systems may be understood by reference to rational subsystems. (I'll return to *akrasia* in particular later in this chapter.)

First, consider again the analogy between a function from *pro tanto* reasons to all-things-considered judgments and a social welfare function. It is well known that certain methods of aggregating the transitive preferences of individuals may yield intransitive social preferences. The simplest illustration of how this may happen is provided by the Voter's Paradox: person $i$ prefers $a$ to $b$ to $c$, person $j$ prefers $b$ to $c$ to $a$, and person $k$ prefers $c$ to $a$ to $b$. Each of them has perfectly transitive, and in this respect rational, preferences. Nevertheless, if we apply the method of majority decision to yield social preference, we get intransitive, thus irrational, results: $a$ is preferred to $b$ by two out of three persons, $b$ to $c$ by two out of three persons, and $c$ to $a$ by two out of three persons. Collective choices may be irrational despite individual rationality.

Intrapersonal analogues of the Voter's Paradox might explain intransitive individual choices in terms of transitive rankings by subsystems, where each subsystem is governed by a discrete *pro tanto* reason and maintains internal consistency. I shall have much more to say about the possibility of this kind of irrationality in later chapters, especially Chapter 12, where I shall try to show how it is possible for persons to avoid a generalized threat of such irrationality deriving from Arrow's Theorem. Nevertheless, while it may be possible to avoid the generalized threat of such irrationality, it is also certainly possible to fall into such irrationality under particular conditions, which is all

I am claiming for present purposes. Since I will consider this sort of case in detail later, here I'll dwell on the next two kinds of case.

Second, there may be intrapersonal analogues of game theoretic problems such as the Prisoner's Dilemma. In cases studied by game theory, people are most often assumed to have different aims rather than a common aim; each person tries to maximize the satisfaction of his own separate goal, rather than to maximize the satisfaction of a common goal. Yet when each person succeeds in doing that act out of those available that is rational in terms of his own goal, all may end up worse off in terms of their own goals than they might have been if each had not behaved rationally. Parfit calls such situations *Each-We Dilemmas.*[3] Looking at such a situation from the collective or group perspective, what is done is irrational: a better solution was available *to the group*—better in terms of the goals of the individual members of the group. Looking at the situation from the individuals' perspectives, what is done is rational: Each individual has done the best *he could do* for himself.

Jon Elster has pursued the thought that some cases of weakness of the will may be understood as intrapersonal analogues of the Prisoner's Dilemma.[4] In my terms, each subsystem of the self may try to maximize the satisfaction of its own goal and may indeed succeed in rationally doing that act out of those available that is rational in terms of its own goal. Nevertheless, all subsystems may end up worse off in terms of their own goals than they might have been if each had not behaved rationally. Looking at the dilemma from the point of view of the system, or person, what is done is irrational; but from the point of view of the subsystems it is rational, as each subsystem served its own goal as best it could.

Parfit and Elster suggest examples of intrapersonal intertemporal Prisoner's Dilemmas (tidying one's room, jogging, refusing drink, in each time period), in which it is better for each temporally identified person-stage not to do the act in question, no matter what the others do, even though it is better for each person-stage if all do it than if all do not. In considering possible intrapersonal analogues, however, I would emphasize that even though only one subsystem may be capable of acting at a given point in time, nevertheless subsystems needn't necessarily be thought of as temporally identified person-stages. Rather, subsystems may be identified functionally, as I argued in the last chapter, in terms of the rational relations among contents of attitudes and their governing reasons for action; and attitudes cannot normally be ascribed in a temporally atomistic manner. The temporal dimension is still essential to the attitudes in terms of the relations among which the split is identified; but the split is carried along through time with the attitudes.[5] For example, consider a possible psychiatric condition with the pay-off structure of that in the Prisoner's Dilemma, in which the act in question for both subsystems is taking a certain drug prescribed as treatment. This possible condition may or may not in fact amount to manic depressive illness (whether it does does not matter for my purposes), but I shall use the labels *manic* and *depressive* to identify the recurring subsystems. Both the manic and the depressive prefer that both take the drug than that neither take the drug; in the latter case the sheer disjointedness of the person's life causes both 'halves' to suffer more than they would in the former case (the strain may break up a marriage, for example). Nevertheless, no matter what the other does, each prefers not to take the drug. The drug causes occasional headaches, and is more effective at damping the manic's over-confident elation, which the manic enjoys, than at raising the depressive's low spirits. If only one 'half' but not the other takes the drug, however, some beneficial effects accrue to the non-taker. Thus each subsystem would like most of all for only the other to take the drug, and each can reason that, whether the other takes the drug or not, it is better off not to.[6]

The first two cases, of systemic intransivity and the Prisoner's Dilemma, have in common that the subsystems which account for the irrationality of the system have *different goals*. However, it may be possible to understand the irrationality of a system in terms of rational subsystems even when the subsystems in question share a *common goal*. It is important to see both what the shared-goal cases have in common with the different-goal cases, and how they differ. I shall first explain what they have in common, and then how they differ.

While in general game theory studies situations in which agents' goals differ, as they do in Prisoner's Dilemmas, nothing in game theory rules out the possibility that agent's goals may coincide, and even that it may be common knowledge that they do so—as, for example, might be the case in a society of Act Utilitarians. Such shared-goal cases form an especially interesting game-theoretic subcategory.[7] Indeed, consideration of such cases helps to reveal a distinction with respect to the unit of agency which cuts across the question of whether goals are different or shared. That is, the shared-goal cases share with the different-goal cases a further and independent dimension of contrast, with respect to the unit of agency. The unit of agency is the unit the causal consequences of the activity of which are in question; the unit may be taken to be the subsystem ('each') or the system ('we'). (The distinction between system and subsystem is of course itself relative: individual persons are subsystems in relation to groups of persons, and systems in relation to conflicting reasons corresponding to different values or periods of time.) The distinction with respect to unit of agency cuts across the distinction between different-goal and shared-goal cases; what the latter have in common is that they admit the former distinction.[8] I shall elaborate.

Each prisoner may evaluate in terms of his different goals the consequences of the alternative acts open to him individually: this is to evaluate alternatives from the *subsystemic point of view* in terms of *differing goals*, namely, the differing goals of the two prisoners. Or each prisoner may evaluate in terms of his separate goals the consequences of the alternative sets of acts open to the prisoners taken as a pair: this is to evaluate alternatives from the *systemic point of view* in terms of the same *differing goals*. The standard kind of Prisoner's Dilemma matrix makes clear how the subsystemic and systemic perspectives can come apart: if *each* does what best serves his goals, *we* do

## DIFFERENT GOALS

You

|   |   | confess | do not confess |
|---|---|---------|----------------|
| I | confess | 3rd best for each | best for me worst for you |
|   | do not confess | worst for me, best for you | 2nd best for each |

FIGURE 8.1

something that fails to serve each of our goals as well as something else we might have done (see Figure 8.1).

A similar contrast may be drawn for shared-goal cases. One may evaluate in terms of shared goals the consequences of individual acts, considered individually and compared with other possible individual acts: This is to evaluate alternatives from the *subsystemic point of view* in terms of the *same goal*. Or one may evaluate in terms of shared goals the consequences of a set of individual acts, considered as a unit and compared with other possible sets of acts: this is to evaluative alternatives from the *systemic point of view* in terms of the *same goal*. The standard kind of matrix employed by those writers, such as Gibbard and Regan, who have demonstrated the distinctness of Act and Rule Utilitarianism, illustrates how the subsystemic and systemic perspectives can come apart even when the goal is shared: if each does as well as he can in terms of our common goal, given what the other has done, we *may* fail to do as well as we can. In the Figure 8.2 matrix, each has done the best thing, given what the other has done, if we both push; but each has also done the best thing, given what the other has done, if neither pushes (see Figure 8.2).

I shall explain further how the distinction with respect to units of agency arises in the shared-goal cases, and how they differ from the different-goal

## SAME GOALS

You

|   |   | push your button | do not push your button |
|---|---|------------------|-------------------------|
| I | push my button | best | equal worst |
|   | do not push my button | equal worst | 2nd best |

FIGURE 8.2

cases. First, however, some explanatory comments that pertain to both the shared-goal and the different-goal cases. There may be intrapersonal analogues of shared-goal cases as well as of different-goal cases, which help us to understand systemic irrationality in terms of rational subsystems.[9] Thus the set of events evaluated from a systemic point of view may be a set of acts performed over some period of time by one person, or it may be a set of acts performed by members of a group of persons. When I speak of a collective unit of agency, I mean in part that the causal consequences of alternative sets of acts of members of a group of persons, with alternative *sets* of acts rather than alternative individual acts taken as units, are evaluated. *Collective action* involves identifying, as well as possible, the group of those prepared to co-operate with whoever else is co-operating (which partially determines the class of actual collective alternatives), and then acting as part of that group, participating in the best collective alternative. This is quite different both from doing the individual act with best consequences, given what the others do, and from doing what would be best were everyone to do it, regardless of what others do. (If someone prefers to speak of a distinct form of assessment of the upshots of individual acts, in terms of their membership relations to collections of acts with good consequences, rather than a collective unit of agency, I have no objection, so long as it is registered that an individual by himself cannot do a "collective act".[10]) The notions of personal action and a personal unit of agency already allow for the possibility and indeed the normality of the corresponding sense of intrapersonal 'collective' agency—it just is personal agency, which reflects the distinctive capacities of persons in the presence of conflicting reasons for deliberation, all-things-considered judgment, and higher-order attitudes.

As I mentioned earlier, I do not claim that intrapersonal analogues of Voters Paradoxes, Prisoner's Dilemmas, or pure coordination problems amount to *akrasia* in particular, but only make the weaker generic claim that they may cast light on individual irrationality. In later chapters, however, I develop the view that all-things-considered judgments, which are acted against in cases of *akrasia* and other forms of practical irrationality, are judgments about the theoretical relationships among the applicable reasons for action. When the latter provide functional subsystemic distinctions in the way that I argued for in the last chapter, then all-things-considered judgments are in effect judgments about the theoretical relationships among subsystems, or systemic judgments; that is, the systemic perspective just is the perspective of all-things-considered judgment.

Now, more on the shared-goal cases. Consider the inadequacy of Act Utilitarianism as expounded by Donald Regan. (For my purposes Act Utilitarianism merely provides an example of *shared-goal individualism*, which involves both a shared goal and the assumption of an individualistic unit of agency. Nothing, for my purposes, turns on the utilitarian character of the shared goal; the structural, game-theoretic considerations my argument depends on are independent of the content of the goal. Thus, my argument could be applied to shared-goal individualism with other goals that may be held in common, e.g., purely self-interested goals. I speak in terms of Act Utilitarianism in particular, rather than of shared-goal individualism in general, when I do, merely because the former provides a familiar example of the latter.) Many Act Utilitarians, each of whom correctly calculates the total utility of the consequences of his *individual* alternatives and succeeds in doing the best he can individually, given what the others do, may nonetheless fail to achieve as high a level of total utility as would be achieved by calculation and maximization of the utilities of the consequences of possible *classes* of acts taken as units.[11] Even when each individual does the best he can in terms of total utility given what the others do, a lower level of utility may be achieved than could be achieved through collective action. This is because games with shared goals may be indeterminate; for example, as in Figure 8.2, there may be more than one way in which we can each do what is best in Act Utilitarian terms, given what the others do. Some of these ways of satisfying Act Utilitarianism may produce better consequences from the collective point of view than others; but the collective point of view is not that of the Act Utilitarian. In some cases Act Utilitarianism may be unable to secure the superior consequences, just because it counsels persons to act as individuals, not as members of a group. Thus, in my more general terms, collective agency may have advantages over individual agency even when all agents share the same goal.

These points are not avoided by the fact that shared-goal individualism would urge an individual, were it within his causal powers to do so, to organize people in order to secure good consequences, or causally to bind his actions to those of others so it is causally impossible for them not to act in the same way. If such an act is in an individual's power, then the matrix has been changed and is no longer as specified. No one claims that shared-goal individualism has undesirable properties in all cases, only in some cases, as specified, which seem perfectly possible. In the cases in question, it is not within any individual's causal powers to obtain the benefits of co-operation through his own acts (or the probability of success is so small as not to be worth the cost, in terms of the shared goal), but it is within the causal powers of a group of co-operators. It's no response to these cases to point out that shared-goal individualism can handle other cases. Moreover, in some situations efforts to organize people may themselves form a coordination problem for shared-goal individualism, so that organization itself may require collective action.

The difference I had in mind between the shared-goal and different-goal cases is this. In the different-goal cases, such as the Prisoner's Dilemma, each may do better in terms of their differing goals, though together they do worse in those terms than they might have; these are Each-We Dilemmas.[12] In these cases, success from the point of view of subsystems may *guarantee failure* from the point of view of systems. But, at least until we move to considering versions of individualism that take subjective probabilities into account, this will not happen in shared-goal cases; success from the point of view of systems will be consistent with success from the point of view of subsystems. Nevertheless, acting from the subsystems' point of view in shared-goal cases may still have a defect (even though in some sense it's a lesser defect than that of

GOALS

| | DIFFERENT | SAME |
|---|---|---|
| SUBSYSTEM (fixed) | e.g.: self-interest without co-operation (each-we dilemmas) | e.g.: Act Utilitarianism (indeterminacy) |
| SYSTEM (fixed) | e.g.: self-interest with fixed hypothetical group agent | e.g.: Rule Utilitarianism, Utilitarian Generalization |
| FLEXIBLE | e.g.: ? | e.g.: Reagan's theory, Co-operative Utilitarianism |

(UNIT OF AGENCY — row label to the left of the table)

FIGURE 8.3

the different-goal cases): success from the point of view of subsystems may *fail to guarantee success* from the point of view of systems.[13] The difference between the different-goal cases and the shared-goal cases is thus the difference between guaranteed failure and failure to guarantee success, from the systemic point of view; or between internal and external negation. Shared-goal cases cannot guarantee systemic success on the basis of subsystemic success because of the indeterminacy they may involve; each of several overall patterns of behaviour may be consistent with successful application of shared-goal individualism by each subsystem, even though one of them clearly involves greater total goal-satisfaction than another, as in Figure 8.2 above. Thus indeterminacy may play a role in the shared-goal cases analogous to the role of each-we dilemmas in the different-goal cases, in allowing the subsystemic and systemic units of agency, for purposes of calculating consequences, to come apart. My point for present purposes is merely that despite the difference I've noted between different-goal and shared-goal cases, the distinction with respect to subsystemic and systemic units of agency can still be drawn for each of them. Subsystemic behaviour motivated by separate goals and subsystemic behaviour motivated by shared goals may both be defective, though in different ways, from the point of view of the system. We can map out this territory, with examples, as in Figure 8.3.

The problem from the systemic point of view in both different-goal and shared-goal cases is to find a way of coordinating individual centers of agency so that collective agency is possible, even when it is not within any one individual's power to accomplish this. There may be intrapersonal versions of both kinds of coordination problems, in which subsystems tend to break away from the personal unit of agency, in pursuit of the consequences of subsystemic acts rather than of those of systemic acts. It is in terms of the difficulties of achieving such intrapersonal coherence that I've suggested we can understand some kinds of irrationality in persons.

## 2. The Irrationality of Taking the Unit of Agency as Fixed

However, at this point an important objection may be made.[14] As Davidson has emphasized, understanding irrationality too well threatens to undermine the sense in which it is irrational after all. And after all, why is it irrational for the individualist in a Prisoner's Dilemma, or in a shared-goal indeterminacy case, to concern himself with the consequences of his own acts considered individually rather than with the consequences of classes of acts? Individual agents, even when they recognize that collective agency would have advantages over individual agency, may naturally tend to revert to considering the consequences of their own acts taken individually, since no individual can by himself *do* the collective act. How can this be irrational? And by the same token, how can personal 'irrationality' understood in terms of rational subsystems be irrational? If there really are effective subsystemic units of agency, then in what sense is the system irrational? The supposedly irrational person is in danger of being no more irrational than the pair of prisoners or the group of benighted Act Utilitarians.

The objection gets something right and something wrong. It's right that, so long as we occupy only the subsystemic point of view, the irrationality will escape us. But nevertheless the irrationality is there to be accounted for: there is *something* irrational about the subsystemic solutions to the Prisoners' Dilemma and to the problem of maximizing total utility. If they are able to act collectively, the prisoners are irrational not to act *as a pair*, and thus do better for themselves; again, if they are able to act collectively, the Utilitarians are irrational not to act *as a group*, and thus do better in terms of total utility. It is no use objecting that people cannot act as members of a group, as this claim is simply false: persons, unlike some other creatures, do have the distinctive capacity for collective action—even when they do not have a shared goal.[15] (I will suggest in section 4 below that this capacity is part of the distinctive capacity of persons for self-determination.) This is not to say that it would be more rational to adopt any particular, fixed collective unit of agency for all purposes. As many writers have pointed out, rigidly following rules irrespective of whether others co-operate in following them may be disastrous.[16] What the objection gets wrong is that it tacitly assumes that *some* unit of agency must be taken as fixed. But insistence on *taking the unit of agency as fixed* itself contributes to the very irrationality that needs to be accounted for in these cases.[17]

In order to capture the irrationality these cases involve, we must allow ourselves to survey the units of agency that are possible in the circumstances at hand and to ask *what the unit of agency, among those possible, should be*.[18] The answer to this question is not determined by whether or not the goal is common, nor can it be inferred from the content of the goal (for example, an individualistic unit of agency cannot be inferred from an egoistic goal); these questions cut across one another. We should then ask ourselves *how we can contribute to the realization of the best unit possible in the circumstances*. This is not the same thing *either* as individually doing what is best, given what the others do (or are likely to do), *or* as doing what would be best were the others to do it (whether or not they will); in neither of these cases can one's act be regarded as part of a collective act. Collective action does not calculate consequences from a fixed unit of agency; rather, it involves first identifying those willing to act collectively, and then *together* doing what's best, given what the non-co-operators do (or are likely to do). But if we tacitly insist that the unit of agency must be fixed, somehow, once and for all, so that the possibility of collective action does not arise, it's no wonder the irrationality the cases intuitively involve seems to elude us. Once we recognize that the question what the unit of agency should be, among those possible, does arise, then the irrationality of certain answers to it may become patent. In the case of the Prisoners, the unit should be the pair; in the case of Act Utilitarian indeterminacy, the unit should be the group. In the case of the irrational person, the unit should be the person, as opposed to a breakaway subsystem. Individual irrationality understood in terms of rational subsystems will only begin to look rational after all if we take the subsystemic unit of agency as fixed and fail to register that the *wrong* unit of agency is operating.

It is true, as Parfit points out in defending the Self-interest theory of rationality against the charge of self-defeatingness, that some theories do not aim to be collective theories of rationality. But it is not enough to stop with this point. An adequate theory of rationality for persons, or self-determining agents, cannot simply take the unit of agency as fixed and refuse to address the question of what it should be. An adequate theory should help us to understand what the appropriate unit of agency is in various circumstances, as, for example, Regan's consequentialist theory of Co-operative Utilitarianism tries to do. A follower of this theory begins by holding himself ready to co-operate with whoever else is willing and able to co-operate. He then identifies the other co-operators and does his part in the best possible pattern of behaviour for the class of co-operators (including himself), in view of the behaviour of the non-co-operators.[19] We cannot, however, understand what makes one unit of agency right for one case and not for another by calculating the consequences of alternatives by reference to some fixed unit of agency; to do so would merely beg the question by embedding the problem of what makes *that* the right unit. (Compare the point made in Chapter 15 section 3 about the inadequacies of certain democratic procedures to determine how the boundaries of a democracy should be fixed.) This is *not* a point against consequentialism, which holds that consequences should be evaluated in terms that give each agent the same goal. (Indeed, Regan, who is a consequentialist, argues—to use my terminology rather than his—that the irrationality of taking the unit of agency as fixed is demonstrated by consequentialism itself.) Even shared-goal evaluation of consequences presupposes a unit of agency, the causal consequences of activity by which are evaluated; even consequentialists, who assume a shared goal, must say something about which unit of agency is the appropriate one to take as the basis of consequentialist calculation under which circumstances.

Two questions thus arise. First, what *does* make a particular unit the right unit under particular circumstances? This is a particular version of more general concerns with how persons should exercise their self-determining capacity, what agents should be like, and what kinds of agents there should be—a version of these concerns that in effect is about boundary questions about agents. But questions about what kinds of agents there should be in general make sense only for a special kind of agent: a self-determining agent, or person. There is no simple or uniform answer to all questions of this kind; there may be both consequentialist and non-consequentialist reasons for there to be certain kinds of agents rather than others, among those possible. What makes the breakaway subsystem the wrong unit of agency in particular cases of individual irrationality, for example, is whatever it is in that case that supports the person's better judgment: a judgment about which of his conflicting reasons, interests, or ends he should identify with under particular circumstances. Such judgments reflect the systemic—here, the personal— point of view. (In Chapters 10 through 12, we shall look at how deliberation may discover support for such judgments by analyzing settled actual and hypothetical cases.) What makes an individual as opposed to some collectivity the wrong unit of agency in particular cases is whatever makes co-operation with the members of some group possible and beneficial, with respect to whatever shared or separate goals are specified, in the circumstances at hand, as it may be in cases with a structure similar to that illustrated in Figure 8.2. This will vary according to one's substantive goals and ethical views. But one fails to understand the radical character of the question if one is tempted to ask: beneficial assuming the unit of agency to be the individual or the group? Again, the question is in effect about *which* possible unit of agency, subsystemic or systemic, *ought* to be realized, given whatever goals are specified; it cannot be non-question-beggingly answered by presupposing that one or another unit is to be taken as given. Nor is it determined merely by the character of the goals in question, by whether they are separate or shared; as I argued above, the question of whether goals coincide or not cuts across that of what the unit of agency should be. The answer may be determined in part by consequentialist considerations; the existence of certain kinds of agency, or qualities of character or motivation, may have better consequences than others.[20] (Analysis of relevant settled and hypothetical cases may also play an important role in deliberation and in arriving at reflective equilibrium when the demands of a collective perspective conflict with those of an individual perspective.)

Second, given that a subsystem cannot *do* a systemic act, what should it do? A subsystem, that is, may not be able by itself to bring about the consequences of the systemic alternatives: its alternatives may not stand in a potentially sufficient causal relationship to the consequences of the system's alternatives. Nor does a subsystemic alternative stand in a potentially causal relationship to the existence of the system, or its acts: *ex hypothesi*, subsystemic acts cannot cause the system to exist, or to act. (Recall that we are not discussing cases in which an individual can cause a system to exist by organizing it. There are such cases, but they are not the cases that prompted this discussion. Moreover, organization itself often requires collective action.) But the acts of the subsystem do stand in a constitutive, as opposed to causal, relationship to the acts of the system. What a subsystem can do is to act as a part of a system. It can help to realize the systemic unit of agency; it does so not through the causal effects of what *it alone* does, but by in part constituting the larger unit of agency.

It is wrong to assume that an act can only be rationally required in virtue of *its* causal consequences;[21] it can also be rationally required in virtue of its constitutive relationship to a valuable form of agency—or, one might say, in virtue of its *constitutive consequences*. The point holds of course when the latter kind of agency is held to be intrinsically valuable, or virtuous; but it important to see that it holds even if the kind of agency in question is held to be valuable only in virtue of its causal consequences. Again, my point is neutral as between consequentialist and non-consequentialist views of evaluation; even if one believes that evaluation of causal consequences of various forms of agency in terms of some goal, as opposed to intrinsic qualities, determines which forms of agency are valuable, one still can (and should) endorse participation in collective action under certain circumstances. That is, we must distinguish the causal consequences of collective action from the causal consequences of an individual act which may stand in a constitutive relationship to collective action: it may be rational to participate in a form of collective agency because of the valuable causal consequences of that kind of agency, even if one's individual act of participation does not in itself have the best possible causal consequences but rather merely helps to realize the valuable form of collective agency in question. (I emphasize that this claim is very different from the claim that what one should do depends on counterfactual propositions about what would be the case were everyone to do such and such, regardless of which others are in fact prepared to act collectively. In the latter cases, one's act is not constitutively related to actual collective alternatives or collective acts with good consequences; since such an act is not part of any collective alternatives or collective acts, it has no "constitutive consequences" to set against its less than optimal individual causal consequences.)

It is also wrong, as a matter of interpretation, to assume that when someone acts as a member of a group he must have made a mistake about the causal consequences of his act on the acts of the other members of the group, or have engaged in magical or superstitious thinking of some kind; such an individualistic assumption in fact distorts familiar forms of human motivation and agency. Someone's reason in acting may rather be that his act bears a constitutive relationship to a valuable form of agency. His contribution to its realization is not a causal one, but that of a part to a whole; it is hardly any less of a contribution, or irrational, on that score. If anything, the relation of part to whole seems more immediate than that of cause to effect. A particular part may not be necessary to the whole, but rather may be an insufficient but necessary component of various possible unneccessary but sufficient ways of realizing the whole.

## 3. Some Illustrations

These comments and their intrapersonal and interpersonal implications may be illustrated by considering and comparing several examples. Consider first someone who does refuses to do an act despite realizing quite clearly that in the unfortunate circumstances that obtain it would have the best causal consequences. He is told by the terrorists, and believes, that they will spare nine of the hostages if he shoots one of them himself. Suppose he refuses to do the act for reasons of integrity, because of the intrinsic character of the act itself and because of the character traits to which it would contribute. He may so refuse while realizing quite clearly the causal consequences of his refusal, but do so because of the constitutive relationship of the act to his own character. I am not saying I would necessarily endorse his decision, but am merely pointing out that it need involve no confusion about causal consequences or superstitious thinking. Nor need it involve any assumption that a single act of killing will cause one to become hardened and callous and to regard people as means—or will cause any other complete character change. Similarly, doing a single courageous act does not *cause* one to be courageous; and while it is a *sign* of courage, it is not *merely* that. Rather, it is *part of what it is* to be courageous. If we become courageous by doing courageous acts, it's because we are what we do—on the whole, of course; but the qualification does not make the relationship a causal one, merely a holistic one. Concern with character of agency is not irrational merely because it is not concern with the causal consequences of individual acts.

Indeed, concern with causal consequences of individual acts, *to the exclusion of* concern with character of agency, I have claimed, may itself be irrational: it may be irrational (even for a consequentialist) to take the unit of agency as fixed rather than to contribute to its realization. The interpersonal versions of these points can be illustrated by reference to the problem of why people do, and should vote. We can describe voting problems in either same goal or different goal terms; for the rest of this section I shall assume a shared-goal framework. One may recognize quite clearly that the chance that one's own act of voting will affect the outcome is so small that its expected value would not outweight its cost, and that it has no tendency whatsoever to cause others to vote (or that, even if it does, these beneficial causal consequences, and those of other acts of organizing people to vote, are also outweighed, in terms of the shared goal, by their costs). One may still vote because one's vote is partly constitutive of a valuable form of collective agency—valuable in terms of its causal consequences; it may be rational to, and irrational not to, co-operate with whoever is co-operating in this form of collective agency. In this case, and the case of courage, one may act despite clearly recognizing the absence of certain causal consequences of one's individual act, in order to participate in a valuable form of agency; in the terrorist case one may refuse to act despite clearly recognizing the presence of certain causal consequences of one's individual act, in order to avoid participating in an abhorrent form of agency.

The distinctiveness and potential rationality of concern with the character of agency may be overlooked. To see this, compare two different interpretations of voting behaviour, one offered by Regan and the other offered by Quattrone and Tversky and endorsed by Elster.[22] Regan provides an interpretation of voting under certain circumstances that shows it to be rationally required by his theory of co-operation, which tells each agent to co-operate, with whoever else is co-operating, in the production of the best consequences possible given the behaviour of non-co-operators. Call this *the co-operative interpretation*. Quattrone and Tversky describe an experiment in which Regan's co-operative interpretation of voting would apply and in which the voting behaviour they report, thus interpreted, would be rational. However, they themselves overlook this interpretation of the behaviour they report and offer a different interpretation, *the diagnostic interpretation*, according to which it is irrational. (Elster seems to endorse the latter interpretation, as well as the view that the behaviour in question is irrational.) I shall argue that the behaviour in question is better interpreted as co-operative behaviour, motivated by a concern to be a part of, do one's part in, participate in (the phrases abound, as the motivation is entirely familiar) a valuable form of collective agency; and that as such it is quite rational.

Subjects in Quattrone and Tversky's experiment were asked to suppose they were citizens of a country whose electorate consisted of 4 million supporters of party A, 4 million supporters of party B, and 4 million non-aligned voters. Subjects were all to suppose that they supported party A, and were asked to decide whether it is worth voting in an important upcoming election; voting in this country was supposed to be costly in time and effort. Subjects were then given one of two theories about who would determine the margin of victory in the election; they cannot ask others directly if they will vote as that is considered impolite.

> Both theories maintained that the victorious party would win by a margin of 200,000 to 400,000 votes. But according to the 'Non-Aligned Voters Theory', party supporters will vote in roughly equal numbers; hence the margin of victory will be determined by the non-aligned voters, who will either swing disproportionately for Party A or for Party B depending on which group of political experts one consulted. In contrast, the Party Supporters Theory held that non-aligned voters will split their vote equally between the two parties. The margin of victory would therefore depend on which of the two parties voted in greater numbers. That is, supporters of one party will be more likely to vote than supporters of the other party, although the political experts did not agree as to which party it would be.[23]

According to the diagnostic interpretation of voting, a voter votes because he reasons that the preferred party can defeat the opposition only if like-minded citizens vote in larger numbers than do unlike-minded citizens, and he regards his single vote as diagnostic of millions of votes, and hence as a sign that the preferred party will win.[24] Quattrone and Tversky point out that causal consequences of individual acts of voting are constant across the two theories subjects received, but that only subjects who received the Party Supporters Theory could regard their decision to vote or not as diagnostic of the decision reached by other Party A supporters. They predict that, because deciding to vote would be diagnostic of a favourable outcome only for subjects exposed to the Party Supporters Theory, those subjects should show a greater willingness to vote than subjects who received the Non-Aligned Voters Theory. Their results confirm this prediction.

There is no doubt that the diagnostic interpretation accounts for the result of this ingenious experiment. However, there is a better interpretation of the fact that the Party Supporter Theory subjects showed greater willingness to vote than the Non-Aligned Voters Theory subjects. The interpretation is better because more charitable; it makes better sense of the behaviour in question. (Diagnostic reasoning, moreover, is not intuitively attractive in certain other cases, which do not admit of an alternative co-operative interpretation. Consider the case in which a gene causes both lung cancer and cigarette smoking.) According to this co-operative interpretation, the subjects implicitly reject the individualist assumption that the unit of agency must be the individual, and ask themselves what the unit of agency should be in their situation. Individualism about agency holds that the rationality of an act is determined by the causal consequences of that individual act only, rather than by the causal consequences of any collective act that it may be a part of; thus if the causal consequences of an individual's acts in two possible situations are held constant, their rationality should not vary along with the contexts of the acts. Quattrone and Tversky's experiment comes close to being a kind of Twin Earth case for rational agency, in which causal consequences are held constant at the level of individual acts but we find intuitively that their rationality nonetheless varies with social context and the possibilities for co-operation.

The subjects who received the Party Supporters Theory, who are not told whether other members of their group will vote in at least the numbers that members of the opposed Party B do, find that as members of Party A they face a co-ordination problem that requires them to act collectively—to co-operate in voting with whoever else in their goal-sharing group is co-operating, given the behaviour of non-co-operators. By contrast, the subjects who received the Non-Aligned Voters Theory are told that members of their group will vote in equal numbers to members of the opposed Party B. They do not thus face a co-ordination problem as members of Party A which requires them to act collectively. Co-operation, as Regan notes, is not merely a matter of ultimate correct behaviour, but of attempting to achieve a jointly valued outcome by co-ordinated behaviour involving motivation to co-operate and a potentially infinite hierarch of reciprocal expectations about the motivations and expectations of others (in the style of Lewis and Schelling); in order for one agent to co-operate with another, the second must be a co-operator himself. The information the Non-Aligned Voters Theory subjects are given does not positively exclude the possibility that the members of Party A who vote will be doing so with co-operative motives and beliefs; but it suggests that they are going to vote in any case—perhaps they will vote because they believe it is their duty, regardless of what other members of their party do. If so, then while those party members who vote may do the right individual act, they do not act co-operatively as part of a group; to be prepared to act thus-and-so regardless of what others do is not to be prepared to act collectively. Thus the Non-Aligned Voters Theory subjects cannot correctly conceive of their own acts of voting as participation in a collective act by Party A.[25] Therefore, the Non-Aligned Voters Theory subjects are more likely to conceive of the problem from a more individualistic point of view, and to act on the basis of calculation of the consequences of their individual acts, given what the others do, rather than to regard their acts as parts of a collective act.[26]

I've claimed in effect that the difference between the two cases resides in their differential amenability to collective action by members of Party A, and that sensitivity to this difference is not irrational. But it may be objected that a similar possibility of collective action is present in the Non-Aligned Voters case, and the subjects are irrational to overlook it: they can regard the non-aligned voters themselves as potential co-operators. There is something in this objection, but it doesn't ultimately have the force it needs. It is more difficult for a Party A member to co-operate with non-aligned voters than with his own party members just because he doesn't know the goal of the non-aligned voters, and thus which way they are motivated to vote if they do vote. If they are all on the other side, after all, one may end up co-operating with no one, or with very few. This possibility that the individual perspective may really be the appropriate one for the case after all isn't present in the Party Supporters Theory case. It isn't true, as the objection suggests, that just any gerrymandered set of voters constitutes a group capable of collective action. Nevertheless, the objection is right to suggest that people should be more imaginative than they usually are in considering the possibilities of co-operation outside their familiar groups.

Why is the co-operative interpretation overlooked? This is a large question and I won't try to answer it properly. But I suspect that individualism about agency is as deeply ingrained a theoretical habit (though not an intuitive habit, as the example shows) as other forms of psychological individualism.[27] Only by recognizing and deliberately distancing oneself from the individualistic tradition for the sake of appraisal can one assess the ways in which it may distort the relationships of human thought and agency to the natural and social environment, and recognize the various respects in which rationality is not an intrinsic property of persons, but depends on their context. As in the anti-individualistic thought experiments of Burge that were discussed in Chapter 5, the importance of causal relations between agents and their environments is not in question, but rather the unit of account: normal rather than particular causal relations may determine the content and hence correctness of particular mental states, and the causal consequences of collections of acts rather particular acts may determine the rationality of particular acts.

Another objection may be made to speaking of the rationality of participating in collective action in the way I have in shared-goal cases. It may be objected that a theory of collective action has no advantages in accounting for the rationality of co-operating over a version of individualism that takes explicit account of each agent's subjective probabilities about what other agents may do.[28] According to such a theory, what is rational for an agent to do depends on the agent's reasonable expectations about what others are likely to do; in arriving at his expectations, the agent should take full advantage of cues about what others are likely to do provided by the salience of alternatives. It might be argued, for example, that in cases such as that in Figure 8.2, such an individualistic theory could obtain the benefits of co-operation as follows. Each agent would reason that the other is significantly more likely to push rather than not to push just because of the salience of the consequence of their both pushing, in respect of its being the best outcome, as opposed to the consequence of their both not pushing. But if the other pushes, then he should clearly push too. Therefore, each would push. Here, individualism's ability to account for the rationality of pushing depends on an independent empirical premise about the salience of the fact that the consequence of their both pushing is the best outcome, but given such a premise it seems to secure the benefits of co-operation without departing from calculation of the consequences of individual acts as a basis for action. Each is attentive to the consequences of what they together do, but only because of the brute empirical salience of certain of those consequences, which feeds into the calculation of the consequences of individual acts, and not as a basis for collective action.[29]

There are several ways to respond to this objection. One is Regan's, which ultimately depends on the distinction he draws between subjective exclusively-act-oriented theories and objective non-exclusively-act-oriented theories. I will not discuss this response here and refer the reader to his discussion.[30]

A rather different way of responding is to admit, for the sake of argument, that individualism may be able to secure the benefits of co-operation in some cases, but point out that there will still be many cases in which co-operation would, intuitively, be rational, but with respect to which a strictly individualistic account of rationality, however explicitly it takes account of subjective probabilities, lacks the resources to display co-operation as rational. And this is all my position requires. So long as there are only a few agents among whom co-operation is possible, perhaps the best outcome will retain its salience and serve to focus each agent's expectations about what the others are likely to do on the same outcome. But as the number of agents increases, the difficulty of finding a basis for prediction of what others will do that justifies co-operative behaviour from an individualistic perspective increases dramatically.

Consider a many-person version of Figure 8.2, in which nearly all voters, except for a few corrupt officials who control the system, share the goal of electoral reform and a common evaluation of the possible outcomes. By far the best results would be obtained if at least 90% vote for electoral reform, since, even given the existing corrupt electoral system, the magnitude of the vote will make it impossible to defer reform yet again. A weak second best outcome would be the result of no more than 10% voting, since mass abstension from voting may be taken as a protest that will eventually spur electoral reform anyway. The worst outcome would result from between 10% and 90% voting, which, given the corrupt electoral system, will permit the *status quo* to continue. Under what assumptions would it be rational to treat voting day as a "day of action" and vote in such a case?

In the absence of any knowledge of the objective probabilities of what others will do, we might start from a principle of insufficient reason with a Bayesian assumption that the subjective probability that any given person will vote is 50%. The assumption that the salience of the best outcome provides a basis for the expectation that any given person is more likely to vote than not seems unjustified in this case. But even if it were, it wouldn't help. Suppose we allow, for the sake of argument, that the brute empirical salience of the best outcome justifies a subjective probability that any given person will vote of, say, 75%; this figure seems to me quite unrealistically high, given the pay-off matrix I have specified. Still, 90% must vote for the best rather than the worst outcome to obtain. The subjective probability that 90% of the voters will vote rapidly becomes miniscule as the number of voters increases, even if there is a 75% subjective probability that each will vote. If there are even minor costs to voting, the individualist voter has no justification for voting in such a case; if she knows that almost all the other voters are also individualists who share her goal, she'll know they have no reason to vote either, and will have to revise the 75% subjective probability that any given person will vote radically downwards. And all the other individualists would be in the same position. We can suppose that there is common knowledge of the pay-off matrix, the shared goal, and the individualism of the agents. But common knowledge will not help them unless extra-rational considerations such as those of salience get them over the 90% threshold to begin with, which is what I am claiming is highly implausible in such a case.[31] In the absence of some such extra-rational considerations as a starting point, strictly individualistic rationality cannot get a grip; it cannot generate the subjective probabilities needed for a step-by-step demonstration of the individualistic rationality of co-operating in such a case.

The basic form of the circularity problem for individualism presented by this case is that individualism can only demonstrate the rationality of voting given high enough subjective probabilities; but the rationality of such high subjective probabilities in turn depends on the rationality of voting. To spell this out: If individualism can justify voting in this case, then it will depend on each person's subjective probabilities about what other people will do. The basis of the needed high subjective probabilities must be either empirical or rational. That is, either each person is justified in believing that the subjective probability of any given person's voting is high enough on empirical grounds (parallel to the "brute empirical salience" of the best outcome in the small Figure 8.2 case), or he must be rationally justified in believing this because of the rationality of voting and the rationality of the voters, common knowledge of these factors, etc. The former, empirical basis I claim is simply lacking in the case as I've described it. The latter rational basis presupposes that voting in this case is rational, which is what individualism is trying to prove. In sum, to avoid depending on an unjustified empirical premise in this case, individualism must depend on rationally based subjective probabilities. But such subjective probabilities are themselves only rational given the rationality of voting in this case. Individualism cannot break into this circle of presuppositions. This argument seems to me to be entirely independent of the content of the shared goal, and is not avoided by common knowledge (which it allows for). As a result, a society almost entirely composed of individualists about agency, despite their shared goal and common knowledge, may be unable to secure the benefits of co-operation that would be available to a society almost entirely composed of people who stood ready to act collectively on voting day. The tendency to slip away from a rigidly individualistic unit of account in such cases in order to account for the rationality of co-operation is laudable; but it should be recognized for what it is. It should not be supposed that the "obviousness" of the best solution means that somehow it *must* be justifiable on an individualistic theory of rationality which takes account of subjective probabilities.

The example brings out the contrast between such an individualistic theory and a theory that admits of the rationality of participation in truly collective action in appropriate circumstances. As Regan puts it, the latter kind of theory

> ... assumes very sensibly that some agents can be counted on to do their part in producing best possible consequences, and that some cannot. What each agent is instructed to do is to figure out which other agents fall into each category. Each agent is then required to join with the other agents who can be counted on to do their part in responding to the behaviour of those agents who can not. The agents who can be counted on to do their part are not required to worry about responding to the behaviour of others who can be counted on. Co-ordination among the co-operators is achieved just because they *do* all do their part. . . . An optimal response by the co-operators to the non-co-operators is achieved because the co-operators are required to respond *as a group* to the behaviour of those who do not co-operate.[32]

This important contrast is implicit in Schelling's own writings. Schelling wishes to understand how, out of a "fluid and indeterminate situation that seemingly provides no logical reason for anybody to expect anything except what he expects to be expected to expect, a decision is reached." He emphasizes that "coordination is not a matter of guessing what the "average man" will do. One is not, in tacit coordination, trying to guess what another will do in an objective situation; one is trying to guess what the other will guess one's self to guess the other to guess, and so on ad infinitum. . . . The reasoning becomes disconnected from the objective situation, except insofar as the objective situation may provide some clue for *a concerted choice*." [My emphasis.] In the mutually recognized response of players to salient features of alternatives, "the fundamental psychic and intellectual process is that of participating in the creation of *traditions*." [Author's emphasis.] "The players must *jointly* discover and mutually acquiesce in an outcome of in a mode of play that makes the outcome determinate. They must *together* find 'rules of the game' or suffer the consequences." [My emphasis.] "The assertion here is *not* that people simply *are* affected by symbolic details but that they *should* be for the purpose of correct play". " . . . [E]ven a normative theory . . . must recognize that rational players may *jointly* take advantage" of the clues provided by salience. [My emphasis.][33]

Schelling is not saying that salience merely provides a basis for individual expectations about what others are likely to do. He uses the language and logic of rational participation in collective action; it is this which salience may make possible. In certain situations an individualistic conception of rationality may be able to exploit clues provided by salience to justify expectations about what others will do and thus obtain the benefits of co-operation. But in the absence, as an empirical matter, of already-established traditions that provide such clues, it cannot tell individuals, as Schelling does, that they ought rationally to "participate in the creation" of them, since such creation is (in some cases at least) a joint, not an individual, enterprise.

I am not objecting to an individualistic approach that its justification of co-operation may depend on the presence of independent empirically based expectations about what others will do. This objection has been decisively rebutted by Lewis and others.[34] It is rather than it cannot provide a rational basis for such expectations which does not already suppose that people have the capacity to and will co-operate, act collectively, which is just to say that they have the convergent mutual expectations in question. Given that they do, individualism can in some cases justify individuals in going along. But this is just to say that the needed expectations may be justified because they are there. If the needed expectations are not there, individuals are not justified, on an individualistic account, in co-operating in the creation of a basis for them. (Of course, an individual might be justified in individual acts of engineering their creation; we are concerned here with circumstances in which this is not possible but co-operation in their creation is possible.) But, as Schelling points out, it is not merely that people in fact *do* co-ordinate their expectations and act accordingly, it is that if they don't they *should* do so, jointly. Even if, as a matter of empirical psychological fact, the best outcome in Figure 8.2 were not salient, consequentialists would be rationally required to co-operate with one another in pushing. Rationality requires collective action in some circumstances, in which an individualistic approach, even one that allows rationality to depend on expectations, cannot account for this requirement.

## 4. Collective Action, Self-determination, and Ethics

It's important not to overstate or strain the analogy between interpersonal and intrapersonal co-ordination. There are undoubtedly critical differences between the two, stemming from the fact that self-determination is distinctive of persons. But the analogy may nevertheless be helpful in structuring the flexibility of self-determining agents; an analogy doesn't have to be perfect to be illuminating and suggestive as far as it goes. Persons may find opportunities for self-determination both within and without. They may look inward, discover conflicting reasons, arrive at judgments about what kind of person they wish to be, and thus "participate in the constitution of their own identities" (to anticipate the discussion of Sandel's views in Chapter 15 section 1). They may also look outwards, and identify more or less with various groups, communities, and practices, and find opportunities for co-operation in collective action. Indeed, as I've suggested in earlier chapters, communities and practices may well supply the raw material of rational personality, the substantive constraints on the contents of the conflicting reasons persons discover when they look inward. Persons exist within a structure of subpersonal and social reasons, which cut across persons and bind them to one another in various respects, a structure that makes rational self-determining agency on the part of persons possible.[35] While there are undoubtedly fruitful analogies to be pursued between the relations of persons to their subsystems and the relations of social groups to the persons who are their members, nevertheless familiar bodily-individuated persons remain the normal units of rational agency; in trying to understand various failures of self-determination, we take the personal unit of agency as our starting point. But this does not entail what I've claimed is irrational, namely, that we take the unit of agency as fixed.

While an individual cannot by herself *do* a collective act, she can identify herself with a coordinated collective agent—to become, in this sense, *public-spirited*—because she realizes that it is a good thing for such collective agency to exist. In doing so, she will be able to act as a member of this group or collective agent—to co-operate with whoever else is co-operating. Of course, not all creatures have the capacity for collective action. The general capacity on the part of persons for participation in collective action—part of the distinctive capacity of persons for self-determination—is enough, however, to provide a sense in which refusal to co-operate and persistence in doggedly individualistic 'rationality' may be irrational. If it is also a good thing for coherent personal agency to exist, then this is likewise enough to provide a sense in which various intrapersonal goings on are irrational. The irrationality of systems has feedback effects on the rationality of subsystems; subsystems that are rational taken out of context may nevertheless suffer from a kind of contextual irrationality. I do not suggest that the perspective of the subsystem is somehow unreal or subject to illusion, or that the conflict between the perspective of the system and that of the subsystems can be eliminated, or that rationality of the system somehow subsumes rationality of the subsystems. Nevertheless, for persons the question arises: what kind of agents, among those possible, should there be, and what kind of agent should I therefore be? Persons can see themselves as various possible kinds of agent, and as co-operating in various forms of collective agency with other individual agents;

and persons can take steps toward realizing certain of these possibilities as opposed to others. They are, that is, self-determining agents, who have the capacity and the responsibility to determine, in part, their own identities.[36] The irrationality of failing to do so cannot be avoided by declining responsibility for who one is, by treating the identities of persons as a fixed brute fact. Persons don't need to allow themselves to be buffeted about by their subsystems; they have the capacity to get the parts of themselves into order. What would not be irrational for a wanton may be irrational for a person, because of the self-determining capacities and responsibilities of persons. Thus the understanding of *akrasia*, intransitivity, and other forms of personal irrationality in terms of the rationality of subsystems does not threaten to undermine the sense in which they are nevertheless forms of irrationality, any more than the understanding of collective irrationality in terms of the rational individual agency undermines the sense in which it is nevertheless a form of irrationality. (I shall have more to say about these matters in later chapters, especially in Part III and in Chapter 15.)

Recall the objection that by explaining the irrationality of systems in terms of rational subsystems, we explain away the irrationality. The response, in sum, has involved rejecting the assumption that an adequate theory of rationality—for persons, at any rate—can take the unit of agency as fixed. This response highlights a particular aspect of a more general point: what cannot be taken as fixed by a theory of rationality for self-determining agents is not just the unit of agency, but, more generally, the character of agents. Such a theory must address questions about what kinds of agents there should be as well as questions about what given kinds of agents should do. Such a theory of practical rationality is an *ethic*. It is distinctive of human beings as persons, as opposed to wantons, that they are self-determining agents; it is correspondingly distinctive of them that they are capable of ethical concern, character improvement and co-operation. To suppose that human beings are wantons is to allow the theoretical tail of maximization with respect to a fixed agent with a fixed character to wag the dog of facts about human nature. The fact that by holding the characters of agents fixed we cannot account for certain forms of co-operative or ethical activity on the part of persons does not show the irrationality of such co-operative or ethical activity. It rather shows the irrationality of thus holding the character of agents fixed and the inadequacy for persons of any theory of rationality committed to doing so.

Note that I make no claim about the relationship between ethics and morality, except that ethics does not sustain the sharp distinction between morality and self-interest as it is usually conceived by post-classical philosophers. The distinction between public and private interests is blurred by the capacities of persons to determine themselves and the constitutive relevance to exercises of this capacity of social practices and forms of life. This book is not about morality; I share Bernard William's sense that there is something peculiar about it. Ethics, in the broadly neo-classical sense I have given, is what is really interesting, what really matters. It displaces the usual philosophical preoccupation with the relationship between morality and self-interest with the view that ethical concern is already in part a concern for oneself, a concern with what kind of a person one should be, while concern for oneself on the part of self-determining agents is already in part ethical.[37]

In Chapters 10 through 12 I shall argue that deliberation is a kind of self-interpretation and self-determination, which aims to arrive at a coherent response to conflicting reasons. The search for coherence as I'll describe it may be carried out at the individual level, as well as at the collective level, by the judiciary, the legislature, various groups, and communities, etc.; in Chapter 15 I shall consider what it is in virtue of which a particular social division of deliberative labour may be democratic. One of the burdens of this section has been to argue that self-determination may also involve surveying the various possible units of agency and determining to participate co-operatively in the appropriate form of collective agency.

## 5. Attributions of *Akrasia*: Conflict and Formal vs. Substantive Constraints on Eligibility

My claims in the previous chapter about the distinction between *pro tanto* and *prima facie* reasons start from the claim that there is no such thing as evidential *akrasia*. This claim may be challenged. Its status is not empirical, nor can it be derived from inductive logic. Rather it's a substantive methodological claim about interpretation, about the constraints on attributions of beliefs as opposed to desires; it is part of a theory of interpretation. The possibility of the akratic structure is characteristic of desires and their relations to conflicting reasons for action, while its absence is characteristic of beliefs and their relations to truth; an attribution of beliefs with the akratic structure would be a bad interpretation. I shall argue that, cases of self-deception aside, we could either be justified in attributing the belief that $-q$ is probable in relation to all the evidence or the belief that $q$ is probable, held for a reason given by some piece of evidence included in all the evidence, but not both. A better interpretation would attribute a simpler kind of mistake, a failure to recognize or remember that the evidence for $q$ is not all the evidence, or perhaps even self-deception or an intent to deceive someone else. The analogous claims, however, cannot be made about reasons for action, for reasons that have to do with the way in which evaluative constraints on eligibility may reflect conflict among reasons for action. The values that provide reasons for action may stand in ultimate conflict, while truth alone ultimately governs what should be believed; because of this, formal and substantive constraints on eligibility interact in such a way that attributions of *akrasia* may be justified, but attributions of evidential *akrasia* cannot be.

Attributions of *akrasia* have to be seen in the context of attributions of irrationality to agents in general. The general rule is: Attribute irrationality with restraint; be as charitable as possible. As Davidson writes, "Making sense of the utterances and behavior of others, even their most aberrant behavior, requires us to find a great deal of reason and truth in them. To see too much unreason on the part of others is simply to undermine our ability to understand what it is they are so unreasonable about".[38]

I've already noted one corollary: since *akrasia* is a kind of inconsistency, attributions of *akrasia* are less eligible than non-akratic attributions, other things equal. It makes little sense to suppose someone could be weak willed in most cases (though of course there may be long-standing cases of akrasia); too many cases of *akrasia* would undermine our grounds for attributing to someone the all-things-considered judgments he supposedly flouts in all these cases. Of course, it's compatible with recognizing a general constraint that agents not be interpreted as doing the wrong thing by their own lights most of the time to admit that the variety of circumstances is such that it will be correct to attribute weak will more often, hence weaker character, to some persons than to others.

Another corollary is that, even if one has to attribute some kind of irrationality to an agent, one should try to make as much sense of him as possible. Some kinds of irrationality are less odd, hence easier to justify attributing, than others. When attributions of *akrasia* are justified, it must be because they make better sense of the agent than alternative attributions of irrationality or mistake would. When someone behaves akratically, he is irrational by his own lights; he recognizes what he ought to do, but fails to do it. That is, he is internally inconsistent; the attribution of such inconsistency stands in tension with formal constraints on eligibility. Given such constraints, why isn't it always simpler to attribute a different view about what he ought to do, namely, the view that he ought to do what he does do? That view may be substantively irrational or mistaken by our lights, of course, but then so may beliefs about what is probable; even so it's better to attribute a belief that's wrong by our lights, or an intent to mislead, or wishful thinking, or something else, than a belief that's irrational by someone's own lights, i.e., evidential *akrasia*. Why isn't the same argument decisive in the case of reasons for action?

Both beliefs about what is probable absolutely and judgments about what should be done, all things considered, are attributed with the aim of producing a coherent picture of a conscious agent whose beliefs and desires continue and develop over time in response to his environment and to the reasons that bear on the alternatives he faces. When these conflict, we attribute to him general views about the relative weights of such values in various circumstances that make sense of the way he behaves in response to conflict, which his all-things-considered judgments reflect. Such attributions reflect not isolated bits of his behaviour, but an on-going complex of behaviours in variously characterized environments. It's in this context that the possibility of attributing *akrasia* arises.

Suppose someone's behaviour seems to justify the attribution to her of a general view that gives the value of good health priority over the value of earned recognition of excellence when they conflict; perhaps she follows her doctor's advice in giving up coffee and cigarettes even though she finds it much easier to work with their help than without. But there are certain bits of behaviour that are at odds with the attribution; perhaps she occasionally disregards her health by working such long hours that she doesn't get enough sleep, even though her doctor has warned her that loss of sleep will delay her full recovery from a serious illness. It may be hard to claim that the person isn't aware of the character of the alternatives when she does this, so we have to arrive an an interpretative judgment about whether to retain the original attribution and consider her behaviour in these cases akratic or to tailor the general view we have attributed to her to fit the odd cases by finding some distinguishing feature of the odd cases. That is, we must decide between, on the one hand, attributing a judgment that, all things considered, she shouldn't work long hours, lose sleep, and undermine her health, even though she goes ahead and does so in order to earn recognition of excellence, and, on the other hand, attributing a different judgment that, all things considered, good health matters more than earning recognition of excellence except where some distinguishing feature of the cases in question is present, so that her behaviour in these cases accords with her better judgment. What could argue against tailoring the all-things-considered judgment so that it favours doing what the agent did do in just the circumstances at hand?

Again, some kinds of irrationality are less odd than others. Substantive constraints on eligibility may underwrite attributions of inconsistency. Perhaps the distinction the tailored attribution draws is ineligible, just doesn't make sense, corresponds to no distinction with respect to the relevant reasons: she only stays up late on Tuesdays. (Compare the pressure on courts to overrule earlier decisions as mistaken rather than to allow unprincipled distinctions between cases to proliferate.) Perhaps it's sometimes acceptable to attribute unreasoned or arbitrary distinctions, but only when the presumption against doing so is outweighed by some special feature of the case—perhaps it involves a slippery slope that demands arbitrary line drawing—or by another constraint, such as the constraint against attributing too many cases of *akrasia*. When too many cases of *akrasia* are the alternative, we may have to attribute gerrymandered, unfamiliar motives; but otherwise we do better to allow attitudes to follow familiar conflicting reasons by attributing an all-things-considered judgment that doesn't draw odd distinctions and also occasionally attributing akratic irrationality. (The fact that the presumption against drawing arbitrary lines is rebuttable will be important in Chapter 12's consideration of how coherence is possible.)

We can construct a parallel case involving beliefs. When all someone knows of relevance to rain is that the barometer is falling he behaves as if he expects rain and when all he knows of relevance to rain is that the sky is red he behaves as if he expects no rain; hence we attribute the beliefs that rain is probable in relation to a falling barometer and no rain is probable is relation to red skies. But when he knows both that the barometer is falling and that the sky is red, he generally behaves as if he expects no rain; hence we attribute to him the belief, which we may agree with, that no rain is probable in relation to a falling barometer and a red sky. Against this background, we consider a bit of odd behaviour: he's looked at the falling barometer and he's been watching the red sky with interest, but he takes his umbrella with him when he leaves the house. An attribution of evidential *akrasia* would retain the attribution of the belief that no rain is probable in relation to a falling barometer and a red sky and add to it attribution of belief that rain is probable, formed on the basis of a subset of the evidence, namely, the falling barometer. But instead we could, for example, revise the first attribution by casting about for some circumstance that distinguishes his behaviour on this occasion: perhaps there are dark clouds in the red sky. Now we may think that it's false that rain is probable in relation to a falling barometer and a red sky with dark clouds, but perhaps he believes it. If there's no such thing as evidential *akrasia*, then we must either cast about for some such circumstance that other bits of behaviour reveal him to believe, however falsely, is relevant to rain, or, alternatively, suppose that he is trying to mislead someone he thinks is observing him, or that he has some other purpose for his umbrella, or that he is deceiving himself because he so wants it to rain, or something of the sort. And in fact what we, or Sherlock Holmes, would do in interpreting such a case would be to pursue these possibilities. The oddness of any candidate distinction we might draw in revising our attributions of what he believes the evidence supports wouldn't push us to attribute evidential *akrasia* instead, but rather to consider the other alternatives. There isn't a live interpretative issue between evidential *akrasia* and alternative attributions, as there was between ordinary *akrasia* and a tailored better judgment.

In both the cases of reasons for action and reasons for belief we may have to weigh formal constraints on eligibility, which count against attributing internal inconsistencies, against substantive constraints, which count against attributing very odd ends, including ends that incorporate very odd distinctions. We've seen in earlier chapters that at some point we must regard interpretations that preserve consistency at the expense of substance as ineligible; substantive constraints are needed if formal constraints are to have any bite. The further point we now make is that a particular way of resolving interpretative issues in favour of inconsistency for the sake of intelligible substance is available when the possibility of ultimate conflict among the governing substantive constraints is admitted, which is not available when such conflict makes no sense. This is the possibility of the akratic structure, which preserves intelligible relations among familiar conflicting reasons for action at the expense of akratic inconsistency, rather than preserving consistency at the expense of substance. The possibility of ultimate conflict among reasons for action provides the rationale for the attribution of *akrasia* as a particular version of the way in which inconsistency may be attributed on the strength of substantive constraints. Attributions of *akrasia* have something in common with the ways in which we can understand irrational collective action in terms of the conflicting interests in individuals; in both cases we can understand systemic irrationality in terms of familiar though conflicting subsystems—reasons or values in the case of *akrasia*, individuals in the case of collective irrationality. We can sometimes best understand what would be irrational as collective action in terms of familiar conflicts of individual interests, even though alternative interpretations would avoid the irrationality by revising our understanding of the interests of the group. Perhaps, for example, the prisoners in the supposed dilemma are really members of a group of activists co-operatively engaged in principled civil disobedience, and accordingly they actually wish to confess their 'crime' and be sentenced accordingly. But in many cases no such revision of the content of the interests in question will have the substantive plausibility of more familiar conflicting individual interests. Similarly, the capacity of the akratic structure to absorb some of the unintelligibility of inconsistency depends on complexity of structure, on intelligible subsystems that can move independently of one another and come into conflict.[39] But when the governing substantive constraints do not admit of such ultimate conflict, the akratic interpretative option would involve pointless complication and hence is not available. In such cases, substantively tolerant interpretations of all-things-considered judgments may be required (as in the case of the distinction between causal and incidental base rates considered in the next section). Alternatively, various forms of inconsistency may be attributed on the strength of substantive constraints. But where substantive constraints cannot come into conflict, by the same token they cannot serve to render attitudes with the akratic structure in particular substantively intelligible as a manifestation of conflict, even though inconsistent.

Note that I am claiming neither that the existence of conflicts among reasons for action may be taken as given and the existence of akratic attitudes inferred from it, nor that the existence of akratic attitudes may be taken as given and the existence of conflict inferred from it. I am claiming that the two issues are interdependent, and that conflict stands in an explanatory relation to *akrasia*; the recognition of each helps us to understand the postulation of the other. Together they make better sense than either would on its own, and shed light on the distinction between belief and desire.

## 6. Some Possible Examples of Evidential *Akrasia* Disposed of: The Warming Effect

I've tried in the last section to provide an interpretative rationale for my claim that there is no such thing as evidential *akrasia*. In this section I shall illustrate the claim by disposing of several cases that might appear to be counterexamples to it. Counterexamples to the claim that there's no such thing as evidential *akrasia* would be cases where an unproblematic interpretation attributes beliefs with the akratic structure and there's no pressure to attribute a motivating wish, allied to a reason that's not a reason for belief, not a piece of evidence. In Pears' terminology, we need a cold case of *akrasia*, in which the akratic structure has no warming effect; otherwise the operative reason won't be one included by the judgment in relation to all the evidence, as the akratic structure requires. A case in which the sum of the evidence is against the beautiful client, but the detective somehow has a hunch she's innocent, won't do.

Consider someone who has devoted her academic career—books, seminars, etc.—to defending the perfect market hypothesis, that markets automatically discount for any available information on the basis of which someone might predict what they will do. Nevertheless, over the past 25 years she's made a fortune on the stock market.[40] What does she believe? Is it that she recognizes that the perfect market hypothesis is probable in relation to all the evidence but that she forms beliefs that guide her actions of buying and selling on a subset of the evidence, namely, the information she has about a particular company's financial state, the likelihood of a merger, etc.? This could be evidential *akrasia*.

But why isn't what's going on here rather just a kind of wishful thinking? She wants to believe that she can make money on the stock market because she wants to make money. This much is straightforward. The odd thing about the case is that the actions that the wishful thinking motivates prove the wishful belief to be correct and disprove the supposedly better founded belief, based on more of the evidence. It may have been better founded at first, but after the first few bouts of wishful thinking have been successful there is more evidence to account for, even though she doesn't seem to have taken this in. The case only seems to present a problem because wishful beliefs are normally false beliefs and don't normally transform themselves, by own their operation, into beliefs that are better founded on all the evidence. Indeed, the person herself may not realize that this has happened, so her wishful beliefs go on being motivated by her wish to make money even though better reasons are available, i.e., evidence that she can make money. What if someone says to her in one of his seminars: "Look, aren't you a counterexample to your own theory?" Now she is forced to adjust her view of what position is supported by all the evidence. She can say *yes*, in which case her wishful beliefs finally obtain their rightful recognition; or she can say *no*, and effectively distinguish her own situation from those addressed by the theory, in which case there is no conflict (perhaps she's just been in index funds). So, there are three possibilities: dogged wishful thinking, theory revision, or distinguishing cases. I don't see under what circumstances evidential *akrasia* would be a better attribution than one of these.

Secondly, consider the peculiar situation of jurors, whose duty in a court of law is to find the facts, when they are faced with a selective exclusionary rule. An exclusionary rule is a procedural rule that excludes a piece of evidence admitted to be relevant to the issues the jury must determine; the reasons for excluding it are often unrelated to the search for the facts. As one court put it, the search for truth is in certain instances subordinated to higher values.[41] These may be constitutional values, such as those embodied in the Fourth Amendment to the U.S. Constitution, which guarantees the right to be free from unreasonable searches and seizures. This right is held to require the exclusion of evidence obtained by means of unlawful search or seizure, even when it and it alone reveals the truth about an issue before the court.

Another example is evidence of a defendant's character, which can't be admitted to show that he acted in conformity with his character in the circumstances at issue. As Cardozo said, "The principle back of the exclusion is one, not of logic, but of policy."[42] The policy is one against requiring someone brought to trial to answer a specific charge to answer for his whole character; a Western liberal government is entitled to determine whether or not he has violated a particular legal proscription, but his unsavoury character and general propensities are his own business.

However—and this is what it means to say an exclusionary rule is selective—evidence of the defendant's character may be admitted for a purpose other than showing he acted in accord with some propensity his character supposedly establishes. For example, it may be admitted to show the defendant's identity, to impeach the credibility of his testimony, or to prove that he had the required motive, opportunity, or intent. Similar selectivity exists for evidence of acts by the defendant similar to that for which he is being tried and of prior convictions. In a trial of a defendant who has several prior convictions of a crime that involves deceit, such as embezzling, evidence of his prior convictions may be excluded for purposes of showing he is likely to have embezzled this time too, but admitted to discredit his testimony, to show he is likely to be lying.

Consider the structure of the jurors' beliefs in the following case: The defendant committed a murder, observed by two witnesses. The defendant was aware of the presence of one of them, but not the other. The first, known witness is found murdered, and the defendant is charged with his murder. At this trial, the prosecution offers the testimony of the second, hidden witness, as to the first murder. As evidence of a capacity for murder or murderous propensity to show the defendant is likely to have committed the second murder as well, it is excluded, but it is admitted to show that he had a motive to commit the second murder, namely, to keep the witness from revealing the first murder. But suppose the known witness had other enemies with reasons to want him out of the way, so that the mere fact that the defendant had a motive too wouldn't distinguish him; it wouldn't be more than circumstantial evidence, and wouldn't be sufficient to establish that he is guilty beyond a reasonable doubt.

Now a plausible pattern of belief about the defendant in the absence of an exclusionary rule would be the following. The first murder supports two suggestions: that the defendant's character is such that he is capable of and prone to murder, and that he had a motive. Thus $ePp$ and $ePm$, where $e$ describes the first murder, $p$ the propensity, and $m$ the motive. Both of these suggestions are relevant to the issue of guilt. Together with the rest of the evidence, the propensity evidence and the motive evidence is sufficient to establish his guilt, beyond a reasonable doubt. Thus $(p \, \& \, m \, \& \, \ldots )Pg$, where $g$ is guilt and $P$ now expresses the required degree of strength of belief, beyond reasonable doubt (*however* the latter phrase is understood—I am not suggesting anything about whether it can be understood in purely statistical terms). But the rest of the evidence along with the motive evidence, with the propensity evidence left out of account, would not be sufficient to establish beyond a reasonable doubt that the defendant is guilty. Thus $-[(m \& \ldots)Pg]$.

The jurors have access to both the propensity evidence and the motive evidence; indeed, the same thing that reveals the motive, namely, the first murder, also reveals the propensity. But the selective exclusionary rule tells them to base their verdict about the defendant's guilt on the motive evidence plus the rest of the evidence, leaving out of account the suggested propensity as an evidential basis for their verdict. Thus in this case they should base a conclusion that it's not the case that the defendant is guilty beyond a reasonable doubt $(-Pg)$ on a subset of the evidence which by itself would warrant such a conclusion, despite the fact that in relation to all the evidence they're aware of a verdict of guilty is warranted.

Can they do this? If so, does this show that something akin to evidential *akrasia* is possible after all? (It wouldn't fit the akratic pattern exactly, since the conclusion is externally negated rather than internally. But it might be close enough to cast doubt on the motivation of my thesis that evidential *akrasia* isn't possible.) It's certainly true that the jury's official role in courts of law is one of determining the facts as opposed to determining what the law requires; so in some sense the jury serves as the court's cognitive faculty and is supposed to arrive at the court's beliefs about the matters of fact at issue. But it's also the case that rules of evidence are rules of law that constrain this process according to reasons of policy or principle that may have nothing to do with the facts of the matter. Exclusionary rules are a liberal version of propaganda, if I can use that term without begging the question of whether they're a good thing; they enforce a kind of institutionalized wishful thinking, except that the motivation isn't provided by a wish but by a legal policy or principle. So they don't provide an example of something akin to *akrasia* of belief; since all the reasons in play aren't strictly truth-related, we don't have a legal analogue of a cold case.

Perhaps this isn't an adequate response to the example. Here are two objections. First, in the example a verdict of not guilty is based on a subset of the existing evidence despite the fact that all the evidence, had it been admissible, would have warranted a verdict of guilty. But the legal policy or principle in play isn't pre-empting the evidence the verdict is based on and doing the real motivating work, as in cases of wishful thinking; all it's doing is suppressing part of the evidence. There is nothing analogous to a desire to believe that the defendant is not guilty; the policy is indifferent to a verdict of guilt or innocence, but hostile to a certain way of arriving at it, to a certain kind of evidence.

Second, it might be objected, we've lost sight of the state of mind of the individual juror, apart from these institutional analogues of belief and desire in the legal system. What's the structure of each juror's beliefs about the defendant? Even if there is a legal policy in play that produces an analogue of wishful thinking for the legal system, the individual juror may have no corresponding desire to motivate a belief related to a subset of the evidence.

If he manages to form such a belief in the face of his recognition that in relation to all the evidence a different belief is warranted, then we have no reason to attribute a motivating wish to him. So perhaps we have got a case of evidential *akrasia* after all.

But I don't think so. In the first place, it may be true that the analogy between propaganda and wishful thinking isn't perfect. However, this doesn't mean that our case is akin to evidential *akrasia*, because it still involves reasons that aren't proper reasons for belief. Most forms of propaganda are hostile to particular conclusions and favour others, whereas exclusionary rules are hostile to certain ways of arriving at conclusions rather than particular conclusions themselves. But it's not surprising that exclusionary rules are a feature of a kind of liberalism that elevates certain procedural values to the role of substantive values. These points go to show variety in the structure of hot cases, or their legal analogues, but not to show that selective exclusionary rules give rise to a cold case, which is what is needed.

Nor, in the second place, do we get such a case by focussing on the individual juror. For the juror is asked for a verdict, not simply for his belief. And he is told that his verdict is not to be arrived at in certain ways; the exclusionary rule applies to the verdict, not necessarily to his beliefs. The verdict is a legal artifact, not a strictly psychological one, and nothing guarantees that an obedient jury's verdict corresponds with the beliefs of the individual jurors; a juror may vote for a verdict of not guilty even though he believes the defendant has done what he's accused of. Moreover, if some adjustment does go on it seems more psychologically plausible to suppose that jurors would adjust their verdict to match their beliefs than that they would adjust their beliefs to match their verdict. Thus, the case still does not provide something akin to a counterexample to my claim.

Consider finally two of the cold cases studied by the psychologists Kahnemann and Tversky, which have been interpreted as showing that experimental subjects are irrational by Bayesian standards in that they sometimes ignore background frequencies or base rates in arriving at judgments of probability. In these cases, the subjects are told that a taxi was involved in a hit and run accident at night and that there are two taxi companies operating in the area, the Green Taxi Company and the Blue Taxi Company. In each case they are asked what the probability is that the taxi involved in the accident was blue rather than green, and are given two opposing pieces of evidence on the basis of which to answer. On the one hand, a witness identified the cab as blue. The court tested the reliability of the witness under the same conditions that existed on the night of the accident and concluded that the witness correctly identified each one of the two colours 80% of the time and failed 20% of the time. (That is, 80% of the time the taxi is green, the witness says it is green, and so forth; *not*: 80% of the time the witness says it is green, it is green.) The two cases are the same with respect to this piece of evidence in favour of the taxi having been blue, but they differ with respect to the evidence in favour of the taxi having been green. In one case the information they are given is that though the two taxi companies are roughly equal in

|  | Witness right: 80% | Witness wrong: 20% |
|---|---|---|
| Taxi Green: 85% | taxi green and witness says it's green: 68% | taxi green and witness says it's blue: 17% |
| Taxi Blue: 15% | taxi blue and witness says it's blue: 12% | taxi blue and witness says it's green: 3% |

FIGURE 8.4

size, 85% of taxi accidents in the city involve green taxis and 15% involve blue taxis. In the other case the information is simply that 85% of the taxis in the city are green and 15% are blue.

In both cases, the problem the subjects have is how the two opposing pieces of evidence balance out. Kahneman and Tversky's view is that the correct answer is the same in the two cases, and it is got by using Bayes' Theorem to combine the prior probability given by the base rates with the probability that the witness was right. This says that the probability that the witness correctly identifies the taxi as blue is the 15% probability of a blue taxi multiplied by the 80% reliability of the witness, or 12%; the probability that the witness correctly identifies the taxi as green is the 85% probability of a green taxi times the 80% reliability of the witness, or 68%; the probability that the witness incorrectly identifies the taxi as blue is the 85% probability of a green taxi times the 20% unreliability of the witness, or 17%; and the probability that the witness incorrectly identifies the taxi as green is the 15% probability of a blue taxi times the 20% unreliability of the witness, or 3%. Thus the witness will identify the taxi as blue correctly 12% of the the time and will identify it as blue incorrectly 17% of the time. So, given both the base rates and the witness' testimony, the probability that the taxi is blue is 12 divided by 29 (12 + 17), or 41%. "In spite of the witness's report, therefore, the hit and run cab is more likely to be Green than Blue, because the base rate is more extreme than the witness is credible"—and by the same amount in each case (see Figure 8.4).

The experimental subjects don't get this answer in either of the two cases; moreover, they answer differently in the two cases. In the first case, where 85% of the taxis involved in accidents are green, they regard the probability that the taxi was blue as considerably less than the reliability of the witness (the median answer is 60%), while in the second, where it's merely that 85% of the taxis in the area are green, they ignore the base rate entirely and equate the probability that the taxi was blue with the reliability of the witness. (If they are told nothing about a witness but only that 85% of the taxis in the area are green and 15% are blue, most say the probability the taxi was blue is 15%.)

While the experimenters' claim that the correct answer is 41% in both cases has generated a great deal of controversy, here I want to focus only on whether the subjects' answers should be interpreted as providing an example of evidential *akrasia*. For the subjects' answers in the first case seem to support the attribution to them of the belief that in relation to all the evidence, the eyewitness testimony and base rate, the probability that the taxi was blue is less than the reliability of the witness; they do seem to recognize the relevance of the base rate information, that in relation to it as well as the witness's reliability the probability of a blue taxi is lower than it is in relation to the witness's reliability alone. In the second case, however, despite the availability of similar base rate information, they may seem to base their belief on a subset of the evidence, that is, on the evidence as to the witness's reliability, leaving the base rate information out. Here, a diagnosis of wishful thinking is implausible. And, by contrast to cases in which subjects are misled by the salience of a piece of information and revise their beliefs when this is pointed out to them, many people have different intuitions about the two cases that stubbornly resist correction. Aren't they precisely forming a belief based on a subset of the evidence in the face of what they recognize to be justified in relation to all the evidence? That is, aren't they forming a belief that it's highly probable that the taxi was blue, based on a subset of the evidence, despite having judged that in relation to all the evidence, both the base rate evidence and the testimony, it's considerably less probable that the taxi was blue?

Again, there's at least one better interpretation, according to which the subjects distinguish the two cases with respect to the weight of the base rate evidence. As the experimenters themselves put it, the base rate in the first case

> . . . is causal because the difference in rates of accidents between companies of equal size readily elicits the inference that the drivers of the Green cabs are more reckless and/or less competent than the drivers of the Blue cabs. This inference accounts for the differential base rates of accidents and implies than any Green cab is more likely to be involved in an accident than any Blue cab. In contrast, the base rate in the other case is incidental because the difference between the number of Blue and Green cabs in the city does not justify a causal inference that makes any particular Green cab more likely to be involved in an accident than any particular Blue cab.

According to the preferred interpretation, the subjects take causal base rate evidence to be weightier, a more reliable indicator of probability, than incidental base rate evidence, and their aims in responding to the experimenters' questions reflect such distinctions of weight or reliability. That is, the preferred interpretation tailors their judgments about what is probable in relation to all the evidence to incorporate the distinction between causal and incidental base rate evidence: in relation to conflicting incidental base rate evidence and testimony, when that is all the evidence there is, it's highly probable that the testimony is correct and the taxi was blue; but in relation to conflicting causal base rate evidence and testimony, when that is all the evidence there is, it's considerably less probable that the testimony is correct and the taxi was blue. Whether it's correct to take an interest in such distinctions is a vexed question; but we cannot determine whether the subjects' beliefs are irrational independently of determining what they are trying to do, what concepts they are trying to apply. Suppose for the sake of argument that the subjects ought not to be interested in distinguishing causal and incidental base rates, ought not to have a conception of probability that reflects such distinctions. Even so, the distinction is quite intelligible, normal, and natural to draw, hence substantively eligible; and we make better sense of the subjects by attributing to them such a mistaken conception and interpreting them as succeeding in doing something they shouldn't be trying to do, than by interpreting them as evidentially akratic. Indeed, support from diverse sources has been given to the view that the evaluation of evidence in courts of law is best understood to involve the assessment of any causal explanatory relationships there may be between the evidence and the events at issue.[43]

I've considered three possible counterexamples to the claim that there's no such thing as evidential *akrasia*, in order to illustrate the difficulty in principle of finding cold cases with the akratic structure, and thus to defend the distinction drawn in the last chapter between *prima facie* and *pro tanto* reasons. In the next chapter I shall put the distinction between *pro tanto* and *prima facie* reasons to use, to throw light on a certain argument from conflicts of values to non-cognitivism.

# 9

# Cognitivism

## 1. The Compatibility of Conflict and Cognitivism

In the last two chapters I've drawn a distinction between *prima facie* and *pro tanto* reasons and defended it against several purported counterexamples. I shall begin this chapter by using the distinction to throw light on a certain argument from conflicts of values to non-cognitivism made by Bernard Williams. The argument assumes that *cognitivism*, or the view that ethical claims express beliefs that aim to be true and are either true or false, commits us to holding that it must be possible to solve ethical conflicts "without remainder" and without leaving ground for rational regret. Since the latter claim is wrong, the argument goes, cognitivism is wrong. Thus Williams writes:

> It seems to me a fundamental criticism of many ethical theories that their accounts of moral conflict and its resolution do not do justice to the facts of regret and related considerations: basically because they eliminate from the scene the ought that is not acted upon. A structure appropriate to conflicts of belief is projected on to the moral cases; one by which the conflict is basically adventitious, and a resolution of it disembarrasses one of a mistaken view which for a while confused the situation. Such an approach must be inherent in purely cognitive accounts of the matter; since it is just a question of which of the conflicting ought statements is true, and they cannot both be true, to decide correctly for one of them must be to be rid of error with respect to the other.[1]

If a structure appropriate to conflicts of belief were projected onto the ethical case only in the sense that conflicting ethical judgments are taken to be analogous to conflicting judgments of relational probability, then it wouldn't be the case that both of the conflicting judgments couldn't be true. It can be true both that rain tomorrow is probable in relation to tonight's falling barometer and that no rain tomorrow is probable in relation to tonight's red sky. Conflicting ethical judgments modelled on relational probabilities could likewise conflict without contradiction. It isn't necessary to depart from the model of *prima facie* reasons in order to restrict agglomerativity and hence to make conflicts, at least of *prima facie* reasons, possible.

But to rest with this point would be to fail to give Williams' argument sufficient credit. The claim that a distinction appropriate to conflicts of belief is projected onto the ethical case is made also in order to explain the way certain ethical theories, which it supposedly turns out must include cognitivist theories, eliminate from the scene the 'ought' that is not acted upon. The elimination may take the form of the denial that rational regret is possible, which Williams emphasizes,[2] or the denial that *akrasia* is possible. The two possibilities go hand in hand. If it makes sense to suppose someone rationally regrets not having brought about a state of affairs, $q$, when he has in fact brought about $-q$, and done so for reasons, then it makes sense to suppose he instead brings about $q$, and does so for the reason to which the regret relates, despite the different, perhaps weightier reasons favouring $-q$. And *vice versa*.

We can accept the connection between a structure appropriate to conflicts of belief and the elimination from the scene of the reason that turns out not to be operative, in the following sense. The structure appropriate to conflicts of belief just is the structure that relates conflicting judgments of relational probabilities and judgments of absolute probability; what's probable absolutely just is what is probable in relation to evidence than which none is better. It is characteristic of *prima facie* reasons that either they turn out to be the operative reasons or they get subsumed. Evidence for $-q$ that is subsumed by evidence for $q$, than which none is better, is subsumed without remainder and retains no residual doxastic force that might give rise to cases of evidential *akrasia*.

Certainty is another matter. No matter how high the probability that $q$, so long as it is merely probable and not certain that $q$, it is possible that $-q$. There's a sense in which, by admitting that $-q$ is possible, one admits a doubt about $q$. So long as we admit that there is a distinction between certainty that $q$ and belief that $q$ which falls short of certainty, we must admit the possibility that $-q$. No degree of probability eliminates this possibility, and it is the gap between the best probabilistic reasons and what actually is the case to which doubt in the face of probabilities relates. But there is no corresponding gap between the best, or weightiest-in-the-circumstances-at-hand, reasons for action and what ought to be done, all things considered, to which regret or *akrasia* relates. What one ought to have done, all things considered, doesn't stand in the same relation to regret as what is actually the case does to doubt. Grounds for regretting an action not done needn't relate to a possibility that the action one in fact did was not what one ought to have done, all things considered. One may have reason for regret even though one is certain that one did what one ought to have done, all things considered. Indeed, the *akrates* fails altogether to do what he is certain one ought to do, all things considered, and does something else entirely, and for a reason. So, if there's an analogue between probabilities and reasons for action, it should not imply correspondence between it being (certainly) the case that $q$ and it being the case that one ought to bring it about that $q$, all things considered. The claim of analogy between probabilities and reasons for action implies not this correspondence, but rather a correspondence between it being probable absolutely that $q$ and it being that case that it ought to be that $q$, all things considered.[3] It's this correspondence that must obtain if the analogy is to be sustained. And it's just the failure of this correspondence to obtain that led me to distinguish *pro tanto* from *prima facie* reasons in previous chapters.

But the distinction between *prima facie* and *pro tanto* reasons brings into question a further premise of Williams' argument, that cognitivist ethical theories must project a structure appropriate to conflicts of belief onto ethical conflicts in the sense that they must treat reasons for action as *prima facie* and adopt the evidential model of conflict. Why should we accept this premise? Having noted the close structural relationship between regret and *akrasia*, and the inability of the evidential model of conflict to handle regret, we have grounds for doubting whether the evidential model will handle *akrasia* either. But this is not to say that we need instead a non-cognitivist model of conflict. The subsystems model of conflict provides an alternative to the evidential model that overcomes its shortcomings with respect to regret and *akrasia*, but they are both cognitivist models.

I've argued that conflicting values are not conflicting pieces of evidence about what ought to be done; they're not *prima facie* reasons for belief about what ought to be done, but *pro tanto* reasons for action. When we deliberate about what ought to be done, all things considered, when values conflict, we aren't trying to arrive at a judgment based on evidence than which none is better, which subsumes all contrary evidence. We don't think that by arriving at a view about what ought to be done we'll resolve the conflict without remainder or remove any possible basis for rational regret or eliminate the possibility of *akrasia*. We're rather trying to describe a coherent set of relationships among the conflicting values, which are still on the scene after we have done so (see Chapters 10 through 13).

If, as the cognitivist claims, we have beliefs about what ought to be done, all things considered (which, I suggest, is some function of conflicting *pro tanto* reasons for action), then perhaps there can also be *prima facie* reasons for belief about what ought to be done, all things considered. Such *prima facie* reasons might be provided by the results of an opinion poll, or, under certain conditions, by voting (see Chapter 15 sections 2 and 3). But there's no need to explain reasons for action in terms of reasons for belief. Indeed, if there are reasons for belief about what ought to be done, then there must be reasons for action, for such belief to be about and for the reasons for such belief to relate to. Thus there's a sense in which the reasons for action are more fundamental than the reasons for belief about reasons for action, and can't be explained by reference to them.

Consider two different ways to find out the answer to a question in a specialized discipline. One would be to master the discipline, do the necessary research, and arrive at an answer oneself. Another would be to consult a panel of experts in the discipline and pool their opinions about the matter.

There is no difficulty in holding that both of these different ways of finding the answer exist, or that both are fairly reliable. One can have reasons for belief about the answer without oneself having immediate reasons to answer the question one way or another, by believing that others have immediate reasons to answer it one way or another. But there have to be reasons to answer one way or another if there are to be reasons for belief about the answer; the latter are ultimately parasitic on the former. Similarly, *prima facie* reasons for belief about what ought to be done, all things considered, are ultimately parasitic on *pro tanto* reasons for action, some function of which determines what ought to be done, all things considered.

None of these claims is inconsistent with cognitivism. There's no reason to suppose that reasons for action must have the same structure as reasons for belief if ethical judgments express beliefs about reasons for action. It may be true that *pro tanto* reasons for action conflict while it is also true that there are truths about what there is *pro tanto* reason for and about what ought to be done when *pro tanto* reasons conflict. It's just this possibility that the distinction between *prima facie* and *pro tanto* reasons draws to our attention. Indeed, truths about *pro tanto* reasons for action must reflect the fact that they conflict not in relation to truth—which is just to say they don't contradict one another—but rather as guides to action. Leszek Kolakowski writes:

> . . . the world of values is not logically dualistic, as opposed to the world of theoretical thought. In other words, there are values that exclude one another without ceasing to be values (although there are no mutually exclusive truths that still remain truths).[4]

This claim may be true, while it is also true that there are truths about values, if truths about conflicting values are not mutually exclusive *in relation to truth*. Cognitivism doesn't require a view of conflicting reasons for action as conflicting pieces of evidence for belief about what ought to be done.[5] So, the fact that reasons for action do permit rational regret and *akrasia*, and thus don't behave as if they were conflicting pieces of evidence for the truth of claims about what ought to be done, does not support non-cognitivism.

Of course, many other considerations bear on the issue between cognitivism and non-cognitivism. In this section I have only tried to establish that ethical cognitivism is compatible with the existence of conflicts among *pro tanto* reasons for action, including ethical reasons. But my claims in earlier chapters about the role of values in interpretation and the determination of the content of preferences suggest the following view. Non-cognitivists are right that there is a necessary connection between claims about what ought to be done and preference, but they often have a one-sided, i.e., subjectivist, conception of this connection. I have argued, against subjectivism, that it's not the case that certain prior and independent preferences determine values and provide reasons for action, but rather that values and reasons for action play a necessary role in determining preferences, so that preference and value are interdependent. The rejection of subjectivism does not in itself commit one to either the cognivitist view that evaluative judgments and judgments about what should be done, all things considered, express beliefs, or the non-cognitivist view that (at least) judgments about what should be done, all things considered, express a special kind of preference, such as extended preference (recall my claim in Chapter 6 that theories of extended preference need not be subjectivist). However, at the end of Chapter 6 I suggested that the distinction between belief and extended preference may not be sharp, or worth quarrelling over—at least for some purposes. Extended preference is certainly not subject to individual volition, and can hardly provide a bastion of psychological individualism and ethical privacy against encroachments by society, reason, and expertise. Nevertheless, there is an issue between cognitivism and non-cognitivism, one of logic rather than politics, which I shall consider in the remainder of this chapter. I shall come down in favour of cognitivism on this issue, and shall then go on in Chapters 10 through 13 to develop a coherence account of judgments about what should be done, all things considered, which will accordingly be cast as a kind of cognitivism and according to which such judgments express theoretical beliefs. Skeptical claims to the effect that ethical beliefs are false or cannot constitute knowledge will be discussed in Chapter 14.

## 2. Frege Against the Proliferation of Force

So far in this chapter I've been defending cognitivism against Williams' argument from conflicts of values by arguing for the compatibility of conflict and cognitivism. But now I shall consider an argument in favour of cognitivism, or, more precisely, against non-cognitivism, the essential form of which is due to Frege (though he applied the argument to a different, analogous issue).

In his article "Negation" Frege argues against a view of assertion and negation as two coordinate ways of judging, one positive, the other negative. That is, he was arguing against the view that there were two different kinds of activity, asserting and denying, such that if one asserts that $p$ and denies that $p$, the content of the speech act is the same in the two cases and the difference between them is in the kind of speech act, or the force of the utterance: one is an assertion, the other is a denial. The view that Frege favours rejects this conception of negation as involving a different kind of force from assertion. When one denies that $p$, on his view, one is doing the same kind of thing, i.e., making an assertion, as one is when one asserts that $p$; it's just that one is asserting a different content, namely, that not $p$.

Frege argued against the proliferation of force in the case of negation by depending on a simple and plausible account of how the familiar type of inference *modus ponens* works. Instances of *modus ponens* are inferences that have the same pattern as the inference: if $p$ then $q$; $p$; therefore, $q$. Frege's argument is as follows. He claims that there are two inferences that "proceed on the same principle". They are:

(1)   If $p$, then $q$; $p$; therefore, $q$

and:

(2)  If not $p$, then not $q$; not $p$; therefore, not $q$

That these two inferences work in the same way plays the role in Frege's argument of a piece of data to which logical theorizing is responsible. But these two inferences could not proceed on the same principle if we "had to recognize a special way of judging for the negative case"—namely, denying, a special kind of linguistic act coordinate with assertion but with the opposite valence. Frege explains how *modus ponens* works in terms of the match between the content of the antecedent of the first premise and the content of the second premise. In inference (1), assertoric force attaches to the first premise as a whole and to the second premise as a whole, and the thought expressed in the second premise coincides with the thought expressed in the antecedent of the first premise.[6] If we were to recognize denying as a different kind of activity from asserting, then in inference (2) assertoric force would still attach to the first premise as a whole, while in the second premise the negation sign would be absorbed into the act of denying. Thus the content of the second premise, namely, that $p$, would no longer coincide with that of the antecedent of the first premise, namely, that not $p$, so that "the inference . . . cannot be performed in the same way". That is, there would be matching contents in the assertion case, but not in the denial case, for the negative aspect would be allocated to the special act of denying and would not show up in the content denied.[7] But since the two inferences evidently do proceed on the same principle, in a way which is straightforwardly accounted for by leaving the negative aspect of negation as part of the content of what is asserted, denying is not a different kind of activity from assertion.

This argument suggests a test of hypotheses to the effect that, despite contrary appearances, a term or phrase is not functioning to express the content of an ordinary assertion, in virtue of which it's true or false in the ordinary way, but rather to signal that some activity other than assertion is going on, perhaps that some attitude other than belief is being expressed. Such hypotheses are to be tested by considering whether they can explain the data, namely, that certain inferences proceed in the same simple way as does inference (1), via the matching of the contents of the second premise and of the antecedent of the first premise. The non-cognitivist puts forward a hypothesis of this kind: despite appearances to the contrary, evaluative terms are not used to express the contents of assertions, in virtue of which such assertions are true or false in the ordinary way; rather they are used to approve, or to commend, or to condemn, or to command, etc. Evaluative terms are not used to express beliefs that are true or false, but rather attitudes of some other kind, states of the will.

## 3. Geach and Dummett on the Proliferation of Force

Thus Michael Dummett claims that it is Frege's doctrine that force "cannot significantly occur within a clause which is a constituent of a complex sentence [such as the antedent of a conditional], but can attach only to a complete sentence as a whole", and that if this doctrine is correct, it would provide "a powerful new method for detecting spurious claims to have identified a new kind of force".[8] Peter Geach in particular has put the doctrine to this use; in "Assertion", he uses appearance in the antecedent of a conditional as a test to rule out various proposals to construe words or phrases as force signs, including a non-cognitivist construal of *wrong* as expressing condemnation.

Geach's argument starts out parallel to Frege's in "Negation": he claims that the phrases "it's true that . . . " and " . . . is wrong" cannot carry a special kind of force because *modus ponens* goes through in the usual way from both premises "If it's true that *p*, then *q*" and "If gambling is wrong, then inviting people to gamble is wrong", which involve neither asserting that *p* nor condemning gambling, respectively. Geach goes on to introduce an extension of Frege's argument for cases involving generality. Consider inferences (3) and (4):

(3)  If it's true that a thing is *F*, then it's *G*
     it's true that *a* is *F*;
     therefore, *a* is *G*.
(4)  If doing a thing is wrong, then getting your little brother to do it is wrong;
     tormenting the cat is wrong;
     therefore, getting your little brother to torment the cat is wrong.

In inferences (3) and (4), "it's true that . . . " and " . . . is wrong" must mean the same thing at each occurrence in order for the inferences to proceed in the same manner as ordinary instances of inferences from universalized conditionals. Yet in the first premise of the respective inferences "it's true that . . . " and " . . . is wrong" cannot function as force signs, for they occur within the scope of a universal quantifier; the inferences certainly do not involve asserting that everything is *F* or condemning all actions. Thus in the second premise of each inference "it's true that . . . " and " . . . is wrong" cannot function as force signs either, or the required matching of contents would not obtain.[9]

In Chapter 10 of his book *Frege*, Dummett engages in a long investigation of the Frege/Geach argument, in the version that does not involve generality. He conducts a systematic search for cases where force signs occur inside the scope of the logical constants; he considers and reconsiders all twelve permutations of the logical constants negation, conjunction, disjunction, and the conditional with assertoric, imperative, and interrogative force. He succeeds in devising interpretations of certain combinations such as to avoid the Frege/Geach point, namely, of assertions, commands, and questions occurring within the scope of the negation sign, and of questions occurring within the scope of conjunction, disjunction, and the conditional. The interpretations of the first three combinations describe new linguistic acts of refusing to perform the familiar linguistic acts, for example, refusal to command; the interpretations of the second three combinations describe linguistic acts that differ from complex questions in the responses they call for, although the appearance of interrogative force in the consequent of a conditional also admits of interpretation as a sealed or suspended question, such that the question only gets asked if the condition obtains. The analogous sealed or suspended assertion and command interpretations are dismissed as appealing to a state of affairs, which obtains when the condition is not met, that renders the utterance neither true nor false, neither obeyed nor disobeyed. Dummett rules this appeal out, claiming that truth and falsity, as well as obedience and disobedience, are fully correlative pairs, at least thus far: the rationale for introducing a gap between truth and falsity relates "not to the use of the sentence by itself to make an assertion", but to the construal of its negation in cases involving bearerless names, or to the law of bivalence, which are not here at issue.[10]

For present purposes, however, Dummett's success in devising interpretations of force signs within the scope of the logical constants is of unclear import; his remarks cut both ways.

On the one hand, he claims that his interpretations of force signs appearing with narrow scope are erratic, admitting neither of a uniform derivation nor of reiteration, and thus do not affect the essential soundness of the Frege/Geach point.[11] Geach's use of appearance in the antecedent of a conditional as a test to rule out proposals to recognize various types of force reflects the important insight that the need to ascribe determinate truth conditions to utterances, rather than mere conditions of justification, is tied to the condition the antecedent expresses. For example, in a future tense conditional statement such as "If nobody will ever understand my work, my life has been in vain", the content "nobody will ever understand my work" appearing in the antecedent must be understood in terms of truth conditions rather than as being used to make a prediction. As Dummett puts it, such cases show that "the occurrence of future-tense statements as constituents in complex sentences . . . forces us to ascribe to such statements a truth-value independent of the existence of conditions which would justify their assertion on their own, i.e. as predictions or expressions of intention".[12]

On the other hand, Dummett suggests that the appearance of sentences of a certain kind in the antecedent of a conditional is not sufficient to show that they have truth-conditions of the ordinary sort rendering them susceptible of assertoric use, since any linguistic act that we might have an interest in eliciting from others lends itself to an interpretation of conditionals in the antecedents of which force indicators do appear. It is just because assertion registers an inner act of adherence, which may be expected to influence actions in some way, that we may well have a use for sentences of the form of: "If I were to assert that $A$, then I should assert that $B$". As Dummett explains, "It would be of interest to say something of this kind in a discussion in which the other person was trying to induce me to assent to his assertion that $B$: by such a conditional utterance, I should indicate to him that he can achieve this if he can first induce me to assent to the assertion that $A$".[13] The linguistic acts represented by ordinary interrogative and imperative force signs do not register any such inner act; hence we're not interested in eliciting such acts from others, nor do we have a use for a form expressing the conditional linkage of two such acts. But the linguistic acts represented, on ascriptivist, prescriptivist, and other non-cognitivist accounts of the kind that Geach is concerned to refute, by words such as *wrong*, *voluntary*, etc., do register a commitment to some course of action or type of conduct that we may well be interested in eliciting from others. *Wrong* is used to condemn, *voluntary* is used to ascribe responsibility, and so on. Hence, a use for a conditional form expressing the conditional linkage of two such acts is readily conceivable. Dummett concludes that Geach's test does serve to distinguish between utterances that we might have such an interest in eliciting, which he calls "quasi-assertions", and those that we have no interest in eliciting. But it does not serve to distinguish between utterances a cognitivist account of which is correct, which have truth conditons of the ordinary sort and to which assertoric force may be attached, and those with some other sort of meaning, or with some other variety of force already attached.[14] So it does not provide the kind of test for proposals to recognize different kinds of force that Geach envisaged.

Geach's response to this argument by Dummett is to point out that Dummett has not taken account of his extension of Frege's "Negation" argument to cases involving generality.[15] Dummett has given interpretations of certain force signs' occurrences in the antecedents of conditionals that allow inferences in the propositional calculus to go through. But he has not dealt with the matter of how to interpret inferences made from quantified complex sentences in which the proposed force signs occur, such as inference (4).

Does our interest in eliciting utterances such as "Getting your liittle brother to torment the cat is wrong" provide a Dummettian interpretation of quantified sentences in which force signs occur, such as "If doing a thing is wrong, then getting your little brother to do it is wrong"? The interpretation would presumably be along the lines of: "If I were to condemn doing a thing, I should condemn getting one's little brother to do it". If Dummett's interpretation of the force signs' occurrence within the antecedent of the conditional is accepted in the first place, it's hard to see what turns on the introduction of the quantifier. The Dummettian interpretation does not involve a failure to heed Geach's warning that the speaker can hardly be taken to be condemning just doing a thing,[16] that is, a failure to get the quantifier outside the scope of both the force signs and the conditional. If, on Dummett's interpretation, an inference from a quantified conditional such as "If doing a thing is wrong, getting your little brother to do it is wrong" must play on both the performative and the descriptive senses of "I condemn", then so will an inference from an unquantified conditional such as "If gambling is wrong, inviting people to gamble is wrong".

Perhaps Geach thinks that consideration of the quantified conditional shows clearly that inferences from conditionals interpreted along the lines Dummett suggests, whether quantified or not, involve an equivocation between performance of a linguistic act and description of performance. In "For any *x*, if I were to condemn doing *x*, I should condemn getting one's little brother to do $x$", "condemn" must be understood to describe a hypothetical act of condemnation, rather than to express condemnation. If this is denied, we may ask to have a thought made out that is distinct from the one in question solely in that "condemn" does occur non-performatively; but there is none such. Thus the claim to a performative reading can be persisted in only at the expense of either conflating the two readings of the quantified conditional, and so undermining their resemblance to the distinctly different performative and descriptive readings of "I condemn", or of denying, implausibly, that a descriptive reading is to be had at all. Once we recognize that in the quantified conditional *wrong* is not being understood along performative lines but along the lines of old-fashioned ethical subjectivism, it is clear that this is also the case in the unquantified condition "If I were to condemn gambling, I should condemn getting others to gamble."

Old-fashioned ethical subjectivist views pre-dated non-cognitivist views such as emotivism and prescriptivism and were decisively refuted by the non-cognitivists themselves, whose views constituted a step forward. Whereas the non-cognitivist theories emphasized the distinction between *description* of anything, including the agent and his attitudes, and other non-descriptive linguistic activities, such as condemning, commending, and commanding, which *express* the agent's attitudes, the earlier subjectivist theories had simply appealed to descriptions of the agent and his attitudes: to say something is wrong is to say one dislikes it, which is to say something about oneself. The standard objection to the earlier theories, which the non-cognitivst accounts wished to avoid, was that they translated away disagreement. Accounts of what we mean when I say something is wrong and you say it isn't are responsible to a piece of linguistic data, namely, that we are disagreeing with one another, contradicting one another; both of our claims cannot be true. But the old-fashioned subjectivist account fails to capture this: if I say that I dislike something and you say that you don't dislike it, we're not contradicting one another at all, and both of our claims can perfectly well be true. Thus the old-fashioned subjectivist account does not capture the logical relations of judgments in question. The advantage of appealing to performance or expression of attitudes instead of description or ascription of them, as non-cognitivists do, is that it avoids attributing compatible truth conditions to the two judgments, and restores their inconsistency—though not in terms of incompatible truth conditions, but rather by moving away from a truth-conditional account altogether.

## 4. The Independence of Frege's Argument from the Availability of Additional Modes of Inference

I have tried to draw out the source of the disagreement between Dummett and Geach. But note that nothing in the explication of the Frege/Geach position need involve denying what is surely correct, namely, that, equivocation or no, an inference of some kind *can* go through from a conditional major premise interpreted along the lines Dummett suggests and a minor premise that involves a performance of an act of condemnation, or some other linguistic act. Dummett is surely right about the usefulness of making assertions about the links that obtain between linguistic acts we might have an interest in eliciting from others. However, by casting his comments as a response to Frege's argument, Dummett seems, at least implicitly, to be identifying inferences from such conditional linkages between linguistic acts as instances of *modus ponens*. But, given the descriptive rather than performative function of "condemn" in the proposed interpretation of the major premise, it is just this identification that would be rejected by someone advancing an argument against non-cognitivist construals of ethical claims parallel to Frege's in "Negation" against the proliferation of force: *modus ponens* involves matching contents; the equivocation between description and performance in the proposed version of the inference keeps the contents from matching; therefore, while there may still be a valid inference, it's not *modus ponens*.

In "Negation" Frege does not deny that an inference goes through if negation is viewed as a special kind of judging, but only that the inference would "proceed on the same principle" as cases of *modus ponens*. This latter denial discredits the view of negation as a special kind of judging, since Frege regards it as clear that the inference from: "If *p*, then *q*", and the inference from: "If not *p*, then not *q*" do proceed on the same principle: this is taken as a piece of data provided by linguistic intuitions, to which theorizing on these matters is responsible (at least, we may add, other things equal, in the absence of some independent reason to 'revise' this datum). Frege's reason for claiming that the inference involving negation construed as a force sign could not proceed on the same principle as do cases of *modus ponens* is that the content of the linguistic act of denying in the minor premise would not coincide with the content of the antecedent of the conditional major premise, as it does in cases of *modus ponens*. This reason is unaffected if we interpret the conditional along the lines Dummett suggests to mean: "If I were to deny that *p*, then I should deny that *q*". The concept of denying contributes to the content of the antecedent of this conditional, but is no part of what is denied by the minor premise.

The same reason operates in favor of the claim that a Dummettian inference, which we can admit to be valid, from the assertion of "If I were to assert that *p*, then I should assert that *q*", and the assertion of "*p*", to the assertion of "*q*", does not proceed on the same principle as inference (1) above. This inference should be distinguished from the following inference, which does proceed on the same principle as inference (1):

(5)  If I assert that *p*, then I assert that *q*;
     I assert that *p*;
     therefore, I assert that *q*.

By contrast, the kind of inference Dummett defends seems to depend on the logical and/or practical oddness of the assertion: "*p*, but I don't assert that

$p$". To avoid this oddness, I seem in some way entitled to go from my assertion of "$p$" to the assertion of "I assert that $p$".[17] Assuming we can go from the counterfactual "If I were to assert that $p$, then I should assert that $q$" to the conditional "If I assert that $p$, then I assert that $q$", we can then go via *modus ponens* in inference (5) to "I assert that $q$", which counts as an assertion of "$q$". All of this may serve to explicate our sense of the validity of the type of inference Dummett defends; and it suggests that *modens ponens* lends the inference support; but it does not support the view that the inference in question simply is a case of *modus ponens*. The inference in question is considerably more complex in form than inference (1), and raises interesting questions about the status of assertions such as "$p$, but I don't assert that $p$" not raised by simple cases of *modus ponens*. Thus, valid though it may be, and dependent on the validity of *modus ponens* though it may be, the Dummettian inference does not proceed in the same simple way as does inference (1). Indeed, the full explanation of the validity of the Dummettian inference seems to presuppose the validity of the simpler form of inference *modus ponens*, as Frege conceived it.

The same reason operates again in favor of the claim that an inference from the assertion of "If I were to condemn gambling, then I should condemn getting other people to gamble", and an act of condemnation of gambling, to an act of condemnation of getting other people to gamble, does not proceed on the same principle as inference (1). However, the following inference (6) does proceed on the same principle as inference (1), just as inference (2) does.

(6)  If gambling is wrong, then getting other people to gamble is wrong
     gambling is wrong;
     therefore, getting other people to gamble is wrong.

The general form of Frege's argument is: The inference purportedly involving a new kind of force is an ordinary case of *modus ponens*; but if it does involve a new kind of force, it can't be an ordinary case of *modus ponens*; therefore, it doesn't involve a new kind of force. This argument cuts against the non-cognitivist proposal to construe occurrences of *wrong* as expressions of non-assertoric force, e. g., acts of condemnation. It does so, moreover, without denying the validity or usefulness of inferences of the kind Dummett suggests. Arguments for the validity and usefulness of such inferences on behalf of non-cognitivist proposals miss their mark unless they either address the reason Frege gave against identifying such inferences as cases of *modus ponens*, or provide independent grounds for denying the Fregean assumption that inferences from premises such as "If gambling is wrong, then inviting people to gamble is wrong" are, as they surely appear to be, ordinary cases of *modus ponens*.

Simon Blackburn has independently proposed a non-cognitivist account of conditional sentences in which ethical propositions occur. He writes: "anybody asserting '$P$ and if $P$ then $Q$' where $P$ attributes worth to a thing expresses his attitude to that thing, and asserts that that attitude involves a further attitude or belief".[18] Blackburn explains that he does not intend the 'assertion' that one attitude involves another as a claim about what attitude someone would express if he were to express the first, but rather as an evaluation of a linking of attitudes.[19] It is important to us not only to evaluate sensibilities (which are functions from beliefs or perceptions to non-cognitive attitudes), but also to evaluate relations between sensibilities. I may disapprove of the combination of an attitude of disapproval of gambling with approval of getting one's little brother to gamble; I express this disapproval by means of the conditional form, which is interpreted to express my approval of disapproval of gambling being linked with disapproval of getting one's little brother to gamble.

For present purposes, Blackburn's view is not very different from the Dummettian view of quasi-assertions. It omits the counterfactual element of the Dummettian interpretation, and instead involves evaluations of linkages of attitudes. But these differences do not affect my arguments above, since inferences from the conditionals Blackburn envisages, however valid, would also involve equivocation between performance or expression and description of performance or expression; indeed, the equivocation is explicit in Blackburn's account. Blackburn's major premise is interpreted to express my approval of disapproval of gambling being linked to disapproval of getting one's little brother to gamble; here, talk of disapproval of gambling serves to pick out a class of attitudes of disapproval, not to express disapproval—as Blackburn puts it, to "*talk about*" an attitude.[20] In the minor premise, however, disapproval of gambling actually gets *expressed*.[21] Like Dummett, Blackburn makes a claim for his interpretation of conditional sentences with ethical antecedents that is surely correct, namely, that when one has expressed one's attitude to a thing and has 'asserted' that the attitude involves a further attitude or belief, that is, has approved of that attitude involving a further attitude or belief, then there is an "inconsistency in not holding the further attitude or belief".[22]

However, Blackburn goes on to claim explicitly that "It is this logical inconsistency which is expressed by saying that *modus ponendo ponens* is valid" from conditional premises with ethical antecedents. But, again, it's just this identification that would be rejected by someone advancing an argument against non-cognitivism parallel to Frege's argument in "Negation". Blackburn has given an explanation of how certain inferences can work; but these inferences, work though they may, are not simple cases of *modus ponens*, at least not on the plausible account that Frege gives of it. Frege's argument appeals to the linguistic intuition about the uniformity of *modus ponens* across these different cases: inferences from conditionals that embed ethical terms work in just the same way as ordinary cases of *modus ponens*, which involve no equivocation. This intuition provides a piece of data to be explained or at least respected; the cognitivist view respects it, and the non-cognitivist view does not.[23] This intuition has a status similar to that the non-cognitivists themselves appeal to in rejecting old-fashioned ethical subjectivism, to the effect that when I say something is wrong and you say it isn't, we are disagreeing and both our claims cannot be true. Consider also the intuition that judgments about pain must mean the same thing in their first-person and third-person uses, which the solipsist fails to respect.

Of course the solipsist can always reject the intuition of uniformity as simply wrong, as the non-cognitivist can reject the intuition of uniformity in the Fregean argument (though it then begins to become unclear what evidence the non-cognitivist hypothesis *is* supposed to be responsible to). It's also possible that Frege's account of *modus ponens* is itself wrong, and that another account shows that ordinary cases of *modus ponens* in fact work in the same way as these special cases, though it's not the way Frege supposed. The uniformity intuition and the account of *modus ponens* support the premises of Frege's argument, which are not beyond doubt. At least, however, the Fregean argument puts the burden on non-cognitivism to show that either the uniformity intuition or Frege's account of modus ponens is wrong, since both seem, at least *prima facie*, correct. Moreover, to count as an argument for non-cognitivism the demonstration that either of the Fregean assumptions fails should not presuppose non-cognitivism, but be independent of it.

I see no motivation independent of non-cognitivism for rejecting the uniformity intuition. The hypothesis that inference (6) really proceeds along the lines Dummett or Blackburn envisages fails to respect the uniformity intuition, since the envisaged types of inference are distinct from *modus ponens* conceived as proceeding in the way Frege suggested, by simple matching of contents.

The non-cognitivist can also respond to the Fregean argument by claiming that Frege's account of *modus ponens* is wrong, and that the correct account of *modus ponens* itself is rather along the lines Dummett, or Blackburn, envisages; we can regard Dummett and Blackburn as having provided alternative accounts of *modus ponens* itself, quite generally, which are more complicated than Frege's but may have other advantages. Now the uniformity intuition is respected, but the non-cognitivist is in danger of undermining his own motivation. The alternative account of *modus ponens* would apply equally to inferences involving acts of asserting, condemning, etc.; in each case, there would be an equivocation between description of performance or expression and performance or expression itself. But now what is the point of the contrast between cognitive and non-cognitive judgments? It is in danger of being lost if it turns out that, even when I make what are, paradigmatically, assertions, the inferences I can draw from them do not depend on the truth-conditions of what I assert but merely on my attitudes about linkages between my own attitudes or performances. We have now abandoned even for uncontroversially assertoric cases the important insight that the need to ascribe determinate truth-conditions to utterances, rather than merely conditions of justification, is tied to the condition the antecedent expresses. We will, in effect, have succeeded in defending a kind of 'non-cognitivism' about assertions as well as about evaluations; since we will have thus treated the two cases in the same way, we will not have motivated a contrast between assertion and evaluation. The defender of 'cognitivism' at this point may simply bow out of the argument, and say that so long as assertion and evaluation are treated in the same way, he does not mind whether the account is labelled "cognitivist" or "non-cognitivist"; his point was simply that they should not be sharply distinguished. As Blackburn puts it, "unasserted contexts show us treating moral predicates like others, *as though* by their means we can introduce objects of . . . belief"; the non-cognitivist must try to explain why we do this.[24] But if the explanation of why we do this entails that our reasons for doing it are in fact just the same as our reasons for treating any other predicate as we do in unasserted contexts, because some type of linkage of attitude account is offered perfectly generally as an account of *modus ponens*, then the non-cognitivist has respected the uniformity intuition at the expense of his favoured distinction between evaluative and other judgments.

## 5. The Objection from Skepticism

Someone might make the following objections, reminiscent of Mackie's error theory. You've made it sound as if the only issue were one about what *we mean* when we make evaluative judgments, about our linguistic usages and intentions. But these usages and intentions aren't self-validating or self-fulfilling. Perhaps it *is* the case, as a matter of what we mean, that *modus ponens* operates uniformly across the evaluative and non-evaluative cases and that Frege's account of how it operates is correct, hence that the cognitivist position about what we mean is correct. It doesn't follow that we actually succeed in doing what we intend to do, that is, making a true evaluative assertion. Our evaluative assertions may be false, or at least may fail to express knowledge.

This objection in fact changes the subject. It admits what I have called "cognitivism", that we do express beliefs which aim at truth in making evaluative judgments, but takes a skeptical view of such beliefs. One might make an analogous point about colours, if one held the view that ordinary colour judgments express beliefs that involve an unjustified pretense to describe reality: we think we are saying something about the world when we say something is red, but all we actually succeed in describing correctly is the way the world looks to us. But note that even if we concede this skeptical point, for the sake of argument, it doesn't establish non-cognitivism about colour judgments, that they express something other than belief or are made to perform linguistic acts other than assertion. The skeptical point rather runs to a distinction between mere belief and belief that succeeds in being knowledge of the way the world is. And parallel comments apply to the evaluative case: even if for the sake of argument we concede the point (which in fact I think we should not concede), that evaluative judgments involve an unjustified pretense to describe reality, this doesn't go to show that they don't express beliefs, or do not make assertions, but only that the beliefs they express don't succeed in constituting knowledge of evaluative truths. The issues raised by the skeptic do not determine the issue of cognitivism, i.e., whether evaluative judgments have assertoric force and express beliefs that aim to constitute knowledge, or rather have some other kind of force and express attitudes other than belief, which is the issue I have addressed in this chapter (except in so far as skepticism rather loses its point if evaluative judgments do not express beliefs). The cognitivist and the skeptic could both be correct; evaluative judgments could have assertoric force, express beliefs, and aim for truth, but fail—they may in fact be false, or fail to constitute knowledge. Skepticism is discussed in Chapter 14. It is impossible to consider adequately whether beliefs about what should be done fail to meet certain conditions for knowledge until one has some account of their truth conditions, which we shall have by the time we get to Chapter 14, namely, a coherence account. Only then will we be in a position to evaluate skepticism.

# III

# RATIONALITY IN THE FACE OF CONFLICTING REASONS

# 10

# Theory

## 1. The Refutation of Conventionalism

In earlier chapters I have argued against centralism and subjectivism, and have defended the view that values may stand in ultimate conflict with one another as well as the possibility of cognitivism given such conflict. In this chapter I shall begin to move from criticism of various views about practical reason to a positive account, but I shall do so by way of a critique of conventionalism, which leads into a coherence account of what should be done when values conflict that is developed and defended in subsequent chapters. The overall strategy is suggested by Hilary Putnam's refutation of conventionalism. Putnam criticizes conventionalist views of distance and translation, but the general principles of his critique may be applied to various centralist doctrines, such as emotivism and legal positivism; his remarks about the way in which coherence may replace convention in determining reference suggests non-centralist alternatives to these doctrines.

In his article "The Refutation of Conventionalism" Putnam discusses Grunbaum's views on distance and a standard version of Quine's views on translation.[1] He labels both views as *conventionalist*,[2] and explains this labelling in terms of a common structure:

> 1. A set of conditions on the use of the notion is given. These conditions are claimed to exhaust the content of the notion being analysed.
> 2. It is proved that these conditions do not determine the extension of the notion.
> 3. Since there are different sets of objects that satisfy the conditions that exhaust the meaning of the notion, there is no fact as to which of the sets of objects is referred to when the notion is used. Reference is fixed, if at all, arbitrarily, by convention.

Putnam argues that conventionalism is negative essentialism. The conventionalist claims that his conditions exhaust the meaning of the notion being analysed.

189

He claims to intuit not just that the constraints in question . . . are *part* of the meaning of the notion . . . , but that *any further condition* that one might suggest *would definitely not be part of the meaning* of the notion in question. . . .

[C]onventionalism is not usually recognized as essentialism because it is *negative* essentialism. Essentialism is usually criticized because the essentialist *intuits too much*. He claims to see that *too many* properties are part of a concept. The negative essentialist, the conventionalist, intuits not that a great many strong properties are part of a concept, but that only a few *could be* part of a concept.[3]

The conventionalist insists that it is essential to whatever is in question that there be no more to it than he allows, with indeterminacy and arbitrary fixing of reference by convention as a necessary consequence. But Putnam argues that the conventionalist cannot defend this view precisely because of an insight of Quine's. "That is the insight that *meaning*, in the sense of reference, is a function of theory, and that the enterprise of trying to list the statements containing a term which are true by virtue of its meaning, let alone to give a list of statements which *exhaust* its meaning, is a futile one." That such a set of statements can not be found does not mean that we must opt for the conventionalist solution. "[R]eference need not be fixed by a convention. It can be fixed by coherence".[4]

In "Two Dogmas of Empiricism" Quine expresses the insight Putnam refers to by noting "our natural tendency to disturb the total system as little as possible", and our "pragmatic inclination", based on "conservativism" and "the quest for simplicity", to "adjust one strand of the fabric of science rather than another in accommodating some particular recalcitrant experience." Quine comments that "in point of epistemological footing the physical objects and the gods differ only in degree and not in kind", and immediately makes an essential qualification: "The myth of physical objects is epistemologically superior to most in that it has proved more efficacious than other myths as a device for working a manageable structure into the flux of experience".[5] Putnam exploits Quine's admission of the superiority, on grounds we may summarize as those of coherence, of certain cultural posits over others, by asking why coherence should not be regarded as providing reason to believe, for example, that the distance between two points or the correct translation of an utterance is such-and-such rather than so-and-so.

To illustrate this suggestion, Putnam first considers a pair of rival conceptions of distance, M1 and M2, each of which satisfies Grunbaum's axioms for a metric. We can regard the axioms as a first attempt to formulate a set of principles or theory that unifies our uses of the notion of distance by displaying them as coherently interrelated. In pursuing maximal coherence, we are looking for the simplest, most powerful set of principles among the various sets we may construct. Power is a matter of sensitivity and coverage in displaying relationships among the group of linguistic practices that includes and forms the context of the practice of employing the particular concept in question. A gain in simplicity with respect to a narrow area of practice can be offset by resulting complications for a broad area of practice; so Putnam compares not only the rival metrics but also the physical theories that go with them for coherence. M1 leads to a Newtonian physical theory; M2 leads to a physical theory with extremely complicated laws, involving computations that cannot in practice be made and counter-intuitive universal forces. Rather than say that there's no fact of the matter as to which is the true geometry plus physics, Putnam asks why we shouldn't say that "distance according to the metric M1 is what we *mean* by distance".[6]

Putnam's second illustration involves a pair of rival translation manuals, both of which, Putnam argues, satisfy Quine's conditions for a translation manual. One gives homophonic translations, while the other has the peculiarity of translating "The distance from the earth to the sun is 93 million miles" as "There are no rivers on Mars" and *vice versa*. What we hear the speaker say is: "The distance from the earth to the sun is 93 million miles; light travels 186,000 miles a second; that is the reason it takes 8 minutes for light from the sun to reach the earth." If there is no fact of the matter as to which translation is required by the set of conditions that exhaust the content of the notion of translation, then we're free to accept either translation. But if we consider our judgments about translation and meaning in the context of judgments that form the data of psychology, sociology, anthropology, etc., we find that contextual coherence again provides a basis for discrimination. The homophonic translation, and not the other, allows us to make straightforward sense of the speaker's reasons for saying what he does. Insistence that there is no fact of the matter as to what the speaker means seems to depend on holding that there's no fact of the matter as to whether standard psychological theory or the highly non-standard psychological theory that attributes a strange inferential connection to the speaker is correct. But again Putnam asks: "If the adoption of one system of analytical hypotheses rather than another permits a great simplification of such sciences as neurophysiology, psychology, anthropology, and so on, then why should we not say that what we mean by 'translation' is *translation according to the manuals that have this property*".[7]

## 2. Emotivism and Legal Positivism as Conventionalism

Putnam claims that the conventionalist ploy is not topic specific, and that the conclusions to which it leads should be viewed as suspect in every area of philosophy; and he suggests that emotivism is a form of conventionalism.[8] Consider the emotivist view that:

1. The constraints that exhaust the content of claims that something ought to be done or that something would be the right thing to do are that they express the speakers' all-things-considered attitude toward an alternative and that the attitude supervenes on a naturalistic description of the alternative.[9] If a judgment about what ought to be done meets these conditions, it can't be disqualified as an ethical judgment in virtue of its content. We do, of

course, consider the content of the judgment in deciding whether these conditions are met, but once we've decided that they are, the judgment can't be disqualified on account of its content.

2. There could always be different and conflicting judgments that satisfy these conditions; for example, a Nazi may express an attitude, corresponding to his fascist values, that meets these conditions and a liberal may express an attitude, corresponding to the value of tolerance, that meets these conditions. Thus the conditions do not determine the extension of the concept of what ought to be done.

3. There is no fact of the matter as to which of the judgments that meet the conditions described is correct. Given what each means, there is no basis on which to judge between the claims of the sincere Nazi and the sincere liberal.

Note that the second element of Putnam's model should not simply be equated with the non-cognitivist feature of emotivism. If the constraints held to exhaust the meaning of *right* or *ought* were such as to allow only one of the competing judgments to qualify as a correct use of the concept, the second element of Putnam's model would not be present, even if the constraints provided a non-cognitivist analysis of ethical judgments. This might be the case, for example, if there are constitutive constraints on the content of universal prescriptions strong enough to decide among competing possible universal prescriptions. Hare's views in his earlier books, *The Language of Morals* and *Freedom and Reason*, seem to conform to the conventionalist pattern. But he argues in *Moral Thinking* that attitudes that are universalizable across changes in personal identity should not conflict. If so, then his account may not be a form of conventionalism or lend itself to Putnam's critique. An emotivism like that suggested by Blackburn in his article "Moral Realism", which incorporates supervenience, may be another example of conventionalism.[10]

Again, coherence provides an alternative to conventionalism. According to a coherence account, what is true of the claims of both a liberal and a Nazi fanatic is that they're claims about what there is reason to do that are responsible to considerations of theoretical coherence. The fascist and the liberal conceptions of what ought to be done stand in the same sort of relationship to one another as the rival metrics and translation manuals in Putnam's examples (and as the estoppel and consideration doctrines in the legal example discussed in Chapter 11). Following Putnam, we can ask: If one conception of what ought to be done in a given situation is associated with the theory or set of principles that displays the greatest degree of coherence among the various specific reason-giving concepts that apply to the alternatives in question, why shouldn't we say that part of what we mean by "right action" is *action in accord with such principles*?

Certain conceptions of the law also fit Putnam's model of conventionalism; conceptions of the law in terms of the command of the sovereign may provide the closest parallel to emotivism and conventionalist forms of prescriptivism, but I shall consider the legal positivist account of the concept of law in terms of a rule of recognition. The elements of Putnam's model present in the legal positivist model are as follows.

> 1. The complex constraint that exhausts the content of the concept of law is that of satisfying the rule of recognition.[11] All rules that meet the conditions set forth in the rule of recognition are equally rules of law, just as all metrics that satisfy Grunbaum's axioms equally provide a measure of distance and all translation manuals that satisfy Quine's conditions on analytical hypotheses equally provide a translation. That these conditions are satisfied is all we mean when we speak of law, distance, or translation.
>
> 2. The constraint that the rule of recognition must be satisfied cannot determine the extension of the concept of law in hard cases or cases that fall in the interstices of the law. Incompatible answers to legal questions may equally satisfy the rule of recognition.
>
> 3. Since incompatible answers to legal questions satisfy the constraint that exhausts the meaning of the notion of law, there's no fact of the matter as to which of the answers is required by law. The choice is a matter for judicial discretion.

We can regard the principle that a rule of law satisfies the rule of recognition, as we did Grunbaum's axioms and Quine's conditions, as a first attempt to formulate a theory that displays the coherence of our judgments employing a particular notion. The rule of recognition attempts to summarize the conditions that must be met by judgments of the form "*p* is a proposition of law." It's not altogether successful, for it leaves decisions in hard cases to judicial discretion. So, the rule of recognition does not determine the extension of the concept of law. But rather than accept the claim of legal positivism to have exhausted the content of this notion, we can again ask: If one decision is in better accord than another with the theory or set of principles that best displays coherence among the specific doctrines that apply to the alternatives in question (such as the estoppel and consideration doctrines in the legal example discussed in the next chapter), why shouldn't we say that part of what we mean by "law" is *decision in accord with such principles*?

## 3. Coherence and the Role of Theory

It's important to note that the suggestion is *not*: to say a certain alternative ought to be done, all things considered, is to say that a particular theory about the relationships among the various values that apply favours that alternative, or which particular theory does the best job of displaying coherence. It is rather: to say a certain alternative ought to be done, all things considered, is to say that the theory that does the best job of displaying coherence favours that alternative; the theory is identified only by the description of it as doing the best job of displaying coherence. Which theory this is is, as a conceptual matter, left open by the claim that a certain alternative ought to be done, all things considered; that is, it is left as a substantive issue, to be determined by theoretical deliberation. A coherence account makes as a conceptual matter merely an existential claim about a theory, namely, that there is some theory displaying coherence among the specific values that apply to the alternatives that does the best job of it, and that theory favours a certain alternative. Recall the point made in Chapter 2 about the scope distinction between claims of supervenience and claims of reduction. Supervenience claims are of the form: "in all possible worlds there is some function . . . ", rather than of the stronger, reductionist form "there is some function such that in all logically possible worlds . . . ." What the coherentist claims is given as a conceptual matter is simply that there is some theory (represented by a coherence function—see Chapter 12) that best displays coherence, not which one it is; he's thus committed to supervenience, as he must be, but not reduction. That is, he is committed to:

$$\Box \; \exists f \; (O_t(\dots) = f[\, O_j(\dots), O_k(\dots), \dots\, ]\,)$$

but not

$$\exists f \; \Box \; (\, O_t(\dots) = f[\, O_j(\dots), O_k(\dots), \dots\, ]\,)$$

The second, stronger, reductionist claim does not follow from the first, any more that it follows from the claim that, as a conceptual matter, someone's utility is some function of his income, that there is some particular function of income such that, as a conceptual matter, his utility is that function of his income. The stronger, reductionist claim gives rise to certain traditional problems, as we shall see below. But the weaker, former claim is not completely lacking in bite, and it leaves openings for responsible skepticism.[12] It means that the claim that a certain alternative ought to be done, all things considered, can be false if the theory that does the best job of displaying coherence does not favour that alternative; which theory this is is to be discovered *a posteriori*, and there's room for argument and disagreement about which it is. But the claim can also be false if there's no theory that displays coherence, if coherence is unobtainable and thus there are no right answers when values conflict. These possibilities of falsehood reflect the substantial status of claims about what should be done, and the scope for responsible skepticism.

There are several immediate favourable points to be made about a coherence account. First, it does not rule out any particular ethical theory, such as utilitarianism. To see this we have to distinguish between utilitarianism offered as an analytical account of concepts such as *ought* and *right* and utilitarianism offered as a theory that displays coherence. In *Freedom and Reason* Hare considers the suggestion that someone is not making an ethical judgment if he isn't prepared to abandon a principle when it conflicts with the most pressing interests of very large numbers of other people. This is in effect to take utilitarianism as an analysis. Hare's response to this suggestion is that a Nazi fanatic is not using this restricted notion in his dispute with a liberal, and yet the two of them are having a substantive dispute; we should consider the dispute they're in fact having, and not simply change the subject.

> To put this restriction upon the use of the word 'moral' is to write some kind of utilitarianism into its definition. . . . If we give the liberal the victory over

the Nazi by means of a definition of this kind, the victory will be in an important sense barren. Both will be left prescribing, universally, different ways of life, and therefore differing about the most fundamental questions that people can differ about.... We should be falling short of our duty as moral philosophers if we just left the Nazi and the liberal each playing his own different game; for there is one game which they are both playing.[13]

A coherence account of the sort suggested by Putnam's remark is less vulnerable to this type of criticism than the suggestion Hare considers. A coherentist's rejection of the view that the conventionalist's constraints exhaust the meaning of the claims both the Nazi and the liberal make does not *eo ipso* force the coherentist to defend the view that their claims can correctly be represented by writing some particular theory, such as utilitarianism, into the definition of *right* or *ought* (any more than Putnam's views about the meaning of *water* or *gold* would have it that their specific chemical compositions are given by their meanings). According to a coherence account, it is in virtue of their answerability to considerations of theoretical coherence that the claims of the liberal and the fanatic can be recognized as claims about the right thing to do at all, and that we can distinguish the true claims among them from the false. The fanatic is making such a claim, and he is having a substantive dispute with the liberal; but his claim is false. A claim using *right* or *ought* is responsible to considerations of theoretical coherence in a way similar to that in which a scientific claim is, in that no particular theory is specified in making a claim. Such a claim merely involves a commitment to make a case for coherence under *some* theory, and may be defeated by a demonstration of incoherence relative to some other theory. As we saw in Chapters 2 and 3, a shared practice of theorizing is required. But if the theory used to display coherence or demonstrate relative incoherence happens to be utilitarianism, this doesn't write utilitarianism into the definition of *right* or *ought*, for it's always open to a non-utilitarian to propose yet another theory, which does an even better job of displaying coherence, in defense of his position.

These remarks suppose that the disputants have mastered, or have access to mastery of, a fair range of the specific reason-giving concepts that apply to the alternatives in question, and that they disagree about how to resolve conflicts among the applicable reasons. On a coherence account, it's only in virtue of shared mastery of various specific reason-giving practices, which provide substantive constraints on eligibility and which the shared practice of theorizing is a practice of theorizing about, that people succeed in disagreeing with one another rather than talking past one another in disputes about what should be done (see again, for example, Chapter 4 section 5). Thus, the role of theory in a coherence account is not that of a central evaluative component which bestows or withholds approval of specific reason-giving practices, which depend on it for their status as reason-giving. The points made in Part I, about the way in which decentralization underwrites the possibility of disagreement and why substantive as well as formal constraints on eligibility are necessary to dispell the threat of radical indeterminacy, apply in full force to a coherence account; keeping them in mind will later help to disarm the 'problem' of the authority of theory (see Chapter 13 section 3). Recall that the point of a coherence account is not to eliminate open-ended theoretical disagreement, but to entitle us to take our theoretical practices with respect to essentially contested concepts at face value in a certain sense, by disarming the skeptic who threatens us with an *a priori* demonstration of radical indeterminacy. We do not need to rule out the possibility that participation in the relevant practice of theorizing may in particular cases itself support, *a posteriori*, an hypothesis of theoretical underdetermination, such as a view that two well-developed theories are equally good. But there is no *a priori* skeptical shortcut to this conclusion; we must engage in theorizing to entitle ourselves to it.[14]

### 4. Coherence, Naturalism, and the Authority of Theory

Since Moore claimed to refute the naturalistic fallacy in *Principia Ethica*, many philosophers have been shy of ethical naturalism, or the view that ethical facts are natural facts. Is a coherence account a form of naturalism? If so, does it succumb to the arguments that have been levelled against naturalism?

My arguments against a subjectivist version of centralism in Chapter 6, to the effect that ethical constraints are among natural constraints on the eligibility of contents, suggest a positive answer to the first question. Since the specific reason-giving concepts that constrain eligibility serve to express natural facts, and since such natural facts are conceptually embedded within a coherence account, a coherence account involves a naturalistic view of reason-giving facts. Thus someone holding a non-centralist conception of specific reason-giving concepts such as *just* and *unkind* and a coherentist conception of the general concepts may claim that it is a natural fact whether or not specific reasons obtain, which the theoretical claims made by the general concepts are about. A coherence account adds a theoretical element to such natural reasons, which comes into its own when they conflict. The theoretical remove of claims made by means of the general concepts allows our coherentist-*cum*-naturalist to make substantive claims about actions described by means of specific reason-giving concepts. Thus he can say "You ought to do the just thing" and be understood as making a substantive claim to the effect that in some particular situation the just act is the one favoured by the theory that best displays coherence among the conflicting specific reasons that apply to the alternatives. Which theory is the best one is a substantive question, and so is precisely what it recommends in particular circumstances. Similarly, it is possible to claim that one ought not to do the just thing without contradicting oneself. Whether one ought or ought not to do the just thing remains an open question, and answers to it make substantial claims.

Arguments against naturalism based on Moore's open-question argument insist on the substantive character of applications of the general concepts to alternatives described naturalistically.[15] Thus, it cannot be correct to claim that *goodness* is synonymous, for example, with *conduciveness to pleasure*, because it is a substantive claim that pleasure is a good thing; the parallel point can be made for any other claim of synonymy between a general ethical term and a specific naturalistic description. But this kind of argument does not work in the same way against a coherence account. The theoretical element in a coherence account leaves open questions about what should be done, all things considered, when reasons conflict, and answers to such questions, substantive. A coherence account is thus analogous in certain respects to accounts of natural kind terms that make them responsible to theory, though the appeal to theory is generalized, reflecting the fact that we have uses for theories which are not strictly causal, or scientific, such as ethical, legal, and aesthetic theories: a coherence account makes the general ethical concepts responsible to theories about values, i.e., to ethical theories, whereas natural kind terms are responsible to causal theories, i.e., to science. However, someone who claims that what Aristotle meant by "water" was in fact $H_2O$, though he didn't realize it because it hadn't yet been discovered that water is $H_2O$, cannot be shown to be wrong by pointing out that the latter was a substantive scientific discovery. Part of the point of this account of natural kind terms is to recognize that metaphysical necessities may be *a posteriori*. The claim is that uses of the term "water", even before such discoveries were made, were such that counterfactual suppositions about circumstances in which such discoveries might be made would reveal the users to intend their uses to be responsible to the revelations of theory.[16]

Nevertheless, the open-question argument may be reproduced at the theoretical level. It could be argued that it must be possible to make a substantive claim to the effect that one ought or ought not to do the action favoured by the theory that best displays coherent relationships among the conflicting specific reasons that apply to the alternatives. Someone who is skeptical about the authority of theory may be wrong, but at least it is a substantive issue whether he is wrong or not. Bernard Williams has recently expressed such a skepticism.[17] He comments on the general enterprise of trying to resolve practical dilemmas by appealing to a structure of ethical principles, a systematic framework, and asks why a set of ideas should be thought to have any special authority over our sentiments and our lives because it has the structure of a theory.

There are several ways one might respond to this objection. One might, for example, respond as follows. "This argument does not have the force of the original anti-naturalistic argument, which depended on recognition that we can indeed use the general ethical concepts to commend alternatives described in particular ways, e.g., as conducive to pleasure. But resistance to particular restrictions on the substantive use of the general ethical concepts does not entail resistance to any such restriction. Nor does whether resistance to a coherence account is appropriate depend on whether descriptions that invoke theories about natural facts count as naturalistic. Each proposed account must be looked at to see if indeed it gives rise to an unacceptable restriction on substantive use. If we are to give an account of the general concepts at all, some such restriction is inevitable. One arises even on non-cognitivist accounts, though it may take a different form owing, for example, to the role of imperatival force in certain such accounts: a universal prescriber cannot make a substantive prescription to the effect that whatever he or she universally prescribes is right, or wrong. The issue here isn't how to avoid a restriction on substantive uses entirely, but rather how to place it where it does not keep us from saying something we might indeed say. Candidates for how to place the restriction are tested in part by how compelling the claims to substantive use are which they rule out. If the claim to substantive use made by an anti-coherentist argument is not compelling, then reproduction of the open-question argument at the level of theory will not damage a co-herence account. It might be argued that this claim is far from compelling, that it is much harder to motivate than the claims about pleasure and other natural properties in the original anti-naturalist argument, that it certainly isn't needed to make room for *akrasia*, and so on. Perhaps it could be dis-approved as nihilistic, anarchic, as threatening wholesale irrationalism.''

But in fact this whole line of response suffers from the assumptions it shares with the objection. An adequate response to the objection would be a more radical one, which rejects these assumptions. To see what is wrong with the above response, compare it with an analogous response to an anal-ogous objection to an account natural kind terms that makes them responsible to theory rather than merely to appearances. Someone might object, that is, that even if it is correct that natural kind terms are responsible to theory rather than merely appearances, it is a substantive philosophical claim that this is so, and someone who denies it is not contradicting himself, even if he is wrong. Of course this is true, and it would be wrongheaded to respond to the point by trying to show that the substantive claim ruled about by the view that natural kind terms are responsible to theory is not compelling. The response should rather be that it is to misconceive the nature of the philo-sophical account of natural kind terms being offered to suppose it would rule any contrary substantive claim as a matter of definition. The account is not being offered as a definition, but as a substantive philosophical account, where what the best philosophical account is is itself responsible to philosophical theorizing about the relevant data, such as intuitions gathered in Twin Earth thought experiments. In order to make a case against the account of natural kind terms as responsible to theory, an objector must dirty his hands with the data, and do some contrary theorizing of his own; the above objection is altogether to quick a way with the account.

The account of natural kind terms that makes them responsible to the revelations of theory, even if the latter are yet unknown, makes it wrong for someone to deny that natural kind terms are in fact responsible to theory and hold them instead responsible only to appearances; a coherence account of the general ethical terms similarly makes it wrong for someone to deny that they are in fact responsible to theory. Thus these accounts rule out certain rival views as incorrect accounts of the relevant terms. But they don't rule these views out as immediately self-contradictory, or render their own positive accounts trivial. It is a substantive philosophical question whether certain terms are responsible to theory or not, and answers to it are not rendered insubstantial because they appeal to data about how competent speakers would use the terms in questions under counterfactual suppositions, i.e., because they appeal to data about meanings. Someone is wrong to deny that natural kind terms are responsible to causal theory, if he is wrong, because the best philosophical theory of natural kind terms reveals that they are thus responsible; just as someone is wrong to deny that water is H2O because the best causal theory reveals that it is. Though the kind of theory appropriately appealed to is different as between the two levels, in neither case is the objector wrong by definition or other than as a substantive matter. Of course, if someone were make the analogous objection yet again, at the third level, to deny that what the best philosophical account of natural kind terms is is itself responsible to philosophical theory, he would indeed be talking nonsense; at this third level, the short way with the objection is finally correct.

The analogous response for a coherence account is now obvious. A coherence account does not offer a definition, but a substantial philosophical account, arrived at as the result of philosophical theorizing such as that carried out in the chapters of this book and others. If a coherence account is wrong, it is so as a substantial philosophical matter, because there is something wrong with the theory or because there is a better theory. The distinction between the role of causal theory in relation to natural kind terms and the role of philosophical theory in relation to accounts of natural kind terms is mirrored in the distinction between the role of ethical theory in relation to the general ethical terms and the role of philosophical theory in relation to accounts of the general ethical terms. The skeptic about the authority of theory cannot win ground against a coherence account merely by pointing out that the authority of theory is a substantial philosophical issue, as this point is altogether compatible with a coherence account. Rather, the skeptic must produce an argument against the theory or a better philosophical theory. If the skeptic now retreats to reproducing his point at the third level, by denying that what the best philosophical account of the general ethical terms is is itself responsible to philosophical theory, he is indeed finally talking nonsense, and, as before, the short way with him is finally appropriate.

Note that I do not suggest that William's own skepticism about the authority of theory falls into these errors; I introduced his skepticism as an example of a position that might be put to certain uses in considering the relationship of a coherence account to certain traditional refutations of naturalism; but these are not Williams' uses of his skepticism. However, I suspect that Williams' problem of the authority of theory may be the result of conceiving the authority of theory to be greater than it can be, compatibly with recognizing the ineliminability of conflicts among reasons. I shall argue in Chapter 13 section 3, that coherence does not amount to strong commensurability, nor does it aspire to eliminate conflict; a coherence account may recognize the authority that theoretical reasons, reasons of coherence and integrity, in fact have in our lives without granting them central reason-giving power in relation to reasons of other kinds and without aspiring to eliminate the conflict between theoretical reasons and reasons of other kinds. However, this way of defusing the problem of the authority of theory must wait until more ground has been covered.


## 5. The Practice of Theorizing

Thus, parallel applications of Putnam's critique may be made to conventionalist analyses of the general ethical and legal concepts. But the position we're left in by the critique needs further positive characterization. It will be filled out in the next three chapters, in which I'll make various suggestions about the nature of the theorizing activity postulated by coherence accounts. Throughout the following discussion of the practice of theorizing, I shall depend on the notion of a linguistic practice that emerges from Wittgenstein's consideration of what it is to follow a rule, and that I invoked in Part I. Such a practice is the exercise of a technique of collecting objects under a concept; mastery of the technique enables one to go on using a concept in the same way. The set of specific reason-giving practices, practices of applying concepts such as *just* and *unkind*, is a subset of the set of all our linguistic practices. However, the rule-following considerations relate no less to the theoretical concept of coherence, as applied to sets of reason-giving practices, than to any other concept. That is, they apply both to the understanding of reasons and to the understanding of the relationships among reasons. Our exercise of the technique of bringing considerations of coherence to bear in puzzling or conflict cases is itself one of our practices. Theorizing when we're in doubt is one of the things we "simply . . . do".[18]

Is this theorizing activity such as to make questions posed in terms of the general ethical and legal concepts susceptible of right answers?[19] In Chapter 3 and Chapter 12 I defend the possibility that it is. But a presupposition of my approach is that any view taken about the matter should be based on attention to the theorizing activity itself, as embodied in our practices, and not on the supposed metaphysical peculiarities of ethical and legal reality. Claims to knowledge, Wittgenstein comments, seem not to "tolerate a metaphysical emphasis";[20] metaphysical disputes arise out of a kind of picture-mongering about our forms of expression that fails to engage with the uses to which we put them. He writes:

> When . . . we disapprove of the expressions of ordinary language (which are after all performing their office), we have got a picture in our heads which conflicts with the picture of our ordinary way of speaking. Whereas we are tempted to say that our way of speaking does not describe the facts as they really are. As if, for example, the proposition "he has pains" could be false in some other way than by that man's *not* having pains. As if the form of expression were saying something false even when the proposition *faute de mieux* asserted something true. For *this* is what disputes between Idealists,

Solipsists and Realists look like. The one party attack the normal form of expression as if they were attacking a statement; the others defend it, as if they were stating facts recognized by every reasonable human being.[21]

Dworkin has forcefully expressed, in the legal context, the Wittgensteinian view that metaphysical imagination and metaphor provide false standards of objectivity and gives rise to spurious dilemmas. His rejection of the no-right-answer thesis about questions of law in hard cases is underpinned by his repudiation of the widespread mistake he dubs the "secret books" picture of legal claims. The latter involves the supposition that if there really are right answers to legal questions that cannot be derived from propositions of law found in actual public books, they must instead derive from secret books, which no one can get at. In deciding hard cases, then, judges must guess at the contents of these secret books. The secret books picture, Dworkin claims, has exercised a great hold over jurisprudential thinking; it lies behind Holmes' famous observation that the law must be found in actual books because it cannot be a "brooding omnipresence", and behind the widespread belief that non-positivists must believe in natural law conceived as the contents of celestial secret books. But this picture is no part of any proper account of how there can be right answers to legal questions even when reasonable lawyers disagree.[22] Once the secret books picture is exposed, the way is open for Dworkin's arguments to the effect that there is room for neither judicial guesswork nor judicial discretion. His account is a kind of coherence account, according to which the concept of law is responsible to legal, political, and ethical theory. The common belabouring of skepticism about secret books and the like is one manifestation of the attraction many lawyers feel toward external skepticism.

> They say, of any thesis about the best account of legal practice in some department of the law, "That's your opinion", which is true but to no point. Or they ask, "How do you know?" or "Where does that claim come from?" demanding not a case they can accept or oppose but a thundering knock-down metaphysical demonstration no one can resist who has the wit to understand. And when they see that no argument of that power is in prospect, they grumble that jurisprudence is subjective only. Then, finally, they return to their knitting—making, accepting, resisting, rejecting arguments in the normal way, consulting, revising, deploying convictions pertinent to deciding which of competing accounts of legal practice provides the best justification of that practice. My advice is straightforward: this preliminary dance of skepticism is silly and wasteful; it neither adds to nor subtracts from the business at hand. The only skepticism worth anything is skepticism of the internal kind, and this must be earned by arguments of the same contested character as the arguments it opposes, not claimed in advance by some pretense at hard-hitting empirical metaphysics.[23]

The parallel view about ethics bears emphasis: The issue of whether there are right answers to questions about what one ought to do when reasons for action conflict is not properly addressed in terms of uncashed metaphors such as those involved in denials that to-be-doneness is somehow 'out there', part of the 'furniture of the universe'. It should rather be addressed by attending to the power, scope, and characteristics of the theorizing about reasons for action in which we engage. If our theoretical practices are such as in principle to determine right answers, or perhaps to approach right answers as limits, then it's not clear why anyone should, or even that anyone really does, care whether the reasons thus arrived at are part of the 'furniture of the universe', whatever that is. The furniture of the universe, along with secret books, are straw men and red herrings. I shall press this line of thought further in Chapter 14.

A persistent adherent of what Williams calls an 'absolute conception' of reality may press an adherent of the practice view to take a stand, perhaps to admit that his view of reasons is profoundly skeptical, not an objectivist view at all. He ought to respond by distinguishing skepticism about the furniture of the universe and associated absolute conceptions, which the Wittgensteinian practice view arguably may express, from skepticism about reasons, which it does not express. Indeed, the former kind of skeptic cannot be the latter kind of skeptic; far from taking a negative stand on the furniture issue or the secret books issue, he doubts that there is any ultimately intelligible issue in the offing to take a stand about. He may thus doubt the power and scope of certain kinds of metaphysical theorizing. But this doubt does not commit him to doubting the power and scope of theorizing about reasons.[24]

In the next chapter I shall descend from the level of theorizing about theorizing to attend to some actual theorizing, an example of what lawyers at their knitting do. I shall go through an example of legal theorizing in detail, abstract its general structure, and then briefly suggest other examples of deliberation for consideration.

# 11

# Deliberation

## 1. A Legal Example

In the last chapter I sketched some background and motivation for coherence accounts in ethics and law, as suggested by Putnam's critique of conventionalism. Such coherence accounts hold that practical judgments about what should be done, all things considered, are responsible to theory. In this chapter I shall examine in detail examples of the kind of theoretical activity, or deliberation, that aims at coherence; the examination will yield a schematic characterization of deliberation that will then, in the following chapter, be evaluated in abstract terms.

The discussion in this chapter will concentrate on a legal example, though an ethical illustration will also be given (and further ethical examples are discussed in Chapters 12 and 13). What is needed for our purposes is simply a case in which the relevant practical reasons—legal doctrines or precedents—conflict, and the court has to decide how to resolve the conflict. The illustration I've chosen, which involves basic principles of contract and tort law, is that of the conflict between the doctrine of bargained-for consideration and the doctrine of estoppel. In fact, the conflict between the two doctrines has long been resolved in most jurisdictions, and the resolution has established another legal doctrine, that of promissory estoppel.[1] In examining the case I shall be trying to illustrate the way in which deliberation about how to resolve the conflict involves analyzing the doctrines that apply to the alternatives and articulating their relationships to one another. I do not claim that the arguments I shall examine are unanswerable, only that they are representative. I shall run through the whole exercise of examining the case twice; the purpose of the first run-though is to give various possible deliberative arguments, and that of the second to stand back from the particular arguments and abstract the general structure of the deliberative process that they illustrate.

The common law doctrine of *consideration* requires an element of bargain or exchange to be present in order for a valid and enforceable contractual relationship to arise. The *Restatement Second of Contracts* says:

(1) To constitute consideration, a performance or a return promise must be bargained for.

(2) A performance or return promise is bargained for if it is sought by the promisor in exchange for his promise and is given by the promisee in exchange for that promise.[2]

In *The Common Law*, Oliver Wendell Holmes describes the requirement this way:

> . . . it is the essence of consideration, that, by the terms of the agreement, it is given and accepted as the motive or inducement of the promise. Conversely the promise must be made and accepted as the conventional motive or inducement for furnishing the consideration. The root of the whole matter is the relation of reciprocal conventional inducement, each for the other, between consideration and promise.[3]

A promise that is not motivated by consideration has no legal consequence in contract. (Consideration is normally a matter of fact, though under some circumstances it might be held that consideration exists as a matter of legal convention—but we needn't worry about such cases.) Thus, the judgment that a promise was made without bargained-for consideration is a reason to hold that the promisor is not legally obligated to make good his promise. He may still be morally obligated, but the law won't hold him to it.

Various suggestions have been made as to the rationale of the consideration requirement.

One suggestion is that "When one receives a naked promise and such promise is broken, he is no worse off than he was. He gave nothing for it, he has lost nothing by it, and on its breach he has suffered no damage cognizable to courts. No benefit accrued to him who made the promise, nor did any injury flow to him who received it".[4]

A second is that "From an economic point of view contracts involving an exchange of values tend to promote an increase in the public wealth. A gift, on the other hand, is a sterile transaction".[5] The economic advantages to society of enforcing promises made for consideration do not follow from enforcing promises made without consideration.

A third suggestion is that business would actually be positively discouraged by the enforcement of all promises:

> . . . the ability to rely on the promises of others adds to the confidence necessary for social intercourse and enterprise . . . .

> Promises constitute modern wealth and . . . their enforcement is thus a necessity of maintaining wealth as a basis of civilization. My bank's promise to pay the checks drawn to my account not only constitutes my wealth but puts it into a more manageable form than that of my personal possession of certain goods or even gold. Still, business men as a whole do not wish the law to enforce every promise. Many business transactions, such as those on a stock or produce exchange, could not be carried on unless we could rely on a mere verbal agreement or hasty memorandum. But other transactions, like those

of real estate, are more complicated and would become too risky if we were bound by every chance promise that escapes us. Negotiations would be checked by such fear. In such cases men do not want to be bound until the final stage, when some formality like the signing of papers gives one the feeling of security, of having taken proper precautions.[6]

The requirement of consideration provides a means of enforcing promises selectively. It eliminates some of the risks of enterprise and negotiation while, by enforcing bargains, it secures the economic benefits of sound risk-taking.

The doctrine of *estoppel* prevents a party from taking unfair advantage of a predicament in which that party's own bad behaviour has placed his adversary.[7] For example, suppose the defendant has deceived the plaintiff in some way and has violated a duty to him by lulling him into a false sense of security, so that the plaintiff has failed to realize that he has a problem. As a result, the plaintiff allows his legal claim against the defendant to run up against a statutory time limit, which requires that legal claims in a certain category be made before a given period of time elapses after the events that give rise to the claim. Because the defendant violated a duty to the plaintiff by lulling him into a false sense of security, the plaintiff's otherwise viable claim against the defendant comes up against the time limit. If the defendant were to defend against the plaintiff's claim by asserting that it is barred by the time limit, he would be exploiting the benefits of his own wrongdoing in deceiving and lulling the plaintiff. If the defendant hadn't deceived and lulled him, he might well have made the claim in time. The estoppel doctrine expresses the sense that this would be unfair, by saying the defendant can be estopped from obtaining the benefits of his own wrongdoing by asserting the limitation. In one such case, the United States Supreme Court commented:

> To decide the case we need look no further than the maxim that no man may take advantage of his own wrong. Deeply rooted in our jurisprudence, this principle has been applied in many diverse classes of cases by both law and equity courts and has frequently been employed to bar inequitable reliance on statutes of limitation.[8]

Now consider circumstances in which these two doctrines may conflict. Suppose a promise is made gratuitously, and the promisee relies on it to his detriment. That is, he acts or forbears in reliance on the promise in such a way that he'll be injured if the promise isn't kept. We don't count the mere loss of the benefits that would have been *constituted by fulfillment* of the promise as loss *in reliance* on the promise. For a reliance loss, the promisee's change of position in anticipation of fulfillment of the promise has itself to be positively detrimental to him, so that if the promise isn't fulfilled he'll be worse off, because of this change of position, than if it had never been made. He wouldn't have changed position this way at all if he hadn't been counting on the promise being fulfilled. We're supposing a case in which a gratuitous promise induces detrimental reliance. Suppose also that the promise is of such a kind that the promisor should reasonably have expected it "to induce action or forbearance on the part of the promisee."[9] He should have realized what might happen. Lastly, suppose the promisor has no particular interest in the promisee's acting as he does in reliance on the promise. He doesn't make the promise in order to induce him to act this way, but purely gratuitously. So, while a promise, of value to the promisee if enforceable, passes from the promisor to the promisee, nothing of value to the promisor passes back to him. Thus the consideration requirement isn't met: the element of bargained-for exchange essential to contractual liability is absent.

Suppose the promisee sues the promisor for failing to fulfill the promise. What decision as to the promisor's liability is favoured by the principles that best display a coherent relationship between the consideration and estoppel doctrines? Is the promisor under a legal obligation to the promisee or not? If so, under what theory? He seems not to be under a contractual obligation. But he has acted irresponsibly in making and then breaking a promise that he should reasonably have expected to induce reliance. Since this makes him a wrongdoer, the principle that the law should not permit a party to take advantage of his own wrongdoing may seem to support holding that the promisor is estopped from asserting that his promise is not binding.

The promisor can make an objection to the effect that the principle that the law should not allow a party to take advantage of his own wrongdoing is limited to cases where the wrongdoer is to be estopped from asserting a position *the availability of which depends on his wrongdoing*. He can admit that in this case he is in the wrong as an *ethical* matter for having broken his promise but argue that nevertheless he is not taking *legal* advantage of his promise-breaking, since if he *had* kept his promise he would no more have bargained for the promisee's reliance than he did as things were. So it's not his wrongdoing in breaking his promise that makes his legal position available to him. By invoking the requirement of bargained-for consideration he is not making promise-breaking a legal expedient, but is simply pointing out that the promisee failed to demonstrate one of the elements essential to contractual liability, and so has not even made out a *prima facie* legal case against him.

This argument by the promisor about how the estoppel principle applies is correct as far as it goes; but it doesn't go far enough. By invoking the requirement of bargained-for consideration he does not turn his promise-breaking in itself to legal advantage. However, the estoppel principle will still apply if we can show that the very circumstances that put what the promisor has done outside of contract, by enabling him to invoke the doctrine of bargained-for consideration, contribute to his wrongdoing. He made a promise, without bargaining for action in reliance on it, but still one that he should, reasonably, have expected to induce reliance. Given that the consideration doctrine denies the promisee a contractual right to performance, in doing this the promisor has induced the promisee to rely to his detriment. This, rather than the promise-breaking in isolation, is the wrongdoing to which the principle applies, that a party should not be able to take legal advantage of his own wrongdoing. This wrongdoing is not independent of the promisor's legal position, but partly constitutes his legal position. And it's just that part of his legal position that's constituted by his wrongdoing that the estoppel doctrine undermines.

Recall the three rationales that inform the requirement of bargained-for consideration. We've already noted that the no-worse-off-than-he-was rationale doesn't apply in this case: the promisee *is* worse off than he was before the promise was made, and not on account of any surprising behaviour on his part. The policy of promoting exchanges of value and hence increases in the public wealth, which supports enforcement of promises made for consideration, does not support enforcement of this non-bargain promise, but neither does it count against enforcement on other grounds. What about the policy of encouraging business, which would eliminate the risk of being bound "by every chance promise that escapes us?" *Should* this risk be eliminated in cases where the promise should reasonably be expected to induce reliance? Consider cases involving the following: a promise to tend someone else's property while he's away, which induces the owner to forbear making other arrangements for its care; a promise to make arrangements for insurance on someone else's property, which induces the owner to forbear making the arrangements himself; a promise to deliver money for someone in time to pay off his debt before it is overdue, which induces the debtor to forbear hiring a courier or delivering it himself; a promise by a wealthy uncle of a substantial sum as a graduation present, on the basis of which the promisee makes arrangements to open a business.[10] Applied to such cases, the principle that no one should be allowed to take legal advantage of his own wrongdoing and the policy of encouraging business by limiting liability to bargains seem to point in different directions. Thus at this point we must step back and look at the contexts in which the estoppel and consideration doctrines operate in order to see how they may be related to one another.

In order better to understand why *some* promises are *not* worthy of enforcement, we can ask the more basic question why *any* promises *are* worthy of enforcement. Various answers to this question have given rise to various measures of what someone is entitled to recover when a promise is enforced.

First: To *avoid unjust enrichment* of a defaulting promisor at the expense of the promisee, we give the promisee *restitution* of the value he has passed to the promisor. In our case, the principle that unjust enrichment should be avoided doesn't apply, since the promisor hasn't received anything of value.

Second: To *undo the harm* that a promisee suffers by relying on a promise, we try to put him in as good a position as he was in before the promise was made.[11] Gardner refers to the principle of undoing harm incurred in reliance as the *tort* idea underlying contract: "one ought to pay for the injuries he does to another. As applied to promises this means that one ought to pay for losses which others suffer in *reliance* on his promises."[12] Williston claims "It may fairly be argued that the fundamental basis of simple contracts historically was action in justifiable reliance on a promise."[13] Gardner, however, insists that the tort idea is in profound and perennial conflict with another fundamental idea, i.e., the bargain idea.

Third: The *bargain* idea, i.e., "that one who gets anything of value by promising to pay an agreed price for it ought to pay the seller the price he agreed."[14] In order to give the promisee the value of the *expectation* the promise created, we try to put him in as good a position as he would have been in if the promisor had fulfilled the promise.

We've thus found that there is a conflict between two background principles of contract law, the tort principle and the bargain principle. How might this conflict bear on the cases we're concerned with, cases of gratuitous promises that induce reasonable-to-expect reliance? In these cases the promisor is protected from liability under the doctrine of consideration by the very gratuitousness of the promise that, in conjunction with reasonable-to-expect reliance and the absence of contractual remedy, exposes him to liability under the doctrine of estoppel. The estoppel doctrine, which functions to make a wrongdoer pay for the harm he causes another by refusing him the legal benefits of his wrongdoing, is a procedural manifestation of the tort principle.

We've seen that the tort principle gives rise to the reliance measure of damages in contract. But the reliance measure of damages is not in fact the normal measure of contractual damages; rather, the expectancy measure is the normal measure of damages. This is a settled aspect of the law. Does this mean that the bargain principle, which supports the expectancy measure, normally has greater weight than the tort principle and should take priority in cases of conflict? If so, then a strategy suggests itself: We might claim that the bargain principle is another manifestation of the policy of encouraging business that motivates the consideration requirement. If the policy of encouraging business accounts for the bargain principle, we may have reason to think that the consideration doctrine outweighs the estoppel doctrine in our cases.

However, this strategy for weighing the two principles against one another does not actually work when we examine it more closely. This is because the normal preference for the expectancy measure is not supported exclusively by the policy of encouraging business. In their article on contract damages, Fuller and Perdue argue that a general preference for the expectancy measure has the indirect effect of protecting promises against reliance losses as well as the effect of facilitating business agreements.[15] That is, the practice of normally granting expectancy is supported by *both* the tort principle *and* the policy of encouraging business. As for the tort principle: expectancy is the best cure for reliance losses because reliance is too hard to calculate, and is the best preventative of reliance losses because, just in virtue of being more definite, it's more capable of enforcement than reliance, so better serves to deter breaches of contract. As for the policy of encouraging business: since proving reliance damages would be too difficult in many cases, a preference for reliance damages would discourage the venturesome business deals that are essential to our economic and credit sytems. Fuller and Purdue write:

> When business agreements are not only made but are also acted on, the division of labor is facilitated, goods find their way to the places where they

are most needed, and economic activity is generally stimulated. These advantages would be threatened by any rule which limited legal protection to the reliance interests. Such a rule would in practice tend to discourage reliance. The difficulties in proving reliance and subjecting it to pecuniary measurement are such that the business man knowing, or sensing, that these obstacles stood in the way of judicial relief would hesitate to rely on a promise in any case where the legal sanction was of significance to him. To encourage reliance we must therefore dispense with its proof.[16]

Since the preference for the expectancy measure is supported by the tort principle as well as by the policy of encouraging business, it does not provide evidence that the latter rationale is the weightier of the two. Thus we cannot derive support from it for the conclusion that the consideration requirement, motivated by the policy of encouraging business, takes priority over the estoppel doctrine, motivated by the tort principle.

In fact, further consideration of the expectancy measure leads to an argument that the tort principle has *greater* weight than the policy of encouraging business in the gratuitous promise cases we're concerned with. Consider the hypothetical question whether, if these cases do give rise to liability, the measure of damages should be expectancy or reliance. Fuller and Perdue suggest that the weight of the policy of encouraging business in favour of the expectancy measure is negligible in these cases.[17] Gratuitous promises that should reasonably be expected to induce reliance do not play a significant role in the systems of credit and finance on which business depends—and what counts as reasonable here does not depend simply on the state of the law with regard to the enforceability of such promises, but on business practices. Business promises for which nothing of value has been received are seldom such as to incline other businessmen to rely to their detriment. People in business don't generally make gratuitous promises to begin with, and they'd have no greater tendency to if such promises became enforceable. Gratuitous promises that should reasonably be expected to induce reliance are generally made in personal contexts removed from the credit and financial sytems. As a result, the business encouragement rationale has little force in favour of granting expectancy in these cases. On similar grounds we can discount its influence in favour of the consideration requirement in these cases. In the personal contexts in which this kind of reliance would be reasonable to expect, the need to protect businessmen against being held to every chance promise is hardly relevant.

Moreover, there are even cases that suggest the tort principle may take priority over the policy of encouraging business in certain types of case *despite* their relevance to business dealings. For example, in a suit for deceit the plaintiff was awarded his reliance losses even though they were *more* than the actual value of the defendant's promised performance, "in other words, although the plaintiff would have had a poor bargain even if the defendant's statements had been true".[18] As a rule, entitling a plaintiff who has made a bad bargain to shift his contractual losses to the defendant is not thought to be a proper penalty for simple breach of contract. The plaintiff would have suffered the loss even if the defendant *had* performed according to contract. The defendant is at fault for the breach, but it's not his fault that the plaintiff made a bad bargain to begin with. Business isn't encouraged by making one contracting party liable on breach for the other's bad bargain, as the increased risk would discourage enterprise. So, though we've seen that the tort principle cuts both ways as regards damages in cases of simple breach of contract, it seems to have special force in favour of reliance where the more-than-merely-contractual wrongdoing of deceit is also involved. There's no similar cutting both ways as regards the consideration requirement and estoppel, but there are two reasons to think that the tort principle does similarly have special force in favour of estoppel in our gratuitous promise cases.

The first reason is that the wrongdoing in these cases does not consist simply of the failure to fulfill a promise, as we noted earlier. That the wrong-doing is more-than-merely contractual makes these cases more like cases of deceit than like cases of simple breach of contract, and we can expect it to trigger the special force tort principle has in undoing reliance injuries that go beyond losses in contract.

The second reason is that cases involving gratuitous promises that should reasonably be expected to induce detrimental reliance do not generally arise in business contexts, as we've noted, while cases involving deceit certainly do. If the tort principle has added force against the policy of encouraging business even in cases of deceit, there's all the more reason to think it has special force in cases that tend to be removed from business dealings.

Arguments such as these determine what the law requires in cases of conflict: arguments about the relationships between the legal doctrines that conflict in application to the alternatives at issue. The aim of such arguments is to articulate these relationships by analyzing actual and hypothetical cases to reveal the types of circumstance that affect the relative weights of principles or purposes associated with each doctrine. In the discussion above, the aims of our arguments have been that "the interrelations of contract, deceit, es-toppel . . . be brought into some coherent pattern" and that "the remedy . . . be adapted to the needs of the particular situation", as Fuller and Perdue put it.[19] The arguments considered support the claim that the tort principle has greater weight than the policy of encouraging business in application to gratuitous promises that induce reasonable-to-expect reliance. (In fact, the doctrine of promissory estoppel that has developed to cover these cases is often regarded as sounding in tort rather than in contract.) But in any given jurisdiction there will be a multitude of actual and hypothetical cases that could throw light on a particular conflict of doctrines; any case has the po-tential to be illuminating whose resolution is influenced by principles or pur-poses associated with the conflicting doctrines.[20] In difficult cases light can travel by indirect routes; in order to take the play out of our theory about how the conflicting doctrines are related, we may have to look to areas of legal practice whose relation to the issue at hand is not obvious. Finding and analyzing cases that display the effect of particular types of circumstance on the weight of the relevant principles and purposes is hardly a mechanical

| C | E |
|---|---|
| −1 | 1 |
| 1 | −1 |

FIGURE 11.1

process; as well as reasoning power, it requires distinctive imaginative capacities, sensibilities, and insight, developed through exposure to, familiarity with, and participation in legal practices.

## 2. A Schematic Characterization of Deliberation: The Deliberative Matrix

We shall now begin the second run-through; we shall go back over our consideration of the promissory estoppel problem and try to extract from it the general character and structure of the kind of theorizing, or deliberation, it illustrates. Various stages of deliberation will be characterized by reference to a schematic representation of the example.

*First*, we specify the problem. This involves giving a partial description of the alternatives. We can label and describe the alternatives in our example as follows.

> 1: gratuitous promises that induce reasonable-to-expect reliance do give rise to liability.

and

> −1: gratuitous promises that induce reasonable-to-expect reliance do not give rise to liability.

Specifying the problem also involves determining which reason-giving practices bear on the alternatives in question and how the alternatives are ranked by each. In our example the doctrines of consideration and estoppel bore on the choice between *1* and *−1*. Letting *C* stand for the consideration doctrine and *E* for the estoppel doctrine, the doctrines rank the alternatives as shown in Figure 11.1.

What reasons bear on the alternatives and how may not be clear; in our example we had to clarify the bearing of the estoppel principle on the alternatives in response to the promisor's objection. The first stage of deliberation requires us to exercise our capacities to perceive the world in disaggregated, *pro tanto* evaluative terms, to engage in ethical or legal scrutiny the aim of which isn't to make decisions on balance but to discover and illuminate what's at stake in the first place. This task may require us first to develop these perceptual capacities, through experience and education, to overcome certain kinds of what Wittgenstein calls aspect-blindness, to learn to see all that it's possible to see about how an alternative might make sense.[21] Through legal education, for example, students acquire distinctively legal perceptual ca-pacites; they learn to spot issues, to perceive patterns of non-legal facts in legal terms, to participate in practices of applying specific, and often conflict-ing, legal concepts.

At the most fundamental level the question of what reasons bear on the alternatives leads back to the considerations about interpretation and charity from Part I. In trying to decide the right thing to say or do in a particular case, we must determine which reasons apply in the circumstances at hand; when they conflict, we consider settled cases, actual or hypothetical cases, in which the relevant reasons also apply, in order to arrive at a theory about how the reasons are related in the circumstances we face. Thus deliberation itself is a kind of interpretation, an effort to make sense of a body of practice as a coherent whole. At this stage specific values and reason-giving practices provide constraints on the eligibility of interpretations; in their absence, the description of the problem would be badly underdetermined, just as, in con-sequence, its resolution by reference to past choices and settled cases would be. These points about the eligibility of interpretations apply to the contents of legal reasons and intentions and the rationality of judicial action, as a special case of their application to the contents of reasons for action and desires and the rationality of intentional action in general. Applied to the legal case, these points yield the decentralized conception of law that I sketched in Chapter 2: recall Dworkin's objections to Hart's master rule analysis and appeal instead to specific legal practices as a starting point for legal analysis.[22] Indeed, important themes are common to Dworkin's recent discussions in *Law's Empire* of the interpretative nature of the concept of law and the literature on the interpretation of action and linguistic action: those of the eligibility of interpretations, principles of charity, the role of agreement on paradigmatic practices, etc. Paradigmatic legal practices con-strain the eligibility of the contents of legal reasons; the status of such practices as legal is not derivative, nor is it the result of legal interpretation, but rather a presupposition of it.

If all the specific reasons that bear on the alternatives favour the same alternative, then we need have no further problem. But this is often not the case. When the applicable reasons do conflict, we must go on to the *second* stage of deliberation, at which we try to articulate the principles and purposes that inform each of the relevant reason-giving practices. Our theorizing at this stage can have a local character, as we try to give separate accounts of the various specific reasons.[23] Some of the needed work may already have been done at the first stage, in the course of clarifying how the various reasons bear on the alternatives. In discussing the doctrines of consideration and estoppel we factored out, respectively, the policy of encouraging business, which I'll label *B*, and the tort principle that one ought to pay for the injuries one does to another, including the losses that others suffer in reasonable reliance on one's promises, which I'll label *T* in Figure 11.2.

At the *third* stage we gather the background data for theorizing about the relationships between the specific reason-giving practices we've analyzed by

| $C\,(\ldots B \ldots)$ | $E\,(\ldots T \ldots)$ |
|:---:|:---:|
| $-1$ | $1$ |
| $1$ | $-1$ |

FIGURE 11.2

looking for other issues on which the principles and purposes that figure in those accounts also have a bearing. These issues may have been decided in actual cases or may be illustrated by hypothetical cases that admit of clear argument or intuition; either way, they have settled outcomes. In the discussion of section 1 three issues were considered to this end: the first was the issue of whether the normal measure of contractual damages should be expectancy or reliance, which has actually been settled; second was the hypothetical question of whether, if gratuitous promises that induce reasonable-to-expect reliance *do* give rise to liability, the measure of damages in these cases should be expectancy or reliance; and third was the issue, on which there are some actual cases, of whether in contract cases that involve deceit and in which reliance losses exceed expectancy the measure of damages should be expectancy or reliance. We can label and describe the alternatives presented by these background issues as follows.

*ne:* the normal measure of contractual damages is expectancy.
*nr:* the normal measure of contractual damages is reliance.
*le:* if gratuitous promises that induce reasonable-to-expect reliance do give rise to liability, then the measure of damages in such cases is expectancy.
*lr:* if gratuitous promises that induce reasonable-to-expect reliance do give rise to liability, then the measure of damages in such cases is reliance.
*de:* in contract cases that involve deceit and in which reliance losses exceed expectancy the measure of damages is expectancy.
*dr:* in contract cases that involve deceit and in which reliance losses exceed expectancy the measure of damages is reliance.

The discussion above suggested that the policy of encouraging business and the tort principle bear on these issues, and that their resolutions are as shown in Figure 11.3 (only the rank order of alternatives *within* pairs of issues in each column is significant, not the rank order *between* pairs of issues).

The partially completed matrix we've constructed by the end of the third stage forms the basis for the theorizing we do at the next stage, the aim of which is to arrive at a coherent way of completing the matrix, i.e., of resolving the conflict in the case at issue. At the *fourth* stage we analyze the settled issues in order to form hypotheses about the relationships between the conflicting reasons. Put into a more schematic form, the reasoning in the above discussion was as follows. Consider the first issue, between *ne* and *nr*. Its resolution in favor of *ne* tells us nothing about the relative weight of *B* and *T* since, despite first appearances, both of them favour *ne*, *T* as well as *B*. But *B* and *T* do conflict in the second issue, over alternatives *le* and *lr*.

| $C(\ldots B\ldots)$ | $E(\ldots T\ldots)$ | Resolution |
|---|---|---|
| $-1$<br>$1$ | $1$<br>$-1$ | ? |
| ne<br>nr | ne<br>nr | ne<br>nr |
| le<br>lr | lr<br>le | lr<br>le |
| de<br>dr | dr<br>de | dr<br>de |

FIGURE 11.3

Resolution in favor of *lr* suggests that *T* outweighs *B* in some kinds of circumstance, which a fuller description of the alternatives *le* and *lr* should reveal. We consider these alternatives and realize that they can be characterized more fully by these propositions, *p* and *q*.

*p*:  the promises these cases involve are of a kind seldom made or relied on in the course of business.

and

*q*:  these cases involve more than merely contractual wrongdoing.

So, resolution of the second issue in favor of *lr* suggests the following hypothesis about the relationship between *B* and *T*: *T* outweighs *B* in certain circumstances, namely, when *p* and *q* obtain. Now go to the third issue: *B* and *T* also conflict over alternatives *de* and *dr*, that is, when *q*, but not *p*, obtains. Resolution of the third issue in favour of *dr* suggests a refinement of the hypothesis: that *q* has the effect of augmenting the weight of the tort principle relative to the policy of encouraging business, independently of *p*. The tort principle is concerned to make persons pay for harm they do to others, whether the harm flows from contractual or other than contractual wrongdoing; but it has added force when the wrongdoing involved is more-than-merely-contractual. We can fill the matrix in to show how we arrived at this hypothesis (see Figure 11.4).

We might also wonder whether the fact that *p* has the effect of diminishing the weight of the policy of encouraging business relative to the tort principle independently of the fact that *q*; if the two effects operate in the absence of one another, the total effect when both *p* and *q* obtain may be that much greater. In order to answer this question we can go back to stage three and find another issue over which *B* and *T* conflict and where the alternatives are characterized by *p*, but not *q*. Consider the alternatives *fe* and *fr*:

*fe*:  in suits brought by foster children for breach of contract to adopt, the measure of damages is expectancy.

| $C(\ldots B\ldots)$ | $E(\ldots T\ldots)$ | Resolution |
|---|---|---|
| $-1$ <br> $1$ | $1$ <br> $-1$ | $?$ |
| *ne* <br> *nr* | *ne* <br> *nr* | *ne* <br> *nr* |
| *le* & *p* & *q* <br> *lr* & *p* & *q* | *lr* & *p* & *q* <br> *le* & *p* & *q* | *lr* & *p* & *q* <br> *le* & *p* & *q* |
| *de* & $-p$ & *q* <br> *dr* & $-p$ & *q* | *dr* & $-p$ & *q* <br> *de* & $-p$ & *q* | *dr* & $-p$ & *q* <br> *de* & $-p$ & *q* |

FIGURE 11.4

and

*fr*: in suits brought by foster children for breach of contract to adopt, the measure of damages is reliance.

In fact this issue is settled in some jurisdictions; suppose we have adopted the Pennsylvania rule that limits recovery by foster children on contracts to adopt to reliance.[24] Then we can add the following row to our stage four matrix (see Figure 11.5). Resolution of this new, fourth issue in favor of *fr* suggests that *p* does have the effect of diminishing the weight of the policy of encouraging business relative to the tort principle independently of *q*.

We thus go back and forth between stages three and four, looking for settled and hypothetical cases that help to qualify and refine our hypotheses about the relationships between the conflicting reasons under various types of circumstance. We do this, of course, with an eye to the circumstances of the issue we actually have to resolve. There's no point at which we can be certain that this process of theorizing has come to an end once and for all; we may think we have exhaustively analyzed all the cases that might have a bearing on the case at issue, but if someone comes up with a new case or a more subtle, or more radical, analysis, our theory may have to be further refined, or even abandoned. The open-endedness

| $C(\ldots B\ldots)$ | $E(\ldots T\ldots)$ | Resolution |
|---|---|---|
| . <br> . <br> . | . <br> . <br> . | . <br> . <br> . |
| *fe* & *p* & $-q$ <br> *fr* & *p* & $-q$ | *fr* & *p* & $-q$ <br> *fe* & *p* & $-q$ | *fr* & *p* & $-q$ <br> *fe* & *p* & $-q$ |

FIGURE 11.5

| $C(\dots B\dots)$ | $E(\dots T\dots)$ | Resolution |
|---|---|---|
| $-1$ | $1$ | $1 \& p \& q$ |
| $1$ | $-1$ | $-1 \& p \& q$ |
| $ne$ | $ne$ | $ne$ |
| $nr$ | $nr$ | $nr$ |
| $le \& p \& q$ | $lr \& p \& q$ | $lr \& -p \& q$ |
| $lr \& p \& q$ | $lr \& p \& q$ | $le \& p \& q$ |
| $de \& -p \& q$ | $dr \& -p \& q$ | $dr \& -p \& q$ |
| $dr \& -p \& q$ | $de \& -p \& q$ | $de \& -p \& q$ |
| $fe \& p \& -q$ | $fr \& p \& -q$ | $fr \& p \& -q$ |
| $fr \& p \& -q$ | $fe \& p \& -q$ | $fe \& p \& -q$ |

FIGURE 11.6

of this theoretical process and its attendant disagreements do not entail the radical indeterminacy I have been concerned to resist in earlier chapters; they leave the extent of any actual theoretical underdetermination a matter that itself must be determined by ongoing theorizing, *a posteriori*. However, in systems of reason-giving practices as rich in data as, for example, the legal system in the United States, the hypothesis that no settled cases could be found or constructed to break some particular theoretical tie may be difficult to support.[25]

At the *fifth* stage we work out the implications of the best theory we've been able to construct for the issue we actually have to decide. In the example we arrived at the hypotheses that when $q$ obtains the weight of the tort principle relative to that of the policy of encouraging business is augmented and that when $p$ obtains the weight of the policy of encouraging business relative to that of the tort principle is independently diminished. Both of these circumstances characterize the cases we have to resolve: cases of gratuitous promises that induce reasonable-to-expect reliance involve other than contractual wrongdoing, and such promises are seldom made or relied on in the course of business. So, we decide that in these cases the tort principle, which motivates the doctrine of estoppel, outweighs the policy of encouraging business, which motivates the doctrine of consideration. The result is that gratuitous promises that induce reasonable-to-expect reliance do give rise to liability.

Figure 11.6 shows the completed matrix. The work that the second, third, fourth, and fifth rows of the matrix do is to help us arrive at a hypothesis, a partial specification of a *coherence function*, which takes us across the first row, from the rankings of the alternatives actually confronting us by the conflicting doctrines of consideration and estoppel to a ranking of these alternatives that reflects what the law requires, all things considered. The hypotheses about the relative weights of the tort principle and the policy of encouraging business when $p$ or $q$ obtains are such partial specifications of a coherence function. The theory such a coherence function aims to represent is that the existence of which is postulated by a coherence account of the general concept of law (or ethics); it is the theory that makes best sense of the relationships among various specific, sometimes conflicting reasons. But, again, which theory this is must be discovered *a posteriori*, through deliberation of the general character we have illustrated.

### 3. Three Sorts of Reason: Deductive, Practical, Theoretical

We've now completed the second run-through of the promissory estoppel problem; we've seen that the deliberative process it illustrates can be conceived as falling into five stages. Note now that at least three kinds of reason may be operative in the deliberative process: ordinary deductive reasons, practical reasons, and theoretical reasons.

In the *first* place, ordinary deductive reasons can operate at any point. For example, in the first stage of deliberation about gratuitous promises we were trying to determine which specific legal doctrines had a bearing on the alternatives in question. I attributed an objection and argument to the promisor that illustrates one sort of contribution that deductive reasoning can make. He argued as follows: only if the availability of a wrongdoer's legal position depends on his wrongdoing should he be estopped from asserting it; the availability of my legal position does not depend on my wrongdoing (i.e., my promise-breaking); therefore, it's not the case that I should be estopped from asserting it. This argument is an instance of the valid inference pattern: only if $p$, then $q$; not $p$; therefore, not $q$. The inference is valid, but, as we saw, the second premise is false: the availability of the promisor's legal position does depend on his wrongdoing, because the promisor's legal position is not independent of his wrongdoing in having induced the promisor to rely to his detriment. A claim to this effect featured in the obvious rebuttal of the promisor's objection, which takes the form of *modus ponens*: if $p$, then $q$; $p$; therefore, $q$. That is, if a wrongdoer's legal position depends on his wrongdoing, then he ought to be estopped from asserting it; the promisor's legal position does so depend; therefore, he ought to be estopped from asserting it. Similarly, the promisor employs deductive reasoning when he argues: only if the element of bargained-for consideration is present does contractual liability arise; the element of bargained-for consideration is not present in the case at hand; therefore, contractual liability does not arise in the case at hand.[26]

These uses of deductive reasoning are obvious and straightforward, but it's important to distinguish deductive reasons from the *second* sort, practical reasons—*pro tanto* reasons for action or legal decision. Logical, i.e., deductive, reasons for beliefs, the content of which concerns reasons for action or decision, cannot be identified with reasons for action or for decision themselves. Deductive reasons for beliefs about reasons for action are reasons of the same kind as deductive reasons for beliefs about anything else; there's nothing distinctive about them *qua* reasons just because the beliefs in question happen to be about actions or legal decisions. When I recognize an inference as a case of *modus ponens*, I have a perfectly general reason to infer from the premises to the conclusion, if the premises are true. The nature of this reason is not changed or transformed according to the content of the propositions involved. By contrast, when I recognize that the availability of a wrongdoer's legal position depends on his wrongdoing, or that the element of bargained-for consideration isn't present, or that an act would be unjust or would violate a right, I have a practical reason, a reason for action or decision. We can regard practical reasons as analogous to deductive reasons in certain respects, but the analogies between them should not be allowed to obscure the fact that they are reasons for different sorts of things: reasons for action or decision on the one hand, and reasons for belief on the other. A capacity to recognize reasons for action or decision cannot be reduced to a capacity to recognize deductive reasons for belief; to pursue such a reduction is to pursue a false explanatory economy.[27]

*Third*, reasons of a theoretical nature operate in the process of deliberation, at each stage. They may be regarded as falling under a generalization of the category of inductive reasons—a generalization, because the theories in question are not necessarily causal, and may provide explanations, interpretations, and understanding that are distinctively legal or ethical. The analysis of settled actual and hypothetical cases constitutes a theoretical practice, which provides reasons to view our specific reason-giving practices as related to one another in certain ways under certain circumstances. Theoretical reasons are reasons for beliefs about the relationships among specific practical reasons; *that* specific practical reasons are related to one another in certain ways by the best account of them may itself constitute a practical reason.

There is interplay between our specific reasons and our theorizing about the relationships among them. We might, for instance, find theoretical reasons to demote a particular kind of reason to a very low priority under certain types of circumstance, so that it only has force when another particular kind of reason, almost always present in those circumstances, is absent. In general, our specific reason-giving practices have to hold their place in a system of reason-giving practices, and are to some extent subject to revision and qualification as our perceptual, imaginative, sympathetic, and theoretical capacities enlarge and develop (though of course limits are provided by substantive constraints on eligibility). This general view has been made familiar by Rawls' descriptions of the two-way technique of arriving at reflective equilibrium, and has been enlarged upon by a number of writers, including Dworkin, Daniels, MacCormick, Norman, and many others. In Daniels' terminology, deliberation seeks wide reflective equilibrium, not narrow. Norman claims that evaluative concepts have their sense only in the context of a system of values.[28] And Dworkin writes about the interplay between legal practices and the principles that figure in legal theories:

. . . the techniques we apply in arguing for another principle do not stand (as Hart's rule of recognition is designed to do) on an entirely different level from the principles they support. Hart's sharp distinction between acceptance and validity does not hold. If we are arguing for the principle that a man should not profit from his own wrong, we could cite the acts of courts and legislatures that exemplify it, but this speaks as much to the principle's acceptance as its validity. . . . If we are asked (as we might well be) to defend the particular doctrine or precedent, or the particular technique of statutory interpretation, that we used in this argument, we should certainly cite the practice of others in using that doctrine or technique. But we should also cite other general principles that we believe support that practice, and this introduces a note of validity into the chord of acceptance. We might argue, for example, that the use we make of earlier cases and statutes is supported by a particular analysis of the point of the practice of legislation or the doctrine of precedent, or by the principles of democratic theory, or by a particular position on the proper division of authority between national and local institutions, or something else of that sort. Nor is this path of support a one-way street leading to some ultimate principle resting on acceptance alone. Our principles of legislation, precedent, democracy, or federalism might be challenged too; and if they were we should argue for them, not only in terms of practice, but in terms of each other and in terms of the implications of trends of judicial and legislative decisions, even though this last would involve appealing to those same doctrines of interpretation we justified through the principles we are now trying to support. At this level of abstraction, in other words, principles rather hang together than link together.[29]

We can express this conception of specific reason-giving practices as standing in a relation of interdependence with theoretical considerations by paraphrasing Wittgenstein: We do not learn the practice of giving reasons by learning rules; we are taught reasons and their connection with other reasons. A totality of reasons is made plausible to us. When we first begin to justify anything, what we justify is not a single action or decision but a whole system of actions and decision. (Light dawns gradually over the whole.)[30]

## 4. An Ethical Example

The legal example involved two conflicting doctrines. To indicate how the account of deliberation I've given would apply to an ethical problem, I'll consider a more complicated problem, where there are three conflicting values. We want an account of deliberation that is general, that will apply to more complicated cases as well as simpler ones.

Consider the pattern of conflict illustrated by the following situation, which is an elaboration of an example given by Amartya Sen in lectures in Oxford: The situation involves three characters. $a$ is a craftsman who has been employed to produce an extraordinarily fine violin; and he has produced an exquisite violin, his masterpiece. $b$, who is $a$'s underpaid apprentice, helped in the work, and $c$, an interested onlooker, did nothing. But we know a bit

| F | G | H |
|:---:|:---:|:---:|
| a | b | c |
| b | c | a |
| c | a | b |

FIGURE 11.7

more about these characters. c is the foremost violinist of the group, a young prodigy. a plays a bit for his own enjoyment, and b is tone deaf. Also, b is poor and dejected, an orphan who has had an unhappy life. c is slightly better off, but certainly cannot afford a violin worthy of her talents. a is well enough off to provide necessities for his household without serious worry, but isn't rich enough to acquire for himself a violin as fine as the one he's made, or take the time away from his employment to make another one for himself, without bringing substantial hardship on his family. Each of them would love to own the violin.

Imagine that a's employer is a distant admirer of a person we'll call *the deliberator*. a's employer has supplied a with materials and paid his wages, and the violin is his legal possession when it comes into existence; he leaves the violin to the deliberator in his will. The employer dies, and the violin goes to the deliberator. She doesn't want to keep it, and she doesn't need the money she would get by selling it. In fact, she's a wealthy philanthropist who gives a great deal of money to various charities anyway. Since she's aware of the history of the violin, and of how very happy each of a, b, and c would be to possess it, she decides that she would do better to give it to one of them than to do anything else with it. I shall suppose that this much is settled. But to which of them should she give it? To a, the craftsman who made it; to b, a's miserable underling; or to c, the young prodigy?

*First*, the deliberator brings various specific reason-giving concepts to bear on the alternatives. She judges that considerations of three sorts, of entitlement, equality, and excellence or perfectionism, have differential bearing on the alternatives. Let's say that value F ranks them according to considerations of entitlement, value G ranks them according to considerations of equality, and value H ranks them according to considerations of excellence or perfectionism. The rankings these values effect are as shown in Figure 11.7.

It's not difficult to find other, perhaps more compelling, examples of this same pattern of conflict. Suppose, as a variation, that the deliberator is a doctor who can treat only one of three urgent cases of the same illness. Her alternatives are to treat a, b, or c. The illness has very similar symptoms and effects in the three cases, and the treatment would be equally successful applied to any of them. The doctor has the following further information about a, b, and c. a is the doctor's own patient of long standing, b has been referred to her by a colleague, and c is a foreigner attending a conference of mathematicians in the doctor's vicinity (which a and b are also attending). b has had a miserable life and suffers from other serious conditions as well; *c* has another less serious complaint, while this is *a*'s only complaint. Finally, *c* promises to make brilliant advances in some branch of pure mathematics if cured of the disease, while *a* has somewhat less talent and *b* somewhat less still. We have the same pattern of conflict in this case as in the violin case. (As an adolescent, I decided that the most important things in life were knowledge, beauty, and kindness, and was preoccupied with trying to figure out which of these three concerns took priority when; they also give rise to similar patterns of conflict.)

Since the applicable reasons in such cases conflict, the deliberator must try to achieve a view about their relationships that will take her from the rankings of the alternatives by the various conflicting reasons to an all-things-considered evaluation.

At the *second* stage the deliberator develops conceptions of entitlement, equality, and excellence. She may consider and evaluate the ideas of Aristotle, Locke, Marx, the difference principle and various forms of contract argument, the distinction between patterned and process principles of entitlement, various formulations of utilitarianism, the principle of diminishing marginal utility, etc. But she needn't master the philosophical literature to deliberate; she can just as well come up with her own accounts of entitlement, equality, and excellence, though in doing so she'll probably light on some of the principles that philosophers discuss. Let's suppose that the deliberator has a Rawlsian bent (though, again, nothing rules out the possibility that some form of utilitarianism provides the best accounts at this stage). Her view of equality depends on a conception of human beings as autonomous ethical agents, and her account of fair entitlements appeals to the contents of a hypothetical contract that would be agreed on by these autonomous selves from behind a veil of ignorance. She thinks that the contractors would be rational to agree on a maximin strategy and the difference principle applied to primary goods. She also accepts psychological generalizations to the effect that self-respect is a primary good and that achieving excellence is a major source of self-respect and of happiness to persons. At this stage the relationship between the difference principle and some perfectionist principle motivated by these generalizations about self-respect is left open. But if they describe salient enough features of human nature the contractors may have reason to subordinate the difference principle to principles of entitlement geared to an incentive structure that reflects some perfectionist principle; this might be rational if it would encourage and reinforce the people's efforts to achieve self-respect through excellence.

At stages *three* and *four* the deliberator tries to specify the relationships of these principles and values. She'll look for other issues they bear on that have intuitive and widely accepted resolutions, and she'll develop and revise hypotheses about the relative weight of the principles in various circumstances. Eventually she'll incorporate her accounts of entitlement, equality, and excellence into a more comprehensive theory that clarifies how the principles that inform these values are related. For example, she may, with Rawls, subordinate a principle of perfectionism by reference to the value of "negative" liberty,[31] at least when conditions permitting informed desires are met. Or, in order to make sense of regret and second-order evaluation, she may adopt a self-realization theory of "positive" freedom[32] that allows a perfectionist principle to outweigh the difference principle in a wide range of circumstances. This latter type of move may require some corresponding adjustment in the conception of the autonomous selves whose equality the veil of ignorance was designed to express in the first place. (For further discussion of related issues, see Chapter 15 sections 1 and 5.)

*Finally*, when the deliberator has developed her theory about entitlement, equality, and excellence as far as she can, she determines which has priority in the particular situation she faces, according to the weighted and qualified principles that figure in her theory.

I've given legal and ethical illustrations of deliberation, but the account of deliberation itself is intended to be quite general, applicable to any practical problem that is a problem about conflicting ends rather than one merely about means. Thus, it applies to problems that involve the conflicting interests of a single person who's not certain what he most wants to do, what would be the best thing for him, all things considered, or what kind of person he really is or should be. In such cases, deliberation involves active self-interpretation and indeed self-determination, not merely passive introspection: the person tries to sort out the various specific interests, ends, and values at stake and, by reference to them, to make sense of what he has done and what he would do under various circumstances, and thus to arrive at a coherent conception of himself as a person, in order to determine what he is to do in the case at hand.

The economist von Mises has written:

> Choosing determines all human decisions. In making his choice man chooses not only between various material things and services. All human values are offered for option. All ends and all means, both material and ideal issues, the sublime and the base, the noble and the ignoble, are ranged in a single row and subjected to a decision which picks out one thing and sets aside another. Nothing that men aim at or want to avoid remains outside of this arrangement into a unique scale of gradation and preference.[33]

The purposes of economists may well justify their habit of taking preference orderings as given and their ordinary lack of interest in how they are arrived at.[34] In principle, however, it's no less problematic to assume that a scale exists on which to read off the resolution of conflicts among the desires and interests of *one* person, than it is to assume there's a scale on which to read off the resolution of conflicts among the desires and interests of *different* persons. When the interests of different people clash, we cannot take the basis for interpersonal comparisons as obvious, but must work to establish it. While the basis for intrapersonal comparisons and the resolution of conflict among his own ends is sometimes clear to a person, in many cases he also must work to arrive at them. Behaviour interpreted as revealing transitive preferences guarantees such a scale for one person only in the unhelpful, *ex post facto* sense in which it does so for society as well. That is, outcomes eventually emerge: individuals eventually do one thing or another, and certain preferences of one group eventually prevail over certain preferences of other groups. But it's no more illuminating to an individual whose ends conflict and who hasn't yet decided what to do to be told that eventually he'll reveal transitive preferences, so he might as well just sit back and wait to see what happens, than it would be illuminating to a society trying to arrive at a just resolution of a conflict of interests among its members to be told the same. Human beings may sometimes act with no coherent conception of what they are doing at all, or may be buffetted about by their subsystems, or may act against their best judgment about what they should do, even when only their own interests are involved; similarly, societies may subsist in chaos and corruption, or may permit unjust arrangements to persist and just arrangements to be flouted. (Recall the example at the beginning of Chapter 8, section 1.) Thus, in determining what to do in part by reference to settled cases, a decision-maker must allow that some of his past decisions have been mistaken; his task is not merely to let some new decision emerge, but to find a way of accounting for settled cases that helps *in arriving at* a resolution of the case at issue, with the aim of getting it right, of correcting for past mistakes and avoiding further mistakes. A coherence account cannot allow that *most* past decisions are mistaken, but this point falls far short of licensing complacency.

The general account of deliberation I've given applies to both legal and ethical reasoning despite the significant differences between them, and the fact that judicial action is a very special kind of action. McCormick comments that "legal reasoning is a special, highly institutionalized and formalized, type of moral reasoning" even though "the very features of institutionalization and formality create important disanalogies".[35] For example, the rules of evidence artificially simplify legal deliberation, perhaps partly as a result of practical pressures to arrive at fair decisions as efficiently as possible. Decisions left to personal ethical deliberation, whether because of their irrelevance to political functions or out of respect for the autonomy of persons, are not subject to the same pressures; no analogous procedural principles operate to render ethical problems managable, and they face us in all their substantive complexity. Thomas Nagel admits the attractions of an approach to ethical problems that emulates the legal system, but concludes that most ethical problems are too complex and untidy to be handled by an advocacy procedure before a tribunal.[36] The examples of legal and ethical deliberation I've discussed reflect the greater demands made by ethical issues: one might develop a coherent conception of entitlement, equality, and excellence in the course of a book or two on the subject, or in the course of years of thoughtful decision-making, but certainly not in the number of pages I have devoted, or a judge might, to setting out a theory about consideration and estoppel. Moreover, a person's cultivation of his capacities to recognize the values at stake under various circumstances, and his efforts at character formation and self-determination, have an aesthetic dimension which cannot, I believe, be separated from the business of ethics, and which is particularly resistent to the kinds of procedures and compartmentalization appropriate to legal deliberation.

We've now considered some of the philosophical background and motivation for a coherence account, as well as illustrations of the way in which deliberation aspires to coherence. My main point in this chapter has been to develop an abstract characterization of deliberation and the search for coherence out of a concrete and detailed example. In the next chapter we shall consider the applicability of various formal conditions to the structure of the deliberative matrix we began to characterize in this chapter. The formal conditions to be considered are suggested by the analogy between deliberation for one individual with conflicting ends and the determination of social choices given conflicting individual preferences. Given various impossibility results in social choice theory, the analogy raises the question whether the kind of coherence sought in deliberation is possible after all.

# 12

# Coherence

## 1. Coherence Accounts and the Existence of Coherence Functions

In the preceding two chapters I've described and argued for a coherence account of the general concepts of ethics and law as an alternative to centralism. A *coherence account* postulates the existence of a theory, sought in deliberation, that best displays as coherent the relationships among specific reasons for action. That is, it involves a claim of the following kind: to say that a certain act ought to be done is to say that it is favoured by the theory, whichever it may be, that gives the best account of the relationships among the various specific reasons (such as ethical values, or legal doctrines and precedents) that apply to the alternatives in question. Coherentist views are held by many and are regarded by many others as a live option.[1] In this chapter I will assume that views of this kind are attractive, and will consider whether or not a certain kind of challenge to them is successful. Since few of the people who hold coherentist views have been worried about this kind of challenge, my claim that it doesn't in the end succeed may not come as a great relief. But perhaps coherentists should have been more worried; it's interesting to see why the challenge does not succeed, and to discover that among the factors that keep it from succeeding are both formal constraints on theories about what ought to be done, in particular a requirement of supervenience, and substantive constraints.

According to coherence accounts, the deliberator's task is to seek the ethical, or legal, theory that best displays coherence. Another way of putting this is to say that deliberation involves a process of constructing hypotheses about the content of a *coherence function*, which represents the theory sought and which takes us from alternatives ranked by specific reasons to all-things-considered rankings in a way that meets certain conditions. In the last chapter I gave examples to support the plausibility of this view. But it is one thing to claim the plausibility of such an account of what deliberators try to do, and another to claim that the coherence functions they seek exist. In order to support the latter claim we have to say more about what they are and the conditions they must meet. Until we have, we cannot dismiss the possibility that, even if our account of their search is correct, deliberators are seeking a chimera. Thus we now turn to consider the possible threat of overdetermination raised and postponed at the end of Chapter 2.

If a coherence account is to allow us to defend the truth of claims about what ought to be done, then at least it has to be the case that the minimal conditions that are reasonable to impose on a coherence function are consistent, so that the function is not, in effect, overdetermined. According to a coherence account, to claim that a certain act ought to be done isn't to say that it's favoured by any given theory, or to say which theory does the best job of displaying coherence, but rather to say that the act is favoured by *the theory that best displays coherence*; which theory this is has to be discovered *a posteriori*. So, the claim is false if the theory that in fact does the best job of displaying coherence doesn't favour the act in question. But it's also false, *inter alia*, if there's no theory that displays coherence because coherence is impossible to obtain. It may be true that deliberators seek coherence but that all of their claims about what ought to be done are false because there's no such thing as coherence.

Note that any claim to objectivity based on a coherence account would embody a rather different conception of objectivity than that John Mackie had in mind when he denied the existence of objective values as part of an error theory.[2] A coherentist's claim to objectivity might well reflect skepticism about the metaphysics that supplies the content of Mackie's denial; it might turn instead on the power and scope of the theoretical activity that plays an essential role in coherence accounts. And this of course would be to follow the Wittgensteinian injunction to make the power and scope of theoretical practices the focus of attention rather than giving rein to metaphysical imagination. But nevertheless, the possibility of error is still there. The very contrast between the conception of objectivity that informs Mackie's denial and a more austere conception of objectivity points up the importance of recognizing that the possibility of error that cuts across them: if claims about what ought to be done are claims about coherence, it is still possible that they are false because there's no such thing as coherence, because our theoretical practices themselves impose conditions that are jointly impossible to meet. I shall argue that, while at first it may look as if there is an alarmingly strong case that this is so, and thus that coherence functions do not exist, the case cannot be made out.

## 2. The Analogy Between Deliberation and Social Choice

It's often assumed that the possibility of rationally resolving one-person conflicts is less problematic in principle than the possibility of rationally resolving conflicts between persons. Bernard Williams has expressed scepticism about this assumption. He points out that

> . . . some one-person conflicts of values are expressions of a complex inheritance of values, from different social sources, and what we experience in

ourselves as a conflict is something which could have been, and perhaps was, expressed as a conflict between two societies. . . . The same point comes out the opposite way round, so to speak: a characteristic dispute about values in society, such as some issue of equality against freedom, is not one most typically enacted by a body of single-minded egalitarians confronting a body of equally single-minded libertarians, but is rather a conflict which one person, equipped with a more generous range of human values, could find enacted in himself.[3]

The analogy between one-person conflict and many-person conflict is sometimes taken to support attempts to model techniques for resolving many-person conflicts on techniques for resolving one-person conflict, on the assumption that the former techniques are no more problematic than the latter. (Recall the views of Harsanyi and Hare, discussed in Chapter 6 section 2.) But the analogy can be turned on its head: it can be taken to support scepticism about the possibility of rationally resolving one-person conflicts, on the assumption that this possibility is no *less* problematic than the possibility of rationally resolving many-person conflicts. At least we should be prepared to take one-person conflict seriously by the discussions of *akrasia* and of the ways in which conflict within a person may be like conflict between persons, in Chapters 7 and 8. If there are grounds for skepticism about the possibility of rationally resolving conflicts between persons, and if conflicts within persons are in many ways like conflicts between persons, then there may be grounds for skepticism about the possibility of rationally resolving conflicts within persons as well. Kenneth Arrow's impossibility result for social welfare functions brought home just how problematic the resolution of many-person conflicts is. And indeed, in the wake of Arrow's result, Kenneth May described an analogous impossibility result for the individual deliberator with conflicting criteria of choice.

Arrow was concerned with the widely held view that social welfare is some function of the conflicting preferences of individuals. He considered the problem faced by a society that tries to aggregate rankings of alternatives by individuals to get a ranking that reflects social welfare, and he demonstrated that we cannot count on transitivity of group preferences even if individual preferences are transitive. May reinterpreted Arrow's result to apply to the problem faced by an individual who trying to arrive at all-things-considered evaluations of alternatives that he ranks in different ways according to different criteria, and May concluded that "we cannot expect individual preferences to be always transitive" even given the transitivity of the rankings of alternatives effected by each criterion.[4] That is, May was concerned with the possibility of functions formally analogous to social welfare functions, but which take as arguments rankings of alternatives generated by various conflicting criteria rather than by various individuals. He claimed that no function exists that meets conditions analogous to Arrow's and takes us from transitive criterial rankings of alternatives to a transitive all-things-considered ranking of them.

Consider again the case of the deliberator who is a doctor who can treat

| Entitlement | Equality | Excellence |
|:-----------:|:--------:|:----------:|
| *a* | *b* | *c* |
| *b* | *c* | *a* |
| *c* | *a* | *b* |

FIGURE 12.1

only one of three urgent cases of the same illness; her alternatives are to treat *a*, *b*, or *c*. The illness has very similar symptoms and effects in the three cases, and the treatment would be equally successful applied to any of them. *a*, *b*, and *c* are all free of family obligations. *a* is the doctor's own patient of long standing, *b* has been referred to her by a colleague, and *c* is a foreigner attending a conference of mathematicians in the doctor's vicinity (which *a* and *b* are also attending). *b* has had bad health all his life, and has several other serious conditions; *c* has another, somewhat less serious complaint, while the illness in question is *a*'s only complaint. Finally, *c* promises to make brilliant advances in some branch of pure mathematics if cured of the disease, while *a* has somewhat less talent and *b* somewhat less still. The deliberator determines that considerations of entitlement, equality, and excellence or perfectionism have differential bearing on the alternatives, and that they rank the alternatives as shown in Figure 12.1.

The relevant criteria in this example are entitlement, equality, and excellence, and the alternatives are ranked with respect to each criterion according to the degree to which they satisfy it; the criteria are directional, such that any one alternative's ranking above a second with respect to a criterion counts *per se* in favour of the first (see condition $P^*$ below). This pattern of conflict is the same as that found in *voters' paradoxes*, where voters are substituted for values: if the three rankings of alternatives were determined, respectively, by three voters, or three groups of voters of the same size, instead of by considerations of entitlement, equality, and excellence, then the method of majority decision would produce an intransitivity. To see this, note that alternative *a* would be ranked higher than alternative *b* by two out of three voters, alternative *b* would be ranked higher than alternative *c* by two out of three voters, and alternative *c* would be ranked higher than alternative *a* by two out of three voters. (Larger voters' paradoxes can be constructed, in which the ratio of voters favouring one of a pair of alternative to those disfavouring it approaches unity.) So, rankings of alternatives arrived at by the method of majority decision may be intransitive, despite the transitivity of rankings of alternatives by individual voters.

Arrow generalized this problem. He showed it arises not *only* for the method of majority decision, but that the possibility of intransitivity, of "collective irrationality", revealed by the voters' paradox exists for *any* method of resolving conflicts between people's preferences, or social welfare function, that meets his conditions. And these conditions he, and many others, regard as fundamental and minimal conditions of rationality. That is, there is no function from individual orderings of alternatives to a social ordering that meets the following conditions (which are the versions of the conditions familiarized by Sen):[5]

> *P (Weak Pareto Principle)*: For any alternatives $x$ and $y$, if all individuals prefer $x$ to $y$ then society prefers $x$ to $y$.
>
> *D (Non-Dictatorship)*: There is no individual such that, for every set of individual orderings, for all alternatives $x$ and $y$, if that individual prefers $x$ to $y$ then society prefers $x$ to $y$.
>
> *U (Unrestricted Domain)*: For any set of alternatives and any set of individuals, the domain of the social welfare function includes all orderings of alternatives by individuals.
>
> *I (Independence of Irrelevant Alternatives)*: For any alternatives $x$ and $y$, if the preferences of all individuals as between $x$ and $y$ remain the same, then the preference of society as between $x$ and $y$ remains the same; that is, the preferences of society as between $x$ and $y$ depend only on the preferences of individuals as between $x$ and $y$.

There is no method of aggregating transitive individual preferences that meets these conditions and that guarantees transitive social preferences. Arrow's proof works by showing that a dictator will emerge from any method of aggregation that meets conditions $P$, $U$, and $I$. Arrow interprets his result to mean that "the doctrine of voters' sovereignty is incompatible with that of collective rationality".[6] Whether the conditions Arrow imposes are really appropriate, and thus what the significance of his result is for liberal democratic theory, are controversial questions. Particularly controversial is condition I, in light of its effect when combined with other conditions of ruling out many methods of arriving at interpersonal comparisons of utility.[7]

However, I shall approach the problem of many-person conflict by way of the problem of conflict for one person. In this chapter I shall not consider the appropriateness of Arrow's conditions or the significance of his result as Arrow originally interpreted it for liberal democracy, but rather the appropriateness of placing conditions analogous to Arrow's on deliberation and the significance of May's reinterpretation of Arrow's result for coherence accounts. (In Chapter 15 section 3, however, I shall try to show how the considerations of this chapter apply to the theory of liberal democracy.) So, for present purposes, consider again the earlier formulation of the doctor's problem as a problem of deliberation for one person with conflicting values. Perhaps the doctor considers a method of deliberation analogous to the method of majority decision, which would tell him just to add up the numbers of criteria that favour each alternative and select the one that's favoured by a majority of criteria. Again, however, this method recommends $a$ over $b$, $b$ over $c$, and $c$ over $a$. May in turn suggests that this possibility of deliberative irrationality can be generalized: intransitive all-things-considered recommendations may be generated by any method of deliberation that meets conditions analogous to Arrow's, with criteria replacing individuals in the formulation of the conditions.

We may regard the majority-of-criteria method of deliberation as crude and unappealing, so we may not be alarmed when it turns out to be inadequate. But the generalized claim, that there's no function from orderings of alternatives by specific criteria to an all-things-considered ordering that meets certain conditions, may indeed be alarming. Just how alarming depends on how fundamental and important these conditions are to the kind of theories or coherence functions that deliberators seek. According to coherence accounts, what ought to be done is some function of the various specific reasons that apply to the alternatives in question; deliberation involves a process of constructing hypotheses about the content of the function. If May's reinterpretation of Arrow's framework accurately represents the constraints on a deliberator who seeks coherence in the face of conflicting reasons, then there is no question but that the sought-after coherence functions do not exist. Conversely, if coherence functions do exist, then *at least one* of the conditions analogous to the conditions that produce Arrow's result does not represent a constraint faced by a deliberator seeking coherence; in order to vindicate a coherence account, we have to show that one of the conditions fails. Which one, however, is not obvious. Thus we must scrutinize the conditions that give rise to May's claim.

Several words of caution: First, May works with variations of Arrow's original conditions, rather than with the conditions $P$, $D$, $U$, and $I$ made familiar by Amartya Sen, whose analogues I shall consider. However, the essential point of May's paper is to suggest that Arrow's result may be interpreted to apply to conflicting criteria as well as to individuals with conflicting preferences, rather than a technical point about the proof of the result in its new application. The semantic alteration does not affect syntactic relations among the conditions in either the original set or the now familiar set. Moreover, the crucial critiques of unrestricted domain and independence apply equally to May's versions of the conditions.

Next, it may be that May never intended his suggestion to be applied to criteria that have the properties of values invoked in the discussion below, in particular, that of supervenience. In so applying it I am not attempting to interpret or criticize May, but only to follow out a line of thought that his suggestion brings to light, whether he intended it to or not. The line of thought is interesting in its own right, since if the application can be made a familiar kind of appeal to coherence in ethics may be undermined.

Finally, since Arrow proved his theorem, many other impossibility results have been obtained. I will consider the analogues of three sets of conditions that produce impossibility results for social welfare functions; these results seem, for reasons that will emerge, especially threatening to coherence accounts. (Of course, I don't claim that there is no threat from any other impossibility result; there may well be threats I haven't noticed.) For each set of analogous conditions, if the conditions in it are indeed constraints on rational deliberation, then non-dictatorial coherence functions don't exist; if not, we must conclude that, despite their attractions, non-lexicographic pluralistic theories, which recognize conflicting values and give priority to different values in different circumstances rather than simply arranging them in a rigid hierarchy, cannot be coherent. The scope of this conclusion, if it were warranted, would be disturbing; not even Rawls' theory of justice is thoroughly lexicographic, as the priority of liberty only sets in after society reaches a certain stage of development.[8]

## 3. The Analogues of Conditions *P* and *D*

The first set of conditions to look at is the set of conditions analogous to Arrrow's but with criteria playing the role of individuals, where the rankings of alternatives by criteria are required to be orderings, hence transitive. The conditions in this set are:

*P\* (Dominance)*: For all alternatives $x$ and $y$, if all criteria rank $x$ above $y$, then $x$ ranks above $y$, all things considered.

*D\* (Non-Dictatorship)*: A coherence function must not give so much weight to one criterion that it outweighs any criterion that conflicts with it under any circumstances; that is, it must not be the case that there is one criterion such that any one alternative's superiority over any other according to this criterion would always result in its superiority all things considered, regardless of how other criteria might rank those alternatives.

*U\* (Unrestricted Domain)*: For any set of alternatives and any set of criteria, the domain of the coherence function includes all orderings of alternatives by criteria.

*I\* (Independence of Irrelevant Alternatives)*: For all alternatives $x$ and $y$, if the rankings of $x$ and $y$ by all criteria remain the same, then the ranking of $x$ and $y$ all things considered remains the same; that is, a deliberator's ranking of a pair of alternatives all things considered depends only on the ranking of those alternatives by all relevant criteria, and not on the rankings of other alternatives.

Consider first $P^*$, the analogue of the weak Pareto principle. $P^*$ just amounts to a principle of dominance, which isn't very controversial (at least not in this kind of context). Against the weak Pareto principle itself well-known objections have been raised by Amartya Sen. His demonstration of the impossibility of Paretian liberalism points up that implicit in the Pareto principle is a certain element of *welfarism*, or neutrality with respect to non-welfare information: at least when all welfare indicators, all individual preferences, favour one alternative over another, then their unanimous recommendation must be followed and non-welfare information such as that adduced by the liberal can't affect their all-things-considered ranking. We might wonder whether Sen's objections to the exclusion of non-welfare information in the face of unanimous welfare indicators carry over in any way to the analogue of the weak Pareto principle, $P^*$? But it seems not. Sen writes:

> . . . it is perhaps worth remarking that the criticism of the Pareto principle under discussion does not dispute the use of 'dominance' as a way of sepa-

rating out non-controversial choices, which do not involve conflicting considerations, from choices that do. If utility were accepted to be the only basis
of moral claim, then the Pareto principle would indeed reflect 'dominance'
of moral claims, and would be—accordingly—quite noncontroversial. The
difficulty, however, arises from accepting other sources of moral claim....
The Pareto principle (i) lists a set of virtues, and (ii) uses dominance of
virtues as the criterion. What is in dispute here is the former, not the latter.[9]

The analogue of the weak Pareto principle, $P^*$, involves no presumption in
favour of reasons of some particular kind, such as reasons of welfare. It merely
says that if all the applicable criteria, whatever they may be, favour one
alternative over another, then their unanimous recommendation must be
followed, and the non-criterial characteristics of the alternatives cannot affect
their all-things-considered ranking. This is an unobjectionable condition to
place on coherence functions. Thus, condition $P^*$ is in force.

What of the analogue of the non-dictatorship condition, $D^*$? May suggests
that if one criterion were to dictate, there would be no deliberative problem.[10]
If one criterion were to outweigh all others in all circumstances, the sought-
after function would be obvious; all our resolutions of past and hypothetical
cases, which the theory is supposed to account for in terms of the relationships
among the relevant criteria, would reflect its dictatorial status. In assuming
that there *is* a deliberative problem we're assuming that no one of the criteria,
the relationships among which are our subject matter, does dictate.

But this argument for $D^*$ is too swift. Someone might object as follows:
The best theory we can construct may tell us that some of our resolutions of
conflicts have been mistaken; we may be akratic, or we may, more simply,
just be wrong, and later realize it. Why couldn't a theory tell us that all
resolutions of conflicts that don't reflect the dictatorship of a particular criterion have been mistaken? Why couldn't it turn out that the correct resolution
would reflect dictatorship?

A theory could tell us this, but $D^*$ might embody a conception of deliberative theorizing governed by familiar theoretical norms according to which
it couldn't be the best possible theory if it did. By telling us that all such
resolutions have been mistakes, a theory that establishes the dictatorship of
a particular criterion achieves simplicity, which is admittedly a theoretical
virtue, but at too great a price in terms of the data the theory is supposed to
account for. We saw in Chapter 8 that attributions of *akrasia* must be the
exception, not the rule, if they are not to undermine the very attribution of
a flouted all-things-considered judgment that they essentially involve. And in
general, charity favours not attributing too many mistakes; if we do, we
undermine the basis for our theorizing. We'll always do better to look for a
theory that doesn't regard so much of the data as flawed as a theory establishing dictatorship does. (We might also impose $D^*$ because we are interested
in whether non-dictatorial theories that meet our other conditions are possible; if they are not, it is worth knowing.)[11]

Note that $D^*$ doesn't rule out utilitarian or other monistic theories. Sophisticated forms of utilitarianism appeal to rules, motives, and/or a separation

of levels in a way that gives utility a role to play within a theory, rather than merely asserting its domination in all conflicts. Such forms of utilitarianism don't simply overrule the claims of justice, for example, but try to account for them within a structured utilitarian theory—at least to a degree that theoretically justifies overriding residual claims that can't be so accommodated. In this sense, a theory that is monistic may still recognize a plurality of values. On a coherence account, utilitarianism is subject, regardless of its monistic character, to the same standards *qua* theory as non-monistic theories; if a form of utilitarianism is to succeed, it has to dominate other theories on theoretical grounds. And nothing in $D^*$ rules out the possibility that some form of utilitarianism may dominate as a theory. We must distinguish the domination of a particular theory about values over others on theoretical grounds from the dictatorial status of a particular value, which may be asserted by a theory about values. $D^*$ merely reflects the view that any theory that did thus assert the dictatorial status of a particular value, without qualification to take account of conflicting values, would be so weak on theoretical grounds as to be out of the running; but utilitarianism doesn't have to be such a theory.

There's a related possible confusion it's important to avoid in thinking about $D^*$. If a hypothesis about the content of a coherence function is successful in accounting for settled cases of conflict, then it provides theoretical justification for using that coherence function to resolve cases at issue. But a coherence function's success and the justification it provides for certain resolutions of conflicts shouldn't be confused with the dictatorship of one of the values the theory is about. If this confusion is made, $D^*$ alone would rule out the possibility of a coherence function, as any successful coherence function could immediately be reinterpreted as a dictatorial argument of a simpler function and thus debarred. To do this would be immediately to reinterpret any particular successful theory about values as itself embodying a particular value, and a dictatorial one to boot (not to mention gimmicky and gerrymandered—see Chapter 13 section 5, on artificial unity). The analogous confusion for social welfare functions doesn't arise because functions of individuals' preferences have no tendency to materialize into individuals whose dictatorial status would be a matter of concern. We can admit that there is interplay between various specific reasons and our theorizing about them, so that the distinction between practical and theoretical reasons isn't absolute, and may admit of differences of degree. But this interplay doesn't render values so obligingly nascent as to obliterate the distinction between practical and theoretical reasons or to undermine the role of specific reason-giving practices in providing substantive constraints on eligibility. A particular hypothesis about the relationships among practical reasons may gradually come to have the discrete character and force of a practical reason itself, but this result isn't an instant consequence of theorizing, and it may require conceptual, perceptual, and phenomenological development.

We may still be worried that this attempted defense of $D^*$ is not enough to justify ruling out certain side-constraint theories, which assert that whenever a given reason applies it trumps other conflicting reasons. However, there is something more fundamentally worrying about $D^*$; these doubts are in effect pre-empted by the fact that dictatorship is defined so that a given dictatorial individual or criterion must dictate over the whole unrestricted domain of sets of orderings. Thus, $D^*$ is implicated in the critique of $U^*$ that follows. $D^*$'s ultimate intelligibility is brought into question by the fact that, as I shall argue in the next section, $U^*$ cannot be given a plausible interpretation. So, we need now to leave off trying to defend $D^*$ and instead to consider $U^*$.

## 4. The Analogues of Conditions $U$ and $I$

The analogues of conditions $U$ and $I$ must be considered together, because of the way in which the logical structures of the two conditions interact. In order to understand this interaction one must realize that in social choice theory these conditions function to involve us in counterfactual suppositions. Condition $U$ requires the social welfare function to apply not just to individuals' actual preference orderings and changes of mind, but to all conceptually possible orderings of alternatives by individuals. The domain of the social welfare function extends over counterfactual states of affairs that are specifically *counterpreferential*; the function is supposed to apply satisfactorily whatever the content of preferences—within the bounds of individual consistency, of course—or, as it's usually put, for all possible profiles of preferences. Condition I applies to this unrestricted domain; as Amartya Sen has explained, much of its power derives from its application across such a domain.[12] Take any possible profile of preferences and the social ordering for that profile; then condition $I$ requires the social welfare function to yield social orderings for other possible preference profiles such that, concerning any two alternatives, if the preferences of all individuals between those two alternatives were to remain the same as in the original profile, then social preference between those two would remain the same as well. That is, the social ordering of the *given* pair of alternatives cannot vary with counterpreferential suppositions about *other* alternatives, so long as individuals' preferences about the given pair remain constant across profiles.

In Chapter 15 I shall discuss the way in which these conditions on social choice embody non-cognitivist assumptions and how they fare under an alternative, cognitivist interpretation of democratic social choice. However, it is first necessary to consider how analogues of these conditions should be interpreted in application to the situation of an individual deliberator with conflicting values. In particular, we must consider what the analogous counterfactual structure is and whether it is acceptable.

Given that conflicting criteria replace individuals with conflicting preferences in the deliberative analogue of the social choice problem, what states of affairs will be analogous to the counterpreferential states of affairs condition $U$ includes in the domain of the social welfare function? Should $U^*$ be interpreted as requiring a deliberator to seek a coherence function that applies across counterfactual suppositions that are specifically *counterevaluative* (or, to use the more general term, *countercriterial*)? This interpretation of $U^*$ is perhaps the most natural analogue, considered from a purely logical point of view, of the normal counterfactual interpretation of condition $U$. Unfortunately, considered from any point of view other than the purely logical, $U^*$ thus interpreted is extremely unattractive as a condition on deliberation; moreover, there is an immediate obstacle to anything other than the counterevaluative interpretation of $U^*$.

We need not take a position on the issue of reducibility, about whether it is conceptually possible that our values have had other content than they in fact have, in order to see what is wrong with the counterevaluative interpretation of $U^*$. The point is that such counterevaluative conceptual possibilities, even if we admit them, are simply irrelevant to our efforts to find the best theory about our values as they are. Perhaps our values might, as a matter of pure logic, have ordered the alternatives differently, but in deliberation we make essential use of what our values actually tell us about various actual and hypothetical cases. Consideration of what our values actually tell us about merely counter*factual* suppositions certainly does provide relevant data for deliberative theorizing, as when we appeal to hypothetical cases; but consideration of counter*evaluative* suppositions does not. Parallel points apply when legal deliberation is in question and the relevant criteria are legal precedents and principles.

The world might have been other than it is in many ways. We expect a scientific theory to tell us what to believe given the data we have about the way the world is; but we do not also expect it to tell us what we ought to have believed if the world had been different in certain significant respects. If the world had been different in certain ways, our theories about it might well have differed as a result. We do not hold it against a scientific theory or against scientific methodology that under some counterfactual assumptions theories might be supported that are inconsistent with the theory that is in fact supported. Similarly, it is to misconstrue the role of the kind of ethical theory sought in deliberation to expect it to tell us what we ought to have done if our values had been other than what they are; if they had been, again, we might well have needed a different, inconsistent, theory.

Perhaps we could find an alternative interpretation of $U^*$ that is not thus at odds with deliberative practice, that avoids the above criticism of $U^*$ by requiring the coherence function to apply to merely counterfactual but not counterevaluative possibilities. But I think not, for there is an immediate obstacle to this project, in the form of a version of the conceptual requirement of the supervenience of values. *Supervenience* requires that, in all conceptually possible worlds, if two alternatives differ in some evaluative characteristic, then they differ in some non-evaluative characteristic as well. If someone says two alternatives are exactly alike except that one is worthy of praise in some particular respect and the other worthy of blame, then he's just confused, he hasn't really understood what he's saying, he's making a conceptual mistake rather than having a substantive disagreement with us. By differentiating between the two alternatives at the evaluative level he's already committed, as a conceptual matter, to agreeing that there must be some non-evaluative difference between them. Now $U^*$ says that the domain of the coherence function includes all orderings of alternatives by criteria. A proof of the emergence of a dictatorial criterion parallel to Arrow's would depend on $U^*$ to guarantee the ability to hold the set of alternatives and the set of criteria constant and vary the orderings of the former by the latter. If we interpret this variation, not as taking us into exotic conceptually possible counterevaluative worlds (the existence of which is asserted by a conceptual irreducibility doctrine and is not denied by a conceptual supervenience doctrine but is, as explained above, irrelevant to deliberative theorizing), but rather as remaining within the merely counterfactual worlds in which our actual values apply, then this variation is just what the doctrine of the supervenience of the evaluative disallows. (If we had colour characteristics instead of evaluative characteristics and shape characteristics instead of non-evaluative characteristics, then such variation would be possible, since colours do not, as a conceptual matter at least, supervene on shapes, in the way that evaluative characteristics supervene on non-evaluative characteristics.) On this interpretation $U^*$ is incompatible with what is widely held to be a minimal conceptual requirement of consistency on the use of evaluative terms. We can shift from one evaluative criterion to another, but a given evaluative criterion cannot vary independently of non-evaluative characteristics.

Thus, on neither interpretation is $U^*$ a reasonable condition to impose on coherence fucntions that take rankings generated by values as arguments and that represent the theories sought in deliberation. Related points may be made about condition $I^*$, which will lead us to consider an alternative route to impossibility results for coherence functions by reference to the literature on single-profile social welfare functions.

Condition $I^*$ has two aspects,[13] only one of which is essential to an impossibility result.

First, the *ordinalist aspect*, which restricts the *quality* of information provided by a criterion about any pair of alternatives—the information has to be ordinal information, merely about how the alternatives are ordered with respect to the criterion, *not* about *how much* better one is than the other. If we want to make use of cardinal information about the degree to which the alternatives satisfy a criterion, we may object to the ordinalist aspect of $I^*$. However, impossibility results are not avoided when $I^*$ is reformulated to allow for cardinal information. Cardinality for each criterion does not give us comparability between criteria; cardinal information tells us to what degree each criterion favours one alternative over another, but that in itself doesn't amount to weighing the different criteria against each other, any more than expected utility functions are automatically interpersonally comparable in virtue of their cardinality. Weighing the conflicting criteria isn't the job of the criteria themselves but is the work the coherence function has to do, and is what impossibility results threaten.[14]

The second aspect is the *irrelevant alternative aspect* proper. This is crucial in precipitating the impossibility result, whether in conjunction with ordinal or cardinal information. It simply says that the ranking of two alternatives all things considered is determined solely by admissible criterial information about those alternatives, and no others; it restricts the *quantity*, but not the quality of admissible information—we can decide to admit either cardinal or only ordinal information, but it has to be only about those two alternatives and no others. This restriction seems difficult to resist: if all admissible criterial information that does concern a pair of alternatives has been taken into account, how could it be helpful to consider criterial information about other alternatives?[15]

But consider the following argument to the effect that a coherence account does require us to resist this restriction. In trying to determine what consistent set of relationships may obtain among our various values—that is, what coherence amounts to—we normally appeal to settled and hypothetical cases other than those at issue. This claim is illustrated by the description of deliberation in the preceding chapter. It's only by theorizing about settled and hypothetical cases that we can give any particular content to a coherence function; a theory has to be *about* something. We analyze these cases in order to determine the relationships among the relevant values, or doctrines and precedents, in various circumstances. (Indeed, appeal to preferences about hypothetical alternatives is also an essential feature of multi-attribute decision theory, for related reasons.) What the relevant values are may ultimately itself be a matter for theorizing, but a starting point is provided by shared specific reason-giving practices and the methodology of charity.[16] We can imagine that we might find the irrelevant alternatives, those not at issue, ranked otherwise by the relevant values than they are in fact. If we were to, it seems that our theory of the relationships among those values and the weights we assign to them under various circumstances might differ as a result, so that our all-things-considered evaluations of the alternatives at issue might vary with the rankings of irrelevant alternatives. But if this were so, then $I^*$ would be violated by a characteristic and normal feature of deliberation, so it couldn't represent a reasonable constraint on deliberation.

However, there are at least two difficulties with this argument against $I^*$, which require us to elaborate and qualify it. Consider exactly what needs to be the case in order for $I^*$ to be violated. There must be a pair of alternatives $a$ and $b$ such that the rankings of $a$ and $b$ by all criteria stay constant while nevertheless the all-things-considered ranking of $a$ and $b$ to which a given coherence function takes us varies, presumably with the criterial rankings of other, 'irrelevant' alternatives.

The first difficulty for the argument against $I^*$ is this. Suppose we were to grant the existence of a pair of alternatives $a$ and $b$ whose criterial rankings stay constant while their all-things-considered ranking varies with counter-criterial variation in the criterial rankings of other alternatives. Even so, the former variation would reflect different hypotheses about the content of a coherence function, hence different functions. But for our purposes $I^*$ must be taken to constrain applications of any given coherence function, not on the process of arriving at that function to begin with; that is, it constrains relations between input and output of one function, not relations between different functions. Deliberation involves the search for a theory about our values as they actually are, not a methodology, a theory about theories. It proceeds by reference to hypothetical cases that may be counterfactual, but not specifically counterevaluative; the function of the hypothetical cases is to reveal more about the values we actually have, not to introduce information about other possible values. In the context of ethical theory, for example, a coherence function represents a substantive theory that takes the relations between given values as its subject matter. If our values had been other than they are or had had different content, we might well have needed a different theory to account for the relationships among them. The parallel point holds about actual legal doctrines and practices and the use of hypothetical cases in legal theory.

$I^*$ is indeed objectionable in application to a methodology as opposed to a substantive theory, as it would require different substantive theories, theories about sets of different conceptually possible values, to rank two alternatives in the same way if the corresponding values in each set rank them the same way. That this is implausible can be seen by considering the way it would apply to two different persons with different sets of conceptually possible values. First, there are difficulties about what the correspondence of values across sets of different conceptually possible values could consist of, or how it could be nonarbitrarily determined. If this correspondence is arbitrarily determined, then it can be rigged so that Condition $I^*$ is satisfied just when the ulterior motives of the theorist dictate. But even if these difficulties could be overcome, the requirement would mean that a value in one theory, or for one person, could not have more weight than its corresponding value in another theory, or for another person, for reasons of coherence *per se*—that is, as a result of its relationships to other values and its role in the theory, or the person's conception of himself, as a whole, as revealed by consideration of alternatives other than the two at issue to which the values also apply. Theories about different values are in part differentiated by just such differences of structure and weight, which are in turn called for by differences in the values the theories are about. The contemplated restriction would indeed frustrate the basic purpose of theorizing about values by reference to hypothetical cases, namely, to arrive at the most coherent possible account of the relationships among those values in particular.

Suppose, then, that $I^*$ is not put forward as a condition on methodologies but a condition on substantive theories. Then the second problem for the argument that I gave four paragraphs back is that, when the criteria involved are values, the supervenience of evaluative on non-evaluative characteristics rules out countercriterial variation, i.e., prevents the criterial rankings of any given set of alternatives from varying at all. (This point is of course closely related to the use of the requirement of supervenience above to block a noncounterevaluative interpretation of $U^*$.) Supervenience says that, as a matter of conceptual necessity, if two alternatives differ in some evaluative characteristic, then they differ in some non-evaluative characteristic as well. The ranking by a given value of a given set of alternatives may not be determined as a conceptual matter, so that counterevaluative suppositions to the effect that the value might have had some other content are not self-contradictory (though, as we've seen, such suppositions are irrelevant to ethical theorizing). But what is determined as a matter of logic is that once that ranking is established for any conceptually possible value, it can't vary (in the way that colour can vary independently of shape). Of course, two different values may conflict about alternatives with given non-evaluative characteristics; if they could not there would be no deliberative problem. But a given value can't 'change its mind' about given alternatives. If it seems to, it must be the case either that value has altered (i.e., there are two different values involved), or that the non-evaluative description of the alternatives, hence the alternatives themselves, have altered; alternatives with different characteristics are different alternatives.[17] Thus, the evaluative rankings of any given pair of "irrelevant" alternatives can't vary. *Ex hypothesi*, the evaluative rankings of the alternatives at issue don't vary, when condition $I^*$ is at issue. But if the evaluative rankings of all alternatives must stay constant, then the all-things-considered ranking of the alternatives at issue can't vary either, as there is nothing for it to vary with. (Of course we can consider different or larger sets of evaluative criteria, but we are now considering $I^*$ applied to a given set of criteria, rather than across sets of different conceptually possible criteria.) That is, if all input to the coherence function is held constant, then its output must be constant as well. As a result, condition $I^*$ can't be violated.[18]

Recall that the impossibility result is preserved if $I^*$ is reformulated to allow for cardinal information with respect to each value. But supervenience guarantees $I^*$ in this guise as well, because it holds cardinal evaluative information about a given set of alternatives constant no less than ordinal evaluative information about a given set of alternatives. If cardinal evaluative information changes, then either the evaluative criterion has changed or the non-evaluative characteristics of the alternatives have changed. The same argument applies whether the evaluative information is ordinal or cardinal. So, supervenience makes it conceptually impossible to violate $I^*$.

However, it's clear that the sense in which $I^*$ is met is trivial; it is met because, if we avoid the counterevaluative interpretations of $U^*$ and $I^*$, then supervenience renders $I^*$ empty at the same time as invalidating any other interpretation of $U^*$. And in fact an analogous charge of triviality is found in the social choice literature dealing with impossibility results for Bergson-Samuelson social welfare functions. The social welfare functions Arrow was concerned with are supposed to apply to whatever preferences people might have (again, within the bounds of individual consistency); one is supposed to be able to go on applying the same social welfare function under various counterpreferential suppositions. But Bergson-Samuelson social welfare functions, by contrast, apply to any one profile of preference orderings, but only one; once the profile is determined, counterpreferential suppositions are not considered. The Bergson-Samuelson approach to social welfare that holds individual preferences constant, while still not imposing any restrictions on their content (again, other than individual consistency constraints), is known as the *single-profile* approach, in contrast to Arrow's *multiple-profile* approach. As Paul Samuelson explains, "here we are in the domain of given individuals' tastes and values and not in the wider and different Arrow domain of all that their tastes and values might be . . . ." "[O]ne and only one of the . . . possible patterns of individual orderings is needed. It could be *any* one, but it is only one." Just as an ethical theory is not concerned with counterevaluative possibilities, but only with the actual content of values, so the Bergson-Samuelson social welfare function can be interpreted not to be concerned with counterpreferential possibilities, but only with the actual content of preferences. Thus, in light of our critique above of the counterevaluative interpretations of $U^*$ and $I^*$, perhaps the single-profile approach rather than the multiple-profile approach provides the correct analogy to deliberation involving values. It shouldn't come as a surprise that Samuelson claims that condition $I$ is automatically met by Bergson-Samuelson social welfare functions, that it is built in from the beginning.[19]

The charge of triviality is made by Sen, against the sense in which condition $I$ is met by Bergson-Samuelson social welfare functions. Sen suggests that condition $I$ is essentially an inter-profile (or what I've been calling counterpreferential) constraint, and that it has to be reformulated in a way that's appropriate for the single-profile approach if we're to be able properly to address the question whether impossibilities arise for Bergson-Samuelson functions.[20] If this is right, and if a coherence function cannot properly be required to apply counterevaluatively, then the analogous point can be made for coherence functions: we need a reformulation of condition $I^*$ appropriate to the noncounterevaluative approach if we're properly to address the question whether impossibility results obtain for coherence functions.

The social choice literature contains two types of suggestion about how to reformulate condition $I$ for the single-profile approach. The first is made by Robert Parks, and by Murray Kemp and Yew-Kwang Ng, and the second is made by Kevin Roberts. These two types of suggestion contribute to the second and third sets of conditions leading to impossibility results whose analogues I shall be concerned with. The question now becomes: do the analogues of conditions needed for single-profile impossibility results represent reasonable constraints on deliberation?

Before going further, however, it may be helpful to summarize the discussion of this section. Against the counterevaluative interpretation of $U^*$ I have argued that we do not in fact, nor should we, expect the kind of theory sought in deliberation to apply counterevaluatively; such a theory is essentially a substantive theory about the values we actually have and their relationships to one another. These relationships may well be revealed by the way the values apply to alternatives other than those at issue, but this theoretical sensitivity would not violate $I^*$ applied to a particular substantive theory about the values we actually have. It may violate $I^*$ applied instead across substantive theories, to a methodology, but this counts against the reasonableness of $I^*$, since the method of considering hypothetical alternatives in order to understand the relationships among the values that apply to the actual alternatives is essential to deliberation. Thus, the character of deliberation as a search for a substantive theory about the relationships among our actual values by consideration of how they would apply to alternatives other than those at issue is incompatible with the counterevaluative interpretations of $U^*$ and $I^*$. The prospects for a noncounterevaluative interpretation of $U^*$ are blocked by the requirement of supervenience, which at the same time renders $I^*$, noncounterevaluatively interpreted, trivial. These difficulties suggested that we might do better to consider conditions appropriate to the single-profile (or, in effect, the noncounterpreferential) approach to social choice; perhaps the single-profile conditions that give rise to impossibility results will have analogues which are not subject to the kind of difficulties we found for counterevaluative $U^*$ and $I^*$, and which still threaten coherence functions.

## 5. The Analogue of Single-profile Neutrality

Parks, and Kemp and Ng, have obtained single-profile impossibility results that depend on a strong reformulation of condition $I$, which amounts to the outright assumption of neutrality with respect to non-welfare information, as follows.

   *N (Neutrality with respect to Non-Welfare Information):* For any alternatives $w$, $x$, $y$, and $z$, if the preferences of all individuals are same as between $w$ and $z$ as they are as between $x$ and $y$, then the preference of society as between $w$ and $z$ must be the same as its preference as between $x$ and $y$.[21]

   The effect of a condition of neutrality is to deprive us of information; if it's neutrality with respect to non-welfare information, as in the social choice context, then it deprives us of all but welfare information, deriving from individual preferences, about the alternatives. In the deliberative context, neutrality with respect to non-criterial information deprives us of all but criterial information about the alternatives. The deliberative analogue of $N$ is $N^*$, as follows.

   *N\* (Neutrality with respect to Non-Criterial Information):* For any alternatives $w$, $x$, $y$, and $z$, if all criteria rank $w$ and $z$ in the same way they rank $x$ and $y$, then $w$ and $z$ must be ranked in the same way, all things considered, as $x$ and $y$.

   How does $N^*$ differ from $I^*$? In order for a neutrality condition to be other than trivially satisfied it is not necessary for the ranking of given alternatives by any individual or any criterion to vary, as the alternatives themselves and thus their characteristics are allowed to vary; the characteristics of $w$ and $z$ may differ from the characteristics of $x$ and $y$ even though all individuals, or criteria, treat $w$ and $z$ in the same way as $x$ and $y$. Neutrality with respect to all but information of the favoured kind requires that such different pairs of alternatives be treated the same way in the final ranking. The difference in logical form that gives the neutrality conditions bite where the independence conditions had none is as follows (where "$xR_i^1y$" means that in situation 1, person or criterion $i$ ranks $x$ at least as high as $y$):

*Independence:*    $\forall x \, \forall y \, (\forall i \, [(xR_i^1y \leftrightarrow xR_i^2y)$
$$\& \; (yR_i^1x \leftrightarrow yR_i^2x)]$$
$$\rightarrow (xR^1y \leftrightarrow xR^2y) \,)$$

*Neutrality:*    $\forall w \, \forall x \, \forall y \, \forall z \, (\forall i \, [(xR_iy \leftrightarrow wR_iz)$
$$\& \; (yR_ix \leftrightarrow zR_iw)]$$
$$\rightarrow (xRy \leftrightarrow wRz) \,)$$

One of the impressive things about Arrow's theorem is that from his seemingly minimal conditions he proves a surprisingly strong result. Much of the labour in his proof of the emergence of a dictator is spent on deriving elements of neutrality from conditions $U$, $P$, and $I$, which are independently attractive as conditions on a social welfare function. But if neutrality is simply assumed from the beginning, it is not so surprising that dictatorship and an impossibility result follow.[22] Indeed, the close relationship between neutrality and dictatorship may in effect be intuitively familiar, at least to those familiar with adjudication. It's recognized among lawyers that there is a tension between the doctrine of *stare decisis* and the requirement that distinctions between cases be "reasoned". Greater resistance to overruling earlier decisions results in greater tolerance of rather more arbitrary distinctions between cases, i.e., greater tolerance of non-neutrality—as, in the past, in the House of Lords.[23] I defended the non-dictatorship condition on *stare decisis* grounds, in effect, that is, by saying we should avoid regarding too many of our earlier decisions as mistaken. The result, at least when certain other requisite conditions are implicitly satisfied, is that the possibility of non-neutrality is admitted. Recall also the way in which we may attribute *akrasia*—a kind of mistake—rather than violate the presumption against drawing arbitrary distinctions.

The very closeness of the relation between conditions $D$ and $N$ suggests an objection to condition $N$. We might think that single-profile impossibility results that just help themselves to neutrality from the beginning are less disturbing than Arrow's result: it's only collectively that the individually attractive conditions $U$, $P$, and $I$ impose the informational parsimony that condition $N$ imposes explicitly. But just because it operates explicitly to deprive us of information, neutrality is immediately unattractive as a canonical constraint on a social welfare function.[24] Analogous thoughts about $N^*$ require us to look carefully at its merits as a condition on reasonable deliberation.

The immediate effect of $N^*$ is to rule out the use of non-criterial information, parallel to the effect of $N$ in ruling out the use of non-welfare information. It says that so long as, for each relevant criteria, the information that each criterion gives us about one pair of alternatives is the same as the information it gives us about another, then the resolution of conflict between criteria has to be the same for both. One criterion cannot outweigh the other for alternatives with certain non-criterial characteristics while the second outweighs the first for alternatives with different non-criterial characteristics;

non-criterial information cannot be invoked in tailoring a theory about the relationships among the various criteria. The theory must weigh the criteria against one another without depending on any non-criterial information about the alternatives.

Thus, an objection to $N^*$ might be that it requires theories about the relationships among values to be gratuitously crude. There's no doubt that we must recognize substantive constraints on eligible distinctions and a presumption against drawing arbitrary lines, but $N^*$ goes further than this. Eligibility is a matter of degree, and the presumption may be rebutted in certain cases. We might sometimes want to distinguish different types of circumstance in describing these relationships without being forced to count such circumstances as having independent reason-giving force. $N^*$ would deprive us of this theoretical flexibility. I shall develop and defend this objection to $N^*$ by means of three counter-objections.

Consider the way non-criterial information is used in this case: The question before a judge is whether or not to admit evidence of two of a defendant's prior felony convictions, both over ten years old, in order to help the jury evaluate the defendant's credibility. A reason to admit the evidence is simply that the evidence is relevant, so it's generally admissible under the rules of evidence. A reason not to admit it is that there's a danger of prejudice to the defendant if the jury comes to see him as a hardened criminal and so not to care much about the possibility of mistakenly convicting him of the crime he is being tried for. The rules of evidence require that evidence be excluded when its potential for prejudice outweighs its probative value. The balancing of these two reasons against one another is achieved by a general rule that excludes evidence of prior convictions that are more than ten years old on grounds that their potential for prejudice is likely to outweigh their probative value. However, the judge might reason as follows: By contrast to the cases for which the general rule was developed, the defendant in this case is being tried for the crime of being a convicted felon in possession of firearms. In these circumstances, "the prejudicial impact of proof of prior convictions is considerably lessened because the jury already knows the defendant had a record. At the same time the value of the evidence to the jury in determining the credibility of the defendant as a witness is somewhat enhanced because a man with a more extensive record is much more likely to know it is unlawful to possess weapons and to guard against the danger". In fact these are the words of a dissenting judge in the 1978 case *U.S. v Sims*. He is appealing to information about the distinctive circumstances of the case to adjust the relative weights of the reasons in play, but these circumstances do not count *per se* as a reason for or against admitting the evidence; rather, they affect the relationship between the reasons.[25] Thus the objection to $N^*$ is that to rule out the appeal to such information would be to reduce drastically and arbitrarily the possibility of finesse in our account of such relationships.

However, this objection is open to a counter-objection, namely, that the objection overlooks a third possibility. Such appeals to apparently non-reason-giving circumstances should not be interpreted *either* as invoking independent reasons *or* as contributing to a theory about the relationships among unqualified reasons. Rather, they should be interpreted as qualifying and refining the reasons we recognize in the first place. For example, Sidgwick writes:

> ... it appears that a clear *consensus* can only be claimed for the principle that a promise, express or tacit, is binding, if a number of conditions are fulfilled: viz. if the promisor has a clear belief as to the sense in which it was understood by the promisee, and if the latter is still in a position to grant release from it, but unwilling to do so, if it was not obtained by force or fraud, if it does not conflict with definite prior obligations, if we do not believe that its fulfilment will be harmful to the promisee, or will inflict a disproportionate sacrifice on the promiser, and if circumstances have not materially changed since it was made. If any of these conditions fails, the *consensus* seems to become evanescent, and the common moral perceptions of thoughtful persons fall into obscurity and disagreement.[26]

Perhaps some of the circumstances Sidgwick mentions figure in essential qualifications of any obligation to keep promises; we appeal to such circumstances in the course of theorizing about the value of keeping promises and refining our view of it.

In response to this first counter-objection we should sharpen the original objection to $N^*$ as follows. We can admit that *some* of our theorizing in effect qualifies or revises our values without being forced to reconstrue *all* our theorizing about values as doing this; the suggested defense of $N^*$ fails to recognize the limits to such qualification and revision. Imagine a case in which the obligation to keep a promise, qualified in the way Sidgwick suggests, comes into conflict with the value of human life. Suppose, for example, that when a promise is made the promisor correctly calculates that keeping it will create an extremely small risk to the life of a third party. After it's made, however, an unlikely event occurs, so that keeping the promise now will create a substantial risk to the life of a third party. In deliberating about such a situation we will consider comparable cases where the two values conflict and there's a settled resolution, and analyze the character of the promises involved and the character of the threat to life involved. In doing so, we're not contributing to an elaborate qualification of the obligation to keep promises or the value of human life or both so that they no longer conflict at all.

This is not a formal claim; it may well be formally possible to reconstrue a successful hypothesis about the content of a coherence function as a single all-purpose highly refined criterion, but this possibility is not to the point. If we do this we immediately have a dictatorial criterion, as I said earlier, but we have not explained how we have arrived at a resolution of the conflict between the values we started with, and this is the task at hand. When the relevant criteria are specific ethical values or legal doctrines or precedents they have discrete and elastic identities, they are not idefinitely malleable; such values provide substantive constraints on the contents of our theories which may not always yield to formal or structural considerations. (Indeed, as we saw in Part I, such substantive constraints are needed if formal constraints are to avoid emptiness.) At some point theorizing about the relationships among such conflicting values ceases to qualify away conflict and takes it as its subject matter. The nature of our values is such that in at least some cases even fully qualified values stand in conflict with one another, so that anything we do will infringe one of them. In these cases we do not decide what to do by transforming our familiar values beyond recognition, or by ignoring them and adopting new ones, but by scrutinizing them, and other cases of conflict where they apply, to discern some coherent set of relationships between them. For any such theory or coherence function, the value of resolving conflicts according to that theory is just as distinct from the values the theory is about as the values are from one another. So the objection to $N^*$, that it would render such theories gratuitously crude, still stands.

But the objection to $N^*$ thus sharpened is in turn open to a second counter-objection, namely, that it misrepresents the considerations that make $N^*$ appropriate, which the first counter-objection appealed to. These considerations need not involve the view that all appeals to non-criterial information serve to qualify away conflict. We may appeal to non-criterial information to determine the extent to which alternatives are supported or discouraged by the relevant criteria, the *intra*-criterial positions of the various alternatives; the criteria can still conflict. But we qualify and revise our criteria so that our use for non-criterial information is reflected in *what the criteria themselves tell us* in various circumstances, as opposed to *the weight we give to what they tell us*. We do not have to go all the way to a single, dictatorial, if highly refined, criterion. That non-criterial information has a role in determining what the criteria tell us about the alternatives does not mean that it has a further role in determining how the criteria weigh against one another in various circumstances. It might be claimed that many assignments of *different* weights to criteria under *different* circumstances could be reconstrued as a *uniform* weighting of criteria plus a *recasting of the criteria to adjust the information they provide in the different circumstances*.[27]

There is also justice in this second counter-objection, but again it goes too far. Many uses of non-criterial information are of the kind it describes, but not all. It would rule out other uses of such information that there is no reason to rule out. Even if the claim about the possibility of reconstrual is correct as a technical matter, the reconstrual may not correctly describe the role of non-criterial information in theories *about given criteria*, in particular, about familiar specific values. It will not always be true that the circumstances affect the information the criteria give us about the alternatives rather than the way we weigh the criteria against one another.

Consider for example a theory about distributive justice. Suppose we're trying to decide how resources should be distributed, and that we take into account conflicting considerations of total welfare, of equality of resources, of equality of welfare, and of responsibility for certain personal traits. As a result of deliberation we arrive at a pluralistic theory that tells us to distribute resources so as to maximize welfare except in two kinds of circumstance: (1) when doing so would leave someone with less than a certain minimum level of resources, below some subsistence level, *or* (2) when doing so would leave a handicapped person with less than a certain minimum level of welfare. A handicapped person is understood to be someone with a characteristic for which he's not responsible that causes him to be brought to a much lower-than-average level of welfare by any given level of resources; if someone cannot walk, for example, he needs more income to reach the same level of overall well-being as most people, because he needs to pay for a wheelchair, etc. In these two kinds of circumstance, when a normal person would be left below a subsistence income or when a handicapped person would be left very badly off, the theory tells us to distribute resources so as to maintain some roughly equal minimum level of resources for everyone and some roughly equal minimum level of welfare for the handicapped.

What is the role in such a theory of the information that a distribution would leave someone at a certain level of resources? It does not tell us that considerations of equality of resources favour it more or less; the distribution may involve more or less *in*equality of resources than some other distribution, which leaves no one at that level. Rather, it tells us that circumstances obtain in which the theory assigns certain relative weights to considerations of total welfare and of equality of resources. Parallel comments apply to the role of the information that a distribution would leave a handicapped person at a certain level of welfare. This information does not tell us that considerations of equality of welfare favour the alternative more or less; again, it may involve more or less *in*equality of welfare than another distribution, which leaves no one at that level. Nor does it tell us that considerations of responsibility favour the alternative more or less. Some talented people are no more responsible for their ability to get to a much higher-than-average level of welfare from a given level of resources than the handicapped are for their handicaps. A distribution, for example, that leaves a handicapped person at a low level might also avoid letting those who are not responsible for their talents to reap and hoard their rewards. The net result might be that it would come closer than any alternative distribution to giving each person just what he deserves, which after all is relative to what others get who are equally deserving. Rather, the information that a distribution would leave a handicapped person at a certain level of welfare tells us that circumstances obtain in which the theory assigns certain weights to considerations of equality of welfare and of responsibility in relation to other evaluative bases of consideration. Moreover, the weightings associated with these theoretically relevant circumstances may themselves come into conflict. For example, perhaps the only alternatives available will either leave someone below the minimum level of resources or leave a handicapped person below the minimum level of welfare. In such a case, further distinctions of circumstance and weight have to be drawn. (We've seen that substantive constraints on the eligibility of distinctions are necessary if mistakes and disagreement are to be possible, but also that eligibility is a matter of degree, and that admitting occasional less eligible distinctions may be preferable to finding too many cases mistaken.) To require any theory to weigh values against one another once and for all, as $N^*$ does, would indeed be to render it gratuitously crude, to prevent if from ramifying into a set of weighting principles to be applied in various circumstances. Perhaps the only moderately complex pluralistic theory I have described can be rejected on substantive grounds, but it should not be rejected out of hand, *a priori*, which would be the effect of $N^*$. Similarly, in the legal context, an acceptable theory about the relationships among conflicting legal precedents or doctrines may be a balancing theory or a trumping theory, or may mix balancing and trumping structures as appropriate to various circumstances.

Finally, a third counter-objection might be made on behalf of $N^*$: it might be claimed that if the use of non-criterial information is not to enrich our understanding of how the given criteria bear on various alternatives, then this supposedly non-criterial information must in effect be functioning as another criterion.[28] If we assign different weights to our values in different circumstances, we must have *reasons* for doing it; the supposedly non-criterial information we use to distinguish these circumstances just reflects such reasons.

For example, the objector might claim that falling below a certain level of welfare is a bad thing in itself. But at least part of the sense in which it is a bad thing is already expressed by the value of welfare itself. Moreover, an acceptable variant of the theory I have described might *unweight* the value of equality of welfare when a more equal distribution would leave someone below an *even lower level*. Decisions about how to allocate medical resources may reflect such an unweighting; doctors often decide to do more for someone who has better prospects than for someone who has worse prospects.[29] The information that certain distributions would leave someone in a band between these two levels of welfare, where the value of equality gets extra weight, hardly counts in itself as a separate and distinct kind of reason for or against them. We need have no other reason for weighing values against one another differently in different circumstances than that by doing so we produce a better, more coherent theory of the cases we're trying to account for.

Furthermore, judgments about what should be done, all things considered, when values conflict, sometimes require us to draw arbitrary lines: consider how we'd determine at what age someone is eligible to vote, or to marry without parental consent, or (assuming we think some abortions are permissible) during what period an abortion is permissible. We should recognize a presumption against drawing arbitrary lines (i.e., substantively ineligible distinctions), such that we are sometimes justified in determining that an earlier decision was mistaken rather than drawing an arbitrary line between cases that would reconcile them. But the presumption is not irrebuttable; in theorizing we may sometimes draw arbitrary lines between cases so as to avoid attributing too many or too serious mistakes. (Recall my discussion of $D^*$ above, and the arguments of Chapter 8 section 2.) There is no reason to deprive ourselves of this theoretical flexibility and the information it requires.[30]

We can resist $N^*$, then, on the grounds that a deliberator may reasonably require access to non-criterial information about the alternatives that $N^*$

denies him. $N^*$ would constitute an undue constraint on theorizing, would deprive us of too much flexibility. We can recognize many of the points made in favour of $N^*$ by recognizing a presumption against relatively ineligible distinctions, without going all the way to $N^*$. Since $N^*$ is not a reasonable constraint to put on coherence functions, impossibility results that follow from $N^*$ do not threaten their existence.

Note that, having rejected condition $N^*$, we cannot proceed to reproduce impossibility results simply by treating non-criterial information as generating additional rankings to which relevant conditions apply, as non-criterial information is not directional in the way needed for application of condition $P^*$. That an alternative might be nearer to one extreme or the other of a ranking generated by non-criterial information would not in itself count for or against it; this is just what it is for information to be non-criterial (see section 2).

## 6. The Analogues of Roberts' Single-profile Conditions

We've seen that the first type of single-profile reformulation of condition $I$, as condition $N$, does not provide an acceptable analogue condition on coherence functions. Next we must consider a second kind of single-profile impossibility result, due to Kevin Roberts. Roberts' result depends both on a mild reformulation of the independence condition $I$, which amounts merely to a requirement that cases that are alike in all respects be treated alike by the social welfare function, and on a potent reformulation of the condition of unrestricted domain, $U$.

Roberts shows to reformulate $I$ without incorporating neutrality with respect to non-welfare information. He does so by partitioning of the set of alternatives into equivalence classes such that all alternatives in any one equivalence class have exactly the same non-welfare characteristics. He then makes use of this partitioning to state his condition, which I've labelled $L$.

$L$ *(Like Cases)*: For any alternatives $w$, $x$, $y$, and $z$, if $x$ and $w$ are members of one equivalence class collecting alternatives with just the same non-welfare characteristics and $y$ and $z$ are members of another, and if the complete specifications of welfare characteristics of $x$, and $y$, respectively, are equivalent (for whatever welfare informational basis, or conceptualization of welfare, may be actually realized) to the complete specifications of welfare characteristics of $w$, and $z$, then the preference of society as between $x$ and $y$ must be the same as its preference as between $w$ and $z$. (Some particular welfare informational base, or conceptualization of welfare, must be taken as actually applicable.)

If $x$ and $w$ are members of one such class and $y$ and $z$ are members of another, then any non-welfare information that might differentiate between or influence a decision between $x$ and $y$ will also apply to a decision between $w$ and $z$, and *vice versa*. In non-welfare respects, $x$ is just like $w$ and $y$ is just like $z$. Thus only welfare information could differentiate the two decisions, to account for a decision in favour of $x$ in one case and a decision in favour of $z$ in the other.[31] Condition $L$ says that if all welfare and non-welfare characteristics of two pairs of alternatives are the same, then the two issues should be resolved in the same way, or that like cases should be treated alike; this is just to require that judgments about social welfare supervene on judgements about individual welfare and all other information.

$L$'s deliberative analogue is $L^*$, as follows.

$L^*$ *(Like Cases)*: For any alternatives $w$, $x$, $y$, and $z$, if $x$ and $w$ are members of one equivalence class collecting alternatives with just the same non-criterial characteristics and $y$ and $z$ are members of another, and if the complete specifications of criterial characteristics of $x$, and $y$, respectively, are equivalent (for whatever criterial information base, or conceptualization of the relevant criteria, may be actually realized) to the complete specifications of criterial characteristics of $w$, and $z$, then the ranking of $x$ and $y$ all things considered must be the same as the ranking of $w$ and $z$ all things considered. (Again, some particular criterial informational base, or conceptualization of the relevant criteria, must be taken as actually applicable.)

$L^*$ says that if all criterial and non-criterial characteristics of two pairs of alternatives are the same, the two issues should be resolved in the same way; this is just to require that all-things-considered evaluations supervene on criterial and non-criterial information. This requirement is difficult to dispute; it is a requirement on any reasonable theory that cases alike in all respects be treated alike, even if non-criterial differences alone may occasionally justify different treatment, as I argued in the last section. We cannot defuse an impossibility threat to coherence functions by resisting $L^*$.

However, Roberts' result depends not only on this mild and indisputable reformulation of independence, but also on a strong reformulation of unrestricted domain. Multiple-profile condition $U$ says that, for any set of alternatives and any set of individuals, the domain of a social welfare function includes *all* orderings of alternatives by individuals; as I explained last time, the move to a single profile means that the domain of the social welfare function is *any one* ordering of alternatives by individuals, but *only one* (as Samuelson says). With this change, Arrow's result eludes us, as his proof of the emergence of a dictator depends on the ability that condition $U$ guarantees to hold the set of alternatives and the set of individuals constant and vary the orderings of the given alternatives by the given individuals.[32] As we have seen, a strong reformulation of independence as neutrality compensates for this change and permits impossibility results to be obtained for a single profile. Roberts provides an alternative route to an impossibility result for a single profile, which avoids neutrality and depends instead on a condition that uses the partitioning into equivalence classes to guarantee the richness of the single-profile domain.

$R$ *(Richness)*: For any ordered triple $[X,Y,Z]$ of equivalence classes, which collect alternatives with just the same non-welfare characteristics, and any ordered triple $[A,B,C]$ of complete specifications of an alternative's welfare characteristics (for some welfare information base, or conceptualization of welfare, equivalent to that actually realized), there exist three distinct alternatives characterized by $A$ and membership in $X$, by $B$ and membership in $Y$, and by $C$ and membership in $Z$, respectively. (Some particular welfare information base, or conceptualization of welfare, must be taken as actually applicable.)[33]

The deliberative analogue of $R$ is $R^*$, as follows.

$R^*$ *(Richness)*: For any ordered triple $[X, Y, Z]$ of equivalence classes, which collect alternatives with just the same non-criterial characteristics, and any ordered triple $[A, B, C]$ of complete specifications of criterial characteristics (for some criterial information base, or conceptualization of criteria, equivalent to that actually realized), there exist three distinct alternatives characterized by $A$ and membership in $X$, by $B$ and membership in $Y$, and by $C$ and membership in $Z$, respectively. (Again, some particular criterial information base, or conceptualization of the relevant criteria, must be taken as actually applicable.)

Intuitively, $R^*$ requires that the set of all alternatives be very rich, in that it contains alternatives with any combination of complete non-criterial characterization and complete criterial characterization we care to specify. Note that $A$, $B$, and $C$ do not each specify information provided by one value; for example, $A$ would not tell us about the justice of alternatives, $B$ something else about them, and so on. Rather, $A$ might tell us that an alternative is ranked thus by justice and thus by kindness and so on. $B$ would then give a different but also complete specification of criterial information, derived from the same set of criteria, about another alternative.

However, while $L^*$ guarantees the supervenience of all-things-considered evaluations on information provided by specific values and all other information, by demanding such a rich set of alternatives $R^*$ fails to respect the supervenience of specific evaluative judgments on non-evaluative information. The combination of $L^*$ and $R^*$ respects the supervenience of the all-things-considered evaluations, but not of the specific evaluations. To see that $R^*$ fails to respect supervenience, let the triple of equivalence classes be $[P, P, P]$ and the triple of specifications of criterial characteristics be $[F, G, H]$, where $F$, $G$, and $H$ are distinct and derive from evaluative characteristics.[34] Then $R^*$ says that, for this choice of triples, which it entitles us to make, there are three distinct alternatives, all with exhaustive non-evaluative specification $P$, but with different evaluative specifications $F$, $G$, and $H$. That is, the complete evaluative specifications for alternatives with just the same non-evaluative characteristics differ. For complete evaluative specifications to differ, at least two values have to differ about them, even if all but one are indifferent between them. If two values differ about two alternatives, then even if one is indifferent at least one must itself distinguish between the two alternatives. So, for the complete evaluative specification of two alternatives to differ, at least one value must itself treat them differently. But if they are exactly the same in non-evaluative respects, this violates supervenience.

An objection might be that all that is needed is for the two alternatives to differ with respect to some other value, though they are alike in non-evaluative respects; two or more values might form a circle of such distinctions between two alternatives with the same non-evaluative characteristics. But then all-things-considered evaluations delivered by the coherence function may be sensitive to evaluative distinctions which no non-evaluative distinctions underlie, which would surely be an objectionable violation of supervenience itself, though pushed up a level.[35]

Perhaps Roberts' result would be preserved if $R^*$ is altered to apply to triples of *distinct* equivalence classes, so that we could not choose $[P, P, P]$. If so, however, we could still get a violation of supervenience by making two applications of condition $R^*$. For example, in the first case we choose $[P, R, S]$ and $[F, G, H]$, and in the second case we choose $[P, R, S]$ and $[G, H, F]$. Then consider the alternative characterized by membership in $P$ and by $F$, and the alternative characterized by membership in $P$ and by $G$. Again, we have alternatives with the same non-evaluative and different evaluative characteristics, which violates supervenience.

It might be suggested that the condition can be met in this case without violating supervenience, just by shifting from one conceptualization of some criterion to another between applications, for example, from a conception of equality of resources to one of equality of welfare.[36] The different conceptualization would then account for the different evaluative specification, without a violation of supervenience. However, the various criterial conceptualizations or informational bases permitted are supposed to be equivalent to the actual, which must be taken as a starting point and held constant while applying the condition. If in fact we give weight to both considerations of equality of welfare and of equality of resources, and neither sort of consideration can be reduced to the other, then the actual conceptualization involves two criteria, and both must feature in any equivalent conceptualization. If we do not give weight to both, or if one does reduce to the other, then any conceptualization equivalent to the actual must reflect this. We must either count both of them or choose between them, consistently. Again, a coherence function represents a substantive theory about the relationships among various values; we must take as a starting point, to theorize about, some definite conception of what those values have to say; if this is left entirely open the theory is deprived of its subject matter. We have to know what equality actually does require, in various settled and hypothetical cases, in order to theorize about what its relationship is to other values; the theory is about the values we actually have, not what they might have been. Thus, we can rule out variation in the conceptualization of criteria between applications as the explanation of the different evaluative specifications. Even the altered condition involves a violation of supervenience.

Perhaps not all criteria we might want to use in a decision problem will be values, such that supervenience holds of them. But we are entitled by $R^*$ to specify any criteria, so we can specify the supervenient criteria, or values, that interest us. Thus we can reject $R^*$ on the grounds that it violates the requirement that evaluative descriptions supervene on non-evaluative de-

MULTIPLE-PROFILE CONDITIONS

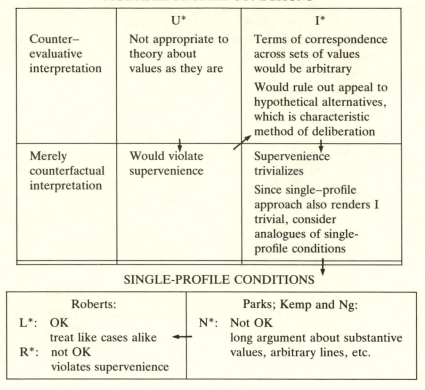

SINGLE-PROFILE CONDITIONS

FIGURE 12.2

scriptions, and so cannot be a reasonable constraint to impose on theories about the relationships among conflicting values. The existence of coherence functions is not threatened by impossibility results that depend on $R^*$.

## 7. Summary and Conclusion

We have now considered the analogues of three sets of conditions that give rise to impossibility results for social choice, and have found good reason to reject some condition in each analogous set as a condition on the kind of theory sought in deliberation about conflicting values. Thus we may conclude that none of these results threaten the existence of coherence functions or undermine a coherence account. We may still hope that coherence functions are not overdetermined by the appropriate constraints on deliberation, and that deliberators are not seeking a chimera. It may be helpful at this point to summarize the arguments that have led to this conclusion.

The impossibility of multiple-profile social welfare functions that meet conditions $P$, $D$, $U$, and $I$ has been shown by Arrow. If coherence functions can reasonably be required to meet formally analogous conditions, then their impossibility will follow. Coherence functions can, arguably, be required to meet conditions $P^*$ and $D^*$. With respect to $U^*$ and $I^*$: when these conditions are interpreted counterevaluatively, they are incompatible with the basic method of deliberation, which involves seeking a substantive theory about the relationships among the values we actually have by considering how they would apply or have applied to alternatives other than those at issue. When these conditions are not interpreted counterevaluatively, however, the requirement of supervenience both invalidates $U^*$ and renders $I^*$ empty. The difficulties of defending these analogues of multiple-profile conditions suggested considering analogues of conditions that produce single-profile impossibilities. We have two suggestions as to how an independence condition may be reformulated in the single-profile literature. By analogy to the first suggestion, we could derive impossibility results by using condition $N^*$, which requires neutrality with respect to non-criterial information. But this is not a reasonable constraint to impose on the theories represented by coherence functions: it would either render them gratuitously crude or would involve the transformation of the substantive values that are its subject matter to an extent that would be incompatible with their discrete characters. By analogy to the second suggestion, we could use condition $L^*$, which merely requires that cases alike in all respects be treated alike. This requirement cannot be resisted. However, to get an impossibility results with this condition we also need to impose a reformulation of condition $U^*$. But the reformulation, $R^*$, violates supervenience, and therefore it is not a reasonable condition to impose on coherence functions. The course of argument summarized in this paragraph is represented in Figure 12.2.

More generally still, the character of the theory sought in deliberation as a substantive theory about specific values made trouble for the counterevaluative interpretation of the multiple-profile conditions and for the neutrality condition, while the requirement of supervenience made trouble for any other interpretation of the multiple-profile conditions and for the single-profile richness condition. In earlier chapters, in particular those of Part I, we found that both substantive and formal constraints on interpretation were needed to defend against a challenge of indeterminacy. In this chapter, we have found that both substantive and formal constraints on the theory represented by a coherence function are needed to defend against a challenge of overdetermination.

# 13

# Commensurability

## 1. Domain Restrictions and Multi-dimensional Conflict

Of the three routes to impossibility results for coherence functions considered in the last chapter, two are blocked by supervenience. The effect of supervenience is to deny us access to a counterevaluative domain, freedom to manipulate what given criteria say about given alternatives without switching alternatives or criteria. How crucial is supervenience in particular to avoiding impossibility results for coherence functions? There are many domain restrictions that avoid impossibility results for social welfare functions, and they've been extensively studied.[1] Perhaps some analogous domain restriction on coherence functions would allow us to block impossibility results without invoking supervenience.

Although many domain restrictions that avoid Arrow's result have been discovered, for present purposes it will suffice to consider the domain restriction originally suggested by Duncan Black and Arrow himself. This is because there is a general problem with domain restrictions as a way of avoiding impossibilities for coherence functions, which the many domain restrictions studied suffer from and which the original domain restriction illustrates: they would avoid impossibility results by stipulating that cohererence functions do not apply to certain hard cases, namely, those involving the multi-dimensional pattern of conflict illustrated in Chapter 11 by the violin example and the example of three cases of an illness.

Black described a property of preference profiles he called *single-peakedness*. He showed that single-peaked preference profiles, or sets of preference orderings, give one alternative a simple majority over every other. One qualification: the profile must contain an odd number of preference orderings, in order to avoid ties. Arrow went on to show that the property of single-peakedness Black described could be used to restrict the domain of a social welfare function in a way that would allow Arrow's conditions, other than $U$, to be met. Simple majority decision meets Arrow's conditions and does not produce intransitivities so long as its domain is restricted to sets of odd-numbered single-peaked orderings. A set of orderings is single-peaked

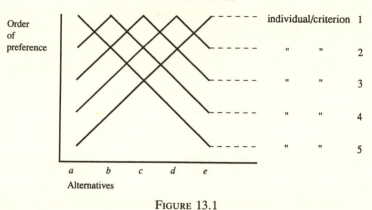

SINGLE PEAKEDNESS

FIGURE 13.1

if there is some particular linear arrangement of the alternatives *a*, *b*, *c*, etc., such that each ordering, when plotted against this particular arrangement of the alternatives, takes on a single-peaked configuration, as shown in Figure 13.1.

This property may at first seem rather formal and abstract, but in fact it gives rigourous expression to an intuitive notion, namely, it expresses a necessary condition for the existence of a single-dimensional spectrum. Black noted that there's a tendency for sets of individual's preferences actually to meet the single-peakedness condition in certain circumstances.[2] Psychologists have interpreted this tendency in terms of *joint qualitative scales*: when what is at issue among individuals is the ideal degree or quantity of some one quality, and each individual decides between any two alternatives according to which is closer to his ideal, then the set of their orderings is single-peaked. Thus the single-peakedness property of sets of preference orderings reflects the intuitive notion that certain issues are, for a given population, one-dimensional. For example, classification of political candidates on a left-right spectrum would give rise to a single-peaked preference profile if people were to disagree about whether the ideal candidate is to the far right, the far left, or somewhere in between, but each person's preferences were determined just by how far each candidate is from his own position on this one left-right scale.[3] (Single-peakedness is a necessary but not a sufficient condition of single-dimensionality; it is conceivable that a profile might happen to be single-peaked accidentally, so to speak; i.e., individual preferences about multi-dimensional issues may just happen to fall into the single-peaked configuration.) To contrapose the "single-dimensional, therefore single-peaked" formula, political issues that do not give rise to a single-peaked profile are of multi-dimensional complexity and cannot be represented in single-dimensional terms such as in terms of a left-right spectrum. (See Chapter 15 section 4, for an expression of skepticism about the existence of a one-dimensional political spectrum.)

While some issues are one-dimensional, so that preference profiles are single-peaked, profiles are not single-peaked for many other, multi-dimensional issues. Often, people disagree about the relations of priority among values that are irreducibly distinct and cannot be commensurated (in the sense developed in the rest of this chapter), so that their disagreement cannot be reduced to disagreement with respect to the ideal quantity of some one value. Thus the general problem with the idea of avoiding impossibility results by restricting the domain of the social welfare function to one-dimensional issues is that doing so constitutes simply putting aside the most difficult issues. Progress with difficulties is not made by averting one's gaze from them. We can make the same point for coherence functions. Domain restrictions would take issues that are not one-dimensional out of the scope of the theory sought in deliberation. But our fundamental values, such as the values of entitlement, equality, and excellence in the problem of what to do with the violin or the problem of whose illness to treat, may give rise to issues that are not single-dimensional. In these examples, there is no single-peaked arrangement of the alternatives. What's at issue is not the ideal magnitude of some single attribute of the alternatives, but how three discrete aspects are related to one another. The various domain restrictions would, in effect, have us not think about these cases, but consider only simpler, one-dimensional cases; the coherence function would simply be silent about them. Thus, domain restrictions do not provide an attractive alternative to supervenience, if we want to avoid having theories riddled with blind spots.[4]

## 2. Transitivity as Commensurability vs. Transitivity as Coherence

If we can resolve conflicts by seeking and finding coherent relationships among the conflicting values, does this mean that the conflicting values are commensurable? I shall argue that the answer is *no*.

In defending the possibility of coherence I've been defending the possibility of rationality in the face of conflicting ends. Fundamental to any conception of the rationality of ends is the requirement that claims about what should be done, all things considered, be transitive. The irrationality May claimed to have pointed up just consists in the intransitivities you can get by applying any function that meets the analogues of Arrow's conditions. In the last chapter I resisted May's conclusion not by denying his assumption of the close connection between transitivity and rationality, but by arguing that certain of the conditions that produce intransitivities are unreasonable constraints on the theories sought in deliberation and represented by coherence functions. But I have not questioned the reasonableness of requiring that such theories not generate intransitivities.

Transitivity is often made out to be tantamount to the commensurability of different ends or values, as well as an essential requirement of rationality in the face of conflicting ends. A dilemma seems to result, that would force us to choose between irrationalism and commensurability: no rationality without transitivity, and no transitivity without commensurability.

There are at least two different kinds of responses to this apparent dilemma. Some, who reject commensurability and suppose that transitivity goes along with it, attempt to mitigate the loss by straining to find a point of view from which transitivity doesn't look so important after all. For example, May argues that transitivity is necessary and in practice sufficient for there to be a single dimension of value, or utility, underlying those preferences: he says that "transitivity holds just when a money price (a utility expressed in money terms) can fully express the preference pattern, at least ordinally. If it were true that 'everything has a price' reflecting its preference status, intransitivity of value judgments could hardly arise." But "where choice depends on conflicting criteria, preference patterns *may* be intransitive". If someone insists that transitivity is part of the definition of 'rational behavior', it becomes questionable "whether rational behavior as so defined has very much importance, either descriptive or normative".[5]

Here are some other examples of this kind of response. James Reynolds and David Paris say that utilitarianism may seem to be the only hope of a rational solution in cases of conflict because transitivity is assumed to be a legitimate criterion of rational choice. They are skeptical about whether conflicting values can be represented adequately in a single dimension, and they advocate a non-utilitarian method of rational choice that involves comparison of each member of a small set of "serious candidates", not with each other two at a time but with all others. They realize this method may produce intransitivities with respect to different sets of serious candidates but do not seem to be bothered by it. Thomas Schwartz also advocates a method of rational choice that allows intransitivities given different sets of alternatives; he requires the method only to order each set of alternatives, not to produce one ordering that holds for all sets. Dennis Packard diagnoses our unhappiness with comparisons that go in circles as due to an assumption that the alternatives compared must have some basic property in common, in terms of which the comparison is made; but, he says, when various different factors are influential, then "cyclical comparatives are not unreasonable". Tom Burns and Dave Meeker remark about Arrow's result that "the 'paradox' arises *because of Arrow's very insistence that 'social choices' satisfy certain conditions or rules of unidimensional nonconflictive rationality*, in particular, that a society or social group knows or behaves as if it knows what is to be chosen first, what second, third, etc., and that it is consistent in this respect". Their view is that "such standards are ... *inappropriate guidelines* to decision-making and action generally", and that "*intransitivities are inherent in multicriteria evaluation and decisionmaking*"[6] (author's emphasis).

However, these responses to the apparent dilemma between irrationalism and commensurability are unpersuasive; they don't give us very strong reasons to override the deep sense that intransitive judgements are irrational.[7] An alternative response to the apparent dilemma is more attractive: other writers have resisted it not by adopting heroic positions about what counts as rational, but by specifying the sense of *commensurability* and exploring the possibilities of pluralism. Thomas Nagel, for example, contrasts the fragmentation of value with the singleness of decision. He writes:

> When faced with conflicting and incommensurable claims we still have to do something—even if it is only to do nothing. And the fact that action must be unitary seems to imply that unless justification is also unitary, nothing can be either right or wrong and all decisions under conflict are arbitrary.

Nagel rejects this seeming implication, and the underlying assumption that we should seek a unitary view of right and wrong. He comments:

> To look for a single general theory of how to decide the right thing to do is like looking for a single theory of how to decide what to believe. . . . it is as irrational to despair of systematic ethics because one cannot find a completely general account of what should be done as it would be to give up scientific research because there is no general method of arriving at true beliefs.

These remarks might seem to favour domain restrictions, but this appearance is dispelled so long as we distinguish the formal unity given by a coherence function with a relatively unrestricted domain from the substantive unity or monistic character of a theory. The issues of whether it's a good thing for a theory to be comprehensive, on the one hand, and monistic, on the other, are two different issues, which cut across one another: a piecemeal coherence function that's a patchwork of local theories but covers all the ground that needs to be covered may be a better theory than one that's monistic but applies only to one-dimensional issues. Nagel warns against letting the lack of unitary justification lead to a false dichotomy between unsystematic intuitive judgments and a unified but artificial decision procedure. "What we need most", he writes, "is a method of breaking up or analyzing practical problems to say what evaluative principles apply, and how".[8]

Bernard Williams questions the link between incommensurability and irrationalism by distinguishing three different kinds of incommensurability from a fourth; only the fourth is clearly irrationalist.[9] A distinction related to Williams' distinctions is made by David Wiggins. In the course of looking for an interpretation of Aristotle that reconciles his recognition of the incommensurability of values with his view of deliberation as aiming at *eudaimonia*, Wiggins writes:

> There is no question here of supposing that there is just one evaluative dimension $\phi$ and one measure $m$ such that $\phi$-ness is all that matters, and all courses of action can be compared with one another by the measure $m$ in respect of $\phi$-ness. What is assumed is only the weaker proposition, which is of the $\forall\exists$ not the $\exists\forall$ form, that for all courses of action there is some measure such that comparison by this measure will establish which is the better course of action in respect of *eudaimonia*, and therefore the greater good. There is no obvious inconsistency between holding this *De Anima* doctrine and main-

taining the thesis of value pluralism or incommensurability in the form of the denial of the ∃∀ sentence.[10]

And Sen and Williams write, in their introduction to the collection of essays *Utilitarianism and Beyond*: "Plural theories which require the maximization of several distinct magnitudes simultaneously can, of course, lead to inconsistency. But the culprit there is not pluralism itself, but the incoherent form of maximization that is adopted." Moreover, "pluralist moralities need not necessarily admit incompleteness"; that is:

> There could be a hierarchy of criteria . . . or a resolving rule if there is a conflict between the different criteria. In these cases, the contrast with 'monist' moralities like utilitarianism does not rest on the issue of completeness as such, but on the way completeness is achieved when it is achieved. In the case of utilitarianism the complete ordering takes the form of simply recording the numerical ordering of some allegedly homogeneous magnitude—total utility, to be exact—whereas for complete plural moralities there is no such homogeneous magnitude with independent descriptive content. ('Moral goodness' does not, of course, have that descriptive content.)[11]

To argue that the conception of rationality as coherence does not entail commensurability, we should follow the lead of this latter group, delimit the sense of *commensurability*, and elaborate the possibilities of pluralism. Since my defense of coherence has presumed that a theory could claim to represent rationality in the face of conflicting ends only by managing to avoid intransitivities, I've already decisively parted company with the first group, who'd resist the inference from rationality to commensurability by expanding the notion of rationality to accommodate intransitivity. I shall argue that coherence does not amount to commensurability by arguing that transitivity does not amount to commensurability. The aim is to avoid the apparent dilemma by reining in the notion of commensurability rather than by expanding the notion of rationality.

In earlier chapters I've developed a non-centralist view of specific reason-giving concepts and a coherence account of the general evaluative concepts. With this non-centralist coherence account in hand, we can see the first response, eagerness to spurn commensurability by rejecting transitivity along with it, as overkill. The first response assumes that transitivity indicates some single dimension of value that underlies and commensurates conflicting values. But from the point of view of my account, there's another natural interpretation of transitivity, as simply a requirement of any decent theory about the relationships among discrete conflicting values. The general concepts used to deliver all-things-considered judgments are not prior to and independent of various specific reason-giving concepts. Rather, they're responsible to theorizing about the relationships among specific values. The transitivity of all-things-considered judgments may simply reflect a feature of theories about the relationships among values and not some common feature of those values themselves. I shall try to explain how this might be true.

If each all-things-considered comparison of two alternatives tells us which is favoured by the best theory about the values that apply to them, then why shouldn't a series of such comparisons form an intransitive chain? The reason is that a good theory about the relationships among the values that apply to any two alternatives has to take into account the way those values apply to other alternatives as well. Recall the way we appealed to settled and hypothetical cases in constructing hypotheses. To decide between two alternatives, the theory only needs to cover the relationships among the values that apply to those alternatives. But those values themselves also apply to other alternatives. Part of the information that concerns one pair of alternatives is information about the relationships among the values that apply to that pair. But all of their applications are potentially relevant to a theory about the relationships among such values, and hence to a decision between that pair. If consideration of other, settled or hypothetical cases reveals that a certain hypothesis would produce an intransitivity, our theoretical project, namely, to find some orderly and coherent method of proceeding in conflict cases, would itself constrain us to find a way of qualifying the hypothesis to avoid the intransitivity. We would not have arrived at a satisfactory theory about the values that apply to that one pair of alternatives until we had found one that would avoid intransitivities when those values were applied to other pairs of alternatives. So, the transitivity of all-things-considered judgments is imposed by the notion of a coherent theory about the relationships among conflicting values, not by some common feature of the values the theory is about. The values are connected by there being a theory about them, but a theory about conflicting values does not necessarily commensurate them or eliminate the conflicts among them. Nor does it have to be monistic; nothing I've said about coherence rules out either pluralistic or monistic theories.

### 3. Conflict, Transitivity as Coherence, and Self-determination

Notice the connection between the conception of transitivity as coherence and certain remarks made by Donald Davidson in "Psychology as Philosophy", namely, that "satisfaction of conditions of consistency and rational coherence may be viewed as constitutive of the range of application of such concepts as those of . . . desire, intention and action", and that "we cannot make good sense of an attribution of preference except against a background of coherent attitudes".[12] On a coherence acount, we can understand how someone, without a change of mind, might choose a over b, b over c, and c over a, by supposing that he acts on discrete, conflicting values, all of which he accepts. He can act on these values, as the *akrates* does, without acting on an all-things-considered judgment; and he may not have arrived at an all-things-considered judgment at all. What we can't understand is someone thinking it better, all things considered, to do a rather than b, b rather than c, and c rather than a. To do what one thinks is best, all things considered, is to act in accord with a view of the relationships among the relevant reasons for action that promises to provide an orderly and consistent method of proceeding when they conflict. But having the kind of reason such a theory provides doesn't make the reasons the theory is about any the less reasons for action, again, as the *akrates* demonstrates. Although one should, all things considered, act in accord with the theory, nevertheless the reasons the theory is about may still conflict with the reasons the theory provides. Reasons for action are *pro tanto*, not *prima facie*; they aren't bits of evidence about what should be done that yield to better, more comprehensive evidence.

Suppose a skeptic about the authority of theory (recall my introduction of such skepticism in Chapter 10 section 4) asks: Why should I act in accord with the theory rather than on one of the conflicting reasons it's about? Does he suppose that an answer to this question might be provided by yet another, higher-order reason, that will eliminate the conflict? One should, all things considered, act in accord with the theory rather than in accord with one of the conflicting values the theory is about; but the sense in which you should is just given by the supposition that it *is* the best account of the relationships among those values. The conceptual relationship between all-things-considered reasons and *pro tanto* reasons does not require them not to conflict, any more than the conceptual possibility that an alternative might be both better in respect of justice and worse in respect of unkindness requires reasons of justice and kindness not to conflict. We can recognize the value of proceeding in an orderly and consistent way according to a theory about the relationships between conflicting values, without thinking that the reason-giving force of the theory somehow subsumes the reason-giving force of the discrete specific values the theory is about. It can be true that a certain act would be just but unkind. It can also be true that the act is favoured by the best theory of justice and kindness; it may *still* be unkind. Unkindness is no more cancelled out by theoretical favour than by justice; once again, as the *akrates* demonstrates in acting for a reason, specific *pro tanto* reasons retain their reason-giving force in the face of contrary all-things-considered judgments. Action-guidingness comes in discrete, specific kinds, among which is the kind provided by theories about the relationships among values and associated reasons of coherence. To complain that such theories give us no reason to act on the reasons they provide rather than on one of the conflicting reasons they're about is to misconstrue their proper role. These theories are about conflicting specific values. They do not eliminate the conflict, which is a feature of the way things are, not merely the way they appear. Rather, they provide a way of proceeding in the face of conflict that has certain virtues, among them transitivity. Reason to proceed thus, namely, coherently, is one kind of practical reason, but it is no more insulated from conflict with other reasons than they are from conflict with one another. And conflict between the reasons of coherence, provided by theories, and other reasons is no more eliminable than conflicts among those other reasons. Even if it made sense to suppose there might be a reason to act on the reason provided by a theory rather than on one of the conflicting reasons the theory is about, such a reason would still conflict with other reasons; a regress would not solve the supposed problem, but merely push it to the next level. The solution to the problem of the authority of theory is to recognize that the supposed problem only arises from demanding the impossible, namely, the elimination of conflict.

Why seek a coherent way of resolving conflicts given that conflict is ineliminable? Recall Davidson's claims about the constitutive role of coherence; charity is not optional or derivative, with respect to either the norms of pattern which embody our conception of coherence and provide formal constraints on interpretation, or the norms of correspondence which provide substantive constraints on interpretation. Those norms of pattern embodied in a conception of coherence in particular play an important role in both the self-determination of individual persons and the personification of communities. The role of reasons of coherence and integrity in a responsible community's determination of its identity has recently been illuminatingly discussed by Ronald Dworkin in his book *Law's Empire*.[13] Here I shall only comment briefly on the role of coherence in individual self-determination. (In Chapter 15 I discuss at greater length the way in which a cognitive conception of individual autonomy emerges from a coherence account, as well as the role of reasons of coherence in a democratic community's determinations of what should be done.)

I have argued that conflicts within persons are in certain respects like conflicts between persons. Persons both are conflicted, fragmented, and seek not to be, seek personal coherence and integrity. The influence of conflicting values on persons is such that they are not always certain what or who they are, or what or who they want to be. However, it is distinctive of persons to reflect on their own values and attitudes, and thus to arrive at judgments about they should do, all things considered, and corresponding higher-order attitudes. In thus seeking coherence they are seeking their very identities as persons, seeking to determine themselves out of the various subsystems responsive and responsible to various conflicting interests and values; in deliberating about what to do they are trying to determine who they really are. Thus deliberation, the search for coherence, is a kind of self-interpretation and self-determination. Interpretation is guided by various constitutive constraints, among them those that constrain us to seek to understand ourselves and others as coherent, as unified persons; but the unity of persons, the coherence they seek, is not more fundamental than or prior to the familiar reason-giving practices that also inform interpretation. Both formal and substantive constraints on interpretation are needed, and neither sort is derivative from the other. Personal coherence is not something that is given by experience or observation, even at a single point in time; it's something that must be achieved. Moreover, it is fragile and sometimes fails to maintain authority over breakaway subsystems. Nevertheless, it's only against a background of the concern with personal coherence and the norms of pattern that embody our conception of coherence that attributions of disunity make sense. The concern with personal coherence is not something we are free to disown entirely, nor is it an appropriate object of empirical skepticism. (Recall the arguments for my claim in Chapter 5 section 5 that constraints on eligibility cannot be provided by empirical correlations between characteristics of alternatives—or patterns of characteristics of alternatives—and the contents of preference somehow independently determined.) Reasons are no more independent of persons than persons are of reasons.

Thus, to ask: "Why should the requirements on a person imposed by the best account of the relationships among the relevant conflicting reasons, i.e., the demands of coherence and integrity, be met, rather than the requirements of one of the conflicting reasons the account is an account of?" is rather like asking: "Why should the requirements imposed on a community by the best account of the relationships among the members of the community, whose legitimate demands often conflict, be met, rather than the requirements of one of the persons or groups who are members of the community?" (Recall the parallel developed in Chapter 8 sections 1 through 4 between conflicts within persons and conflicts between persons.) It may be tempting to say that such questions can have no answer until they are addressed to a given, fully characterized agent, whose actions are in question: a person with specified preferences, or a community of a specified sort. But this response misses the deeper point of such questions, which is to insist that the questions arise: who in fact is the relevant agent, and who should it be? What kind of agents are we, and what kind should we be? Qualities of agency are not entirely fixed, but are in part our own creation, and we are thus responsible for our *selves*. Such questions would have no force if the identities of agents were entirely fixed, and no ethical questions arose about them; the tempting rebuttal would then be correct. But such questions do have force, and that is because the identities of agents are not entirely fixed, but in part for them to determine. For *persons*, questions about what kind of an agent to be, whether to identify one's *self* with certain groups, or certain values, must arise. It cannot be a problem *that* they arise, for it is a distinctive feature of personhood that they do. This is not to say that such questions are easy to answer. But the difficulty of answering them does not in turn give rise to the question: Should I be a *person* at all? The latter question does not arise; any reason for a negative answer to it would be self-defeating, since the desire to become a wanton, even if efficacious (someone might arrange to have the relevant bits of his brain removed), is itself a mark of a person.[14]

## 4. The Constitutive Status of Coherence and the Possibility of Pluralism

From the point of view of a non-centralist coherence account, transitivity has a role as a constraint on theories about the conflicting reasons for which we act, theories that display conflicting reasons as coherently related. Transitivity needn't be seen as reflecting some underlying common feature of those reasons that commensurates them. The availability of the view of transitivity I've suggested means that transitivity cannot simply be equated with commensurability for the sake of arguing that coherence amounts to commensurability. There's a danger of obscuring the view of transitivity I've suggested, though, if we misinterpret the role of coherence functions as epistemic.[15] This mis-interpretation would naturally go with a view of specific reasons for action as *prima facie* rather than *pro tanto*, as pieces of evidence about what should be done, where the latter is independently understood. A coherence function, on this view, would *reveal* to us what should be done rather than *constitute* it; its complexity would be an epistemic matter and compatible with the unitary character of what it revealed.

By contrast, I've given coherence a constitutive role. On a coherence account the appeal to theory doesn't just reveal what should be done, but is partly constitutive of it, is involved in our very understanding of the notion of what should be done. As a result, the question whether commensurability obtains, or whether some monistic theory of values is correct, waits on the results of theorizing. Coherence *may* amount to commensurability if the best theory turns out to be monistic, but if so this will be a substantive theoretical result. As I explained in Chapter 12 section 3, the non-dictatorship condition on coherence functions does not rule out monistic theories. The success of a monistic theory about the relationships between values should not be confused with the dictatorship of one of the values the theory is about. Rather, a monistic theory requires the maximization of a "homogeneous magnitude with independent descriptive content", as Sen and Williams put it;[16] more-over, monism can be a matter of degree. Forms of utilitarianism that appeal to rules, motives, or a separation of levels are examples of more or less monistic theories. Only if the best theory is monistic does coherence amount to commensurability in this sense; but coherence also leaves the possibility of pluralism open.

### 5. Monism, Pluralism, and Substantive vs. Formal Unity: An Example

The contrast between monistic and pluralistic coherence functions does not turn on the possibility of formally representing the search for coherence as the maximization of some one magnitude. Rather, it turns on whether such formal unity corresponds to substantive unity. It may be technically possible to construe many pluralistic theories as maximizing some complex theoretical magnitude.[17] But this possibility does not make for commensurability in any interesting sense, but a merely formal, *ex post* unity. Such merely formal unity does not *per se* bestow any independent descriptive or explanatory unity on the magnitude constructed, but merely dangles from the pluralistic sub-stance of the theory.

Consider an example of a pluralistic theory construed to display formal unity. I shall continue with the theory of distributive justice that I described in Chapter 12 section 5 when considering the neutrality condition. The al-ternatives to be evaluated are:

*a*: everyone gets income $Y$
*b*: everyone gets income $\frac{1}{2}Y$

| W | ER | EW | R | Resolution |
|---|-----|-------|-----|------------|
| c | a,b | d | e | e |
| d | e | e | d | d |
| e | c,d | a,b,c | a,b | a |
| a |  |  | c | c |
| b |  |  |  | b |

FIGURE 13.2

c: 90% get income $2Y$ and 10% get income $\frac{1}{2}Y$

d: 90%, who are brought to a welfare level of approximately $v$ by an income of $Y$, get income $Y$; the remaining 10%, who are either handicapped or have expensive tastes and are brought to a welfare level of approximately $v$ by an income of $2Y$, get income $2Y$

e: everyone gets income $Y$ except the handicapped, who get income $Y + n$.

The relevant values include considerations of total welfare ($W$), of equality of resources ($ER$), of equality of welfare ($EW$), and of responsibility for certain personal traits ($R$). Suppose we have deliberated and arrived at a theory that tells us to distribute resources so as to maximize welfare except in two kinds of circumstance, namely, when by doing so we would either leave someone with less than a certain minimum level of resources or would leave a handicapped person with less than a certain minimum level of welfare. Recall that a handicapped person is understood for these purposes to be someone with a characteristic that he's not responsible for and that causes him to be left at a much lower-than-average level of welfare by any given level of resources. When either of these circumstances obtain, the theory tells us to distribute resources to maintain a certain roughly equal minimum level of resources for everyone and a certain roughly equal minimum level of welfare for the handicapped. Now suppose that the various specific values and the theory we've arrived at through deliberation order the alternatives as shown in Figure 13.2.

Our theory is pluralistic insofar as it fixes relationships among the relevant considerations without appealing to some unitary standard, as a theory would, for example, that simply told us to foster motives and dispositions the prevalence of which would maximize welfare. It would be natural to describe the theory as an egalitarian form of liberalism. It seeks to distribute means without constraining ends by recognizing certain rights—economic rights, and rights to basic capabilities or their most feasible substitutes. However, it would be possible to redescribe the theory so that it simply tells us to maximize a certain constructed magnitude, into which we've built the desired relationships between $W$, $ER$, $EW$, and $R$.

To illustrate, here is one way such a magnitude might be constructed. Call the magnitude to be constructed "$T$". The relationship our theory specifies between $W$ and $ER$ can be obtained, or very nearly, by extrapolating from a familiar assumption, namely, the diminishing marginal utility of income. For example, we could set $T$ equal to the sum of the logarithms to some base $b$ of the income allocated to each person. The allocation of income between persons that maximizes $T$ is at the point where the derivatives of the logarithms of different person's incomes are equal; $T$ is maximized by equalizing marginal $T$. But the derivative curves of logs have a shape that restricts the circumstances in which sacrifices of $ER$ are allowed. The restriction in the circumstances in which inequality of income will maximize $T$ reflects the economic rights the theory recognizes. Since a log function to any base always includes the point $(1,0)$, its boomerang-shaped derivative curve always falls precipitously from infinite $T$ as the income allocated to a given person approaches the point $(1,0)$; and after that point it gradually levels out and approaches zero $T$, as shown in Figure 13.3. So for levels of income down to and around whatever we stipulate as the unit level, the loss of $T$ from shifting income away from a given person will be measurable, and, if the person already has a large income, negligible. Suppose one alternative allocation leaves some with less and others with more than they have in the *status quo*; say it leaves the richer with less and the poorer with more than at present. A loss of $T$ from one person due to a loss of income in the elbow of his derivative curve near the unit point can be balanced by a gain of $T$ from another person or persons; as the derivative curve approaches the horizontal axis, for higher levels of income, these trade-offs are easier and easier to justify under the theory. But for levels of income below the unit point, they become harder and harder to justify, since $T$ falls rapidly to negative infinity with very small reductions in the income allocated to a given person. It's very hard to justify an allocation that leaves someone below the subsistence level; again, a reflection of economic rights. So, the elbow in the derivative curve at the stipulated unit point acts as a barrier to trade-offs, except where enough $T$ is at stake to overtake the log curve as it plummets to negative infinity.

Thus we can build consideration of equality of resources or income into the magnitude we're trying to maximize, $T$, so as to mimic what our pluralistic theory tells us. The section of derivative curve to the left of the elbow reflects the greater weight of considerations of $ER$ under certain circumstances and the section to the right of the elbow reflects the greater weight of considerations of total welfare, $W$, under other circumstances. There's scope for further fine tuning. The behaviour of $T$ for income levels above the unit level can be made more responsive to considerations of total welfare by setting the base $b$ for each person to reflect comparisons of welfare at higher income levels. If the two people competing for resources are $A$ and $B$, we can set the base $b$ for each in such a way that the values of marginal $T$ for $A$ and $B$ are equal, hence total $T$ is maximized, at an allocation that respects the minimum income level for each of them but which also takes into account the fact that one of them—$B$ in the diagram—may have a flatter $T$ curve, reflecting his lower capacity for enjoyment at higher income levels (see Figure

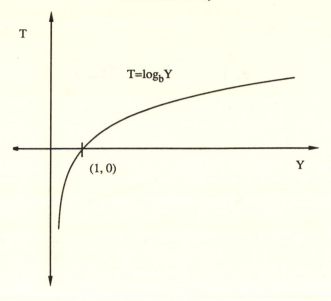

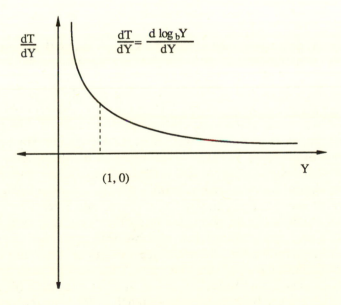

FIGURE 13.3

13.4). Suppose that *B* has champagne tastes, and beer makes him less happy than it makes *A*; *A* is a more efficient generator of welfare from a given amount of income. Expensive tastes are like handicaps except—and this is the essential difference—that we are considered responsible for them, so they do not give rise to special privileges. Thus resources about the minimum income level are allocated so as gradually to favour those with a greater

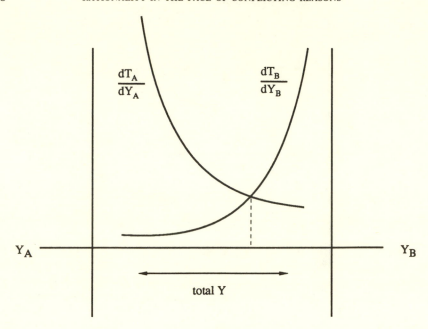

FIGURE 13.4

capacity to enjoy things, though if resources are so scarce that the economic rights of the competitors clash, then resources are divided equally, as in Figure 13.5.

Now we have built two of the four relevant considerations, $W$ and $ER$, into $T$. What about $EW$ and $R$? We have to tinker further with $T$ to incorporate our theory's treatment of $EW$ and $R$ in relation to $W$ and $ER$. The pluralistic theory we're mimicking constrains welfare maximization not only by the economic rights of everyone but also by the rights to minimum levels of well-being of the handicapped, people who are brought to a lower level of welfare by a given income owing to characteristics they're *not* responsible for. So, the theory allows considerations of $EW$ to come into force when levels of welfare fall below a certain point, but even then only if considerations $R$ permit. As I said, the welfare levels of those with expensive tastes, which they're held responsible for, are not objects of our theory's concern, only those of the handicapped. If someone starves because he can't afford *foie gras* and truffles and can't bear hamburgers and potatos, that's his problem; but if he goes hungry because it costs so much to feed his seeing-eye dog, he's entitled to extra help. As we left it, the unit of resources constraint enforces a minimum defined in terms of income; but it doesn't do anything to hold up minimum levels of well-being for the handicapped. We can fix this by introducing a constant into the log function for each person that relocates the elbow of the derivative curve to reflect handicaps, and thus to support minimum levels of well-being for the handicapped. The new magnitude $T$ to be maximized would be the sum of the $\log_b (x + c)$ functions for each person;

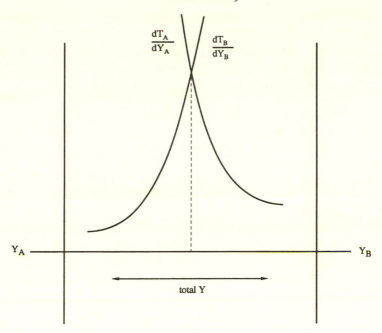

$\frac{dT_A}{dY_A}$     $\frac{dT_B}{dY_B}$

$Y_A$                                        $Y_B$

total Y

FIGURE 13.5

the constant $c$ would be chosen for each person in such a way as to measure the special needs of the handicapped and to distinguish them from the burden of expensive tastes. So, if a handicapped person is brought to roughly the same level of well-being by the income $d$ that most people are brought to by the unit level of income, we raise the trade-off barrier for the handicapped person accordingly by setting $c = 1 - d$ for him and $c = 0$ for the others.

All of this shows that we can indeed construct a magnitude that is being maximized when we act in accord with our pluralistic theory. The magnitude $T$ is the sum of the logs, to some base $b$ for each person, of his income plus some constant $c$ for each person. However, we have to stipulate the unit level of income to reflect economic rights at some minimum level, and we have to arrive at a list of constants $b$ and $c$ for each person, chosen to reflect comparisons of welfare at income levels above the minimum level of income, in the case of $b$, and, in the case of $c$, to reflect levels of welfare at minimum income levels as well as the distinction between handicaps for which a person isn't responsible and expensive tastes for which he is. Our construction of a single magnitude that artificially unifies these various considerations does not eliminate the need to determine the level of economic rights and the lists of constants $b$ and $c$ for each person, and these determinations are still going to be based on considerations of $W$, $ER$, $EW$, and $R$. This is the kind of case I had in mind when I said that the formal unity achieved by construction of a single magnitude may merely dangle from the pluralistic substance of a theory. A distinction remains between theories that are pluralistic in this substantive sense and theories of which the substance, not merely the form, is monistic.

If a claim to the effect that commensurability follows from a conception of rationality as coherence is only intended as a claim about commensurability in the weak sense of merely formal unity, such as that provided by $T$, then a coherentist who wants to deny commensurability in some more substantial sense and to defend a pluralistic theory needn't be worried by it. The weak sense of commensurability is not one that motivates pluralists to resist a supposed dilemma between commensurability and irrationalism; weak commensurability is compatible with substantive pluralism.

With a coherence account now in hand, we will turn in the next chapter to issues concerning skepticism about what should be done that were deferred from earlier chapters.

# IV

# KNOWLEDGE OF WHAT SHOULD BE DONE

# 14

# Skepticism

## 1. Taking Stock

We have now a coherence account according to which ethics and philosophy of mind are continuous: reasons stand to intentional action in general much as meanings stand to linguistic action in particular. Deliberation about what to do when reasons conflict is at once self-interpretation and self-determination. The account dovetails with views to the effect that the capacity for higher-order attitudes is distinctive of persons: in attributing to ourselves such attitudes we determine our own identities. In developing this account we have dealt with two related sources of skepticism about the exercise of interpretation that is central to it.

*First*, the question of indeterminacy: might the data to be interpreted not determine a best theory, a right interpretation? In particular, might there always be radically too many eligible interpretations, such that nothing we intend fixes the way we should go on as interpreters? This difficult question is central to many philosophical problems and not merely to those discussed in this book; it is at the heart of my lengthy discussion of objectivity, disagreement, and constraints on interpretation in Part I, one of the upshots of which is to dispel the threat of radical indeterminacy (if not occasional, livable-with underdetermination).

*Second*, the question of possibility: might the constraints on interpretation be so stringent as to be impossible for any theory to satisfy? If so, then claims about what the best theory recommends would be false because nothing could be such a theory. The solution to this problem in Chapters 12 and 13 is related to the solution to the first problem: it essentially involves recognizing that constraints on interpretation are substantive as well as formal. Supervenience is a formal constraint, but the argument against neutrality in Chapter 12 appealed to the specific, not-indefinitely-malleable content of the values by reference to which events are intelligible as action. Moreover, the relevance to the theoretical exercise of specific values, as opposed to all conceptually possible values, motivates the arguments about the domain and independence conditions. It may be helpful now to review in a somewhat more schematic

273

and less detailed way how this is so, which I shall do in section 2 (but readers already satisfied on this second question can omit this review).

In the context thus set, I'll go on in further sections to consider what scope there is for skepticism about claims to knowledge of what should be done, and the nature of debunking explanations in particular, drawing on recent discussions of skepticism by John Mackie, Robert Nozick, and Bernard Williams. Finally, I'll suggest that the right response to skepticism bears on the justification of democracy. The suggestion will be pursued in the next and final chapter, in which a cognitive conception of democracy will be developed.

## 2. The Modal Structure of Deliberation, the Existence of a Best Theory, and Skepticism

Consider again, from a somewhat loftier viewpoint, the role of the unrestricted domain and independence conditions in social choice theory and their significance in the context of deliberation. If preferences are understood to be determined prior to and independently of values and judgments about what ought to be done, which latter are some kind of construction out of them, then one might reasonably want such a logical construction to apply regardless of the content of the preferences (so long as they're consistent). The content of actual preferences may be such and such, but actual preferences have no special significance. A social welfare function that in effect constitutes evaluative judgments out of prior preferences should work for counterpreferential possibilities as well, since all preferential possibilities are on equal footing. This aspiration is embodied in the condition of unrestricted domain, $U$.

The parallel aspiration in the context of deliberation, in which one is trying to arrive at an all-things-considered judgment by coming to understand the alternatives one faces in terms of the specific values that constrain the interpretation of events as intelligible action, is embodied in condition $U^*$. But this parallel aspiration ultimately makes no sense. The deliberator is looking for illumination of the relationships among the values that actually apply; counterevaluative conceptual possibilities are not on an equal footing with the content of actual values, and indeed are quite irrelevant to his purposes. To suppose that all counterevaluative possibilities are on a equal footing with actual values seems to involve supposing that the content of the applicable specific values is itself somehow subject to the independent will, so that all conceptual possibilities must be catered for. But the determination of the will is the very exercise in question! Thus the aspiration to unrestricted domain would seem to involve some unreconstructed subjectivist assumptions about the content of the will being both unconstrained and unproblematically given. Rejection of such subjectivist assumptions was the starting point for the view that deliberation is a kind of self-interpretation, necessarily subject to substantive evaluative constraints. Moreover, if the deliberator's problem were not one of finding a substantive theory but rather one of finding a methodology to apply no matter what substantive values were taken to be relevant, consideration of the methodology of interpretation would itself bring us to recognize the necessity of substantive constraints—as it did in Chapter 4 above.

So, condition $U^*$, understood to require a coherence function to handle counterevaluative suppositions as well as merely counterfactual alternatives in which actual values apply, may be rejected as a condition on deliberation. And even if we waive considerations about substantive constraints on interpretation and admit conceptually possible counterevaluative suppositions, condition $I^*$ applied to such counterevaluative suppositions is subject to further objections, as explained in Chapter 12. Consider what it would require. Suppose, just for the sake of argument, we have different sets of different conceptually possible values, which may be quite unrelated across sets and which may not make sense by reference to familiar values; there are sane human values, mad human values, Martian values, Alpha Centaurian values, and so forth. Each set is the basis for all-things-considered judgments about what to do when its member values conflict, and condition $I^*$ constrains, not separate theories, one for each set, that guide such judgments, but rather a methodology—one overall process that applies to all the sets of values, perhaps producing theories along the way, one process that ultimately yields all-things-considered judgments. $I^*$ requires this process to rank two alternatives in the same way if the corresponding values in different sets of values that apply to those alternatives rank them the same way. But what does such correspondence of different conceptually possible values amount to, and how is it to be determined? What does it mean for the human value of justice to correspond to some member of the set of Martian values, which, *ex hypothesi*, may not make sense in terms of our values? If the terms of the correspondence are arbitrary, can't we tinker with them so as to affect whether or not all-things-considered rankings satisfy condition $I^*$? Moreover, to require that if the applicable values in one set rank two alternatives in the same way as the applicable but different, corresponding values in another set, then resolution of the conflict must be the same across the two sets, would rule out the characteristic technique of deliberation as described in Chapter 11, namely, the appeal to and analysis of settled and hypothetical cases other than those at issue, to reveal and test the relationships among the particular values that apply. If, counterevaluatively, we were to find the 'irrelevant alternatives' ranked otherwise by the relevant values than they actually are, we might well find our theory of the relationships among those values in various circumstances would differ accordingly, and hence our all-things-considered judgments about the alternatives at issue.

Thus, neither $U^*$ nor $I^*$ can be sustained if understood to apply counterevaluatively. Instead, we may consider applying them within one set of conceptually possible values, namely, actual values, and requiring our theory about those values to cope with counterfactual but not counterevaluative suppositions. However, we run into immediate trouble with $U^*$ on this interpretation: it would allow us to hold the set of alternatives and the set of values constant, and vary the orderings of the former by the latter, which, so long as we are not making counterevaluative suppositions, is just what supervenience rules out. The relationships between evaluative and non-evaluative characteristics is unlike the relationship between colours and shapes, in that the former cannot vary independently of the latter. We also run into a kind of trouble with condition $I^*$ thus interpreted: it is impossible to violate because it's trivialized. If it's not possible for the evaluative rankings of any alternatives, either those at issue or other 'irrelevant' alternatives, to vary, then neither can all-things-considered judgments about them vary. The trivialization of $I^*$ under this interpretation seems analogous to the trivialization of the original condition $I$ as applied within the single-profile approach to social choice. Thus we were prompted to examine reformulations of condition $I$ in ways appropriate to the single-profile approach, with the thought that perhaps analogous reformulations would be appropriate to deliberation that does not range across counterevaluative possibilities. Perhaps analogous reformulations would yet produce impossibility results and so sustain skepticism about coherence.

The analogue of the first kind of single-profile reformulation we considered involved condition $N^*$. The argument against condition $N^*$ was complex and I shall not recapitulate in detail, but it ultimately turned on the way in which the discrete identities of familiar specific values provide constraints on eligibility. If it is the relationships among *those* values that the deliberator seeks to understand and if a theory *about them* cannot always reasonably be required to satisfy condition $N^*$, then it is not to the point that it may be formally possible to construct other 'values' such that a theory about them would always satisfy $N^*$; this would be changing the subject.[1] The rejection of $N^*$ is compatible, however, with recognizing a presumption against violations of $N^*$: other things equal, better not to draw arbitrary distinctions. In fact, I argued for such a presumption in discussing *akrasia*. But since other things may not be equal, the presumption was not to be irrebutable, which condition $N^*$ would make it. So, we can accept many of the points made in favour of $N^*$ by recognizing such a presumption, but still reject $N^*$.

The analogue of the second kind of single-profile impossibility result we considered involved two new conditions, $L^*$ and $R^*$. $L^*$ was unobjectionable, making all-things-considered evaluations a function of, or supervenient upon, criterial and non-criterial characteristics of alternatives taken together. However, $R^*$ required a domain so rich as to violate the supervenience of criterial on non-criterial characteristics; and here, within one profile, there is no question of counterevaluative supposition. $R^*$ required there to exist alternatives with exactly the same non-evaluative characteristics and different complete specifications of evaluative characteristics, which means that at least one value arbitrarily distinguishes between alternatives alike in non-evaluative respects, or fails to supervene. Thus, neither type of single-profile impossibility result gives rise to an analogous result for deliberation.

We have failed to produce impossibility results for coherence functions by analogy to either the multiple-profile or the single-profile approach. We have considered in detail and from several angles a threat to the existence claim made by a coherence account, namely, a threatened proof of non-existence, and have not seen it materialize; have we thus shifted the burden of proof to those ontological skeptics who wish to deny that there is such a thing as what ought to be done, all things considered? In this context, what further scope is there for skepticism? Note that the existence claim made by a coherence account, which has so far emerged unscathed, is such as to be susceptible of truth or falsity, and that the falsity of the existence claim has all along been allowed to be epistemically possible. The skeptic cannot object that we have conducted a defense merely by appealing to meanings, which may not apply to anything. Even if the non-existence of coherence functions could be demonstrated, this wouldn't be a matter of meaning, but a substantive result, just as Arrow's mathematical result itself is.

The skeptic may reply that mere abstract mathematical existence, the existence of an abstract entity, a function representing a theory, is not what he is denying, but rather the existence of something more concrete. But if so, he is in danger of stalking a straw man: of denying something which objectivism need not assert, which in no way follows from the denial that prior and independent preferences determine values, and which is not clearly intelligible to begin with.[2] There are truths about such things as meanings, beliefs, numbers, values, theories, and explanations; and one can perceive the meaning, the value, or the number of something concrete, or grasp its explanation; but is the meaning, the value, the number, or the explanation itself concrete? It's not clear what could be meant by supposing they might be. Such things are abstract entities, which provide a rational, but nonetheless natural—as reason is itself natural—framework for natural events, including human actions, a framework that needs no pretense to supernatural underpinnings, a natural order naturalized.

The ontological skeptic is now bound to feel there has been a sleight of hand. However, a critical difficulty in this area is that of identifying a sharp issue, finding a nonmetaphorical proposition that one party actually wishes to assert and the other to deny (as opposed to diagnose or reinterpret or deny the presuppositions of). The difficulty of finding a sharp issue here suggests there may be more agreement between traditional opponents than they recognize. But let's try another tack. We've seen that, according to a coherence account, for a claim about what ought to be done to be correct, there must exist a best theory of the sort we've been concerned with, and the best theory must favour the alternative it's claimed ought to be done. A skeptic may claim that our beliefs about what ought to be done do not track the truth about it, either with respect to the existence of the best theory or with respect to the alternatives it favours, because we are very bad at discovering what ought to be done, are subject to systematic error, deception, or illusion. (Of course, no one would deny occasional, or even very frequent, error; the error in question must be pervasive.[3]) If so, then even if the best theory claimed to exist by a coherence account does indeed exist, our beliefs about what ought to be done would not constitute knowlege. John Mackie claims that his skepticism is of an ontological rather than linguistic variety, but certain of his arguments for skepticism suggest that epistemic considerations are critical; and Bernard Williams has recently expressed skepticism about the possibility of knowledge of what ought to be done, all things considered. I shall focus on their discussions in attempting to sharpen a skeptical issue.


### 3. The Error Theory, and the Link to Psychological States

Mackie puts forward an error theory about objective values. He holds that the ordinary user of ethical concepts means to say something about whatever he characterizes in ethical terms "as it is in itself", and that what he says to this effect is in fact false:

> The ordinary user of moral language means to say something about whatever it is that he characterizes morally, for example a possible action, as it is in itself . . .

> If second order ethics were confined, then, to linguistic and conceptual analysis, it ought to conclude that moral values at least are objective: that they are so is part of what our ordinary moral statements mean: the traditional moral concepts of the ordinary man as well as of the main line of Western philosophers are concepts of objective value. But it is precisely for this reason that linguistic and conceptual analysis is not enough. The claim to objectivity, however ingrained in our language and thought, is not self-validating. It can and should be questioned. But the denial of objective values will have to be put forward not as the result of an analytic approach, but as an 'error theory', a theory that although most people in making moral judgments impiicitly claim, among other things, to be pointing to something objectively prescriptive, these claims are all false.[4]

However, given the multiplicity of senses of the term *objectivity* in common usage, it is not clear what the error is supposed to be. What exactly is it to characterize something 'as it is in itself'? Until we know this we can't judge whether (1) most people do indeed attempt to do so in using ethical concepts, or (2) if so, they are wrong to do so. It is important to recognize that an error theory requires both these conditions to be met for the same conception of objectivity. That is, it requires, for some conception of objectivity, (1) that the attribution to people of claims of objectivity is correct, and (2) that the claims thus attributed are in fact false. I shall call (1) *the attribution condition* and (2) *the falsity condition*. However, there is tension between these two conditions: the satisfaction of one condition tends to interfere with the satisfaction of the other, when the conception of objectivity is held constant. I shall consider several interpretations of Mackie's claim, and shall argue that claims that are false are not plausibly attributed to the ordinary user of ethical concepts to begin with, while claims that may perhaps be plausibly attributed are not false.

Consider *first*, briefly, the suggestion that to characterize something 'as it is in itself' is to characterize it in a way that is not conceptually linked to psychological states—to the motivation of action, or to the content of experience. If the ordinary user of ethical concepts claimed to be characterizing things in a way that is not conceptually linked to the motivation of action, at least defeasibly or holistically, then he would be making an error, just as the ordinary user of terms for secondary qualities would be making an error if he claimed to be characterizing things in a way that is not conceptually linked to the content of experience. Thus the falsity condition would be met. But neither claim *is* made by the ordinary user; if the error theory's attribution of a claim to characterize things as they are in themselves is interpreted this first way, the attribution condition is not met. Ethical terms and secondary quality terms *are* conceptually linked, as they are ordinarily understood and used, to psychological states; if they also carry claims to characterize objects as they are in themselves, these claims must be interpreted in some sense other than as claims to characterize objects in a way not linked to psychological states. Mackie might disagree on the attribution issue, as he seems to hold an error theory in the case of secondary qualities as well as ethics.[5] However, despite its (possibly) Lockean credentials, the view that most people think secondary qualities have no conceptual links to the content of experience, or mistake secondary for primary qualities, seems if anything even more immediately implausible than the view that most people think ethical concepts have no conceptual link to psychological states; and in any case I take it to have been adequately refuted by, for example, McGinn, and McDowell.[6] No doubt there is much more to be said on this subject, but I shall not try to say it. I shall put this large set of issues aside and shall not consider either such attributions, which I believe to be implausible, or error theories that depend on them, any further here.

## 4. In Pursuit of Error: Various Suppositions About Explanatory Primacy

Consider a *second* interpretation of the supposed error. Perhaps to characterize objects as they are in themselves is to characterize them in terms of concepts with explanatory primacy. *Explanatorily primary* concepts are those ultimately identified "across all theories which converge upon what are destined to be agreed upon (by us or any other determined tribe of natural researchers) as the fundamental principles of nature". Such concepts "will always pull their weight in all explanatorily adequate theories of the world", and hence are "fit to survive". They feature in what Williams has called the *absolute conception* of the world.[7] There is a sense of the term *realist* in which someone may be said to be a realist with respect to a given concept if he believes it would feature in such ideal causal theories; in this sense, Mackie was an anti-realist in that he held that ethical concepts would not feature in such theories. Perhaps the error theory should be interpreted to involve the attribution to the ordinary user of ethical concepts the realist view that ethical concepts do have explanatory primacy, do properly feature in the absolute conception.

A terminological objection may be made. There is some precedent for using the term "realist" in this way. However, if one also, reasonably, believes there are truths about viewpoints, courage, national moods, auras of sanctity, ironical insights, twinges of pain, and so on, which presumably would not feature in an absolute conception of the world, one is left saying something like: reality isn't all there truly is, or: there is more to truth than to reality. This may sound paradoxical. Thus it would be preferable to use "*scientific realism*" in place of "realism", since this makes matters clearer, and there is no hint of paradox about the common-sensical claim that the aspects of reality described by science—even by an ultimate science—aren't all there are. Of course one could stipulate that the aspects of reality described by science are all there are by loading the concept of truth with an explanatory primacy test as well as the term "scientific reality". But this would be a revisionary and inconvenient stipulation, since evidently in the ordinary sense of "truth" there are lots of truths that wouldn't feature in an absolute conception of the world or in ideal causal explanations. Moreover, it would be to close an open question: to make true by stipulation the substantive thesis, the denial of which certainly does not involve self-contradiction, that the causal-explanatorily-primary, or scientific reality, occupies the whole of reality. In short, we need one way of talking that does incorporate an explanatory primacy test, namely, talk of scientific reality, and another that does not, namely, ordinary talk of truth and falsity. There is no point in making both ways of talking do the same job.

Suppose the error theorist responds (perhaps somewhat indignantly!) to this version of the open-question argument by insisting that of course he is not making his claim true by stipulation, any more than someone who claims that water is $H_2O$ does. Rather he is making a substantive metaphysical claim to the effect that the truths about reality cited in ideal causal explanations are indeed all the truths there are, in the ordinary sense of truth, and that the ordinary person, who believes the contrary, is in error. He has now purchased a plausible attribution of belief to the ordinary person at the price of the truth of the belief in question; common beliefs in truths about particular viewpoints, for example, are not in the least undermined by the supposition that viewpoints play no role in ideal causal explanations.[8] The attribution condition is now met, but not the falsity condition. Again, the error eludes us.

But perhaps some argument could be given to underwrite the equation of the causal-explanatorily primary and reality, which would show that we're wrong to believe any propositions about viewpoints, for example, are literally true after all. The equation of $H_2O$ and water is underwritten by causal explanation; scientific explanation of the behaviour of water uses the chemical formulation "$H_2O$". But it is very difficult to see how the equation of the causal-explanatorily-primary and reality could be underwritten by causal explanation without begging the very question at issue. Moreover, scientific explanation does not itself use the concept of the causal-explanatorily-primary. Perhaps some other kind of (philosophical) explanation does;

but this just illustrates the point that reality is not revealed solely by causal-explanatory primacy. Reality is revealed by various different kinds of theorizing, not all of them scientific or strictly causal. For example, the truth about what the law really is in a particular case is determined by means of legal theorizing. Nevertheless, legal theory is not science; nor is legal explanation of cases causal explanation, even though it does formulate and test hypotheses against the data provided by other precedents and hypothetical cases. The exclusive superiority of scientific reality so far remains safely ineffable; a scientist would not be speaking scientifically if he tried to express it (though to be fair I've never met one who thought we should give up legal theory).[9]

Let us assume for the sake of argument that ethical concepts do not in fact have explanatory primacy, would not feature in an ideal causal theory or an absolute conception of the world, that *scientific anti-realism* about them, in this specific sense, is correct. I do not in fact need to take a position on this issue. For reasons to do with the very idea of an absolute conception which I shall come to, I think it is better not to take a position on this issue in the course of ordinary uses of ethical terms. Moreover, it is unnecessary to do so in order to make various points about cognitivism, objectivity, and knowledge. There are simply several different issues here, which cut across one another and should not be run together. (I have tried to make this clear, in relation to my overall divide-and-conquer strategy, by assigning to each of the terms *objectivism*, *cognitivism*, and *scientific realism* a distinct and independent sense. I have endorsed objectivism about ethics in several early chapters, and ethical cognitivism in Chapter 9, and I shall below defend the possibility of ethical knowledge; but I have not endorsed scientific realism about ethics. Obviously, no particular way of labelling the issues is essential, so long as the issues are kept distinct.) For example, an assumption of scientific anti-realism does not settle the issue of cognitivism, about whether ethical judgments express beliefs or attitudes of some other kind. Concepts used to express beliefs need not be explanatorily primary, as of course colour concepts are not. Nor does scientific anti-realism settle the question of whether beliefs, for example, about colours, could constitute knowledge. Nor is scientific anti-realism incompatible with objectivism in the sense described in Part I, which amounts to the rejection of the subjectivist view that prior and independent preferences somehow determine values. Nevertheless, the view that values do not feature in ideal scientific explanations is immediately extremely plausible and unsurprising, and has been favourably viewed by those who do not advertise themselves as skeptics about ethics.[10] So it will be of interest to assume that scientific anti-realism in this sense is correct, for the sake of argument, and see where this gets us in regard to skepticism.

This assumption is not of immediate help in establishing an error theory, since the attribution to the ordinary user of ethical concepts of the claim to characterize objects in terms of explanatorily primary concepts is again extremely implausible. Indeed, the implausibility of the attribution is directly related to the plausibility of the view that values do not feature in scientific explanations. When someone claims that a particular action would be unjust we have no reason to believe he means anything like that the concept of justice has explanatory primacy, that it would feature in some ideal scientific theory or causal explanation. Nor does he mean that it would not do so; he simply does not address the issue. Either attribution would be, apart from the prospect of finding an error, quite gratuitous.

Next, consider a *third* possible interpretation of the supposed error. Could the error be that the ordinary user of ethical concepts *ought* to aspire to use only concepts with explanatory primary, even if he does not in fact? Surely not; he is wise to refrain from taking on issues about the absolute conception of the world as part of the ordinary use of ethical terms, as they are irrelevant to his purposes. They are of course extremely interesting in their own right, but there is nothing to prevent any erstwhile ordinary user of ethical terms from pursuing these issues about the absolute conception in their own right. Thus I am not echoing Rorty's "don't care"; nor am I urging us, in a way that Williams regards as self-defeating, not to be interested in whether science describes a world that is there independently of us.[11] I am rather claiming that we should not suppose that our uses of ethical concepts do, or ought to, involve us in claiming or denying that they feature in an absolute conception of the world. The supposition involves a wild category mistake: this is simply not what we're up to in using them, nor should we be. (Does anyone really think we are? Who are those to whom ethics even begins to seem to be a branch of natural science?[12])

But nevertheless let's suppose for the sake of argument that our concepts do carry false claims to explanatory primacy, and consider the consequences. This supposition gives us a *fourth* possible interpretation of the error theory. There is, however, no evident reason to confine the supposition to ethics, to suppose that ethical concepts do carry claims to explanatory primacy while logical concepts or colour concepts, for example, do not. Given the general presence of the claim to explanatory primacy, the consequent risk of error would be widespread, even apart from worries about the very notion of an absolute conception. Logical concepts might perhaps pull their weight in the ultimate scientific theory, but ethical and legal concepts, and colour and sensation concepts, would not. And what of respectable concepts with no conceptual ties to psychological states, such as that of (absolute) simultaneity? If we really were in the unfortunate position of making generalized claims to explanatory primacy, the most effective way to avoid the risk of widespread error would be to revise our concepts so as to drop these claims and to adopt agnosticism with respect to explanatory primacy, *except when there is reason explicitly to address the issue*. The progress of science would of course be in no way impeded by such agnostic 'revision'.

An alternative would be to try to avoid the error by conforming our concepts to the requirements of scientific economy imposed by the claims to explanatory primacy they carry. Revision would presumably proceed in stages, according to category of concepts lacking explanatory primacy. At each stage, a first component of the revised meanings of concepts in a given category, such as the category of reasons for action, colours, shapes, etc., would be postulated to express the causal role of concepts in that category according to the ideal theory. At the same stage, the extensions of the various unrevised concepts falling into that category would be matched by the extensions of the second postulated component of the revised meanings, to be specified without employing concepts in that category that lack explanatory primacy. The revision process would stop only when the two components of the revised meaning of every concept in each category could be specified using only explanatorily primary concepts.

There are several disadvantages to this program for revision that would not attach to the rival agnostic 'revision'. First, we may have practical difficulties in correctly identifying explanatorily primary concepts in advance of having arrived at ideal scientific theories; but on the second proposal we would remain in error until we succeeded in doing so. Second, the proposal would respond to false claims that concepts feature in an absolute conception by in effect affirming the appropriateness of the goal of refraining from the use of all but explanatorily primary concepts. But far from being desirable, attaining such a goal would constitute a radical impoverishment of our lives and would handicap us in the pursuit of many interests: the many non-explanatorily-primary concepts we have serve many purposes in our lives. Third, there is little theoretical agreement on exactly what it is for a concept to have explanatory primacy, what grounds there are for thinking this or that set of concepts has explanatory primacy, or even on whether the absolute conception of the world ultimately makes sense.[13] To build a particular position on these matters into all our ordinary talk about other things is to build in a pervasive and unnecessary risk of error. The rival agnostic program for revision would avoid these difficulties and sources of possible error simply by eliminating any general claims to explanatory primacy. This would be achieved without the substantial and impractical changes of understanding required by the alternative. Agnostic revision would not affect our interests in causal explanation, which would remain compelling, and it would not in any way hinder the work of scientists, or the work of metaphysicians, who would continue to argue explicitly about the absolute conception and explanatory primacy. Agnosticism with respect to explanatory primacy would no more interfere with the work that ethical concepts must do than with the work that colour concepts must do: judgments using these concepts would have the same purposes and uses as before, and neither our capacities to make them nor the point of doing so would be undermined.[14] The search for ideal scientific theories and ordinary uses of ethical and other concepts could carry on peacefully coexisting under the agnostic program.

But of course there is no need for agnostic 'revision' because in fact we already follow the agnostic program. We do, and, if we didn't already, we should. Thus it is no criticism of what ordinary users of ethical concepts say to point out that ethical concepts do not have explanatory primacy. Moreover, ethical theory is transparently not a kind of scientific theory, even though ethical and scientific theorizing may have broad principles of the construction and testing of generalizations in common. Theorizing in ethics contributes to

our understanding of ourselves and of others as persons, and to the determination of the relations among our ends and values, of what we ourselves
and our communities should be like and should do; these are not among the
purposes of scientific theorizing. It would not be in the least inconsistent with
ordinary uses of ethical concepts to respond to someone who rehearsed these
points by saying: It may very well be true that ethical concepts do not subserve
our interests in causal explanation and prediction, but this can hardly be
disturbing, since we have many other interests in addition to these: we seek
to understand, evaluate, and decide, as well as to predict. Someone does not
make a mistake merely because in making ethical judgments he does not use
a concept, namely, the concept of explanatory primacy, whose applications
in such cases preoccupy the error theorist.

As a *fifth* possible interpretation of the error theory, we should perhaps
reconsider the possibility that there is some incompatibility between scientific
anti-realism about values and some other widely held beliefs or assumptions
about values: perhaps with objectivism, or with cognitivism. I addressed this
possibility briefly a few pages back, but more can be said. I said above that
the assumption of scientific anti-realism about ethics is compatible with the
rejection of subjectivism. The objectivist view developed in Part I above, that
the understanding of action in terms of beliefs and preferences is already
value-laden, is a view about the concept of intentional action as applied to
persons, or self-interpreting animals: in order for it to be warranted to regard
certain events as the acts of persons, it must be possible to attribute beliefs,
preferences, and higher-order attitudes that make those events intelligible as
the acts of persons, and in making such attributions, we do and should assume
that agents generally desire things that are valuable in various respects, and
distinguish among their various desires in these respects. Thus, *if* we apply
the concepts of a person and of intentional action, we will naturally use
evaluative concepts.[15] It does not follow that it is necessary that these concepts
be applied by sentient creatures at all, or necessary that they actually apply
to anything; there might not have been any persons. Of course, in fact there
are persons—we are they—and perhaps it can be argued that it is pragmatically
necessary for us to apply these concepts.[16] However (and this is why objectivism is compatible with scientific anti-realism in ethics), it is a still different
question whether we must use the concept of action and its associated cluster
of reason-giving concepts in ideal scientific theories.[17] The answer to this
question may be *no*, so that scientific anti-realism about action, attitudes, and
values is correct, while the objectivist view of the relation between preference
and value may also be correct. Again, for my purposes I do not need to
endorse such scientific anti-realism, but merely to point out its compatibility
with objectivism. And, again, scientific anti-realism about values does not
entail anti-realism about values *tout court*.

Even if reasons for action are causes of action, reason-giving descriptions
of events as actions may not be appropriate to the laws of ideal scientific
causal explanations. If they are not, nothing whatsoever will follow about
whether we should be interested in understanding events as the acts of per-

sons. The explanation of action is not *just* causal explanation, but a special kind of explanation, namely, rational explanation. The particular kind of understanding of reality given by a rational explanation depends on the use of reason-giving descriptions, and may not be preserved by redescription in terms appropriate to scientific explanation. Our interest in rational explanation and understanding of one another does not depend on whether reason-giving concepts feature in ideal scientific causal theories, any more than our interest in understanding music depends on whether the concepts of harmony or modulation feature in ideal scientific causal theories. As McGinn writes in a related context, of the manifest image and the scientific image, "neither view can serve the purposes of the other, and neither can be construed as setting a standard which the other can be criticised for failing to meet."[18] We go in for explanations of reality of many kinds, which do not depend for their interest on being approximations to ideal scientific causal theories, and which simply are not in competition with science. It would seem rash to claim that we should not have these interests, or that they are something to be ashamed of, and indeed the source of these odd prescriptions would be mysterious. Again, their source certainly could not be science itself; to suppose it might be would be to anthropomorphize science in a most unscientific way. *Why* then should we suppress these interests? What reason could there be for giving up law, ethics, music theory, etc.? If it were merely that we should not imagine that non-scientific explanation is scientific, or suitable to the absolute conception, no one will dissent. Has anyone ever seriously doubted that only a scientific causal theory could hope to explain scientifically and causally our attaining that theory itself? But there is a large gap between these truisms and the view that often seems to follow in their wake, namely, that reality is "no more than" scientific reality, or that there isn't any kind of understanding of reality worth having except that provided by scientific explanation. We can accept that realism about $X$ requires that $X$ do some worthwhile explanatory work, without accepting that this must be scientific explanatory work, unless we do believe that only scientific explanation is worthwhile.

Consider, for example, Blackburn's reaction to the sort of points about explanation made by McDowell. McDowell claims that the kind of explanation to which values are relevant is rational explanation, explanation that makes sense of the thing explained (as opposed to merely causally explaining it), renders it intelligible (as opposed to merely predictable), which we seek as a part of self-understanding.[19] McDowell defends the interest and relevance of such explanations against a restriction to explanations from a more external standpoint, such as those provided by science, which restriction would deprive us of a kind of intelligibility to which we aspire. He questions the presumption that scientific explanation is uniquely linked to reality and issues about realism. He does not argue *against* an interest in causal and scientific explanation, but *in favour of* something else that scientific explanation cannot displace, that is, for a generous conception of explanation which does not exclude explanation of the making-sense kind. Blackburn, at cross purposes, comments that the something else is "by itself . . . quite inert", and "goes no way toward disallowing [!] another, wider, explanatory interest which these answers quite fail to engage", which seeks causal explanation. But the question is not one of disallowing an interest in causal explanation, but rather of preventing something else from being disallowed in favour of causal explanation. The something else needn't be "by itself", so there is no threat whatsoever to an interest in causal explanation. Blackburn considers whether it could be held that his explanatory interests are unjustified, and comments that there can never be an *a priori* right to claim that our activity in making certain judgments permits of no explanation; you just have to try the various explanations out. This sounds very similar in motivation to the kind of liberality McDowell urges when he asks why we should deprive ourselves of a kind of intelligibility to which we aspire, but Blackburn makes the point in defending an interest in causal explanation as if the two were incompatible.

Perhaps revealing is Blackburn's response to the suggestion that phenomenology (for example, understanding fear, as we all know and feel it) is the philosopher's business, while causal explanation is the scientist's: he complains that "the trouble then is that the philsopher gets to say nothing" about reality and "the only philosophical activity left is playing variations on the theme of everything being what it is and not another thing".[20] No reason for upholding a unique link between scientific causal explanation and reality is explicitly given, but the implication is that he thinks there isn't any kind of understanding of reality worth having but that provided by causal explanation, that making sense, the interpretative understanding of ourselves and others, and phenomenology, cannot contribute to the understanding of reality. So the value of any kind of understanding of reality that does not feature in the absolute conception, does not pull its weight in ideal causal theories, really is being challenged, implicitly. But the challenge can't stand being made explicit, because it's simply baffling to claim that causal understanding is the only kind worth having.

Moreover, if it were true without qualification that causal explanation is better left to scientists, the consequence (if it were one) that this would leave philosophers with nothing to do could hardly count as a compelling reason for philosophers to go in for causal explanation. The case would have to be that philosophy can actually contribute to causal explanation, as well as to other kinds of explanation. There is a great deal of interest to questions about how, as a causal matter, we come to have concepts and behaviours that mark just those distinctions that ours mark. Human beings perceive only a certain segment of a larger spectrum of wavelengths as colour, and certain distinctions within that segment, while other creatures perceive other distinctions, as well as magnetic fields and the direction of the polarization of light.[21] Certain patterns of 'altruistic' behavior are common in certain species, others in others. But the kind of puzzlement about such facts that calls for scientific explanation survives philosophical accounts, however successful, of the concepts of colour, or altruism. Moreover, neither the raising nor the answering of such scientific questions about colour discriminations, for example, requires a particular philosophical account. The descriptions in terms of wavelength appropriate to investigation of the causal basis of our capacity to perceive colour are equally available, for example, to the non-centralist and the centralist about colours. (Recall from Chapters 2 and 3 that the non-centralist holds that the general concept of colour is not independent of specific colour concepts and their relationships to one another, while the centralist accounts for the specific colour concepts in terms of a prior general concept of colour.)

If it can be made the object of causal explanation that we see certain wavelengths and not others as colours, perhaps it can likewise be made the object of causal explanation that we see certain natural events and not others as intentional acts or as providing reasons for action. By rejecting the subjectivist view that preference is conceptually independent of and prior to values, we in no way preempt or displace science; whether a given distribution of reason-giving status to features of the world is a conceptual matter or is an appropriate object of attempts at causal explanation depends on the way the world is described. Reason-giving concepts, with their conceptual ties to action, do not float free of the familiar physical world; they do not describe a different or queer world, but the same world, in a different way, as the site of the intelligible acts of persons. The objectivist about values is no less capable than the subjectivist of describing the world in terms appropriate to science.

## 5. In Pursuit of Error: Explanatory Primacy and Debunking Explanations

So far, I've argued that the ordinary user of ethical concepts does not in fact make any claim with respect to their explanatory primacy or lack thereof in everyday applications of such concepts; that there is no reason to make any such claim for many purposes; that if such a claim were made indiscriminately, it should be dropped; and that scientific anti-realism about values is nevertheless compatible with believing that there are values, with ethical cognitivism, and with the rejection of subjectivism. No error has yet been flushed out of our five possible interpretations of the error theory.

However, the possibility of causal explanations of our uses of certain concepts suggests a way in which the notion of explanatory primacy might lead less directly to an error theory. If ethical concepts are not explanatorily primary, then ethical concepts do not feature in the ideal lawlike generalizations that causally explain our uses of ethical concepts. Thus, presumably some sociobiological-cum-game-theoretic, or psychological, or neurophysiological explanation, or some combination of such explanations, may in principle be found of our uses of ethical concepts, which makes the use of ethical concepts in the ideal causal theory unnecessary. Mackie, however, faults ethical values for their epistemological *in*accessibility:

When we ask the awkward question, how we can be aware of this authoritative prescriptivity, of the truth of these distinctively ethical premises or of the cogency of this distinctively ethical pattern of reasoning, none of our ordinary accounts of sensory perception or introspection or the framing and confirming of explanatory hypotheses or inference or logical construction or conceptual analysis, or any combination of these, will provide a satisfactory answer.[22]

Of course, Mackie is not faulting ethical values *both* for the explicability *and* for the inexplicability of our awareness of them. In order for Mackie's comment not to be in tension with the view that ethical concepts are not explanatorily primary, hence that our uses of them can be explained by a theory that does not use ethical concepts, we must assume that whatever might scientifically explain our uses of ethical concepts would be *independent*, in some sense, of what he claims would be inaccessible to explanation. Otherwise, the explanation implied by the claim that ethical concepts are not explanatorily primary would itself belie the claim that awareness of ethical values is inaccessible to explanation. Suppose we have a sociobiological-cum-game-theoretical explanation of some prevalent ethical belief that $e$, say the belief that $X$-ing is unjust. Why does this explanation itself not describe a mechanism by which we become aware of the truth that $X$-ing is unjust? The assumption would seem to be that our belief that $X$-ing is unjust can be explained whether or not it is true that $X$-ing is unjust, that the explanation shows that if it were not true that $X$-ing is unjust, we would still believe it. Such an explanation would aim to *debunk* the belief it explains by showing that even if the belief just happened to be true, it wouldn't constitute knowledge. Thus Simon Blackburn and Bernard Williams both press the need to address in the case of purported evaluative knowledge the general requirement for knowledge put forward by Nozick that if it hadn't been true that $p$, the knower wouldn't have believed that $p$.[23]

The necessity of this counterfactual tracking condition for inferential knowledge has been questioned, since it carries with it failure of deductive closure, which arguably is an undesirable attribute in inferential knowledge.[24] But skeptical challenges to knowledge often depend on this condition, as in: if you were a brain floating in a tank on Alpha Centauri being stimulated to believe you were living on Earth, you would still believe you weren't in the tank; so you don't know that you're not.[25] Certainly debunking arguments often assume that some such tracking condition holds, as the point of the debunking explanations is often to show that even if the belief thus explained weren't true, we'd still believe it, so it can't be knowledge.

Consider then a *sixth* possible interpretation of the error theory. Perhaps the error made by the ordinary user of ethical concepts is not in believing ethical concepts to have explanatory primacy themselves, but in believing that our applications of them cannot be explained in a way that thus debunks them. In particular, perhaps he falsely believes that it is not the case that: we would believe that $X$-ing is unjust whether or not it were true that $X$-ing is unjust. That Mackie may have had something like this in mind is suggested by his argument from relativity in support of the error theory. As he writes,

> Disagreement on questions in history or biology or cosmology does not show that there are no objective issues in these fields for investigators to disagree about. But such scientific disagreement results from speculative inferences or explanatory hypotheses based on inadequate evidence, and it is hardly plausible to interpret moral disagreement in the same way. Disagreement about moral codes seems to reflect people's adherence to and participation in different ways of life. The causal connection seems to be mainly that way round: it is that people approve of monogamy because they participate in a monogamous way of life rather than that they participate in a monogamous way of life because they approve of monogamy. . . . Of course there have been and are moral heretics and moral reformers, people who have turned against the established rules and practices of their own communities for moral reasons and often for moral reasons that we would endorse. But this can ususaly be understood as the extension, in ways which, though new and unconventional, seemed to them to be required for consistency, of rules to which they already adhered as arising out of an existing way of life. In short, the argument from relativity has some force simply because the actual variations in the moral codes are more readily explained by the hypothesis that they reflect ways of life than by the hypothesis that they express perceptions, most of them seriously inadequate and badly distorted, of objective values.[26]

There is little I should wish to resist in this passage, until we reach the last sentence. But what isn't immediately clear is why Mackie thinks the considerations he adduces here support an error theory. In offering them in support of an error theory, he seems to be assuming that if you can causally explain an evaluative belief without referring to or applying the values the beliefs are about, but in other terms, then you've defeated some claim evaluative beliefs carry. Without this assumption, there is a gap between the considerations he adduces here and the support for the error theory he wishes to derive from them. I've argued the supposed erroneous claim cannot be a claim that evaluative concepts feature in causal explanations; but perhaps it might be instead be a claim that evaluative beliefs can't be explained in such a way as to be debunked, that is, so as to show that even if they weren't true we'd believe them.

There would be little point in predicating an error theory on the assumption that someone who knows that *e* must know, or even believe, that he knows that *e*, or in particular must know, or even believe, that if it weren't true that *e* he wouldn't believe *e*, since this assumption is highly controversial. If certain of Nozick's externalist claims about knowledge are correct, someone who has an ethical belief that *e* need not believe that if *e* weren't true he wouldn't believe that *e*; so if the latter counterfactual is false, and his ethical belief is not knowledge, his ethical belief may nonetheless be true. That is, he does not hold a false belief, as postulated by an error theory, merely because he has a belief that does not constitute knowledge. Nozick allows that it may be necesary for knowledge that the believer not believe that it is not the case that if his belief weren't true he wouldn't believe it. So someone who believes his ethical belief has been debunked, even though he is wrong, would not have knowledge; but it is hardly going to be of comfort to an error theorist that misguided skepticism can destroy knowledge. Nozick doubts even that it's necessary for knowledge that a person's belief be in equilibrium, such that knowledge of the causes of his belief would not lead him no longer to have it.[27]

## 6. The Possibility of Evaluative Knowledge: Mere Lack of Explanatory Primacy Does Not Debunk

At this point it may be most fruitful to give up trying to reconstruct some element of ordinary ethical claims that makes them erroneous, and pursue directly the skepticism about the possibility of ethical knowledge suggested by Mackie's argument and raised explicitly by Blackburn and Williams. An important issue raised by the possibility of debunking explanations goes beyond the mere truth or falsity of ethical beliefs to whether or not an ethical belief could constitute knowledge, and in particular could meet the condition that if it weren't true, it wouldn't be believed. Do the kind of explanations of ethical beliefs Mackie envisages show that they do not meet this condition?

Williams' remarks on the possibility of ethical knowledge suggest complications.[28] He argues that, while tracking and knowledge may be possible of ethical truths that involve applications of what he calls *thick* concepts (and what I have called specific reason-giving concepts), tracking and knowledge at the general, reflective, all things considered level are not possible. I shall examine the kinds of consideration he offers in support of this view. However, we should notice at once that there is a tension between the suggestion that causal explanations, such as sociobiological explanations, of our uses of ethical concepts interfere with tracking, hence debunk ethical knowledge claims, and Williams' view. This is because such explanations seem to work best for the specific concepts, such as reciprocity, chastity, etc. Williams allows that such explanations at the level of specific concepts may have something in common with explanations of our capacities to perceive the world in terms of secondary qualities, which help us to understand how we have evolved "so that the physical world will present itself to us in reliable and useful ways". This kind of understanding does not undermine claims to knowledge, and may even support them.[29] In order to understand how this might be so, we must look more closely at the tracking relationship. But first we must try to understand why Williams admits this possibility for the specific concepts, and denies it at the reflective level.

Williams begins by making out a sensible distinction between science and ethics with respect to convergence. Scientific enquiry aims to converge on answers such that the best explanation of the convergence involves the idea that these answers represent how things are. We are on familiar ground here: concepts with explanatory primacy are such that ideal causal explanations of the beliefs of those who employ those concepts would feature those concepts. Of course, only a causal theory could hope causally to explain belief in itself. This much is fine. I should want to add the thought I expressed in the last section: "And of course ethics aims at no such thing". But this is not the other half of Williams' distinction. Rather, he says that "in the area of the ethical, at least at a high level of generality, there is no such coherent hope", and also that "ethical thought has no chance of being everything it seems".[30] That is, he seems not to be merely pointing out that science aims to discover true propositions featuring explanatorily primary concepts and ethics doesn't, which we should be happy to concede, at least for the sake of argument, but supposing that ethics does too, and is doomed to failure. I have already argued that this understanding of ethics cannot be defended. It's false that ethics has "no hope of being everything it seems", not because it seems to describe reality in explanatorily primary terms and it really does so after all, but because it doesn't seem to do so to begin with, nor should it. Ethics simply doesn't have the aspirations with respect to the explanation of convergence Williams' attributes to it. Thus it embodies no error on this score.

Williams goes on to caution that his points about explanatory primacy, convergence, and the absolute conception of the world "relate to science, not to all kinds of knowledge" and that the point is not to contrast ethics and knowledge but ethics and science. He admits that we may have perspectival knowledge, knowledge of secondary qualities picked out by non-universal perceptual capacities, and ethical knowledge involving the thick concepts, so that it may be no accident that we have true beliefs in these areas. His discussion of how it is possible for beliefs employing thick ethical concepts to track the truth does not invoke the absolute conception, explanatory primacy, or convergence; there is no supposition that specific ethical concepts feature in causal explanations of why we go in for applying them.[31] He then returns to the question of whether ethical knowledge at the general, reflective, all-things-considered level may be possible and comments that we need some account of what tracking the truth at this level will be. In this context, I find his next remarks very puzzling: "The idea that our beliefs can track the truth at this level must at least imply that a range of investigators could rationally, reasonably, and unconstrainedly come to converge on a determinate set of ethical conclusions"; "if it [such a process] is construed as convergence on a body of ethical truths which is brought about and explained by the fact that they are truths—this would be the strict analogy to scientific objectivity—then I see no hope for it." In particular, he sees no hope of extending to the reflective level the considerations that made knowledge possible at the level of the thick concepts. Williams "cannot see any convincing theory of knowledge for the convergence of reflective ethical thought on ethical reality in even a distant analogy to the scientific case", nor a convincing analogy with mathematics. Thus we cannot understand ethical reflection as a process that can hope to arrive at knowledge.[32]

Why, when he reaches the general ethical concepts, does Williams in effect revert to an equation of science and knowledge that he has earlier repudiated?

Why should tracking require anything about the explanation of convergence and/or explanatory primacy just at this point? There is nothing in the idea of tracking that requires the proposition believed to feature in causal explanations of why it is believed of a kind appropriate to science. This is one kind of non-accidental link between truth and belief, but Nozick introduces his counterfactual tracking account of knowledge as an improvement upon a causal theory of knowledge, and comments that causal linkage may be merely one way of realizing a more general linkage that constitutes knowledge.[33] Nor is there any apparent motivation for an explanation-of-convergence requirement independent of a demand for explanatory primacy and a tacit equation of knowledge and science; such a requirement would rule out the possibility of knowledge of how essentially contested concepts apply, and that is just what is in question.

Williams' claim that "the idea that our beliefs can track the truth at this level must at least imply that a range of investigators could rationally, reasonably, and unconstrainedly come to converge on a determinate set of ethical conclusions" should not be accepted. What can be supposed for the sake of argument to be necessary for some person's general ethical belief to constitute knowledge, without begging the relevant questions for our purposes, is *not* that a range of investigators could reasonably and unconstrainedly come to converge on it, or that any convergence there may be have any particular explanation, but rather that if the proposition believed weren't true the person in question wouldn't believe it (and, perhaps we should add, that if it were he would). Such counterfactuals might hold of some particular person's beliefs even though there was no reason to think disagreement in all things considered judgments about what to do would ever come to an end, or that, if it were to, this would be causally explained by the truth of the believed propositions. The failure of these convergence conditions does not *per se* undermine the knowledge of those who possess it; the failure of these conditions may be determined, indeed overdetermined, by many factors other than universal lack of knowledge. To ignore this is to assume (optimistically? or on political grounds?) too great a degree of uniformity, or potential uniformity, among persons and their situations; one person's knowledge does not depend on another's capacity for it. The failure of the convergence conditions would impugn knowledge only when all differences among the investigators relevant to their capacity for knowledge in particular areas could with justification be assumed away. But such justification would itself require an account of knowledge and would not depend on facts about convergence; so it's not clear what work the convergence conditions are doing.

Some people might simply be better at discovering truths about what should be done, all things considered, than others (who might be better at discovering other kinds of truth); and even within the former domain, some people might be better at discovering the truth in certain subsets of the domain, and others in others.[34] Moreover, someone's knowledge in one domain does not necessarily depend on his knowledge in other domains. Someone who forms beliefs by a method that works for some sorts of propositions but not others, and who applies it indiscriminately, *may* nonetheless have knowledge of propositions of the former sorts.[35] The causal explanation of how he comes to have these knowledge-constituting beliefs might describe the causes of his having the particular constitution which, under another description, amounts to a sensibility which provides a reliable method of discovering the truth in these cases. But for the method to be reliably linked to the truth of these propositions it is not necessary for these propositions to appear in the causal explanation of why he believes them or why he has the sensibility.

For example, some people have very specific agnosias, or recognitional disabilities. Perhaps the most familiar is prosopagnosia, or inability to recognize faces, on the part of someone whose vision is otherwise unimpaired. Consider a hypothetical example in which someone has the capacity to recognize various fruits, and the capacity to recognize pictures of most things, but is unable to recognize pictures of fruit in particular, despite verbal competence with descriptions of pictures of fruit.[36] Such a person's inability to recognize pictures of fruit reliably by looking would not in the least undermine her knowledge, acquired by looking, that something is a picture of a cat. No doubt there is some neurophysiological-cum-evolutionary explanation to be found of the general convergence of opinions about pictures of fruit and of the agnosiac's specific recognitional incapacity. But we need not insist that the explanation essentially depend on use of the concept of a picture, in order to attribute to the agnosiac knowledge that something is a picture of a cat, or to others knowledge that something is a picture of a mango. The links required for knowledge, between truths about pictures of fruits or non-fruits and beliefs about pictures of fruits or non-fruits, respectively, may hold even though the convergence conditions are not met.

How can it be known in particular cases when the links between belief and truth needed for knowledge hold or fail to hold? There are various points to be made that I shall discuss below in section 10 and in Chapter 15, in considering the way the division of epistemic labour figures in the justification of democracy. For example, we generally expect people to be better at arriving at true beliefs when they do not already have very strong desires to believe one thing rather than another.[37] But for present purposes, of defending the possibility of ethical knowledge against skepticism, a critical point is that we may not know that these links hold; knowledge on the tracking account requires that the links hold, but it does not require that it be known that the links hold. As Nozick says, "If there is an external fact to which we are linked, then eventually the linkage must turn external".[38]

Of course these remarks do not relieve us from the obligation to say something about what the linkage would amount to in the case of general ethical concepts. Williams and Blackburn are right to say that we need some account of tracking the truth here.[39] My aim so far in this section, however, has been to consider whether causal explanations of the uses of ethical concepts that do not feature those concepts necessarily interfere with tracking by showing that even if the belief weren't true we would still believe it.

Williams himself has provided some reason to doubt they must have this effect, in conceding the possibility of knowledge for the specific ethical concepts where sociobiological explanations, for example, are at their most plausible. I don't know whether a neurophysiological or sociobiological explanation could be given of deliberation and the pursuit of coherence. It's not difficult to see that the requirement of "articulate consistency", as Dworkin calls it, could have a stabilizing function in law and politics.[40] More generally, deliberation and the pursuit of coherence is intimately bound up with the creation of our identities as persons, self-interpreting subjects with second- and higher-order attitudes as opposed to mere wantons; there may, for all I know, be interesting things to be said about why creatures that go in for these activities have evolved, about the effects and the causal role of such complicated attitudes, though perhaps under different descriptions. If so, however, it will not necessarily follow that such explanations show that beliefs about what should be done, all things considered, would be held whether or not they were true and thus do not constitute knowledge.

### 7. The Debunker's Dilemma, Horn 1: The Problematic Status of Counterevaluative Suppositions

What kind of explanation of a belief about what should be done, all things considered, *would* show that even if it were false, it would be believed? It would need to be one that positively supported Mackie's assumption, namely, that what explained the belief was *counterfactually independent* (not merely conceptually) of the truth of the belief. (As we'll see, it is important that conceptual independence does not entail counterfactual independence, as in the case of the relations between particular ethical and non-ethical propositions.) In order to appraise this counterfactual independence claim, we'll need to depend on some understanding of what the truth of such a belief involves, counterfactual independence from which is at issue. I'll depend on the coherence account I've given of all-things-considered judgments about what should be done, which Williams denies can express knowledge. We can approach the connection between the counterfactual independence claim and the coherence account by first considering a particular kind of response to attempts to debunk ethical knowledge.

Responses of the kind I have in mind try to show that the attempt to apply the counterfactual condition is misguided because of the problematic status of counterfactuals with impossible antecedents. Such reponses to skepticism appeal to the impossibility of the antecedent of counterfactuals such as "if it weren't true that $e$, it wouldn't be believed that $e$", where $e$ is some necessary truth of ethics. Ronald Dworkin has made this kind of argument, and it is also suggested by various remarks Nozick makes. In the case of knowledge of a necessary proposition of mathematics, to require that if it weren't true, so and so wouldn't believe it, involves evaluating a counterfactual with an impossible antecedent, and Nozick doubts that a theory of counterfactuals can handle such cases satisfactorily. If the world were so different that the impossible were true, how can we say what else would be true, or which possible worlds would be closer or further away? He suggests that in these cases only the other, positive member of his pair of tracking conditions for knowledge, that if it were true that *e*, so and so would believe it, applies, and that if ethical truths are necessary the same holds for ethical knowledge. Then it would not be a requirement of ethical knowledge that if the ethical belief weren't true it wouldn't be believed, and the debunking strategy is undermined from the very beginning; we can evaluate neither claims that if the impossible were true it wouldn't be believed nor claims that if the impossible were true it would be believed. Moreover, Nozick says that some ethical truths at least are more like necessary truths than like contingent ones. However, Nozick seems to be unwilling to put exclusive weight on this argument in defending the possibility of ethical knowledge, as he considers seriously the possibility that sociobiological explanations of ethical beliefs undercut the tracking of ethical truth by ethical belief by showing that if the beliefs weren't true, we'd still believe them.[41]

The above argument may be correct, but I too am unwilling to rely on it exclusively to undermine the debunking strategy. The matter of whether ethical truths are necessary is complicated. It's not clear that they are necessary in many cases that are the target of debunking tactics, and in particular in the cases I'm especially concerned with here, namely, cases involving claims about what should be done, all things considered, which are the target of Williams' skepticism. Values have a non-optional role in the interpretation of action and the attribution of all-things-considered judgments, and specific ethical truths appear in a special kind of explanation of action, rational explanation, as do specific truths about mental states. Is this enough to make specific ethical truths necessary in some sense? Specific truths about mental states don't seem to be necessary. Even if general principles such as "slavery is unjust" are necessary, it's still questionable whether "what he did was perfectly fair" is necessary, or, "even so, it was the wrong thing to do, all things considered", on occasions when these claims are true. At any rate, I don't wish to be committed to defending their necessity. What should thus be said about purported debunking explanations in these cases?

## 8. The Debunker's Dilemma, Horn 2, Preliminaries: Projection vs. Interpretation, and the Explanation of Supervenience

Some ethical truths may be necessary in some sense, but I shall not take a position on this question. I shall rather try to show that it is not necessary for ethical truths to be necessary in order to defend the possibility of ethical knowledge. Certainly we shouldn't want the possibility of knowledge of truths about what should be done, all things considered, to depend on the assumption that they are conceptual necessities. Is there really nothing we can say about

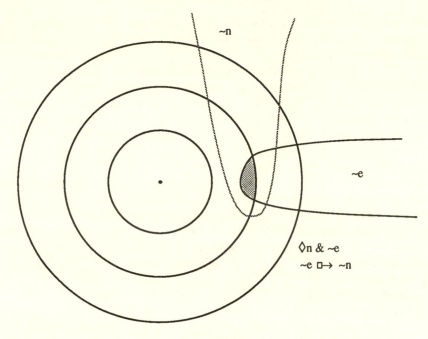

FIGURE 14.1

what would be the case if, as may be conceptually possible, at least, they were false?

Consistent with the denial that ethical truths are conceptually necessary is the conceptual doctrine that the evaluative characteristics of alternatives supervene on, or are some function of, their non-evaluative characteristics. It is not a conceptually necessary truth that slavery, as identified by its non-evaluative characteristics, is wrong, all things considered (though it may be necessary in some other sense), but supervenience requires that if it weren't wrong there would be some further difference between slavery in our world and slavery in the close conceptually possible world we've imagined. The irreducibility of concepts in one set to concepts in another does not entail their counterfactual independence. That is, it may be conceptually possible that slavery, just as it is in non-evaluative respects, is not wrong, all things considered; and it may also be true that if slavery weren't wrong, all things considered, it wouldn't be just as it is in non-evaluative respects. Schematically, where $a$ is some alternative, $E(\ )$ is some ethical characteristic of $a$, and $CN(\ )$ is some complete specification of the non-ethical characteristics of $a$ ("CN" for "complete non-ethical"), let the proposition that $e$ be the proposition that $E(a)$, and the proposition that $n$ be the proposition that $CN(a)$. Then it is possible that $n$ and not $e$; and if it were not that $e$ then it would not be that $n$.

Figure 14.1 illustrates this state of affairs, in the style of David Lewis' *Counterfactuals*. The counterevaluative worlds in which $n$ and not-$e$ are farther away from the actual world at the center, in which $n$ and $e$, than are the merely counterfactual worlds in which not-*n* and not-*e*; the concentric circles indicate the distance, or degree of dissimiliarity, of possible worlds from the actual world.[42]

Similar patterns of conceptual relationships between propositions of different kinds are not unusual, though they may have different explanations in different cases. Consider:

> 1. The relationship between propositions about melody, harmony and modulation, and propositions about frequencies.[43]
>
> 2. The relationship between propositions about faces and their expressions and propositions about the physical characteristics and configuration of bones, muscles, skin, etc. at the front of someone's head. (I shall say more about this case below, in section 10.)
>
> 3. The relationship between propositions about the truth or meaning of sentences or utterances and propositions about the physical characteristics of certain marks or sounds (holding context constant).[44]
>
> 4. The relationship between propositions about mental states or events, and those about behavioural states or events: If the person hadn't wanted to have an umbrella just in case it rained and believed it was unlikely to rain, he wouldn't have behaved like that in those circumstances; nevertheless, it's conceptually possible for him to have behaved just as he did in those circumstances while not minding getting wet and believing the odds of rain were even. The counterpsychological, so to speak, worlds in which this is the case are further away than those in which he neither wanted to have the umbrella just in case it rained, which he judged unlikely, nor behaved the way he did.[45]
>
> 5. The relationship between propositions about theory, explanation, or interpretation, and those that describe the data. If the best theory/explanation/interpretation of such and such didn't say that such and such, the data would have to be different in some way; nevertheless, the data don't entail what the best theory/explanation/interpretation is, so it's conceptually that the data are exactly the same, yet the best theory/explanation/interpretation is different. The countertheoretical worlds are further away.[46]

For purposes of understanding the supervenience of ethical judgments, given their role in interpretation, the last case is the most suggestive. I have argued in Chapters 10 through 13 that ethical theories, represented by coherence functions, properly do take account of counter*factual* possibilities, involving hypothetical alternatives to which the relevant values apply, but not counter*evaluative* possibilities. Given the role of specific values in structuring and constraining the interpretation and deliberative self-interpretation of persons that I've argued for, the greater distance of counterevaluative worlds from the actual world may be a special case of the greater distance of countertheoretical worlds from the actual world.[47] In particular, an explanation is suggested of why evaluative characteristics of possible acts supervene, as a matter of conceptual necessity, on nonevaluative, though no particular correlations between evaluative and nonevaluative characteristics are conceptually necessary. A coherence account reflects the fact that evaluations of alternatives play an essential role in the rational explanations of choices among possible acts, explanations that render these natural events intelligible as the intentional acts of persons. According to such an account, a claim about what should be done, all things considered, is a claim that there is some best theory about the specific values that apply and the alternatives, both actual and hypothetical, they apply to, that favours a certain possible act. We have seen in Chapter 12 that what should be done is some function of the specific evaluative and non-evaluative characteristics of alternatives. In simple, non-conflict cases, a specific evaluative concept by itself can explain why someone did something, can provide a reading of a natural event as an intentional act. For specific evaluative concepts to play this explanatory role, the specific evaluative characteristics of alternatives must themselves be some function of their non-evaluative characteristics. Thus, what should be done, all things considered, must itself be some function of the non-evaluative characteristics of the alternatives. Moreover, the claim that the value of one variable is a function of the value of another, or that truths of one sort are a function of truths of another sort, entails that a relationship of counterfactual dependence holds between the two: if the value of the function were different, the argument would have to be different (though if the argument were different, the value of the function might nevertheless be the same).

Supervenience follows directly from this functional relationship, which itself follows from the relationship between propositions about the best theory/explanation/interpretation and propositions about what is explained or interpreted:[48] if it were not the case that the best theory says what it actually does say, the data about the alternatives would have to be different in some non-evaluative respect. (The supervenience of propositions about best theories on data is not inconsistent with the possibility of moderate *a posteriori* underdetermination of theory, which I have admitted in developing a coherence account. The latter possibility merely requries that "best theory" in the existential claim made by the coherence account and in the supervenience claim be understood to include equal-best theories in such cases. As was the case in my development of a coherence account in earlier chapters, my talk of best theories in the rest of this chapter should be understood in this way.) If one mode of description carries claims about the best theory or way of making sense of events described in another mode, the former must be some function of the latter. If characteristics of the former sort are some function of characteristics of the latter sort, then if there were some difference between the alternatives with respect to the former characteristics, there would also be some difference between them with respect to the latter characteristics.[49] For example, if slavery weren't wrong, it wouldn't be just as it is in non-evaluative respects, or to revert to the earlier schematism, if it were not that $e$, then it would not be that $n$.

If a coherence account is correct, then claims about what ought to be done manifest supervenience as a conceptual matter for the same reason that claims about the best theory do, which is compatible with the lack of entailment of any particular theory by the data. The role of evaluative characteristics of alternatives in making it possible to understand the natural world as the site of personal agency would necessitate supervenience, but not correlations between particular evaluative and non-evaluative characteristics. (I do not rule out the possibility that a stronger relation than supervenience may hold between specific evaluative concepts and the concepts they supervene on, even though I do rule out the corresponding possibility for all-things-considered judgments. However, *at least* supervenience holds for specific concepts, and the point here is merely that an explanation of supervenience is available that doesn't depend on any stronger relationship's holding.)

There is a source of possible misunderstanding about the way in which propositions about the best theory/explanation/interpretation supervene on data. I'm not taking the position which Simon Blackburn is arguing against when he claims that the relation between theoretical facts and evidence for them is not like, hence cannot explain, the relation of supervenience in ethics:

> Suppose we imagine a total phenomenal description of a world, giving an answer to every possible question about what is observed or would be observed under any circumstances. Suppose that this . . . description does not as a matter of conceptual necessity entail the truth of any particular scientific theory . . . it merely affords evidence for it, whilst leaving open the possibility of other and perhaps conflicting theoretical truths . . . . Just because of this there is no conceptual pressure to suppose that whenever we have [the phenomenal description] we must have the same [particular theoretical truth]. Nor is there any reason to suppose that if one part of a world is phenomenally just like another, there must be the same underlying [particular theoretical truths].[50]

By contrast, the explanation of supervenience afforded by a coherence account does not depend on the identification of any particular best theory, only on an appeal to the best theory (whatever it may be).

As was explained in Chapter 10 section 3, a coherence account does not depend on claims of the form: there is some best theory, or function representing a theory, such that it is conceptually necessary that what should be done, all things considered, is favoured by this theory. It can admit that this is not the case, and thus that for any theory, or function representing a theory, it's conceptually possible that what should be done, all things considered is not favoured by that theory. So open questions remain open. But all this is compatible with the claim that a coherence account does involve, and which provides the explanation of supervenience, namely, that it's conceptually necessary that there is some best theory, or function representing a theory, such that what should be done, all things considered, is favoured by that theory.

In general, of course, claims of the form: it's necessary that there is some function such that . . . , do not entail claims of the form: there is some function such that it's necessary that . . . . Again, for example, we might have good reasons for claiming that, necessarily, utility is some function of income, while having no reason to claim that there is any particular function such that, necessarily, utility is that function of income.[51] In a coherence account, it is the appeal to the best theory, whatever that may be (giving the existential quantifier narrower scope than the necessity operator), that explains supervenience without reducibility.

Simon Blackburn has claimed that it is difficult for a realist about values, as opposed to a projectivist, to explain the combination of supervenience and irreducibility.

> To make the peculiarity of the view evident we can put it like this. Imagine a thing A which has a certain set of naturalistic properties and relations. A also has a certain degree of moral worth, say, it is very good. This, according to the realist, reports the existence of a state of affairs: A's goodness. Now the existence of this state of affairs is not entailed by A being as it is in all naturalistic respects. That is, it is logically possible that A should be as it is in all naturalistic respects, yet this further state of affairs not exist. But if that's a logical possibility, why isn't it a logical possibility that A should stay as it is in all naturalistic respects, when it was once good, and cease to be good? The existence of the naturalistic facts doesn't guarantee, logically, the moral state of affairs, so why should their continuation give a logical guarantee of the continued existence of the moral state of affairs? . . . Supervenience becomes, for the realist, an opaque, isolated, logical fact, for which no explanation can be proferred.[52]

I'm not certain I understand the distinction he intends between what he refers to as "realism" and his favoured alternative, projectivism, so I'm not certain whether I'm in disagreement with him at this point or not. I suspect that Blackburn's issue between realism and projectivism does not coincide with any of the distinct issues I have addressed: not the objectivist/subjectivist issue, nor the scientific realist/scientific anti-realist issue, nor the cognitivist/non-cogntivist issue, nor the issue about tracking.[53] I shall, however, try to clarify the relationship of the explanation of supervenience I've given to the error theory, the rejection of subjectivism and the possibility of ethical knowledge.

Recall that for ethical purposes it does not matter *per se* whether evaluative propositions feature in causal explanations of evaluative beliefs or not, since in making evaluative claims we are not claiming that they do, nor should we be. Thus we make no error if they do not. Nothing I have said in explaining supervenience casts doubt on this conclusion.

Note that the explanation of supervenience I have given does not depend on or lead to subjectivism, the view that values are determined by preferences conceived as prior and indendepent. Rather, the explanation of supervenience derives from a coherence account, developed as an alternative to subjectivism, and ultimately from considerations about interpretation that result in the rejection of subjectivism and support the view that evaluative constraints are among the constitutive constraints on interpretation, in virtue of which preferences have determinate content at all. An argument to the contrary may be suggested by remarks made by Colin McGinn about Davidson's doctrine of anomalous monism, which also combines supervenience and irreducibility doctrines. He writes:

> ... what are we to make of those irreducible mental properties of the brain ... ? They are said to be fixed by physical properties of the brain, but how *can* they be, given their categorial difference from physical properties? What kind of dependence is this? What is its explanation? ... I suspect that Davidson does not get himself worked up about these questions because of a more or less tacit instrumentalism about mental ascriptions: to have mental properties is to be interpretable by the ascription of mental predicates—having a mind is as much dependent upon the interpreter as the interpretee. Suppose one were such an instrumentalist: then one would not be excessively concerned about how the physical properties of a subject fix his mental properties, since these latter properties are possessed, as it were, only by courtesy—they are projected onto the subject by the interpreter. I think this kind of instrumentalism does alleviate the worry about irreducible mental properties—but at an obvious cost. The question to worry about is: can one rest content with anomalous monism if one believes that mental properties are objectively determined?[54]

But note the transition McGinn makes from the plural or social nature of interpretative practices to a view of mental properties as possessed only by courtesy, or projected, with the implication that projection is somehow arbitrary, as opposed to being objectively determined. This transition must be puzzling to anyone whose very understanding of objectivity depends on the public and social character of interpretation, as Davidson's does,[55] and as mine does. The only obvious cost of Davidson's view seems to be an individualistic conception of the mental as an autonomous realm, independent of the natural and social environments of agents, and his view of objectivity emerges from the rejection of such a conception of the mental.[56]

Blackburn certainly thinks an explanation of the combination of supervenience and irreducibility in the ethical case can be given. He thinks supervenience can be explained in terms of the constraints on the proper 'projection' of attitudes, and that our purpose in projecting value predicates may demand that we respect it.[57] So, his explanation appeals to constraints on projection, and mine to constraints on interpretation; what does the difference amount to? I'm not certain, but will hazard some guesses. (I certainly do not attribute these views on the relationship between projection and interpretation to Blackburn. But if the contrast cannot be drawn in some such way, then projection is just another name for interpretation, and my arguments in Part I about the relations between preference and values in support of objectivism apply to projection.)

Projection may be a subjectivist business. Constraints on projection sound as if they might be: formal rather than substantive, or at least not evaluative; optional; subject to or expressive of value-independent preferences; or discovered through empirical investigation of independently determined contents rather than constitutive. Interpretation, by contrast, is not a subjectivist business. Constraints on interpretation are: substantive as well as formal; evaluative; not optional; and play a constitutive role in the very process of determining the will; they are not the subject of empirical generalizations about independently determined contents (in the sense explained in Chapter 5 section 5).[58] However, nothing Blackburn says makes it more plausible for the subjectivist to explain supervenience in terms of constraints on projection than for the objectivist to explain it in terms of constraints on interpretation. Indeed objectivism and subjectivism don't differ over the need for such a formal constraint, but rather over the issue of further substantive and especially evaluative constraints and over the relations between preference and values and the rest of the world. The subjectivist has the world determining preferences first, so to speak, and then preferences determining values (through projection), whereas the objectivist holds that preferences and values arrive 'in the world' together, with persons. But an explanation of supervenience as a formal constraint is in the offing either way. The need to explain the combination of supervenience and irreducibility does not determine an issue between projection and interpretation, or between subjectivism and objectivism. Thus a subjectivist-projectivist approach has no advantages on this score over an objectivist-interpretationalist approach.

Blackburn considers the perceptual model as the rival to projectivism in ethics. However, perhaps the supervenience constraint on interpretation can help to make sense of talk of ethical perception. Perception cannot be conceived to have as its objects only scientific reality and the characteristics of the world conceived absolutely, so that one is only perceiving something if it features (in the right way) in the causal explanation of one's experience or belief, and otherwise one is projecting. If perception were conceived this narrowly, then one could not perceive the evaluative characteristics of actions, but neither could one perceive modulations, or facial expressions, or colours, or many things we ordinarily think we do perceive. Blackburn does not take this implausibly restrictive line about perception. Rather he sensibly suggests that it is necessary for genuine cases of perception to support counterfactuals such as "If it hadn't been red, I wouldn't have believed it was".[59] Thus, if someone wishes to defend the perceptual model it will be necessary (though not sufficient) to defend the possibility of ethical knowledge, which will involve considering the relationship between the counterfactuals supported by the doctrine of supervenience, and the counterfactuals sustained by the causal explanations of belief offered by the would-be debunker of knowledge. (I should add that, while defending the perceptual model in ethics is not my project here, it seems to me more plausible in relation to specific ethical judgments than in relation to all-things-considered judgments.)

## 9. The Debunker's Dilemma, Horn 2, Concluded: The Counterfactual Independence Assumption Exposed and the Naturalist Alternative

So we return to the question how it could be shown that we would hold some ethical belief even if it weren't true. Would a sociobiological explanation of the belief show this? We've seen that the irreducibility, as a matter of conceptual necessity, of ethical concepts to non-ethical concepts that feature in causal explanations of the uses of those concepts, does not entail the functional or counterfactual independence of the ethical and non-ethical characteristics.[60] Mackie's assumption that what scientifically explains our ethical beliefs would be independent of what he regards as inaccessible to explanation, namely, awareness of ethical truth, cannot be sustained merely by conceptual irreducibility.[61] Thus, a causal explanation of an ethical belief that does not feature ethical concepts does not *per se* show that we would have the belief whether or not it were true. A causal explanation of an ethical belief does not, merely by not using ethical concepts, show that our belief would not be counterfactually sensitive to the difference between the state of affairs in which the belief is true and that in which it is false. It may be plausible in some cases that among the non-ethical characteristics on which ethical characteristics supervene are characteristics that feature in causal explanations of our ethical beliefs. If variation with respect to ethical characteristics entails variation with respect to these non-ethical characteristics, why should we assume that our ethical beliefs nonetheless remain constant? Someone's ethical beliefs might be causally explained in terms of, hence vary along with, concepts on which ethical concepts supervene. Whatever would argue against this possibility would also give us a reason to think he'd hold some ethical belief whether or not it were true, but an explanation of the belief does not do this merely in virtue of not using ethical concepts. We must further distinguish among such explanations those that debunk and those that do not.

We've seen that Williams considers it most difficult to make out the possibility of knowledge and tracking for beliefs about what should be done at the general, reflective, all-things-considered level, so let's look at them in particular. A coherence account of judgments about what should be done, all things considered, postulates that there is some function of evaluative and non-evaluative characteristics of alternatives that represents a best theory about values, a theory sought in deliberation, where deliberation is conceived as a sense-making exercise, a process of self-interpretation and self-determination. On this view, for an all-things-considered judgment to be true, is for there to be a theory that's best and that supports the alternative judged right. To suppose that some such judgment were false, and consider whether or not a deliberator would still make it, involves us in supposing counterfactually that any theory that's best doesn't support the alternative in question, or, equivalently, that any theory that does support it isn't best.

This counterfactual supposition would be satisfied if there were no best theory at all. It would also be satisfied if there were a best theory but it did not support the alternative judged best. In this latter case we might think that what varies may be either what the best theory is along with which alternative it supports, or merely which alternative the best theory it supports. But these are not really different possibilities. Either way, the best theory will say something different about what should be done than the deliberator actually believes is said by the best theory. If his actual belief is in fact true, the theory that makes it true and that is best cannot be the same theory as the theory that is best in our counterfactual supposition, since the two theories say different things. We are thus supposing that whatever theory is best in the actual world, which we can label with the descriptive shorthand "*BT*", is not best in some counterfactual world, and that some other theory is, or perhaps that there is no best theory at all. What is important is that we are considering what would be the case in near possible worlds (not in far, countertheoretical though conceptually possible worlds) in which whatever theory is best in the actual world is not the best theory.

Consider the supposition that *BT* is not best but another theory is, which supports a different alternative. If *BT* were not the best theory and another theory were, would the deliberator believe that the best theory supports the alternative he favours, which we can call "*a*"? *BT* is identified by its content. If the best theory about the alternatives were to have a different content, the data about some alternatives would, in near possible worlds, be different in some way: either the evaluative or non-evaluative characteristics of the alternatives would be different. And if their evaluative characteristics were different, their non-evaluative characteristics would be different too, since any evaluative characteristic can by itself, in simple cases not involving conflict, provide explanations of why people do things. So, in any case, if the best theory were to have a different content, the alternatives would be different in some non-evaluative respects. If these differences were to obtain, would the deliberator still believe that the best theory supports alternative *a*? He might well not; these differences might play a role in the causal explanation of his deliberated beliefs about what alternative the best theory supports.

I suggested that *BT* cannot be identified by part of its content but not all of it, so that there is no separate possibility in which *BT* is the best theory but does not support *a*. Someone might reject this claim, but my point does not depend on it. Consider the supposition that, while *BT* is the best theory, it does not support alternative *a*. Would the deliberator still believe that the best theory supports alternative *a*? Again, if the best theory were not to support the alternative it actually supports, some alternatives to which the theory applies would, in near possible worlds, be different in some way that might well cause him to have appropriately different deliberated beliefs.

Now consider the supposition that there is no best theory at all. Would the deliberator believe there was? He might not; there might be reliable connections, even though he might be unaware of them, between the existence of a best theory and his belief that there is a best theory. If there were no best theory, that would be because the requirements of a best theory were not compatible. If, as a matter of mathematical fact, the requirements of a best theory are compatible, then to suppose such requirements are not compatible is to suppose the requirements are *different*, incompatible requirements. (The very same requirements can't be mathematically compatible in one world and mathematically incompatible in another close world.) But it is plausible that, if the requirements of a best theory were different, our deliberative theorizing and its role and function in our lives would be accordingly different. It might well be that important (evolutionary, sociological, whatever) roles and functions that our deliberative theorizing actually serves would not be served by this alternative kind of deliberation (indeed, this may be part of a causal explanation of the fact that we don't go in for the alternative kind of deliberation), and that as a result we would not believe that there was a best theory.[62]

Thus, it is possible for a belief that the best theory supports a particular alternative to meet the tracking condition. Beliefs about what the best theory or interpretation is may be reliably correlated with facts about what the best theory or interpretation is even though such facts themselves are not stated by the causal explanation of the belief.

To make the point schematically: Consider the conceptual relationships among various claims, where the proposition that $n$ gives a complete non-evaluative specification of the act which the ethical proposition that $e$ is about:

> *that* some particular ethical proposition, $e$ for short, is true;
> *that* some particular person or group believes that $e$, or $Be$ for short;
> *and* that the fact that $c$ (not the fact that $e$) ideally causally explains[63] the fact that $Be$, so that the counterfactuals "if it were the case that $c$, it would be the case that $Be$" and "if it weren't the case that $c$, it wouldn't be the case that $Be$" hold;
> *and* that ethical characteristics of actions supervene on non-ethical characteristics, so that the counterfactual "if it weren't the case that $e$, it wouldn't be the case that $n$" holds.

So far we've got: if it were not that $e$, it would not be that $n$, and if it were not that $c$, it would not be that $Be$. What is the relationship between not-$n$ and not-$c$? If the fact that $n$ is involved in the ideal causal explanation given by $c$, it may be true that if it were not that $n$, it would not be that $c$. That is, the non-evaluative characteristics on which the ethical description of the action supervenes may be among those that feature in the causal explanation of the ethical belief. It will not of course follow that the ethical description features in the causal explanation of the belief, but it may nevertheless be true that if it were not that $e$, it would not be that $Be$. In other words, the assumption made by the debunker that what causally explains the belief is counterfactually independent of its truth may not hold. Figure 14.2 illustrates how the debunker's counterfactual independence assumption might be false. Note that this situation is not logically guaranteed; nor would we want it to be. (It would not be logically guaranteed even if there were no question about the relationship between $n$ and $c$, simply because chains of counterfactuals are not *necessarily* transitive.[64]) Figure 14.3 illustrates, by contrast, how the debunker's assumption of counterfactual independence might be true. It is an open question so far whether either picture is correct; neither the causal explanation nor the doctrine of supervenience nor the combination allows us to bypass the substantive question of whether or not particular ethical beliefs are sensitive to ethical truth. And in order to evaluate this sensitivity one must employ some conception of what that truth might

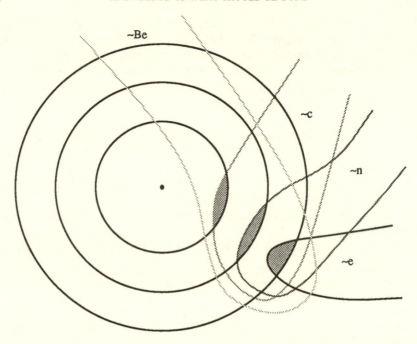

FIGURE 14.2   How the debunker's assumption might be false

involve or could not involve, even if one does not know what the truth is in
a particular case. If the debunker operates tacitly with a supernatural conception of ethical truth, then a naturalistic explanation of ethical beliefs may
indeed support the counterfactual independence assumption and the second
picture; but the remedy here is for the debunker to resist the temptation to
set up a supernaturalist straw man, whom the debunker's naturalist opponents
have no need to defend. If the debunker merely assumes that the second
picture is correct, he is in effect merely assuming that the tracking condition
for knowledge is not met, which is what the debunking explanation is supposedly trying to show.

   Debunking explanations of the kind we are considering aim to exploit the
negative tracking condition for knowledge given by Nozick, that if it weren't
true we wouldn't believe it. Thus it will be interesting to compare my argument
with Nozick's discussion of the skeptic's attempt to exploit this condition by
putting forward skeptical possibilities such as that you are deceived by a
demon or in a tank on Alpha Centauri having one's brain stimulated by
scientists with purposes of their own. Nozick sums his discussion up as follows:

> A belief's somehow varying with the truth of what is believed is not closed
> under known logical implication. Since knowledge that $p$ involves such var-
> iation, knowledge also is not closed under known logical implication. The
> skeptic cannot easily deny that knowlege involves such variation, for his
> argument that we don't know that we're not floating in that tank, for example,

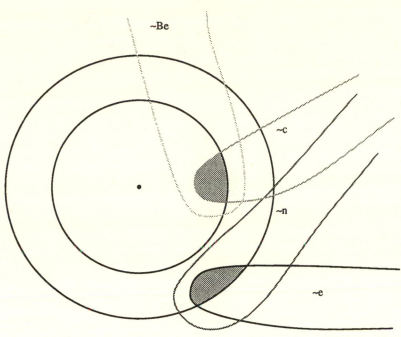

FIGURE 14.3  How the debunker's assumption might be true

uses the fact that knowledge does involve variation. ("If you were floating in the tank you would still think you weren't, so you don't know that you're not.") Yet, though one part of his argument uses that fact that knowledge involves such variation, another part of his argument presupposes that knowledge does not involve any such variation. This latter is that part that depends upon knowledge being closed under known logical implication, as when the skeptic argues that since you don't know that . . . you are not floating in the tank, then you also don't know, for example, that you are now reading a book. That closure can hold only if the variation does not. The skeptic cannot be right both times. According to our view he is right when he holds that knowledge involves such variation and so concludes that we don't know, for example, that we are not floating in that tank; but he is wrong when he assumes knowldge is closed under known logical implication and concludes that we know hardly anything.[65]

It's not clear that Nozick's development of this strategy against skepticism at large is ultimately successful. It clearly relies on the point about non-closure of knowledge under known logical implication, and there are serious difficulties with the consequences of non-closure which it's not clear can be resolved merely by distinguishing inferential and non-inferential knowledge. I shall not recount these difficulties here.[66] At any rate, as a result of these difficulties radical skepticism may not be routed by Nozick's argument. However, we have seen in Chapter 5 that there are reasons, to do with the way in which contents are determined, to be less confident than Nozick is that the radical skeptic's skeptical possibilities are ultimately intelligible. Of course a version of the demon or tank story can be told especially for ethics; and, similarly, as I've suggested in Part I and in Chapter 10 section 5, there are reasons to doubt the intelligibility of radical ethical skepticism. However, the argument I have given in this chapter is not intended to defuse such versions of skepticism at large, when they are aimed at ethics in particular. Rather, it has a more limited purpose of defending against undiscriminating attempts to debunk ethical knowledge by alluding to plausible, real-world causal explanations, such as sociobiological explanations, of ethical beliefs, or ideal versions of such explanations. Of course, defense of the possibility of ethical knowledge against an insufficiently selective debunking strategy does not amount to a positive demonstration of knowledge.

The relation of my strategy to Nozick's can be expressed by saying that I have been trying to show that causal explanations of ethical beliefs do not, *merely* in virtue of the fact that ethical propositions do not feature in them, play the role of the deceiving demon or the scientists manipulating the tank on Alpha Centauri.[67] Such skeptical possibilities have the counterfactual independence, or counterdependence, of the truth of the belief and its cause positively built into them: the scientists have purposes of their own; the demon is supposed to be deceitful. If we suppose the scientists to be concerned, above all, to give their subjects true beliefs, or a Leibnizian God instead of a demon, these characters would cease to play their proper role in undermining knowledge.[68] If we suppose, fantastically, that the tanks on Alpha Centauri are somehow the products of evolution, counterfactual independence of the beliefs they produce and happenings on Earth is no longer positively built into the story, but it's hard to doubt. However, if the 'tanks' (or skulls?) are on Earth and are somehow the products of evolution, we begin to approach the situation we are in with sociobiological explanations of particular ethical beliefs: neither counterfactual sensitivity nor counterfactual independence is built in automatically in all cases. That which causally explains our beliefs and their truth may be counterfactually related as facts about particles are to facts about waves; or as physical descriptions of sound are to truths about harmony and modulation; or as data are to truths about theories about such data. We may not know enough to say they are definitely related in any of these ways; but neither, so far, do we know enough to say they are not, that, for example, they are rather related in the way that self-deceptive desires to believe are to truth. Thus the imagined causal explanations do not positively debunk in the way the skeptic's possibilities may. Moreover, if error presupposes a general background of veridicality in the ways that Davidson, Burge, and others claim, then the burden of proof is on the debunker to come up with a positively debunking explanation to underwrite skepticism in particular areas. I have no doubt that this is possible to do in many areas; my point here is simply that it is not done *merely* by giving a causal explanation that does not feature the propositions, belief in which is thus explained. There must in addition be some reason for supporting the counterfactual independence assumption in particular cases. Skepticism can't avoid the tedium of examining the influences on particular evaluative beliefs by appealing to an undiscriminating debunking effect.

I emphasize that I do not hold, nor does my argument require me to hold, the view that the counterfactual account fully captures whatever relation of dependence between truth and belief is required for knowledge (of which I do not pretend to have given a positive account). I have been arguing by reference to a counterfactual tracking account because Williams poses his challenge in terms of tracking and because debunking arguments are usually expressed in terms of counterfactuals. However, a discriminating debunker may wish to press some kind of justification condition, at least for inferential knowledge, and may try to show by means of a debunking explanation that such a condition is not met. I have no objection to such a strategy. I would merely insist that one does not show a justification condition to fail, any more than a counterfactual tracking condition, *merely* by giving a causal explanation of the belief in question, in which the propositions believed do not do causal explanatory work. (Consider mathematical knowledge.) There must be some further reason, which a discriminating debunker would elaborate, to believe that the causal explanation *excludes* the possibility of justification; it is not enough that the causal explanation does not itself *provide* a justification of the belief.

## 10. Discriminating Debunking and Selective Skepticism

To debunk a belief it is not sufficient to show that it can be causally explained by propositions that do not include the proposition believed. But of course some explanations do debunk; how can we distinguish those causal explanations that debunk from those that do not? Let's now consider various examples to see what further there may be to say about the conditions under which explanations do or do not debunk.

The case of facial expressions is similar in some ways to the ethical case. Wittgenstein writes that it "belongs to the concept of emotion" that we "describe a face immediately as sad, radiant, bored, even when we are unable to give any other description of the features".[69] Moreover, no proposition about what a face expresses is entailed by any proposition that describes it in strictly physical terms. Yet is is also true, and something one must realize in order to understand expressions of emotion, that two faces cannot have identical physical descriptions while one has, say, a radiant expression and the other a bored expression: if the radiant face were not to look radiant, there would have to be something different about it in physical terms as well. The conjunction of the conceptual irreducibility and supervenience claims here is not puzzling. Nor are claims to perceive emotional expressions debunked by causal explanations of the widespread perception of expressive significance in certain specific configurations of the facial muscles.[70] That is, such an evolutionary explanation does not show the counterfactual independence of the causes of my belief that some face expresses anger from the truth of the belief, does not show that even if the face didn't express anger, I'd believe it did anyway. The concepts describing physical configurations of faces on which expressions of emotion supervene may also feature in causal explanations of beliefs about facial expression. In the absence of some reason to think otherwise, which such causal explanations *per se* do not provide, it is natural to suppose that the relation between facial expression concepts and those on which they supervene is as in Figure 14.2, rather than as in Figure 14.3. It may be true that if certain reactions to certain configurations of the facial muscles were not adaptive, I wouldn't believe that so-and-so's face expressed anger. But it may also be true that if it didn't express anger, there would be something different about its physical configuration such that I wouldn't believe it did.

Is any reason to doubt this line of thought provided by a more complete causal explanation, which explains the physiological conditions of the perception of faces as well as its evolution? Consider other specific kinds of agnosia. People with facial agnosia, or prosopagnosia, can in some sense see perfectly well—they can read—but they cannot recognize faces. The condition seems to involve some deficiency in the right hemisphere of the brain, and it can come on very suddenly.[71] Another form of agnosia, which seems to involve a left hemisphere deficiency, is described as follows:

> The typical patient is a person over the age of 50 who suddenly becomes unable to understand spoken language, to repeat spoken words and to write from dictation. In contrast, he still can speak, read and write spontaneously quite well. These patients show such a severe impairment of all performances involving auditory language input that they tend to be mistaken for deaf persons. . . . However, they are not at all deaf, at least in the sense that pure-tone audiometry is virtually normal. This condition, which is conspicuous and rather rare, has been defined as 'pure word deafness' . . . precisely to stress the fact that the defect was limited to the perception of spoken language. These patients complained first and foremost that they could not perceive what people said to them.[72]

Studies of such cases may enable us to say such things as: if his right hemisphere had not been in such and such condition, he would not have believed that her face expressed sorrow. Or: if her left hemisphere had not been in such and such condition, she would not have believed that the sound the headwaiter made meant that her table was ready. And it is not very plausible that facts about facial expression, or facts about what utterances mean, supervene on facts about the state of anyone's right or left hemisphere; a difference in the state of one person's right or left hemisphere could not account for a difference in another person's facial expression or meaning. However, we still haven't got a debunking explanation of beliefs about facial expression or meaning, just because of the way in which facts about the state of someone's right or left hemisphere may themselves be explained in evolutionary terms. Very crudely, if human beings' hemispheres hadn't happened to have been in certain states, certain survival-enhancing behavioural effects wouldn't have followed, and if that causal relationship hadn't held, it wouldn't be the case that human beings' right hemispheres were generally in certain states in the present. Description of the survival-enhancing effects involves descriptions of behavioural interactions of a kind that descriptions of facial expression or meaning may indeed supervene on. Thus we can understand actual cases of right or left hemisphere deficiency as involving an inability to perceive faces, or meanings.

Consider this claim: If the judge weren't a member of a group subject to discrimination, she wouldn't believe that affirmative action was right. It cuts both ways: whether a belief in affirmative action is true or not cannot depend on whether the believer is a member of such a group or not, and moreover being a member of such a group might make someone want to believe that affirmative action was right because it would be in her interests or those of her friends and family. On the other hand, we also can understand how being a member of such a group might give someone special insight about whether or not it is right. If she hadn't been a member of such a group, she wouldn't have had certain first-hand experiences of discrimination, and thus would not have as much evidence on the basis of which to arrive at judgments about what remedies are warranted. In a case like this we have to try to separate the influences on her belief in virtue of which it would not track its truth, such as the desire to believe affirmative action was right, from those influences in virtue of which it might well, such as the special insights gained from experience. We would consider, for example, what she believes when her desires to believe and her insights based on experience diverge.[73] Similar remarks apply to the claim: If he weren't of draft age, he wouldn't believe conscription was wrong. Being of draft age may make the wrong of forced military service especially vivid; but would he still believe it was wrong if the alternative were working in a ghetto for two years instead, or something else which he doesn't believe would be wrong but which would not be in his interest? Conscientious objectors could prove their good faith in this way. These kinds of explanation do not debunk automatically, but they suggest further considerations that might. Such explanations might turn out not to debunk the belief at all, but to be quite compatible with the claim to knowlege, so they should not simply be used as shorthand for the further considerations. However, it's of interest to note that if the further considerations do debunk, they will do so without necessarily depending on the truth or falsity of the belief. We don't need to know whether affirmative action is right or wrong in order to know that a self-interested desire to believe one way or another will not track the truth of the matter. Similarly, we do not need to know that particular constitutional theory is right or wrong in order to know that beliefs about constitutional rights on the part of a judge that vary with the economic or social status of the parties do not track the truth. Those responsible for evaluating the suitability of certain judicial candidates may properly consider such debunking influences on the candidates' beliefs without necessarily themselves taking a position on the truth or falsity of those beliefs.

But consider: If he weren't president of a tobacco company, he wouldn't believe that smoking is harmless. Or: If he weren't white, he wouldn't believe apartheid was right. Or: If he weren't Aryan, he wouldn't believe that the Nazis' final solution was right. In these cases, it is very difficult to stand back and weigh the self-interested influences on belief against any possible special insight, in order to evaluate whether the dominant influence is truth-tracking or not, because it is difficult to understand what the special insight could amount to, how the beliefs in question could possibly track the truth. In these cases our determination of whether the belief is debunked or not cannot be kept strictly separate from our outright evaluation of its truth-value. Someone might believe affirmative action is wrong, but not consider the judge's belief in it to be debunked by her being a member of the group subject to discrimination, because of the possibility of special insight and because of integrity in holding to her beliefs even when they do not serve her interests. But we can't really make sense of a similar attitude toward the president of the tobacco company because we cannot take the possibility of special insight seriously. Similarly, even if the Nazi supporter were willing to go to the gas chamber if he turned out to be Jewish, we'd regard him as a misguided fanatic rather than respecting his integrity. In these cases the explanation of the belief is not really doing the work in debunking the claim to knowledge; rather it's being done by the strength of the reasons supporting our own contrary belief.

Thus, we should distinguish between cases of debunking in which we do depend on our own evaluation of the truth-values of the beliefs in question, and cases in which we do not, but rather depend on higher-order judgments. Here are some more examples of the latter: If he hadn't been so afraid of hearing that his son had been killed in the war that he threw the telegram away unopened, he would not still believe that his son was alive. If Geraldine Ferraro had not worn a pink dress during the debate, the voter wouldn't have believed that she would not be as good a Vice President as George Bush. These explanations debunk, and they do so in a way that does not depend on our already knowing the truth, only on our knowing that whatever it is, beliefs thus motivated will not track it; if they are true, it will be an accident. We may suspect that the son is in fact still alive and that the telegram was sent out of malice; but the father's belief does not constitute knowledge because it is a self-deceptive belief caused by a desire to believe the son alive. George Bush might be better as Vice President than Geraldine Ferraro would be; but a belief based on a quirky subliminal prejudice cannot track the truth of the matter.

Let's return to two of the examples: If the judge hadn't had friends and family who would benefit from affirmative action, she wouldn't have believed it was right (assume we've considered the special insight theory and found it not to hold up for this particular person, on the basis of her record). And: if Ferraro hadn't worn a pink dress during the debate, the voter wouldn't have believed Bush was a better choice for Vice President. Suppose we don't know whether affirmative action is right or wrong, or whether Ferraro or Bush would be a better Vice President, but nevertheless need to make decisions on these matters. Suppose further that we want to choose reliable methods (or at least avoid unreliable methods) of decision in each case, because our aim is that the methods yield all-things-considered judgments about what to do that constitute knowledge (or at least that they not yield judgments that do not constitute knowledge). The debunking explanations then are able to give us some guidance about what methods are appropriate. Even though we don't know the right answer in each case, we know that it's not going to vary according to whether the judge's friends and family benefit, or with the colour of Ferraro's dress. Insofar as it's practicable, we'll do well to exclude the influences of such debunking factors from the methods used to reach decisions in these cases. In general, we'd like to assign methods to sets of issues such that the methods yield knowledge about how those issues should be resolved. But in cases where we're not certain which methods would do this at least we can be skeptical of certain methods that we know would yield results that vary independently of the truth. If we want to know the truth about what should be done in these cases, we should not rely on opinions formed in these ways—on the opinions of judges or of voters subject to these debunking influences. Similarly, we should be cautious and critical of our own views in circumstances in which self-deception or the distortion of our beliefs by our desires is antecedently likely.

I began this chapter by asking what further scope there was for skepticism, given the failure of one strategy, deriving from impossibility results, for making out claims that there is no such thing as what ought to be done, all things considered. Our consideration of epistemological skepticism has finally yielded an answer: those explanations that positively debunk, by showing that the causes of someone's belief about what should be done vary independently of its truth, or, more generally, that some condition for knowledge is not met, indicate the proper scope for skepticism. That scope will depend on the circumstances that particular sorts of debunking explanation allude to. Given a normal distribution of various desires, interests, abilities, insights, quirks, and prejudices, most people won't be right all of the time, and many people may form reliable or justified beliefs—or at least undebunked beliefs—on some types of issue but not on other types. It may be easier to avoid debunked beliefs than positively to identify expertise. Moreover, we should expect these divisions of issues into types to cut across one another, and for people to disagree in complex ways—not for their judgments to converge. However, this diversity of opinion can be turned to epistemic advantage;[74] the proper response to the skepticism debunking explanations support will be to seek generalizations about the circumstances in which beliefs about certain types of issues are debunked, and to devise a division of epistemic labour accordingly. I shall begin the next chapter by considering how this general kind of response of skepticism and its institutional manifestations might produce an epistemic justification of democracy, and shall go on to consider the relationship of such a conception of democracy to standard assumptions in social choice theory, and to the values of autonomy, liberty, and equality.

# 15

# Autonomy and Democracy

## 1. Autonomy Without Subjectivism

In this final chapter I shall try to put the foundational questions addressed in preceding chapters into the context of political philosophy. The attempt will be speculative and rather sketchy, and the arguments of preceding chapters do not turn on acceptance of the arguments of this chapter. I do not say "into the social context" since the basis of the account I've given in the philosophy of mind has involved social context all along, as a constitutive matter. A non-centralist coherence account is a practice account; reason-giving practices are in part socially determined, and their undebunked status as reason-giving is compatible with their existence in the natural world and their being, under certain descriptions, objects of causal explanation.[1] The aim in this chapter will be to connect the preceding material with various issues in political theory, in particular those concerning autonomy and democracy. The framework I have developed leads to a view of autonomy free of subjectivism, and to a distinctive recasting of certain issues about the value of liberal democracy, which calls into question certain assumptions prevalent among theories of liberal democracy. The renewed conception of democracy that emerges has, I believe, philosophically sounder foundations and stronger links to the value of autonomy than do the conceptions that share these assumptions.

In Part I, I argued against the subjectivist view that preference determines value, and went on, in Part III, to develop an alternative to subjectivism, a coherence account. The latter replaces the subjectivist view of the relation between preference and value with an interdependence doctrine, but does not press a contrary, or Platonist, view of the relation.[2] I shall begin this chapter by describing a contrast between a subjectivist conception of autonomy and one yielded by the coherence account I have given, or, more properly, by a family of views of which mine is a member. The contrast I wish to draw between cognitivist and subjectivist conceptions of autonomy is related to, and indeed owes much to, contrasts drawn by Charles Taylor and Michael Sandel. It is thus useful to begin by reviewing Taylor's comparison of the radical choices of a simple weigher with the self-interpretations of a strong evaluator, and Sandel's comparison of voluntarist and cognitive conceptions of agency.

One of the earliest influences on a subjectivist conception of autonomy is the work of Thomas Hobbes. Hobbes aspired to what he conceived to be a scientific view of man; he wished to account for man, as Galileo had for the universe, as "matter in motion". Motion towards an object he called "desire", motion from an object "aversion". All the particular qualities of passion that prompt action he reduced to quantity and direction of motion to or from, in terms of which he then defined good and evil: "whatsoever is the object of any man's Appetite or Desire, that is it, which he for his part calleth good: And the object of his Hate, and Aversion, Evill". Hobbes' account of practical reasoning, or deliberation, as a taking of "the whole summe" of the quantities of desire and aversion inspired by the various aspects and consequences of an act[3] has been reproduced, in hedonistic, behaviouristic, and other variations, throughout the utilitarian tradition and modern welfare economics. All appetites and aversions are on the same level; there are no significant qualitative differences among them, and the problem is merely one of totting them up to get a net quantity, which determines good and evil. The individual's ultimately ungrounded volitions or choices are the source both of the characterizations of the alternatives under which they are desirable and of the balance of desirabilities between alternatives. The Hobbesian deliberator Taylor calls a *simple weigher*. According to Taylor, an influential strand of thought in more recent times has tried to understand the deliberator's capacity to determine his own preferences in terms of radical choice, the evaluatively ungrounded choice of values, as opposed to choice that presupposes values, recognition of the validity of which is not optional. The agent of radical choice chooses as a simple weigher (when what he does can be understood as choosing at all, rather than mere lurching). His private exercise of self-determination, at least, is supposed to be unproblematic for ethical and political theory; problems for the latter concern how to resolve conflicts between the preferences of different individuals.[4]

Against conceptions of deliberation and autonomy in terms of simple weighing, such as are found in the Hobbesian view and in theories of radical choice, Taylor sets the view that "Social theories require a conception of the properly human life which is such that we are not assured it by simply being alive, but it must be developed and it can fail to be developed; on this basis they can argue that society or a certain form of society is the essential condition of this development", and that evaluation consists in the "sensitivity to certain standards, those involved in the peculiarly human goals" such that "The sense of self is the sense of where one stands in relation to these standards, and properly personal choice is one informed by these standards." By contrast, the Hobbesian view involves "rejecting utterly all such talk of forms or qualities of life which are properly human". And whereas a simple weigher can supposedly assess his motivations merely by attending to his desires and what he feels like more, Taylor's *strong evaluator* distinguishes his various desires qualitatively and forms higher-order desires by reflecting on which of his desires to identify with, on the kind of being he is and is to become. His deliberations do not merely take a given set of desires, character, and personal identity for granted, but actively form them; deliberation for a strong evaluator is at once a cognitive exercise, of self-interpretation, and an exercise of autonomous agency, of self-determination.[5]

Sandel draws a related contrast between the *voluntarist* sense of agency, which takes the identity of the subject as somehow antecedently given and relates the self to the ends or goods it desires through the will, and the *cognitive* sense of agency, which conceives the identity of the subject as the product rather than the premise of its agency. In the cognitive sense of agency, the agent participates in the constitution of its own identity as a subject, in the light of ends and goods already before it; "agency consists less in summoning the will than in seeking self-understanding". "I ask, as I deliberate, not only what I really want but who I really am." Where the self is not prior to its ends, the relevant question is "who I am, how I am to discern in this clutter of possible ends what is me from what is mine"; the challenge to the agent is "to sort out the limits or the boundaries of the self, to distinguish the subject from its situation, and so to forge its identity".[6]

If the subject is conceived as prior to its ends, by contrast, as in the voluntarist sense of agency, Sandel claims that this kind of self-knowledge and self-determination is not possible; reflection on the relative intensity of desires and how to satisfy them "looks inward in a sense but not all the way in":

> It takes as its objects the contingent wants and desires and preferences of the self, but not the self itself.... it cannot reach the self qua subject of desires.... Because this sort of deliberation is restricted to assessing the desires of a subject whose identity is given (unreflectively) in advance, it cannot lead to self-understanding in the strong sense which enables the subject to participate in the constitution of its identity.

Deliberation about ends becomes what Sandel calls "an exercise in arbitrariness, what Taylor describes as "a pure leap into the void" by "a kind of extensionless point". Agency in the cognitive sense is needed for self-determination to be possible. Sandel writes:

> While the contours of my identity will in some ways be open and subject to revision, they are not wholly without shape. And the fact that they are not enables me to discriminate among my more immediate wants and desires; some now appear essential, others merely incidental to my defining projects and commitments.... While the notion of constitutive attachments may at first seem an obstacle to agency—the self, now encumbered, is no longer strictly prior—some relative fixity of character appears essential to prevent the lapse into arbitrariness.[7]

It would not serve present purposes to set out in greater detail or to evaluate Taylor's or Sandel's objections to subjectivist conceptions of deliberation and self-determination, as I have given my own arguments against subjectivism in earlier chapters. However, in light of my arguments about the need for substantive constraints on interpretation and on the search for coherence, Taylor's and Sandel's remarks should have a certain resonance. I have argued against subjectivism that substantive as well as formal constraints on interpretation are needed to make determinate sense of the very idea of preference that decision theory invokes; these constraints themselves cannot be determined by prior and independent preferences, and they include evaluative constraints. However, they may, and often do, involve distinct and conflicting values, such that self-interpretation requires deliberation about ends. The theory of deliberation I have given is an ethic (in the sense explained at the end of Chapter 8 section 4), or a theory of rationality for persons, self-interpreting and self-determining agents, whose efforts to interpret themselves are constrained in various ways, but whose characters are not entirely fixed. Such deliberation involves the search for a coherent set of relationships among the relevant values, which presupposes substantive as well as formal constraints; again, it is at once a cognitive exercise and an exercise of self-determination. Thus we have seen, in effect, that autonomous agency is possible, and is really only possible, without subjectivism, in the context set by substantive as well as formal constraints on self-interpretation.

A rather abstract way of putting this conception of autonomy as self-determination, which I shall elaborate in later sections, is as follows. The notion of autonomy essentially involves horizontal as well as vertical divisions within society. *Horizontal divisions* reflect formal and substantive distinctions *within* agents, among the various values and circumstances that inform their desires and beliefs; while *vertical divisions* reflect distinctions *between* agents, loci of deliberation and the search for coherence. (The lines of division, rather than the arrangement of things divided, are described as horizontal or vertical.) Horizontal distinctions may be of many different kinds, and they may cut across different agents, thus binding them together, and may cut between groups of agents with conflicting loyalties; but without horizontal distinctions the element of *determination* is missing from self-determination. Vertical distinctions, between agents, are primarily those between biological individuals; but other units of agency are also possible, such as the family and other groups, and substantial questions about the vertical distinctions proper to the conceptualization of a given social problem should not be begged by simply assuming the the biological individual is the only relevant agent for all purposes. (As I argued above in Chapter 8 sections 1 through 4, it is irrational for persons to take the unit of agency as fixed, as well as to take the character of agency as fixed in other respects.[8]) Equally, vertical distinctions are indispensable to autonomy; without them the element of *self* is missing from self-determination.[9] Moreover, the two kinds of distinction stand in no reductionist relation to one another but are inextricably interdependent; indeed, the impulse running throughout political philosophy to make one fundamental at the expense of the other should be circumspectly avoided, as a potential source of dehumanizing extremism and aspect-blindness. Theories that give pride of place to vertical distinctions between persons, such as many contract and libertarian theories, I shall call *vertical theories*, while those that give pride of place to horizontal distinctions, such as those of Plato and Marx, who are primarily concerned that the right part of the soul, or of society, dominate, I shall call *horizontal theories*. Exclusively vertical theories run the risk of blindness to evaluative distinctions and truths; exclusively horizontal theories run the risk of blindness to the value of autonomous agency. Only social theories that avoid both reductionist extremes, and which admit both horizontal and vertical distinctions as equally fundamental, as, in their different ways, those of Mill, Sen, and Taylor do, are what I shall call *fully structured*.[10] The idea of a fully structured social theory is a natural extension of the idea of an ethic. I fill out these remarks below in section 5. In section 6 I consider certain implications of a fully structured theoretical framework for issues of distributive justice, and suggest that within such a framework the quality of the education and opportunities for self-development and self-realization which a society provides its members assumes central importance.

The stage is set for the rather general considerations of sections 5 and 6 by detailed arguments given in sections 2 through 4. In sections 2 and 3 I develop a cognitive conception of democracy and consider its relation to social choice theory; in section 4 the relationships between democracy and the value of autonomy are considered. Before going on to these matters, however, it will be helpful to make some further points that emerge from a coherence account about the value of autonomy and its relationship to the various specific reasons and values which are among the substantive constraints that a coherence account presupposes.

Deliberation about conflicting ends involves a search for coherence, which is a kind of self-interpretation-and-determination. It is in deliberating about ends that an agent exercises his or her autonomy; the value of autonomy emerges immediately from the need for deliberation and the search for coherence. Thus, to ask what the relationship of the value of autonomy is to the values that deliberators theorize about is in effect to ask what the relationship of the value of coherence is to the values deliberators theorize about. And this is a question that has already been addressed, in Chapter 13; I shall review the points made there in the present context.

Recall that a coherent theory about the relationships between conflicting *pro tanto* values does not subsume their reason-giving force or eliminate the conflict; unkindness, for example, is no more cancelled out by considerations of coherence than by those of justice. Considerations of coherence may give us reason to do the just thing rather than the kind thing, but they cannot themselves give us reason to act on considerations of coherence rather than on the *pro tanto* reason with which they conflict. Their role is not to eliminate conflict between other reasons, and they are no more insulated from conflict with other reasons than other reasons are from conflict with one another. A regress of higher-order reasons will not solve the supposed problem of conflict either, but merely relocate it. The solution is to recognize that the supposed problem only arises from demanding the impossible, namely, the elimination of conflict.

The deeper understanding we now have of the way in which the search for coherence may constitute an exercise of self-determination dovetails into the points made in Chapter 13 about why we seek a coherent way of resolving conflicts when conflict is eliminable and the constitutive role of coherence. Agents both are conflicted and seek personal coherence; in the presence of conflicting values, an agent may be uncertain what kind of a person he is or wants to be, and in seeking coherence he may be trying to determine his very identity as a person in relation to various subsystems responsible to conflicting values. Thus, deliberation is a kind of self-interpretation, and as such is constrained in various ways. We are constrained to seek to understand ourselves and others as coherent agents in relation to various specific values; neither the search for coherence nor the values in terms of which it is carried out are optional for persons. And these constraints go together; the identities of agents are not more fundamental than or prior to the values that inform interpretation; we are able to understand agents as coherent only in conjunction with understanding of these values. (Indeed, sometimes the latter may exert such a pull that the assumptions we take as a starting point about the individual unit of agency may be suspended, as in cases of split personality or collective agency, though it is only against the background of the normal starting point assumptions, which locate agency in the biological individual, that the exceptional cases make sense.) Moreover, this understanding of ourselves is something we must achieve, the result of cognitive activity. Thus, the value of autonomy is inextricably bound up with the values that make it possible. Though autonomy has a special role in relation to other values, and indeed in making human beings distinctive among animals as self-interpreting animals, or persons, it is still one value among others, which may conflict with it. Finally, it is not *per se* a threat to the value of individual autonomy to recognize, as Taylor puts it, that "The community is also constitutive of the individual, in the sense that the self-interpretations which define him are drawn from the interchange which the community carries on".[11]

Given these points, we can disarm a complex of important objections to the conception of self-determination in terms of higher-order attitudes about the relationships among ends associated with given forms of life. The first move characteristic of this complex of objections is made, for example, by Campbell, in his essay "In Defense of Free Will". He points out that every historic self has an hereditary nature consisting of a group of inborn propensities, which with equipment the self just *happens* to be born; similarly, every self is born and bred in a particular environment, not of his own choosing. Insofar as the self's choices manifest the causal influence of hereditary and environmental influences not of his own choosing, they are not self-determined. "Surely we must admit that every particular act of choice bears the marks of the agent's hereditary nature and enviromental nurture; in which case a free act, in the sense of an act determined solely by the self, must be dismissed as a mere chimera". Campbell thus operates with a conception of self-determination which would require the self, as the *sole* source of self-determining choices, to be prior to and independent of the human nature and forms of life which, I have argued, stand in a constitutive relation to the self and its choices. Because actual selves are stamped by heredity and environment, he thinks that they cannot be truly self-determining.

Campbell allows the "Self-determinist", of which he takes T. H. Green to be a typical example, a stock reply to his criticism: "He urges that these factors, heredity and environment, are not, in so far as their operation in willing (and therefore in conduct proper) is concerned, 'external' to the self at all". Willing, properly understood, is such that no end can be willed by the self except as conceived by the self as a good for the self; thus the self in willing is essentially self-determining, moved by its own conception of its good. "Inherited nature and environmental circumstance do play their part; but not as factors external to the self. They can function only in so far as their suggestions are, as it were, incorporated by the self in its conception of its own good".

Campbell, however, will have no truck with the externalizing—the naturalizing and socializing—of the self; he doesn't so much argue against it as simply baulk at it. He writes, "Let us grant that inheritance and environment can operate in willing only in the medium of the self's conception of its own good. But then let us ask, how is the self's conception of its own good constituted? . . . It seems certain . . . that the self's conception of its own good is influenced directly by its particular inheritance and enviroment. But to admit this surely involves the admission that external determination enters into choices. It may be true that the self's choices are always determined by its own conception of its own good. But if what it conceives to be its own good is always dependent, at least partly, upon inheritance and enviroment, as external facts, then it is idle to deny that the self's choices are externally influenced likewise". This passage suggests the failure to distinguish causal from constitutive relations, or, more precisely, of the causation of particular mental states from the individuation of their contents in terms of normal causal relations, which Burge warns against, in arguing against psychological individualism. (Recall his arguments in "Individualism and Psychology", as discussed in Chapter 5.) Campbell asks how the self's conception of its good is *constituted*, but does not allow that nature and social environment could possibly provide the answer to the question at a constitutive level, and construes them as answers to a question about causation, which leaves them in a strictly external role.[12] He refuses to consider them in a constitutive role at all, and simply relegates them again to the category of that which is external to the self.

Certainly, an account is needed of how the line is drawn between that which is external to the self and that which is not, an account that does not have the consequence that action in accordance with the self's determination of itself is simply automatic. I have put forward a coherence account of deliberation as self-determination, which provides a way of meeting this need. We have seen that it does not make action in accordance with self-determination automatic; *akrasia* is possible. My account is indebted to Frankfurt's views on the importance to persons of certain higher-order attitudes, which Taylor calls "strong evaluations", by which they identify themselves differentially with various given ends. But now we meet a more sophisticated version of Campbell's objection, made by Frankfurt himself. In the course of examining which of the passions in a person's history are external to him, and what the conditions of their externality are, Frankfurt considers the suggestion that "a passion is unequivocally ours when it is what we want to feel, or are willing to feel, while a passion whose occurrence in us we disapprove of is not strictly ours". He makes various qualifications of the position, but then puts forward what he considers to be a fatal objection to the suggestion, namely, that it fails to account for the fact that attitudes toward passions are as susceptible to externality as passions themselves:

> The fact that a person has a certain attitude toward a passion can be construed as determining either the internality or the externality of the passion, surely, only if the attitude in question is itself genuinely attributable to him. An attitude in virtue of which a passion is internal, or in virtue of which a passion is external, cannot be merely an attitude that a person finds within himself; it must be one with which he is to be identified. But given that the question of attribution arises not only with regard to a person's passions, but also with regard to his attitudes toward his passions, an infinite regress will be generated by any attempt to account for internality or externality in terms of attitudes. For the attitude that is invoked to account for the status of a passion will have to be an internal one; its internality will have to be accounted for by invoking a higher-order attitude—that is, an attitude toward an attitude; the internality of this higher-order attitude will have to be accounted for in terms of an attitude of a still higher order; and so on. This precludes explication of the concepts of internality and externality by appealing merely to the notion of orders of attitudes.[13]

This objection to understanding autonomy in terms of higher-order attitudes bears a certain resemblance to objections to the notion of extended or highest-order preference as somehow attributable to a featureless ego or bare self, which must determine the ordering of extended alternatives involving lower-order preferences. The objection is that as we follow the regress up through the orders of preference, the self becomes thinner, barer, more featureless; either the regress never ends, or perhaps we are finally left, at the highest order, with a mere extensionless point. Either way, it is difficult to see how the result of this regress could be a meaningful exercise of self-determination. In the case of extended preference, we saw that the objection could be met; the notion of extended preference requires a theory of human nature and primary goods, and need not depend on the postulation of ineffectual featureless egos. Neither does the understanding of self-determination in terms of higher-order attitudes give rise to a regress from which the bare self continually retreats, denying its imprimatur to the exercise. This is because the self is itself in part the creation of the continuing exercise; the question of attributing the entire exercise to the self cannot arise. The self is the result of activity in relation to given forms of life, so it is not *merely* given; but the activity is itself part of the world, as constituted by natural and social relationships, not an elusive vanishing point, the limit of a regress. No doubt thoughtful persons engage in higher than second-order exercises of self-determination (e.g., wanting and trying to become more spontaneous), but in doing so they elaborate and deepen their personalities from within themselves; their autonomy does not depend on the last step, which others may not take, but on the distinctive first step, in which the person begins to take form. Before we get very far into the regress, the self is already with us. Persons are self-interpreting animals, but they are animals, and stand in constitutive relationships to a natural and social world; indeed, their personhood is itself a natural fact, a product of the natural and social world, and stands in no tension with its own status as such. Personhood depends on the capacity for reflection on and evaluation of one's own attitudes, for self-interpretation and self-determination, not on self-postulation *ex nihilo*.

Perhaps the response to Frankfurt's objection can be made clearer by emphasizing the coherentist character of autonomy. The familiar contrast between coherentist and foundationalist conceptions of knowledge has an analogue in the contrast between a coherentist conception of autonomy, and one which requires the imprimatur of a bare self at the end of the regress, which would provide the kind of foundation for the exercise of self-determination which Campbell and Frankfurt seem to be after in the passages discussed. Just as a foundation in certainty to validate the entire structure of knowledge is not needed, the determination by the self of the entire structure of the self is not needed. We can mend and improve the body of knowledge from within it, plank by plank; but we cannot get off the boat. Similarly, we can determine ourselves, exercise our autonomy, in relation to given forms of life by depending on certain of them as a basis for criticism and revision of others; but we must always occupy ourselves in the process. Self-determination does not depend on detaching ourselves from the whole of what we *are*.

Given the cross-hatched framework of fully structured social theories, the question naturally arises what the relationship is between the autonomy of such in part socially constituted persons and democracy. The answer will be complex, as the relationship is complex, and must begin with a discussion of democracy.

## 2. The Cognitive Value of Democracy

In earlier chapters we have found that values conflict, and that though we try to make coherent decisions about what should be done, our success in doing so does not eliminate the conflict; nor does the value of seeking coherence depend on a presupposition that conflict can be eliminated. We've also seen that 'the problem of the authority of theory' is not a problem, because the value of coherence, served by theory, still itself conflicts with the values coherently related by theory; nor does the value of seeking coherence depend on an assumption that this cross-level conflict can be eliminated. Nevertheless, we've seen that, even granting these points, which serve in some sense to correct our aspirations, there are still considerable epistemic obstacles to the search for coherence, as indicated by successful debunking explanations of beliefs about what should be done. However, these very epistemic difficulties suggest the broad form of a defense of democracy, in terms of its cognitive value. I shall begin to develop this suggestion by considering two prevalent assumptions rejected by a cognitive conception of democracy. Many alternative conceptions of liberal democracy are characterized by one, or both, of these two assumptions.

The first is that the votes of citizens of a democracy are responsible to[14] their own preferences about what is to happen rather than their beliefs about what should be done, all things considered; the attainment of knowledge is not an aim or function of democracy, but rather the fulfillment of preferences. This noncognitivist assumption dominates social choice theory, which takes the individual orderings the aggregation of which is at issue to represent individual preferences, not beliefs (although the preferences may be sanitized in some way, to remove anti-social preferences, preferences based on false beliefs, etc.). Certain important conditions employed in social choice theory, as we shall see in the next section, are in tension with a view of the aggregation of individual orderings as aiming for knowledge of what should be done, since these conditions admit debunking influences. In welfarist or preference-based theories, the basic aims of democractic institutions are to elicit individual preferences and to provide procedures for regulating them when they conflict so that the greatest degree of overall preference satisfaction is achieved; according to more subtle versions of this kind of view, these aims are more or less heavily qualified and constrained under various circumstances so that rights are respected.

The second assumption is that it is essential to liberalism that, as Dworkin puts it, "political decisions must be, so far as is possible, independent of any particular conception of the good life, or of what gives value to life." According to Dworkin, if they are not, they do not respect what Dworkin takes to be the central value of liberalism, that of equal concern and respect for the members of society.[15] Rawls writes that his conception of justice as fairness "presents itself not as a conception of justice that is true, but one that can serve as a basis of informed and willing political agreement between citizens viewed as free and equal persons". Given the existence of "conflicting and incommensurable conceptions of the good", a fundamental feature of modern culture that social theory must recognize, we secure this agreement by trying, "so far as we can, to avoid disputed philosophical, as well as disputed moral and religious, questions. We do this not because these questions are unimportant or regarded with indifference, but because we think them too important and recognize that there is no way to resolve them politically.... Philosophy as the search for truth about an independent metaphysical and moral order cannot, I believe, provide a workable and shared basis for a political conception of justice in a democratic society".[16]

It should be emphasized that neither Dworkin nor Rawls advocate ethical noncognitivism; however, they restrain the cognitive aims of the task of institutional design, for political reasons, namely, as a matter of equal concern and respect for each person's conception of the good, and in order to secure political agreement among free and equal persons; democratic institutions are not, so far as possible, to be premissed on disputed propositions about what gives value to life or to be conceived as means of arriving at knowledge of truths about the good. Dworkin comments that "liberalism cannot be based on skepticism. Its constitutive morality provides that human beings must be treated as equals by their government, not because there is no right and wrong in political morality, but because that is what is right".[17] Rawls would refrain from judgments about what gives value to life even in respect of the comprehensive moral ideals of autonomy and individualism that are often associated with liberalism:

> The absence of commitment to these ideals, and indeed to any particular comprehensive ideal, is essential to liberalism as a political doctrine. The reason is that any such ideal, when pursued as a comprehensive ideal, is incompatible with other conceptions of the good, with forms of personal, moral, and religious life consistent with justice and which, therefore, have a proper place in a democratic society. As comprehensive moral ideals, autonomy and individuality are unsuited for a political conception of justice.

Understood in terms of these substantive ideals, "liberalism becomes but another sectarian doctrine".[18] Rawls goes on to comment that such ideals may be among the more prominent doctrines in the overlapping consensus that justice as fairness seeks to identify as a basis for political agreement; but then again they may not.

I agree with Dworkin and Rawls that a principled lack of commitment to ideals of the good life is characteristic of a certain conception of liberal democracy, and this is the second prevalent assumption I wish to mark. I believe that conceptions of liberal democracy characterized by either or both of these two assumptions may be coherent, and do not subscribe to claims to the effect that they harbour contradictions. Nevertheless, I shall argue in favour of a different conception of liberal democracy, which gives the value of autonomy the distinctive role Dworkin gives to the value of equality (though I shall eventually argue, in section 6, that autonomy involves intrinsic distributional requirements). I put it forward as a rival to conceptions characterized by either or both of these assumptions, a rival view of what liberal democracy should be. Perhaps it will strike some as not a *liberal* theory of democracy, in virtue of its unrestrained cognitivism. I'm not attached to the label, and I'm not concerned to defend the boundary between interpretation and reform. However, there are precedents, in the theories of Green and Mill, for example, for regarding the view I develop as involving a competing conception *of* liberalism, rather than as competing *with* liberalism.

Many different conceptions of liberal democracy involving either or both of these prevalent assumptions may be found, ranging from elitist revisionary theories to participatory theories; the presence, either explicit or implicit, of either or both of these two assumptions cuts across other issues that divide many theorists of liberal democracy.[19] However, these assumptions tend to cut short any serious consideration of a cognitive conception of democracy, according to which voters express their beliefs about what should be done, not their own preferences, and democratic institutions provide a means of arriving at knowledge of what should be done. Burke, of course, famously spoke to the electors of Bristol as follows:

> My worthy colleague says, his will ought to be subservient to yours. If that be all, the thing is innocent. If government were a matter of will, yours, without question, ought to be superior. But government and legislation are matters of reason and judgment, and not of inclination. . . .
>
> Parliament is not a congress of ambassadors from different hostile interests; which interests each must maintain, as an agent and advocate, against the other agents and advocates; but Parliament is a deliberative assembly of one nation, with one interest, that of the whole; where, not local purposes, not local prejudices ought to guide, but the general good, resulting from the general reason of the whole.[20]

And since Burke a few theorists have suggested or held cognitive views of democracy; they must include John Stuart Mill as well as several contemporary writers.[21] In this context I cannot attempt a survey or classification of cognitive views of democracy; however, it's as well to keep in mind that there are substantial points of difference among them, for example, about the unity of the good to be discovered and pursued. I shall draw on material from preceding chapters to argue that a cognitive conception need not provide a foothold for intolerance and totalitarianism, but rather can turn disagreement within society about the relations between conflicting values to advantage, within a democratic division of epistemic labour.

Note the role, in the contrast drawn above between the prevalent assumptions about liberal democracy and a cognitive conception, of suppositions about the unity of the good and the nature of conflict: Burke, on the cognitive side, assumes the nation has one interest, while Rawls, on the other side, emphasizes conflict between different particular conceptions of the good held by different persons, conflict located primarily between persons, rather than conflict between qualitatively different goods located equally within persons. Rawls' view that the absence of commitment to ideals such as that of autonomy is essential to liberalism, if the latter is not to become merely another sectarian doctrine, turns on the description of such ideals as comprehensive: "any such ideal, when pursued as a comprehensive ideal, is incompatible with other conceptions of the good".[22] The common supposition that, although different persons' conceptions of the good may be conflicting and incommensurable, the good itself must be conceived by each person as something unitary and comprehensive which does not admit of conflict, or at least in such a way that, whatever intrapersonal conflicts may exist, they are sharply distinguished in their nature and/or significance from interpersonal conflicts, has distorted what's at issue between the conceptions characterized by one or both of the prevalent assumptions and a cognitive conception. Arguments for the former often depend on a conception of the alternatives as characterized by this supposition about unity and conflict; but without this supposition, the cognitive value of self-determination comes into its own and a cognitive conception of democracy is able to do justice to many of the liberal motivations of the prevalent assumptions. We have seen in earlier chapters that cognitivism and conflict are compatible; conflicts between values cut across persons as well as between them, and may unite them to one another as well as divide them. The presence of horizontal as well as vertical distinctions within a fully structured theory allows us to see the aims of democracy, as an exercise of collective self-determination, in cognitive terms, which nevertheless provide a basis for characteristically egalitarian and liberal positions, such as support for principles of redistributive justice and individual autonomy.[23]

I supposed at the end of the last chapter that the members of some community seek knowledge of what should be done in certain cases and that they thus seek to base decisions on beliefs about what should be done that track the truth. For them to succeed in this aim it is necessary, but not sufficient, that the beliefs on which decisions are based are not positively debunked. It is, of course, not enough for a belief to constitute knowledge that it be true, and it may often be possible to know that a certain class of beliefs do not in general track the truth and hence do not constitute knowledge, even if one does not know the truth about particular issues under dispute. That is, even in the absence of knowledge of the truth, beliefs about certain kinds of issues, which have been formed in certain ways or under certain circumstances, may be known to be debunked, as the result of self-deception, wishful thinking, prejudice, deceit, propaganda, advertising, or some other kind of deliberate manipulation, a kind of sour grapes reaction, illusion, common inferential error, etc.[24] The members of such a community should seek to exploit this possibility by designing procedures and institutions that effect a division of epistemic labour in accordance with generalizations about the circumstances in which beliefs about certain types of issues are debunked, or likely to be. *First*, they should seek to divide authority on various kinds of issues among institutions and procedures not so much in accordance with positive expertise about what should be done, which may be very hard to identify in the absence of knowledge of the truth about it, but so as to avoid relying on debunked (or debunkable—I intend "debunked" to include "debunkable") beliefs. *Second*, they should actively foster the capacity for deliberation and the formation of undebunked beliefs. These two epistemic precepts provide a basis for institutional design and agenda and domain division. If the procedures and institutions that result are democratic, then democracy is of cognitive value. And in fact it is, according to the cognitive theory of democracy; democracy is more likely to lead to the right answer than alternative forms of government, because it is less likely to lead to disastrously wrong answers, which those recommended by the forces that debunk beliefs are likely to be, and because it preserves the conditions in which the search for right answers can continue, that is, the conditions of autonomous deliberation.

I shall refer to these two precepts of the cognitive conception of democracy as Millian, as they are closely related to the claim made by Mill to have obtained "a foundation for a two-fold division of the merit which any set of political institutions can possess":

> It consists partly of the degree in which they promote the general mental advancement of the community, including under that phrase advancement in intellect, in virtue, and in practical activity and efficiency; and partly of the degree of perfection with which they organize the moral, intellectual, and active worth already existing, so as to operate with the greatest effect on public affairs.[25]

Note the essentially cognitive basis of Mill's argument for free debate and adversarial procedures:

> ... the true opinion abides in the mind, but abides as a prejudice, a belief independent of, and proof against, argument—this is not the way in which truth ought to be held by a rational being. This is not knowing the truth. . . . But on every subject on which difference of opinion is possible, the truth depends on a balance to be struck between two sets of conflicting reasons.
>
> . . . [Someone who would do justice to the arguments] must be able to hear them from persons who actually believe them; who defend them in earnest, and do their very utmost for them. He must know them in their most plausible and persuasive form; he must feel the whole force of the difficulty which the true view of the subject has to encounter and dispose of; else he will never really possess himself of the portion of truth which meets and removes that difficulty. Ninety-nine in a hundred of what are called educated men are in this condition; even of those who can argue fluently for their opinions. Their conclusion may be true, but it might be false for anything they know: they have never thrown themselves into the mental position of those who think differently from them, and considered what such persons may have to say; and consequently they do not, in any proper sense of the word, know the doctrine which they themselves profess. . . . nor is it ever really known, but to those who have attended equally and impartially to both sides, and endeavored to see the reasons of both in the stongest light. So essential is this discipline to a real understanding of moral and human subjects, that if opponents of all important truths do not exist, it is indispensable to imagine them, and supply them with the strongest arguments which the most skilful devil's advocate can conjure up.[26]

And note that disagreement among the members of society is regarded by Mill as of indispensable cognitive value, rather than as undermining the possibility of conceiving of democracy in terms of a search for the truth.

I shall explain the relationship of the two Millian precepts of institutional design to a cognitive conception of democracy and to debunking explanations. For certain types of issue certain institutional arrangements and decision procedures may be more reliable, or less unreliable, than others as guides to the truth; the variety of possible domain and agenda divisions is enormous, ranging from reliance solely on one individual's opinion about self-regarding alternatives through systems of checks and balances among judicial, legislative, and executive branches of government, and divisions of jurisdiction according to subject matter, to the occasional direct referenda. A good reason for the overall design of institutions and allocation of authority among them to have a liberal democratic character, in the sense that authority is thoroughly divided and individual autonomy is cultivated and respected, rather than an authoritarian character, may be that certain of such arrangements best exploit disagreement within society, so as to provide undebunked sources of evidence about what should be done when values conflict. The cognitive value of democracy in any given society is relative to other possible methods of social decision making, but this does not make democracy merely a means to an independent cognitive end, any more than personal autonomy is; social self-determination that is specifically democratic, in the sense above specified, is constitutively and not merely instrumentally related to the value of individual autonomy. In this respect, a democratic division of epistemic labour is a way of realizing as well as discovering what ought to be the case. Of course the value of individual autonomy may itself conflict with other values; but neither the value of individual autonomy, to which democracy is thus constitutively related, nor the instrumental epistemic value of democracy, as a way of discovering what ought to be the case, need be absolute for democracy to be well and thoroughly justified.[27]

Nevertheless, not just any thorough division of authority will sustain this judgment of relative cognitive value; some divisions will work better than others, and many may result, in a wide range of circumstances, in chaos, inconsistency, and/or manipulation, as the social choice literature has illustrated.[28] Indeed, Aristotle wrote:

> For it is possible that the many . . . may yet taken all together be better than the few, not individually but collectively. . . . For where there are many people, each has some share of goodness and intelligence, and when these are brought together, they become as it were one multiple man with many pairs of feet and hands and many minds. . . . But it is not at all certain that this superiority of the many over the good few is to be found in every people and every large majority.[29]

Judgments of relative cognitive value informed by debunking explanations provide a basis for determining choices among alternative divisions of authority within a democracy. It is quite compatible with the cognitive value of democracy and with the value of democracy as a kind of self-determination that it matters how well a particular division of authority fits a particular society; from the perspective of the cognitive conception it is unreasonable to rely on any given set of democratic institutions and division of authority regardless of the history and character of the society and the various influences on the beliefs of members of the society.[30]

In considering an epistemic contribution to the justification of democracy, we should recall several points about the distinction between *prima facie* and *pro tanto* reasons. Conflicting values are not conflicting pieces of evidence about what to do; they are not *prima facie* but *pro tanto* reasons. When we deliberate and construct theories about conflicting values, we are not trying to arrive at a judgment based on evidence than which none is better. Coherence functions do not have an epistemic role, of leading us to what should be done, but a constitutive role. There may be *prima facie* reasons for belief about what ought to be done in addition to *pro tanto* reasons for action, but we understand neither *pro tanto* reasons nor reasons to do this or that all things considered in terms of *prima facie* reasons. Recall the two different ways to find the answer to a question: one is to do the research yourself, the other is to ask qualified persons what they think. Both ways of finding the answer may be quite reliable; but ultimately the research has to be done by someone for there to be answers at all. Similarly, *prima facie* reasons for action are ultimately parasitic on *pro tanto* reasons and reasons of coherence.

The suggestion is that democracy may be justified in part by the view that, in conditions of free and open debate, the division of authority over various kinds of issue between individual decision makers, various branches and levels of local government, the whole electorate, the legislature, the executive branch, the judiciary (itself perhaps with divided jurisdiction), etc., has epistemic value. For many issues, under the right conditions, taking votes, like taking polls of qualified opinions, may provide an undebunked source of evidence about what ought to be done, and the suggestion extends easily to the case where elected representatives are held responsible to the opinions of their constituents.[31] We need not choose once and for all between the position that an elected representative should remain faithful to the views of his constituents and the position that he should exercise his own best judgment.[32] Rather, the aim should be to design institutions so that each constraint applies under appropriate circumstances, i.e., when it is less likely to be subject to debunking forces than alternative decision-making mechanisms. Each method of finding answers to questions about what should be done may be quite reliable in the right circumstances. Ultimately, however, the value of the evidence from any given source, including the public, about what should be done, hence its status as providing *prima facie* reasons to act, depends on the quality of the deliberative exercise which underlies that evidence.[33] Hence the importance, on a cognitive conception of democracy, of the two principles of institutional design and agenda and domain division: avoid relying on evidence about what should be done derived from debunked beliefs, and foster the capacity for deliberation and the formation of undebunked beliefs. The cognitive value of a democratic division of epistemic labour is ultimately parasitic on the widespread capacity and willingness of citizens to deliberate responsibly about what should be done, all things considered.

In effect I am suggesting a reversal of the roles normally assumed to be played by values, on the one hand, and the votes of citizens, on the other, in relation to what ought to be done. Philosophers have often regarded values as providing *prima facie* reasons for action, evidence about what should be done,[34] while social choice theory provides tacit resistence to a view of the votes of citizens as providing evidence about what ought to be done. By contrast, I am suggesting that we resist the view that values provide evidence about what ought to be done and that we instead view voting as a more or less reliable source of such evidence. A cognitive conception of democracy gives a critically important role to the education of citizens and makes considerable demands on citizens, as voters or in whatever capacity they contribute to the democratic decision-making process, greater demands certainly than do many conceptions that involve either or both of the prevalent assumptions; citizens are obliged to express not their own preferences, but rather their well-considered beliefs about what should be done. These demands may be regarded as unrealistic in the sense that most citizens of most actual democracies do not live up to them. However, there is another, perhaps more important sense in which these demands are realistic: if democracy is to work in the long run, the importance of attempting to meet them had better be recognized.[35]

These remarks are not to be understood as implying the sharp dichotomy between the matters concerning only the interests of one individual and matters of ethical and political concern arising from conflicts between the interests of different individuals, which I have repudiated in earlier chapters. My position remains a version of the classical view according to which individual preferences and interests cannot ultimately be understood independently of public values and shared reason-giving practices. Recognition within a fully structured social theory that conflicts of value occur within persons as well as between them means that the ethical domain extends to intrapersonal as well as interpersonal conflicts. The traditional conception of morality as a realm in which conflicts between prior and independent individual interests are adjudicated is rejected in favour of a neo-classical concept of ethics, as explained at the end of Chapter 8 section 4. Nevertheless, it is possible to distinguish the scope of considerations appropriate to deliberative efforts at individual self-determination and those appropriate to citizens in their role as sources of evidence about what a society should do and what kind of a society it should be. Indeed, it is not sensible not to do so; many issues of collective self-determination, of what society should do and what kind of society it should be, cannot be reduced to issues of individual self-determination, insofar as the most effective units of agency differ. There are alternatives, which involve public goods, or the consequences of classes of acts, which are only alternatives for a society or a collective agent, not for an individual, or a collection of individual agents each calculating and evaluating the consequences of his or her individual acts, however impartially. Recognizing and providing decision procedures for such collective alternatives is one of the basic tasks of domain and agenda division and institutional design in a democracy. But a prior point is that the search for knowledge of what should be done across an entire social agenda may itself give rise to possibilities of collective action and co-operation within a democratic division of epistemic labour, which would require citizens to respect the undebunked contributions of others to the epistemic enterprise, even though they may not agree with them.

For a citizen to deliberate about which of such collective alternatives should be done with regard solely to their bearing on the alternatives he faces as an individual agent is for him to fail fully to live up to the demands of citizenship in an autonomous society, even though he may take some ethical considerations into account; individualism with respect to agency, and in particular, with respect to the activity of deliberation, remain all too possible even though the traditional sharp dichotomy between matters of individual interest and matters of moral and political concern be rejected.[36] (This is in effect just to apply the point made in Chapter 8 sections 1 through 4 that the issue about the unit of agency cuts across the issue about what the relationships between the goals of different persons are.) Indeed, an aspect of the ethics of self-determination concerns the circumstances in which the individual ought to abandon the exclusively individual unit of agency and to act as part of a group, to become, literally, public-spirited.[37] However, the distinction between such individualistic self-centredness and the co-operative public-spiritedness worthy of citizens is drawn very differently from, for example, a distinction between self-interested and 'moral' preferences, or between personal and extended preferences, premised on subjectivism. (See the discussion of extended preference and subjectivism in Chapter 6. Further comments on the relationships between individual autonomy and democracy are to be found below in section 4.)

None of this is to deny that considerations of total welfare conceived as a function of individual interests should figure in the deliberations of voters. However, to hold as some utilitarians do that society should simply maximize total welfare is to hold a particular substantive ethical position, rather than a view about how society can best discover what it should do. As such, it has to be defended against other substantive ethical positions, including pluralistic views of what society should do in which such a conception of welfare may also play an important role. As Thomas Nagel comments, "utilitarian theory ... has a great deal to contribute if it is not required to account for everything".[38]

It may be objected that there is a difficulty of incentive-compatibility with the suggestion that votes should be used to express beliefs about what should be done rather than preferences; beliefs expressed in elections the outcome of which affects the voters' interests all too likely to be debunked.[39] Of course, judgments about the differential liabilities of votes within various domains and with respect to various agenda to debunking influences must be arrived at on the cognitive view; but similarly in other conceptions of liberal democracy issues on which certain voters' preferences are antecedently likely to be what Dworkin calls "external" must be assigned to a different domain (see the discussion below in section 3.) There is no difficulty about incentive compatibility special to the cognitive conception when it comes to arriving at such judgments of differential liability of votes to be disqualified. The objection is rather more general: that, across the board, people do not need incentives to express their preferences, since doing so will, at least under many conditions, conduce to their getting what they want, while they do need incentives to express their beliefs about what should be done, which under a wide range of conditions may not be in their interests or what they prefer.

The reply is twofold, and involves applications of the two Millian epistemic precepts, of, first, dividing authority in accordance with epistemic considerations, considering actual conditions and debunking influences, and, second, aiming to improve actual conditions and check debunking influences by fostering deliberative capacities.

First, the general objection can be disarmed by assimilating incentive-compatibility issues to the issues of institutional design and agenda and domain division which require differential judgments of liability to debunking influences. Many elections are such that any one individual's vote has a negligible chance of affecting the outcome. Even if we assume that a voter will vote for what is in his interests, if he votes at all, it may not be worth someone's while, given his goals, to go to the polls and cast his vote; indeed, this is regarded as a problem for many conceptions of liberal democracy.[40] Moreover, the circumstances for collective action with respect to self-interested goals may not obtain. In such cases there is no strong argument from self-interest *against* going to the polls to vote for what one believes should be done, assuming there is some public-spirited motivation independent of self-interest *in favour of* doing so. These cases should be identified and given general characterizations in the course of designing institutions and dividing institutions and domains, and the conditions that give rise to them cultivated. Circumstances in which someone's vote will have a non-negligible effect on an outcome that directly affects certain of his interests are at least *prima facie* debunking; note that in this respect elections in which the number of voters is large may have an advantage over elections in which the number of voters is small.[41] Moreover, the votes of members of an organized group, acting as a unit, may have a non-negligible effect on an outcome that directly affects the members of the group. Thus debunking explanations provide an argument, within the cognitive conception, for regulating the activities of political pressure groups, to ensure that the kind of dispersion and decentralization of influence compatible with the undebunked status of votes is maintained, and for regulating the conduct and financing of election campaigns, to limit the extent to which money can buy political influence, that is, political advertising (as opposed to publicly funded pamphlets and debates). Both pressure groups and privately funded political advertising may make considerable sense when the point of democracy is conceived to be maximizing total welfare as constituted by the satisfaction of preferences expressed by voting; pressure groups and market mechanisms may arguably express intensity of preference, at least under certain conditions. But it is much harder, within a cognitive conception of democracy, to argue that they are compatible with, let alone contribute to, the epistemic responsibilities of the electorate and the legislature—much harder than to argue, as Mill does, for the essential epistemic function of open and free debate.[42]

Second, the deliberative capacity and public-spiritedness of citizens should be cultivated, so that positive motivation to participate is present. In circumstances in which the influence of each person's vote on certain of his own interests is negligible, both the cognitive conception and the alternatives to it must say something about what should motivate citizens to vote. In the face of knowledge that one's own vote will have a negligible effect on the outcome, I suggest that, as a psychological matter, the appeal to co-operative public-spiritedness is at least as likely to succeed in getting people to vote for what they believe should be done as the appeal to self-interest is to get them to vote for what they would personally prefer. The latter appeal often has a kind of pointlessness in its own terms, conducive to apathy, which the former does not.[43]

Furthermore, in shared-goal cases, voters may be more likely to participate when they can readily conceive of their acts of voting as participation in collective action than when they simply calculate the consequences of their acts in individualistic terms; recall the differential voting response of the two groups of subjects in the experiment by Quattrone and Tversky discussed in Chapter 8 section 3. The importance of the rejection of individualism about agency for the theory of democracy is that it opens the way to consideration of voting and others forms of democratic activity as participation in collective action.[44] A co-operative cognitive theory of democracy would expand the range of possibilities for collective action by conceiving of the goal of such participation in cognitive terms, in particular, in terms of a collective deliberative search for knowledge of what should be done, rather than in non-cognitive terms, that is, in terms of the satisfaction of self-interested preferences. Co-operation with respect to the former rather general shared goal may be possible when it is not possible with respect to self-interested goals. If a shared goal of citizens is to discover the truth about what should be done, they may come to understand that they may collectively do better in their efforts to achieve knowledge by co-operating through voting within a democratic division of epistemic labour than by each relying exclusively on his own efforts to discover the truth across the entire agenda. Without for a moment giving up their own beliefs as individuals or their responsibilities as citizens to arrive at them as thoughtfully as possible, they may thus have good reason for epistemic co-operation. Thus, the cognitive conception is subject to no special difficulties on the score of incentive compatibility, and may even have some advantages in this respect.

## 3. Tracking, Debunking, and the Democratic Division of Epistemic Labour

The analogy between social welfare functions and coherence functions, which represent the theories sought by deliberation, was originally introduced in order to consider whether impossibility results for social welfare functions constituted a threat by analogy to a coherence account and to throw light on just what coherence amounts to. For the analogy between social welfare functions and coherence functions to constitute a threat to a coherence account, it would only be necessary for conditions formally analogous to those that produce impossibility results for social welfare functions to hold for coherence functions, and, as we saw, they do not; it would not be necessary for social welfare functions and coherence functions to have the same theoretical role. In fact their respective theoretical roles, as I have characterized them, may make impossibility results for functions of orderings generated by citizens, given their epistemic role, less disturbing than impossibility results for functions of orderings generated by values, given their constitutive role, would be.

Recall that on the account I have given, coherence functions have conceptual status, in the sense that they provide a way of filling out the noncentralist view that the right thing to do is not conceptually prior to and independent of specific values. The claim that there is a coherence function from specific values to the right thing to do that meets certain conditions is an expression of the constitutive relationships between the right thing to do and those values. (As already explained, this conceptual relationship does not involve any particular coherence function, but an existential claim.) Many social choice theorists would seem to assume a rival view, namely, that social welfare functions express a constitutive relationship between individual preferences and the right thing for society to do, a relationship implicitly taken to underlie and justify democratic procedures. But I have also suggested an alternative, cognitive conception of democracy, according to which individual voters provide more or less reliable evidence about the right thing to do; their relationship to the right thing to do is epistemic rather than constitutive. Arrow associates a related view, which he says that he regards as fundamentally different from his own, with Rousseau; it should also be associated with Mill. Arrow writes:

> In this aspect, the case for democracy rests on the argument that free discussion and expression of opinion are the most suitable techniques of arriving at the moral imperative implicitly common to all. Voting, from this point of view, is not a device whereby each individual expresses his personal interests, but rather where each individual gives his opinion of the general will.

> This model has much in common with the statistical problem of pooling the opinions of a group of experts to arrive at a best judgment; here, individuals are considered experts at detecting the moral imperative.[45]

This different view of the nature of the relationship between various individuals' rankings of alternatives and social decisions may affect our interpretation of various formal conditions and results of social choice theory. Of course, if the epistemic interpretation of the relationship between individual rankings and the right thing to do is adopted, then impossibility results for social choice are still highly relevant to democratic theory and must be taken into account: assertions of the cognitive value of voting must be qualified in accord with the limitations of various voting methods that impossibility results reveal. Indeed, impossibility results take on a new and significant role in designing a democratic division of epistemic labour under the cognitivist interpretation. Certain social choice conditions, I shall suggest, are rendered attractive by non-cognitivist presuppositions; a cognitive view, by contrast, provides an explicit and principled epistemological basis for rejecting or restricting trouble-making conditions.

Democratic theorists have argued for institutional limitations to majoritarian methods of decision on various grounds. For example, consider Dworkin's argument from equal concern and respect that external preferences, preferences that are meddlesome or partial in that they are directly about what happens to others and whether they get what they want rather than about what happens to oneself, should be excluded from the social calculus. The rights of citizens limit the extent to which the external preferences of majorities can dictate to minorities; they thus limit the legislative role and fall under the special protection of the judiciary. Dworkin suggests a general theory of rights, namely, that the concept of a political right "allows us to enjoy the institutions of political democracy . . . and yet protects the fundamental rights of citizens . . . by prohibiting decisions that seem, antecedently, likely to have been reached" through the influence of external preferences.[46] Given that arguments for limitations to majoritarian methods are familiar, the fact that the cognitive conception gives rise to such limitations cannot be urged against it selectively; clearly, what matters is the nature of the limitations it gives rise to. As we shall see, a cognitive conception provides a new interpretation of and basis for already familiar limitations, such as that urged by Dworkin.

By contrast with the epistemic guidance provided by impossibility results within a cognitive conception of democracy, impossibility results that pertain to a function the existence of which is postulated by an account of what something *is*, not merely how you *find* it, would undermine the account. In the latter posture, one could not simply absorb the point by qualifying one's claims for the merits of the account. A coherence account is one such account, according to which specific values are not more or less dependable guides to what should be done, but are primarily constitutive of it. Evidence about what should be done can remain fairly good evidence without being foolproof, since we may have an independent grasp of what it is evidence for. But coherence functions are supposed to reflect something about the very way we conceive of what should be done, not just tell us how to find it. If impossibility results could be derived from reasonable conditions on coherence functions, this would support scepticism about the existence of such a thing as what ought to be done. And in general, impossibility results for functions whose arguments are interpreted to have a constitutive role are more threatening than for functions whose arguments have an epistemic role. Thus, impossibility results in social choice theory are less threatening to a cognitive conception of democracy than to the conception held by Arrow and many social choice theorists; epistemic value can be circumscribed without being undermined.[47]

What sort of limitations to the epistemic role of voting are suggested by impossibility results for social choice? Both the considerations about tracking and debunking that occupied us in the last chapter, and the conditions that give rise to impossibility results in social choice, concern the structure of attitudes, including their counterfactual variation. These attitudes are beliefs about what should be done in the former case, but are normally regarded as preferences in the latter case. I have suggested we consider a cognitivist conception of democracy, so let us reinterpret the social welfare function as a social knowledge function (though the emphasis will be at least as much on avoiding false claims to knowledge as arriving at positive knowledge), and the social choice conditions as conditions on ways of arriving at beliefs about what should be done on the basis of the beliefs of citizens, and then consider how these conditions interact with concerns about tracking and debunking. The interaction will prove to be illuminating and also reassuring: among the conditions that produce intransitivities are some which there is independent reason to regard as incompatible with a view of democratic procedures as having cognitive value. The value of democracy is thus not undermined by impossibility results; rather the results give a particular and rigorous expression to the general precept that epistemic labour ought to be divided within a democracy in such a way that, so far as possible, reliance on debunked beliefs is avoided. We already know that we must violate the Arrow conditions in some way to avoid possible inconsistency. But while a non-cognitive conception of the problem of social choice makes Arrow's conditions attractive, a cognitive conception provides principled motivation for and guidance in the necessary departure from them.

I shall consider first the way in which the multiple-profile conditions $U$ and $I$, interpreted to apply to beliefs about what should be done, all things considered, rather than preferences, interact with considerations about tracking and debunking. Then I shall do the same for the single-profile conditions $N$ and $R$; and finally I shall consider the epistemic significance of Sen's Paretian Liberal result.

Condition $U$ requires that a given social knowledge function apply whatever the content of the beliefs of citizens about what ought to be done happens to be. That is, the same function must apply when given voters change their minds about whether a particular alternative would be better, all things considered, than another, and must apply to counterfactual situations in which their beliefs about the same alternatives are different. Such a social knowledge function is not expected to work only for a particular society, in a way that takes built-in account of its particular history and character and the various influences on the beliefs of various groups of its citizens; it is perfectly general, and is supposed to be able to cope with all possible opinions that each citizen might hold. A function that has such an unrestricted domain of application, which applies to all possible profiles of beliefs held by citizens, and also meets Arrow's other conditions, will produce intransitive recommendations for some profile of beliefs, and may be subject to agenda manipulation such that the result arrived at is not independent of the path taken to it, that is, the order in which the alternatives come up on the political agenda.[48]

In order for a social knowledge function to aim to track the truth on the basis of different possible sets of beliefs, it must depend on some information other than merely what their content is, information relevant to whether or not beliefs held by citizens in various capacities and circumstances about certain kinds of alternatives and issues vary counterfactually with the truth value of such beliefs. (Only evaluative beliefs about general kinds of alternative can vary counterfactually with the truth of the beliefs, since evaluative truths about fully specified alternatives cannot vary counterfactually, but only counterevaluatively, compatibly with supervenience. See Chapter 12.) Perhaps such a function could represent the process of taking account of all possible histories and characters of society and influences on the beliefs of citizens; thus it would not embody any particular set of institutions, but would provide a recipe for designing institutions. The information it would draw upon would include information about the likely reasons for, and irrational causes of, beliefs about certain kinds of issue in various circumstances; are they, for example, likely to be the product of wishful thinking, or propaganda, or to be motivated by meddlesomeness or spite, as in Sen's Prude-and-Lewd example? We cannot assume that an explanation debunks merely because it does not positively display the covariation of truths and beliefs, but we may be justified in assuming that truths of certain kinds cannot vary with certain causal factors that give rise to beliefs, even if we do not know particular truths of the kind in question; an evolutionary explanation of beliefs about facial expression, for example, may not debunk, whereas an explanation of beliefs in terms of manipulation by mad scientists—or politicians—with purposes of their own would debunk. We may be justified in assuming that, whatever the truth is, it cannot vary with *that*.[49] Thus debunking information may support views about the relation between the contents of certain beliefs and their truth-value, even though their truth-value is unknown.

In the actual world, the nominee for Justice believes it is better to have an affirmative action policy in a particular context than not to. But under what circumstances would she not believe it was better? In order for a social knowledge function to apply to an unrestricted domain of counterfactual situations in which her beliefs are different, it must have some way of ascertaining whether circumstances obtain in which her beliefs about alternatives of certain kinds vary independently of truths about them. It might, for example, want to distinguish cases in which, if the candidate were not to have family and friends who would benefit from affirmative action, she would not believe it was right, from cases in which if she had not had certain first-hand experiences of discrimination and its effects, she would not believe affirmative action was right. The social knowledge function might regard her beliefs about such issues as inappropriate to rely upon in the former case, but not in the latter, and institutional constraints on judicial appointments might reflect such distinctions.

Or, a social knowledge function might distinguish the case in which, if the vice-presidential candidate had been blonde, the voters would have believed that her opponent would be more effective as Vice-President, from the case in which if she had been not been correct in claiming during the debate that her opponent's figures about AFDC spending were substantially wrong, the voters would have believed that her opponent would be more effective as Vice-President. (By the way, in fact Ferraro was correct when she claimed during the 1984 debate that Bush's figures were substantially wrong.) Or it might distinguish the case in which if a particular presidential candidate's make-up had been better during the televized debate, the voters would have believed he would make a better president than his opponent, from the case in which if the first candidate had led his opponent to contradict himself about the circumstances under which he would use nuclear weapons, the voters would have believed the first candidate would make a better president than his opponent. Or it might distinguish the case in which if the first candidate had been able to afford colour television commercials instead of black and white, the voter might have . . . , and so on. Some such distinctions might be reflected in regulations of the form and financing of campaign activity, others indirectly in the education of citizens in their responsibilities as voters.[50]

Just because the tracking condition for knowledge, which debunking explanations may negate, characterizes the relationship between the content of beliefs and the truth, a social knowledge function sensitive to tracking concerns cannot be purely internalist in the sense that it cannot depend solely on information about the content of beliefs, but rather must be sensitive to external information about the reliability of beliefs about certain kinds of issue in certain circumstances, such as is reflected in the above distinctions. However, this sensitivity, needed to avoid relying on debunked beliefs, violates condition $I$, which would require the social knowledge function to deliver the same recommendations on a particular issue in both of two possible situations in which the contents of all beliefs in the domain about that particular issue are the same, regardless of distinctions between the two situations with respect to the possibly debunking etiology of beliefs about issues of that kind. Thus a cognitive conception of the problem of social choice provides epistemological justification for resistance to condition $I$. Note that externalist (in Nozick's sense[51]) insistence on the importance of the relationship between the contents of beliefs and the truth is the cognitive analogue of Sen's insistence on the importance to social choice of non-welfare information; both views hold that information just about the contents of attitudes is inadequate.[52]

That condition $I$ constitutes an epistemic handicap at odds with a cognitive conception of democracy is confirmed by its contribution to the generation of inconsistent recommendations by a social knowledge function. That is, if condition $I$ were in force, along with the other conditions that produce Arrow's impossibility result, the possibility of intransitive recommendations would arise. If democratic procedures are to have cognitive value, institutions must be designed so as to provide as inputs to decision procedures beliefs that are, as far as possible, undebunked, well-informed and well-considered, not subject to arbitrary change. Some persons or group of persons or institution or level or branch of government may be a reliable source of such beliefs for certain circumstances and types of issue, and others for others. A social knowledge function that would place equal reliance on all possible opinions in an unrestricted domain irrespective of their sensitivity to the truth cannot include institutional procedures, and choices among institutional arrangements, which function to divide epistemic labour in accordance with such distinctions, as may be called for in particular societies and circumstances.

This is *not* to deny that all conflicting beliefs that may be held should be freely and forcefully expressed. As Mill claims, open debate among adversaries plays an essential role in allowing the decision makers' beliefs to approach the status of knowledge, as in the case of judges who decide a case after hearing evidence and arguments from both sides. There is no incompatibility between the free expression of fundamental disagreement and many methods of domain and agenda division. The critical point is not simply that all opinions in an unrestricted domain cannot vary with the truth, but that we can distinguish, among those which in fact do not, those that are debunked from those that, for all we know, might constitute knowledge, the reasons for which can contribute along Millian lines to the search for the right answer.[53] In dividing domains and agendas in accordance with such distinctions a social knowledge function does not restrict the domain of possible opinions, but does rely on opinions selectively, thus violating condition *I*.

Of course, many have written on the topic of agenda and domain division within democratic states. Mill's remarks suggest a cognitive ground for such divisions, while others have urged them on independent grounds.[54] Thus Dahl writes:

> The proper scope of a democratic organization—the matters it may properly place on its agenda for decision—is dependent on the domain of the organization, that is, on the nature of the demos. Matters that are proper for one demos, such as the citizens of a province, are not necessarily proper for another demos, such as the citizens of a village.
>
> ... democratic control requires an appropriate demos.
>
> ... both fundamental rights and social utility provide adequate grounds for holding that different matters should often be subject to control by different bodies of citizens—just as they are by the governments of municipalities, states, and the nation.[55]

The point to be emphasized is that domain and agenda divisions, and the principles of choice among alternative divisions, take on a new significance when viewed in the light of the interacting considerations which derive from a cognitive conception of democracy, on the one hand, and the results of social choice theory, on the other.

It may be objected that choices among alternative domain and agenda divisions cannot be made except by prejudging the substance of the issues and delegating authority merely to get the desired result. On its face, the objection is implausible; as we saw in the last chapter, it is often easier to determine that certain beliefs do not vary with the truth than to determine what the truth is. For a social knowledge function to exploit such information when it is available is not for it to prejudge the substance of issues; moreover, when issues happen to involve fundamental constitutional values, there may be no objection to a social knowledge function that does prejudge their substance.[56] However, the objection can be reformulated so as to raise the important question of the sense in which domain and agenda divisions may be considered democratic: so far we have discussed the division of epistemic labour, but not what it is in virtue of which some such divisions might be termed more democratic than others. I shall return to this question after discussing the conditions that give rise to two further impossibility results.

Another immediate objection, however, is that the divisions effected by institutions and procedures that function to avoid reliance on debunked beliefs and cultivate the epistemic value of disagreement may not be sufficient to avoid impossibility results. Responsible disagreement within subdomains may still provide a domain rich enough to support impossibility results. Assuming we have already exploited debunking information to the full, if we now violate condition $I$ again by dividing the domain still further our choice of how to do so may determine the result. We will then have to choose between tolerating a possibility of intransitivity and restricting the domain so as to determine a solution. If we reject the latter option as undemocratic, then the cognitive value of democracy must be qualified by the overall probability of such intransitivities within subdomains. However, the cognitive value of democracy does not need to be unqualified; it may still be considerably greater than that of the alternatives, including that of rigging the domain and agenda divisions so as to determine solutions. Moreover, non-overlapping assignments of agendas to subdomains may have the effect of checking or isolating intransitivities.[57]

Consider now the possibility of a social knowledge function that applies only to a single profile of beliefs instead of to all possible beliefs. The epistemic critique of multiple-profile condition $I$ extends to single-profile condition $N$ (see Chapter 12). We have seen that some persons or institutions in the domain may have reliable methods of forming beliefs for some types of issues and not for others. But a social knowledge function that reflects such epistemic distinctions by dividing the domain into subdomains and the agenda according to types of issue, and placing more reliance on opinions from a given subdomain for some issues and some circumstances than for others, violates condition $N$.

Recall the second kind of single-profile result we considered in Chapter 12, obtained by Roberts, which avoided a neutrality condition such as $N$ but depended on a strong domain condition, $R$; consider the cognitive interpretation of $R$ and its epistemic implications. Original condition $R$ requires there to be alternatives with exactly the same non-welfare characteristics and different welfare characteristics. On the cognitive interpretation, what I shall call *doxastic characteristics*, which reflect all beliefs with respect to what would be better to do, all things considered, in relation to each alternative, replace welfare characteristics, and non-doxastic characteristics, which include all other characteristics, replace non-welfare characteristics. $R$ then requires there to be alternatives with exactly the same non-doxastic characteristics, but different doxastic characteristics.

For two alternatives to have different doxastic characteristics, at least two people must have different beliefs about which would be better, which in turn means that at least one person must himself distinguish between the two alternatives. But if they have just the same non-doxastic characteristics, then at least one person must be evaluating differently alternatives with exactly the same non-doxastic characteristics. Why would someone do this? Perhaps, except for the fact that he distinguishes them, the alternatives are exactly alike, so that by distinguishing them he violates supervenience. He might be drawing a fundamentally arbitrary distinction, one which there is no reason for, between alternatives, treating exactly like cases differently. Perhaps he does not realize he is doing so, but at any rate, as a result he must be wrong about at least one of the alternatives. This kind of arbitrariness on the part of an individual voter or other source of opinions in the single profile could make condition $R$ hold, so that Roberts' impossibility result obtains and the possibility of intransitivity arises.

It may not worry social choice theorists who conceive of democracy in noncognitivist terms if preferences turn out to be fundamentally arbitrary; they may think it irrelevant whether there are reasons for preferences. On a cognitive conception, however, the fact that opinions may be fundamentally arbitrary tends to undermine their reliability as sources of evidence about what should be done. Beliefs that we know to vary across alternatives independently of the truth about them do not track the truth; and we can know that beliefs violate supervenience even if we do not know the truth about what should be done. Members of a profile of beliefs that do vary independently of the truth with respect to certain kinds of issue may be debunked; we should attempt to divide the domain and agenda so as to avoid relying on them. We would not expect a poll of expert opinions to provide reliable evidence if the experts were not arriving at their opinions responsibly, for good reasons. Similarly, we should expect voting to be a less reliable guide to the truth about what should be done when the opinions of the voters may be fundamentally arbitrary; the expectation is confirmed by the contribution of such arbitrariness would make, via condition $R$, to the generation of inconsistent recommendations by a social knowledge function.

A cognitive conception of democracy, again, makes demands on citizens; voters and other decision makers must strive to avoid arbitrariness, and must be encouraged to express thoughtful and reasoned opinions through their votes.[58]

There is another way in which condition $R$ could be met, however. Perhaps the person who distinguishes alternatives with just the same non-doxastic characteristics points to someone else's different beliefs about them to justify his own; this might involve debunking influences on beliefs such as unwarranted deference, or, if the ranking is reversed, spite, or meddlesomeness, as in Sen's example of Prude and Lewd.[59] If straw votes or opinion polls are taken, each person could point to another person's distinction between the two as the reason for his own different treatment of them. Thus individual arbitrariness would be avoided, but only by the whole set of everyone's distinctions forming a great circle, each person pointing to another's distinction to justify his own.

But there are still epistemic problems with this way of meeting condition $R$. First, these opinions would be external, in a cognitive extension of Dworkin's sense; a procedure based on beliefs held for reasons that include deference, spite, and meddlesomeness, which thus are debunked, is unlikely to be a reliable guide to what should be done. Second, a kind of indeterminacy may arise, if each person's reason for thinking what he does about two alternatives is what someone else thinks about them; who gets there first? Finally, we have still got collective arbitrariness: a ranking of alternatives determined by votes that distinguish between alternatives only with respect to others' votes about them may well end up itself distinguishing between alternatives that are exactly alike except with respect to votes. We are looking for circumstances in which voting provides relatively reliable evidence about what should be done. But facts about what should be done are evaluative, thus supervenient, facts; there must be further, underlying differences between alternatives that differ in evaluative respects. For this constraint to be met, is it enough for the only difference between alternatives to be that people have different opinions about them? It seems reasonable to hold that responsible difference of opinion about whether $a$ or $b$ should be done requires there to be some distinction between $a$ and $b$ other than those that hold merely in virtue of the fact that some opinion distinguishes between $a$ and $b$; on a cognitive conception of democracy, voting shows us what should be done not because what should be done is determined by people's opinions about it, but because their opinions about it are (relatively) reliable. But we are supposing in this paragraph and the last that condition $R$ is met in such a way that such doxastic differences are the only differences between the alternatives. A voting procedure that relies on opinions that meet condition $R$ in this way, such as deferential or spiteful opinions, is epistemically unsound, as is confirmed, again, by the contribution of condition $R$ to generating inconsistencies.

Finally, consider an epistemic interpretation of Sen's result, the impossibility of Paretian liberalism, which depends on conditions $U$, $P$, and the condition of *Minimal Liberalism*. In Sen's illustration about whether Prude, Lewd, or no one should read the scurrilous book, Prude and Lewd both agree, each for his own meddlesome reasons, that it would be better for Prude to read the book than for Lewd to read it; hence by condition P their unanimous preferences must be respected. But each is given control over the choice between reading it himself or leaving it unread, by the condition of *Minimal Liberalism*, which demands that at least two individuals should have their personal preferences reflected in social preference over one pair of alternatives each, that is, there are at least two persons and two distinct pairs of alternatives such that one of these two individuals is decisive over one of the pairs and the other over the other. (Someone is decisive over a pair of alternatives $x$ and $y$ just when, if he prefers $x$ to $y$, then society prefers $x$ to $y$, and if he prefers $y$ to $x$, then society prefers $y$ to $x$.)[60] The result is that every alternative is socially worse than some other. (The result is an impossibility for social decision functions, of which less is demanded than of social welfare functions: merely acyclic choice among the alternatives rather than an ordering of them.)

How does the result bear on the suggestion that a social knowledge function should work by delegating authority over various types of issues to various sources of opinion on what should be done, in accord with epistemic considerations? We might reasonably hold, as a special case of the general strategy of domain and agenda division, that each person's own opinion is the best source of evidence about what should be done with respect to certain personal issues. And, more generally, we may think of the two or more individuals postulated by the Liberalism condition as the various sources of opinion, branches of government, or jurisdictions to which authority is delegated with respect to various issues in accordance with epistemic considerations; if we do so, however, the cognitive conception of democracy may seem to face an obstacle in the form of Sen's result.

However, the suggestion that the domain and agenda divisions recommended by the cognitive conception may in effect satisfy a cognitive version of the condition of Minimal Liberalism, so that Sen's result is in force, overlooks the way in which that condition interacts with condition $U$. In Sen's proof, one assignment of agenda to sub-domains, that is, of one pair of alternatives to one individual and another to another, is supposed to hold across the whole of the unrestricted domain. But we cannot simply assume that one way of dividing epistemic labour will have cognitive value across the whole of an unrestricted domain of possible beliefs; we are aiming to divide agenda and domain *in the light of knowledge* about the likely influences on beliefs about certain issues under certain circumstances and in particular societies, *not irrespective of* such knowledge, once and for all. We may grant that the domain is unrestricted, while aiming, by choices both between institutions and within institutions, to divide it differently in different cases. But a social knowledge function that is thus sensitive to information about the reliability of various sources of evidence within the domain, the recommendations of which vary with the influences on the domain, over however unrestricted a range of possibilities, does not meet the Minimal Liberalism condition, which requires that one way of dividing authority be in effect throughout the entire domain. Thus, initial appearances to the contrary, the division of epistemic labour recommended by the cognitive conception of democracy does not in effect satisfy a cognitive version of the Minimal Liberalism condition, so does not land us with a version of Sen's result.

But it may be objected that, while this response may work at the level of institutional design and the division of authority among jurisdictions and branches of government, it will not handle the problem Sen's result poses for a cognitive conception with regard to the very special delegations of authority over personal or self-regarding alternatives to individuals. At least for some such alternatives and some individuals, which is all Minimal Liberalism requires, respect for the value of autonomy would seem to require that one delegation of authority—namely, of authority over those alternatives to those individuals—work across the entire unrestricted domain, irrespective of debunking and other epistemic information.

However, we can respond to this point by focussing in turn on the epistemic significance of condition $P$, and in particular by putting together two points that have already been made. The first is the point made by Sen and alluded to in the discussion of condition $P^*$ in Chapter 12, that condition $P$ itself incorporates a weak form of welfarism, or neutrality with respect to non-welfare information, in that it rules out dependence on non-welfare information in the special case in which everyone's utility rankings coincide.[61] The second is the point made above, that the epistemological emphasis on the relationship between beliefs and the truth is the cognitive version of Sen's emphasis on non-welfare information; information about the content of beliefs or preferences alone is inadequate. Sen's result suggests that the importance of non-welfare information is such that it may provide a basis for challenging even the very limited welfarism incorporated in condition $P$. He writes: "It is not my contention that the libertarian rights should invariably prevail over Paretian judgements, but that there are cases when this makes evident sense. The decision may have to be conditioned on other features, e.g., the *motivation* underlying the utility rankings".[62] We might aim, for example, to suspend condition $P$ when preferences, however unanimous, are motivated by deference, spite, or meddlesomeness; the cognitive version of the point is evidently that even unanimous opinions about what should be done may be debunked in certain circumstances, for example, when they are likely to be thus motivated, or to be the product of false information or propaganda. The aim thus to limit the application of condition $P$ to certain agendas, which may not overlap with the agendas assigned to individuals, is the promised cognitively motivated version of Dworkin's aim to exclude certain preferences from majoritarian procedures.[63] Equally we might, and do, aim to avoid delegating authority over certain self-regarding alternatives to individuals who have become addicted to mind-altering drugs, or to children or the mentally infirm. Sen suggests a preferentist version of the carefully-designed-division-of-labour response to his result when he writes:

> It is also possible to argue that whether a certain condition on a CCR [collective choice rule, including social welfare functions and social decision functions] such as the Pareto principle, or minimal liberalism, is a good condition or not might depend much on what patterns of individual preferences would actually hold, and not on what patterns are logically conceivable. A condition may be fine for a CCR with a certain restricted domain and another may be alright for a CCR with a different restricted domain, and given a possible conflict between the two, we might choose with an eye to the likely sets of individual preferences. It is possible to argue for a CCR that satisfies condition P over a domain [X] and satisfies [the condition of

Minimal Liberalism] over a domain [Y], with [X] and [Y] having some, but not all, common elements.[64]

The distinctive contributions of the cognitive conception of democracy to this approach are the two Millian epistemic precepts of institutional design and the division of labour noted in the previous section: avoid relying on evidence about what should be done derived from debunked beliefs, and foster conditions that give rise to the capacity for deliberation and the formation of undebunked beliefs.

Finally, however, we must return to the issues deferred earlier: in what sense do certain divisions of epistemic labour count as *democratic*? Indeed, are not such divisions essentially *un*democratic? The second question is prior and must be addressed first. The answer to it is *no*; and seeing why it must be no helps to understand the answer to the first question, that the value of autonomy provides the sense in which certain divisions are democratic and others not.

What is the basis for the common view that certain delegations of authority over certain agenda which thereby take those matters out of the hands of the majority and their representatives, are *per se* undemocratic? We have discussed the conflict between liberal delegations of authority to individuals and the 'democratic' Pareto principle, and briefly remarked upon the frequently made charge that judicial review is undemocratic; less frequently discussed, but perhaps more revealing, is the issue of whether the system of overlapping organizational units characteristic of federalism is undemocratic. The three topics of liberalism, judicial review, and federalism each present a special case of the general issue of how jurisdiction— the assignment of agenda to some subset of decision-makers within society—is to be determined. As Dahl writes, "while relatively autonomous organizations are not sufficient for democracy *per se*, they are a necessary element in a large scale democracy, both as a prerequisite for its operation and as an inevitable consequence of its institutions"; but this point raises the issue of how such organizations can be entitled within a democracy to a certain range of authority as against the total population and its representatives. Such delegations of authority are incompatible with the equal influence of each citizen's opinions about what should be done on the final decision. Even when each of a number of organizations has equal influence on certain outcomes, as the states do in the U.S. Senate, unless each organization represents the same number of citizens, equality among organizations will conflict with equality among individuals.[65]

If we rule out large-scale direct democracy and admit the need to divide authority between citizens and various intermediate organizations, institutions, and branches of government, how is this conflict to be resolved? How, that is, should the balance be struck between procedures that do give each citizen in the society equal opportunity to influence the decision and those that do not, and should the latter be avoided as far as possible as *per se* undemocratic? To slip into thinking that the answer to the last question must be *yes* is to succumb to a fallacy similar to those, exposed by Dahl and Whelan, involved in supposing that the principle that each citizen should have equal influence can 'democratically' determine jurisdictional conflicts and boundary issues.

Dahl is concerned in *Dilemmas of Pluralist Democracy* to examine the extent to which various problems of pluralist democracy can be attributed to insufficient democratization. He considers whether jurisdictional conflicts, disagreements over how agenda and domain should be divided and authority delegated, can be resolved by ordinary 'democratic' procedures for resolving political disputes, such as majority rule, and notes that "a difficulty lies close beneath the surface: Democratic procedures by which particular demos? A majority of what persons?" He considers the proposal that jurisdictional conflicts should be solved by democratic procedures among the largest group of citizens all of whose interests are affected in a significant way. Even if one concedes the point that the determination of whose interests are affected will be a bit arbitrary (a concession that Whelan does not make, as we shall see), this principle will be inadequate when the jurisdictional conflict involves questions about the fundamental rights of some included minority. "What makes the majority principle morally acceptable (when it is acceptable) is one's judgment that the demos consists of persons who are roughly equal in their qualifications for deciding the matters on the agenda of the association. But what if a demand for autonomy by a minority calls that very judgment into question by asserting a fundamental right or a claim to freedom that the existing demos is not qualified to decide?" However, if we agree that under such circumstances it may be necessary to grant the minority a degree of autonomy with respect to a certain agenda, the question immediately arises whether this grant of autonomy will not itself result in oppression by the newly autonomous group of yet another group. If so, we cannot resolve this conflict by appealing to the principle that every jurisdictional conflict should be settled by democratic procedures among the largest number of citizens whose interests are involved, as this was the point at which we started. An appeal to majoritarian procedures or to the principle that every citizen's views ought to have equal influence cannot satisfactorily resolve such jurisdictional conflicts; it is not more democratic *per se* to give control over local issues to national majorities than to local majorities, and control by local majorities is incompatible with the equal influence of each citizen on a national scale. Moreover, democracy does not demand that the demos of any *one* of the various possible organizational units be given ultimate control over the entire agenda; the best arrangement might well be, as Dahl puts it, "a complex system with several or more layers of democratic government, each operating with a somewhat different agenda".[66]

In his article "Federalism and the Democratic Process", Dahl writes:

> The fact is that one cannot decide from *within* democratic theory what constitutes a proper unit for the democratic process. Like the majority principle, the democratic process *presupposes* a unit. *The criteria of the democratic*

*process presupposes the rightfulness of the unit itself.* If the unit itself is not a proper or rightful one, then it cannot be made rightful simply by democratic procedures.[67]

While I agree with the logic of his position, I should like to dissent from the implications of certain elements of his formulation of it. If issues about whether various possible divisions of authority are more or less democratic, are understood simply in terms of the majority and equal influence principles applied to the most inclusive demos, then it is true that democratic theory cannot itself tell us which divisions are proper. But democratic theory should not be understood in this simple way; therefore, democratic theory may allow us to discriminate among various possible divisions of authority with respect to how democratic they are. The first step is to get past thinking that any departure from the simplest kind of democracy is *per se* a departure from democracy. It is no more undemocratic *per se* to divide agenda and domain and delegate authority within a society than it is undemocratic *per se* to set the boundaries of a society less inclusively rather than more inclusively; we should not be beguiled by the salient simplicity of certain democratic arrangements, those within simple, unitary systems, into believing them salient in respect of democracy as well. We must get past the point of supposing that the obvious difficulty, namely, that people will disagree about how divisions of authority within society should be drawn, somehow shows that such divisions are *per se* undemocratic. For people will also disagree about how the boundaries of society should be drawn; but this does not make drawing boundaries *per se* undemocratic. Particular boundaries may be drawn more or less democratically; persons outside a given boundary are not necessarily irrelevant to concerns of democracy, and exclusion may amount to repression and exploitation, which is none the more democratic for being kept at a distance. The boundaries of a democracy should not be taken as absolutely fixed or exogenously given; the question whether it is more democratic to draw a particular boundary more or less inclusively is a substantive question, which turns on the circumstances of particular cases. I believe we should allow that certain boundaries may be less democratic than others, and certain divisions of authority less democratic than others; but we cannot understand the basis for such distinctions by reference to the above simple understanding of democracy.[68]

If the majority and equal influence principles cannot play the key role in democratic theory of determining how jurisdictional disagreements should be resolved, what principles should decide them? Various principles suggest themselves. Perhaps authority should be divided in a way that is conducive to the good life; but in whose opinion conducive to the good life? Perhaps all people who will be affected by the resolution of issues of a certain kind should have a voice in their resolution; but who is to judge which people are affected and which are not? As Whelan explains,

> ... before a democratic decision could be made on a particular issue (by those affected), a prior decision would have to be made, in each case, as to

who is affected and therefore entitled to vote on the substantive issue—a
decision, that is, on the proper bounds of the relevant constituency. And
how is this decision, which will be determinative of the ensuing substantive
decision, to be made? It too should presumably be made democratically—
that is, by those affected—but now we encounter a regression from which
no procedural escape is possible.[69]

Perhaps authority ought to be divided in accordance with the two epistemic
precepts that I have suggested, following Mill; but of course the same problem
arises for this suggestion, namely, that people will disagree about how to
apply these precepts. The point is, however, that the same problem arises
for *any* suggestion that attempts to extract us from the regress Whelan describes, not merely for the two precepts I have suggested. Even views requiring
principles of division that would be agreed upon by all under special conditions
of ignorance, since of course they will not be agreed upon under ordinary
conditions, are subject to disagreement about which principles would be
agreed upon, or rationally agreed upon, under those conditions (witness the
disagreement about what would be rationally agreed on in Rawls' original
position); or to disagreement about what the special conditions should be.
Since the regress cannot be escaped procedurally, by reference to the simple
understanding of democracy, whatever means we adopt to escape it will
involve in effect taking a substantive position about how authority ought to
be divided, on the basis of some principle and despite the fact that people
may well disagree about how that principle should be applied, as well as about
the position that invokes that principle to begin with. Since responsibility for
taking such a substantive position cannot be avoided, it should be recognized
openly so that substantive deliberation may occur among whatever parties
are responsible as a matter of fact; otherwise, the "danger is that the claim
to scientific neutrality can cover an uncritical disregard for actual normative
assumptions".[70]

   Is there any sense in which certain substantive positions about how authority ought to be divided are more democratic than others? Once we have
distanced ourselves from the simple understanding of democracy, we can see
that the answer may be *yes*. The sense in which certain divisions of authority
are more democratic than others ultimately depends on the relationship of
the principles of division to the value of individual autonomy.[71] This remains
true within a cognitive framework: if one conceives of divisions of authority
as divisions of epistemic labour, it is still with respect to the value of individual
autonomy that some divisions of epistemic labour are more democratic than
others. Thus democracy is compatible with domain and agenda divisions based
on epistemic considerations in which debunking explanations play a large
role. In the next section I shall attempt to explain the complex role of the
value of autonomy within a cognitive theory of democracy.

## 4. Democracy and Autonomy

It may seem that there are two elements in a cognitive theory of democracy
which threaten to come apart, the cognitive element and the democratic

element. Given that there are many ways of dividing authority within society that are not democratic, some of which may conceivably be of greater epistemic merit than democratic arrangements that respect and foster the value of individual autonomy, there seem to be two separable and potentially conflicting responses to the question how authority ought to be divided, the response that gives ultimate priority to epistemic concerns and the response that gives ultimate priority to the value of individual autonomy. We might think of a cognitive theory of democracy as making cognitive success the end and democratic arrangements which respect and foster individual autonomy as merely the means to this end, hence as affirming a version of the end/means distinction Schumpeter assumes when he claims that "democracy is a political method, that is to say, a certain type of institutional arrangement for arriving at political . . . decisions and hence incapabale of being an end in itself, irrespective of what decisions it will produce under given historial conditions".[72] But if we do think of a cognitive theory in this way, then the theory does indeed threaten to decompose, and the importance of respecting individual autonomy is rendered disturbingly contingent.

However, we should *not* think of the cognitive theory of democracy in this way. The view of autonomy and the democratic divisions of authority that respect and foster it as merely means to an independent cognitive end, which gives rise to this threat, is rejected by the cognitive conception of democracy that I am developing. Recall that democracy is constitutively and not merely instrumentally related to the value of individual autonomy; thus it is a way of realizing as well as of discovering what ought to be the case. Of course, the value of autonomy may conflict with other values, and part of what we are trying to determine in deliberating about what we ought to do all things considered is the relationships between autonomy and other values. But we need not deny the possibility of conflict between autonomy and other values, or give autonomy absolute priority over other values in all circumstances, in order to claim that a democratic division of authority, which respects and fosters the value of autonomy, is justified on a cognitive basis, at least under a very wide range of historical conditions.[73] Neither the value of autonomy, to which democracy is constitutively related, nor the instrumental epistemic value of democracy, need be absolute for democratic divisions of authority to be decisively better in cognitive terms than the alternatives.

The cognitive theory of democracy makes two substantive claims involving autonomy. *First*, epistemologically sound divisions of authority within society, which avoid relying on opinions that are likely to be debunked and which foster the conditions that allow undebunked opinions to arise, and thus are more likely than alternative arrangements to lead to the truth about what should be done, will, at least under a very wide range of circumstances, be democratic. That is, they will be divisions of authority that respect and foster the value of individual autonomy and the associated capacity for deliberation. Of course, there are many different ways of dividing authority democratically; the claim is not that all of them are likely to be of cognitive value, but that the divisions of authority that are of cognitive value are likely to be democratic, or, contraposing, that undemocratic divisions are likely not be of cognitive value, but to be especially subject to debunking influences. Thus democratic arrangements build respect for autonomy into the political system in part for *instrumental* reasons relating to the goal of achieving a system with cognitive value.

*Second*, democratic divisions of authority at the same time help to *realize* the value of autonomy. They thus have an important advantage over undemocratic arrangements. Autonomy is not, of course, the only value society seeks to realize, and it may conflict with others; but it is nevertheless a weighty value and plays a distinctive role for persons as self-interpreting animals. Democratic arrangements, despite the fact that they are characterized in terms of their respect for autonomy, have notoriously pluralistic tendencies and no intrinsic tendency to exclude values other than autonomy; indeed, as we saw in section 1, the notion of autonomy or self-determination essentially involves horizontal distinctions, between qualitatitively distinct and conflicting values, as well as vertical distinctions; it has a logically higher-order character in relation to other substantive values, and would not make sense at all as an isolated value. But nondemocratic arrangements, characterized in terms of their absence of respect for autonomy, do have an intrinsic tendency to exclude the value of autonomy. Thus, even though autonomy is by no means unique, fundamental, of highest priority, or central among substantive values, it does, by virtue of its higher-order logical relation to other values, have a unique capacity to provide the political basis of pluralism. Perhaps it is logically possible that under certain circumstances an undemocratic division of authority, such as that envisaged by Plato, would be more likely than any democratic scheme to lead to the truth about what should be done. However, for this to be the case, the truth led to (unless it were that autonomy and the capacity for deliberation ought to be fostered and democracy instituted) would have to involve it being the case that the value of autonomy is not merely less weighty than other values in certain kinds of case, but very nearly entirely weightless; and since this is almost certainly not true, the logical possibility we have admitted is little more than that. The supposition of the epistemological value of undemocratic arrangements has a tendency to defeat itself, not as a matter of logic, but because of the constitutive link between the substantive value of autonomy, which any epistemologically justified political arrangement must account for, and democracy; this is the large grain of truth in Mill's comments:

> It is not much to be wondered at if impatient or disappointed reformers, groaning under the impediments opposed to the most salutary public improvements by the ignorance, the indifference, the intractableness, the perverse obstinacy of a people, and the corrupt combinations of selfish private interests armed with the powerful weapons afforded by free institutions, should at times sigh for a strong hand to bear down all these obstacles and compel a recalcitrant people to be better governed. But (setting aside the fact that for one despot who now and then reforms an abuse, there are ninety-nine who do nothing but create them) those who look in any such direction for the realization of their hopes leave out of the idea of good

government its principal element, the improvement of the people themselves. One of the benefits of freedom is that under it the ruler cannot pass by the people's minds and amend their affairs for them without amending them.

> Truth gains more even by the errors of one who, with due study and prep-
> aration, thinks for himself, than by the true opinions of those who only hold
> them because they do not suffer themselves to think. Not that it is solely,
> or chiefly, to form great thinkers, that freedom of thinking is required. On
> the contrary, it is as much and even more indispensable, to enable average
> human beings to attain the mental stature which they are capable of.[74]

My conception of liberal democracy, like Mill's, gives autonomy the status of a virtue, and respect for the autonomy of persons the role of a substantive value itself, rather than merely the formal role of regulating the intersections of preferences in a way as neutral as possible with respect to substantive values; both are committed to the view that it's an intrinsically good thing for people to work through problems for themselves, even if they often arrive at questionable results.

If the cognitive theory of democracy were to confine itself to the first of the two claims put forward in the two preceding paragraphs, it would indeed be subject to the objection that respect for autonomy does not merely have value as a means to an independent end. But, given the second claim, it is not subject to this objection; autonomy plays the role of a substantive value, and not merely an instrumental role, within the theory. One of the aims of democracy must be to protect and sustain the social conditions, the public reason-giving and delibera-tive practices, that make the virtue of autonomy possible.[75]

The substantive role of autonomy within the cognitive theory of democracy is also to be contrasted with the procedural role of liberty within various concep-tions of liberal democracy, according to which substantive values, including that of autonomy, are eschewed, and liberal procedures seek to protect liberty by guaranteeing that as many individuals as possible can realize as many of their ends as possible, except insofar as they may frustrate the purposes of others. Liberty thus negatively conceived, as a matter of the absence of obstacles to ac-tion aimed at the fulfillment of preferences, including obstacles presented by other people's interfering preferences, is contrasted in Berlin's essay "Two Concepts of Liberty" with positive conceptions of liberty, which take auton-omy, self-determination, as a good in itself.[76] The notion of autonomy I have de-veloped is a member of the family of positive conceptions, and has, as we've seen, a substantive role within a cognitive conception of democracy: efforts at self-interpretation and self-determination are themselves valuable, though again the value of autonomy may itself conflict with other values.

Theories according to which negative freedom is the only kind that matters, or the only kind that is properly of political concern, eschew questions about conflicts within persons which call for qualitative and evaluative distinctions among our various desires and purposes, for deliberative efforts to understand the relationships among them and so to understand what we truly want, who we truly are—to realize ourselves; it leaves out what Sandel describes as "the capacity of the self through reflection to participate in the constitution of its identity". Indeed, just because they leave no scope for questions of intra-personal structure and value in the name of freedom, they are supposed to lessen the danger, associated by Berlin with positive conceptions, that I may be forced to realize my 'true' self in the name of freedom. Taylor is especially insightful in diagnosing the appeal to liberals of the negative conception of liberty—and its dangers, in turn. Unlike negative conceptions, positive conceptions of liberty as self-determination do give rise to further questions about human nature and how the self is to be understood, and they may leave room for grandiloquent answers that threaten the freedom of the poor ordinary person: persons are essentially species beings, members of this class or that, this race or that. Such persons can be forced to realize their true nature, even if that means doing away with their false natures. So totalitarianism mas-querades as liberation. As Taylor says, it may seem more prudent to deny the conceptual resources that allow these questions to arise, to fight the Totalitarian Menace by digging in at the natural frontier of the negative/positive issue on the negative side. More prudent, that is, than engaging the enemy on open ground, where one will have to fight to discriminate the good from the bad among conceptions of human nature, the person and self-realization, to argue, for example, for the importance of individual autonomy as against various collectivist or classist notions of self-realization. Rather than defend liberal ideals on substantive grounds, it seems easier to cut all the nonsense off at the start, declare all self-realization views to be meta-physical hogwash and stick to the tough-minded view of liberty as the absence of external obstacles to action aimed at the fulfillment of preferences, what-ever they may be.[77]

According to Taylor, the apparently safe route, of avoiding substantive debate with the enemy in openly evaluative terms by digging in at the Maginot Line between negative and positive conceptions on the negative side, and thus basing liberalism in neutrality with respect to substantive as opposed to procedural values, actually endangers liberalism, for several reasons. This apparently safe route

> . . . is misguided not only because it involves abandoning some of the most inspiring terrain of liberalism, which is concerned with individual self-realization, but also because the line turns out to be untenable. The first step . . . to a view of freedom as the ability to fulfil my purposes, and as being greater the more significant my purposes, is one we cannot help taking. Whether we must also take the second step, to a view of freedom which sees it as realizable or fully realizable only within a certain form of society; and whether in taking a step of this kind one is necessarily committed to justifying the excesses of totalitarian oppression in the name of liberty; these are ques-tions which must now be addressed.

The implication is that the greatest dangers of totalitarianism and fanaticism may lie in not addressing these questions, not seeing to it that they are answered responsibly, rather than by brute political forces, since they cannot be headed off. The substantively correct choice among positive conceptions of liberty *must* occupy us, as the attempt to evade the choice is doomed. And, in instrumental political terms, the likelihood that the correct choice will be made and individual autonomy respected is reduced by sacrificing the wide appeal of positive ideals of individual self-determination and respect for the autonomy of others, as expounded by Mill, for example, for an uninspiring proceduralism. Thus the ideal of autonomy may demand the protection of negative freedoms, and the demand thus motivated may be at its strongest. That is, it may be true not only that the best means of protecting the possibility of autonomy and positive freedom may be respect for negative freedom, a point that has often been made, but also that the best means of protecting negative freedom may be cultivation of respect for autonomy and positive freedom; respect for negative and for positive freedom may be instrumentally related to one another, and mutually supporting.[78] These points cannot be met by the claim, however true, that the value of autonomy is controversial, that not everyone endorses it. The merits of proceduralism, and of neutrality with respect to substantive values, are at least as controversial; the issue between the view that substantive evaluative assumptions should be avoided and the value of autonomy is itself a substantive issue. The aim of liberal democracy should not be to avoid controversy or to find a basis that excludes it, but rather to exploit it within a democratic division of epistemic labour.

Note that the rejection of psychological individualism, and the constitutive role of social practices in determining the eligibility of the contents of the mind, do not argue in favour of collectivist political doctrines; to the contrary, as I have developed their implications, they have naturally given a special role to the autonomy of individual agents, or persons. But the appeal to social practices must be made at the right, deep enough level, and the constitutive (rather than *merely* causal) character of their role recognized, so that the arbitrary will at the root of subjectivism, and the false sophistication of skepticism, which are the real threat to respect for the autonomy of persons, are thoroughly exorcized. In Chapter 14 we saw that a naturalistic and social conception of mind and value exposes the often unwarranted assumption that the mere conceptual independence of propositions that causally explain our uses of evaluative concepts from evaluative propositions brings in its wake some stronger counterfactual independence, or even incompatibility. The dangerous illusion of an easy and unselective debunking effect that seems to dissolve ethical constraints is thus an artifact of the skeptic's preconceptions. In brief: A standard form of the Totalitarian Menance is subjectivism plus skepticism at the fundamental level and undemocratic, collectivist substantive ideals. By contrast, my view rejects subjectivism and skepticism at the fundamental level and gives respect for the autonomy of agents a distinctive and substantive role in the justification of democracy.

There are several reasons why the coherence account I have given, while based on the rejection of subjectivism, yet provides no intellectual foothold for intolerance and fanaticism. Recognition of the decentralization of the realm of value and of the permanent possibility of conflict among values undermines the basis for intolerance of questionable results. All-things-considered judgments made in the face of conflicting values are theoretical judgments about the relationships among the values that conflict, forced out of us by the fact that we must decide what to do, despite the conflict. Theoretical judgments of this kind would not need to be made if conflict could always be eliminated. Fanaticism based on the conviction that one has finally got it right is deflated, because getting it right just is muddling through, deciding what to do when we know ahead of time we cannot win on all counts. As Berlin says, that we can't have everything is a necessary, not a contingent truth. Berlin connects the existence of conflicting and incommensurable values with the central importance of liberty:

> The world that we encounter in ordinary experience is one in which we are faced with choices between ends equally ultimate, and claims equally absolute, the realization of some of which must inevitably involve the sacrifice of others. Indeed, it is because this is their situation that men place such immense value upon the freedom to choose; for if they had assurance that in some perfect state, realizable by men on earth, no ends pursued by them would ever be in conflict, the necessity and agony of choice would disappear, and with it the central importance of the freedom to choose. Any method of bringing this final state nearer would then seem fully justified, no matter how much freedom were sacrificed to forward its solution.

The belief, more than any other, that Berlin holds responsible for tyrannies, slaughters, deprivations of liberty, and violations of the person, is the belief that ultimately all ends, all goods, all values must be compatible.[79]

As I argued in preceding chapters, we can reject the no-ulimate-conflict view as well as subjectivism and non-cognitivism. We can thus agree with Berlin about the important connection between conflict and liberty without retreating to the negative conception of liberty, by recognizing that conflict between values and hence within persons is as fundamental as conflict between persons. Democratic procedures for the fair resolution of conflicts between persons, which respect individual autonomy, cannot be securely justified while the fundamental character of conflict within persons, the basis for the importance to persons of individual exercises of self-determination, is unrecognized.

Furthermore, the view that claims of right and wrong are responsible to considerations of theoretical coherence means that no such claim is in principle immune to, above, or below, rational criticism; the effort of critical attention can't be avoided simply by allocating a problem to the realms of ethics or politics, as is so often done with the over-used excuses "But, you're making a value judgment", or "I don't want to make a value judgment." If a coherence account is correct, our views about right and wrong commit us to reasoned criticism of even repugnant claims and to evaluation of our own ethical views in a critical spirit; and if a cognitive conception of democracy is correct, value judgments, including judgments concerning the virtue of autonomy, should not be a merely private matter, but a public matter. There is a deep-rooted instinct among Western liberals to withhold criticism from those whose positions we disapprove of: sincere criticism is a kind of attention that we don't readily grant. More often, so long as those with opposing views do us no harm we simply refrain from engaging them in argument, and if their views produce harmful behaviour we punish it without attending to its source. A person's ethical views—sometimes even those that lead criminals to commit crimes—are regarded as his own business, something to which he is entitled, though of course he has to accept the social consequences of acting on them. The instinct to resist criticism and self-examination, to demand ethical privacy and security, is similarly deep-rooted. It's not clear to what extent these instincts are a popular reflection of claims in favour of subjectivism, skepticism, or neutrality with respect to values, and to what extent they rather express the substantive political value of respect for autonomy even when other, conflicting values are at stake. However, these instincts can be guided by recognition that the latter is their proper source, not the former, and is perfectly capable of accommodating them. If claims of right and wrong are responsible to considerations of theoretical coherence, these instincts must be defended on substantive grounds, in terms of the relationships between the value of autonomy and self-determination, and the other conflicting values at stake. The difficulty and complexity of the task of arriving at and evaluating theories about conflicting values is essentially at odds with fanatical claims to know the right answer intuitively. Rather, the character of the task lends itself, in a way that I have sketched above, to a democratic division of epistemic labour, and the hopes for success depend on the full and widespread development of the deliberative and critical capacities, and of the autonomy and public-spiritedness, of citizens. Concepts of virtue and criticism thus have an essential role to play within the theory of liberal democracy.

Finally, the view that an adequate social theory must be fully structured, in the sense of giving an equally basic, non-derivative status to both horizontal and vertical distinctions, rejects the ubiquitous polarization of political options into left and right—not in the way that centrist views do, but rather by condemning altogether the notion of a left-right spectrum, or any other one-dimensional analysis of political issues, as explanatorily inadequate and theoretically sterile. The belief in such a spectrum is one of the most widely suffered delusions of modern times, and one most urgently in need of a dose of hearty skepticism, since it can prevent the full complexity and range of political possibilities, including the possibility of fully structured theories, from being appreciated. As we saw in Chapter 13 section 1, the single-peakedness of a set of alternatives is a necessary condition for there to be a single spectrum, in terms of which one can explain disagreement about what should be done as involving underlying disagreement about how far left or right on which we should be. We have seen that a wide range of issues about what should be done fail to have this property. Therefore, there is in fact no such single political spectrum; views which assume that there is lack the resources to illuminate political issues which reflect the ineliminable conflict of a plurality of qualitatively distinct values or to justify decisions about what to do in the

face of such conflict. Moreover, the distortion imposed by the supposition of
a single spectrum is not minor but of the essence. Horizontal distinctions,
and conflicts within persons, are as fundamental as vertical distinctions, and
conflicts between persons. Political conflicts are not simply the result of disagreement about whether this class or that class should have more or less of
some one thing; they often reflect more fundamental, ineliminable conflicts
between essentially different values, which members of one or another class
only happen to represent more or less, and which a person "equipped with
a more generous range of human values", as Williams puts it, may find in
conflict within himself.[80] There is no hope for eliminating such conflicts by
removing or suppressing or reeducating the members of some class, for the
values they represent will find other representatives; they have, so to speak,
a life of their own. The obsession with placing options on a left-right spectrum
makes it more difficult to grasp this salutary fact, and its democratic
implications.

### 5. Personality and Polity: The Convergence to Full Structure

I believe that there is a direction of development in political theory, which
may be characterized as the convergence, from both horizontal and vertical
theories, toward full structure. The movement from more or less horizontal
theories toward fully structured theories can be illustrated, for example, by
the relationship of classical political thought to the liberalism of T. H. Green;
and the movement from more or less vertical theories toward full structure
can be illustrated in the progression from classical contract theories through
the Rawlsian conception of justice to the information-rich conception of justice in terms of the capabilities of persons put forward by Sen.[81] It would be
of interest to canvass thoroughly such developments. It would also be of
interest to catalogue and relate various types of vertical distinction, conceptions of collective agency and the possibilities of overlapping units of agency;
as well as the various types of horizontal distinction that have been proposed
and that may be among the resources of fully structured theories, including:
classical, psychoanalytic, and functional distinctions among the parts of the
soul; distinctions between debunked and undebunked evaluative beliefs; between higher and lower pleasures; between self-regarding and other-regarding
preferences; between preference as is and as corrected for various mistakes
of fact and reasoning; between personal and extended preferences; between
preferences of different degrees of urgency; between preferences whose gen-
esis does, and does not, call their rationality into question; etc. But these
would be large taxonomic projects indeed; I must put them off, and here
shall merely illustrate the convergence by reference to two recent discussions
of Rawls' theory of justice, by Michael Sandel and Martha Nussbaum.

Rawls famously criticizes utilitarianism for conflating different persons'
systems of desires as if they belonged to one superperson, and thus failing to
respect the separateness of and distinctions between persons. The theoretical

device of the original position in Rawls' theory does serve to respect the distinctions between persons. But Sandel in turn calls into question what he takes to be Rawls' assumption that the important distinctions for political theory cut primarily between persons, rather than within them as well, are vertical but not horizontal. He suggests that even from the perspective of the contractors in the original position, who are behind the veil of ignorance and thus deprived of knowledge of the contingent features that distinguish them from one another, distinct interests and values conflict while yet each making compelling claims; and that the source of the problem each one faces in deliberating about which principles of justice to adopt is not merely uncertainty as to what he will turn out to be like, given the interpersonal conflicts in prospect once the veil is lifted, but involves intrapersonal conflicts as well. Thus, even behind the veil of ignorance there is scope for theorizing about how conflicts should be resolved, and for disagreement among the contractors (we made a related discovery about the scope for disagreement about the theory of human nature required by the conception of extended preference in Chapter 6); conflict and the value of self-determination both have their place here, within the person. Sandel writes:

> The appropriate description of the moral subject may refer to a plurality of selves within a single, individual human being, as when we account for inner deliberation in terms of the pull of competing identities . . . .

> While Rawls does not reject such notions explicitly, he denies them by implication when he assumes that to every individual person there corresponds a single system of desires, and that utilitarianism fails as a social ethic in mistakenly applying to society the principles of choice appropriate for one man. Since he takes for granted that every individual consists of one and only one system of desires, the problem of conflating desires does not arise in the individual case . . . .

> For Rawls, utilitarianism goes wrong not in conceiving the good as the satisfaction of arbitrarily given desires undifferentiated as to worth—for justice as fairness shares in this—but only in being indifferent to the way these consummations are spread across individuals.

However, Sandel calls for further explanation of why to each person there corresponds just one system of desires, exactly what such a system is, and why it is wrong to conflate them:

> Is a 'system of desires' a set of desires ordered in a certain way, arranged in a hierarchy of relative worth or essential connection with the identity of the agent, or is it simply a concatenation of desires arbitrarily arrayed, distinguishable only by their relative intensity and accidental location? If it is the second, if a system of desires means nothing more than an arbitrary collection of desires accidentally embodied in some particular human being, then it is unclear why the integrity of such a 'system' should be taken so morally and metaphysically seriously. If desires can properly be conflated within persons, why not between persons as well?
> If, on the other hand, what makes a *system* of desires is a hierarchical

ordering of qualitatively distinguishable desires, then it would be no more justifiable to 'conflate' desires within a person than between persons.... The tendency to conflate desires, whether within persons or between them, would reflect the failure to *order* them, or to acknowledge the qualitative distinctions between them. But this failure cuts across the distinction between individual and social choice, for there is no reason to suppose that a 'system of desires' in *this* sense corresponds in all cases to the empirically-individuated person. Communities of various sorts could count as distinct 'systems of desires' in this sense, so long as they were identifiable in part by an order or structure of shared values partly constitutive of a common identity or form of life. From this point of view, the utilitarian failure to take seriously the distinction between persons would appear a mere symptom of its larger failure to take seriously the qualitative distinctions of worth between different orders of desires.[82]

In my terms, Sandel is thus criticizing what he takes to be a primarily vertical theory for failing to recognize the importance of horizontal distinctions. While I could not agree more about the importance of the latter, however, it is not clear to me that a theory quite close to that of Rawls in many respects could not accommodate their importance, and emerge as fully structured. We can see how this might be done by considering a critique that moves in the opposite direction from Sandel's critique of Rawls: Aristotle's critique of Plato's horizontal theory for failing to recognize the importance of vertical distinctions. The Aristotelian position, as set out by Martha Nussbaum, shows that, while there may be no reason to assume a "system of desire" corresponds in *all* cases to the individual person, there is good reason to assume that it does so in a very wide range of cases, reason provided by the value of individual autonomy. Nussbaum presents Aristotle's views in the context of questioning and strengthening Rawls' conception of the good of self-respect, and in effect provides a response to Sandel's points at the same time; a summary of her arguments follows in the next three paragraphs.

Plato, Aristotle, and Rawls share the view that self-respect is a primary good, something each person must have in order to live well. But Platonic self-respect is achieved by submission of agents to reason and law; if the rational capacities are well-developed in certain agents, but not in others, in whom contrary forces are not controlled by reason, then self-respect, the avoidance of shame, demands of the latter that they be ruled by the former, who represent their true, higher self. Those supposedly free agents within whom reason is shrunken and disordered appetites rage out of control are in fact the most shameful of slaves. What matters on Plato's view is that appetite be ruled by reason, and not *whose* appetites are ruled by *whose* reason; the importance of getting the parts of the soul (and, indeed, a mass view of soul may be appropriate to Plato) in order is paramount and the value of getting one's *own* soul in order *oneself* negligible, as "the unity of the biological person is only a deceptive envelope". Thus the conditions of self-respect must be secured through politically imposed order; if we stop seeing ourselves as associated with a particular body, we will be less prone to resist rational rule from 'outside'. The distribution of the good of self-respect among persons reduces to the ordering of the parts of the soul. (Here is the danger Berlin fears; horizontal theories ride roughshod over vertical distinctions between "poor empirical selves".[83])

Aristotle's hylomorphic view of the soul as the form or functional organization of the living body, by contrast, recognizes the natural distinctions between persons effected by their separate bodies; and he regards a person's capacity to get his *own* soul into order, his autonomy, as essential to self-respect. Both the Platonic and the Aristotelian conceptions of self-respect, however, are objective conceptions, as against Rawls' apparently subjective conception, which makes self-respect a matter of one's *sense* of the worth of one's life plan, one's *feeling* of capacity to carry it out, to which the objective value of my pursuits and the truth of my beliefs about them are not relevant. Nussbaum argues by reference to examples, in particular that of the happy slave, that Rawls' theory actually needs a conception of self-respect with objective components, with some distinction between felt and genuine self-respect, so that a situation may be acknowledged to be shameful for an agent even though he feels no shame. She warns against empirically dubious generalizations about the level of autonomy most people feel a need for; one of the worst features of slavery is that it may make slaves content with their lot. The case for justice should not be rested on what most people can learn not to feel ashamed of, or even to like. Aristotle's critique of Plato's views illustrates the relationship between a conception of self-respect with the needed objective components and the value of autonomy.

The critique has several strands. Aristotle's hylomorphism is more egalitarian with respect to the parts of the soul than Plato's view, and recognizes "no good reason not to make the development and flourishing of all our bodily human nature a part of our conception of the human good". But this by itself does not eliminate the threat to self-respect posed by uncontrolled appetites, and we must look further in support of autonomy, to Aristotle's conception of human nature and personality, and his vision of what is in effect one version of a fully structured polity. By aiming for excessive unity in society, Plato destroys its ability to foster and sustain the distinctive capacity of human beings, as political animals by nature, to participate in an organization of autonomous persons who share its public, deliberative life, that is, to develop and exercise their own capacities for deliberation and self-determination, and to share in the deliberative tasks of the polity. The exercise of the capacity of persons for self-determination is necessary for objective self-respect, even if the need for autonomy is not felt, and it is frustrated by Platonic relegation of persons to parthood.[84] Plato is right that self-respect has objective components, which allow a distinction between felt and genuine self-respect; but he is wrong to miss out one of the most important of the objective components of self-respect, namely, autonomy. Rawls wishes to avoid dependence on metaphysical, as opposed to political, conceptions of human personality, as well as endorsement of substantive values, including that of autonomy.[85] However, Aristotle shows that the value of autonomy emerges naturally from a political conception of human personality, once the need for objective self-respect is admitted.

Thus we have found good reason, in this conception of human nature and personality, and also, I would argue, in the complementary conception of a fully structured polity characterized by a democratic division of deliberative labour, to give special respect to the "system of desires" associated with each person, that is, to individual autonomy. We can do so without ignoring the importance of horizontal distinctions, and without retreating to a primarily vertical theory: the insistence on objective self-respect characteristic of a horizontal theory such as Plato's itself leads, on Nussbaum's interpretation of Aristotle, to the value of autonomy. While it would be crudely anachronistic and quite wrong to regard Aristotle, who condoned slavery, as a theorist of liberal democracy, nevertheless he had certain proto-liberal insights, and the theory of liberal democracy can make selective use of Aristotelian elements. Thus we can respond to Sandel's critique of liberalism both from within liberalism, and in Aristotelian terms. The importance of full structure can be demonstrated from the direction of either vertical or horizontal theory.

### 6. Intrapersonal Structure and Distributive Justice

Nussbaum argues that Plato's denial of hylomorphism "appears to be an important step in the direction of his denial of our common views about separateness", and in his disregard for the value of autonomy.[86] A related claim is made by Derek Parfit, about the relationship between conceptions of personal identity, the separateness of persons, and principles of distributive justice.

Recall Rawls' criticism of classical utilitarianism for not recognizing the distinctness of persons, for treating the desires of different people as if they were the desires of one superperson, with the result that the importance of distributions across persons is neglected. Of course, income *may* be distributed across persons by classical utilitarianism as a result of the dimimishing marginal utility of income; but there is no guarantee even of this, and at any rate concern with the distribution of utility itself across persons is not thus catered for. Classical utilitarianism holds, in effect, that social welfare is a linear function of individual utility, that the marginal social welfare of utility does not diminish; it treats marginal utilities rather than persons as the relevant units for purposes of treating like cases alike.

Parfit suggests, in response to Rawls' criticism, that the classical utilitarian's lack of concern with the distribution of utility across persons

> ... may derive, not from the conflation of persons, but from their partial disintegration. It may rest on the view that a person's life is less deeply integrated than we mostly think. Utilitarians may be treating benefits and burdens, not as if they all came within the same life, but as if it made no moral difference where they came.

This belief may be supported by the view that the unity of each life, and hence the difference between lives, is in its nature less deep.

If we adopt an atomistic and reductionist view of personal identity,

> ... we regard the existence of a person as ... involving nothing more than the occurrence of interrelated mental and physical events.

> If we are ... atomists about people, we can then more plausibly reject ... the demand for fair shares. We may tend to focus less upon the person, the subject of experience, and instead focus more upon the experiences themselves.[87]

Parfit's suggestion is that a sub-personal focus may tend to undermine or weaken concern with the distribution of well-being across persons. In this section I shall briefly point out several possible sources of resistance to this tendency that themselves arise from considerations of intrapersonal structure. Since these sources of resistance would be intrapersonal to begin with, if they obtain at all, they would be proof against the kind of partial distintegration Parfit considers; a subpersonal focus would thus not weaken distributional concern. That is, certain principles of intrapersonal structure concern the way in which personal coherence is constructed out of its components; if these principles themselves have implications that support concerns with distribution across persons, then the fact that personal coherence is constructed out of components will have no tendency to undermine such distributional concerns.[88]

My points may be somewhat oblique in relation to Parfit's suggestion, however, for two reasons. First, the intrapersonal structure I have focussed on is that of propositional attitudes and the values that inform them rather than that of experiences. This is because I believe that personal coherence is largely a matter of relations among conflicting attitudes and values, discovered through self-determining deliberation, rather than a matter of relations among experiences. And second, the intrapersonal structure I have focussed on concerns the coherence of persons at a point in time as much as their coherence over time. In his recent book *Reasons and Persons* Parfit develops a reductionist view of the unity of a person over time. However, he seems to take as unproblematic the unity of consciousness at a point in time when he writes: "This unity does not need a deep explanation. It is simply a fact that several experiences can be *co-conscious, or be the objects of a single state of awareness*".[89] By contrast, my focus on understanding unity in terms of attitudes, rather than in terms of experiences, makes it impossible to take unity at point in time as unproblematic. It emerges from the discussion of *akrasia* in Chapters 7 and 8 that the contents of component attitudes at given points in time cannot be identified independently of contents at other points in time. The focus on attitudes rather than experiences binds considerations of coherence at a point in time and considerations of coherence over time together. Indeed, the rejection of the notion of attitudes at points in time as the atoms[90] out of which personal coherence is constructed is in some ways analogous to the rejection of psychological individualism: in both cases the claim is that the individuation of the supposed atoms in fact depends on context—on temporal, or social and environmental, surroundings. I suspect that the rejection of context-independent individuation may be appropriate for experiences as well as attitudes, but that is another topic.

Structural principles, principles of coherence that constrain interpretation and deliberation, are not optional; persons are fragmented and conflicted, but it is their nature as persons to seek a coherent interpretation of themselves and thus to determine their selves. Personal coherence is not unproblematically given by experience or open to observation, but must be achieved through the exercise of autonomy in the cognitive sense. Some human beings may achieve it to a greater degree than others, and some may fail altogether, or not even try to begin with, in the manner of wantons; the constraints on interpretation are loose and multifarious enough to accommodate all these possibilties in particular cases. Nevertheless, the general role of considerations of personal coherence in constraining interpretation and deliberation is not something we are free to abjure altogether. There is, I believe, a connection between this general conception of personal coherence and autonomy, on the one hand, and concern with distributive justice, though the connection is admittedly rather loose. I shall first attempt to sketch this connection, and then shall go on to make several further and much more specific points about the relationship of particular intrapersonal principles, of separability, independence, and Sure Thing, to questions of distributive justice. These points taken together come nowhere close to providing a conception of distributive justice, but are intended rather in the way of incidental remarks about the ways in which certain views of intrapersonal structure canvassed in this book may support concern with certain aspects of distributive justice.

First, the general connection. I've already commented on the way in which the value of autonomy or self-determination emerges out of a coherence account of self-interpretation and deliberation. And we've seen that the value of autonomy has intrinsic distributional requirements, in tracing Aristotle's reasons for rejecting the Platonic conception of self-respect. The virtue of autonomy cannot be realized through Platonic parthood, but requires each person to exercise his own capacity for deliberation, to determine himself. Thus the distribution of the good of self-respect, objectively conceived, cannot reduce to an ordering of the parts of the soul reflected in a political order in which some, the representatives of reason, cultivate themselves and control the subservient representatives of spirit and appetite. Aristotle did hold that education and leisure for self-realization must be the privilege of the few, supported by the labour of the many. Those who perform the needed labour will not have the leisure required for self-development and a good life, even though they have the capacities for virtue and self-respect; they labour in darkness so that some others may realize themselves. But Nussbaum argues that this "is a dark spot in Aristotle's political theory—a point concerning which he himself is evidently insecure and unhappy" and that, unlike Plato, he concedes that injustice is being done to these labourers.[91] And T. H. Green argues that it is implicit in the value placed by the Greeks on self-realization that this distributive injustice should be condemned, even at the cost of the loftiest forms of self-development of the privileged:

> Human society indeed is essentially a society of self-determined persons. There can be no progress of society which is not a development of capacities on the part of persons composing it, considered as ends in themselves. But in estimating the worth of any type of virtue ... We must enquire whether any apparent splendour in that virtue is due to a degradation of human society outside the particular group, or whether, on the contrary, the virtue of the few takes its character from their assistance in the struggle upward of the many.

> If (as would seem to be the case) the free play of spiritual activity in the life of the Greek citizen, with its consequent bright enjoyableness, depended partly on the seclusion of the Greek communities from the mass of mankind, partly on their keeping in slavery so much of the mass as was in necessary contact with them ... then, whatever value we may ascribe to the highest type of Greek life, as suggesting an ideal of 'liberty, equality and fraternity', afterwards to be realised on a wider scale, we cannot regard its exemption from the impeding cares, which the intercommunication of mankind on terms of recognized equality brings with it, as constituting a real superiority.

Green holds that the understanding of the good in terms of the realization of the capacities of the human soul is as correct for us as it was for Aristotle, but that in order to contribute to this realization we must be conscious of

> ... claims upon us on the part of other men which, as we now see, must be satisfied in order to any perfecting of the human soul, but which were not, and in the then state of society could not be, recognised by the Greek philosophers.

When the Greek philosophers told the citizen

> that the object of his life should be duly to fulfil his function as a man, or to contribute to a good consisting in a realisation of the soul's faculties, they were directing him to an object which in fact was common to him with all men, without possibility of competition for it, without distinction of Greek or barbarian, bond or free. Their teaching was thus, in its own nature, of a kind to yield a social result which they did not themselves contemplate, and which tended to make good the practical shortcomings of their teaching itself.[92]

The general connection I wish to draw between the value of autonomy and concern with distributive justice has something in common with these views of Green on the distributive implications of the ideal of self-realization. However, I think we should go further than Green did, and say more about what gives rise to concern with the distribution as well as the total amount of the virtue in question. Recognition of the "claims upon us on the part of other men" does not *per se* give rise to this concern, any more than recognition of other persons as sources of utility *per se* gives rise to concern with the distribution of utility. It is not hard to see the intrinsic distributional demands made by recognition that determination of oneself, as opposed to determination by others, has substantive value. But Aristotle got this far. We can go further, and hold that the higher reaches of self-determination pale in significance beside the wider distribution across persons of exercises of the basic capacity for it.[93] It is especially bad, on such a view, to deny the most fundamental exercises of autonomy.

There are two ways to interpret this claim. It could be a claim, in effect, that the value, all things considered, of autonomy diminishes at the margin, as a person exercises more and more autonomy. Or it could be a claim that autonomy itself, as opposed to the marginal value, all things considered, of it, diminishes at the margin as an individual fusses over himself more and more, detaches himself fastidiously from more and more of his given ends, and ascends through the orders of attitudes. This second claim gives a stronger reading to the intrinsic distributional requirements of autonomy than Aristotle did. Both interpretations seems defensible, and they are not incompatible. The first I shall touch on below, in discussing holistic relations among conflicting values. The second, however, we have already seen reason to support, in section 1 of this chapter, where I discussed points made by Campbell and Frankfurt in light of Taylor's views on strong evaluation and Sandel's comments on the cognitive sense of agency. There I argued that the exercise of autonomy involves depending on certain of our values as a basis for criticizing and revising others, but not detachment from all of them, and that autonomy does not depend on a regress into higher and higher order attitudes, but on the first step. Perhaps pursuing the regress further than is usual does result in increased autonomy; but it seems plausible to hold that after the first crucial step to second-order attitudes autonomy increases at an ever diminishing rate as the regress proceeds, and perhaps even to hold that eventually further pursuit of the regress ceases to increase autonomy at all but rather becomes priggish or neurotic self-obsession. The point is an instance of a general point with respect to classical and self-realization ethics: *excessive* or exclusive concern with one's character tends to be self-defeating. (Perhaps this is the grain of truth in Pritchard's objection to classical ethics; however, the qualifications are essential, and allow ample scope for political theories which give an important place to concern with education, autonomy, and self-realization.[94])

Given the intrinsic distributional requirements of autonomy, an emphasis on the value of autonomy within liberal democratic theory entails the fundamental importance of the thorough distribution of the means to autonomy in the form of human capital: basic physical capacities and health, as well as higher education, a tradition of deliberative discussion, and a wide variety of opportunities for self-development, what Aristotle called *schole*.[95] Theories of distributive justice that concentrate entirely on the distribution of income or utility but do not concern themselves with the uses made of income or the sources of utility thus fall critically short. In particular, the crucial role of education in distributive justice is unduly neglected. A society in which education for all but a small percentage ends before maturity, whether voluntarily or not, or one in which opportunities for self-development and objective self-respect are spurned and the vast majority choose to plug into pleasure machines, drugs, or their psychological equivalent in the form of mindless consumerism, while members of a small elite or governing group manipulate beliefs and desires or maintain the conditions which the majority 'enjoy'— such societies do not live up to the titles 'democratic', 'liberal', 'just', or 'egalitarian'. Here a conception of liberal democracy as tied to the value of autonomy parts company with the aspiration to neutrality with respect to ideals: conceptions of the good which make personal autonomy impossible do not deserve respect.

Next, I shall make three points about the relationship of particular intra-personal principles to issues of distributive justice. (My discussion will invoke decision-theoretic principles and issues raised in Part I above, especially in Chapter 4; in particular, subsection I will relate roughly to issues about Mutual Preferential Independence, subsection II to issues about the Independence Axiom, and subsection III to issues about the Sure-Thing Principle.)

I. Recall the discussion of the relation between equality and welfare in Chapter 13, in the context of an examination of the notion of commensurability. There I explained the familiar point that equality of resources, or income, can be obtained by maximizing a quantity that diminishes at the margin with the amount of income each person has. The diminishing marginal utility of income reflects the common view that utility is not a linear function of income, that the more income someone has the less utility he derives from another unit of income, so that the maximization of utility itself may favour a relatively equal distribution of income. I also distinguished, following Dworkin and Sen, equality of resources or income from equality of welfare or utility itself; it may be held that the distribution of utility across persons itself is of value in a sense not reducible to the value of equality of income or resources. Such views may be expressed in terms of the diminishing marginal social welfare of utility: social welfare is not a linear function of utility, and the higher someone's utility, the less his additional utility adds to social welfare, so that the maximization of social welfare itself may tend to favour a relatively equal distribution of utility. Standard examples of functions that incorporate distributional requirements with respect to utility or welfare would have us maximize the product, or the sum of the logs, of different persons' incomes, or utilities, rather than their sum. However the relevant functions may be convoluted, and in certain sub-domains may be nonlinear in the opposite direction, such that the marginal utility of income increases.

The distinction between the claim that the utility is not a linear function of income and the claim that social welfare is not a linear function of utility is in some respects analogous to the distinction between the two interpretations of the distributional claim about autonomy made above; and both distinctions concern distributional effects with respect to persons. The analogy I've pursued in Chapter 12 between social welfare functions and coherence functions, between relations between persons and relations between values, suggests in turn a similar distinction concerning distribution with respect to specific values. Compare the claim that the marginal social welfare of utility is not constant, that social welfare is not a linear function of utility, with the claim that a coherence function is not, in effect, a linear function of specific values. The latter claim has an analogous effect on the distribution of satisfaction across different values. Just as how much one person's utility contributes to social welfare may depend on the levels of other persons' utilities, how much one value's satisfaction matters, all things considered, may depend on the levels of other values' satisfaction. The relations among certain values may be holistic and complementary, so that variety with respect to them is itself of value, and equal distribution across them is favoured, while among others it is such as to favour an unequal distribution.

For example, the coherence theorist might claim that the values of autonomy and economic equality, equality of resources, are complementarily related. Just as unit increases in utility may get more weight in terms of social welfare the lower the absolute level of utility of the person to whom the increase accrues, unit increases in economic equality and in respect for autonomy may get more weight, all things considered, the lower the absolute levels of equality and autonomy, respectively. Thus, if society is doing quite well in terms of autonomy, it should concentrate on economic equality, and vice versa. At a more personal level, recall also my examples of failure of Mutual Preferential Independence from Chapter 4 section 4 of complementary relations between the degrees to which one's career and one's home life are flourishing, etc. It might also be plausible for the coherence theorist to claim that certain forms of excellence behave rather differently, in that unit increases in excellence get more weight, all things considered, the higher the absolute level of excellence. It may be worthwhile for a society to make sacrifices in the level of autonomy realized in order to cultivate those rare artistic talents of potentially millennial importance, but not to raise somewhat the general level of mediocre talent. In general, then, the effect of allowing departures from a linear coherence function is that the function of specific values to be maximized may favour alternatives in which greater or lesser relative equality obtains of the extent of satisfaction of different values; it is to allow the interaction of values with respect to what should be done, all things considered.

Of course, in order for this effect to be distinct from non-linearity internal to the values themselves (as, analogously, diminishing marginal social welfare of utility may be distinct from diminishing marginal utility of income), the extent to which various specific values are satisfied by various alternatives must be understood independently of the all-things-considered evaluation.[96] But I have argued at length in Chapter 12, in discussing the neutrality condition and various examples, that they may be thus independently understood. The precise form of the coherence function with respect to the relations among various values is left to the results of deliberation. But the coherence function that best accounts for all-things-considered judgments about settled cases may be a non-linear function of certain specific values even though it's possible to reconstrue it as a linear function of different 'criteria', even though we could to tailor the criteria so that they automatically reflect the results of deliberation without the coherence function departing from linearity. Similarly, social welfare may be a non-linear function of individual utility even though it is possible to reconstrue it as a linear function of a revised conception of utility that reflects even more pronounced diminishing marginal utility of income than did the conception of utility we started out with. That is, we can reconstrue diminishing marginal social welfare of individual utility as even more sharply diminishing revised-utility of income and thus keep social welfare a linear function of revised-utility. There is a certain amount of theoretical play in the concept of individual utility, to be sure, but there are limits to the amount of technical tinkering and revision we can do without distorting our independent understanding of individual well-being. Thus the technical possibility of reconstruing social welfare as a linear function of something else does not provide grounds for objecting to the view that social welfare is a non-linear function of individual utility, as we understand it. The parallel points apply to reconstrual of a non-linear coherence function of certain specific values as a linear function of other made-up criteria. We may, likewise, have an independent understanding of specific values such that the coherence function that represents our all-things-considered evaluations is a non-linear function of those values, even though it may be reconstrued as a linear function of something else.[97]

I have emphasized that values may conflict even for one person because the extent to which this is true is often overlooked. However, I do not need to deny that individuals and classes of individuals may sometimes identify with and strive to satisfy some particular value. Consider now cases where some class of persons comes in this way to represent the claims of some particular value, and another class those of a different value.[98] Suppose that the coherence function is in effect a non-linear function of those values, such that it favours relative equality of the extents to which they are satisfied. It follows that it will favour relative equality of the extents to which the claims of the two classes that represent these values are met. If the relations among certain specific values are complementary in the sense that a coherence function is not a linear function of them, and if particular persons or classes of persons characteristically identify with and strive to satisfy those values, then a relatively equal distribution across those values may entail a relatively equal distribution of satisfaction across those persons or classes of persons. Thus, under certain conditions concern with the equality of distribution between classes may be derivative from the complementary relations among the values they strive to satisfy. I do *not* suggest that this is the only or even a major source of egalitarian concern, only that it is one possible source among others. Perhaps it can be argued that in fact this possibility is realized in certain familiar cases; some classes or groups may characteristically represent the demands of autonomy, others those of equality, others those of excellence of various kinds, others those of charity, etc. But my present point is merely that *if* it is, we can be as atomistic as we like about persons without affecting this source of the value of equal distribution across persons, in the ordinary bodily sense (given that it is normally by means of the acts of persons in the ordinary bodily sense that values are satisfied); thus, such a source of egalitarian concern would have the attraction to egalitarians of being immune to the threat Parfit sees as deriving from a sub-personal focus. To the extent that complementary relations among values may hold intrapersonally and the concern with distribution across persons may be derivative from the complementary relations among values, such distributional concern is proof against atomism about persons. Complementarily related values are equally so for one person at one time, one person at different times, different persons at one time, or different persons at different times. Even if, as Parfit suggests, we focus on experiences rather than subjects of experience, we can claim that the different values whose satisfaction those experiences reflect are complementarily related to one another.

I have argued that a complementary relation among values, analogous to the complementary relation among individual utilities expressed by the notion of diminishing marginal social welfare of utility, may have distributional consequences across persons or classes of persons who represent and strive to satisfy those values, and that such distributional consequences would not be subject to the undermining effect of a sub-personal focus. And I have defended the distinctions between complementary relations among values and non-linearity internal to the values themselves, and between complementary relations among individual utilities and non-linearity (with respect to income, for example) internal to individual utilities themselves. However, so far I have said nothing to defend the position that complementary relations among individual utilities do in fact obtain, that marginal social welfare of individual utility in fact diminishes—a position that would evidently have immediate and powerful distributional consequences. I shall not actually argue outright in favour of this position, but I shall examine a way in which it might be supported, by reference to arguments about certain principles of intrapersonal structure. Again, if it can be thus supported, the strongly egalitarian results would be proof against the undermining effects of a sub-personal focus, as their source would be intrapersonal to begin with.

II. The relevant intrapersonal principles for these purposes were discussed in Chapters 4 and 5: the Independence and Sure-Thing Principles. I shall first consider the Independence axiom and the distinction between risk and certainty, and shall then go on to consider the Sure Thing Principle and the distinction between risk and uncertainty. It is widely recognized that attitudes toward risk and toward equality are intimately connected; the former are used to measure utilities in expected utility theory in such a way that diminishing marginal utility of income is identified with risk aversion with respect to income, i.e., the preference for the actuarial value of a gamble over the gamble itself. It is also recognized that the debate over the Independence and Sure-Thing Principles may have consequences for issues of distributive justice in general, and in particular for the issue about whether the distribution of utility itself may be a proper object of concern.[99] That is, there may be a link between the position that the distribution of utilities (as opposed to income) across possible outcomes may be a proper object of concern in itself in such a way that personal preferences may properly fail to satisfy Independence or Sure Thing, and the position that the distribution of utilities among persons may be a proper object of concern in itself. This link is brought to light by considering approaches to distributive justice that involve supposing that one has an equal chance of being anyone in society or that one does not know who one is.

Harsanyi is perhaps the staunchest defender of the position that the marginal social welfare of utility does not diminish. He himself links his position to the axioms of expected utility theory in two ways.

First, he offers a proof that social welfare is a weighted sum of individual utilities that depends on the assumption that both individual decision making and social choice satisfy the assumption of expected utility theory (as well as the assumption that social welfare can be written as an increasing function of individual expected utilities).[100] Diamond has taken issue with the axiom that social choice must satisfy the Sure Thing Principle, though he accepts it for individual decision making. However, as we saw in Chapters 4 and 5, the normative adequacy of Sure Thing and Independence has been brought into question for individual decision making as well (for example, by Allais, Hagen, McClennan, etc.), and the resources and rigour of utility theory without these axioms have been demonstrated to be far greater than may have been appreciated in the past (for example, by Machina). Thus, even if we decline to take a stand with Diamond against Sure Thing for social choice (perhaps on the grounds that such a stand would be so immediately connected to the egalitarianism at issue as not to provide an independent argument for it), we may be persuaded to reject Independence or Sure Thing as normative for individual decision. Thus the obstacle Harsanyi's proof presents to concern with the distribution of utilities would be removed (though I emphasize that to remove an obstacle to a certain kind of egalitarianism is not to provide a positive argument for such egalitarianism).

Second, Harsanyi suggests that there is a "close formal similarity" between the view that social welfare may be a non-linear function of individual utilities and the view that the utility of a lottery ticket may be a non-linear function of its possible utility outcomes (as opposed to its possible monetary outcomes). (Recall my discussion in Chapter 4 section 3.) He argues that the former view is incorrect for reasons closely analogous to those that make the latter view incorrect. If it turns out that the latter view is not incorrect after all, then any support the attack on egalitarianism with respect to individual utilities gains from the analogy is undermined.

Here are the details. In the first chapter of his book *On Economic Inequality*, Sen considers the way in which utilitarianism, with no concern for the distribution of utilities, would distribute a given amount of income between two people, one of whom derives half as much utility as the other from any given level of income, say, because he is crippled. Since the handicapped person is an inefficient generator of utility, utilitarianism would leave him with both less income and less utility than the other person. The case suggests that the distribution of utility between persons may be a relevant aspect of the problem of income distribution. Harsanyi comments that Sen's view would thus, in contrast to his own, make social welfare depend not only on the mean value of various individuals' utility levels, but also on their dispersion, that is, would make it a non-linear function of individual utilities.

> . . . the utility-dispersion argument about social welfare, which underlies Sen's theory, shows a close formal similarity to what I shall call the utility-dispersion argument about lotteries, viz. to the view that the utility of a lottery ticket should depend not only on its expected (mean) utility, but also on some measure of risk, i.e., on some measure of dispersion among its possible utility outcomes. Therefore, so the argument runs, the utility of a lottery ticket must be a nonlinear function of these possible utility outcomes.
>     Yet the utility-dispersion argument about lotteries is known to be mistaken . . .

According to Harsanyi, concern with the dispersion of possible monetary outcomes is legitimate, and is catered for within expected utility theory; but concern with the dispersion of possible utility outcomes is not legitimate.

> The basic reason for this lies in the fact that the utility of any possible money income is measured by the decision-maker's von-Neumann-Morgenstern utility function, which already makes appropriate allowance for his attitude toward risk. For instance, if he has a negative attitude toward risk then his utility function will display decreasing marginal utility for money (i.e. it will be strictly concave in money). Thus, his risk aversion will already be fully reflected in the utilities he assigns to various possible incomes, and therefore, also, in his expected utility associated with the lottery ticket. Hence, it would be unnecessary and inadmissible double-counting if we made an allowance for the decision-maker's risk aversion for a second time, and made his utility for a lottery ticket dependent, not only on its expected utility, but also on the dispersion in achievable utilities.

Indeed, the latter would be inconsistent with the axioms of expected utility theory. Harsanyi goes on to argue that "Sen's utility-dispersion argument about social welfare succumbs to the same objection as the utility-dispersion argument about lotteries does: it is an illegitimate transfer of a mathematical relationship from money amounts, for which it does hold, to utility levels, for which it does not". The argument that the transfer is illegitimate in the case of Sen's position in particular, however, appeals to an example, involving a child with "an unlucky temperament" rather than a cripple, which he seems to think intuitively supports the conclusion he wishes to reach, namely, that the distribution of utilities is irrelevant.[101] No argument is given to distinguish the case from Sen's case, involving a cripple, in which intuition favours Sen's position. But even if we agree with Harsanyi about his example, Sen only needs a single counter-example to Harsanyi's position to show that the distribution of utilities may be relevant to distributive justice; he doesn't need to show that it is in every case. So the argument against Sen's position comes

| | 10% | 10% | 10% | 10% | 10% | 10% | 10% | 10% | 10% | 10% |
|---|---|---|---|---|---|---|---|---|---|---|
| A | $1000 | $1000 | $1000 | $1000 | $1000 | $ 0 | $ 0 | $ 0 | $ 0 | $ 0 |
| B | $ 400 | $ 400 | $ 400 | $ 400 | $ 400 | $ 400 | $ 400 | $ 400 | $ 400 | $ 400 |
| C | $1000 | $ 0 | $ 0 | $ 0 | $ 0 | $ 0 | $ 0 | $ 0 | $ 0 | $ 0 |
| D | $ 400 | $ 400 | $ 0 | $ 0 | $ 0 | $ 0 | $ 0 | $ 0 | $ 0 | $ 0 |

FIGURE 15.1

down to whatever support is provided by the analogy to the illegitimacy of the utility-dispersion argument about lotteries.

In a case considered by Tversky, discussed in Chapter 4, "the utility of a positive outcome appears greater when it is certain than when it is embedded in a gamble", an effect which cannot be accounted for in terms of risk aversion understood as diminishing marginal utility of income.[102] (See Tversky's case in the Table of 'Observed Violations' for that chapter.) The dispersion of utility across possible outcomes is linked to the distribution of probabilities: utility is maximally dispersed across possible outcomes (and utility *levels* are minimally dispersed) in the case of certainty, i.e., when the utilities of all possible outcomes are the same, just as utility is maximally dispersed across persons (and utility *levels* are minimally dispersed) when the utilities of all persons are the same. A concern with certainty *per se* is thus in a certain sense analogous with a concern with equality of utility *per se*; and the link is closer still within approaches to distributive justice that involve supposing one has an equal chance of being any member of society. We can see this if we think of the alternatives in Tversky's case as shown in Figure 15.1, where A and B, and C and D, are the two pairs of alternatives, and each column presents outcomes with a 10% probability (instead of outcomes that apply to 10% of the population).

The Independence axiom, recall, does not dictate the choice between A and B or between C and D, which is left to individual attitudes to risk. But it does require that if A is preferred to B, then C be preferred to D, and so on, since C and D are just uniform probabilistic transformations of A and B. But from the point of view of concern with the distribution of utilities across possible outcomes, the difference between A and B is greater than the difference between C and D. The dispersion of utility levels across possible outcomes is at its absolute minimum in alternative B, the case of certainty where the utility of every possible outcome is the same, and the difference between A and B is thus significant; whereas the difference between C and D is hardly dramatic in respect of the dispersion of utilities. In fact most subjects prefer B to A and C to D.[103]

If certainty is an object of concern in its own right, then, *pace* Harsanyi, concern with the dispersion of utilities is not double counting, because the allowance made by the von Neumann-Morgenstern utility function for attitude to risk is not adequate to reflect it; perhaps some form of non-expected utility function is needed. A nonlinear function of the utilities of different possible outcomes could reflect an individual's preference to lower the dispersion of utility levels across outcomes and the distinctive value of certainty, just as a nonlinear function of utilities of individuals reflects a social preference to lower the dispersion of utility levels across persons and the distinctive value of equality with respect to utility. There is nothing intrinsically inconsistent about such a preference; it is only inconsistent with the axioms of expected utility theory. But to assume that the only 'appropriate' allowance for attitude to risk is that made by expected utility theory is to assume that people should not be concerned with certainty *per se*, that any legitimate concern with risk must be reducible to that allowed for by expected utility theory and cannot conflict with the principle that expected utility ought to be maximized.[104] Given the availability of elegant and powerful alternative formalisms of non-expected utility theories, this is a substantive, rather than a merely formal, assumption. Perhaps the assumption is correct, but it needs substantive argument at the all-things-considered level in view of the intelligibility of the concern with certainty *per se*, and the prevalence of it suggested by data gathered by Allais, Tversky, and others. Machina has emphasized that worries about Dutch books and money pump arrangements do not support it, and that Independence axioms may be given up without giving up transitivity; and he and others have done much to provide attractive and rigorous alternatives to expected utility theory's treatment of attitudes to risk. Consistency does not require lack of concern with dispersion of utilities unless expected utility theory is assumed to be superior to the alternatives, which is just what is in question. My claim is not that no convincing argument could possibly be given for the all-things-considered conclusion that people should not be concerned with the dispersion of utilities. It's rather that a substantive position should not be disguised as a demand for 'mere' consistency; an all-things-considered conclusion should not be built into the formal structure of a theory of rationality. We are entitled to ask, as a substantive matter, on what basis the expected utility theorist claims that people should not be concerned, if only at the *pro tanto* level, with something that evidently it is normal and natural for people to be concerned with? We can refrain from falling back on mottos about the indisputability of tastes. Nevertheless, the amount of independent leverage expected utility theory provides for arguments against concern with distribution of utilities is limited. (Again, I emphasize that to remove an obstacle to a certain kind of egalitarianism, as I have tried to do in this subsection, is not to provide a positive argument for such egalitarianism.)

In Chapters 4 and 5 we saw that apparent violations of Independence and Sure Thing could often be avoided by reindividuating the alternatives or reinterpreting the contents of the preferences in question, and that the issue between axiom-conservativism and data-conservatism turns on substantive constraints on the eligibility of interpretations. The distinction between *consequences known with certainty* and *uncertain or risky consequences* seems to be eligible. But it may be doubted that this particular reinterpretation of the contents of preferences, to incorporate explicitly concern with certainty and thus with the dispersion of utilities among the possible outcomes of a gamble, should be seen as a way of preserving the formal structure of expected utility (as opposed to providing a way of developing an alternative formal structure). Lack of concern with the dispersion of utilities is a distinguishing formal feature of expected utility theory, and to set form and content at odds with one another might seem to be asking for trouble. At any rate such a re-interpretation could not serve Hansanyi's purposes. The analogous suggestion would allow the distribution of utility across persons to be an explicit concern of social choice, which would be to concede Sen's point.

III. Finally, the intrapersonal eligibility of a further distinction, that between *known risks* and *uncertainty*, and, more generally, the intelligibility of concern with the amount and quality of the information on which one's assessments of probabilities are based, may be brought to bear on certain criticisms of Rawlsian egalitarianism. I shall first sketch a difficulty for Rawls' claim that a maximin principle applied to primary goods emerges from the original position. Then I shall explain the distinction between risk aversion and aversion to uncertainty, as it emerges from the work of Ellsberg and others. Finally, I shall indicate the way in which the distinction between risk and uncertainty may be drawn by contractors in the original position and the way in which aversion to uncertainty may be assumed to operate independently of any assumption about attitude to risk.

I argued in Chapter 6 that a theory of extended preference depends on a theory of human nature. Since personal preferences have been incorporated into extended alternatives, it would be selective double-counting to allow some one person's personal preferences to determine the extended preference ordering; and since the extended preference ordering provides a measure of interpersonal utility, we cannot appeal to the latter in advance of the determination of extended preference. Following Kolm, I used the term "human nature" as a blanket term to cover whatever it is that determines extended preferences and supplies constraints on eligibility. I went on to suggest that something like a theory of primary goods would form a part of a theory of human nature. Rawls indicates related reservations about the notion of interpersonally comparable utility as it might feature in the reasoning for the principle of average utility in the original position.[105]

However, this is only one part of Rawls' critique of the reasoning for the principle of average utility. Another important line of thought in Rawls' critique concerns the notion of probability rather than that of utility, as it would feature in the conditions of the original position. Rawls resists the use of the principle of insufficient reason to translate his stipulation of the contractors' ignorance of the particular positions they will occupy in society into an assumption that each has an equal probability of occupying each particular position.[106] If the equiprobability assumption were made, and if difficulties with the measurement of interpersonal utility were waived, then expected utility theory would support the choice of the principle of average utility. But Rawls' contractors are in a position of radical uncertainty about the positions they will occupy, as distinct from a position in which they know that each has an equal objective probability of occupying each position. They do not treat uncertainty as if it were known risk; they distinguish between the two, in some way such that a solution other than the principle of average utility emerges: Rawls argues that a maximin principle applied to primary goods would be chosen. However, Rawls also claims that the assumption of a particular attitude to risk should be no part of the characterization of the original position; attitudes to risk may vary, and are to be respected as part of each person's personal conception of the good. How can he demonstrate the rationality of resistance to the equiprobability assumption and to the principle of average utility without assuming a particular attitude to risk, namely, risk aversion? If this question can be answered satisfactorily, it is then a further question whether the maximin principle in particular would emerge instead of the principle of average utility.

I shall try to indicate the way in which concern with the quality and amount of information on the basis of which one acts may support Rawlsian resistance to the equiprobability assumption and the principle of average utility, in the absence of any assumption of risk aversion. Daniel Ellsberg and others have demonstrated that such concern, and a general preference to act on more information rather than less, on known risks rather than under uncertainty, is widespread and dependable; their experimental results are remarkably robust. Even in the face of arguments against the behaviour in question that spell out the way in which it appears to violate one or another axiom, most subjects decide, in Samuelson's phrase, to satisfy their preferences and let the axioms satisfy themselves.[107] Again, I say 'appears' because formal inconsistency may be avoided by reindividuating the alternatives to reflect the distinction between known risk and uncertainty; for example, in various articles Gardenfors, Sahlin, and Goldsmith have developed a generalization of Bayesian decision theory that reflects this distinction. Thus, requirements of formal consistency alone do not support the substantive claim that people *should not* be interested in the difference between known risk and uncertainty, *should not* prefer to act on more and better quality information.[108] Indeed, it is difficult to deny that it is better *pro tanto* to act on the basis of more information than on the basis of less; the eligibility of the distinction is clear, and it might even be claimed that, unlike risk aversion, the aversion to acting under ignorance or uncertainty, the preference to act on more and better quality information (or, as Goldsmith and Sahlin put it, the importance of second-order probabilities) is a distinctive mark of personhood.[109] Several examples may help to illustrate the point.

In Ellsberg's examples, subjects are given the choice between bets, some involving an urn containing variously coloured balls in unknown proportions, others involving an urn containing variously coloured balls in known proportions, where use of a principle of insufficient reason would ascribe the same expected utility to both bets. Subjects dependably avoid the former bets in favour of the latter, even when factors other than the distinction between uncertainty and known risk are held constant in such a way that *if* those other factors exhausted the relevant considerations the subjects's choices would be inconsistent. In one case, Urn I contains 100 red and/or black balls in an unknown ratio, and Urn II contains exactly 50 red and 50 black balls. Subjects are asked whether they would rather bet on drawing red from Urn I or black from Urn I; then whether they would rather bet on drawing red from Urn II or black from Urn II. Typically, they are indifferent in these cases. However, when they are asked whether they would prefer to bet on drawing red from Urn I or red from Urn II, and whether they would prefer to bet on drawing black from Urn I or black from Urn II, most prefer the bets involving Urn II.

In another of Ellsberg's cases, an urn is known to contain 30 red balls and 60 balls that are either black or yellow; the proportion of black to yellow balls is unknown. Subjects are asked whether they would prefer to bet on a red ball being drawn from the urn or a black ball being drawn, where in either case if a yellow ball is drawn they get nothing. They are then asked whether they would prefer to bet on either a red or a yellow ball being drawn, or on either a black or a yellow ball being drawn. The most frequent pattern of response is to prefer to bet on red rather than black in the first choice, and to prefer to bet on either black or yellow rather than either red or yellow in the second case. (See Table 4.1 at the end of Chapter 4.) Such choices, which seem to violate the Sure-Thing Principle, can be explained by supposing that the subjects are not willing to apply the principle of insufficient reason, that they do indeed distinguish known risk from uncertainty, and prefer acting on the former.

Such aversion to uncertainty cannot be captured in terms of ordinary risk aversion (or what Sahlin calls *outcome risk aversion* as opposed to *epistemic risk aversion*[110]). This can perhaps be illustrated most clearly by reference to an example suggested by Gardenfors and Sahlin. Consider a pair of tennis matches on which one is invited to bet. In the first match, the subject has a great deal of information about the two players; she knows all about the results of their previous matches, knows their present physical and mental condition, etc. On the basis of all this information she judges that the odds are 50/50. However, since she is offered a bet on one of the two players on very favourable terms, so that she wins a great deal more if she wins than she loses if she loses, she accepts the bet. Note that however risk-averse, in the ordinary sense, she is, the terms of the bet accepted have been favourable enough to compensate for her risk aversion. In the second match, by contrast, the subject has no information whatsoever about the players. If she is offered the very same terms as she accepted in the first bet, she may well nevertheless decline the second bet. If so, this cannot be accounted for in terms of risk aversion, as the latter has already been allowed for in the terms of the first bet. Rather, it would seem to reflect aversion to uncertainty, to which one is exposed in acting on unreliable probability judgments, based merely or largely on ignorance.

Thus, account must be taken of a widespread substantive preference to act on reliable probability judgments, based on more and better quality evidence and to avoid acting in ignorance or under uncertainty. In the absence of information of sufficient quality, people may simply decline to bet at all.[111]

If they are forced to bet, they may choose to minimize the uncertainty they face, independently of whether they are averse to risk. Someone averse to uncertainty but not to risk will not simply treat ignorance of probabilities as a warrant for assigning equal probabilities to alternatives. If he does not know who he will be when the veil of ignorance is lifted, he will *not* nevertheless behave as if he did know that he had an equal chance of being anyone; even if he is not averse to risk, he may try to minimize uncertainty. Indeed, someone who is risk prone, such as a gambler, may precisely like taking known risks and the element of gamesmanship, of trying to beat the odds, it involves, which he may find altogether lacking in situations of uncertainty.

The distinction between risk aversion and uncertainty aversion would vindicate Rawls' claim that he does not need to assume the contractors in the original position to be risk averse, even though he holds that they should not operate under an equiprobability assumption. Rawls need not assume risk aversion to resist the equiprobability assumption, as it would be sufficient to assume uncertainty aversion, which Ellsberg and others have shown to be far more widely shared than risk aversion. Given the fact that Rawls' theory entitles the contractors to knowledge of psychological generalizations, such an assumption may be altogether justified; in my terms, the value of information may reasonably feature in a theory of human nature. I do not attribute such an assumption to Rawls, but merely suggest that the eligibility of the distinction between known risk and uncertainty, and the very widespread preference to act on the basis of more information rather than less and aversion to acting under uncertainty as opposed to risk, support Rawls' in his resistance to applications of the equiprobability assumption to the original position. Since the latter would open the way to the principle of average utility with its unconcern for distribution *per se*, we again have a case in which the structure of intrapersonal decision theory bears on issues of distributive justice.

I said it is a further question whether the maximin principle would emerge from the original position instead of the principle of average utility. The preceding points about the basis for resistance to the equiprobability assumption in the original position hold independently of what I shall go on to suggest in this paragraph, namely, that uncertainty aversion might, in the absence of any known risks relating to specified goods that might compete with the attractions of certainty and outweigh uncertainty aversion, account for the choice of the maximin principle. Such uncertainty aversion would not have to be assumed to be stronger than other motivations; that is, in conditions in which the need to act under uncertainty was conjoined with the taking of known risks in relation to specified goods, there would be no assumption that aversion to uncertainty outweighed other motivations. The rational choice in particular circumstances would depend on the degree of uncertainty aversion and the weight given to it in relation to other motivations, and in the general case solutions other than maximin may be justified. However, when there are no known risks relating to specified goods to set against aversion to uncertainty, as is the case in the original position, maximin behaviour may be justified as the closest one can come to avoiding uncertainty. Suppose one has no information whatsoever about which position one will occupy, and consider the way in which the choice to distribute a fixed amount of goods absolutely equally would avoid uncertainty: if one knows that each position that one might occupy will be the same and one knows the total amount of goods to be distributed, then one has avoided uncertainty with respect to those goods altogether. Now relax the assumption of a fixed amount of goods: if goods are nevertheless to be distributed absolutely equally, then even if one does not know what the level of the common position that will be, one has at least avoided as much uncertainty as it is possible to avoid. At this point, however, it might be argued that maximin is superior to absolute equality, since it permits only positive deviations from the certain minimum— the only surprises will be bonuses, not penalities. Uncertainty as to whether one will or will not receive a bonus might be regarded as a tolerable deviation from the certainty of an unknown minimum. Thus maximin may emerge from the aversion of contractors to uncertainty, independently of their attitudes to risk.

John Harsanyi has kindly pointed me to Raiffa's discussion of the Ellsberg results. Harsanyi objects that, since Raiffa has shown that a decision-maker can, by using a mixed strategy, costlessly transform a situation of uncertainty into a situation of risk, he can never have any reason to prefer (strictly) a situation of risk over an otherwise similar situation of uncertainty.[112] How does this objection bear on the application I make of the risk/uncertainty distinction to the original position? I don't think it undermines my application, for reasons I shall explain.

First I must explain Raiffa's simple and elegant transformation technique, and then I will explain why it does not apply in the original position.

Raiffa offers subjects two gambles. In the first, they are given an urn containing just 50 red balls and 50 black balls. They guess red or black, and then draw a ball without looking. If they've guessed correctly, they get $100; if they haven't, they get nothing. It doesn't matter whether red or black is drawn; so long as they've guessed correctly, they win. The game is played just once. Subjects are asked how much they would be willing to pay to play this game.

The second gamble is just like the first, except that the urn contains an unknown number of red and/or black balls—all red, all black, or any mixture of the two, and none of any other colours. The procedure and payoffs are the same as in the first game.

Most subjects are risk averse and offer below the actuarial value of the first gamble; answers around $30 are common. But most subjects offer more for the first than the second gamble, reflecting the distinction between risk and uncertainty, and a distinct additional aversion to the latter; $35 for the first and $5 for the second would be typical. A few offer the same amount for the two gambles. The Savage axioms say that regardless of whether one is more or less risk averse, the two gambles should be worth the same thing. How to persuade the majority who distinguish them that they are worth the same thing?

Raiffa finds the following argument persuasive. "Suppose you withdraw a ball from the urn with unknown composition but do not look at its color. Now toss a fair (unbiased) coin and call "red" if heads, "black" if tails. The "objective" probability of getting a match is now .5 and therefore it is just as desirable to participate in the second game as in the first".[113] Thus the second game, apparently involving uncertainty, is transformed into a game equivalent to the first, involving risk.

Let us suppose, for the sake of argument, that this transformation technique is unobjectionable and that it does not beg the question. We must still ask: Can the persons in the original position make use of this transformation technique? The answer, I think, is *no*. A series of steps will lead us from this case to something approaching their situation, and reveal how the two differ.

A. Consider first a negative version of the pair of gambles. If you guess correctly which ball is drawn you remain at the status quo; if you don't, you must pay $100. How much would you pay to avoid facing this situation, i.e., to insure against losing the $100? The remaining aspects of the gambles are held constant. Someone averse to risk might be willing to pay more than the expected value of the first gamble, i.e., − $50, to mitigate the risk. Say he's willing to pay $60. But someone averse to uncertainty as well might be willing to pay even more than that to avoid the second gamble. Just the change from prizes and amounts one is willing to pay to have a chance at them, to losses and amounts one is willing to pay to avoid the chance of them, does not affect Raiffa's analysis. The transformation technique still applies, and if distinguishing the two gambles was irrational in the original case, it is here as well.

B. Now consider the following pair of situations. In the first, there are again 50 black and 50 red balls in the urn. However, the loss of $100 is tied to drawing a black ball, not to your guessing correctly what colour the ball will be. In the second situation, again, you do not know the proportions of black and red balls, and again the loss of $100 is tied to drawing a black ball. You are asked how much you would be willing to pay to avoid being put in each of these situations.

The transformation technique no longer works in the same way. Once you've drawn the ball from the urn of unknown composition, the outcome is fixed, although you don't know what it is until you look. But you cannot now reintroduce an objective 50/50 risk by flipping a coin; you are not asked to guess which colour the ball will be, only to draw one and take your chances against its being black. There are many possible risks you might be facing— many possible distributions of red and black balls. But you don't know which of these possible risks is the actual risk; thus you face uncertainty, or a kind of higher-order risk, a risk about which risks are the ones you actually face. In the original case, you could eliminate this higher-order risk by the coin-flipping ploy. But if losses are the consequence of drawing a black ball rather than of guessing incorrectly, there's nothing to flip a coin over, and no way to transform the uncertainty into risk.

C. Next, consider a pair of urns filled with 100 tickets instead of with black and red balls. In the first case, on half the tickets the word "status quo" is written; on the other half the word "poor" is written. These words stand for circumstances which are set out in full detail elsewhere. The status quo circumstances are the same as those you would be in if you were to avoid this gamble altogether. If you do face this gamble, which ticket you draw will determine which circumstances are yours. Suppose you have some given degree of risk aversion—it may be none at all. Accordingly, you determine how much you are willing to pay to avoid facing this gamble; i.e., how much insurance you are willing to pay to avoid this 50/50 risk of being poor.

In the second case, there are again 100 tickets on which "status quo" or "poor" is written, but they are in unknown proportions. Otherwise, the situation is the same. How much would you now be willing to pay to avoid having to play this game? It seems perfectly reasonable to be averse to the uncertainty this case involves and to be willing to pay more to avoid the situation than you were in the first case. As in the B cases, the transformation technique doesn't work. Once you've drawn the ticket from the urn of unknown composition, the outcome is fixed, although you don't know what it is until you look. You cannot now reintroduce an objective 50/50 risk by flipping a coin; you are not asked to guess what the ticket will say, only to draw one and take your chances against its saying "poor". Again, there are many possible risks you might be facing—many possible distributions of "status quo" and "poor" tickets. But you don't know which of these possible risks is the actual risk; thus you face uncertainty, or a kind of higher-order risk, a risk about which risks are the ones you actually face. And again, in the original case, you could eliminate this higher-order risk by the coin-flipping ploy. But if losses are the consequence of drawing a ticket that says "poor" rather than of guessing incorrectly, there's nothing to flip a coin over, and no way to transform the uncertainty about what your situation will be into risk.

D. Finally, we come to a situation closer to that of the contractor in the original position. In this case, the subject is not asked to guess what his identity and situation are, and given a prize, or protected from a loss, if he guesses correctly. He is a (relatively) bare subject, and (consistently with the requirements of the theory of human nature) his identity and situation themselves constitute the prize, or the loss, and will be determined by a drawing from an urn containing tickets on which are written the names of all N people in society. In the first case, then, he has an equal chance of being any one of the N people in the resulting society. He is asked not how much he is now willing to pay to avoid this situation—how could he say, since he doesn't have a *status quo*?—but what principles should govern the distribution of goods, measured in monetary terms, among the N people. He does not have a status quo in the sense the person in the C cases did, but he must still determine how much he would be willing to sacrifice in various possible outcomes in order now to avoid the possibility of the bad outcomes. He thus pays to avoid risk, to the extent he is risk averse, by in effect borrowing against his position in various possible outcomes. But let's suppose he is not risk averse, and that he is willing to adopt an average maximizing principle to govern the resulting society.

In the second case, his identity and situation are not determined by a drawing from an urn containing N different names, so that he has an equal chance of having anyone's identity and situation. Rather, they have already been fixed, somehow (perhaps by an already accomplished drawing by Nature from an urn of completely unknown composition). He has a full-fledged identity; he is not a bare subject (not even relatively bare). Though his identity and situation are already determined, however, the contractor doesn't know what they are; he hasn't yet 'looked to see' because the veil of ignorance conceals his true position. He cannot transform the uncertainty he faces about his identity and situation into risk by a transformation technique analogous to the coin flipping technique. He does not get a prize or a loss for guessing correctly who he is; who he is *is* the prize or the loss. If he guesses correctly that he is poor, or handicapped, he is still poor, or handicapped. (I assume that the suggestion would not seriously be put forward that the randomizing strategy should be applied to the choice between all possible principles of justice that might turn out to benefit someone.) In this case he may be willing to borrow more than in the first case against his position in various possible outcomes, to avoid some degree of the uncertainty he faces about what his prize or loss will be.

It is true that how much someone is willing to borrow against his possible positions affects the value of being who he turns out to be; in a sense, then, his prizes and losses vary with how much he is willing to borrow, as reflected in his choice of principles to govern society. Some who chooses a maximin principle rather than an average principle has in effect borrowed more against his possible positions, and thus reduced the prizes associated with certain positions. But the amount you are willing to pay to gamble also affects the net value of the position you end up in if you win.

The point here is simply that for purposes of applying the distinction between risk and uncertainty to the Rawlsian situation, Raiffa's transformation technique doesn't work (not that he claimed it did!), and the distinction still holds. Rawls' contractors may not be in exactly the situations of uncertainty depicted in case C or case D, but those cases are more representative of their situation in these respects than is case A, in which Raiffa's technique may be appropriate.

I have examined, in addition to the intrinsic distributional requirements of the value of autonomy, three ways in which intrapersonal structure bears on issues of distributive justice: firstly, by way of complementary relationships among representative values, secondly, by way of the eligible distinction between certainty and either known risks or uncertainty, and, thirdly, by way of the eligible distinction between known risks and uncertainty. I have not endorsed claims to the effect that an adequate account of distributive justice can be given in terms of the distribution of utility or even of primary goods, at least if the latter are restrictively understood; I agree with Sen that richer information than welfarism admits is needed about the uses of income and the sources of utility, and that the distribution of exercises of basic capacities is of great importance—as indeed I have argued above with respect to autonomy in particular. My remarks merely draw attention to possibilities of removing certain obstacles to concern with the distribution across persons of utility and/or primary goods as elements in a theory of distributive justice. Again, since these possibilities derive from consideration of decision-theoretic issues about separability and independence and from claims about intrapersonally eligible distinctions, they are immune to the effect of a sub-personal focus in undermining distributional concerns.

A further issue raised by my discussion under II and III above, however, is why it should be appropriate in the first place to describe the original position, or more generally the position from which certain fundamental decisions with respect to distributive justice are made, as involving uncertainty about who one is rather than an equal chance of being anyone. What is the ultimate justification for the claim that the former supposition rather than the latter enables us to adopt the right perspective for purposes of a theory of distributive justice? If my argument in subsection II is correct, even the supposition that I have an equal chance of being anyone may yield a fair degree of egalitarianism. But nevertheless, it seems to me that the question of greater significance for distributive justice is not one about what I would decide, given an equal chance of being anyone, but rather one about what I would decide, given uncertainty about who I am. Many people, though certainly not all, seem to share this intuition. I do not have anything approaching a full justification to offer in support of it, and will merely sketch two suggestions about what may underlie it.

First, the supposition that 'I' might have an equal chance of being anyone seems to require, for its sense, a subject, not yet identified as any person in particular, to whom probabilities of being particular persons can be attached. I suspect this of being a case in which language carries us along into mistakenly assuming we can make sense of a construction, because there is, so to speak, grammatical space for it, which in fact does not make sense. At least I find it hard to see how, short of postulating a 'bare', metaphysical, or noumenal self, such a construction can make sense; and such a postulation merely transfers the doubts about making sense to notions of the metaphysical self. How, moreover, could any such metaphysical self have reason to base its decisions on probabilistic considerations, which gain appeal from consideration of the long run of cases, when the only decision it is called upon to make is a one-off decision in which its entire life is at stake?[114]

Secondly, the supposition that I have an equal chance of being anyone suggests that only one possibility among those considered will actually be realized, just as would be the case in an individual decision problem in which there were equal chances of various possible mutually exclusive outcomes. In such a case, as is often emphasized in arguments for the Independence

Axiom (see Chapter 4 section 3), I will only ever get one outcome, or another; never several together. However, when the possibilities in question are all human lives, and all of them will in fact be lived, the suggestion that the realization of one possibility in any sense excludes the realization of the others is disturbing; it goes well beyond an assumption of mutual disinterest. The metaphysical parallel between a life being *mine* (rather than anyone else's), and a possible state of affairs being *actual* (rather than merely possible), seems to be in tension with the important and common-sensical view that all of the lives under consideration are equally actual or real, whether or not they are mine. By contrast, the merely epistemic supposition that I do not know who I am suggests no such disturbing metaphysical parallel, and is in no tension with recognizing the reality of the points of view of others besides myself.

What the imposition of ignorance about who I am does function to do very effectively, however, is to exclude many debunking influences from affecting my decision. While I cannot develop this suggestion here, perhaps the significance of imposing radical uncertainty in theories of distributive justice is to be found in a cognitive conception of the task of such theories, as contributing to the deliberative, democratic search for knowledge of what should be done.

# EPILOGUE

I shall not try to summarize the complex argumentative themes and structure of this book, as I did in the introductory chapter (though that survey may mean more to readers who have got this far than to readers starting out). I will merely comment on certain implications of one of my main themes.

I have tried to develop the sense in which the capacities of persons for practical theorizing reflect their personality: the deliberative pursuit of coherence given conflicting values and the higher-order attitudes to which it may give rise are marks of the distinctive capacity of persons for self-interpretation and self-determination. By focussing on the important role of theoretical rationality, however, I do not intend to elevate theoretical values above others. By becoming explicitly aware of the often implicit role and influence of theoretical considerations in our lives, we may be better able to demystify our own theoretical positions, recognize their proper limitations, and check their imperialistic ambitions. Theories are finally responsible to us, not we to them. Awareness of how deeply theories reflect us and the conflicts we face should, I hope, help us to put an end to the dangerous tendency to treat theories as religions, and help us to recognize that wars of theory are no more justified than wars of religion. Practical theorizing should take the form of thoughtful, workmanlike design and tinkering, and should accept as its starting point a generous conception of the conflicting values that are its subject matter. Theoretical reflexes, especially in the realm of political values, are ultimately a sad category mistake.

# NOTES

## Notes to Chapter 2. Objectivity

1. See Wiggins, "Truth, Invention, and the Meaning of Life", at pp. 361–362. See also Harman, *The Nature of Morality*, Chapter 1. For further discussion of realism and scientific realism, see Chapter 14, especially section 4.

2. See, for example, Hare, *Freedom and Reason* (but compare *Moral Thinking*); Hintikka, "Some Main Problems in Deontic Logic", p. 99, and " 'Prima Facie' Obligations and Iterated Modalities", pp. 232–233; and compare: Searle, " 'Prima Facie' Obligations", p. 248; Scotch and Jennings, "Non-Kripkean Deontic Logic", sections 4 and 5; Lemmon, "Deontic Logic and the Logic of Imperatives", pp. 50–51; Castaneda, "On the Semantics of the Ought-to-Do", pp. 687–689.

3. See, for example, Rawls, *A Theory of Justice*; Daniels, "Wide Reflective Equilibrium and Theory Acceptance in Ethics"; Dworkin, *Taking Rights Seriously*, pp. 87, 104–109, 119–122, 126–127, 159–168, 283, and "No Right Answer?".

4. *Pace* Blackburn in "Moral Realism". Indeed, the source of the supervenience of attitudes on the characteristics of their objects may itself be the theoretical or explanatory role of attributions of attitudes; see and compare McGinn, *The Character of Mind*, pp. 29–36. There is further discussion of Blackburn's views in Chapter 14 on skepticism.

5. Note that I suggest giving narrow scope to the existential quantification with respect to a theory about specific values, *not* to designations of the specific values the theory is about. To the contrary, the anti-centralist, anti-subjectivist position I develop in the rest of Part I demands, in effect, that designations of the specific values that provide substantive constraints on eligibility be given wide scope.

6. For explanation of the standard deontic operator, see Hintikka's work, such as "Some Main Problems in Deontic Logic".

7. John McDowell has expressed skepticism about such purely descriptive components, on Wittgensteinian grounds; see especially his "Non-cognitivism and Rule-Following". See also, for example, *Zettel*, I:225, and Wittgenstein's notes, as quoted by Malcolm in *Ludwig Wittgenstein: A Memoir*, pp. 49–50.

In some cases, that someone perceives an alternative in non-reason-giving terms co-extensive with an applicable reason-giving concept tends to undermine attributions to him of the reason-giving concept. We can and do distinguish the behaviour and attitudes of someone who does an action because it is socially required from the behaviour and attitudes of a Julien Sorel, the hero of Stendal's *The Red and the Black*, who does what he does because it falls under his formula for 'socially required action' and he wants to be accepted in society. We rely on this distinction in recognizing that someone is a social climber. The very fact that the social climber's reasons include his perception that an action falls under this formula plus a desire to do such actions allows us to distinguish him from someone who naturally does what he perceives to be socially required. If the latter sort of person explains his action by saying what he did was socially required, it would be to distort his reason for acting to take this as meaning that he thought the action was 'socially required' and wanted to do whatever is 'socially required'; it would be just as much of a distortion to attribute the perceptions of the naturally courteous and correct person to the social climber. If there is a state of mind in which both these sorts of perceptions are had simultaneously, it is a rather special, ironical one; normally one has either one or the other, but not both.

8. This point receives further discussion in Chapter 10 section 4. See and compare Searle on "ought" and promising, in *Speech Acts*, Chapter 8.

9. For related suggestions in the more general context see McDowell, "Singular Thought and the Extent of Inner Space"; compare Rorty on whether Davidson is correct to regard his own position as a realist one, or rather as "beyond realism and anti-realism", in "Pragmatism, Davidson and Truth".

10. See and compare Premack, "On the Abstractness of Human Concepts", pp. 436, 447.

11. See Hart, *The Concept of Law*, pp. 91–92.

12. See *Riggs v. Palmer*; *Henningson v. Bloomfield Motors, Inc.*; Dworkin, *Taking Rights Seriously*, pp. 23–4, 28–9.

13. Dworkin, *Taking Rights Seriously*, p. 40–42.

14. See Wright, *Wittgenstein on the Foundations of Mathematics*, Chapters 4 and 5, esp. pp. 58, 61. On the parallel point for calculation, see pp. 68–69.

15. Wittgenstein, *Remarks on the Foundations of Mathematics*, I:156; I:5; VII:31. See also I:4, VI:16; and see *Philosophical Investigations*, I:164, and *On Certainty*, section 47.

16. Wittgenstein, *Remarks on the Foundations of Mathematics*, III:74. Compare Burge, as cited in note 20 to this chapter, who argues that whether someone visually represents a crack or a shadow may depend on what the normal cause of his physiological state is, in his ordinary activities; an intrinsic physiological state that in one environment would constitute a misrepresentation of a crack as a shadow would in another environment constitute a correct perception of a crack as a crack. The physiological state is not magically self-interpreting; it gets the representational content it has from its normal relations to the environment. If normal interactions with the environment were such as to determine that it represents a crack rather than a shadow, it would be absurd to regard it as misrepresenting a crack as a shadow. The presence of a crack to be discerned is like a table to be measured; the normal relations that determine the content of a visual representation are like the significance of the yard-stick as a measure. In discerning that something is a crack, one does not lay the 'fitness' of one's method of visual representation of cracks open to criticism as well as laying the accuracy of one's particular judgment open to criticism. One method of measurement or representation isn't intrinsically superior to another, apart from empirical success. We must establish and accept some method of representation of cracks before we can evaluate the truth of particular representations, given that method, of cracks. The practices that establish methods of representation and thus determine the contents of particular representations are not subject to challenge by uses of those very representations.

17. See Davidson, "True to the Facts", in *Inquiries into Truth and Interpretation*, p. 49.

18. See McDowell, "Wittgenstein on Following a Rule", section 12.

19. Wittgenstein, *Remarks on the Foundations of Mathematics*, VII:39; see also

VII:40. See and compare Kripke, *Wittgenstein on Rules and Private Language*, p. 59n and passim; and Quine, *Word and Object*, pp. 24–25.

20. For related remarks, see Davidson, "A Coherence Theory of Truth and Knowledge", in *Inquiries into Truth and Interpretation*; Burge, "Individualism and Psychology", esp. pp. 40–43, and "Cartesian Error and the Objectivity of Perception".

21. For a project related to that set out in this paragraph, see Sabina Lovibond's *Realism and Imagination in Ethics*.

22. Dummett, *Frege*, pp. 360, 362. See also p. 352ff, and Wright, *Wittgenstein on the Foundations of Mathematics*, p. 70ff.

23. Peacocke, *Holistic Explanation*, p. 215. See and compare Hornsby, "Physicalist Thinking and Behaviour".

24. See *Philosophical Investigations*, I:337; *Remarks on the Foundations of Mathematics*, p. 335; *The Brown Book* II.14. See also Seabright, "Understanding Cultural Divergence: a Wittgensteinian Paradox".

25. See *Philosophical Investigations*, I:202.

26. "A Coherence Theory of Truth and Knowledge", p. 317, in Le Pore, editor, *Truth and Interpretation*. See also Burge, "Cartesian Error" and "Individualism and Psychology".

27. For his understanding of the term, see Burge, "Cartesian Error and the Objectivity of Perception", pp. 118–119. Beware of the difference between Burge's and Fodor's uses of the term 'individualism'; see Fodor, "Individualism and Supervenience", p. 250ff, on the distinction between what he calls 'methodological solipsism' and what he calls 'individualism', and Davies' reply under the same title, p. 267, on the relation between Fodor's and Burge's uses of the term 'individualism'. I follow Burge's terminology rather than Fodor's. See also Hornsby, "Physicalist Thinking and Behaviour", on a world-conditioned notion of behaviour.

Burge's own work on mental states is located here at the second stage; his claims are motivated primarily by thought experiments rather than by explicit consideration of the indeterminacy problem sketched at the first stage. Nevertheless, recognition of the problem and of the resultant need for constraints is clearly present in his work; see especially the comments on lack of unique fit and environmental constraints in "Cartesian Error and the Objectivity of Perception", and "Individualism and Psychology". Burge also sees Wittgenstein's work as a precursor to his own; see his "Individualism and the Mental", and see Pettit's "Wittgenstein, Individualism and the Mental".

28. See, of course, "The Very Idea of a Conceptual Scheme", in *Inquiries into Truth and Interpretation*.

29. It may help to clarify what is going on at the second stage of argument to note explicitly the order of entailment between various denials: the denial of psychological individualism, the denial of the independence of mind from world, whether mind is conceived in individualistic or social terms, and the denial of the dualism of mind and world, of "organizing system and something waiting to be organized" (as Davidson puts it in "The Very Idea of a Conceptual Scheme"). The latter denial is one of independence in both directions—of mind from world, and of world from mind; it is the strongest of the three denials, yielding a generalized view of the mind and world as interdependent, which entails the former two denials. But one could deny psychological individualism without either denying the independence of mind conceived in social terms from the world, or denying the dualism of mind and world altogether. And one could deny the independence of mind from world without

denying in all respects the independence of world from mind. My concern is primarily with the middle level—with denying the independence of mind from world, though that denial may ultimately be motivated by the more radical rejection of mind-world dualism. I shall advocate the view that mind and world are interdependent in a particular respect, at least: namely, that preferences and values are interdependent.

30. Lewis, "Radical Interpretation", *Philosophical Papers*, p. 112; see also his "New Work for a Theory of Universals", pp. 371–377. For comments about the normative constraints on the concept of belief, see Williams, "Deciding to Believe", in *Problems of the Self*, p. 148ff. Compare Wiggins, "Freedom, Knowledge, Belief and Causality", p. 143ff; and Edgley, *Reason in Theory and Practice*, Chapters 3, 5. See also Wittgenstein, *Remarks on the Foundations of Mathematics*, I:131, 133.

31. In general, values provide reasons that are substantive rather than formal, and ultimate rather than instrumental. Of course there are formal and instrumental reasons as well. I often use "reasons" to refer to reasons provided by values in particular, however.

32. Davidson, "Psychology as Philosophy", *Essays on Action and Events*, pp. 229, 234.

33. See Ramsey, "Truth and Probability", p. 177ff.

34. In fact this remark rather understates the problem, which is more fully and generally developed beginning in Chapter 4. Appealing for a merely ordinal conception of preference at this point will not avoid the problem; see Chapter 4 on the way in which substantive constraints on the contents of preference are needed even to make sense of a merely ordinal conception of preference according to which preferences are not, or should not be, intransitive.

35. Here I am indebted to Paul Seabright and Huw Dixon. See Davidson, "Psychology as Philosophy", *Essays on Actions and Events*, p. 236, and Seabright's discussion of Davidson's criticism of Ramsey in his Oxford M.Phil. thesis in economics, *Uncertainty and Ignorance in Economics*, p. 17ff. See also Dennett, "Intentional Systems", *Brainstorms*, p. 19; Fellner, "Distortion of Subjective Probabilities as a Reaction to Uncertainty", p. 678; MacCrimmon and Larsen, "Utility Theory: Axioms vs. Paradoxes", p. 397.

36. Davidson, "Psychology as Philosophy", *Essays on Actions and Events*, p. 237.

37. See and compare Peacocke, *Holistic Explanation*, pp. 31, 54, 190–191. Peacocke claims that an assumption of rationality, however broadly construed, is not sufficient to enable us to apply the concepts of belief and desire, but that we need "a theory of regularity of such nonrational factors as the constancy and change of underived desires (desires that are not derivative from other desires) over time, and the connection of sensory stimuli physically characterized with the formation of beliefs": "the supposition of rationality and what is believed at a given time have no particular consequences for empirically possible sequences of actions until we adjoin a theory of the agent's underived desires over time, and have also an account of such matters as the connection of his beliefs with sensory stimuli" pp. 190–191. We seem to be differing not so much over the content of the necessary assumptions as about whether it is correct to describe them as assumptions about rationality. Assumptions about the content of the agent's underived desires I am describing as assumptions of their substantive rationality. Assumptions about the connections of an agent's beliefs with sensory stimuli are among those that must be made if we are to follow Davidson's methodological advice to interpret so as to "make native speakers right when plausibly possible, according, of course, to our own view of what is right". "Radical Interpretation", *Inquiries into Truth and Interpretation*, at p. 137. Assumptions of both these

kinds ought to be included in any conception of the charity that Davidson urges on us.

Throughout this book I use the term "substantive" in a sense that may perhaps be less familiar to philosophers than to lawyers, to mean roughly *concerning issues of substance or content rather than form, procedure, or consistency*. This usage is not, I recognize, ideal, but the alternatives seem to me worse. "Content-related" is awkward. "Substantial" suggests importance, which formal issues may have and substantive issues, in my sense, may lack. "Material" is confusingly ambiguous.

38. Davidson, "Mental Events", *Essays on Action and Events*, p. 222.

39. Davidson, "Radical Interpretation", *Inquiries into Truth and Interpretation*, p. 137.

40. See Dworkin on this distinction, in *Law's Empire* (see his index under "skepticism"). See also Searle, *Speech Acts*, footnote, p. 186.

41. Davidson, "Thought and Talk", *Inquiries into Truth and Interpretation*, pp. 169–170. See also Wright, *Wittgenstein on the Foundations of Mathematics*, p. 329.

42. Wittgenstein, *On Certainty*, section 139.

### Notes to Chapter 3. Disagreement

1. Williams, "The Truth in Relativism", *Moral Luck*, p. 135.

2. While thinking about how to answer this question, it may be helpful to keep in mind the distinction between non-centralism and certain familiar forms of relativization. A non-centralist coherence account holds there are conceptual relations between claims about what should be done, all things considered, and a list of specific reasons. But whether this is true or not cuts across the question of whether certain reasons are relativized in the way that agent-relative reasons and legal reasons are: the form of such a reason includes an essential reference to its scope of application. (See, e.g., Nagel, *The View from Nowhere*, p. 153.) A particular legal precedent doesn't pretend to provide a legal reason in systems other than the one to which it belongs; laws are laws in particular countries and not others. There's nothing we seem to want to disagree about that such relativization keeps us from disagreeing about. For example, claims about what the law is in one country don't contradict claims about what it is in another country. Even when jurisdiction is contested and the jurisdictions have conflicts of law rules that would resolve the conflict differently, we don't disagree if I say that the conflicts of law rule in one jurisdiction is such and such and you say that the conflicts of law rule in the other jurisdiction is something else. If we want to disagree we must talk about what ought to be done when conflicts of law rules conflict, or what the law ought to be in each jurisdiction; but this we are free to do.

Granted that claims about the law are relativized in this way, the question whether a non-centralist account of them is correct remains; the two questions are independent of one another. The relativization of claims about the law to particular legal systems doesn't entail that a non-centralist account of the conceptual relationships between the specific and the general concepts within any given legal system is correct; and if non-centralism about reasons for action is correct, this doesn't entail that such reasons must be agent-relative or relativized in the way that legal reasons are. A centralist account of legal concepts doesn't threaten their relativization; and, finally, we aren't constrained to be centralists about agent-neutral reasons for action.

3. See, for example, Wittgenstein, *Philosophical Investigations*, I:185; *Remarks on the Foundations of Mathematics*, I:149ff; *The Blue and Brown Books*, p. 97; compare *Norman*, Reasons for Action, p. 128.

4. Stroud, "Wittgenstein and Logical Necessity", pp. 493, 489. See also Wittgenstein, *Philosophical Investigations*, II:xii.

5. Wittgenstein, *Philosophical Investigations*, I:337.

6. On *grue* and *quus*, see, respectively, Goodman, "The New Riddle of Induction", in *Fact, Fiction and Forecast*, and Kripke, *Wittgenstein on Rules and Private Language*, section 2.

7. Stroud, "Wittgenstein and Logical Necessity", p. 492.

8. Wright, *Wittgenstein on the Foundations of Mathematics*, pp. 69, 70.

9. See, for example, Trigg, *Reason and Commitment*, pp. 66, 71, 123–124.

10. Wittgenstein, *Philosophical Investigations*, I:242.

11. Wittgenstein, *Remarks on the Foundations of Mathematics*, VI:39.

12. *Philosophical Investigations*, I:241.

13. *Remarks on the Foundations of Mathematics*, VI:49. See also VI:30, VII:2, 43.

14. *Remarks on the Foundations of Mathematics* VI:48; III:37. See also I:5, 136.

15. See and compare Bennett on presupposing competence, *Locke, Berkeley, Hume*, p. 13ff.

16. *Philosophical Investigations*, II:xi, p. 217.

17. See and compare McDowell, "On the Sense and Reference of a Proper Name", pp. 168, 174–175, 177; and Kripke, *Wittgenstein on Rules and Private Language*, p. 44. See Wittgenstein, e.g., *The Brown Book*, i.14–17; ii.24–25.

18. See especially Davidson's "A Coherence Theory of Truth and Knowledge", in Le Pore, editor, *Truth and Interpretation*. Compare, also in Le Pore's volume, McGinn's "Radical Interpretation and Epistemology", where he seems to urge on Davidson a strategy the failure of which he in effect concedes to Wittgenstein, in his book *Wittgenstein on Meaning* (see especially Chapters 1 and 3).

19. Wittgenstein, *Remarks on the Foundations of Mathematics* I:113.

20. Wittgenstein, *Remarks on the Foundations of Mathematics* VI:19. See also VI:39.

21. Wittgenstein, *Philosophical Investigations* I:198. See also *On Certainty*, section 44.

22. For closely related remarks, see Burge, "Cartesian Error", pp. 122–135.

23. See Wittgenstein, *The Brown Book* I.40; II.5.

24. See, for example, Strawson, *Individuals*, pp. 112ff; Wittgenstein, for example, *The Blue Book*, pp. 3, 33ff; see also Hampshire, *Thought and Action*, p. 74ff. And again, see Hornsby, "Physicalist Thinking and Behaviour".

25. Wittgenstein, *Philosophical Investigations*, I:201–202. Here and in what follows I am indebted to John McDowell's views in "Non-Cognitivism and Rule-Following", and especially in "Wittgenstein on Following a Rule". Compare Kripke, *Wittgenstein on Rules and Private Language*, section 2.

26. Kripke, *Wittgenstein on Rules and Private Language*, pp. 66, 68–69.

27. Social practices provide constitutive constraints on the interpretation of individuals and the ascription of content to them. However, to anticipate the remarks at the end of Chapter 5 section 3, I do not suggest that Wittgenstein is committed to the view that constraints on interpretation must be social, as opposed to natural, in origin. Or, more accurately, I don't see that he's committed to seeing a persons's relations to his social environment and his relations to his natural environment as *opposed* sources of constititutive constraints on interpretation, though of course there are differences between the two kinds of constraint. Wittgenstein undeniably concentrates on the case of determination by social practices, but what he says is in harmony

with the view that someone's social environment is part of his natural environment, and of social practices as natural phenomena. For related remarks, see Seabright, "Explaining Cultural Divergence: A Wittgensteinian Paradox"; Pettit, "Wittgenstein, Individualism and the Mental", and Pettit and McDowell's introduction to *Subject, Thought and Context*.

It's interesting to compare Aristotle's emphasis on activity with Wittgenstein's on practices. See, e.g., *Nicomachean Ethics* IX.7. And see X.5, where he gives activity an individuating role in relation to kinds of pleasures: "For this reason pleasures seem, too, to differ in kind. For things different in kind are, we think, completed by different things . . . we think that activities differing in kind are completed by things differing in kind. Now the activities of thought differ from those of the senses, and both differ among themselves, in kind; so, therefore, do the pleasures that complete them".

28. Davidson, "On the Very Idea of a Conceptual Scheme", in *Inquiries into Truth and Interpretation*, pp. 196–197.

29. Wright, *Wittgenstein on the Foundations of Mathematics*, pp. 68, 72.

30. Wittgenstein, *Remarks on the Foundations of Mathematics* VI:28.

31. Wittgenstein, *On Certainty*, section 630.

32. Wittgenstein, *On Certainty*, section 673.

33. See *Zettel*, I:354, 346. I am indebted here and in what follows to E. M. Fricker and indirectly to Gareth Evans for suggestions made in conversation about the usefulness of a distinction between sensory and articulated predicates in interpreting Wittgenstein. See her *Rules and Language: An Examination of Some of Wittgenstein's Arguments*, p. 81ff. See also Wittgenstein's remarks at *Zettel* I:331, 332, 353, 362 and *Remarks on Colour*, III:73 and *passim*.

34. Wittgenstein, *Remarks on Colour*, I:66, III:154, III:42, III:88.

35. Wittgenstein, *Remarks on Colour*, I:14, III:127, III:86. Wittgenstein seems to think that green is a primary colour, rather than a mixture of blue and yellow.

36. Wittgenstein, *Zettel*, I:368. See also I:369, 266ff; compare I:257: Wittgenstein responds to the question "Would it be possible to discover a new colour?" by pointing out that "a colour-blind man is in the same situation as we are, his colours form just as complete a system as ours do; he doesn't see any gaps where the remaining colours belong".

37. Wittgenstein, *Remarks on Colour*, III:106.

38. Wittgenstein, *Philosophical Investigations* II:xi, p. 226. See also *Zettel* I:393; *Remarks on the Foundations of Mathematics* VII:43.

39. Wittgenstein, *Remarks on Colour* III:293. Compare *Remarks on the Foundations of Mathematics* I:5; see also III:75.

40. Wittgenstein, *Remarks on the Foundations of Mathematics* I:116. See also Wittgenstein's comments in *Lectures and Conversations on Aesthetics, Psychology and Religious Belief*, pp. 61–63; compare Jonathan Lear, "Leaving the World Alone", pp. 389–390; Edgley, pp. 79–82. For related remarks on the general sensory concepts of taste and of pain, see *Zettel* I:366–367, 380–381. That the distinction between substantive and conceptual difference admits of degrees is implicit in Wittgenstein's remarks about gradual diachronic changes in language games. See *On Certainty*, sections 63, 256; *Remarks on the Foundations of Mathematics* IV:30.

41. Wittgenstein, *Remarks on the Foundations of Mathematics* VII:43.

42. Wittgenstein, *Philosophical Investigations* I:164. See also *The Blue Book*, p. 17.

43. Wittgenstein, *Remarks on the Foundations of Mathematics* VI:16; see also *Philosophical Investigations* I:185.

44. See and compare Burge, "Intellectual Norms and Foundations of Mind" on how contest, substantive disagreement, and mistakes about sofas are possible.

45. Wittgenstein, *On Certainty*, sections 156 and 74.

46. Wittgenstein, *Lectures and Conversations*, p. 59. See also pp. 61–63, and *On Certainty*, section 255.

47. Gallie gives an artificial example involving the concept *champion*, and also the examples *democracy, the Christian life, art*; see his "Essentially Contested Concepts". Wittgenstein gives as an example of such a concept that of the genuineness of an expression of feeling; see *Philosophical Investigations* II:xi, p. 227.

48. Here we might apply what Burge says about disagreement in "Intellectual Norms" to his contract example from "Individualism and the Mental", to yield an account of *contract* as an essentially contested concept.

49. Gallie, p. 175.

50. See Gallie, pp. 172, 176–177, 190.

51. Wittgenstein, *Philosophical Investigations* I:217. See also McDowell, "On the Sense and Reference of a Proper Name", p. 177.

52. Williams, "Wittgenstein and Idealism", *Moral Luck*, p. 160.

53. See and compare Dennett, *Brainstorms*, p. 10. The examples are from: Anscombe, *Intention*, pp. 70–71; and Parfit, *Reasons and Persons*, section 46, respectively. Nagel's example of a desire for there to be parsley on the moon Parfit regards as an excellent whim, and quite intelligible as such—unlike, for example, wanting there to be parsley in the sea. See Nagel, *The Possibility of Altruism*, p. 45. Here I am indebted to Derek Parfit.

54. See Wittgenstein, *Remarks on Colour* III:293; *Philosophical Investigations*, p. 226.

55. Burge makes a particular version of this point, about perception, when he writes: "Most perceptual representations are formed and obtain their content through regular interaction with the environment. They represent what, in some complex sense of 'normally', they normally stem from and are applied to. It makes no sense to attribute systematic perceptual error to a being whose perceptual representations can be explained as the result of regular interaction with a physical environment and whose discriminative activity is reasonably well adapted to that environment." "Cartesian Error", p. 131. Compare Jonathan Lear, who writes: "we cannot step outside our form of life and discuss it like some *objet trouvé*. Any attempt to say what our form of life is like will itself be part of the form of life; it can have no more than the meaning it gets within the context of its use." Lear, "Leaving the World Alone", p. 385. Lear also finds affinities between the positions of Wittgenstein and Davidson. See p. 392n.

See and compare Williams, "Wittgenstein and Idealism", *Moral Luck*, p. 146, 150, 161, 163 and passim; and Wittgenstein, *Tractatus Logico-Philosophicus* 5.6–5.64. Williams argues that relativism is not the result of Wittgenstein's views about the determination of meaning by practices, and suggests that the transcendental idealism of the *Tractatus* is implicit in pluralized form in the later work of Wittgenstein. Williams contrasts Wittgenstein's transcendental solipsism, which "coincides with pure realism" and is expressed by the idea that "the limits of my language are the limits of my world", with idealism "regarded just as a kind of aggregative solipsism", which might be expressed by "the confused idea that the limits of each man's language are the limits of each man's world" and which "is indeed ridiculous." He goes on to point out that relativism represents an aggregative solipsism of the pluralised form that might be expressed by the similarly confused idea that the limits of each society's language are the limits of its world. Relativism is likewise to be contrasted with the position led to by the transcendental arguments of Wittgenstein's later philosophy, arguments which aim to establish the possibility of determinate meaning. The later position, which Williams regards as idealist, shares the characteristics of the solipsism of the *Tractatus*: that we are "driven to state it in forms which are required to be understood, if at all, in the wrong way", and that it, "when its implications are followed out strictly, coincides with pure realism." I think there is much that's correct in Williams' interpretation, but would resist the view that Wittgenstein's later arguments, for all their transcendental character, lead to idealism. For grounds for resistance, see Harrison, "Transcendental Arguments and Idealism"; and see my further discussion in Chapter 5 section 4.

56. Davidson, "On the Very Idea of a Conceptual Scheme", *Inquiries into Truth and Interpretation*, p. 198. Compare: Quine, *Word and Object*, pp. 24–25; Putnam, *Reason, Truth and History*, p. 52.

57. Davidson, "On the Very Idea of a Conceptual Scheme", *Inquiries into Truth and Interpretation*, p. 197.

58. Davidson, "The Very Idea of a Conceptual Scheme", *Inquiries into Truth and Interpretation*, pp. 197–198.

59. Wittgenstein, *On Certainty*, section 599.

## Notes to Chapter 4. Preference

1. For example, see Burge, "Individualism and Psychology" and "Cartesian Error and the Objectivity of Perception".

2. Support for the view of values as natural derives both from the arguments of the chapter on subjectivism, and from the discussion in the chapter on skepticism, section 9, which exposes the debunker's counterfactual independence assumption and suggests a naturalist alternative.

3. On the total interpretative project, that is, the project of interpreting someone's linguistic behaviour along with his intentional behaviour in general, see Davidson's "New Basis for Decision Theory". Compare Jeffrey, *The Logic of Decision*, p. 59.

4. See Davidson, "Knowing One's Own Mind". See and compare Evans, *The Varieties of Reference*, pp. 225–227: "in making a self-ascription of belief, one's eyes are, so to speak, or occasionally literally, directed outward—upon the world. If someone asks me 'Do you think there is going to be a third world war?', I must attend, in answering him, to precisely the same outward phenomena as I would attend to if I were answering the question 'Will there be a third world war?' I get myself in a position to answer the question whether I believe that by putting into operation whatever procedure I have for answering the question whether p."

"So when the subject wishes to make absolutely sure that his judgment is correct, he gazes again at the world (thereby producing, or reproducing, an informational state in himself); he does not in any sense gaze at, or concentrate upon, his internal state."

5. Wittgenstein, *Philosophical Investigations* I.258; see also I.237.

6. See Raiffa, *Decision Analysis*, p. 75.

7. On this distinction, see Harsanyi, "Von Neumann-Morgenstern Utilities, Risk Taking, and Welfare".

8. See Broome, "Rationality and the Sure-Thing Principle", on this point.

9. "Expressing Evaluations", p. 19; and see "A New Basis for Decision Theory", p. 92, on norms of correspondence, "which are concerned with the truth or correctness of particular beliefs and values" and which counsel the interpreter "to interpret agents

he would understanding as having, in important respects, beliefs that are mostly true and needs and values the interpreter shares or can imagine himself sharing if he had the history of the agent and were in comparable circumstances". See also Burge, "Cartesian Error", p. 131.

10. Compare Peacocke, *Holistic Explanation*, pp. 215–216.

11. But beware: terminology is not standardized in this area, and various formulations of closely related axioms and conditions are given different names; "substitution" and "separability" conditions may be postulated rather than independence conditions. I here follow Keeney and Raiffa's terminology.

Independence, Sure-Thing, and Mutual Preferential Independence can all be understood by reference to the economic conception of *strong separability*: Mutual Preferential independence involves strong separability for preferences with respect to different criteria of choice, whereas Independence and Sure-Thing involve strong separability for preferences with respect to goods in different possible worlds. Here I am indebted to John Broome. On separability in general and in expected utility theory, see Deaton and Muellbauer, *Economics and Consumer Behavior*, Chapters 5 and 14. See also Green, *Consumer Theory*, Chapter 10.

12. As well as requiring this additive form, Independence requires in effect that the utility of each possible world be a function just of features of that world; it thus presupposes a distinction between features that are properly features of one possible world rather than of another.

For further comments on the Independence Axiom and the significance of its violation see, e.g., Tversky, "A Critique of Expected Utility Theory", pp. 164–166; McClennan, "Sure-Thing Doubts", pp. 120–121; Machina, " 'Expected Utility' Analysis without the Independence Axiom", p. 278, and Machina, "Economic Theory of Individual Behavior Toward Risk", pp. 7–8. See also Hagen's "Introductory Survey", pp. 14, 22; Menges, "Comparison of Decision Models and Some Suggestions"; Hagen's comments at pp. 6–7, in "Paradoxes and Their Solutions"; Fellner, "Distortion of Subjective Probabilities as a Reaction to Uncertainty", p. 673.

13. On linearity, see Machina, "Generalized Expected Utility Analysis", p. 266, and " 'Rational' Decision Making", p. 166. For more on the parallel between issues about expected utility and issues about distributive justice, see Machina, " 'Expected Utility' Analysis Without the Independence Axiom", section 5.2; Rothschild and Stiglitz, "Some Further Results on the Measurement of Inequality", pp. 198–199; and see Chapter 15.6.

14. Again, see Chapter 15.6.

15. On exclusivity, complementarity, and independence, see von Neumann and Morgenstern, *Theory of Games and Economic Behavior*, pp. 17–18, 27; Allais, "The So-Called Allais Paradox and Rational Decisions under Uncertainty", pp. 466–467, 540, 594ff; McClennan, "Sure-Thing Doubts"; Deaton and Muellbauer, *Economics and Consumer Behavior*, Chapter 14.2. The latter display sensitivity to the 'problem' of eligibility in their emphasis on the crucial assumption that "consequences be fully specified so as to contain everything of interest to the agent" and their comment that this proviso is not satisfied in many applications; see pp. 389, 394.

16. Tversky, "Critique of Expected Utility Theory", p. 164.

17. Tversky, "Additivity, Utility and Subjective Probability", p. 178. Whether this constraint is compatible with the sense in which desirabilities may determine probabilities in Jeffrey's theory is not clear to me; see *The Logic of Decision*, pp. 75–77.

18. See Davidson, for example, in "Mental Events", *Essays on Actions and Events*, p. 217.

19. Tversky, "Critique of Expected Utility Theory", p. 166. This requirement seems to be violated in Tversky's case, for example, as discussed in section 5.

20. The independence requirement in expected utility theory is one example of a general kind of requirement imposed in what's known as simultaneous conjoint measurement theory. In general, if there is an effect that seems to depend on several factors, conjoint measurement tries to find measures of those factors in such a way that the overall effect is the sum, or some other simple function, such as the product, of the separate effects as measured. The measures are functions that rescale, or transform, the original factors in order to obtain the simple functional structure sought in relation to the overall effect, but the measures must preserve certain essential properties of each factor. Thus decision theory looks for measures of the separately identifiable factors of belief and preference which show how behaviour depends on them. See Tversky, "Additivity, Utility and Subjective Probability", pp. 176–178; Luce and Tukey, "Simultaneous Conjoint Measurement", pp. 3, 5–6; Luce, "Conjoint Measurement", p. 328. The point of conjoint measurement is to represent how an effect, such as behaviour, depends on a simple relationship between measures of separately identifiable factors.

21. See Keeney and Raiffa, *Decisions with Multiple Objectives*, pp. 90–91; see also Luce and Tukey, "Simultaneous Conjoint Measurement", p. 7.

22. This would be, in effect, to move from the approach in Chapter 3 in Keeney and Raiffa's book to the approach in Chapters 4 through 6.

23. Compare Keeney and Raiffa, *Decisions with Multiple Objectives*, pp. 114, 256–257.

24. See Goodman, "The New Riddle of Induction", in *Fact, Fiction and Forecast*.

25. See Keeney and Raiffa, *Decisions with Multiple Objectives*, Chapters 4–6, especially the helpful geometrical illustrations on p. 254, and the following material on the possibility of transforming the criteria or attributes so that the inter-attribute utility independence conditions are met.

26. Jeffrey gives a clear account of why linear transformations do not matter in Chapter 2 of his *Logic of Decision*.

27. Compare Jeffrey on computing desirabilities and on his Desirability Axiom, *The Logic of Decision*, sections 5.4, 5.5.

28. See, for example, various articles in Allais and Hagen, editors, *Expected Utility Hypotheses and the Allais Paradox*, especially Allais' "The Foundations of a Positive Theory of Choice Involving Risk and a Criticism of the Postulates and Axioms of the American School"; Tversky, "A Critique of Expected Utility Theory"; Kahneman and Tversky, "Prospect Theory"; on rats, see Battalio, Kagel and MacDonald, "Animal Choices over Uncertain Outcomes".

29. The relevant entries in the bibliography under Broome, Kahneman and Tversky, Machina, Tversky, and the three collections edited by Allais and Hagen, Hagen and Wenstop, and Stigum and Wenstop are good places to begin.

30. "To demonstrate, note that if B is chosen over A then, under utility theory (with $U(0)=0$), we obtain $U(400)>1/2U(1,000)$. On the other hand, if C is chosen over D, we obtain $1/10U(1,000)>1/5U(400)$, a contradiction." See Tversky, "Critique of Expected Utility Theory", p. 165.

31. See Tversky, "A Critique of Expected Utility Theory", p. 166.

32. See Broome, "Rationality and the Sure-Thing Principle", p. 20ff; related

points are made by Eells, *Rational Decision and Causality*, pp. 39–40; Tversky, "A Critique of Expected Utility Theory", p. 170ff, and others. But see and compare Hansson, "The Decision Game—The Conceptualisation of Risk and Utility".

33. See Sen, "Information and Invariance in Normative Choice", section 5.

34. Samuelson, "Probability, Utility and the Independence Axiom", pp. 676–677; see also Samuelson, "Utility, Preference and Probability", in, Samuelson, *Collected Scientific Papers of Paul A. Samuelson*, Stiglitz, editor, p. 136; Machina, "'Rational' Decision Making", p. 173.

35. Tversky, "Additivity, Utility and Subjective Probability", p. 198. See also Hagen, "Paradoxes and Their Solutions", p. 8; and see especially the illuminating article "Utility Theory: Axioms vs. Paradoxes", by MacCrimmon and Larson, on the relations among various axiomatizations and paradoxes, pp. 394–397, and *passim*.

36. See Machina, *The Economic Theory of Individual Behavior Toward Risk*, p. 101; see also his " 'Expected Utility' Analysis", p. 305. For the hardy: *mixture dominance* says that if A and B are both preferred to C, then so will be any probability mixture of A and B. *Symmetry* says that if B is indifferent to a 50% chance of A plus a 50% chance of C, then: a p% chance of A plus a (1-p)% chance of C is indifferent to a 50% chance of A plus a 50% chance of B if and only if a (1-p)% chance of A plus a p% chance of C is indifferent to a 50% chance of C plus a 50% chance of B.

37. On this possibility, see Hagen, "Paradoxes and Their Solutions", pp. 11–12.

## Notes to Chapter 5. Interpretation

1. See Putnam, "The Meaning of 'Meaning' ", *Mind, Language and Reality*, for the origin of the slogan.

2. Savage, *The Foundations of Statistics*, p. 101.

3. See Samuelson, "Probability, Utility, and the Independence Axiom", p. 677.

4. See Broome, "Rationality and the Sure-Thing Principle", section 9.

5. Lewis, "New Work for a Theory of Universals", pp. 375–377; see also his article "Putnam's Paradox".

6. Here I follow McDowell's arguments in favour of the latter view, in his "Wittgenstein on Following a Rule".

7. See Kripke, *Wittgenstein on Rules and Private Language*, pp. 40–44. And see, for example, Wittgenstein, *The Brown Book*, I.14–17; II *passim*. See also Pettit, "Wittgenstein, Individualism, and the Mental", on why "the lesson applies in the first person case as well as in the third", p. 450.

8. See Putnam, "The Meaning of 'Meaning' ", in his *Mind, Language and Reality*, and Burge, "Individualism and the Mental", esp. pp. 77ff.

9. But see Davidson, "Knowing One's Own Mind", on this point.

10. Wittgenstein, *Remarks on the Foundations of Mathematics* VI:33. But see Davidson, "Knowing One's Own Mind", for reservations about the "in the head" jargon and an argument that "the mere fact that ordinary mental states and events are individuated in terms of relations to the outside world has no tendency to discredit mental-physical identity theories as such." P. 452.

11. See Burge, "Intellectual Norms and Foundations of Mind." For an example of theorizing about what contracts really are, see Chapter 11 section 1. Pettit describes a Wittgensteinian variation on the anti-individualistic thought experiments that does not depend on any misunderstanding on the part of the subject or on the complexity of the concepts in question. See Pettit, "Wittgenstein, Individualism, and the Mental". He concisely rehearses familiar Wittgensteinian considerations which show that the determination of content needed for there to be a difference between mistakenly

following one rule and following a different rule, for it to be possible for someone to go wrong—or right—cannot be provided by unconstrained interpretation, whether from the third-person perspective or the first-person perspective; introspection of 'what it's like inside' cannot provide the necessary constraints. See, e.g., Wittgenstein, I:188. For more on the Wittgensteinian overtones of Burge's insistence on the constitutive role of the community in an individual's mental life, see McDowell and Pettit's introduction to *Subject, Thought and Context*, p. 10ff.

12. Burge, "Cartesian Error and the Objectivity of Perception", p. 129.

13. Burge, "Individualism and Psychology", pp. 16–17. See also Pettit, "Wittgenstein, Individualism and the Mental", p. 447.

14. Burge, "Cartesian Error and the Objectivity of Perception", pp. 130–131 (see also pp. 125–128), and Burge, "Individualism and Psychology", p. 35 (see also pp. 32–37).

15. See Pettit and McDowell's introduction to *Subject, Thought and Context*, for comments on the differences.

16. I pointed out in note 28 to Chapter 2 that Davidson's rejection of the independence of mind from world entails, but is more radical than, the rejection of psychological individualism, since Davidson would also reject a socialized version of the independence. As far as I can see, Burge's arguments do not require the latter. While there are important differences between Davidson's and Burge's views, in his most recent articles, Burge seems to be moving closer to Davidson's views in several respects. Given the purposes of my exposition here, I shall not try to map out these relationships. See also note 20 below.

17. See especially Burge's remarks about lack of unique fit and constraints running through "Cartesian Error" and "Individualism and Psychology", and the criticism in the former article of the representative theory of perception and the notion that representations might represent in virtue of intrinsic similarties to their objects.

18. See Davidson, "A Coherence Theory of Truth and Knowledge", in Le Pore, editor. *Truth and Interpretation*, pp. 317–318.

19. See Blackburn, *Spreading the Word*, pp. 60–61; Nagel, *The View From Nowhere*, ch. VI (though in places Nagel's concern with antiskeptical consequences *per se* seems to cut across my concern here with whether the route to them is idealistic or not); see also Williams, "Wittgenstein and Idealism", in *Moral Luck*.

20. Davidson, "A Coherence Theory of Truth and Knowledge", in Le Pore, editor, *Truth and Interpretation*, pp. 313, 317. There are, again, important differences between Davidson, Burge, and Lewis. Despite their differences, there is nevertheless significant common ground in the appeal to constitutive constraints on the eligibility of contents.

In a footnote to the above article on p. 318 Davidson notes a tension between his view and the causal theories of reference of Putnam and Kripke. "Those theories look to causal relations between names and objects of which speakers may well be ignorant. The chance of systematic error is thus increased. My causal theory does the reverse by connecting the cause of a belief with its object." See also McGinn, "Radical Interpretation and Epistemology", in Le Pore, editor, *Truth and Interpretation*, and "Charity, Interpretation and Belief". Rorty's contribution to the Le Pore collection, "Pragmatism, Davidson, and Truth", is illuminating on the relationship between what he calls the Kripkean "building-block" approach to reference, and Davidson's views. See also Putnam's views in *Meaning and the Moral Sciences* and in *Reason, Truth and History*; and see Lewis' critique of Putnam in "Putnam's Paradox".

See Davidson, "Knowing One's Own Mind", for comments on the relations between his views and those of Burge. See Pettit and McDowell's introduction to *Subject, Thought and Context* on the relations among Putnam, Burge and Wittgenstein; and see Pettit, "Individualism, Wittgenstein and the Mental", on Burge and Wittgenstein. For a different view, see McGinn, *Wittgenstein on Meaning*.

21. See, for example, Davidson's "The Very Idea of a Conceptual Scheme", pp. 196–197, and "The Method of Truth in Metaphysics", pp. 200, 213, in *Inquiries into Truth and Interpretation*. And compare McDowell's reading, in his "Wittgenstein on Following a Rule", of Wittgenstein's remark at *Philosophical Investigations* I.201, "What this shews is that there is a way of grasping a rule which is not an interpretation."

I emphasize again that constraints on eligibility, or principles of charity, avoid radical indeterminacy, not moderate underdetermination. The premise is not that moderate underdetermination does not obtain—it may well—but that radical indeterminacy does not obtain; if it did, empirical methods would be of no use, as Goodmanesque riddles of induction demonstrate. See Lewis, "Putnam's Paradox", p. 223; and *passim* on how an objective inegalitarianism with respect to the eligibility of contents can avoid going the way of "just more theory" worries about indeterminacy of interpretation; compare Davidson, "Reality Without Reference", in *Inquiries into Truth and Interpretation*.

22. Compare McDowell's Wittgenstein, in "Wittgenstein on Following a Rule", with Nagel's, in *The View From Nowhere*, pp. 105–109, and Kripke's, in *Wittgenstein on Rules and Private Language*. Even Kripke's skeptical Wittgenstein is clear that the paradox about content is not an epistemological problem; it is not a problem about how we, from the outside, *know* what the content of someone else's mind is. It is rather a problem about how there can *be* such a thing as determinate content, even when all the facts, introspective included, are in. The skeptic claims that even if God could see into our minds, he would not see what was meant. See *Kripke, Wittgenstein on Rules and Private Language*, pp. 14–15, 21, 38, 41–44.

23. But compare Lewis in "Putnam's Paradox"; and McGinn, "Radical Interpretation and Epistemology", and, in effect against McGinn, see Rorty, "Pragmatism, Davidson, and Truth". See also Bolton's argument to the effect that "life is no idea", in "Life-form and Idealism".

24. See Harrison, "Transcendental Arguments and Idealism", in Vesey, editor, *Idealism Past and Present*, for a rebuttal of the claim that transcendental arguments import idealism; see also Malcolm, "Wittgenstein and Idealism", in the same collection. See also Seabright, "Explaining Cultural Divergence: A Wittgensteinian Paradox", on the role of causal explanation in a Wittgensteinian view of social science; and the pieces on "The Disappearing 'We' " and "The Allure of Idealism", by Jonathan Lear and Barry Stroud, respectively.

25. A point famously made by Kripke, *Naming and Necessity*, pp. 266, 270–273, in Davidson and Harman, editors, *Semantics of Natural Language*. And Wittgenstein writes: "we are not doing natural science; nor yet natural history—since we can also invent fictitious natural history for our purposes." *Philosophical Investigations*, p. 230.

26. But see Burge in "Intellectual Norms and Foundations of Mind" for qualifications.

27. See Burge on Marr's theory of vision, "Individualism and Psychology".

28. Burge writes that "states and events are individuated so as to set the terms for specific evaluations of them for truth and other types of success. We can judge directly whether conative states are practically successful and cognitive states are veridical. . . . Theories of vision, of belief formation, of memory, learning, decision-making, categorization, and perhaps even reasoning all attribute states that are subject

to practical and semantical evaluation *by reference to standards partly set by a wider environment.*" Burge, "Individualism and Psychology", p. 25. On individualism and teleology, see Martin Davies, "Individualism and Supervenience". For some thought-provoking parallel lines of thought, see Richard Dawkins' fascinating book *The Extended Phenotype.*

29. On higher-order attitudes and the concept of a person, see Frankfurt, "Freedom of the Will and the Concept of a Person"; Taylor, *Human Agency and Language,* and *Philosophy and the Human Sciences* (especially on the explanation and understanding of self-interpreting animals); Dennett, "Conditions of Personhood", in *Brainstorms,* and "The Panglossian Paradigm Defended"; Davidson, "Rational Animals"; with respect to knowledge, see Goldsmith and Sahlin, "The Role of Second-Order Probabilities in Decision Making"; Sahlin, "On Second Order Probabilities and the Notion of Epistemic Risk", and *Secondary Levels in Decision Making.* Compare Aristotle, *Nicomachean Ethics* I.7. On the relation between the biological and functional elements in a theory of human nature, see Wiggins, *Sameness and Substance,* Chapter 6. Note that the naturalism I espouse in this book is not what Wiggins refers to as Ethical Naturalism, and repudiates, but is rather more akin to the view of nature's role in ethics which he himself espouses; see especially section 11 of Wiggin's Chapter 6.

30. See, for example, "Cartesian Error".

31. See, of course, Davidson, "Actions, Reasons and Causes", "Causal Relations", and "Mental Events", in *Essays on Actions and Events.*

32. In Goodman, *Fact, Fiction and Forecast.* See also Putnam in *Meaning and the Moral Sciences* and *Reason, Truth and History,* and Lewis on "Putnam's Paradox".

33. Even Fodor admits that "commonsense attitude ascriptions aren't—or, rather, aren't *solely*—in aid of causal explanation"! "Individualism and Supervenience", p. 243n. The "solely", I would suggest, *can* make room for the view that the reasons for which things are done *are causes,* even though many species of *causal explanation* would not provide the particular kind of understanding that understanding of someone's reasons provides and which commonsense attitude ascriptions are in aid of.

See also Dworkin, *Law's Empire,* p. 51ff, on constructive interpretation and on why "the interpretation of social practices . . . is *essentially* concerned with purposes rather than mere causes"; the discussion of human understanding and its relation to science in the pieces on following a rule and the social sciences by Charles Taylor and Philip Pettit, in Holtzman and Leich, editors, *Wittgenstein: To Follow a Rule*; Pettit's comments on the distinction between regularizing and normalizing explanation, in "Broad-Minded Explanation and Psychology", p. 38ff; and McCulloch, on the relation between superpsychology and folk psychology, in "Scientism, Mind, and Meaning".

34. See Fodor, "Methodological Solipsism Considered as a Research Strategy in Cognitive Psychology", in *Representations,* p. 228ff.

35. See McClennan, "Sure-Thing Doubts", p. 130.

36. See especially Taylor, "Interpretation and the Sciences of Man", and "Understanding and Ethnocentricity", in *Philosophy and the Human Sciences.*

37. See and compare Kim, "Pscyhophysical Laws", p. 386.

38. In this respect I suspect that Wittgenstein's views of the relations among reason, society and nature are further from Hume's, and closer to Aristotle's and Hegel's, than some commentators have suggested. See McGinn, *Wittgenstein on Meaning,* pp. 39ff, 57, 86ff, etc.; and Taylor, "Hegel's Philosophy of Mind", in *Human Language and Agency.*

39. This is a theme that runs throughout the two volumes of Taylor's *Philosophical Papers*.

## Notes to Chapter 6. Subjectivism

1. See Broome, "Rationality and the Sure Thing Principle". For discussion of a related example, see Sen, "Rationality and Uncertainty".

2. Harsanyi, "Non-Linear Social Welfare Functions", *Essays*, pp. 70–71.

3. On this point see also the essays by McDowell, Taylor, and Pettit, in Holtzman and Leich, editors, *Wittgenstein: To Follow a Rule*, on what Pettit describes as the difference between evaluation and prescription, in relation to human understanding and social science.

4. Davidson, "Belief and the Basis of Meaning", in *Essays on Truth and Interpretation*, p. 147.

5. Tversky, "A Critique of Expected Utility Theory", pp. 172–173.

6. See Harsanyi, *Rational Behavior*, Chapter 4, and *Essays*, Part I; Rawls, "Social Unity and Primary Goods"; Kolm, *Justice and Equite*, pp. 28ff, 79ff (as cited by Rawls in "Social Unity and Primary Goods"); Arrow, "Extended Sympathy and the Possibility of Social Choice"; Mackie, *Ethics*, Chapter 4; Hare, *Moral Thinking*, Part II.

7. See Kant, *Foundations of the Metaphysics of Morals*, p. 59; *Critique of Pure Reason*, pp. 19, 26, 33ff; see also pp. 31, 35, etc.

8. Kant, *Critique of Practical Reason*, p. 45.

9. Kant, *Critique of Practical Reason*, p. 72; see also p. 35.

10. See, for example, Harrison, "Kant's Examples of the First Formulation of the Categorical Imperative"; and Taylor, *Hegel and Modern Society*, pp. 72–84. For Hegel's famously influential comments about "this unrestricted possibility of abstraction from every determinate state of mind which I may find in myself . . . my flight from every content as from a restriction", see the Introduction to the *Philosophy of Right*, especially paragraphs 5, 6, 7, 14, 15, 29, 30.

11. See Nell, *Acting on Principle*, esp. Chapters 2, 3, 5, 6, 7; and Herman, "The Practice of Moral Judgment".

12. Harsanyi, *Rational Behavior*, p. 53; see also Rawls, "Social Unity and Primary Goods", section VI; Arrow, "Extended Sympathy and the Possibility of Social Choice"; Hare, *Moral Thinking*, Chapter 6; Mackie on third level universalizability, in *Ethics*, Chapter 4.

13. See my discussion of the role of hypothetical alternatives in deliberation in Chapters 11 and 12; and see, for example, Keeney and Raiffa, *Decisions with Multiple Objectives*, *passim*.

14. See Harsanyi, *Rational Behaviour*, pp. 57–60; Kolm, cited in Rawls, "Social Unity and Primary Goods", pp. 174n, 178; Arrow, "Extended Sympathy and the Possibility of Social Choice", pp. 224–225. See also and compare Stigler and Becker's conception of preferences that "are the same to all men", or at least do not "differ importantly between people", in "De Gustibus Non Est Disputandum", p. 76, and *passim*. Stigler and Becker's position is representative of a distinctive feature of American high culture: its refusal (or failure) to recognize the importance of the distinction between someone's character and the commodities he possesses (—despite the fact that American popular culture is all too susceptible to the difference).

15. Harsanyi, *Rational Behavior*, p. 51.

16. Harsanyi, in *Rational Behavior*, p. 52, and in "Morality and the Theory of Rational Behavior", p. 55.

17. See Harsanyi, *Rational Behavior*, p. 54. See also Sahlin, "Preference Among

Preferences as a Method for Obtaining a Higher-Ordered Metric Scale", on higher-order preferences as an alternative method of establishing an intrapersonal utility measure.

18. Kolm, as cited and translated in Rawls, "Social Unity and Primary Goods", p. 174n.

19. Harsanyi, *Rational Behavior*, pp. 58–60, and *Essays*, pp. 16–17, 50ff.

20. Hare, *Moral Thinking*, pp. 108–110; see also p. 128.

21. That is, the first person case is regarded as unproblematic, in the Cartesian tradition. Indeed, the extended preference approach to the problem of interpersonal comparisons can be seen as a version of the solution by analogy to the problem of other minds, in that it postulates that the basic psychological reactions of others, including the intensities of their preferences, are much the same as my own would be under like conditions. See and compare Harsanyi, "Morality and the Theory of Rational Behaviour", section 5; Davidson, "Judging Interpersonal Interests"; and Strawson's seminal argument that no 'problem of other minds' can be solved by analogy to the first person case, as "one can ascribe states of consciousness to oneself only if one can ascribe them to others", in Strawson, *Individuals*, p. 100, and Chapter 3, *passim*. I would like to, but cannot here, argue that Davidsonian charity is no relative of the argument from analogy, and does not run afoul of Strawsonian considerations.

Compare also MacKay, "Extended Sympathy and Interpersonal Utility Comparisons", on the supposed epistemic advantages of the reduction of interpersonal to first-person intrapersonal comparison, pp. 314–315, 320–322. MacKay casts doubt on the claim that I can know that if I were in some situation then I would prefer that $p$, only if I now prefer that if I were in that situation then $p$, and points out that imagining satisfying counterfactual conditions is not actually satisfying them. Thus *Wittgenstein*: "The balance on which impressions are weighed is not the impression of a balance." *Philosophical Investigations* I:259; see also I:265.

22. Compare: Borgelin, "States and Persons", p. 91ff: Sandel, *Liberalism and the Limits of Justice*, on radically disembodied selves, e.g., pp. 21, 79, etc.

23. See Wittgenstein, *Zettel* I:537, 540–541, on one such representative concern:

You say you attend to a man who groans because experience has taught you that you yourself groan when you feel such-and-such. But as you don't in fact make any such inference, we can abandon the justification by analogy.

It is a help here to remember that it is a primitive reaction to tend, to treat, the part that hurts when someone else is in pain; and not merely when oneself is—and so to pay attention to other people's pain-behaviour, as one does not pay attention to one's own pain behaviour.

But what is the word "primitive" meant to say here? Presumably that this sort of behaviour is prelinguistic: that a language game is based on it, that it is the prototype of a way of thinking and not the result of thought.

24. See Ellsberg, "Risk, Ambiguity, and the Savage Axioms"; Roberts, "Risk, Ambiguity, and the Savage Axioms: Comment", especially the note on p. 335; and the "Reply" by Ellsberg; and see Fellner, "Distortion of Subjective Probabilities as a Reaction to Uncertainty", especially p. 680. Compare Harsanyi, *Essays*, p. 84, note 2.

25. See and compare Frankfurt, "Freedom of the Will and the Concept of a Person"; Taylor, on strong evaluation in "What is Human Agency?", and other essays, in *Human Agency and Language*; Aristotle, *Nicomachean Ethics*, book I.

26. *Nicomachean Ethics* II.1.

27. But see Pettit's distinction between the grasp independence and the guideline dependence of content, in "Wittgenstein, Individualism and the Mental". Where it is appropriate to maintain guideline dependence but not grasp independence, indeterminacy of content may be an alternative to regarding the odd man out either as inconsistent in virtue of drawing ineligible distinctions, or as consistent in virtue of eligible distinctions he fails to draw.

28. See Frankfurt, "Freedom of the Will and the Concept of a Person". See also my discussion of attributions of *akrasia* in Chapter 8.

Rawls suggests that the notion of the one true extended preference ordering "defines persons as what we may call 'bare persons'. Such persons are ready to consider any new convictions and aims, and even to abandon attachments and loyalties, when doing this promises a life with greater overall satisfaction, or well-being, as specifed by a public ranking. The notion of a bare person implicit in the notion of shared highest-order preference represents the dissolution of the person as leading a life expressive of character and of devotion to specific final ends and adopted (or affirmed) values which define the distinctive points of view associated with different (and incommensurable) conceptions of the good." "Social Unity and Primary Goods", pp. 180–181. See also Borgelin, "States and Persons". I have argued that the notion of extended preference requires a theory of human nature—as its proponents generally seem to recognize—and that an adequate theory of human nature must allow for the importance to persons of deliberative and evaluative exercises of higher-order preference and character formation. Perhaps this latter point is less generally recognized by proponents of extended preference. But nevertheless, it seems that some of Rawls' comments about the notion of extended preference may be excessively harsh, and should really be directed toward the inadequate theories of human nature and personality which typically do, but don't necessarily have to, accompany it. The extended preference device *per se* may be salvaged from such inadequate theories; although I have argued that when it allows for the importance of character formation, etc., it can no longer provide support for subjectivism.

29. Unrestricted domain is required as well; for more detailed discussion, see Chapter 13. And see Sen, *Choice, Welfare and Measurement*, pp. 80–83, and essays 13 and 14, as well as "Liberty and Social Choice", pp. 25–26.

30. Sen, *Choice, Welfare and Measurement*, p. 82. See also Taylor on strong evaluation and self-interpretation, throughout his *Philosophical Papers*.

31. See Taylor, "Understanding and Explanation in the *Geisteswissenschaften*", and his *Philosophical Papers*, on the way in which the evaluative language of self-understanding identifies the explananda of social theories in a way that makes human understanding, and criticism of what has been understood possible.

32. The fostering and preservation of the conditions in which such disagreements and arguments can flourish I take to be one of the essential tasks of democracy; see section 10 of this chapter, and Chapter 15.

33. But see Chapters 11 through 13 on the role of settled cases, actual and hypothetical, in deliberation about what should be done, all things considered; and see Dworkin, *Law's Empire*, especially Chapter 6, on the value of integrity and the personification of the community.

34. But for considerations favouring cognitivism, see Chapter 9.

35. Here I am sympathetic to something like Williams' distinction between ethics and morality, and share his sense of the peculiarity of the latter. See *Ethics and the Limits of Philosophy*, pp. 6ff, 174ff; compare the end of Chapter 8.1. On the classical

view of the interdependence of ethics and self-interest see Norman, *The Moral Philosophers*, part I; McDowell, "The Role of *Eudaimonia* in Aristotle's Ethics".

36. Wittgenstein writes: "I am not saying: if such-and-such facts of nature were different people would have different concepts (in the sense of a hypothesis). But: if anyone believes that certain concepts are absolutely the correct ones, and that having different ones would mean not realizing something that we realize—then let him imagine certain very general facts of nature to be different from what we are used to, and the formation of concepts different from the ususal ones will become intelligible to him". *Philosophical Investigations*, p. 230.

37. On the role of human nature, see also the suggestive remarks by Strawson, *Individuals*, p. 112.

38. See Harsanyi, "Morality and the Theory of Rational Behaviour", p. 55.

39. Wittgenstein, *Philosophical Investigations* I:337. In neither case, of course, is this to say that the world and forms of life could not have been at all different, as Wittgenstein's consideration of odd ways of going on amply shows.

### Notes to Chapter 7. Conflict

1. I use *ought* and *should* at large in the way that they are ordinarily used: they are not *stipulatively* restricted to the expression of all-things-considered judgments, either self-interested or ethical, but may be used to express whatever evaluative judgments provide reasons for action (including all-things-considered judgments). Indeed, one of my purposes in this chapter is to show that issues of substance are at stake in understanding the relationships between *ought* and *should* at large, and *ought* and *should, all things considered*, in particular, which are not appropriately addressed by stipulation. I often use *reasons* as short for *reasons for action*.

2. See Williams, "Ethical Consistency", *Problems of the Self*, p. 180; Lemmon, "Deontic Logic and the Logic of Imperatives", p. 47.

3. Compare Chisholm on the unity of consciousness, *The First Person*, p. 88.

4. See von Wright, *Norm and Action*, p. 148; and Williams, "Consistency and Realism", *Problems of the Self*, pp. 197–200. I do not deny that reasons of the same kind, (e.g., toothache avoidance) but with different periods of application (e.g., short term vs. long term) may conflict, and may give rise to *akrasia*. Similarly, reasons for individual action may conflict with reasons for collective action, and may perhaps give rise to *akrasia*; see Chapter 8, Section 1. My concern in this chapter, however, is with issues that *still* arise with respect to reasons for action that *cannot* be distinguished by relativity to different time periods or different agents in this way. With respect to such reasons (e.g., all one's various longest-term, self-interested reasons, some of which will be of the same kind, others of which will be of different kinds), the two options sketched in the text, and the distinction between *prima facie* and *pro tanto* reasons developed in section 3, still apply. See also note 7 on obligations to different people.

5. Again, holding other possible sources of conflict constant, such as relativization to different periods of application, agents, or objects of obligation. I will not recite this unwieldy qualification every time it is appropriate, but readers should keep it in mind.

6. Compare Scotch and Jennings, "Non-Kripkean Deontic Logic"; Ross, *The Right and the Good*, p. 24. Schotch and Jennings defend the principle that *ought* implies *can* at the expense of unrestricted agglomerativity (which they call complete aggregation) by distinguishing substantive from formal moves in moral theory:

> . . . there are no demonstrations in moral philosophy that absolute obligations cannot conflict; certainly the existence of a distinction (which we grant) between

these and prima facie obligations does not, by any stretch of the imagination, prove that the 'no conflict' position is correct. It is mere stipulation to insist that of two apparently conflicting obligations one will finally emerge as absolute and override the other, prima facie, one. As Russell remarks: 'the method of postulating what we want has many advantages; these are the same as the advantages of theft over honest toil'.

Until there is a convincing argument against the possibility of moral conflict (in the light of ordinary moral experience could any such argument be convincing?) we must keep an open mind. With seemly restraint we insist only that moral theory at least recognize their possibility.

Suppose then that we wish to capture formally some features of general moral reasoning. . . . We would certainly want to include among our deontic principles [the principle that *ought* implies *can*], because that principle cuts across all moral theories. Were one to adopt . . . the principle . . . of complete aggregation [the same as unrestricted agglomerativity], one would then be committed to the view that if both a and b ought to be the case then a and b are consistent. This clearly flies in the face of our resolution to keep an open mind concerning conflicting obligations. To put the matter brutally, there can be no deontic logic which takes as a primitive law, the principle . . . [of unrestricted agglomerativity]. Pp. 155–156.

7. Consider Rawls' views on the relationship between justice and utility, or Sen's on the inconsistency of Paretian liberalism. Foot claims that obligations to keep promises may conflict with one another other than apparently, while Sidgwick suggests that conflicting promises are like marriages to different people in that only one can be valid at a time. Surely obligations to respect the autonomy of others or to preserve human life may conflict, when the autonomy or life of more than one person is involved, and the obligations aren't merely apparent. But perhaps relativization of obligations to different persons as well as immediately to different kinds of reason renders the agglomeration principle inapplicable; perhaps respect for the autonomy of others just does require us to treat them as distinct sources of reasons. It's not clear that obligations to respect autonomy (or to preserve life) may conflict when the autonomy (or life) if only one person is involved; here we may well be right to take the second option and say: respect for that person's autonomy demands one thing or demands another, but not both. See and compare Slote, "Selective Necessity and the Free-will Problem", p. 12; Marcus, "Moral Dilemmas and Consistency", p. 125; Foot, "Moral Realism and Moral Dilemma", p. 383; Sidgwick, *Methods of Ethics*, p. 311.

Again, my concern is not to deny the possibility of conflict with respect to reasons for action that may be of the same kind but yet be distinguishable with respect to time periods, agents, or objects of obligation. My concern is rather with the further possibility of conflict, and corresponding distinctions of kind, with respect to reasons not distinguishable in the former ways.

8. Compare Castaneda, "On the Semantics of the Ought-to-Do", pp. 687–692; Scotch and Jennings, section 5; Marcus, "Moral Dilemmas and Consistency", p. 134; Searle, " 'Prima facie' Obligations".

9. *Pace* Hintikka, who claims that by using different symbols for different kinds of obligation, rather than by defining different kinds of obligation in terms of one primitive notion, we obscure the logical relationship between them; see " 'Prima facie'

Obligations and Iterated Modalities", p. 232. The logical relationships between specific *pro tanto* reasons and all-things-considered judgments are more complex than Hintikka's notation registers. See Chapter 12.

10. For alternatives and some criticisms of them, see Hintikka, " 'Prima Facie' Obligations and Iterated Modalities", and "Some Main Problems of Deontic Logic"; the exchange between Bergstrom and Hintikka in *Theoria*; Searle, " 'Prima facie' Obligations"; Lewis, *Counterfactuals*, Chapter 5.1.

11. Both with respect to probabilities and reasons for action, the propositions expressed by $q$, $-q$, $e$, and $r$ may be taken to indicate your favourite *relata*: states of affairs (in which it rains, in which the act is done), events (its raining, the doing of the act), or whatever. I have been sloppy on this point for the sake of ease of expression and because I don't think it affects my argument.

12. See Chisholm, "Practical Reason the the Logic of Requirement"; Davidson, "How is Weakness of the Will Possible?" in *Essays on Action and Events*, pp. 37–38; Hempel, *Aspects of Scientific Explanation*, p. 64.

13. See Davidson, "How is Weakness of the Will Possible?", *Essays on Actions and Events*, p. 37.

14. For reason to doubt such independent specifiability, see McDowell, "Non-Cognitivism and Rule-Following".

15. Davidson, "How is Weakness of the Will Possible?", *Essays on Actions and Events*, p. 39.

16. Here I am indebted to Mark Sainsbury.

17. See Pears, *Motivated Irrationality*, pp. 73–74, 178–181.

There are other differences between desire and belief that may be explained by our admitting the possibility of ultimate conflict between reasons for action but not between reasons for belief. For example, I can consciously desire to desire that not $q$ (for one reason) without ceasing to desire that $q$ (for another reason), but I can't consciously believe that I believe that not $q$ and consciously believe that $q$. Furthermore: if I believe that if $p$ then $q$ and I intend that $p$, it doesn't necessarily follow that I intend that $q$. One might speculate that if reasons for action could not conflict, intention would be imputed to known consequences of what one intends; it is not so imputed just because we recognize that conflict may be unavoidable. But if we switch the operators, the intention does follow: if I intend that if $p$ then $q$ and I believe that $p$, then I intend that $q$. Consider the use of an innocent bystander by a terrorist to shield himself against police fire: he does not intend that a shot be fired, but he believes one will be and intends that if a shot is fired it kill the innocent bystander rather than him. If a shot is fired and the innocent bystander is killed, the terrorist would be regarded as having intended that the bystander be killed. The example is due to Marianne Constable.

18. Chisholm, "Practical Reason and the Logic of Requirement", p. 50; and see pp. 10, 14, 52–53; Hempel, *Aspects of Scientific Explanation*, pp. 63ff, 394ff; Carnap, *Logical Foundations of Probability*, pp. 211ff, 253ff; Mackie, *Truth, Probability and Paradox*, pp. 167, 195–197, 228–229.

19. Compare Ross, *The Right and the Good*, pp. 19–20, 28–29, 41; Marcus, "Moral Dilemmas and Consistency", pp. 124–125; Castaneda, "Imperatives, Oughts and Moral Oughts", p. 287ff.

20. The subscript "$t$" relates to considerations of *t*heoretical coherence associated with all-things-considered judgments. See Part III.

21. Further illumination of these cryptic remarks is to be found in Chapter 15.

Compare Sandel, *Liberalism and the Limits of Justice*, p. 167; Berlin, *Four Essays on Liberty*, p. 133; Nussbaum, "Shame, Separateness, and Political Unity", in Rorty, editor, *Essays on Aristotle's Ethics*, p. 406.

How is the issue whether conflicting reasons for action are *prima facie* or *pro tanto* related to the question of centralism, discussed in Chapter 2? To represent conflicting reasons as *prima facie* is to preserve their ultimate unity, whereas to represent them as *pro tanto* is to allow that they may conceivably be reasons of different kinds and may ultimately conflict with one another, in the way that different person's wills may ultimately conflict. The centralist view that the general concepts are prior to specific reason-giving concepts would seem to prompt the representation of the reason-giving force of specific concepts as uniform, as expressed in some way by the general concepts: acts of this kind have a tendency to be right, or that an act is of this kind is good evidence for its being right, or something along those lines. But the non-centralist interdependence view leaves the uniformity question open. A non-centralist about reasons for action may want to allow that different specific reasons for action can ultimately conflict, so not represent them uniformly. But we might want to be non-centralists about reasons for belief, and so reject the view that general concepts of truth and validity are prior to and independent of various specific reasons for belief, yet still maintain some kind of consistency constraint on ultimate reasons for belief, and thus represent them uniformly. This is a matter of the unity of the truth, rather than its priority and independence. The unity issue cuts across the priority issue to this extent: centralism supports a unitary conception of reasons as *prima facie*, but non-centralism permits reasons to be conceived as either *prima facie* or *pro tanto*. If we believe independently that reasons are not *prima facie* but rather are *pro tanto* (as we may in the case of reasons for action), this would cut against a centralist view of them. But if we believe independently that they are *prima facie* (as we may in the case of reasons for belief), this would not cut against a non-centralist account of them.

22. "Paradoxes of Irrationality"; Pears, *Motivated Irrationality*, especially Chapters V and VIII. See also Aristotle, *Nicomachean Ethics*: "for where objects differ in kind the part of the soul answering to each of the two is different in kind", book VI, section 1; see also book IX, section 4, on the analogy between relations between persons and relations within persons.

### Notes to Chapter 8. *Akrasia*

1. *Nicomachean Ethics* VII.11.
2. See Arrow, *Social Choice and Individual Values*, second edition, p. 105.
3. Parfit, *Reasons and Persons*, p. 33ff.
4. In his "Weakness of the Will and the Free Rider Problem". See and compare Parfit, *Reasons and Persons*, section 34. See also McClennan's remarks on the possibility of intrapersonal co-ordination in Allais Paradox situations, and its relation to the co-operative resolve that may be called for in Prisoner's Dilemmas, in his "Prisoner's Dilemma and Resolute Choice", in Campbell and Sowden, editors, *Paradoxes of Rationality and Cooperation*.
5. This might seem to approach the idea of a split personality; but the latter involves in addition each personality having some of the attributes of deliberative coherence characteristic of personality, so that the split persists into the higher-order attitudes. Subsystemic divisions *per se*, by contrast, are first-order and are, in the normal case, the basis for the pursuit of deliberative coherence out of which personality emerges. Both types of case are possible.

I thus seem to differ with Elster over why the temporal dimension is essential to the intrapersonal cases; see the assertions in sections I, VI, and VII of his "Weakness of Will and the Free Rider Problem" about the "indivisibility of persons", which I do not accept, at least not for the purposes he puts them to. He discusses different-goal cases, but what he says about the role of time seems more appropriate to shared-goal cases; see note 9.

Jean Hampton has pointed out to me, with respect to examples of purported intrapersonal Prisoner's Dilemmas involving strictly temporally identified person-stages, that it may be hard to see why it should be better for the earlier person-stages if all do than if all do not tidy, jog, or whatever.

6. What is supposed is a pay-off matrix such that the manic and the depressive have the following preference orderings with respect to drug-taking:

| Manic: | Depressive: |
|---|---|
| D does, M does not | D does not, M does |
| D does, M does | D does, M does |
| D does not, M does not | D does not, M does not |
| D does not, M does | D does, M does not |

However, it might also be possible to analyze such a case in terms of repeated Prisoner's Dilemmas and reputation effects.

7. See Schelling, *The Strategy of Conflict*, on the importance of pure coordination problems, esp. pp. 54ff, 71ff, and Chapter 4. He writes that "the limiting case of pure coordination isolates the essential feature of the corresponding nonzero-sum game" and explains: "It is to be stressed that the pure-coordination game is a game of strategy in the strict technical sense. It is a behavior situation in which each player's best choice of action depends on the action he expects the other to take, which he knows depends, in turn, on the other's expectations of his own. This interdependence of expectations is precisely what distinguishes a game of strategy from a game of chance or a game of skill. In the pure-coordination game the interests are convergent; in the pure-conflict game the interests are divergent; but in neither case can a choice of action be made wisely without regard to the dependence of the outcome on the mutual expectations of the players." "The essential game-of-strategy element is . . . : the best choice for either depends on what he expects the other to do, knowing that the other is similarly guided, so that each is aware that each must try to guess what the second guesses the first will guess the second to guess and so on, the the familiar spiral of reciprocal expectations", pp. 86–7; see also p. 70. And see Lewis, *Convention*.

8. See and compare Regan, *Utilitarianism and Co-operation*, pp. 132–3.

9. Intrapersonal versions of the shared-goal problems he addresses are considered by Regan in *Utilitarianism and Co-operation*, at pp. 40–41, 150, etc. The distinction between subsystems now becomes essentially intertemporal, since differing goals do not serve to distinguish subsystems. Recall my comments on Elster in note 5.

10. See Regan in *Utilitarianism and Co-operation* on collective agency at, e.g., pp. 134–135, 144–145, 178, 186–187, 207–208, 211, and *passim*. He speaks of joint efforts, shared tasks, common projects and undertakings, taking part in group activity, and discusses what it means for a theory to direct an individual to participate in a group action. The comments he makes on the page I've cited must be understood in terms of the conception of Co-operative Utilitarianism which he develops, and in particular in terms of the distinction he draws between "subjective exclusively act-oriented", such as a "subjective" (his use of this term is very different from mine) version of Act Utilitarianism, which takes subjective probabilities about what others will do into account, and "objective non-exclusively act-oriented" theories, such as

Co-operative Utilitarianism. Given the Davidsonian conception of rationality in terms of beliefs and desires I have developed in Part I, I am most concerned with theories of rational action that do take explicit account of agents' beliefs; see the discussion of versions of individualism that take account of subjective probabilities in section 3.

With respect to different-goal cases, see Gauthier, "Maximization Constrained: The Rationality of Cooperation", pp. 78–83, on the distinctive character of action based on joint strategies.

11. See Gibbard, "Rule Utilitarianism: An Illusory Alternative?"; and Regan, *Utilitarianism and Co-operation*, especially Chapter 4.

12. See Parfit, *Reasons and Persons*, p. 91.

13. These points have been made clearly and at length by Regan, Parfit, and others; I refer readers to whom they are not familiar to their discussions. See, e.g., Parfit, *Reasons and Persons*, sections 21, 26, 33; and Regan, *Utilitarianism and Co-operation*, Chapters 2, 3, and *passim*.

However, as indicated, these claims must be qualified with respect to versions of individualism that take into account subjective probabilities. In the shared-goal electoral reform example discussed in section 3, for example, individualistic rationality *may* guarantee failure from the collective point of view. In that case, if the subjective probability of any given person's voting is not sufficiently high to justify voting in individualistic terms, then even if more than 90% do in fact vote, voting will not have been individualistically rational. Here I am indebted to Derek Parfit.

14. It was made to me by David Charles

15. As Schelling emphasizes in *The Strategy of Conflict*.

16. See Gibbard, "Rule Utilitarianism: Merely an Illusory Alternative?", p. 219. See also Regan in *Utilitarianism and Co-operation* on what's wrong with Rule Utilitarianism and Utilitarian Generalization (see especially Chapters 5, 6, 7), and on how Co-operative Utilitarianism constitutes an improvement over the latter two theories as well as over Act Utilitarianism.

17. See and compare Regan in *Utilitarianism and Co-operation* on what is desirable about the property of adaptability, and on why theories such as Act and Rule Utilitarianism, which in effect take the unit of agency as fixed, must fail to have this desirable property. A theory is *adaptable* iff, in any situation involving choices by any number of agents, the agents who satisfy the theory in that situation produce by their acts taken together the best consequences that they can possibly produce by any pattern of behaviour, given the behaviour of agents who do not satisfy the theory. His own theory, Co-operative Utilitarianism, advocates co-operating with whoever else is co-operating in the production of best consequences. It does not take the unit of agency as fixed, in my sense, and it is adaptable.

18. Regan, developing suggestions made by Schelling with respect to pure co-ordination games, in effect provides one way of answering this question, by determining who else besides oneself, or how many others, stand ready to co-operate, with whoever else is co-operating, in producing the best consequences possible, given the behaviour of non-co-operators. See Regan, *Utilitarianism and Co-operation*, p. 134, 198. The heart of his discussion involves showing how it is possible to determine the class of persons who stand ready to co-operate with whoever else is co-operating, without becoming trapped in an endless regress or a fruitless indeterminacy.

19. See Regan, *Utilitarianism and Co-operation*, e.g., p. 137, and *passim*.

20. As motive utilitarians recognize. See Regan's Chapters 8 through 12 for a carefully-worked out consequentialist answer in terms of co-operation with whoever else is co-operating.

21. Compare Quattrone and Tversky, "Self-Deception and the Voter's Illusion", p. 55. Consider also individual gambles that form part of a systematic gambling strategy that will, as a statistical matter, pay off in the long run.

22. See Regan, *Utilitarianism and Co-operation*, under 'voting' in index; compare Quattrone and Elster, "Self-Deception and the Voter's Illusion"; and Elster, "Weakness of the Will and the Free Rider Problem".

23. See Quattrone and Tversky, "Self-Deception and the Voter's Illusion", p. 50.

24. The reasoning involved in the diagnostic interpretation is similar in certain respects to that found in evidential decision theory for "one-box" solutions to Newcomb's Problem. (See Campbell and Sowden's introduction to *Paradoxes of Rationality and Cooperation*.) I would argue, but cannot do so here, that varying intuitive responses across a range of cases that equally admit of evidentialist reasoning are better explained in terms of a temptation to participate in collective action than in terms of a temptation to evidentialism.

25. On these points see Regan, on what co-operative action requires, *Utilitarianism and Co-operation*, pp. 124–130.

26. Regan writes: "Act-utilitarianism tells each agent in effect to take the behaviour of all others as given. Rule-utilitarianism and utilitarian generalization, in their pure forms, tell each agent in effect to ignore others' behaviour entirely. Only CU [Co-operative Utilitarianism] embodies an approach to others' behaviour which emphasizes constantly that, whoever the agents are who are willing to try to produce the best consequences possible, they are engaged in a common project.

. . . To be sure, act-utilitarianism requires each agent to engage, when he has the opportunity, in behaviour which will improve others' behaviour or which will increase the likelihood of desirable co-ordination. . . . But there is still a fundamental dichotomy between the agent's own behaviour and everyone else's. The point of view embodied in the act-utilitarian's ultimate criterion of right behaviour is the point of view of one agent alone. It is not the point of view of an agent who is participating in a joint effort.

. . . The follower of CU neither ignores other co-operators' behaviour nor treats it as merely part of the circumstances in which he acts. Instead, he identifies his fellow co-operators and then self-consciously joins in a shared effort to produce the best possible consequences. . . . I suggest that [an] aspect of taking others seriously as persons may be viewing one's own behaviour and other co-operators' behaviour as equally contributions to a common undertaking." See *Utilitarianism and Co-operation*, pp. 207, 208, 211.

For related points about different-goal cases, see Sen, "Goals, Commitment and Identity."

27. See Elster, "Weakness of Will and the Free Rider Problem", who considers intrapersonal analogues of the behaviour of Quattrone and Tversky's Party Supporters. In the Party Supporter's case the subjects are supposed to have reasoned: If I do it, others will, so I will. In the intrapersonal analogue, someone reasons: If I do it now, i.e., refrain from drinking, I'll do it later, so I'll do it now. Elster considers that in the absence of causal connections between the acts in question, the reasoning is arguably rational in the intrapersonal case because of the way in which earlier choices may affect one's self-image or conception of the kind of person one is. But he regards the reasoning in the interpersonal case as clearly irrational, and does not consider the way in which concern with the quality of agency may provide an interpretation of the behaviour in question which renders it too arguably rational. The difference, he simply asserts at several points, is due to the "indivisibility of persons."

28. Derek Parfit has made this objection. See and compare Harsanyi, "Use of

Subjective Probabilities in Game Theory", and "The Tracing Procedure"; Bernheim, "Rationalizable Strategic Behavior"; Pearce, "Rationalizable Strategic Behavior and the Problem of Perfection; Myerson, "Refinements of the Nash Equilibrium Concept"; van Damme, "Refinements of the Nash Equilibrium Concept".

29. The work that salience, and expectations of what one another will do in this argument could also be done by specifying payoffs in Figure 8.2, so that the gap between the best and second-best outcomes is significantly greater than that between the second best and worst outcomes. If this difference is large enough, it may be rational for each to push even if neither could begin by assuming each was at least as likely to push as not, and this in turn would give each a reason to believe the other would indeed push:

You

|  | push your button | do not push your button |
|---|---|---|
| push my button | best e.g., 1,000 utiles each, 2,000 total | equal worst e.g., 0 utiles each |
| do not push my button | equal worst e.g., 0 utiles each | 2nd best e.g., 1 utile each, 2 total |

(Left margin label: I)

Alternatively, it may be argued, each of a pair of Bayesians may begin by assuming that the other is as likely to push as not. Each will, then, independently of the specific magnitudes of the pay-offs, prefer a 50% chance of the best outcome plus a 50% chance of the worst outcome to a 50% chance of the second-best outcome to a 50% chance of the worst outcome, and so will both push. See Regan, *Utilitarianism and Co-operation*, pp. 25–26.

Again, however, I do not claim that individualism is inadequate in all cases, only in some. In the electoral reform voting case discussed below, the gaps between the pay-offs may be assumed not to support the first of the above arguments. Moreover, as I argue below, the second, Bayesian argument will not work, given the many-person structure of that case.

30. See Regan, *Utilitarianism and Co-operation*, pp. 24–26, 119, 167, 173–174, and especially p. 189. On a related point for different-goal cases, see Gauthier's remarks "Maximization Constrained" on the distinctness of what he calls "straight-forward maximization" and "constrained maximization", pp. 78–83, 91–93; the latter may support the rationality of co-operation under conditions in which the former would not.

31. See Aumann, "Agreeing to Disagree". Aumann proved that if two people have the same priors, and their posteriors for a given event A are common knowledge, then these posteriors must be equal.

In general, the necessary calculations of expectations may depend on the magnitudes specified in the pay-off matrix, not just on the ordering of possible outcomes. I have abstracted from this aspect of the problem for the sake of ease of presentation, since magnitudes can evidently be specified to suit my argument. See also note 29.

32. Regan, *Utilitarianism and Co-operation*, p. 144. My emphasis. Compare, for example, Downs, pp. 29, 151, 152, 250, 267–268.

33. See Schelling, *The Strategy of Conflict*, pp. 70, 92–93, 98, 106–108.

34. See Lewis, "Utilitarianism and Truthfulness".

35. See and compare my claims in Chapter 15 about full structure: what I there call vertical distinctions, which cut between persons, and horizontal distinctions, which cut within and across persons, are equally fundamental.

36. Note that I do not claim that persons have the capacity to determine their own identities *entirely*; indeed, I find the suggestion that they might fairly unintelligible, for reasons put forward in the discussion of Campbell's incompatibilism in Chapter 15, section 1. I argue in Chapter 15 that social and environmental constraints on self-understanding are not only not a threat to autonomous personhood, but necessary to it.

37. Thus Aristotle: "Those who use the term as one of reproach ascribe self-love to people who assign to themselves the greater share of wealth, honours, and bodily pleasures.... So those who are grasping with regard to these things gratify their appetites and in general their feelings and the irrational element of the soul; and most men are of this nature (which is the reason why the epithet has come to be used as it is—it takes its meaning from the prevailing type of self-love, which is a bad one); justly, therefore, are men who are lovers of self in this way reproached for being so. That it is those who give themselves the preference in regard to objects of this sort that most people usually call lovers of self is plain; for if a man were always anxious that he himself, above all things, should act justly, temperately, or in accordance with any other of the virtues, and in general were always to try to secure for himself the honourable course, no one would call such a man a lover of self or blame him.

But such a man would seem more than the other a lover of self; at all events he assigns to himself the things that are noblest and best, and gratifies the most authoritative element in himself and in all things obeys this; and just as a city or any other systematic whole is most properly identified with the most authoritative element in it, so is a man; and therefore the man who loves this and gratifies it is most of all a lover of self.

[H]e may even give up actions to his friend; it may be nobler to become the cause of his friend's acting than to act himself. In all the actions, therefore, that men are praised for, the good man is seen to assign to himself the greater share in what is noble. In this sense . . . a man should be a lover of self." *Nicomachean Ethics* IX.8.

Gauthier's account of the rationality of constrained maximization (which involves choices of dispostions to choose) in different-goal cases is in certain respects complementary to my argument about shared-goal cases. He too emphasizes the importance of recognizing the capacity of persons for self-determination in an adequate theory of human rationality. He writes: "there is a further significance in our appeal to a choice among dispositions to choose for we suppose that the capacity to make such choices is itself an essential part of human rationality. We could imagine beings so wired that only straightforward maximization [which does not involve reflection on and choice among dispositions to choose] would be a psychologically possible mode of choice in strategic contexts. Hobbes may have thought that human beings were so wired, that we were straightforward maximizing machines. But if he thought this, then he was surely mistaken. At the core of our rational capacity is the ability to engage in self-critical reflection. The fully rational being is able to reflect on his standard of deliberation and to change that standard in the light of reflection". (Compare my claims in the last paragraph of Chapter 6.3.) Gauthier also comments on the way in which the traditional distinction between self-interest and morality is blurred by a conception of rationality adequate to persons. See his "Maximization Constrained", p. 90.

38. Davidson, "Belief and the Basis of Meaning", in *Inquiries into Truth and Interpretation*, p. 153.

39. See and compare Davidson, who writes in "Paradoxes of Irrationality": "To constitute a structure of the required sort, a part of the mind must show a larger degree of consistency or rationality than is attributed to the whole. Unless this is the case, the point of the analogy with social interaction is destroyed." And: "What is called for is organized elements, within each of which there is a fair degree of consistency, and where one element can operate on another in the modality of nonrational causality", pp. 300, 301.

40. I owe this example to Paul Seabright.

41. *U.S. v. Beechum*, p. 148.

42. *People v. Zackowitz*, p. 97.

43. See Kahneman and Tversky, Essays 8, 10 and 34 in *Judgment Under Uncertainty: Heuristics and Biases*, Kahneman, Slovic, and Tversky, editors, especially pp. 156–158; Cohen: *The Probable and the Provable*; "On the Psychology of Prediction: Whose is the Fallacy?", and the resulting exchange with Kahneman and Tversky; "Are People Programmed to Commit Fallacies?"; "Can Human Irrationality Be Experimentally Demonstrated?", with commentary, author's response, and continuing commentary; Thomson, "Remarks on Causation and Liability"; Goldsmith, "Studies of a Model for Evaluating Judicial Evidence"; Gardenfors, "Probabilistic Reasoning and Evidentiary Value".

Other related cases are discussed in the literature. Suppose you have either dangerous disease A or equally dangerous disease B but you don't know which, and the treatments for them are incompatible. If 85% of the people with either one or the other have disease A and 15% have disease B, but a 20% reliable test administered to you says you have disease B, which treatment would you choose to have? (This example is due to L. J. Cohen.) Or, suppose a bishop with no motive to lie and 99.99% reliable eyesight draws the winning lottery ticket and then destroys it, and reports that it was ticket #1,598,017. Do you believe him, or does the prior improbability of that ticket being drawn (out of say two million) outweigh the reliability of his eyesight?

I make further related arguments about some of Ellsberg's experiments, which concern the distinction between known risk and uncertainty rather than the distinction between causal and incidental base rates, in Chapter 15 section 6.

### Notes to Chapter 9. Cognitivism

1. Williams, "Ethical Consistency", in *Problems of the Self*, p. 175; see also "Consistency and Realism", pp. 204–205; and Berlin, "Two Concepts of Liberty", in *Four Essays on Liberty*, pp. 167–172.

2. See Williams, "Ethical Consistency", *Problems of the Self*, p. 172ff.

3. See Peacocke, "Intention and Akrasia" and Davidson's reply, in the same volume; see also Charles, "Rationality and Irrationality".

4. Kolakowski, "In Praise of Inconsistency", p. 234.

5. Compare Foot, "Moral Realism and Moral Dilemma"; Guttenplan, "Moral Realism and Moral Dilemmas".

6. The inference depends in no way on what Dummett calls the "wholly superfluous" content-stroke. See Dummett, *Frege*, pp. 314–315; see also pp. 255–256; see

also and compare Hare, "Meaning and Speech Acts", in *Practical Inferences*, pp. 82, 87, 92.

7. Frege, "Negation", in *Logical Investigations*, pp. 46–47. Compare Searle, *Speech Acts*, pp. 136–141.

8. Dummett, *Frege*, p. 327. See also Frege, "Compound Thoughts", in *Logical Investigations*.

9. See Geach, "Assertion", in *Logic Matters*, pp. 262, 268.

10. See Dummett, *Frege*, pp. 345–348; compare Geach, "Critical Notice", p. 441.

11. See Dummett, *Frege*, p. 348.

12. Dummett, *Frege*, pp. 350–351.

13. Dummett, *Frege*, p. 351.

14. See Dummett, *Frege*, pp. 351–354.

15. See Geach, "Critical Notice", p. 439.

16. See Geach, "Assertion", p. 269.

17. On how to account for the Moore paradoxes and performative antinomies, see, *inter alia*, Hintikka, *Knowledge and Belief*, p. 64ff; and Lakoff, "Pragmatics in Natural Logic". See also Hintikka on the performative reading of the *cogito*, in "*Cogito, Ergo Sum*: Inference or Performance?".

18. Blackburn, "Moral Realism", p. 121.

19. In correspondence, and in *Spreading the Word*, pp. 192–195.

20. See Blackburn, *Spreading the Word*, p. 194.

21. See Blackburn, *Spreading the Word*, p. 193.

22. See Blackburn, "Moral Realism", p. 121; *Spreading the Word*, p. 195.

23. Thus, Blackburn's account of "the Frege point", which he claims is "very simple" (*Spreading the Word*, pp. 189–190), does not really do it justice. It is not enough to meet Frege's point to give, as Blackburn puts it, "any account at all of these [unasserted] contexts" (p. 191); it must be one which respects the uniformity intuition.

24. See Blackburn, *Spreading the Word*, p. 191.

## Notes to Chapter 10. Theory

1. The standard version is distinguishable, according to Putnam, from the real Quine's views; see especially p. 177ff of "The Refutation of Conventionalism", *Mind, Language and Reality*.

2. The term *conventionalism* may be a misleading label for some of the doctrines that fit Putnam's model; see note 10. The use I make of Putnam's critique of conventionalism in pursuing an alternative to centralism does not depend on any particular view of the relationship between conventionalism and centralism; for present purposes, the connection between them is simply that they have a salient common alternative: a non-centralist coherence account.

3. Hilary Putnam, "The Refutation of Conventionalism", *Mind, Language and Reality*, at pp. 163–164.

4. Putnam, "The Refutation of Conventionalism", *Mind, Language and Reality*, pp. 159–165.

5. Willard Van Orman Quine, "Two Dogmas of Empiricism", *From a Logical Point of View*, pp. 44–46.

6. Putnam, "The Refutation of Conventionalism", *Mind, Language and Reality*, pp. 164–168.

7. Putnam, "The Refutation of Conventionalism", *Mind, Language and Reality*, pp. 168–171.

8. Putnam, "The Refutation of Conventionalism", *Mind, Language and Reality*, pp. 155, 163–164.

9. See Blackburn, "Moral Realism", especially section II; but compare his later work on "quasi-realism".

10. See Hare, *Moral Thinking*, p. 171 and Chapters 5 and 10 generally. Thus Hare may have given a way of refuting forms of emotivism that are conventionalist in Putnam's sense by appealing to universalizability and without appealing to coherence; however, for grounds for doubt that the materials Hare allows himself are sufficient to avoid the indeterminacy problem, see my discussion in Chapter 6. In developing Putnam's suggestions about coherence, I shall depend on substantive constraints on eligiblity as well as formal constraints, such as supervenience, to show that coherence is possible. If Hare's strategy does succeed, however, and if there is no sense in which attitudes may supervene on naturalistic descriptions of alternatives without also being universalizable across changes in personal identity, as Hare also suggests, then the implications of Blackburn's view may not be conventionalist in Putnam's sense either.

On the other hand, Putnam's model may apply to some forms of certain cognitivist accounts, such as ethical intuitionism, or subjectivism. It may seem odd to suggest that subjectivism is a form of conventionalism, since the point of subjectivism seems to be to claim that the meaning of the general ethical concepts is such as to render them applicable or not entirely in virtue of facts about the individual speaker. However, emotivism, which Putnam himself suggests does fit his model, similarly translates away apparent substantive disagreement; the cognitivist/non-cognitivist distinction does not seem to be crucial here. Perhaps the model is misnamed; instead of convention, judicial discretion, or nothing at all, may decide between apparently conflicting judgments. But such a misnomer would be of little consequence. The point is that coherence can do what is needed, not that it ousts convention in particular.

11. See Hart, *The Concept of Law*, pp. 89–107 and 144–150, and Dworkin on legal positivism, in *Taking Rights Seriously*, p. 17ff. But note the limitations of Hart's sympathy for rule-skepticism, e.g., p. 150.

12. "Responsible" in the sense in which internal skepticism is, and external skepticism is not, responsible. See Dworkin, *Law's Empire*, pp. 76–86.

13. Hare, *Freedom and Reason*, p. 163; see also p. 162.

14. Compare Dworkin on the role of legal paradigms, in *Law's Empire*, e.g., pp. 63, 91, 138, etc. See and compare Putnam on the possibility of *empirical* undetermination that remains even after the conventionalist's threatened *proof* of indeterminancy has failed, in "The Refutation of Coonventionalism", *Mind, Language and Reality*.

15. See, for example, Hare, *The Language of Morals*, Chapter 5; *Moral Thinking*, pp. 18, 69.

16. See and compare Putnam, *Reason, Truth and History*, p. 208; Moore, *Principia Ethica*, p. 40.

17. See Williams, *Ethics and the Limits of Philosophy*, p. 99 and ch. 6, *passim*, and also Williams' review of Parfit's *Reasons and Persons, London Review of Books*, 7–20 June 1984, penultimate paragraph.

18. See Wittgenstein, *Philosophical Investigations* I:199–202, 217, etc. Compare Dworkin on legal practices, in *Taking Rights Seriously*, pp. 87, 104–109, 119–122, 126–127, 159–168, 283 (but see also Nickel, "Dworkin on the Nature and Consequences of Rights", pp. 1119–1123; and Dworkin, "Seven Critics", p. 1258). See also *Law's*

*Empire*, pp. 62ff, 90ff, etc., where the apparent influence of Wittgenstein's views is even more noticeable.

19. For Dworkin's views on this question, see Dworkin, "No Right Answer?", pp. 58–84; "Justice and Rights", in *Taking Rights Seriously*, pp. 159–168; and Dworkin on Munzer in "Seven Critics", pp. 1241–1250. And see Putnam, "The Refutation of Conventionalism", *Mind, Language and Reality*, pp. 178–183.

20. Wittgenstein, *On Certainty* I:482.

21. Wittgenstein, *Philosophical Investigations* I:402. See also I:137, 271.

22. Dworkin, "Seven Critics", pp. 1248–1249. It is interesting to consider the parallels between the way in which the secret books conception of the law gives rise to skepticism about right answers to legal questions and the way in which a Cartesian conception of the mind gives rise to skepticism about other minds.

23. Dworkin, *Law's Empire*, pp. 85–86.

24. Higher-order forms of skepticism may render certain lower-order forms pointless: consider the real Quine's insistence that his hypothesis is not that there's no fact of the matter about correct translation, but that there's no fact of the matter as to whether or not there's a fact of the matter. See Putnam, "The Refutation of Conventionalism", *Mind, Language and Reality*, p. 177.

### Notes to Chapter 11. Deliberation

1. *Restatement*, 2nd, Contracts, section 90, p. 215.
2. *Restatement*, 2nd, Contracts, section 75, p. 149.
3. Holmes, *The Common Law*, pp. 293–294.
4. *Davis & Co. v. Morgan*, p. 733.
5. See Fuller and Eisenberg, *Basic Contract Law*, p. 110.
6. Cohen, "The Basis of Contract", pp. 573–574.
7. Prosser, *Handbook of the Law of Torts*, p. 691.
8. *Glus v. Brooklyn Eastern Terminal*, p. 762.
9. *Restatement*, 2nd, Contracts, section 90, p. 215.
10. See Corbin, *Corbin on Contracts*, sections 207–208.
11. See Fuller and Perdue, "The Reliance Interest in Contract Damages", pp. 53–54.
12. Fuller and Eisenberg, *Basic Contract Law*, p. 114.
13. Williston and Thompson, *A Treatise on the Law of Contracts*, vol. 1, section 139, p. 502.
14. Fuller and Eisenberg, *Basic Contract Law*, p. 114.
15. Fuller and Perdue, "The Reliance Interest in Contract Damages", p. 66ff.
16. Fuller and Perdue, "The Reliance Interest in Contract Damages", pp. 61–62.
17. Fuller and Perdue, "The Reliance Interest in Contract Damages", pp. 64–65.
18. See Fuller and Perdue, "The Reliance Interest in Contract Damages", p. 77; and *Wallace v. Hallowell*.
19. Fuller and Perdue, "The Reliance Interest in Contract Damages", pp. 419, 405.
20. This point will be relevant to the discussion of condition I* in Chapter 12 section 4, and also to Chapter 13 section 2, especially the final paragraph of the section.
21. See Aristotle on the need for the perceptiveness born of experience as well as for deliberative ability, e.g., *Nicomachean Ethics* VI.11.
22. See Dworkin, *Taking Rights Seriously*, pp. 40–42.
23. Compare Nagel, "The Fragmentation of Value", in *Mortal Questions*, p. 139.

See, for example, Sen's account of welfare in terms of partially comparable preferences, in *Collective Choice and Social Welfare*, Chapter 7 section 4.

24. See Fuller and Perdue, "The Reliance Interest in Contract Damages", p. 399.

25. Methods of deliberation closely related to the method of reasoning I have sketched have been advocated, discussed, and illustrated by various writers. Rawls' conception of reflective equilibrium is perhaps the most familiar case in point (see *A Theory of Justice*, pp. 20ff, 48ff, etc.); see his "Outline of a Decision Procedure for Ethics" for his earlier views and his "The Independence of Moral Theory" for his later views. References to Dworkin's views about reasoning from coherence may be found in the notes to Chapter 10; recent developments are to be found in *Law's Empire*, especially in the chapters on integrity. See also Daniels, "Wide Reflective Equilibrium and Theory Acceptance in Ethics"; Feinberg, "Justice, Fairness and Rationality", section III; MacCormick, *Legal Reasoning and Legal Theory*, Chapter VII; Scheffler, "On Justification and Commitment". The final chapter of Norman's book *Reasons for Action* provides a detailed illustration of coherentist argument for radical ethical reform with a firm basis in traditional values.

See also the very interesting work on computer modelling of legal reasoning with cases, both actual and hypothetical, by Edwina Rissland and her student Kevin Ashley, as reported, for example, in Ashley's dissertation, *Modelling Legal Argument: Reasoning with Cases and Hypotheticals*. My schematization, applied to legal deliberation, may be compared to that employed by the program HYPO developed by Rissland and Ashley. While there are many differences of detail between the two approaches, I don't believe there is any incompatibility in principle between them. The role of HYPO's "dimensions" is similar to the role of my propositions $p$, $q$, etc. in the analysis of actual and hypothetical settled cases at stage four. Perhaps I try to say a bit more than Rissland and Ashley do about the role of hypotheticals in reaching legal conclusions, in that the answers to hypothetical questions feed back into the resolution of the case at issue via the coherence function, but again I don't believe that what I say is incompatible with their approach. Perhaps the most striking difference is that over whether to use favourableness to conflicting legal doctrines or favourableness to plaintiff as opposed to defendant, as the basic means of organizing the data. Often, within a narrowly limited area of the law, such as trade secrets law, plaintiffs will typically represent one legal doctrine, and defendants another, so that the two approaches are in principle quite similar. However, the doctrine-oriented rather than party-oriented method of organization may have advantages when one comes to generalize beyond a narrowly limited area of the law, so that plaintiff and defendant no longer typically represent particular legal doctrines. By organizing the cases according to legal doctrines directly rather than plaintiffs' and defendants' positions, one may hope to keep theoretical score as one moves from one area of law to another in which the same doctrines apply, and to bring insights about the relationships between legal doctrines from one area to the next.

Of course, different ways of perceiving what legal doctrines apply will yield different analyses, but that is the way the law is, and an analysis that reflects this relativity of conclusion to starting point may be illuminating. Moreover, we can in principle start with as many different legal doctrines as we think may be relevant; again, there is no need to restrict the number of reasons weighed against one another by the coherence function to two.

26. See also MacCormick, *Legal Reasoning and Legal Theory*, Chapter II.

27. Compare Anscombe on the illusory virtues of the practical syllogism as it's often conceived: "Contemplating the accounts given by modern commentators, one

might easily wonder why no one has ever pointed out the mince pie syllogism: the peculiarity of this would be that it was about mince pies, and an example would be 'All mince pies have suet in them—this is a mince pie—therefore etc.' " See Anscombe, *Intention*, section 33, page 58.

28. See Norman, *Reasons for Action*, pp. 89–90.

29. Dworkin, *Taking Rights Seriously*, p. 41.

30. See Wittgenstein, *On Certainty*, sections 140–141. See also Scheffler, "On Justification and Commitment", for a detailed view of how this interaction ought to be characterized.

31. See Rawls, *A Theory of Justice*, section 50.

32. See, for example, Taylor, "What's Wrong with Negative Liberty", in *Philosophy and the Human Sciences*.

33. von Mises, *Human Action*, p. 3.

34. But see Broome, "Choice and Value in Economics".

35. MacCormick, *Legal Reasoning and Legal Theory*, p. 272.

36. Nagel, "The Fragmentation of Value, in *Mortal Questions*, p. 140.

## Notes to Chapter 12. Coherence

1. See and compare: Daniels, "Wide Reflective Equilibrium and Theory Acceptance in Ethics"; Dworkin: "No Right Answer?"; "Seven Critics", p. 1258; *Taking Rights Seriously*, pp. 87, 104–109, 119–122, 126–127, 159–168, 283; Feinberg, "Justice, Fairness and Rationality", section III; MacCormick, *Legal Reasoning and Legal Theory*, Chapter VII; Rawls, *A Theory of Justice*, pp. 20ff, 48ff; Scheffler, "On Justification and Commitment".

2. See Mackie, *Ethics*, pp. 33–35.

3. Williams, "Conflicts of Values", at pp. 222–223.

4. May, "Intransitivity, Utility, and the Aggregation of Preference Patterns", p. 13; see also pp. 3, 5–7, 9–10. See also and compare Tversky, "Intransitivity of Preferences"; Luce and Raiffa, *Games and Decisions*, pp. 318, 342ff; and Kelsey, *Topics in Social Choice*.

5. See Arrow, *Social Choice and Individual Values*, Chapter 3, pp. 59–60, 96–97ff; Sen, *Collective Choice and Social Welfare*, pp. 37–38; Sen, *Choice, Welfare and Measurement*, pp. 164–165, 230–231.

6. Arrow, *Social Choice and Individual Values*, p. 60.

7. See Sen, *Collective Choice and Social Welfare*, Chapter 7.

8. See Rawls, *A Theory of Justice*, pp. 151–152, 542.

9. Sen, *Choice Welfare and Measurement*, p. 346. On the impossiblity of Paretian liberalism, see Sen, *Collective Choice and Social Welfare*, Chapters 6 and 6*; *Choice, Welfare and Measurement*, pp. 248ff, 285–326, 341–346; "Liberty and Social Choice".

10. See May, "Intransitivity, Utility, and the Aggregation of Preference Patterns", p. 12.

11. See and compare Keeney and Raiffa, *Decisions with Multiple Objectives*, pp. 77–78.

12. See Sen, *Choice, Welfare and Measurement*, p. 240.

13. See Sen, *Collective Choice and Social Welfare*, pp. 89–90.

14. In the social choice literature, condition $I$ is reformulated to allow for cardinal information within the framework of *social welfare functionals*, which may take as arguments cardinal non-comparable representations of individuals' preferences. See Sen's conditions $\bar{I}$, $\bar{C}$ and $\bar{M}$, *Collective Choice and Social Welfare*, Chapter 8*.2.; see also Chapter 8.2, and his *Choice, Welfare and Measurement*, pp. 230–231. For sim-

plicity I have stated the conditions and their analogues in terms of criterial orderings of alternatives, but my arguments do not preclude richer criterial information.

It is not an objection to condition $I^*$ reformulated to allow coherence functionals to take as arguments cardinal representations of criterial information that such representations do not provide intercriterial comparisons. Again, it is the job of the coherence *function*, not its *arguments*, to provide an account of the relationships among conflicting values and the circumstances under which certain values outweigh others. The question is whether or not $I^*$ represents a reasonable constraint on functions whose job is to provide such comparisons.

15. See and compare: May, "Intransitivity, Utility, and the Aggregation of Preference Patterns", pp. 9–10; Arrow, *Social Choice and Individual Values*, pp. 27–28; Sen, *Collective Choice and Social Welfare*, pp. 37–38.

16. See and compare Dworkin, on the values of integrity and coherence in legal deliberation, and the role of paradigms and paradigmatic legal practices, in *Law's Empire*, as in his index.

17. See Kevin Roberts, "Social Choice Theory: The Single-Profile and Multi-Profile Approaches", p. 444, who notes with respect to condition $I$: "There can be no change in non-welfare characteristics because these are embodied in states at the outset."

18. Formally, supervenience may be stated as follows, where $x$ and $y$ range over alternatives, or possible acts, and $\Psi$ ranges over non-evaluative specifications of an alternative's characteristics: For any evaluative specification (including ordinal relational specifications and cardinal specifications) of an alternative's characteristics $\phi$, it is conceptually necessary that $\forall x \, \forall y \, [(\phi x \, \& \, -\phi y) \rightarrow \exists \Psi \, (\Psi x \, \& \, -\Psi y)]$. I of course presuppose that different values may supervene on the same set of non-evaluative characteristics, and that such different values may conflict; thus different evaluative criteria may of course differ with respect to alternatives that have the same non-evaluative characteristics. Note that I do not claim that all criteria, in all decision problems, must be evaluative and hence conceptually supervenient; for example, I do not rule out the possibility that a decision problem might be structured so as to have a colour as a criterion, which distinguishes between two boxes identical except with respect to colour. (If colour supervenes it does so as a matter of physics, not conceptual necessity.) A criterion merely provides information, which may be ordinal or cardinal, about the degree to which alternatives have some criterial characteristic that counts for or against them; whether a criterial characteristic must supervene on other characteristics of the alternatives is a further question. However, evaluative criteria, for example, justice, must be supervenient on non-evaluative characteristics. Our interest in decision problems that do involve evaluative criteria, for example in the context of Rawlsian reflective equilibrium, hardly needs defense. Furthermore, while values are supervenient criteria, supervenient criteria may not be values; there may be substantive as well as formal conditions on values, i.e., conditions on their content.

The supervenience of one set of concepts or properties on another is a much discussed topic in ethics and philosophy of mind. For a sample of the large literature see Hare, *Freedom and Reason*, Chapters 2, 3, and *Moral Thinking*, Chapters 5, 6, 7, 10; Mackie, *Ethics*, Chapter 4; Sen, "Information and Invariance in Normative Choice", section 6; Blackburn, "Supervenience Revisited", *Spreading the Word*, Chapter 6, and "Moral Realism"; Kim, "Supervenience and Nomological Incommensurables"; Haugeland, "Weak Supervenience"; Lewis, "Is the Mental Supervenient on the Physical?". See Hare, Mackie and Blackburn on the conceptual or logical necessity of the supervenience of evaluative concepts. Note that supervenience does not entail the reduction of evaluative to non-evaluative characteristics (compare the supervenience of the characteristic of being a table on fundamental physical characteristics); see Blackburn and Kim.

In arguing that supervenience guarantees $I^*$, I assume that alternatives with different non-criterial characteristics are different alternatives. Other assumptions could be made that would themselves guarantee $I^*$ and that might seem to make the appeal to supervenience superfluous; but it is not superfluous when we come to reject condition $R^*$.

19. See Samuelson, "Reaffirming the Existence of 'Reasonable' Bergson-Samuelson Social Welfare Functions", p. 82; and "Arrow's Mathematical Politics", pp. 43, 47, 48–49. See also Roberts, "Social Choice Theory: the Single-Profile and Multiprofile Approaches", p. 443.

20. See Sen, *Choice, Welfare and Measurement*, pp. 251–256.

21. See Kemp and Ng, "On the Existence of Social Welfare Functions, Social Orderings and Social Decision Functions", p. 60; and Parks, "An Impossibility Theorem for Fixed Preferences: A Dictatorial Bergson-Samuelson Welfare Function", p. 448. See also Kemp and Ng, "More on Social Welfare Functions: The Incompatibility of Individualism and Ordinalism", pp. 89–90.

22. See Sen, "Social Choice Theory"; see also Samuelson, "Reaffirming the Existence of 'Reasonable' Bergson-Samuelson Social Welfare Functions".

23. See Hart and Sacks, *The Legal Process*, problems 12 and 21.

24. See Samuelson, "Reaffirming the Existence of 'Reasonable' Bergson-Samuelson Social Welfare Functions", for a forceful presentation of a similar line of thought.

25. Engel, J., dissenting in *U.S. v. Sims*.

26. Sidgwick, *The Methods of Ethics*, p. 311.

27. See Keeney and Raiffa, *Decisions with Multiple Objectives*, Chapter 5.7; recall also the discussion of the need for substantive constraints in Part I, especially Chapter 4, section 4.

28. Recall and compare the arguments discussed in Chapters 4 and 5 that counterexamples to the Sure-Thing principle or the Independence axiom can be avoided by properly individuating possibilities to reflect whatever motivates the apparent violation. See Broome, "Rationality and the Sure-Thing Principle", and Tversky, "A Critique of Expected Utility Theory".

29. See Griffin, "Equality: On Sen's Weak Equity Axiom", p. 282.

30. Compare the arguments of this section with Dworkin's views on checkerboard laws, coherence, and integrity, in *Law's Empire*, Chapter 6.

31. See Kevin Roberts, "Social Choice Theory: The Single-Profile and Multi-Profile Approaches", p. 443.

32. See Sen, *Collective Choice and Social Welfare*, pp. 43–44; see also Sen, *Choice, Welfare and Measurement*, p. 251ff.

33. See Kevin Roberts, "Social Choice Theory: The Single-Profile and Multi-Profile Approaches", pp. 442–443.

34. $F$, $G$, and $H$ are analogous to Roberts' $b1$, $b2$ and $b3$, which are the values for different alternatives of some function $v$, equivalent to the function that captures the welfare information actually realised, of one entire profile of preferences. Thus $b1$, $b2$, and $b3$ each reflect the preferences of all the individuals the profile includes, and do not each relate to a different individual.

35. The analogous complaint about condition $R$ is that it requires someone to have different preferences with respect to alternatives that have just the same non-welfare characteristics. It may not worry some social choice theorists that as a result

some preferences must be fundamentally arbitrary or meddlesome. However, if an epistemic justification is contemplated for democratic adherence to the recommendations of a single-profile social welfare function, perhaps such fundamental arbitrariness should be a cause for concern. That opinions about what ought to be done are fundamentally arbitrary may tend to undermine epistemic justifications for relying on them; such justifications might require opinions to be sensitive to the truth and might not hold irrespective of the content or accuracy of the opinions. Compare Arrow, *Social Choice and Individual Values*, pp. 85, 105. See and compare the discussion of arbitrary votes and votes that form a circle of distinctions in Chapter 15 section 3.

36. This would be analogous to shifting from one *v* to another between two applications of Roberts' condition. See Kevin Roberts, "Social Choice Theory: The Single-Profile and Multi-Profile Approaches", pp. 342–343.

## Notes to Chapter 13. Commensurability

1. For surveys of such domain restrictions, including single-peakedness, single-cavedness, value restriction, limited agreement, and extremal restriction, see Murakami, *Logic and Social Choice*, Chapter 6; Pattanaik, *Voting and Collective Choice*, Chapters 4–7; and Sen, *Collective Choice and Social Welfare*, Chapter 10.

2. See Duncan Black, *The Theory of Committees and Elections*, p. 9.

3. See Arrow, *Social Choice and Individual Values*, pp. 75–76; Coombs, "Psychological Scaling without a Unit of Measurement", and "Social Choice and Strength of Preference"; Luce and Raiffa, *Games and Decisions: Introduction and Critical Survey*, p. 353ff; and Sen, *Collective Choice and Social Welfare*, p. 167.

4. See Sen, *Collective Choice and Social Welfare*, pp. 167–169. Perhaps supervenience can itself be considered a kind of domain restriction; but, if so, this point would affect only the wording, not the substance, of my argument in this section.

Note that my criticism of domain restrictions here is not in tension with the suggestions I make about domain and agenda division in accordance with anti-debunking considerations in Chapter 15 section 3. The latter constitute a violation of Condition I, not Condition U. Even if my remarks were interpreted to involve a violation of Condition U, however, the deeper point is that I suggest a principled epistemological basis for domain and agenda division with respect to multi-dimensional disagreements. The type of domain restrictions I criticize in Chapter 13 section 1 lack such a principled basis, and merely put such disagreements aside.

5. See May, "Intransitivity, Utility, and the Aggregation of Preference Patterns", pp. 5, 7, 8.

6. See Reynolds and Paris, "The Concept of 'Choice' and Arrow's Theorem", pp. 364–367; Schwartz, "Rationality and the Myth of the Maximum", pp. 102, 105–106 (compare Wiggins, in "Weakness of Will, Commensurability, and the Objects of Deliberation and Desire", p. 268, on a distinction related to that drawn by Schwartz); Packard, "A Note on Wittgenstein and Cyclical Comparatives", p. 39; Burns and Meeker, "Conflict and Structure in Multi-Level Multiple Objective Decision-Making Systems", pp. 90–91 (authors' emphasis).

I do not include work by Loomis and Sugden on regret theory here because the conception of regret they develop, and the intransitivities they aim to explain and justify, seem to me essentially to involve uncertainty or risk. It is not clear to me whether, or how, their approach to intransitivity would generalize to the cases I am concerned with, in which the consequences of alternative acts are known with certainty.

7. See Raiffa, *Decision Analysis*, p. 78, on the way in which intransitive judgments leave one open to money pumping arrangements.

8. See Nagel, "The Fragmentation of Value", *Mortal Questions*, pp. 134–139. I have tried to describe such a method in my account of deliberation. See also section 5 of this chapter. Compare Rawls, "Outline of a Decision Procedure for Ethics", p. 189. However, it may be more natural to read Nagel's remarks as casting doubt on the value of pursuing coherence as here conceived at all, rather than on the value of an unrestricted domain or of monism.

9. See Williams, "Conflicts of Values", in Ryan, editor, *The Idea of Freedom*, p. 227.

10. Wiggins, "Weakness of Will, Commensurability, and the Objects of Deliberation and Desire", p. 268. For other versions and uses of the distinction in this context, see Schwartz, "Rationality and the Myth of the Maximum", pp. 105–106; and Reynolds and Paris, "The Concept of 'Choice' and Arrow's Theorem", p. 368.

11. Sen and Williams, Introduction to *Utilitarianism and Beyond*, pp. 17, 18. See also Sen, "Plural Utility".

12. Davidson, "Psychology as Philosophy", *Essays on Actions and Events*, p. 237. See also Davidson, McKinsey, and Suppes, "Outlines of a Formal Theory of Value", p. 145.

13. Dworkin claims that legal norms of coherence and integrity reflect the personification of the community. It is his view that the responsibility of the community as a whole to treat its members in a coherent and principled way is not *conceptually* (also, I would add, not *normatively*) derivative from individual responsibilities. It is quite compatible with this view to admit that *causal* explanation of the phenemenon of communal integrity *may* proceed according to an individualistic method. In particular, Dworkin's view is not in tension with efforts at causal explanation of norms of coherence such as the fascinating work on on signal detection theory and *stare decisis* by Ronald Heiner. Heiner argues that the reliability of judges at using information will drop as it becomes more distant from the experience provided by their past decisions; given the relative likelihoods of Type I and Type II errors at different response levels, in order to maintain a required level of reliability, judges must be less likely to respond to novel than to familiar kinds of information and argument. This pattern of behaviour on the part of judges will select for legal arguments with a strong connection to past decisions. The conceptual and normative claim is made at a different level of description from that of causal explanation, and serves different interests; thus it can be true both that norms of coherence and integrity that reflect the personification of the community are not derivative, and that causal explanations can be given of the process and function of such personification. See Chapter 14 on the compatibility of causal and normative understanding.

Kenneth Kress has argued that the emphasis put by coherence accounts such as Dworkin's with past decisions and deference to precedent makes for retroactive applications of the law. Retroactivity may occur when settled law is changed by intervening cases between the occurrence of the events being litigated and the adjudication of them, since at adjudication the most coherent account of settled cases will be responsible to actual cases decided after the occurrence of the events litigated. I would argue in response, but cannot do so here, that Kress's argument does not cut against coherence accounts in particular but rather gives rise to a general dilemma: either present practice with respect to the precedential effect of intervening cases involves retroactivity, or our thinking about the role of hypothetical cases within the doctrine of precedent is in need of revision. If the revisionionary conception of precedent that would give equal weight to settled hypothetical and actual cases and would thus avoid retroactivity is rejected, then we must choose between accepting the retroactivity of

present practice with respect to intervening cases, and changing present practice so
as to give intervening cases prospective effect only. However, this dilemma is already
implicit in U.S. Supreme Court jurisprudence, and nothing in a coherence account
*per se* prevents us from making any of these choices. See *Stovall v. Denno*; *Desist v.
U.S.*, especially Harlan's dissent; *Shea v. Lousianna*, especially White's dissent. The
Court divides over the problem of intervening cases, and moreover seems to change
its own position. *Stovall* and *Desist* come down in favour of nonretroactivity by
refusing to apply the intervening decisions to pending cases in which the relevant
events of police conduct occurred prior to the intervening decisions. However, Harlan's
dissent in *Desist*, favouring precedent over nonretroactivity, becomes the Court's
position in *Shea*, where White dissents, arguing on nonretroactivity grounds. A nice
self-referential problem of intervening cases about the problem of intervening cases,
the logic of which I will not even attempt to untangle!

It should be kept in mind that the degree to which the Court is willing to consider
and countenance intervening case retroactivity in the criminal procedure context,
where police reliance on earlier cases is in question, may well not generalize. That
is, an acceptable degree of retroactivity with respect to police reliance, which cuts in
*favour* of criminal defendants, may not be acceptable in general, that is, where the
intervening case might cut *against* criminal defendants and undermine *their* reliance
rather than police reliance, or where it might change the positions of civil litigants.
It would be interesting to develop an integrated view of retroactivity doctrine within
and without the criminal procedure context, and to try to isolate the special effects
of the criminal procedure context on retroactivity doctrine, but I cannot do so here.

14. For further discussion of self-determination, see Chapter 15. See also and
compare, Taylor, *Human Language and Agency*, part I, and "Responsibility for Self",
in *Philosophy and the Human Sciences*; Glover, "Self-Creation"; Sen, "Goals, Commitment and Identity".

15. Compare the distinction drawn by Dworkin between the natural and constructive models of coherence, in "Justice and Rights", *Taking Rights Seriously*, p. 160ff.
He writes: "The natural model insists on consistency with conviction, on the assumption that moral intuitions are accurate observations; the requirement of consistency
follows from that assumption. The constructive model insists on consistency with
conviction as an independent requirement, flowing not from the assumption that these
convictions are accurate reports, but from the different assumption that it is unfair
for officials to act except on the basis of a general public theory that will constrain
them to consistency, provide a public standard for testing or debating or predicting
what to do, and not allow appeals to unique intuitions that might mask prejudice or
self-interest in particular cases. The constructive model requires coherence, then, for
independent reasons of political morality", pp. 162–163. See also Dworkin, *Law's
Empire*, on consistency and integrity, as in index. Compare also Daniels, "Wide
Reflective Equilibrium and Theory Acceptance in Ethics", p. 276ff.

16. Sen and Williams, Introduction to *Utilitarianism and Beyond*, p. 18.

17. See Fishburn, "Utility Theory", p. 343 and *passim*; Hwang and Yoon, *Multiple
Attribute Decision Making*, *passim*, and Nozick, *Anarchy, State and Utopia*, p. 29n.

### Notes to Chapter 14. Skepticism

1. Compare Nozick, *Philosophical Explanations*, p. 256n.
2. See Wittgenstein, *Philosophical Grammar*, p. 374.
3. See Dworkin on internal vs. external skepticism, in *Law's Empire*, as in index.
4. Mackie, *Ethics*, pp. 33–35.
5. See Mackie, *Problems from Locke*, pp. 15–16.

6. See McGinn, *The Subjective View*, pp. 76, 114, 118; McDowell, "Values and Secondary Qualities". See also Dummett, "Common Sense and Physics". Note that I am not claiming that ethical concepts and colour concepts are strictly analogous; see again the points of comparison in Chapters 2 and 3.

7. The quotations are from Wiggins, "Truth, Invention, and the Meaning of Life", p. 362; and see Williams, *Descartes*, pp. 65–77, 211–212, 239, 245–249, 301–303, and *Ethics & the Limits of Philosophy*, p. 139.

8. See Nagel, *The View from Nowhere*; see also Strawson, "Perception and Its Objects".

9. See and compare Strawson, "Perception and Its Objects", p. 59; Putnam, *Meaning and the Moral Sciences*, p. 108.

10. See McDowell, "Values and Secondary Qualities", p. 118; McGinn, *The Subjective View*, p. 148; Nozick, *Philosophical Explanations*, p. 399.

11. See Rorty in "The World Well Lost", *The Consequences of Pragmatism*, p. 12; compare Williams on Rorty, in *Ethics and the Limits of Philosophy*, p. 137–138.

12. See Williams, *Ethics and the Limits of Philosophy*, p. 135.

13. For further references see Rorty, "World Well Lost", *The Consequences of Pragmatism*; Williams, *Ethics and the Limits of Philosophy*, Chapter 8.

14. Compare Wittgenstein, *Zettel* I:414, and *Philosophical Investigations* I:271.

15. See Nozick, *Philosophical Explanations*, pp. 547–549.

16. See Strawson, "Freedom and Resentment", *Freedom and Resentment*; and Wolff, "The Importance of Free Will". See and compare Rorty's review of Taylor's *Philosophical Papers*, "Absolutely Non-Absolute".

17. Compare von Wright, *Explanation and Understanding*, p. 72.

18. McGinn, *The Subjective View*, p. 127.

19. See McDowell, "Values and Secondary Qualities", pp. 118–120; for much more along this line of thought, see and compare Taylor, "Self-Interpreting Animals", in *Human Agency and Language*, and *passim*.

20. Blackburn, "Errors and the Phenomenology of Value", p. 18.

21. See Blakemore, *Mechanics of the Mind*, p. 90. See also Hirsch, "The Tunable Seer: Activity-Dependent Development of Vision".

22. Mackie, *Ethics*, pp. 38–39.

23. See Blackburn, "Errors and the Phenomenology of Values", p. 16–18; Williams, *Ethics and the Limits of Philosophy*, p. 143, 151; Nozick, *Philosophical Explanations*, Chapter 3.

24. See Forbes, "Nozick on Skepticism".

25. See Nozick, *Philosophical Explanations*, p. 209.

26. Mackie, *Ethics*, p. 37.

27. On these points see Nozick, *Philosophical Explanations*, pp. 245ff, 280ff; 196 (compare Williams, *Ethics and the Limits of Philosophy*, p. 148); 350, 715.

28. I must admit at the outset that I am not at all confident I have understood the crucial chapter, "Knowledge, Science and Convergence", of his book *Ethics and the Limits of Philosophy*. An example of one of the things I am puzzled by is why he identifies as objectivist a view of the specific ethical concepts (pp. 146–147) that comes very close to what I have called centralism and have claimed goes hand in hand with subjectivism, given the close conceptual connections between the general ethical concepts and expressions of the will. Can we be so much at cross purposes in our very understandings of what objectivity involves?

29. See Williams, *Ethics and the Limits of Philosophy*, pp. 149–150; See also Nozick, *Philosophical Explanations*, pp. 317, 326.

30. Williams, *Ethics and the Limits of Philosophy*, pp. 135–136.

31. See Williams, *Ethics and the Limits of Philosophy*, pp. 139; 142–143; but cf. p. 150.

32. Williams, *Ethics and the Limits of Philosophy*, pp. 151–152.

33. See Nozick, *Philosophical Explanations*, pp. 170–171.

34. See Chapter 15 section 3, on agenda and domain division and, more generally, on the idea of a democratic division of epistemic labour.

35. See Nozick, *Philosophical Explanations*, p. 184; Peacocke, *Thoughts*, pp. 130, 136ff; Forbes, "Nozick on Skepticism", pp. 47–48.

36. This is not an actual case, but one I have supposed to illustrate my point. However, it is close enough to an actual fruit-and-vegetable-specific deficit case discussed by Hart, Berndt, and Caramazza in "Category-Specific Naming Deficit Following Cerebral Infraction" to be absolved of the charge of science-fictional extravagance. Here I am indebted to Ros McCarthy and Nicholas Rawlins.

37. See Nozick, *Philosophical Explanations*, pp. 213–214, 324–325.

38. Nozick, *Philosophical Explanations*, p. 281; see also pp. 246, 280–283.

39. Williams, *Ethics and the Limits of Philosophy*, p. 151; Blackburn, "Errors and the Phenomenology of Values", pp. 16–18.

40. Dworkin, *Taking Rights Seriously*, pp. 162–163; compare Williams, *Ethics and the Limits of Philosophy*, p. 99ff. See especially Heiner, "Uncertainty and Rule-Governed Behavior: On the Evolution of Legal Procedure".

41. See Nozick, *Philosophical Explanations*, pp. 186, 322, 545; and 342ff. See also David Lewis, *Counterfactuals*, pp. 24–25, on why he believes a theory of counterfactuals does not need to discriminate in truth value between different counterfactuals with impossible antecedents and is fairly content to let them all be vacuously true.

42. See Lewis, *Counterfactuals*, pp. 10–11, 16–18; Nozick, *Philosophical Explanations*, pp. 173; 200; 322: "what the antecedent [if the act were not right or best] . . . supposes is that something is different about the act or about the context in which it is done, so that the act then is not right—however, it is not supposed that the nature of rightness itself has changed in any way."

43. See Jacobs, *Understanding Harmony*, especially the first several chapters.

44. Compare Nozick, *Philosophical Explanations*, p. 539; Davidson, "Mental Events", *Essays on Actions and Events*, pp. 214–215.

45. Compare Nozick, *Philosophical Explanations*, pp. 218, 220; Searle, *Intentionality*, pp. 265–266.

46. Compare Nozick, *Philosophical Explanations*, p. 538, 262, 269.

47. We are thus bringing a notion of evaluative possibility—a kind of decentralized version of deontic possibility—to bear on judgments of distance from the actual world, *within* the logic of counterfactuals. Compare Lewis, *Counterfactuals*, Ch. 5.1.

48. See and compare Davidson, "Thought and Talk", *Inquiries into Truth and Interpretation*, p. 159: "The Material Mind", *Essays on Actions and Events*, pp. 253–254; Sen, "Information and Invariance in Normative Choice", section 6.

49. Note that the counterfactual conditionals entailed by the relationship of functional dependence themselves entail the corresponding material conditionals, which can be contraposed. Since the explanation of supervenience makes its obtaining a matter of the conceptual role the supervenient concepts play, the initial functional dependence claim is prefaced by a conceptual necessity operator, which these transformations preserve. (The conceptual necessity of the counterfactual relationship between sets of concepts, which supervenience involves, should not be confused with conceptual links between particular concepts from those sets; the conceptual independence of particular concepts from each of those sets is compatible with the con-

ceptual necessity of the counterfactual relationship between sets of concepts. This is just to say that irreducibility is compatible with necessary supervenience.) Thus we can ultimately get from the conceptual role of propositions about the best theory to claims of the general form:

$$\Box \exists N \ ( \ \forall x \ (Nx \to Ex) \ ),$$

where *"E"* is some particular ethical characteristic of a given alternative and *"N"* ranges over specifications of that alternative's non-ethical characteristics.

To spell out the steps:

To say an alternative has some ethical characteristic $E$ is, as a conceptual matter, to say that there is some function such that its ethical characteristics are a function of its non-ethical characteristics. This is to say that:

$$\Box \exists N \ ( \ \forall x \ (-Ex \ \Box\!\!\to -Nx) \ ), \text{ which entails:}$$
$$\Box \exists N \ ( \ \forall x \ (-Ex \to -Nx) \ ), \text{ which entails:}$$
$$\Box \exists N \ ( \ \forall x \ (Nx \to Ex) \ ).$$

Thus, merely intra-conceptually-possible-world supervenience, as expressed in the last line and appealed to in the argument against $R^*$ in Chapter 12, derives from the stronger inter-conceptually-possible-world supervenience claim involved in the notion of a function. Recall that counter*factual* but not counter*evaluative* conceptual possibilities were relevant to the functional dependence relation studied in Chapter 12.

Note that while counterfactuals cannot in general be contraposed, the notion of functional dependence may well be such as to exclude the cases in which contraposition would fail. Functional counterfactual dependence does seem to permit contraposition: it holds not only that if the value of the function were different the argument would be different, but that if the argument were the same the value would be the same. If so, we could also derive:

$$\Box \exists N \ (\forall x \ (Nx \ \Box\!\!\to Ex) \ ).$$

50. Blackburn, *Spreading the Word*, p. 187.

51. See also Davidson, "Causal Relations", *Essays on Actions and Events*, pp. 159–160.

52. See Blackburn, "Moral Realism", pp. 110–111.

53. Perhaps Blackburn's issue doesn't arise if one follows Davidson in rejecting the conception of the mind as independent of the world. I argue in Chapter 5 section 4, that this rejection itself does *not* constitute a kind of idealism.

54. McGinn, "Weak Wills".

55. As expressed, for example, in "The Method of Truth in Metaphysics", sect. 1, and in "Thought and Talk", pp. 169–170 (both in *Inquiries into Truth and Interpretation*); in "Judging Interpersonal Interests", p. 205; in "Rational Animals", and in remarks in a Trinity Term 1985 seminar in Oxford.

56. Compare McGinn, "The Structure of Content", pp. 254–255, and Burge, "Individualism and the Mental".

57. See Blackburn in *Spreading the Word*, p. 186; "Moral Realism", p. 114–115.

58. Thus the rejection of an individualistic view of the mental is extended to the will, as we saw in Part I. But this is in no way incompatible with holding that the non-optional constraints on interpretation allow for and at times demand critical and imaginative revision of existing reason-giving practices.

59. See Blackburn, "Errors and the Phenomenology of Values", pp. 16–18; compare *Spreading the Word*, p. 182.

60. Recall Putnam, *Reason, Truth and History*, p. 208.

61. See and compare Nozick, *Philosophical Explanations*, p. 328.

62. Note that it cannot be objected to the argument of this paragraph that it fails to meet Nozick's requirement that the method by which the belief is arrived at be held constant under the counterfactual supposition, since the belief that there is a best theory is meta-deliberative and is not itself arrived at by deliberation of the kind in question. The argument of the immediately preceding paragraphs is not open to the objection, of course, because it does hold the method, namely, deliberation, constant. In versions of the argument applied to specific ethical beliefs rather than all-things-considered ethical beliefs, the method held constant would involve a combination of deliberation and taking apparent ethical perceptions as of the specific values in question at face value. See Peacocke, *Thoughts*, p. 137.

63. The non-extensional relation " . . . causally explains . . . " should be distinguished from the extensional relation " . . . causes . . . ". See Chapter 5 section 6; and see Davidson, "Causal Relations", *Essays on Actions and Events*, pp. 161–162; Mackie, *The Cement of the Universe*, ch. 10; Strawson, "Causation and Explanation".

64. See Lewis, *Counterfactuals*, p. 32ff, Nozick, *Philosophical Explanations*, p. 249; Wright, "Keeping Track of Nozick".

65. Nozick, *Philosophical Explanations*, pp. 208–209.

66. See Forbes, "Nozick on Scepticism"; and Peacocke, *Thoughts*, Chapter 9. As Peacocke notes, related points were made by Kripke in his 1985 Gareth Evans Memorial Lecture.

67. See and compare Nozick, *Philosophical Explanations*, pp. 328, 345.

68. See Unger, "Experience and Factual Knowledge"; compare Peacocke, *Thoughts*, p. 138.

69. Wittgenstein, *Zettel* I:225.

70. See Salzen, "Perception of Emotion in Faces".

71. See Hecaen, "The Neurophysicology of Face Recognition".

72. Vignolo, "Auditory Agnosia", p. 4.

73. See Nozick, *Philosophical Explanations*, pp. 182–184, 213–214.

74. See and compare E. A. Ross, *The Principles of Sociology*, pp. 164–165, cited in Miller, "Pluralism and Social Choice", pp. 735–736.

### Notes to Chapter 15. Autonomy and Democracy

1. See Green, *Prolegomena to Ethics*, book II; Irwin, "Reason and Responsibility in Aristotle"; Taylor, "Agency", section 3, in *Human Agency and Language*; compare Holden, "Liberal Democracy and the Social Determination of Ideas", in Pennock and Chapman, editors, *Liberal Democracy*; Rawls, *A Theory of Justice*, section 40.

2. See Taylor, *Human Language and Agency*, p. 11, on the need to avoid spurious dichotomies.

3. Hobbes, *Leviathan*, Chapter VI.

4. See Taylor, "What is Human Agency?", in *Human Agency and Language*, pp. 23ff, 29ff; Taylor, "What's Wrong with Negative Liberty", in *Philosophy and the Human Sciences,* pp. 218ff, 223ff; see also *Sandel, Liberalism and the Limits of Justice*, pp. 30, 124.

5. See Taylor, "Atomism", *Philosophy and the Human Sciences*, p. 201; "What is Human Agency?", and "The Concept of a Person", p. 105, in *Human Agency and Language*.

6. See Sandel, *Liberalism and the Limits of Justice*, pp. 58–59, 119–132, 144, 152–165, 178–180; see also Taylor, various essays in *Human Agency and Language*,

pp. 41–42, 81, 85–86, 112; and compare Rawls, "Justice as Fairness: Political, Not Metaphysical", section V.

7. See Sandel, *Liberalism and the Limits of Justice*, pp. 58, 159, 180; and see Taylor, "What is Human Agency?", in *Human Agency and Language*, p. 35. In Chapters 6 and 9 I treated subjectivism and non-cognitivism as separable doctrines, raising separable issues, whereas Sandel's voluntarist conception of agency seems to involve elements of both.

8. See and compare, e.g., Strawson, *Individuals*, p. 114; Taylor, "Hegel's Philosophy of Mind", in *Human Language and Agency*, p. 93; Sen, "Goals, Commitment, and Identity".

9. See Nussbaum, "Shame, Separateness, and Political Unity: Aristotle's Criticism of Plato", p. 413ff, on the relations between Plato's dualism and his indifference to autonomy, on the one hand, and Aristotle's hylomorphism and his concern with autonomy, on the other.

10. See and compare Taylor, *Human Agency and Language*, p. 11; Pennock's introduction to Pennock and Chapman, editors, *Liberal Democracy*, p. 2.

11. Taylor, *Human Agency and Language*, p. 8; see also "Atomism", *Philosophy and the Human Sciences*, pp. 204–209; and Pennock, "Epilogue: Some Perplexities Further Considered", in Pennock and Chapman, editors, *Liberal Democracy*, p. 422.

12. Campbell, *In Defence of Free Will*, pp. 38–39. Though perhaps what Campbell understands by "constituted" is not what is now understood by it.

13. Frankfurt, "Identification and Externality", pp. 244–248. Compare Frankfurt's earlier remarks in "Freedom of the Will and the Concept of a Person", pp. 16–17. See also and compare Wiggins, "Towards a Reasonable Libertarianism".

14. This phrasing is intended to make room for Downs' views and various views about strategic voting as not directly expressive of preference as nevertheless noncognitivist in character; see Downs, *An Economic Theory of Democracy*, pp. 48, 152ff, etc.

15. Dworkin, "Liberalism", p. 127; see also p. 134.

16. Rawls, in "Justice as Fairness: Political, not Metaphysical", pp. 230, 245.

17. See Rawls, "Social Unity and Primary Goods", p. 183; Dworkin, *Law's Empire*, pp. 440–441, note 19; compare Ely, *Democracy and Distrust*, pp. 54, 58–59. Any tension between the role of ethical and political theory in Dworkin's theory of adjudication and his understanding of liberalism is resolved by the doctrine that within such theory claims of right, derived from the fundamental value of equal concern and respect, trump claims of policy. See *Taking Rights Seriously*, especially "Hard Cases".

18. Rawls, "Justice as Fairness: Political, not Metaphysical", pp. 245–246.

19. For examples, see, Dahl, *A Preface to Democratic Theory*, ch. 4, Dahl, *Dilemmas of Pluralist Democracy*, p. 6; Bacharach, *The Theory of Democratic Elitism*, p. 3; Ely, *Democracy and Distrust*, pp. 54, 58–59, 78, 82; Lively, *Democracy*, pp. 10, 36, 115; Riker, *Liberalism Against Populism* (whose claim that populism and liberalism as he understands them exhaust the possibilities for democracy seems to overlook the very possibility of a cognitive conception), pp. 239–241, but cf. note 2, pp. 291; Levine, "A Conceptual Problem for Liberal Democracy", pp. 302–303, 309. And see Sandel, *Liberalism and the Limits of Justice*, p. 1; Winston, "Toward a Liberal Conception of Legislation", pp. 326–327, 329; Hart, "Between Utility and Rights".

20. Edmund Burke, Speech to the electors of Bristol, p. 447.

21. For a sample of work that displays awareness of or support for the possibility of a cognitive conception of democracy, see Braybrooke, "A Public Goods Approach to the Theory of the General Will"; Birch, *Representation*, pp. 14, 39, 53, 124, and

especially Chapters 5 and 6; Lively, *Democracy*, p. 125; Nelson, *On Justifying Democracy*, pp. 100–121; Holden, "Liberal Democracy and the Social Determination of Ideas", section IX; Hallowell, *The Moral Foundation of Democracy*, pp. 29, 31, 34, 43–45, 58–59, 68–88, 118–126; Pennock, "Epilogue: Some Perplexities Further Considered", pp. 415, 417, 420, and Pennock, *Democratic Political Theory*. I conceive my arguments in this chapter as an effort to proceed where something like Macpherson's second model of democracy, which he calls Developmental Democracy, left off, in the light of subsequent discussion, insights and criticisms, and continuing dissatisfaction with alternative models. See Macpherson, *The Life and Times of Liberal Democracy*.

22. See Rawls, "Justice as Fairness: Political, not Metaphysical", pp. 240, 245–246, 248–249; and see section 5 of this chapter. I shall argue in section 5 that intrapersonal conflicts are indeed relevant to Rawls' enterprise.

23. See Braybrooke, "A Public Goods Approach to the Theory of the General Will"; see also the extended characterization of basic goods that Winston suggests would be of concern to "progressive liberals", in "Toward a Liberal Conception of Legislation", pp. 334–335.

24. See and compare Elster, *Sour Grapes*, ch. 3, 4; see also Holden, "Liberal Democracy and the Social Determination of Ideas", section VIII.

25. Mill, *Considerations of Representative Government*, pp. 27–28. Compare Aristotle, who writes: "That which is genuinely and not just nominally called a state must concern itself with virtue. Otherwise the state-partnership is a mere alliance . . . and under such conditions Law becomes a mere contract or . . . 'a mutual guarantee of rights', and quite unable to make citizens good and just, which it ought to do. The state is intended to enable all, in their households and their kinships, to live *well*, meaning by that a full and satisfying life. . . . that good life, which is the purpose of the state . . . means living happily and nobly." *Politics* III.9; see also VII.1. See also Aristotle in the *Politics* on the advantages of the version of mixed constitution he there favours, the polity, especially when designed to fit a particular society so as to divide the labour of governing it effectively, according to its character and human resources. Other points of similarity between Mill and Aristotle are their emphases on the dangers of government motivated by class or sectarian interests, and on the political importance of education.

26. Mill, Chapter II of *On Liberty*, pp. 35–37; see also p. 47. And see Schauer, "Free Speech and the Argument from Democracy", especially pp. 242, 247–248, 251, and note 4.

27. See also Nussbaum, "Shame, Separateness and Political Unity", and sections 4 and 6 of this chapter, below; and see Schauer, "Free Speech and the Argument from Democracy", on why the "argument from democracy" in favour of free speech is not wholly distinct from the "argument from truth", but rather an important variation on it; pp. 251–252.

28. For a general survey and references, see Riker, *Liberalism Against Populism*, *passim*; compare Miller, "Pluralism and Social Choice"; see also Dahl, *Dilemmas of Pluralist Democracy*, Chapter 3 and *passim*; Birch, *Representation*, pp. 109–110.

29. Aristotle, *Politics* III.11, as translated by T. A. Sinclair; Barry, *Political Argument*, pp. 292–293; Hallowell, *The Moral Foundation of Democracy*, pp. 29, 43–44, 121; Schumpeter, *Capitalism, Socialism and Democracy*, p. 264.

30. See Holden, "Liberal Democracy and the Social Determination of Ideas", pp. 303–304; compare Dahl, *Dilemmas of Pluralist Democracy*, p. 166.

31. See Braybrooke, "A Public Goods Approach to the Theory of the General Will"; Black, *The Theory of Committees and Elections*, pp. 164–165.

32. See Birch, *Representation*, Chapters 1, 3, 4; Pennock, "Epilogue", p. 418; compare Ely, *Democracy and Distrust*, pp. 78–82.

33. See and compare Pennock, "Epilogue", pp. 417–418; Schumpeter, *Capitalism, Socialism and Democracy*, pp. 275, 283; See Hallowell, *The Moral Foundation of Democracy*, p. 120ff.

34. See Ross, *The Right and the Good*; Williams, "Ethical Consistency", in *Problems of the Self*; and Davidson, "How is Weakness of the Will Possible?", in *Essays on Actions and Events*.

35. See Mill, *Considerations on Representative Government*, pp. 133–135; compare Schumpeter, *Capitalism, Socialism and Democracy*, pp. 251–253, 258–263, 269, 290–295; Lively, *Democracy*, p. 42; Dahl, citing Kinder and Kiewiet, in *Dilemmas of Pluralist Democracy*, p. 162; Downs, *An Economic Theory of Democracy*, part III.

36. See and compare Pennock, introduction to *Liberal Democracy*, Pennock and Chapman, editors, p. 2; Pateman, *Participation and Democratic Theory*, p. 29ff; Dahl, *Dilemmas of Pluralist Democracy*, Chapter 7.

37. Recall the arguments and references of Chapter 8, sections 1–4, and the end of section 3 of Chapter 13. See also Braybrooke, "A Public Goods Approach . . . ", and Taylor, "Hegel's Philosophy of Mind", *Human Agency and Language*, p. 93.

38. Nagel, "The Fragmentation of Value", in *Mortal Questions*, pp. 136–137; See also Taylor, "The Diversity of Goods", *Philosophy and the Human Sciences*, p. 235.

39. Here I am indebted to Paul Seabright.

40. See Downs, *An Economic Theory of Democracy*, Chapters 3, 14.

41. Compare Madison in *The Federalist Papers*, no. 10, on the advantages of republics in controlling the evil effects of factionalism.

42. From this point of view Schumpeter gets it exactly wrong when he writes: "The psycho-technics of party management and party advertising, slogans and marching tunes, are not accessories. They are the essence of politics". *Capitalism, Socialism and Democracy*, p. 283. But compare p. 263. See also Lively, *Democracy*, pp. 43, 142–143; Dahl, *A Preface to Democratic Theory*, pp. 68–69. I realize that the arguments of this paragraph fail to address the role of insincere strategic expressions of beliefs, which is certainly relevant here.

43. See and compare Downs, *An Economic Theory of Democracy*, pp. 119, 188–189, 265–268.

44. However, it is important to distinguish individualism about agency, as I have explained it in Chapter 8 sections 1 through 4, from political individualism, which affirms the substantive value of individual autonomy. A conception of democracy that rejects individualism about agency need not, and I believe should not, reject political individualism. Indeed, as I develop the idea of a co-operative cognitive conception of democracy in the rest of this chapter, it naturally gives a special role to respect for the substantive value of individual autonomy. Political individualism in this sense may be better served by a co-operative cognitive theory of democracy than by theories of democracy that presuppose individualism about agency and noncognitivism.

45. Arrow, *Social Choice and Individual Values*, p. 85; see also Braybrooke, "A Public Goods Approach to the Theory of the General Will". John Broome has suggested to me that Arrow, and social choice theory in general, fail adequately to distinguish taste and judgment, or self-interested preference and moral opinion, with respect to their appropriateness as input to social choice mechanisms. In my view,

any such blurring would be natural given a non-cognitivist view of values, which may be widely held among social choice theorists. The distinction which I take Arrow to be drawing in the passage cited, however, is between non-cognitivist and cognitivist views of social choice; he disassociates himself from the latter, even if he allows ethical judgments construed non-cognitively to function as input to social choice mechanisms. The cognitive view of social choice theory I advocate entails rejection of *both* the view that only self-interested preferences are appropriate input to social choice mechanisms and the view that 'ethical' as well as self-interested preferences may be appropriate input; that is, I am rejecting common assumptions of both such views.

46. Dworkin, "Reverse Discrimination" and "What Rights Do We Have?", in *Taking Rights Seriously*, especially pp. 234, 275–277; see also his "Liberalism", p. 134.

47. Compare Sen, "Social Choice Theory: A Re-examination", sections 1, 6 and 7, in *Choice, Welfare and Measurement*; Riker, *Liberalism Against Populism*, p. 238–246; Schumpeter's foreshadowing skepticism, *Capitalism, Socialism and Democracy*, pp. 251, 263.

48. See Riker, *Liberalism Against Populism*, pp. 187, 192.

49. See and compare Elster, *Sour Grapes*, Chapters III, IV.

50. See Mill, *Considerations of Representative Government*, pp. 26–27.

51. On externalist epistemology, see Nozick, *Philosophical Explanations*, pp. 265, 280–283.

52. See and compare Sen, *Choice, Welfare and Measurement*, pp. 315, 317; Elster, *Sour Grapes*, p. 137–140; Lively, *Democracy*, pp. 102–103.

Borda-type rank order voting point systems are also sensitive to information other than than provided by attitudes toward the pair of alternatives at issue. But the character of such sensitivity, when motivated by externalist epistemology, is rather different from that produced by rank order voting point systems. For example, consider the beliefs of Lewd, namely, that it would be better for Prude to read the book than for Lewd to read it, and better for Lewd to read it than no one. A rank order voting point scheme, interpreted cognitively, would presumably treat Lewd's belief that it would better for Prude to read the book rather than no one as stronger evidence about what ought to be done than his belief that it would be better for Lewd himself to read it rather than no one. But a voting scheme designed to avoid debunking influences such as spite and meddlesomeness would make just the reverse weighting of the evidential values of the two beliefs in question.

53. Compare Schauer, "Free Speech and the Argument from Democracy", on the basis for "Special concern for freedom to discuss public issues and criticize government decisions and officials"; he writes that "The next advance in free speech theory may come when we recognize and incorporate into our thinking the fact that different categories of discourse bring different considerations into play, and may require different forms of legal protection", pp. 252–253.

54. See Mill, *Considerations of Representative Government*, pp. 25–28. See also and compare Hamilton and Madison in *The Federalist Papers*, numbers 10, 17, 23, 37, 47, and especially, with respect to sensitivity to anti-debunking considerations as a basis for agenda and domain divisions, 48, 49, 51, 62, 63, 70 and 78. Work in progress by Iain McLean of University College, Oxford, suggests that Condorcet's cognitivist views on social choice were influential with Jefferson and Madison, and were regarded by them as highly significant with respect to the problems faced by their emerging nation.

55. Dahl, *Dilemmas of Pluralist Democracy*, pp. 85, 203–204; compare *Preface*

*to Democratic Theory*, Chapter 1, against the Madisonian conception of the division of power, and Chapters 3, 5, on polyarchy and government by minorities. Compare also Riker's taste for "different methods in different circumstances", *Liberalism Against Populism*, p. 113.

56. Compare Ely, *Democracy and Distrust*, pp. 92–93. One of the issues to be addressed in formulating a social knowledge function, of course, would be the appropriate trade-off between avoiding debunked input and output and capturing undebunked input and output. But this is a general problem about knowledge, and not a problem especially for the notion of a social knowledge function.

57. See and compare Braybrooke, "Can Democracy be Combined with Federalism or with Liberalism?", pp. 113–114.

58. Compare Arrow, *Social Choice and Individual Values*, pp. 85–105.

59. Sen, *Collective Choice and Social Welfare*, p. 83; *Choice, Welfare, and Measurement*, essays 13, 14, especially p. 310.

60. See Sen, *Collective Choice and Social Welfare*, pp. 79–80, 87–88.

61. Sen, *Choice, Welfare and Measurement*, pp. 241ff, 294ff, 341ff.

62. Sen, *Choice, Welfare and Measurement*, p. 342.

63. See also Braybrooke, "Can Democracy be Combined with Federalism or with Liberalism?", on non-overlapping agenda assignments and relativized unrestricted domain, pp. 113–114.

64. Sen, *Collective Choice and Social Welfare*, p. 86; but compare *Choice, Welfare and Measurement*, p. 310.

65. Dahl, *Dilemmas of Pluralist Democracy*, pp. 36, 49; see also pp. 82–84, 99–100.

66. See Dahl, *Dilemmas of Pluralist Democracy*, pp. 86–87, 93–94, 106–107.

67. Dahl, "Federalism and the Democratic Process", pp. 103–104; see also Braybrooke, "Can Democracy be Combined with Federalism or with Liberalism?", pp. 113–114.

68. See and compare Whelan, "Prologue: Democratic Theory and the Boundary Problem", pp. 14–16, 20, 22, 26–27, 31; Beitz, "Procedural Equality in Democratic Theory". Compare also the arguments of this paragraph with the arguments of Chapter 8 section 1, to the effect that questions arise about what the unit of agency should be and that the unit of agency should not be taken as fixed.

69. See Whelan, "Prologue: Democratic Theory and the Boundary Problem", p. 19; see also Dahl, "Federalism and the Democratic Process", p. 104.

70. Lively, *Democracy*, p. 147.

71. See Beitz, "Procedural Equality in Democratic Theory", especially pp. 75, 87; compare Whelan, "Prologue: Democratic Theory and the Boundary Problem", pp. 37ff, 40.

72. Schumpeter, *Capitalism, Socialism and Democracy*, p. 242; compare Bachrach, *The Theory of Democratic Elitism*, pp. 18, 94.

73. See and compare Lively, *Democracy*, pp. 31, 131–132.

74. Mill, *Considerations of Representative Government*, p. 41; see also pp. 25, 37; *On Liberty*, p. 33.

75. See Taylor, *Philosophy and the Human Sciences*, pp. 205–210; Lively, *Democracy*, pp. 131–141; Pateman, *Participation and Democratic Theory*, p. 29.

76. See Berlin, "Two Concepts of Liberty", in *Four Essays on Liberty*, p. 153n.

77. See Sandel, *Liberalism and the Limits of Justice*, pp. 144, 152–153; Taylor, "What's Wrong with Negative Liberty", in *Philosophy and the Human Sciences*.

78. See Taylor, "What's Wrong with Negative Liberty", in *Philosophy and the*

*Human Sciences*, p. 229; see also and compare: Hallowell, *The Moral Foundation of Democracy*, pp. 43–44; Smith, "Liberalism and Judicial Reveiw", p. 222, for the view that process-based constitutional theories are unsatisfactory both as theory and in terms of popular support. For an extreme version of a kind of liberalism that demands respect for negative freedom in service of an ideal of individual self-determination, see von Humboldt, *The Limits of State Action*.

79. See Berlin, "Two Concepts of Liberty", in *Four Essays on Liberty*, pp. 167, 168, 170. Compare Lively, *Democracy*, p. 121.

80. See Dahl, *Dilemmas of Pluralist Democracy*, pp. 61–62, 210.

81. See especially Sen's essay "Equality of What?", in *Choice, Welfare and Measurement*.

82. See Sandel, *Liberalism and the Limits of Justice*, pp. 63, 122–128, 166–167, 178. Rawls' emphasis on conflicting and incommensurable conceptions of the good associated with each person continues in recent work, such as "Justice as Fairness: Political not Metaphysical".

83. See Berlin, "Two Concepts of Liberty", *Four Essays on Liberty*, p. 133.

84. See Nussbaum, "Shame, Separateness, and Political Unity: Aristotle's Criticism of Plato", *passim*.

85. See Rawls, "Justice as Fairness: Political, not Metaphysical".

86. Nussbaum, "Shame, Separateness, and Political Unity", p. 411.

87. Parfit, "Later Selves and Moral Principles", pp. 153, 158, 160; see also *Reasons and Persons*, Chapter 15.

88. Compare Sen, "Utilitarianism and Welfarism", p. 470: "My difficulty with Parfit's argument that the rejection of the 'simple view' provides some defense for the utilitarian unconcern with *inter*personal distribution arises partly from the belief that the moral intuitions dealing with *intra*personal distribution which are referred to in this defense depend heavily on the acceptance of the 'simple view'. When we reject the 'simple view', the case for revising our moral beliefs on *intra*personal distribution is very strong." Sen is speaking here of intrapersonal distribution across different time periods in the life of the same person, whereas my concerns are with intrapersonal distribution across conflicting values, whether at the same or different time periods, and with intrapersonal distribution of probabilities across outcomes.

89. See Parfit, *Reasons and Persons*, p. 250.

90. I do not attribute such atomism with respect to attitudes to Parfit. As I have tried to indicate, his concerns are to some extent orthogonal to mine.

91. See Nussbaum, "Shame, Separateness, and Political Unity", pp. 420–421.

92. See Green, *Prolegomena to Ethics*, sections 267–285, especially pp. 324, 325, 331–332, 337.

93. Holding population constant.

94. See Pritchard, "Duty and Interest". For discussion of, and an effective response to, Pritchard's objection, see Norman, *The Moral Philosophers*, Chapter 4. Compare Elster, *Sour Grapes*, Chapter II. I find unpersuasive Elster's assertion (e.g., pp. 91, 100) that what he calls 'narcissistic political theories' such as Mill's, which give an important role as a political goal to the education of citizens, the cultivation of character, self-realization, etc., must be self-defeating. His view of the difficulties of self-determination and of techniques for becoming a certain kind of person (see especially pp. 43–60) strikes me as somewhat exaggerated, and suggests an essentially Cartesian conception of the self as the given, an internal core of awareness that regards its own actions as from a distance. The essential insight of Aristotle, Hegel, Wittgenstein, and behavioural therapy, that, to put it crudely, one is what one does, is lost.

Moreover, even if one were to grant Elster's claims at the level of individuals, which I do not, the self-defeatingness of goals of character formation and self-realization at the level of social institutions and their design would not not follow from their self-defeatingness as individual goals.

95. See especially Aristotle, *Politics*, books VII, VIII. Compare Lindsay, *The Modern Democratic State*, pp. 241, 245–246. von Humboldt's extreme laissez-faire position, which severely limited the state's area of proper concern even with respect to education, was nevertheless born of concern to protect negative freedom *as a means to* the development of individual autonomy. It seems to me seriously misguided as an instrumental matter.

96. This distinction is not reflected by Mutual Preferential Independence, which operates in an ordinal framework; compare the way in which the distinction between Additive Utility Independence and Mutual Utility Independence opens up within a cardinal framework, in Keeney and Raiffa, *Decisions with Multiple Objectives*, Chapter 5.

97. The point is made by Sen, with respect to the distinction between a concern with the distribution of utility and a concern with the distribution of income:

> Even when utility is the sole basis of importance there is still the question as to whether the size of *marginal* utility, irrespective of *total* utility enjoyed by the person, is an adequate index of moral importance. It is, of course, possible to define a metric on utility characteristics such that each person's utility scale is coordinated with everyone else's in a way that equal social importance is simply 'scaled' as equal marginal utility. If interpersonal comparisons of utility are taken to have no descriptive content, then this can indeed be thought to be a natural approach. No matter how the relative social importances are arrived at, the marginal utilities attributed to each person would then simply reflect these values. . . . the essence of [this type of exercise] consists in using a scaling procedure such that marginal utility measures are automatically identified as indicators of social importance.
>
> This route to utilitarianism may meet with little resistance, but it is non-controversial mainly because it says so little. A problem arises the moment utilities and interpersonal comparisons thereof are taken to have some independent descriptive content, as utilitarians have traditionally insisted that they do. There could then be conflicts between these descriptive utilities and the appropriately scaled, essentially normative, utilities in terms of which one is 'forced' to be a utilitarian.

"Equality of What?", in *Choice, Welfare, and Measurement*, pp. 355–356. See also the distinction between mutual utility independence and additive utility independence, in Keeney and Raiffa, *Decisions with Multiple Objectives*, Chapter 5. On the role of linearity and additive separability assumptions in multi-dimensional utility theory, see: Edwards and Tversky, *Decision Making*, pp. 255–256; Keeney, "An Illustrated Procedure . . . ", p. 100ff; Shepard, "On Subjectively Optimum Selections . . . ", p. 270: and *passim*; Hull, Moore and Thomas, "Utility and its Measurement", p. 76ff.

98. See again Williams, "Conflicts of Values", pp. 222–223.

99. See, for example, Harsanyi, *Essays*, especially essays II, IV and V; Diamond, "Cardinal Welfare, Individualistic Ethics, and Interpersonal Comparison of Utility: Comment"; Sen, *Choice, Welfare, and Measurement*, pp. 204–205; Machina, " 'Expected Utility' Analysis without the Independence Axiom", section 5.2.

100. See Harsanyi, "Cardinal Welfare, Individualistic Ethics, and Interpersonal Comparisons of Utility", in his *Essays*, p. 11ff.

101. See Harsanyi, "Nonlinear Social Welfare Functions", *Essays*, pp. 72–77. But compare the later "Von Neumann-Morgenstern Utilities, Risk-Taking, and Welfare", in which he connects Von Neumann-Morgenstern utilities with an outcome-oriented as opposed to process-oriented position. See also my discussion in Chapter 4 section 3.

102. See Tversky, "Critique of Expected Utility Theory", pp. 164–166. The Independence axiom here violated imposes the requirement that (a) the utility of each possible world be a function just of features of that world, as well as the requirement of (b) additivity, or linearity. See Chapter 4, note 12. In the text I interpret the violation to involve a violation of linearity, since this interpretation is relevant to Harsanyi's position and is invoked by his suggestion of a "close formal similarity" to issues about utility egalitarianism. My argument does not depend on rejecting the alternative interpretation of the violation as one of requirement (a). But the parallel Harsanyi suggests seems to depend on consideration of linearity violations, which is why I focus on that interpretation of Tversky's case.

103. Complementarity effects may also be seen in cases not involving certainty: consider the combination of a preference for a .75 chance of a million dollars over a .60 chance of five million with a preference for a .04 chance of five million over a .05 chance of one million. Such a combination may still be interpreted as reflecting a concern with the distribution of utilities across outcomes: intuitively, such distributional concerns are aroused by the first choice to a much greater degree than by the second choice. The intuition may be clearer for the analogous pairs of choices concerning the distribution of wealth across percentages of the population (assuming identical utility functions): the difference between 75% of the population having a million dollars and 60% having five million is of much greater significance from the point of view of a concern with egalitarian distribution than the difference between 5% having one million and 4% having five million.

104. Vickers, commenting on Tversky's data, writes:

> Aristotle's account of deliberation allows for conflict in the soul. Not only is there the conflict of appetite and reasoned desire, but practical principles which are worthy and accepted may conflict with each other. Deliberation in this case consists in weighing the particular circumstances in the light of these principles. . . .
>
> From the point of view of utility theory, on the other hand, there is but one practical principle: Act so as to maximize the expectation of the utility of consequences. There can thus be no conflict of practical principles. Whatever looks to be conflict of principles . . . will be analyzed in terms of preferences among . . . propositions . . . accompanied . . . by subjective probabilities. Given such preferences and probabilities, the right action is determined by the computation of the expectation of the utility of consequences. Apparent conflict dissipates in a sufficiently logically fine analysis of the propositions . . . .
>
> The incompatibility of these two views of deliberation has always seemed to be more in spirit than in fact. The aristotelian points to the obviousness of conflict and the possiblity of weakness of will, the utility theorist responds by discussing the reconciliation of conflicting desires . . . In general the utility theorist converts what the aristotelian calls a practical principle into propositions

and preferences, and thus provides a unified standard for deliberation, arguing the while that whatever account the aristotelian will offer of deliberation can be more fully and precisely given in utility theoretic terms.

It is precisely from this point of view that Allais' and Tversky's data seem to me striking and important. For they give an instance of a practical principle ('Avoid unnecessary risk.') which apparently cannot be converted into propositions and preferences. The obstacle to such conversion is that the moral neutrality of risk seems to be an a priori principle of utility theory." See Vickers, "Utility and its Ambiguities", pp. 306–308.

These remarks suggest that if expected utility theory were to succeed in its aim of commensuration (in the substantial sense distinguished from the weak sense in Chapter 13 section 5), the notion of a non-linear function of the utilities of different outcomes would make little sense: if only one uniform thing, which incorporates any value or disvalue risk may have, for one person at one time, is at issue, and more of it is better, then may be hard to see how questions of distribution get a grip at all or how anything other than the sum of the expected utilities of each possible outcome could be a matter of concern. If so, the fact that they do get a grip and something else is a matter of concern argues against the supposition that expected utility theory succeeds in its aim of commensuration.

105. See Rawls, *A Theory of Justice*, pp. 173–175.

106. See Rawls, *A Theory of Justice*, pp. 154–155, 164–175.

107. See Ellsberg, "Risk, Ambiguity, and the Savage Axioms", pp. 643–646, 650–651, 656–660 and *passim*; Roberts, "Risk, Ambiguity, and the Savage Axioms: Comment", p. 335n; Goldsmith and Sahlin, "The Role of Second-Order Probabilities in Decision-Making"; Gardenfors & Sahlin, "Unreliable Probabilities, Risk Taking, and Decision Making", and "Decision Making with Unreliable Probabilities"; Sahlin, "On Second-Order Probabilities and the Notion of Epistemic Risk". L. J. Cohen has made related claims about the importance of the weight of evidence in many articles.

108. See also Gardenfors and Sahlins, "Unreliable Probabilities, Risk Taking, and Decision Making", pp. 364–365, on the way in which the Dutch book theorem depends on assuming the willingness of people to bet; and see Ellsberg, "Risk, Ambiguity, and the Savage Axioms", p. 663.

109. See Goldsmith and Sahlin, "The Role of Second Order Probabilities in Decision Making", p. 459.

110. As Sahlin explains in "On Second Order Probabilities and the Notion of Epistemic Risk", p. 102, it is the epistemically risk-averse subject who violates Savage's Sure Thing Principle.

111. See Gardenfors and Sahlin, "Unreliable Probabilities, Risk Taking, and Decision Making", p. 365.

112. Personal communication. See Raiffa, "Risk, Ambiguity, and the Savage Axioms: Comment". For a critical discussion of Raiffa's use of the interpretation of the Independence Axiom as a commutativity principle, see McClennan, "Sure-Thing Doubts", section 4.

113. Raiffa, "Risk, Ambiguity, and the Savage Axioms: Comment", p. 693.

114. See Allais, "The So-Called Allais Paradox and Rational Decisions under Uncertainty", pp. 490, 502ff.

# BIBLIOGRAPHY

ALLAIS, Maurice, "The Foundations of a Positive Theory of Choice involving Risk and a Criticism of the Postulates and Axioms of the American School", in Allais and Hagen, editors, *Expected Utility Hypotheses and the Allais Paradox*.

ALLAIS, Maurice, "The So-Called Allais Paradox and Rational Decisions Under Uncertainty", in Allais and Hagen, editors, *Expected Utility Hypotheses and the Allais Paradox*.

ALLAIS, Maurice, and HAGEN, Ole, editors, *Expected Utility Hypotheses and the Allais Paradox* (Dordrecht, Reidel, 1979).

ANSCOMBE, G. E. M., *Intention*, second edition (Oxford, Blackwell, 1976).

ARISTOTLE, *The Nicomachean Ethics*, David Ross, translator (London, Oxford University Press, 1972).

ARISTOTLE, *The Politics*, T. A. Sinclair, translator (Harmondsworth, Middlesex, Penguin Books, 1962).

ARROW, Kenneth J., "Extended Sympathy and the Possibility of Social Choice", *American Economic Review Papers and Proceedings* (1977).

ARROW, Kenneth J., *Social Choice and Individual Values*, second edition (New Haven and London, Yale University Press, 1963).

ARROW, K. J., and INTRILIGATOR, M., editors, *The Handbook of Mathematical Economics*, vol. 3 (Amsterdam, North Holland, 1985).

ASHLEY, Kevin D., Modelling Legal Argument: Reasoning with Cases and Hypotheticals, Ph.D. dissertation (University of Massachussetts, Dept. of Computer and Information Science, submitted 1987).

AUMANN, R., "Agreeing to Disagree", *The Annals of Statistics* (1976).

BACHRACH, Peter, *The Theory of Democratic Elitism* (London, University of London Press, 1969).

BARRY, Brian, *Political Argument* (London, Routledge and Kegan Paul, 1965).

BATTALIO, Raymond C., KAGEL, John H., MacDONALD, Don N., "Animal Choices Over Uncertain Outcomes: Some Initial Experimental Results", *American Economic Review* (1985).

BEARDSMORE, R. W., *Moral Reasoning* (London, Routledge & Kegan Paul, 1969).

BEITZ, Charles R., "Procedural Equality in Democratic Theory: A Preliminary Examination", in Pennock and Chapman, editors, *Liberal Democracy*.

BENNETT, Jonathan, *Locke, Berkeley, Hume: Central Themes* (Oxford, Clarendon Press, 1971).

BERGSTROM, Lars, "Hintikka on 'Prima Facie' Obligations", *Theoria* (1974).

BERGSTROM, Lars, "Reply to Professor Hintikka", *Theoria* (1975).

BERLIN, Isaiah, *Four Essays on Liberty* (Oxford, Oxford University Press, 1969).

BERNHEIM, B. Douglas, "Rationalizable Strategic Behavior", *Econometrica* (1984).

437

BIRCH, A. H., *Representation* (London, Macmillan, 1971).

BLACK, Duncan, *The Theory of Committees and Elections* (Cambridge, Cambridge University Press, 1971).

BLACKBURN, Simon, "Errors and the Phenomenology of Value", in Honderich, editor, *Morality and Objectivity*.

BLACKBURN, S. W., "Moral Realism", in *Morality and Moral Reasoning*, John Casey, editor (London, Methuen, 1971).

BLACKBURN, S. W., "Reply: Rule-Following and Moral Realism", in Holtzman and Leich, editors, *Wittgenstein: To Follow a Rule*.

BLACKBURN, Simon, *Spreading the Word* (Oxford, Clarendon Press, 1984).

BLACKBURN, Simon, "Supervenience Revisited", in Hacking, editor, *Exercises in Analysis*.

BLAKEMORE, Colin, *Mechanics of the Mind* (Cambridge, Cambridge University Press, 1977).

BLASS, Elliott M., editor, *Handbook of Behavioral Neurobiology*, vol. 8 (New York, Plenun Press, 1986).

BOLTON, Derek, "Life-form and Idealism", in Vesey, editor, *Idealism Past and Present*.

BORGLIN, Anders, "States and Persons—On the Interpretation of Some Fundamental Concepts in the theory of Justice as Fairness", *Journal of Public Economics* (1982).

BRAYBROOKE, David, "Can Democracy be Combined with Federalism?", in Pennock and Chapman, editors, *Liberal Democracy*.

BRAYBROOKE, David, "A Public Goods Approach to the Theory of the General Will", in *Unity, Plurality and Politics*, J. M. Porter and R. Vernon, editors (London, Croom Helm, 1986).

BROADBENT, D. E., and WEISKRANTZ, L., editors, *The Neurophsychology of Cognitive Function* (London, The Royal Society, 1982).

BROOME, John, "Choice and Value in Economics", *Oxford Economic Papers* (1978).

BROOME, John, "Rationality and the Sure-Thing Principle", in *Rationality, Self-Interest and Benevolence*, Gay Meeks, editor.

BURGE, Tyler, "Cartesian Error and the Objectivity of Perception", in Pettit and McDowell, editors, *Subject, Thought, and Context*.

BURGE, Tyler, "Individualism and the Mental", in *Midwest Studies in Philosophy*, vol. IV, French, Uehling and Wettstein, editors.

BURGE, Tyler, "Individualism and Psychology", *Philosophical Review* (1986).

BURGE, Tyler, "Intellectual Norms and Foundations of Mind", *Journal of Philosophy* (1986).

BURKE, Edmund, *Speech to the Electors of Bristol, Works*, vol. 1 (London, Bohn's Standard Library, 1887).

BURNS, Tom R., and MEEKER, Dave, "Conflict and Structure in Multi-Level Multiple Objective Decision-Making Systems", in Hooker, Leach and McClennan, editors, *Foundations and Applications of Decision Theory*.

CAMPBELL, C. A., *In Defence of Free Will* (London, George Allen & Unwin, 1967).

CAMPBELL, Richmond, and SOWDEN, Lanning, editors, *Paradoxes of Rationality and Cooperation: Prisoner's Dilemma and Newcomb's Problem* (Vancouver, University of British Columbia Press, 1985).

CARNAP, Rudolp, *Logical Foundations of Probability* (London, Routledge and Kegan Paul, 1950).

CASTANEDA, Hector-Neri, "Imperatives, Oughts and Moral Oughts", *Australasian Journal of Philosophy* (1966).

CASTANEDA, Hector-Neri, "On the Semantics of the Ought-to-Do", in *Semantics of Natural Language*, Donald Davidson and Gilbert Harman, editors (Dordrecht, Reidel, 1972).

CHARLES, David, "Rationality and Irrationality", *Proceedings of the Aristotelian Society* (1982–83).

CHISHOLM, Roderick, *The First Person* (Brighton, Harvester Press, 1981).

CHISHOLM, Roderick, "Practical Reason and the Logic of Requirement", in *Practical Reason*, Stephan Korner, editor (Oxford, Blackwell, 1974).

COHEN, L. Jonathan, "Are People Programmed to Commit Fallacies?", *Journal for the Theory of Social Behaviour* (1982).

COHEN, L. Jonathan, "Can Human Irrationality Be Experimentally Demonstrated?", with Open Peer Commentary, Author's Response, and Continuing Commentary, *The Behavioral and Brain Sciences* (1981, 1983).

COHEN, L. Jonathan, "On the Psychology of Prediction: Whose is the Fallacy?", *Cognition* (1979).

COHEN, L. Jonathan, *The Probable and the Provable* (Oxford, Clarendon Press, 1977).

COHEN, L. Jonathan, "Twelve Questions about Keyne's Concept of Weight", *British Journal for the Philosophy of Science* (1985).

COHEN, Morris R., "The Basis of Contract", 46 *Harvard Law Review* 553 (1933).

COOMBS, Clyde H. "Psychological Scaling Without a Unit of Measurement", *Psychological Review* (1950).

COOMBS, Clyde H., "Social Choice and Strength of Preference", in Coombs, Thrall and Davis, editors, *Decision Processes*.

COOPER, Wesley E., NIELSEN, Kai, and PATTEN, Steven C., *New Essays on John Stuart Mill and Utilitarianism* (Guelph, Ontario, *Canadian Journal of Philosophy*, supplementary volume, 1979).

CORBIN, Arthur Linton, *Corbin on Contracts* (St. Paul, Minnesota, West Publishing Company, 1952).

DAHL, Robert A., *Dilemmas of Pluralist Democracy: Autonomy vs. Control* (New Haven and London, Yale University Press, 1982).

DAHL, Robert A., "Federalism and the Democratic Process", in Pennock and Chapman, editors, *Liberal Democracy*.

DAHL, Robert A., *A Preface to Democratic Theory* (Chicago, University of Chicago Press, 1956).

DANIELS, Norman, "Wide Reflective Equilibrium and Theory Acceptance in Ethics", *Journal of Philosophy* (1979).

DAVIDSON, Donald, "A Coherence Theory of Truth and Knowledge", in Le Pore, editor, *Truth and Interpretation*.

DAVIDSON, Donald, *Essays on Actions and Events* (Oxford, Clarendon Press, 1982).

DAVIDSON, Donald, "Expressing Evaluations" (Kansas, The Lindley Lecture, University of Kansas, 1982).

DAVIDSON, Donald, *Inquiries into Truth and Interpretation* (Oxford, Clarendon Press, 1984).

DAVIDSON, Donald, "Judging Interpersonal Interests", in Elster and Hylland, editors, *Foundations of Social Choice*.

DAVIDSON, Donald, "Knowing One's Own Mind", *American Philosophical Society Proceedings and Addresses* (1987).

DAVIDSON, Donald, "A New Basis for Decision Theory", *Theory and Decision* (1985).

DAVIDSON, Donald, "Paradoxes of Irrationality", in *Philosophical Essays on Freud*, *Wollheim and Hopkins*, editors.

DAVIDSON, Donald, "Rational Animals", in Le Pore and McLaughlin, editors, *Actions and Events*.

DAVIDSON, Donald, and HARMAN, Gilbert, editors, *Semantics of Natural Language*, (Dordrecht, Reidel, 1972).

DAVIDSON, Donald, McKINSEY, J. C. C., and SUPPES, Patrick, "Outlines of a Formal Theory of Value", *Philosophy of Science* (1955).

DAVIES, Graham, ELLIS, Hadyn, and SHEPHERD, John, editors, *Perceiving and Remembering Faces* (London, Academic Press, 1981).

DAVIES, Martin, "Individualism and Supervenience", *Proceedings of the Aristotelian Society*, supplementary volume (1986).

DAVIS & CO. v. MORGAN, 117 Ga. 504; 43 S.E. 732 (1903).

DAWKINS, Richard, *The Extended Phenotype* (Oxford, Oxford University Press, 1982).

DEATON, Angus, and MUELLBAUER, John, *Economics and Consumer Behavior* (Cambridge, Cambridge University Press, 1980).

DENNETT, Daniel C., *Brainstorms* (Brighton, Harvester Press, 1981).

DENNETT, Daniel C., "Intentional Systems in Cognitive Ethology: The 'Panglossian Paradigm' Defended", *The Behavioral and Brain Sciences* (1983).

DESIST v. U.S., 394 U.S. 244 (1969).

DIAMOND, Peter A., "Cardinal Welfare, Individualistic Ethics, and Interpersonal Comparison of Utility: Comment", *Journal of Political Economy* (1967).

DONEY, Willis, editor, *Descartes: A Collection of Critical Essays* (Notre Dame, University of Notre Dame Press, 1967).

DOWNS, Anthony, *An Economic Theory of Democracy* (New York, Harper and Brothers, 1957).

DUMMETT, Michael, "Common Sense and Physics", in McDonald, editor, *Perception and Identity*.

DUMMETT, Michael, *Frege: Philosophy of Language* (London, Duckworth, 1973).

DWORKIN, Ronald, *Law's Empire* (London, Fontana Press, 1986).

DWORKIN, Ronald, "Liberalism", in *Public and Private Morality*, Hampshire, editor.

DWORKIN, Ronald, "No Right Answer?", in *Law Morality and Society: Essays in Honour of H. L. A. Hart*, Hacker and Raz, editors.

DWORKIN, Ronald, "Seven Critics", 11 *Georgia Law Review* 1201 (1977).

DWORKIN, Ronald, *Taking Rights Seriously* (London, Duckworth, 1977).

EDGLEY, Roy, *Reason in Theory and Practice* (London, Hutchinson University Library, 1969).

EDWARDS, Ward, and TVERSKY, Amos, editors, *Decision Making: Selected Readings* (Harmondsworth, Penguin, 1967).

EELLS, Ellery, *Rational Decision and Causality* (Cambridge, Cambridge University Press, 1982).

ELLSBERG, Daniel, "Risk, Ambiguity, and the Savage Axioms" and "Reply", *Quarterly Journal of Economics* (1961).

ELSTER, Jon, editor, *The Multiple Self* (Cambridge, Cambridge University Press, 1986).

ELSTER, Jon, *Sour Grapes* (Cambridge, Cambridge University Press, 1983).

ELSTER, Jon, "Weakness of the Will and the Free Rider Problem", *Economics and Philosophy* (1985).

ELSTER, Jon, and HYLLAND, Aanund, *Foundations of Social Choice Theory* (Cambridge, Cambridge University Press, 1986).

ELY, John Hart, *Democracy and Distrust* (Cambridge, Mass., Harvard University Press, 1980).

EVANS, Gareth, *The Varieties of Reference*, edited by John McDowell (Oxford, Clarendon Press, 1982).

FEINBERG, Joel, "Justice, Fairness and Rationality", 81 *Yale Law Journal* 1004 (1972).

FEIWEL, George R., editor, *Arrow and the Ascent of Modern Economic Theory* (New York, New York University Press, 1987).

FELLNER, William, "Distortion of Subjective Probabilities as a Reaction to Uncertainty", *Quarterly Journal of Economics* (1961).

FISHBURN, Peter C., "Utility Theory", *Management Science* (1968).

FODOR, Jerry, "Individualism and Supervenience", *Proceedings of the Aristotelian Society*, supplementary volume (1986).

FODOR, Jerry A., *Representations* (Brighton, The Harvester Press, 1981).

FOLLESDAL, Dagfin, and HILPINEN, Risto, "Deontic Logic: An Introduction", in Hilpinen, editor, *Deontic Logic: Introductory and Systematic Readings*.

FOOT, Philippa, "Moral Realism and Moral Dilemma", *Journal of Philosophy* (1983).

FORBES, Graeme, "Nozick on Scepticism", *Philosophical Quarterly* (1984).

FRANKFURT, Harry, "Freedom of the Will and the Concept of a Person", *Journal of Philosophy* (1971).

FRANKFURT, Harry, "Identification and Externality", in Rorty, editor, *The Identities of Persons*.

FREGE, Gottlob, *Logical Investigations*, translated by P. T. Geach and R. H. Stoothoff (Oxford, Blackwell, 1977).

FRENCH, Peter, UEHLING, Theodore, and WETTSTEIN, Howard, editors, *Midwest Studies in Philosophy*, vol. IV (Minneapolis, University of Minnesota Press, 1979).

FRICKER, E. M., *Rules and Language: An Examination of Some of Wittgenstein's Arguments* (Oxford, B.Phil. Thesis, 1979).

FULLER, Lon L., and EISENBERG, Melvin Aron, *Basic Contract Law*, third edition (St. Paul, Minnesota, West Publishing Co., 1972).

FULLER, L. L., and PERDUE, William R., Jr., "The Reliance Interest in Contract Damages", 46 *Yale Law Journal* 52, 373 (1936–1937).

GALLIE, W. B., "Essentially Contested Concepts", *Proceedings of the Aristotelian Society* (1955–1956).

GARDENFORS, Peter, "Probabilistic Reasoning and Evidentiary Value", in *Evidentiary Value*, Gardenfors, Hansson and Sahlin, editors.

GARDENFORS, Peter, HANSSON, Bengt, and SAHLIN, Nils-Eric, editors, *Evidentiary Value*, Library of Theoria no. 15 (Lund, Gleerups, 1983).

GARDENFORS, Peter, and SAHLIN, Nils-Eric, "Decision-Making with Unreliable Probabilities", *British Journal of Mathematical and Statistical Psychology* (1983).

GARDENFORS, Peter, and SAHLIN, Nils-Eric, "Unreliable Probabilities, Risk Taking, and Decision Making", *Synthese* (1982).

GAUTHIER, David, "Maximization Constrained: The Rationality of Cooperation", in Campbell and Sowden, editors, *Paradoxes of Rationality and Cooperation*.

GEACH, Peter, "Critical Notice", *Mind* (1976), pp. 436–449.

GEACH, Peter, *Logic Matters* (Oxford, Blackwell, 1972).

GIBBARD, Allan, "Rule-Utilitarianism: Merely an Illusory Alternative?", *Australasian Journal of Philosophy* (1965).

GLOVER, Jonathan, "Self-Creation", *Proceedings of the British Academy* (1983).

GLUS v. BROOKLYN EASTERN TERMINAL, 359 U.S. 231; 79 S. Ct. 760 (1959).

GOLDSMITH, Robert W., "Studies of a Model for Evaluating Judicial Evidence", *Acta Psychologica* (1980).

GOLDSMITH, Robert W., and SAHLIN, Nils-Eric, "The Role of Second-Order Probabilities in Decision Making", in Humphreys, Svenson, and Vari, editors, *Analysing and Aiding Decision Processes*.

GOMBAY, Andre, "What Is Imperative Inference?", *Analysis* (1967).

GOODMAN, Nelson, *Fact, Fiction and Forecast*, 3rd edition (Hassock, Sussex, Harvester Press, 1979).

GREEN, H. A. John, *Consumer Theory* (Harmondsworth, Middlesex, Penguin, 1971).

GREEN, T. H., *Prolegomena to Ethics*, 5th edition (Oxford, Clarendon Press, 1907).

GRIFFIN, James, "Are There Incommensurable Values?", *Philosophy and Public Affairs* (1977).

GRIFFIN, James, "Equality: On Sen's Weak Equity Axiom", *Mind* (1981).

GUTTENPLAN, Samuel, "Moral Realism and Moral Dilemmas", *Proceedings of the Aristotelian Society* (1979–80).

HACKER, P. M. S., *Insight and Illusion: Wittgenstein on Philosophy and the Metaphysics of Experience* (Oxford, Oxford University Press, 1975).

HACKER, P. M. S., and RAZ, J., editors, *Law Morality and Society: Essays in Honour of H. L. A. Hart* (Oxford, Clarendon Press, 1977).

HACKING, Ian, editor, *Exercises in Analysis* (Cambridge, Cambridge University Press, 1985).

HAGEN, Ole, "Introductory Survey", in Allais and Hagen, editors, *Expected Utility Hypotheses and the Allais Paradox*.

HAGEN, Ole, "Paradoxes and Their Solutions", in Stigum and Wenstop, editors, *Foundations of Utility and Risk Theory with Applications*.

HAGEN, Ole, and WENSTOP, Fred, editors, *Progress in Utility Theory* (Dordrecht, Reidel, 1984).

HALLOWELL, John H., *The Moral Foundation of Democracy* (Chicago, University of Chicago Press, 1954).

HAMILTON, Alexander, MADISON, James, and JAY, John, *The Federalist Papers* (New York, Mentor, 1961).

HAMPSHIRE, Stuart, editor, *Public and Private Morality*, editor (Cambridge, Cambridge University Press, 1978).

HAMPSHIRE, Stuart, *Thought and Action*, new edition (London, Chatto and Windus, 1982).

HANSSON, Bengt, "The Decision Game—The Conceptualisation of Risk and Utility", *Proceedings of the Wittgenstein Society* (1980), volume on Ethics.

HARE, R. M., "Descriptivism", in *Essays on the Moral Concepts* (London, Macmillan, 1972).

HARE, R. M., *Freedom and Reason* (Oxford, Clarendon Press, 1963).

HARE, R. M., *The Language of Morals* (Oxford, Oxford University Press, 1952).

HARE, R. M., *Moral Thinking: Its Levels, Method, and Point* (Oxford, Clarendon Press, 1981).

HARE, R. M., *Practical Inferences* (London, MacMillan, 1971).

HARE, R. M., "Supervenience", *Proceedings of the Aristotelian Society*, supplementary volume (1984).

HARMAN, Gilbert, *The Nature of Morality: An Introduction to Ethics* (New York, Oxford University Press, 1977).

HARRISON, Jonathan, "Kant's Examples of the First Formulation of the Categorical Imperative", in Wolff, editor, *Kant: A Collection of Critical Essays*.

HARRISON, Ross, "Transcendental Arguments and Idealism", in Vesey, editor, *Idealism Past and Present*.

HARSANYI, John C., *Essays on Ethics, Social Behavior, and Scientific Explanation* (Dordrecht, Reidel, 1976).

HARSANYI, John C., "Morality and the Theory of Rational Behaviour", in Sen and Williams, editors, *Utilitarianism and Beyond*.

HARSANYI, John C., *Rational Behavior and Bargaining Equilibrium in Games and Social Situations* (Cambridge, Cambridge University Press, 1977).

HARSANYI, John C., "The Tracing Procedure: A Bayesian Approach to Defining a Solution for n-Person Noncooperative Games", *International Journal of Game Theory* (1975).

HARSANYI, John C., "Use of Subjective Probabilities in Game Theory", in Stigum and Wenstop, editors, *Foundations of Utility and Risk Theory with Applications*.

HARSANYI, John C., "Von Neumann-Morgenstern Utilities, Risk Taking, and Welfare", in *Arrow and the Ascent of Modern Economic Theory*, Feiwel, editor.

HART, Henry M., and SACKS, Albert M., *The Legal Process* (Cambridge, Mass., Harvard Law School mimeograph, 1958).

HART, H. L. A., "Between Utility and Rights", in *The Idea of Freedom*, Ryan, editor.

HART, H. L. A., *The Concept of Law* (Oxford, Clarendon Press, 1961).

HART, John, Jr., BERNDT, Rita Sloan, and CARAMAZZA, Alfonso, "Category-specific Naming Deficit Following Cerebral Infarction", *Nature* (1 August 1985).

HAUGELAND, John, "Weak Supervenience", *American Philosophical Quarterly* (1982).

HECAEN, Henry, "The Neurophysiology of Face Recognition", in *Perceiving and Remembering Faces*, Davies, Ellis and Shepherd, editors.

HEGEL, F., *Philosophy of Right*, T. M. Knox, translator (Oxford, Clarendon Press, 1942).

HEINER, Ronald A., "Uncertainty and Rule-Governed Behavior: On the Evolution of Legal Procedure" (Princeton, Institute for Advanced Study, 1985, typescript).

HELLER, Walter P., STARR, Ross M., and STARRETT, David A., editors, *Social Choice and Public Decision Making: Essays in Honor of Kenneth J. Arrow*, vol. 1 (Cambridge, Cambridge University Press, 1986).

HEMPEL, Carl G., *Aspects of Scientific Explanation* (New York, Free Press, 1965).

HENNINGSON v. BLOOMFIELD MOTORS, INC., 32 NJ 358, 161 A2d 69 (1960).

HERMAN, Barbara, "The Practice of Moral Judgment", *Journal of Philosophy* (1985).

HILPINEN, Risto, editor, *Deontic Logic: Introductory and Systematic Readings*, (Dordrecht, Reidel, 1971).

HILPINEN, Risto, editor, *New Studies in Deontic Logic: Norms, Actions and the Foundations of Ethics* (Dordrecht, Reidel, 1981).

HINTIKKA, Jaakko, "Cogito, Ergo Sum: Inference or Performance?", in Doney, editor, *Descartes*.

HINTIKKA, Jaakko, "Comment on Professor Bergstrom", *Theoria* (1975).

HINTIKKA, Jaakko, *Knowledge and Belief* (Ithaca, Cornell University Press, 1962).

HINTIKKA, Jaakko, " 'Prima facie' Obligations and Iterated Modalities", *Theoria* (1970–1971).

HINTIKKA, Jaakko, "Quantifiers in Deontic Logic", *Societas Scientiarum Fennica Commentationes Humanarum Litterarum* (1957).

HINTIKKA, Jaakko, "Some Main Problems of Deontic Logic", in *Deontic Logic: Introductory and Systemic Readings*, Risto Hilpinen, editor (Dordrecht, Reidel, 1971).

HIRSCH, Helmut V. B., "The Tunable Seer: Activity-Dependent Development of Vision", in Blass, editor, *Handbook of Behavioral Neurobiology*, vol. 8.

HOBBES, Thomas, *Leviathan*, Francis B. Randall, editor (New York, Washington Square Press, 1964).

HOFSTADTER, Albert, and McKINSEY, J. C. C., "On the Logic of Imperatives", *Philosophy of Science* (1939).

HOLDEN, Barry, "Liberal Democracy and the Social Determination of Ideas", in Pennock and Chapman, editors, *Liberal Democracy*.

HOLMES, Oliver Wendell, *The Common Law* (Boston, Little, Brown and Company, 1963).

HOLTZMAN, Steven H., and LEICH, Christopher M., editors, Wittgenstein: *To Follow a Rule* (London, Routledge & Kegan Paul, 1981).

HONDERICH, Ted, editor, *Essays on Freedom of Action* (London, Routledge and Kegan Paul, 1973).

HONDERICH, Ted, editor, *Morality and Objectivity* (London, Routledge & Kegan Paul, 1985).

HOOK, Sidney, editor, *Human Values and Economic Policy: A Symposium* (New York, New York University Press, 1967).

HOOKER, C. A., LEACH, J. J., and McCLENNAN, E. F., *Foundations and Applications of Decision Theory*, Volume I: Theoretical Foundations (Dordrecht & Boston, Reidel, 1978).

HORNSBY, Jennifer, "Physicalist Thinking and Behaviour", in Pettit and McDowell, editors, *Subject, Thought and Context*.

HULL, J. C., MOORE, P. G., and THOMAS, H., "Utility and its Measurement", in Kaufman and Thomas, editors, *Modern Decision Analysis*.

HULSE, Stewart H., FOWLER, Harry, and HONIG, Werner K., editors, *Cognitive Processes in Animal Behavior* (Hillsdale, New Jersey, Lawrence Erlbaum Associates, 1978).

HUMPHREYS, P. C., SVENSON, O., VARI, A., editors, *Analysing and Aiding Decision Processes* (Amsterdam, North-Holland, 1983).

HWANG, Ching-Lai, and YOON, Kwangsun, *Multiple Attribute Decision Making* (Berlin, Springer-Verlag, 1981).

IRWIN, T. H., "Reason and Responsibility in Aristotle", in Rorty, editor, *Essays on Aristotle's Ethics*.

JACOBS, Robert L., *Understanding Harmony* (London, Oxford University Press, 1958).

JEFFREY, R. C., *The Logic of Decision* (New York, McGraw-Hill, 1965).

KAHNEMAN, Daniel, SLOVIC, Paul, and TVERSKY, Amos, editors, *Judgment Under Uncertainty: Heuristics and Biases* (Cambridge, Cambridge University Press, 1982).

KAHNEMAN, Daniel, and TVERSKY, Amos, "Prospect Theory: An Analysis of Decision Under Risk", *Econometrica* (1979).

KANGER, Stig, "New Foundations for Ethical Theory", in Hilpinen, editor, *Deontic Logic: Introductory and Systematic Readings*.

KANT, Immanuel, *Critique of Practical Reason*, Lewis White Beck, translator (Indianapolis, Bobbs-Merrill Company, 1956).

KANT, Immanuel, *Foundations of the Metaphysics of Morals*, Lewis White Beck, translator (Indianapolis, Bobbs-Merrill Company, 1959).

KAUFMAN, Gordon M., and THOMAS, Howard, editors, *Modern Decision Analysis* (Harmondsworth, Penguin, 1977).

KEENAN, Edward L., editor, *Formal Semantics of Natural Language* (Cambridge, Cambridge University Press, 1975).

KEENEY, R. L., "An Illustrated Procedure for Assessing Multi-Attributed Utility Functions", in Kaufman and Thomas, editors, *Modern Decision Analysis*.

KEENEY, Ralph L., and RAIFFA, Howard, *Decisions with Multiple Objectives: Preferences and Value Tradeoffs* (New York, Wiley & Sons, 1976).

KELSEY, D. *Topics in Social Choice* (Oxford, D.Phil. thesis, 1982).

KEMP, Murray C., and NG, Yew-Kwang, "More on Social Welfare Functions: The Incompatibility of Individualism and Ordinalism", *Economica* (1977).

KEMP, Murray C., and NG, Yew-Kwang, "On the Existence of Social Welfare Functions, Social Orderings and Social Decision Functions", *Economica* (1976).

KIM, Jaegwon, "Causality, Identity, and Supervenience in the Mind-Body Problem", in *Midwest Studies in Philosophy*, vol. IV, French, Uehling, and Wettstein, editors.

KIM, Jaegwon, "Psychophysical Laws", in Le Pore and McLaughlin, editors, *Actions and Events*.

KIM, Jaegwon, "Supervenience and Nomological Incommesurables", *American Philosophical Quarterly* (1978).

KOLAKOWKSKI, Leszek, "In Praise of Inconsistency", in *Marxism and Beyond* (London, Pall Mall Press, 1968).

KOLM, S. C., *Justice et Equité* (Paris, Editions du centre national de la recherche scientifique, 1972).

KORNER, Stephan, editor, *Practical Reason* (Oxford, Blackwell, 1974).

KRESS, Kenneth J., "Legal Reasoning and Coherence Theories: Dworkin's Rights Thesis, Retroactivity, and the Linear Order of Decision", 72 *Calif. Law Review* 369 (1984).

KRIPKE, Saul A., "Naming and Necessity", in Donald Davidson and Gilbert Harman, editors, *Semantics of Natural Language*.

KRIPKE, Saul A., *Wittgenstein on Rules and Private Language* (Cambridge, Mass., Harvard University Press, 1982).

LAKOFF, George, "Pragmatics in Natural Logic", in *Formal Semantics of Natural Language*, Keenan, editor.

LE PORE, Ernest, editor, *Truth and Interpretation: Perspectives on the Philosophy of Donald Davidson* (Oxford, Blackwell, 1986).

LE PORE, Ernest, and McLAUGHLIN, Brian, editors, *Actions and Events: Perspectives on the Philosophy of Donald Davidson* (Oxford, Blackwell, 1985).

LEAR, Jonathan, "The Disappearing 'We' ", *Proceedings of the Aristotelian Society*, supplementary volume (1984).

LEAR, Jonathan, "Leaving the World Alone", *Journal of Philosophy* (1982).

LEMMON, E. J. "Deontic Logic and the Logic of Imperatives", *Logique et Analyse* (1965).

LEMMON, E. J., "Moral Dilemmas", *Philosophical Review* (1962).

LEVINE, Andrew, "A Conceptual Problem for Liberal Democracy", *Journal of Philosophy* (1978).

LEWIS, David, *Convention* (Oxford, Blackwell, 1969).

LEWIS, David, *Counterfactuals* (Cambridge, Mass., Harvard University Press, 1973).

LEWIS, David, "New Work for a Theory of Universals", *Australasian Journal of Philosophy* (1983).

LEWIS, David, *Philosophical Papers*, vol. 1 (New York, Oxford University Press, 1983).

LEWIS, David, "Putnam's Paradox", *Australasian Journal of Philosophy* (1984).

LEWIS, David, "Utilitarianism and Truthfulness", *Australasian Journal of Philosophy* (1972).

LEWIS, Harry A., "Is the Mental Supervenient on the Physical?", in *Essays on Davidson*, Vermazen and Hintikka, editors.

LINDSAY, A. D., *The Modern Democratic State* (London, Oxford University Press, 1943).

LIVELY, Jack, *Democracy* (Oxford, Blackwell, 1975).

LOOMES, G., and SUGDEN, R., "Regret Theory: An Alternative Theory of Rational Choice Under Uncertainty", *Economic Journal* (1982).

LOVIBOND, Sabina, *Realism and Imagination in Ethics* (Oxford, Blackwell, 1983).

LUCE, R. Duncan, "Conjoint Measurement", in Hooker, Leach, and McClennan, eds, *Foundations and Applications of Decision Theory*.

LUCE, R. Duncan, and RAIFFA, Howard, *Games and Decisions: Introduction and Critical Survey* (New York, John Wiley & Sons, 1957).

LUCE, R. Duncan, and TUKEY, John W., "Simultaneous Conjoint Measurement", *Journal of Mathematical Psychology* (1964).

MacCORMICK, Neil, *Legal Reasoning and Legal Theory* (Oxford, Clarendon Press, 1978).

MacCRIMMON, Kenneth R., and LARSEN, Stig, "Utility Theory: Axioms vs. Paradoxes", in Allais and Hagen, editors, *Expected Utility Hypotheses and the Allais Paradox*.

MACHINA, Mark J., *The Economic Theory of Individual Behavior Toward Risk: Theory, Evidence and New Directions* (Stanford University, Institute for Mathematical Studies in the Social Sciences, 1983).

MACHINA, Mark J., "'Expected Utility' Analysis Without the Independence Axiom", *Econometrica* (1982).

MACHINA, Mark J., "Generalized Expected Utility Analysis and the Nature of Observed Violations of the Independence Axiom", in Stigum and Wenstop, editors, *Foundations of Utility and Risk Theory with Applications*.

MACHINA, Mark J., "'Rational' Decision Making Versus 'Rational' Decision Modelling?", book review, *Journal of Mathematical Psychology* (1981).

MacKAY, Alfred F., "Extended Sympathy and Interpersonal Utility Comparisons", *Journal of Philosophy* (1986).

MACKIE, J. L. *The Cement of the Universe* (Oxford, Clarendon Press, 1980).

MACKIE, J. L. *Ethics: Inventing Right and Wrong* (Harmondsworth, Penguin, 1977).

MACKIE, J. L., *Problems from Locke* (Oxford, Clarendon Press, 1976).

MACKIE, J. L., *Truth, Probability and Paradox* (Oxford, Clarendon Press, 1973).

MacPHERSON, *The Life and Times of Liberal Democracy* (Oxford, Oxford University Press, 1977).

MALCOLM, Norman, *Ludwig Wittgenstein: A Memoir* (New York, Oxford University Press, 1978).

MARCUS, Ruth Barcan, "Iterated Deontic Modalities", *Mind* (1966).

MARCUS, Ruth Barcan, "Moral Dilemmas and Consistency", *Journal of Philosophy* (1980)

MAY, Kenneth O., "Intransitivity, Utility, and the Aggregation of Preference Patterns", *Econometrica* (1954).

McCLENNAN, Edward F., "Prisoner's Dilemma and Resolute Choice", in Campbell and Sowden, editors, *Paradoxes of Rationality and Cooperation*.

McCLENNAN, Edward F., "Sure-Thing Doubts", in Stigum and Wenstop, editors, *Foundations of Utility and Risk Theory with Applications*.

McCULLOCH, Gregory, "Scientism, Mind, and Meaning", in Pettit and McDowell, editors, *Subject, Thought and Context*.

McDONALD, G. F., editor, *Perception and Identity*, (London, Macmillan, 1979).

McDOWELL, John, "Non-Cognitivism and Rule-Following", in Holtzman and Leich, editors, *Wittgenstein: To Follow a Rule*.

McDOWELL, John, "On the Sense and Reference of a Proper Name", *Mind* (1977).

McDOWELL, John, "The Role of Eudaimonia in Aristotle's Ethics", in Rorty, editor, *Essays on Aristotle's Ethics*.

McDOWELL, John, "Singular Thought and the Extent of Inner Space", in Pettit and McDowell, editors, *Subject, Thought and Context*.

McDOWELL, John, "Values and Secondary Qualities", in Honderich, editor, *Morality and Objectivity*.

McDOWELL, John, "Virtue and Reason", *The Monist* (1979).

McDOWELL, John, "Wittgenstein on Following a Rule", *Synthese* (1984).

McGINN, Colin, *The Character of Mind* (Oxford, Oxford University Press, 1982).

McGINN, Colin, "Charity, Interpretation, and Belief", *Journal of Philosophy* (1977).

McGINN, Colin, "Radical Interpretation and Epistemology", in Le Pore, editor, *Truth and Interpretation*.

McGINN, Colin, "The Structure of Content", in Woodfield, editor, *Thought and Object*.

McGINN, Colin, *The Subjective View* (Oxford, Clarendon Press, 1983).

McGINN, Colin, "Weak Will", review of *Essays on Davidson: Actions and Events*, Vermazen and Hintikka, editors, *London Review of Books* (5 September 1985).

McGINN, Colin, *Wittgenstein on Meaning: An Interpretation and Evaluation* (Oxford, Blackwell, 1984).

MEEKS, Gay, editor, *Rationality, Self-Interest and Benevolence* (Cambridge, Cambridge University Press, forthcoming).

MENGES, Gunter, "Comparison of Decision Models and Some Suggestions", both in *Expected Utility Hypotheses and the Allais Paradox*, Allais and Hagen, editors.

MERRILL, G. H., "The Model-Theoretic Argument Against Realism", *Philosophy of Science* (1980).

MILL, John Stuart, *Considerations of Representative Government* (New York, Liberal Arts Press, 1958).

MILL, John Stuart, *On Liberty* (Northbrook, Illinois, AHM Publishing Corporation, 1947).

MILLER, Nicholas R., "Pluralism and Social Choice", *American Political Science Review* (1983).

MONTEFIORE, A., editor, *Philosophy and Personal Relations* (London, Routledge & Kegan Paul, 1973).

MOORE, G. E., *Principia Ethica* (Cambridge, Cambridge University Press, 1971).

MURAKAMI, Y., *Logic and Social Choice* (London, Routledge & Kegan Paul, 1968).

MURDOCH, Iris, *The Sovereignty of Good* (London, Routledge & Kegan Paul, 1970).

MYERSON, R. B., "Refinements of the Nash Equilibrium Concept", *International Journal of Game Theory* (1978).

NAGEL, Thomas, *Mortal Questions* (Cambridge, Cambridge University Press, 1979).

NAGEL, Thomas, *The Possibility of Altruism* (Oxford, Clarendon Press, 1975).

NAGEL, Thomas, *The View From Nowhere* (Oxford, Oxford University Press, 1986).

NELL, Onora, *Acting on Principle* (New York, Columbia University Press, 1975).

NELSON, William T., *On Justifying Democracy* (London, Routledge & Kegan Paul, 1980).

NG, Yew-Kwang, *Welfare Economics: Introduction and Development of Basic Concepts* (London, Macmillan, 1979).

NICKEL, James W., "Dworkin on the Nature and Consequences of Rights", 11 *Georgia Law Review* 1115 (1977).

NISBETT, Richard, and ROSS, Lee, *Human Inference: Strategies and Shortcomings of Social Judgment* (Englewood Cliffs, New Jersey, Prentice-Hall, 1980).

NORMAN, Richard, *The Moral Philosophers* (Oxford, Clarendon Press, 1983).

NORMAN, Richard, *Reasons for Action: A Critique of Utilitarian Rationality* (Oxford, Blackwell, 1971).

NOZICK, Robert, *Anarchy State and Utopia* (New York, Basic Books, 1974).

NOZICK, Robert, *Philosophical Explanations* (Cambridge, Mass., Harvard University Press, 1984).

NUSSBAUM, Martha Craven, "Shame, Separateness, and Political Unity: Aristotle's Criticism of Plato", in Rorty, editor, *Essays on Aristotle's Ethics*.

PACKARD, Dennis Jay, "A Note on Wittgenstein and Cyclical Comparatives", *Analysis* (1975).

PARFIT, Derek, "Later Selves and Moral Principles", in *Philosophy and Personal Relations*, Montefiore, editor.

PARFIT, Derek, *Reasons and Persons* (Oxford, Oxford University Press, 1984).

PARKER v. RANDOLPH, 442 U.S. 62 (1979).

PARKS, Robert P., "An Impossibility Theorem for Fixed Preferences: A Dictatorial Bergson-Samuelson Welfare Function", *Review of Economic Studies* (1976).

PATEMAN, Carole, *Participation and Democratic Theory* (Cambridge, Cambridge University Press, 1970).

PATTANAIK, P. K., *Voting and Collective Choice* (Cambridge, Cambridge University Press, 1971).

PEACOCKE, Christopher, *Holistic Explanation: Action, Space, Interpretation* (Oxford, Clarendon Press, 1979).

PEACOCKE, Christopher, "Intention and Akrasia", in *Essays on Davidson*, Vermazen and Hintikka, editors.

PEACOCKE, Christopher, *Thoughts: An Essay on Contents, Aristotelian Society Series,* vol. 4 (Oxford, Blackwell, 1986).

PEARCE, David G., "Rationalizable Strategic Behavior and the Problem of Perfection", *Econometrica* (1984).

PEARS, David, *Motivated Irrationality* (Oxford, Clarendon Press, 1984).

PENNOCK, J. Roland, *Democratic Political Theory* (Princeton, Princeton University Press, 1979).

PENNOCK, J. Roland, "Epilogue: Some Perplexities Further Considered", in Pennock and Chapman, editors, *Liberal Democracy*.

PENNOCK, J. Roland, and CHAPMAN, John W., editors, *Liberal Democracy* (New York and London, New York University Press, 1983).

PEOPLE v. ZACKOWITZ, 254 N.Y. 192, 172 N.E. 466 (1930).

PETTIT, Philip, "Broad-Minded Explanation and Psychology", in Pettit and McDowell, editors, *Subject, Thought and Context*.

PETTIT, Philip, "Evaluative Realism and Interpretation", in Holtzman and Leich, editors, *Wittgenstein: To Follow a Rule*.

PETTIT, Philip, "Wittgenstein, Individualism, and the Mental", in Weingartner, editor, *Epistemology and Philosophy of Science*, Proceedings of the Seventh Annual Wittgenstein Symposium.

PETTIT, Philip, and McDOWELL, John, editors, *Subject, Thought and Context* (Oxford, Oxford University Press, 1986).

PHELPS, Edmund S., editor, *Economic Justice* (Harmondsworth, Penguin, 1973).

PHILLIPS, D. Z., and MOUNCE, H. O., *Moral Practices* (London, Routledge & Kegan Paul, 1969).

PITCHER, George, editor, *Wittgenstein: The Philosophical Investigations* (New York, Doubleday & Company, 1966).

PREMACK, David, "On the Abstractness of Human Concepts: Why it Would Be Difficult to Talk to a Pigeon", in Hulse, Fowler and Honig, *Cognitive Processes in Animal Behavior*.

PRITCHARD, H. A., "Duty and Interest", Inaugural Lecture (Oxford, Oxford University Press, 1928).

PROSSER, William L., *Handbook of the Law of Torts* (St. Paul, Minnesota, West Publishing Company, 1971).

PUTNAM, Hilary, *Meaning and the Moral Sciences* (London, Routledge & Kegan Paul, 1978).

PUTNAM, Hilary, *Mind, Language and Reality* (Cambridge, Cambridge University Press, 1975).

PUTNAM, Hilary, *Realism and Reason* (Cambridge, Cambridge University Press, 1983).

PUTNAM, Hilary, *Reason, Truth and History* (Cambridge, Cambridge University Press, 1981).

QUATTRONE, George A., and TVERSKY, Amos, "Self-Deception and the Voter's Illusion", in Elster, editor, *The Multiple Self*.

QUINE, Willard Van Orman, *From a Logical Point of View* (New York, Harper & Row, 1963).

QUINE, Willard Van Orman, "On Empirically Equivalent Systems of the World", *Erkenntnis* (1975).

QUINE, Willard Van Orman, *Word and Object* (Cambridge, Mass., The M.I.T. Press, 1964).

RAIFFA, Howard, *Decision Analysis* (Reading, Mass., Addison-Wesley, 1968).

RAIFFA, Howard, "Risk, Ambiguity, and the Savage Axioms: Comment", *Quarterly Journal of Economics* (1961).

RAMSEY, F. P., "Truth and Probability", *The Foundations of Mathematics* (London, Kegan Paul, 1931).

RAWLS, John, "The Independence of Moral Theory", *Proceedings of the American Philosophical Association* (1974–75).

RAWLS, John, "Justice as Fairness: Political not Metaphysical", *Philosophy and Public Affairs* (1985).

RAWLS, John, "Outline of a Decision Procedure for Ethics", *Philosophical Review* (1951).

RAWLS, John, "Social Unity and Primary Goods", in Sen and Williams, editors, *Utilitarianism and Beyond*.

RAWLS, John, *A Theory of Justice* (Cambridge, Mass., Belknap Press of Harvard University Press, 1971).

RAZ, Joseph, editor, *Practical Reasoning* (Oxford, Oxford University Press, 1978).

REGAN, Donald, *Utilitarianism and Co-operation* (Oxford, Oxford University Press, 1980).

RESTATEMENT of the Law, Second, Contracts, (St. Paul, Minnesota, American Law Institute Publishers, 1973).

REYNOLDS, James F., and PARIS, David C., "The Concept of 'Choice' and Arrow's Theorem", *Ethics* (1979).

RIGGS v. PALMER, 115 N.Y. 506, 22 NE 118 (1889).

RIKER, William H., *Liberalism Against Populism* (San Francisco, Freeman and Co., 1982).

ROBBINS, Lionel, "Interpersonal Comparisons of Utility: A Comment", *Economic Journal* (1938).

ROBERTS, Harry V., "Risk, Ambiguity, and the Savage Axioms: Comment", *Quarterly Journal of Economics* (1963).

ROBERTS, Kevin W. S., "Social Choice Theory: The Single-Profile and Multi-Profile Approaches", *Review of Economic Studies* (1980).

RORTY, Amelie Oksenberg, ed, *Essays on Aristotle's Ethics* (Berkeley and Los Angeles, University of California Press, 1980).

RORTY, Amelie Oksenberg, *The Identities of Persons* (Berkeley, University of California Press, 1976).

RORTY, Richard, "Absolutely Non-Absolute", review of Charles Taylor's Philosophical Papers, *Times Literary Supplement*, 6 December 1985.

RORTY, Richard, *The Consequences of Pragmatism* (Minneapolis, University of Minnesota Press, 1982).

RORTY, Richard, "Pragmatism, Davidson and Truth", in Le Pore, editor, *Truth and Interpretation*.

ROSS, Alf, *Directives and Norms* (London, Routledge & Kegan Paul, 1968).

ROSS, David, *The Right and the Good* (Oxford, Clarendon Press, 1930).

ROSS, E. A., *The Principles of Sociology* (New York, Century, 1920).

ROTHSCHILD, Michael, and STIGLITZ, Joseph E., "Some Further Results on the Measurement of Inequality", *Journal of Economic Theory* (1973).

RYAN, Alan, Editor, *The Idea of Freedom: Essays in Honour of Isaiah Berlin* (Oxford, Oxford University Press, 1979).

SAHLIN, Nils-Eric, "On Second Order Probabilities and the Notion of Epistemic Risk", in Stigum and Wenstop, eds, *Foundations of Utility and Risk Theory with Applications*.

SAHLIN, Nils-Eric, "Preference Among Preferences as a Method for Obtaining a Higher-Ordered Metric Scale", *British Journal of Mathematical and Statistical Psychology* (1981).

SAHLIN, Nils-Eric, *Secondary Levels in Decision Making* (Doctoral Dissertation, Lund University, 1984).

SALZEN, Eric A., "Perception of Emotion in Faces", in *Perceiving and Remembering Faces*, Davies, Ellis, and Shepherd, editors.

SAMUELSON, Paul A., "Arrow's Mathematical Politics", in *Human Values and Economic Policy: A Symposium*, Sidney Hook, editor (New York, New York University Press, 1967).

SAMUELSON, Paul A., *The Collected Scientific Papers of Paul A. Samuelson*, J. E. Stiglitz, editor (Cambridge, Mass., MIT Press, 1966).

SAMUELSON, Paul A., "Probability, Utility, and the Independence Axiom", *Econometrica* (1952).

SAMUELSON, Paul A., "Reaffirming the Existence of 'Reasonable' Bergson-Samuelson Social Welfare Functions", *Economica* (1977).

SANDEL, Michael, *Liberalism and the Limits of Justice* (Cambridge, MA, Cambridge University Press, 1982).

SAVAGE, Leonard, *The Foundations of Statistics*, 2nd edition (New York, Dover, 1972).

SCHAUER, Frederick, "Free Speech and the Argument from Democracy", in Pennock and Chapman, editors, *Liberal Democracy*.

SCHEFFLER, Israel, "On Justification and Commitment", *Journal of Philosophy* (1954).

SCHELLING, Thomas, *The Strategy of Conflict* (Cambridge, Mass., Harvard University Press, 1960).

SCHUMPETER, Joseph A., *Capitalism, Socialism and Democracy*, 5th edition (London, George Allen & Unwin, 1976).

SCHWARTZ, Thomas, "Rationality and the Myth of the Maximum", *Nous* (1972).

SCOTCH, Peter K., and JENNINGS, Raymond E., "Non-Kripkean Deontic Logic", in Hilpinen, editor, *New Studies in Deontic Logic*.

SEABRIGHT, Paul, "Explaining Cultural Divergence: A Wittgensteinian Paradox", *Journal of Philosophy* (1987).

SEABRIGHT, Paul, *Uncertainty and Ignorance in Economics* (Oxford M. Phil. thesis, 1982).

SEARLE, John R., *Intentionality* (Cambridge, Cambridge University Press, 1983).

SEARLE, John, "'Prima Facie' Obligations", in *Philosophical Subjects*, Zak van Straaten, editor (Oxford, Clarendon Press, 1980), and in *Practical Reasoning*, Joseph Raz, editor (Oxford, Oxford University Press, 1978).

SEARLE, John R., *Speech Acts: An Essay in the Philosophy of Language* (London, Cambridge University Press, 1977).

SEN, Amartya K., *Choice, Welfare and Measurement* (Oxford, Blackwell, 1982).

SEN, Amartya K., *Collective Choice and Social Welfare* (San Francisco, Holden-Day, 1970).

SEN, Amartya, "Goals, Commitment, and Identity", *Journal of Law, Economics and Organization* (1985).

SEN, Amartya, "Information and Invariance in Normative Choice", in *Social Choice and Public Decision Making: Essays in Honor of Kenneth J. Arrow*, vol. 1, Heller, Starr, and Starrett, editors.

SEN, Amartya, "Liberty and Social Choice", *Journal of Philosophy* (1983).

SEN, Amartya, *On Economic Inequality* (Oxford, Clarendon Press, 1973).

SEN, Amartya K., "Plural Utility", *Proceedings of the Aristotelian Society* (1980–1981).

SEN, Amartya, "Rationality and Uncertainty", *Theory and Decision* (1985).

SEN, Amartya K., "Social Choice Theory", in *The Handbook of Mathematical Economics*, vol. 3, Arrow and Intriligator, editors.

SEN, Amartya, "Utilitarianism and Welfarism", *Journal of Philosophy* (1979).

SEN, Amartya, and WILLIAMS, Bernard, *Utilitarianism and Beyond* (Cambridge, Cambridge University Press, 1982).

SHEA v. LOUISIANNA, 105 S.Ct. 1065 (1985).

SHEPARD, R. N. "On Subjectively Optimum Selections among Multi-attribute Alternatives", in Edwards and Tversky, *Decision Making*.

SIDGWICK, Henry, *Methods of Ethics*, 5th edition (London, Macmillan, 1893).

SLOTE, Michael, "Selective Necessity and the Free-will Problem", *Journal of Philosophy* (1982).

SMART, J. J. C., and WILLIAMS, Bernard, *Utilitarianism: For and Against* (Cambridge, Cambridge University Press, 1973).

SMITH, David G., "Liberalism and Judicial Review", in Pennock and Chapman, editors, *Liberal Democracy*.

STIGLER, George J., and BECKER, Gary S., "De Gustibus Non Est Disputantdum", *American Economic Review* (1977).

STIGUM, Bernt, and WENSTOP, Fred, editors, *Foundations of Utility and Risk Theory with Applications* (Dordrecht, Reidel, 1983).

STOVALL v. DENNO, 388 U.S. 293 (1967).

STRAWSON, P. F., "Causation and Explanation", in Vermazen and Hintikka, editors, *Essays on Davidson*.

STRAWSON, P. F., *Freedom and Resentment and Other Essays* (London, Methuen, 1974).

STRAWSON, P. F., *Individuals: An Essay in Descriptive Metaphysics* (London, Methuen, 1959).

STRAWSON, P. F., "Perception and Its Objects", in McDonald, editor, *Perception and Identity*.

STROUD, Barry, "The Allure of Idealism", *Proceedings of the Aristotelian Society*, supplementary volume (1984).

STROUD, Barry, "Wittgenstein and Logical Necessity", in *Wittgenstein: The Philosophical Investigations*, Pitcher, editor.

TAYLOR, Charles, *Hegel and Modern Society* (Cambridge, Cambridge University Press, 1979).

TAYLOR, Charles, *Human Agency and Language: Philosophical Papers*, vol. 1 (Cambridge, Cambridge University Press, 1985).

TAYLOR, Charles, *Philosophy and the Human Sciences: Philosophical Papers*, vol. 2 (Cambridge, Cambridge University Press, 1985).

TAYLOR, Charles, "Understanding and Explanation in the Geisteswissenschaften", in Holtzman and Leich, editors, *Wittgenstein: To Follow a Rule*.

THOMSON, Judith Jarvis, "Remarks on Causation and Liability", *Philosophy and Public Affairs* (1983).

THRALL, R. M., COOMBS, C. H., and DAVIS, R. L., editors, *Decision Processes* (New York, John Wiley, 1954).

TRIGG, Roger, *Reason and Commitment* (Cambridge, Cambridge University Press, 1973).

TVERSKY, Amos, "Additivity, Utility, and Subjective Probability", *Journal of Mathematical Psychology* (1967).

TVERSKY, Amos, "A Critique of Expected Utility Theory: Descriptive and Normative Considerations", *Erkenntnis* (1975).

TVERSKY, Amos, "A General Theory of Polynomial Conjoint Measurement", *Journal of Mathematical Psychology* (1967).

TVERSKY, Amos, "Intransitivity of Preferences", *Psychological Review* (1969).

TVERSKY, Amos, and KAHNEMAN, Daniel, "The Framing of Decisions and the Psychology of Choice", *Science* (1981).

UNGER, Peter, "Experience and Factual Knowledge", *Journal of Philosophy* (1967).

UNITED STATES v. BAILEY, 439 F. Supp. 1303 (W.D. Pa. 1977), reversed in 581 F.2d 341 (3d Cir. 1978).

UNITED STATES v. BEECHUM, 582 F.2d 898 (5th Cir. 1978), cert. denied 440 U.S. 920 (1979).

UNITED STATES v. SIMS, 588 F.2d 1145 (1978).

van DAMME, Eric, "Refinements of the Nash Equilibrium Concept", Lecture Notes in Economics and Mathematical Systems series (Berlin, Springer-Verlag, 1983).

van STRAATEN, Zak, editor, *Philosophical Subjects* (Oxford, Clarendon Press, 1980).

VERMAZEN, Bruce, and HINTIKKA, Merrill, editors, *Essays on Davidson* (Oxford, Clarendon Press, 1985).

VESEY, Godfrey, editor, *Idealism Past and Present*, Royal Institute of Philosophy Lecture Series 13 (Cambridge, Cambridge University Press, 1982).

VICKERS, J. M., "Utility and its Ambiguities", *Erkenntnis* (1975).

VIGNOLO, L. A., "Auditory Agnosia", in *The Neurophsychology of Cognitive Function*, Broadbent and Weiskrantz, editors (London, The Royal Society, 1982).

von FRASSEN, Bas C., "Values and the Heart's Command", *Journal of Philosophy* (1973).

von HUMBOLDT, Wilhelm, *The Limits of State Action*, edited and with introductory essay by J. W. Burrow (Cambridge, Cambridge University Press, 1969).

von MISES, Ludwig, *Human Action: A Treatise on Economics*, third edition (Chicago, Henry Regnery Company, 1949).

von NEUMANN, John, and MORGENSTERN, Oskar, *Theory of Games and Economic Behavior* (Princeton, Princeton University Press, 1947).

von WRIGHT, Georg Henrik, *Explanation and Understanding* (London, Routledge and Kegan Paul, 1971).

von WRIGHT, Georg Henrik, *Norm and Action: A Logical Inquiry* (London, Routledge & Kegan Paul, 1963).

WALLACE v. HALLOWELL, 56 Minn. 501; 58 N. W. 292 (1894).

WEINGARTNER, Paul, editor, *Epistemology and Philosophy of Science*, Proceedings of the Seventh Annual Wittgenstein Symposium (Vienna, Holder-Pichler-Tempsky, 1983).

WHELAN, Frederick G., "Democratic Theory and the Boundary Problem", in Pennock and Chapman, editors, *Liberal Democracy*.

WIGGINS, David, "Freedom, Knowledge, Belief and Causality", in *Knowledge and Necessity*, Royal Institute of Philosophy Lectures, vol. 3, 1968–1969 (London, MacMillan, 1970).

WIGGINS, David, *Sameness and Substance* (Oxford, Blackwell, 1980).

WIGGINS, David, "Toward a Reasonable Libertarianism", in Honderich, editor, *Essays on Freedom of Action*.

WIGGINS, David, "Truth, Invention, and the Meaning of Life", *Proceedings of the British Academy* (1976).

WIGGINS, David, "Weakness of Will, Commensurability, and the Objects of Deliberation and Desire", *Proceedings of the Aristotelian Society* (1978–1979).

WILLIAMS, Bernard, "Conflicts of Values", in Ryan, editor, *The Idea of Freedom*.

WILLIAMS, Bernard, "A Critique of Utilitarianism", in Smart and Williams, *Util-*

*itarianism: For and Against* (Cambridge, Cambridge University Press, 1973).

WILLIAMS, Bernard, *Descartes: The Project of Pure Inquiry* (Harmondsworth, Middlesex, Penguin, 1978).

WILLIAMS, Bernard, *Ethics and the Limits of Philosophy* (London, Fontana Press, 1985).

WILLIAMS, Bernard, *Moral Luck* (Cambridge, Cambridge University Press, 1981).

WILLIAMS, Bernard, *Problems of the Self* (Cambridge, Cambridge University Press, 1973).

WILLIAMS, Bernard, review of Derek Parfit, *Reasons and Persons*, in *London Review of Books*, 7–20 June 1984.

WILLIAMS, "The Truth in Relativism", *Proceedings of the Aristotelian Society* (1974–1975).

WILLISTON, Samuel, and THOMPSON, George J., *A Treatise on the Law of Contracts*, revised edition (New York, Baker, Voorhis & Company, 1936), volume 1.

WINSTON, Kenneth I., "Toward a Liberal Conception of Legislation", in Pennock and Chapman, editors, *Liberal Democracy*.

WITTGENSTEIN, Ludwig, *The Blue and Brown Books* (Oxford, Blackwell, 1975).

WITTGENSTEIN, Ludwig, "Lecture on Ethics", *Philosophical Review* (1965).

WITTGENSTEIN, Ludwig, *Lectures and Conversations on Aesthetics, Psychology and Religious Belief*, compiled from notes taken by Yorick Smythies, Rush Rhees and James Taylor, Cyril Barrett, editor (Oxford, Blackwell, 1978).

WITTGENSTEIN, Ludwig, *On Certainty*, G. E. M. Anscombe and G. H. von Wright, editors, Denis Paul and G. E. M. Anscombe, translators (Oxford, Blackwell, 1977).

WITTGENSTEIN, Ludwig, *Philosophical Grammar*, Rush Rhees, editor, Anthony Kenny, translator (Oxford, Blackwell, 1974).

WITTGENSTEIN, Ludwig, *Philosophical Investigations*, G. E. M. Anscombe, translator (Oxford, Blackwell, 1976).

WITTGENSTEIN, Ludwig, *Remarks on Colour*, G. E. M. Anscombe, editor, Linda L. McAlister and Margarete Schatte, translators (Oxford, Blackwell, 1977).

WITTGENSTEIN, Ludwig, *Remarks on the Foundations of Mathematics*, G. H. von Wright, R. Rhees, G. E. M. Anscombe, editors, G. E. M. Anscombe, translator (Oxford, Blackwell, 1978).

WITTGENSTEIN, Ludwig, *Tractatus Logico-Philosophicus*, D. F. Pears and B. F. McGuinness, translators (London, Routledge & Kegan Paul, 1961).

WITTGENSTEIN, Ludwig, *Zettel*, G. E. M. Anscombe and G. H. von Wright, editors, G. E. M. Anscombe, translator (Oxford, Blackwell, 1967).

WOLFF, Robert Paul, editor, *Kant: A Collection of Critical Essays* (London, Macmillan, 1968).

WOLFF, Susan, "The Importance of Free Will", *Mind* (1981).

WOLLHEIM, Richard, and HOPKINS, James, editors, *Philosophical Essays on Freud* (Cambridge, Cambridge University Press, 1982).

WOODFIELD, Andrew, editor, *Thought and Object: Essays on Intentionality* (Oxford, Clarendon Press, 1982).

WRIGHT, Crispin, "Keeping Track of Nozick", *Analysis* (1983).

WRIGHT, Crispin, *Wittgenstein on the Foundations of Mathematics* (London, Duckworth, 1980).

# Index

Bold numbers refer to pages on which definitions and principles are given.